THE LOEB CLASSICAL LIBRARY

FOUNDED BY JAMES LOEB, LL.D.

EDITED BY

† T. E. PAGE, C.H., LITT.D.

E. CAPPS, PH.D., LL.D.   † W. H. D. ROUSE, LITT.D.

. A. POST, L.H.D.   E. H. WARMINGTON, M.A., F.R.HIST.SOC.

PLATO

THE STATESMAN
PHILEBUS
ION

PLATO

WITH AN ENGLISH TRANSLATION

THE STATESMAN · PHILEBUS

BY

HAROLD N. FOWLER, Ph.D.

PROFESSOR OF GREEK, WESTERN RESERVE UNIVERSITY

ION

BY

W. R. M. LAMB, M.A.

SOMETIME FELLOW OF TRINITY COLLEGE, CAMBRIDGE

LONDON
WILLIAM HEINEMANN LTD
CAMBRIDGE, MASSACHUSETTS
HARVARD UNIVERSITY PRESS
MCMLXII

First printed 1925
Reprinted 1939, 1942, 1952, 1962

Printed in Great Britain

CONTENTS

	PAGE
PREFACE	vii
GENERAL INTRODUCTION	ix
THE STATESMAN	1
PHILEBUS	197
ION	401
INDEX	448

v

PREFACE

THE Greek text of the *Statesman* and the *Philebus* is based upon the Codex Clarkianus (B) and the Codex Venetus (T). Deviations from the text as given in one or other of these MSS. are noted in the margin at the foot of the page. In most instances disagreement between these two MSS. and occasionally readings found in inferior MSS. or in ancient quotations, as well as emendations offered by modern scholars, are noted, even when they have not affected the text chosen. The following abbreviations are employed :—

B = Codex Clarkianus or Bodleianus, written A.D. 895.

T = Codex Venetus, Append. class. 4, cod. 1 ; twelfth century.

W = Codex Vindobonensis 54, Suppl. graec. 7.

D = Codex Venetus 185.

G = Codex Venetus, Append. class. 4, cod. 54.

btw = later hands of BTW.

PREFACE

The brief introductions aim merely at supplying such information as may in some measure aid the reader to appreciate these particular dialogues.

HAROLD N. FOWLER.

The text here given of the *Ion* is based on the recension of Schanz. Two modern corrections are adopted and noted at 533 D and 539 E. The introduction and notes are intended to give only immediate help in understanding the dialogue.

W. R. M. LAMB.

GENERAL INTRODUCTION

PLATO was born in 427 B.C. of Athenian parents who could provide him with the best education of the day, and ample means and leisure throughout his life. He came to manhood in the dismal close of the Peloponnesian War, when Aristophanes was at the height of his success, and Sophocles and Euripides had produced their last plays. As a boy he doubtless heard the lectures of Gorgias, Protagoras, and other sophists, and his early bent seems to have been towards poetry. But his intelligence was too progressive to rest in the agnostic position on which the sophistic culture was based. A century before, Heracleitus had declared knowledge to be impossible, because the objects of sense are continually changing; yet now a certain Cratylus was trying to build a theory of knowledge over the assertion of flux, by developing some hints let fall by its oracular author about the truth contained in names. From this influence Plato passed into contact with Socrates, whose character and gifts have left a singular impress on the thought of mankind. This effect is almost wholly due to Plato's applications and extensions of

A 2

his master's thought ; since, fortunately for us, the pupil not only became a teacher in his turn, but brought his artistic genius into play, and composed the memorials of philosophic talk which we know as the Dialogues. Xenophon, Antisthenes, and Aeschines were other disciples of Socrates who drew similar sketches of his teaching : the suggestion came from the " mimes " of the Syracusan Sophron, —realistic studies of conversation between ordinary types of character. As Plato became more engrossed in the Socratic speculations, this artistic impulse was strengthened by the desire of recording each definite stage of thought as a basis for new discussion and advance.

When Plato was twenty years old, Socrates was over sixty, and had long been notorious in Athens for his peculiar kind of sophistry. In the *Phaedo* he tells how he tried, in his youth, the current scientific explanations of the universe, and found them full of puzzles. He then met with the theory of Anaxagoras,—that the cause of everything is " mind." This was more promising : but it led nowhere after all, since it failed to rise above the conception of physical energy ; this " mind " showed no intelligent aim. Disappointed of an assurance that the universe works for the best, Socrates betook himself to the plan of making *definitions* of " beautiful," " good," " large," and so on, as qualities observed in the several classes of beautiful, good and large material things, and then employing these propositions, if they

x

appeared to be sound, for the erection of higher hypotheses. The point is that he made a new science out of a recognized theory of "ideas" or "forms," which had come of reflecting on the quality predicated when we say "this man is good," and which postulates some sure reality behind the fleeting objects of sense. His "hypothetical" method, familiar to mathematicians, attains its full reach and significance in the *Republic*.

The Pythagoreans who appear in the intimate scene of the *Phaedo* were accustomed to the theory of ideas, and were a fit audience for the highest reasonings of Socrates on the true nature of life and the soul. For some years before the master's death (399 B.C.) Plato, if not a member of their circle, was often a spell-bound hearer of the "satyr." But ordinary Athenians had other views of Socrates, which varied according to their age and the extent of their acquaintance with him. Aristophanes' burlesque in the *Clouds* (423 B.C.) had left a common impression not unlike what we have of the King of Laputa. Yet the young men who had any frequent speech with him in his later years, while they felt there was something uncanny about him, found an irresistible attraction in his simple manner, his humorous insight into their ways and thoughts, and his fervent eloquence on the principles of their actions and careers. He kept no school, and took no fees ; he distrusted the pretensions of the regular sophists, with whom he was carelessly confounded ; moreover, he professed

to have no knowledge himself, except so far as to know that he was ignorant. The earliest Dialogues, such as the *Apology*, *Crito*, *Euthyphro*, *Charmides*, *Laches*, and *Lysis*, show the manner in which he performed his ministry. In rousing men, especially those whose minds were fresh, to the need of knowing themselves, he promoted the authority of the intellect, the law of definite individual knowledge, above all reason of state or tie of party; and it is not surprising that his city, in the effort of recovering her political strength, decided to hush such an inconvenient voice. He must have foreseen his fate, but he continued his work undeterred.

Though he seems, in his usual talk, to have professed no positive doctrine, there were one or two beliefs which he frequently declared. Virtue, he said, is knowledge; for each man's good is his happiness, and once he knows it clearly, he needs must choose to ensue it. Further, this knowledge is innate in our minds, and we only need to have it awakened and exercised by "dialectic," or a systematic course of question and answer. He also believed his mission to be divinely ordained, and asserted that his own actions were guided at times by the prohibitions of a "spiritual sign." He was capable, as we find in the *Symposium*, of standing in rapt meditation at any moment for some time, and once for as long as twenty-four hours.

It is clear that, if he claimed no comprehensive theory of existence, and although his ethical reliance

on knowledge, if he never analysed it, leaves him in a very crude stage of psychology, his logical and mystical suggestions must have led his favourite pupils a good way towards a new system of metaphysics. These intimates learnt, as they steeped their minds in his, and felt the growth of a unique affection amid the glow of enlightenment, that happiness may be elsewhere than in our dealings with the material world, and that the mind has prerogatives and duties far above the sphere of civic life.

After the death of Socrates in 399, Plato spent some twelve years in study and travel. For the first part of this time he was perhaps at Megara, where Eucleides, his fellow-student and friend, was forming a school of dialectic. Here he may have composed some of the six Dialogues already mentioned as recording Socrates' activity in Athens. Towards and probably beyond the end of this period, in order to present the Socratic method in bolder conflict with sophistic education, he wrote the *Protagoras, Meno, Euthydemus,* and *Gorgias.* These works show a much greater command of dramatic and literary art, and a deeper interest in logic. The last of them may well be later than 387, the year in which, after an all but disastrous attempt to better the mind of Dionysius of Syracuse, he returned to Athens, and, now forty years of age, founded the Academy ; where the memory of his master was to be perpetuated by continuing and expanding the

Socratic discussions among the elect of the new generation. The rivalry of this private college with the professional school of Isocrates is discernible in the subject and tone of the *Gorgias*. Plato carried on the direction of the Academy till his death, at eighty-one, in 346 ; save that half-way through this period (367) he accepted the invitation of his friend Dion to undertake the instruction of the younger Dionysius at Syracuse. The elder tyrant had been annoyed by the Socratic freedom of Plato's talk : now it was a wayward youth who refused the yoke of a systematic training. What that training was like we see in the *Republic*, where true political wisdom is approached by an arduous ascent through mathematics, logic, and metaphysics. Plato returned, with less hopes of obtaining the ideal ruler, to make wonderful conquests in the realm of thought.

The *Meno* and *Gorgias* set forth the doctrine that knowledge of right is latent in our minds : dialectic, not the rhetoric of the schools, is the means of eliciting it. The method, as Plato soon perceived, must be long and difficult : but he felt a mystical rapture over its certainty, which led him to picture the immutable " forms " as existing in a world of their own. This feeling, and the conviction whence it springs—that knowledge is somehow possible, had come to the front of his mind when he began to know Socrates. Two brilliant compositions, the *Cratylus* and *Symposium*, display the strength of the conviction, and then, the noble fervour of the

feeling. In the latter of these works, the highest powers of imaginative sympathy and eloquence are summoned to unveil the sacred vision of absolute beauty. The *Phaedo* turns the logical theory upon the soul, which is seen to enjoy, when freed from the body, familiar cognition of the eternal types of being. Here Orphic dogma lends its aid to the Socratic search for knowledge, while we behold an inspiring picture of the philosopher in his hour of death.

With increasing confidence in himself as the successor of Socrates, Plato next undertook, in the *Republic*, to show the master meeting his own unsatisfied queries on education and politics. We read now of a " form " of good to which all thought and action aspire, and which, contemplated in itself, will explain not merely why justice is better than injustice, but the meaning and aim of everything. In order that man may be fully understood, we are to view him " writ large " in the organization of an ideal state. The scheme of description opens out into many subsidiary topics, including three great proposals already known to Greece,—the abolition of private property, the community of women and children, and the civic equality of the sexes. But the central subject is the preparation of the philosopher, through a series of ancillary sciences, for dialectic ; so that, once possessed of the supreme truth, he may have light for directing his fellow-men. As in the *Phaedo*, the spell of mythical revelation is

brought to enhance the discourse of reason. The *Phaedrus* takes up the subject of rhetoric, to lead us allegorically into the realm of " ideas," and thence to point out a new rhetoric, worthy of the well-trained dialectician. We get also a glimpse of the philosopher's duty of investigating the mutual relations of the " forms " to which his study of particular things has led him.

A closer interest in logical method, appearing through his delight in imaginative construction, is one distinctive mark of this middle stage in Plato's teaching. As he passes to the next two Dialogues, the *Theaetetus* and *Parmenides*, he puts off the aesthetic rapture, and considers the ideas as categories of thought which require co-ordination. The discussion of knowledge in the former makes it evident that the Academy was now the meeting-place of vigorous minds, some of which were eager to urge or hear refuted the doctrines they had learnt from other schools of thought; while the arguments are conducted with a critical caution very different from the brilliant and often hasty zeal of Socrates. The *Parmenides* corrects an actual or possible misconception of the theory of ideas in the domain of logic, showing perhaps how Aristotle, now a youthful disciple of Plato, found fault with the theory as he understood it. The forms are viewed in the light of the necessities of thought: knowledge is to be attained by a careful practice which will raise our minds to the vision of all parti-

culars in their rightly distinguished and connected classes.

Plato is here at work on his own great problem :— If what we know is a single permanent law under which a multitude of things are ranged, what is the link between the one and the many ? The *Sophist* contains some of his ripest thought on this increasingly urgent question : his confident advance beyond Socratic teaching is indicated by the literary form, which hardly disguises the continuous exposition of a lecture. We observe an attention to physical science, the association of soul, motion, and existence, and the comparative study of being and not-being. The *Politicus* returns to the topic of state-government, and carries on the process of acquiring perfect notions of reality by the classification of things. Perhaps we should see in the absolute " mean " which is posited as the standard of all arts, business, and conduct, a contribution from Aristotle. The *Philebus*, in dealing with pleasure and knowledge, dwells further on the correct division and classification required if our reason, as it surely must, is to apprehend truth. The method is becoming more thorough and more complex, and Plato's hope of bringing it to completion is more remote. But he is gaining a clearer insight into the problem of unity and plurality.

The magnificent myth of the *Timaeus*, related by a Pythagorean, describes the structure of the universe, so as to show how the One manifests

itself as the Many. We have here the latest reflections of Plato on space, time, soul, and many physical matters. In the lengthy treatise of the *Laws* he addresses himself to the final duty of the philosopher as announced in the *Republic* : a long habituation to abstract thought will qualify rather than disqualify him for the practical regulation of public and private affairs. Attention is fixed once more on soul, as the energy of the world and the vehicle of our sovereign reason.

Thus Plato maintains the fixity of the objects of knowledge in a great variety of studies, which enlarge the compass of Socrates' teaching till it embraces enough material for complete systems of logic and metaphysics. How far these systems were actually worked out in the discussions of the Academy we can only surmise from the Dialogues themselves and a careful comparison of Aristotle ; whose writings, however, have come down to us in a much less perfect state. But it seems probable that, to the end, Plato was too fertile in thought to rest content with one authoritative body of doctrine. We may be able to detect in the *Timaeus* a tendency to view numbers as the real principles of things ; and we may conjecture a late-found interest in the physical complexion of the world. As a true artist, with a keen sense of the beauty and stir of life, Plato had this interest, in a notable degree, throughout ; but in speaking of his enthusiasm for science we must regard him rather as a great inventor of

sciences than as what we should now call a scientist. This is giving him a splendid name, which few men have earned. Some of his inventions may be unrealizable, but it is hard to find one that is certainly futile. There are flaws in his arguments: to state them clearly and fairly is to win the privilege of taking part in a discussion at the Academy.

W. R. M. LAMB.

————

[NOTE.—*Each of the Dialogues is a self-contained whole. The order in which they have been mentioned in this Introduction is that which agrees best in the main with modern views of Plato's mental progress, though the succession in some instances is uncertain.*]

BIBLIOGRAPHY

The following give useful accounts of Socratic and Platonic thought :—

T. Gomperz : *The Greek Thinkers*, vols. ii. and iii. Murray, 1901–5.

W. Lutoslawski : *The Origin and Growth of Plato's Logic*. Longmans, 1897.

R. L. Nettleship : *Philosophic Lectures and Remains*. 2 vols. Macmillan, 2nd ed., 1901.

D. G. Ritchie : *Plato*. T. and T. Clark, 1902.

J. A. Stewart : *The Myths of Plato*. Macmillan, 1905.

„ „ *Plato's Doctrine of Ideas*. Clarendon Press, 1909.

A. E. Taylor : *Plato*. Constable, 1911.

A. M. Adam : *Plato : Moral and Political Ideals*. Camb. Univ. Press, 1913.

H. Jackson : *Presocratics, Socrates and the Minor Socratics, Plato and the Old Academy* (Cambridge Companion to Greek Studies). Camb. Univ. Press, 1905.

The following are important editions :—

J. Adam : *The Republic*. 2 vols. Camb. Univ. Press, 1902.

W. H. Thompson : *The Phaedrus*. Bell, 1868.

„ „ *The Gorgias*. Bell, 1871.

R. D. Archer-Hind : *The Phaedo*. Macmillan, 2nd ed., 1894.

„ „ *The Timaeus*. Macmillan, 1888.

J. Burnet : *The Phaedo*. Clarendon Press, 1911.

L. Campbell : *The Theaetetus*. Clarendon Press, 1883.

„ „ *The Sophistes and Politicus*. Clarendon Press, 1867.

E. S. Thompson : *The Meno*. Macmillan, 1901.

THE STATESMAN

INTRODUCTION TO *THE STATESMAN*

THE *Statesman* or *Politicus* is in form a continuation of *The Sophist*. Socrates, Theodorus, the Eleatic Stranger, and Theaetetus meet again, and the Stranger is ready to proceed to discuss the Statesman as he had discussed the Sophist on the previous day. As in the *Theaetetus* and *The Sophist*, other hearers are supposed to be present, and one of them, the young Socrates, now takes the place of Theaetetus as interlocutor. But in this dialogue, as in *The Sophist*, the dramatic form is hardly more than a convention. The Stranger delivers a thinly disguised lecture.

The process of acquiring knowledge of reality by classification of things by means of division is carried on here, as in *The Sophist*, and the importance of the dialectic method is emphasized. The doctrine that virtue and art find their standard in the absolute mean appears here for the first time, foreshadowing the teachings of Aristotle.

The subject of the dialogue, apart from its insistence upon method, is the State, quite as much as the Statesman. Plato maintains that the King or the Statesman may do good to the citizens against their will, even by violence, at least in theory; but

2

in the world as it is, he finds three chief kinds of government,—by one ruler, by the few, and by the many. A divine and perfect ruler might rule without laws, but human governments can be only imitations of the divine; in them, therefore, laws are necessary. The best government is found to be a monarchy with laws; the government of the few is intermediate; but democracy has little power for good or ill; it is therefore the least good of lawful governments and the least bad of governments without law.

The long mythical tale of the reversed motion of the world and the consequent reversal of the processes of life contains serious teachings concerning the relations of God to the universe and to man, but is not an attempt to solve all the difficulties that arise in connexion therewith. The division of property, as it appears in the state, into classes is original and illuminating. This dialogue, like *The Sophist*, is rather hard reading, but is an important part of the body of Platonic doctrine.

ΠΟΛΙΤΙΚΟΣ

[Η ΠΕΡΙ ΒΑΣΙΛΕΙΑΣ, ΛΟΓΙΚΟΣ]

ΤΑ ΤΟΥ ΔΙΑΛΟΓΟΥ ΠΡΟΣΩΠΑ

ΣΩΚΡΑΤΗΣ, ΘΕΟΔΩΡΟΣ, ΞΕΝΟΣ, ΣΩΚΡΑΤΗΣ Ο ΝΕΩΤΕΡΟΣ

Ι. ΣΩ. Ἦ πολλὴν χάριν ὀφείλω σοι τῆς Θεαιτήτου γνωρίσεως, ὦ Θεόδωρε, ἅμα καὶ τῆς τοῦ ξένου.

ΘΕΟ. Τάχα δέ, ὦ Σώκρατες, ὀφειλήσεις ταύτης
τριπλασίαν, ἐπειδὰν τόν τε πολιτικὸν ἀπεργάσωνταί
σοι καὶ τὸν φιλόσοφον.

ΣΩ. Εἶεν· οὕτω τοῦτο, ὦ φίλε Θεόδωρε, φήσομεν
ἀκηκοότες εἶναι τοῦ περὶ λογισμοὺς καὶ τὰ γεωμε-
τρικὰ κρατίστου;

B   ΘΕΟ. Πῶς, ὦ Σώκρατες;

ΣΩ. Τῶν ἀνδρῶν ἕκαστον θέντος[1] τῆς ἴσης ἀξίας,
οἳ τῇ τιμῇ πλέον ἀλλήλων ἀφεστᾶσιν ἢ κατὰ τὴν
ἀναλογίαν τὴν τῆς ὑμετέρας τέχνης.

ΘΕΟ. Εὖ γε νὴ τὸν ἡμέτερον θεόν, ὦ Σώκρατες,
τὸν Ἄμμωνα καὶ δικαίως, καὶ πάνυ μὲν οὖν

---

[1] θέντος Heindorf : θέντες BT.

4

THE STATESMAN

[or ON KINGSHIP; logical]

CHARACTERS

Socrates, Theodorus, the Stranger, the Younger
Socrates

soc. Really I am greatly indebted to you, Theodorus, for my acquaintance with Theaetetus and with
the Stranger, too.

theo. Presently, Socrates, you will be three times
as much indebted, when they have worked out the
statesman and the philosopher for you.

soc. Indeed! My dear Theodorus, can I believe
my ears? Were those really the words of the great
calculator and geometrician?

theo. Why, what do you mean, Socrates?

soc. When you rated sophist, statesman, and
philosopher at the same value, though they are
farther apart in worth than your mathematical
proportion can express.

theo. By Ammon, our special divinity,[1] that is a
good hit, Socrates; evidently you haven't forgotten

[1] Theodorus was from Cyrene, not far from the oasis of
Ammon.

μνημονικῶς ἐπέπληξάς μοι τὸ περὶ τοὺς λογισμοὺς
ἁμάρτημα. καὶ σὲ μὲν ἀντὶ τούτων εἰς αὖθις
μέτειμι· σὺ δ' ἡμῖν, ὦ ξένε, μηδαμῶς ἀποκάμῃς
χαριζόμενος, ἀλλ' ἑξῆς, εἴτε τὸν πολιτικὸν ἄνδρα
C πρότερον εἴτε τὸν φιλόσοφον προαιρεῖ, προ-
ελόμενος διέξελθε.

ΞΕ. Ταῦτ', ὦ Θεόδωρε, ποιητέον, ἐπείπερ ἅπαξ
γε[1] ἐγκεχειρήκαμεν, καὶ οὐκ ἀποστατέον πρὶν ἂν
αὐτῶν πρὸς τὸ τέλος ἔλθωμεν. ἀλλὰ γὰρ περὶ
Θεαιτήτου τοῦδε τί χρὴ δρᾶν με;

ΘΕΟ. Τοῦ πέρι;

ΞΕ. Διαναπαύσωμεν αὐτὸν μεταλαβόντες αὐτοῦ
τὸν συγγυμναστὴν τόνδε Σωκράτη; ἢ πῶς συμ-
βουλεύεις;

ΘΕΟ. Καθάπερ εἶπες, μεταλάμβανε· νέω γὰρ
ὄντε ῥᾷον οἴσετον πάντα πόνον ἀναπαυομένω.

D ΣΩ. Καὶ μὴν κινδυνεύετον, ὦ ξένε, ἄμφω ποθὲν
ἐμοὶ ξυγγένειαν ἔχειν τινά. τὸν μέν γε οὖν ὑμεῖς
κατὰ τὴν τοῦ προσώπου φύσιν ὅμοιον ἐμοὶ φαίνεσθαί
φατε, τοῦ δ' ἡμῖν ἡ κλῆσις ὁμώνυμος οὖσα καὶ ἡ
258 πρόσρησις παρέχεταί τινα οἰκειότητα. δεῖ δὴ τούς
γε ξυγγενεῖς ἡμᾶς ἀεὶ προθύμως διὰ λόγων ἀναγνω-
ρίζειν. Θεαιτήτῳ μὲν οὖν αὐτός τε συνέμιξα χθὲς
διὰ λόγων καὶ νῦν ἀκήκοα ἀποκρινομένου, Σωκρά-
τους δὲ οὐδέτερα· δεῖ δὲ σκέψασθαι καὶ τοῦτον.
ἐμοὶ μὲν οὖν εἰς αὖθις, σοὶ δὲ νῦν ἀποκρινέσθω.

ΞΕ. Ταῦτ' ἔσται. ὦ Σώκρατες, ἀκούεις δὴ Σω-
κράτους;

ΝΕΟΣ ΣΩ. Ναί.

ΞΕ. Συγχωρεῖς οὖν οἷς λέγει;

ΝΕ. ΣΩ. Πάνυ μὲν οὖν.

[1] γε] τε ΒΤ.

your mathematics, and you are quite right in finding fault with my bad arithmetic. I will get even with you at some other time; but now, Stranger, I turn to you. Do not grow tired of being kind to us, but go on and tell us about the statesman or the philosopher, whichever you prefer to take first.

STR. That is the thing to do, Theodorus, since we have once begun, and we must not stop until we have finished with them. But what shall I do about Theaetetus here?

THEO. In what respect?

STR. Shall we give him a rest and take his school-mate here, the young Socrates, in his place? What is your advice?

THEO. Make the change as you suggest. They are young, and if they have a chance to rest by turns, they will bear any labour better.

SOC. And besides, Stranger, it seems to me that they are both related to me after a fashion; one of them anyhow, as you say, looks like me in his cast of countenance, and the other has the same name and appellation, which implies some sort of kinship. Of course we ought always to be eager to get acquainted with our relatives by debating with them. Now I myself had an argument with Theaetetus yesterday and have been listening to his answers just now, but I do not know Socrates in either way and must examine him, too. But let him reply to you now; my turn will come by and by.

STR. Very well; Socrates, do you hear what Socrates says?

Y. SOC. Yes.

STR. And do you agree?

Y. SOC. Certainly.

B ΞΕ. Οὐ τὰ σὰ κωλύειν φαίνεται, δεῖ δὲ ἴσως ἔτι ἧττον τἀμὰ διακωλύειν. ἀλλὰ δὴ μετὰ τὸν σοφιστὴν ἀναγκαῖον, ὡς ἐμοὶ φαίνεται, τὸν πολιτικὸν ἄνδρα[1] διαζητεῖν νῷν· καί μοι λέγε πότερον τῶν ἐπιστημόνων τιν' ἡμῖν καὶ τοῦτον θετέον, ἢ πῶς;

ΝΕ. ΣΩ. Οὕτως.

2. ΞΕ. Τὰς ἐπιστήμας ἄρα διαληπτέον, ὥσπερ ἡνίκα τὸν πρότερον ἐσκοποῦμεν;

ΝΕ. ΣΩ. Τάχ' ἄν.

ΞΕ. Οὐ μὲν δὴ κατὰ ταὐτόν γε, ὦ Σώκρατες, φαίνεταί μοι τμῆμα.

ΝΕ. ΣΩ. Τί μήν;

C ΞΕ. Κατ' ἄλλο.

ΝΕ. ΣΩ. Ἔοικέ γε.

ΞΕ. Τὴν οὖν πολιτικὴν ἀτραπὸν πῇ τις ἀνευρήσει[2]; δεῖ γὰρ αὐτὴν ἀνευρεῖν, καὶ χωρὶς ἀφελόντας ἀπὸ τῶν ἄλλων ἰδέαν αὐτῇ μίαν ἐπισφραγίσασθαι, καὶ ταῖς ἄλλαις ἐκτροπαῖς ἓν ἄλλο εἶδος ἐπισημηναμένους πάσας τὰς ἐπιστήμας ὡς οὔσας δύο εἴδη διανοηθῆναι τὴν ψυχὴν ἡμῶν ποιῆσαι.

ΝΕ. ΣΩ. Τοῦτ' ἤδη σόν, οἶμαι, τὸ ἔργον, ὦ ξένε, ἀλλ' οὐκ ἐμὸν γίγνεται.

D ΞΕ. Δεῖ γε μήν, ὦ Σώκρατες, αὐτὸ εἶναι καὶ σόν, ὅταν ἐμφανὲς ἡμῖν γένηται.

ΝΕ. ΣΩ. Καλῶς εἶπες.

ΞΕ. Ἆρ' οὖν οὐκ ἀριθμητικὴ μὲν καί τινες ἕτεραι ταύτῃ συγγενεῖς τέχναι ψιλαὶ τῶν πράξεών εἰσι, τὸ δὲ γνῶναι παρέσχοντο μόνον;

ΝΕ. ΣΩ. Ἔστιν οὕτως.

---

[1] τὸν πολιτικὸν ἄνδρα W : πολιτικὸν τὸν ἄνδρα BT.
[2] ἀνευρήσει] ἂν εὑρήσῃ B : ἂν εὑρήσει T.

STR. There seems to be no objection on your part, and I suppose there should be still less on mine. Well, then, after the sophist, I think it is our next duty to seek for the statesman; so please tell me: should we rank him also among those who have a science, or not?

Y. SOC. Yes.

STR. Must the sciences, then, be divided as when we were examining the sophist?

Y. SOC. Perhaps.

STR. In that case, Socrates, I think the division will not be along the same lines.

Y. SOC. How will it be?

STR. Along other lines.

Y. SOC. Very likely.

STR. Where, then, shall we find the statesman's path? For we must find it, separate it from the rest, and imprint upon it the seal of a single class; then we must set the mark of another single class upon all the other paths that lead away from this, and make our soul conceive of all sciences as of two classes.[1]

Y. SOC. This, Stranger, is now your affair, I think, not mine.

STR. And yet, Socrates, it must be your affair, too, when we have found the path.

Y. SOC. Quite true.

STR. Are not arithmetic and certain other kindred arts pure sciences, without regard to practical application, which merely furnish knowledge?

Y. SOC. Yes, they are.

[1] *i.e.* one class is to be separated and then all the rest are to be marked as one other class—the familiar division into two parts.

ΞΕ. Αἱ δέ γε περὶ τεκτονικὴν αὖ καὶ σύμπασαν χειρουργίαν ὥσπερ ἐν ταῖς πράξεσιν ἐνοῦσαν Ε σύμφυτον τὴν ἐπιστήμην κέκτηνται, καὶ συναποτελοῦσι τὰ γιγνόμενα ὑπ᾽ αὐτῶν σώματα πρότερον οὐκ ὄντα.

ΝΕ. ΣΩ. Τί μήν;

ΞΕ. Ταύτῃ τοίνυν συμπάσας ἐπιστήμας διαίρει, τὴν μὲν πρακτικὴν προσειπών, τὴν δὲ μόνον γνωστικήν.

ΝΕ. ΣΩ. Ἔστω σοι ταῦθ᾽ ὡς μιᾶς ἐπιστήμης τῆς ὅλης εἴδη δύο.

ΞΕ. Πότερον οὖν τὸν πολιτικὸν καὶ βασιλέα καὶ δεσπότην καὶ ἔτ᾽ οἰκονόμον θήσομεν ὡς ἓν πάντα ταῦτα προσαγορεύοντες, ἢ τοσαύτας τέχνας αὐτὰς εἶναι φῶμεν, ὅσαπερ ὀνόματα ἐρρήθη; μᾶλλον δέ μοι δεῦρο ἕπου.

ΝΕ. ΣΩ. Πῆ;

259 ΞΕ. Τῇδε· εἴ τῴ τις τῶν δημοσιευόντων ἰατρῶν ἱκανὸς ξυμβουλεύειν ἰδιατεύων αὐτός, ἆρ᾽ οὐκ ἀναγκαῖον αὐτῷ προσαγορεύεσθαι τοὔνομα τῆς τέχνης ταὐτὸν ὅπερ ᾧ συμβουλεύει;

ΝΕ. ΣΩ. Ναί.

ΞΕ. Τί δ᾽; ὅστις βασιλεύοντι χώρας ἀνδρὶ παραινεῖν δεινὸς ἰδιώτης ὢν αὐτός, ἆρ᾽ οὐ φήσομεν ἔχειν αὐτὸν τὴν ἐπιστήμην ἣν ἔδει τὸν ἄρχοντα αὐτὸν κεκτῆσθαι;

ΝΕ. ΣΩ. Φήσομεν.

Β ΞΕ. Ἀλλὰ μὴν ἥ γε ἀληθινοῦ βασιλέως βασιλική;

ΝΕ. ΣΩ. Ναί.

ΞΕ. Ταύτην δὲ ὁ κεκτημένος οὐκ, ἄντε ἄρχων ἄντε ἰδιώτης ὢν τυγχάνῃ, πάντως κατά γε τὴν τέχνην αὐτὴν βασιλικὸς ὀρθῶς προσρηθήσεται;

10

STR. But the science possessed by the arts relating to carpentering and to handicraft in general is inherent in their application, and with its aid they create objects which did not previously exist.

Y. SOC. To be sure.

STR. In this way, then, divide all science into two parts, calling the one practical, and the other purely intellectual.

Y. SOC. Let us assume that all science is one and that these are its two forms.

STR. Shall we then assume that the statesman, king, master, and householder too, for that matter, are all one, to be grouped under one title, or shall we say that there are as many arts as names? But let me rather help you to understand in this way.

Y. SOC. In what way?

STR. By this example: If anyone, though himself in private station, is able to advise one of the public physicians, must not his art be called by the same name as that of the man whom he advises?

Y. SOC. Yes.

STR. Well, then, if a man who is himself in private station is wise enough to advise him who is king of a country, shall we not say that he has the science which the ruler himself ought to possess?

Y. SOC. We shall.

STR. But certainly the science of a true king is kingly science?

Y. SOC. Yes.

STR. And will not he who possesses this science, whether he happen to be a ruler or a private citizen, rightly be called " kingly," when considered purely with reference to his art?

ΝΕ. ΣΩ. Δίκαιον γοῦν.

ΞΕ. Καὶ μὴν οἰκονόμος γε καὶ δεσπότης ταὐτόν.

ΝΕ. ΣΩ. Τί μήν;

ΞΕ. Τί δέ; μεγάλης σχῆμα οἰκήσεως ἢ σμικρᾶς αὖ πόλεως ὄγκος μῶν τι πρὸς ἀρχὴν διοίσετον;

ΝΕ. ΣΩ. Οὐδέν.

C ΞΕ. Οὐκοῦν, ὃ νῦν δὴ διεσκοπούμεθα, φανερὸν ὡς ἐπιστήμη μία περὶ πάντ' ἐστὶ ταῦτα· ταύτην δὲ εἴτε βασιλικὴν εἴτε πολιτικὴν εἴτε οἰκονομικὴν τις ὀνομάζει, μηδὲν αὐτῷ διαφερώμεθα.

ΝΕ. ΣΩ. Τί γάρ;

3. ΞΕ. Ἀλλὰ μὴν τόδε γε δῆλον, ὡς βασιλεὺς ἅπας χερσὶ καὶ ξύμπαντι τῷ σώματι σμίκρ' ἄττα εἰς τὸ κατέχειν τὴν ἀρχὴν δύναται πρὸς τὴν τῆς ψυχῆς σύνεσιν καὶ ῥώμην.

ΝΕ. ΣΩ. Δῆλον.

ΞΕ. Τῆς δὴ γνωστικῆς μᾶλλον ἢ τῆς χειρο-
D τεχνικῆς καὶ ὅλως πρακτικῆς βούλει τὸν βασιλέα φῶμεν οἰκειότερον εἶναι;

ΝΕ. ΣΩ. Τί μήν;

ΞΕ. Τὴν ἄρα πολιτικὴν καὶ πολιτικὸν καὶ βασιλικὴν καὶ βασιλικὸν εἰς ταὐτὸν ὡς ἓν πάντα ταῦτα ξυνθήσομεν;

ΝΕ. ΣΩ. Δῆλον.

ΞΕ. Οὐκοῦν πορευοίμεθ' ἂν ἐξῆς, εἰ μετὰ ταῦτα τὴν γνωστικὴν διοριζοίμεθα;

ΝΕ. ΣΩ. Πάνυ γε.

ΞΕ. Πρόσεχε δὴ τὸν νοῦν, ἂν ἄρα ἐν αὐτῇ τινα διαφυὴν[1] κατανοήσωμεν.

ΝΕ. ΣΩ. Φράζε ποίαν.

---

[1] διαφυὴν D : διαφυγὴν BT (γ erased in T).

v. soc. At least he has a right to be.

str. And surely the householder and the master of a family are the same.

y. soc. Yes, of course.

str. Well, so far as government is concerned, is there any difference between the grandeur of a large house and the majesty of a small state?

y. soc. No.

str. Then as for the point we were just discussing, it is clear that all these are the objects of one science, and whether a man calls this the art of kingship or statesmanship or householding, let us not quarrel with him.

y. soc. By no means.

str. But this is plain, that any king can do little with his hands or his whole body toward holding his position, compared with what he can do with the sagacity and strength of his soul.

y. soc. Yes, that is plain.

str. Shall we say, then, that the king is more akin to the intellectual than to the manual or the practical in general?

y. soc. Certainly.

str. Shall we, therefore, put all these together as one—the political art and the statesman, the royal art and the king?

y. soc. Obviously.

str. Then we should be proceeding in due order if we should next divide intellectual science?

y. soc. Certainly.

str. Now pay attention to see if we can perceive any natural line of cleavage in it.

y. soc. Tell us of what sort it is.

E   ΞΕ. Τοιάνδε. λογιστική πού τις ἡμῖν ἦν τέχνη.

ΝΕ. ΣΩ. Ναί.

ΞΕ. Τῶν γνωστικῶν γε, οἶμαι, παντάπασι τεχνῶν.

ΝΕ. ΣΩ. Πῶς δ' οὔ;

ΞΕ. Γνούσῃ δὲ λογιστικῇ τὴν ἐν τοῖς ἀριθμοῖς διαφορὰν μῶν τι πλέον ἔργον δώσομεν ἢ τὰ γνωσθέντα κρῖναι;

ΝΕ. ΣΩ. Τί μήν;

ΞΕ. Καὶ γὰρ ἀρχιτέκτων γε πᾶς οὐκ αὐτὸς ἐργατικὸς ἀλλὰ ἐργατῶν ἄρχων.

ΝΕ. ΣΩ. Ναί.

ΞΕ. Παρεχόμενός γέ που γνῶσιν ἀλλ' οὐ χειρουργίαν.

ΝΕ. ΣΩ. Οὕτως.

260   ΞΕ. Δικαίως δὴ μετέχειν ἂν λέγοιτο τῆς γνωστικῆς ἐπιστήμης.

ΝΕ. ΣΩ. Πάνυ γε.

ΞΕ. Τούτῳ δέ γε, οἶμαι, προσήκει κρίναντι μὴ τέλος ἔχειν μηδ' ἀπηλλάχθαι, καθάπερ ὁ λογιστὴς ἀπήλλακτο, προστάττειν δὲ ἑκάστοις τῶν ἐργατῶν τό γε πρόσφορον, ἕως ἂν ἀπεργάσωνται τὸ προσταχθέν.

ΝΕ. ΣΩ. Ὀρθῶς.

ΞΕ. Οὐκοῦν γνωστικαὶ μὲν αἵ τε τοιαῦται ξύμπασαι καὶ ὁπόσαι ξυνέπονται τῇ λογιστικῇ, κρίσει
B δὲ καὶ ἐπιτάξει διαφέρετον ἀλλήλοιν τούτω τὼ γένη;

ΝΕ. ΣΩ. Φαίνεσθον.

ΞΕ. Ἆρ' οὖν συμπάσης τῆς γνωστικῆς εἰ τὸ μὲν ἐπιτακτικὸν μέρος, τὸ δὲ κριτικὸν δι-

14

STR. Of this sort. We recognized a sort of art of calculation.

Y. SOC. Yes.

STR. It is, I suppose, most certainly one of the intellectual arts.

Y. SOC. Of course.

STR. And shall we grant to the art of calculation, when it has found out the difference between numbers, any further function than that of passing judgement on them when found out?

Y. SOC. No, certainly not.

STR. Every architect, too, is a ruler of workmen, not a workman himself.

Y. SOC. Yes.

STR. As supplying knowledge, not manual labour.

Y. SOC. True.

STR. So he may fairly be said to participate in intellectual science.

Y. SOC. Certainly.

STR. But it is his business, I suppose, not to pass judgement and be done with it and go away, as the calculator did, but to give each of the workmen the proper orders, until they have finished their appointed task.

Y. SOC. You are right.

STR. Then all such sciences, and all those that are in the class with calculating, are alike intellectual sciences, but these two classes differ from one another in the matter of judging and commanding. Am I right?

Y. SOC. I think so.

STR. Then if we bisected intellectual science as a whole and called one part the commanding and the

15

αἱρούμενοι προσείποιμεν, ἐμμελῶς ἂν φαῖμεν δι-
ῃρῆσθαι;

ΝΕ. ΣΩ. Κατά γε τὴν ἐμὴν δόξαν.

ΞΕ. Ἀλλὰ μὴν τοῖς γε κοινῇ τι πράττουσιν
ἀγαπητὸν ὁμονοεῖν.

ΝΕ. ΣΩ. Πῶς δ᾽ οὔ;

ΞΕ. Τούτου τοίνυν μέχριπερ ἂν αὐτοὶ κοινωνῶμεν,
ἐατέον τά γε τῶν ἄλλων δοξάσματα χαίρειν.

ΝΕ. ΣΩ. Τί μήν;

C 4. ΞΕ. Φέρε δή, τούτοιν τοῖν[1] τέχναιν ἡμῖν
τὸν βασιλικὸν ἐν ποτέρᾳ θετέον; ἆρ᾽ ἐν τῇ κριτικῇ,
καθάπερ τινὰ θεατήν, ἢ μᾶλλον τῆς ἐπιτακτικῆς
ὡς ὄντα αὐτὸν τέχνης θήσομεν, δεσπόζοντά γε;

ΝΕ. ΣΩ. Πῶς γὰρ οὐ μᾶλλον;

ΞΕ. Τὴν ἐπιτακτικὴν δὴ τέχνην πάλιν ἂν εἴη
θεατέον εἴ πῃ διέστηκεν. καί μοι δοκεῖ τῇδέ πῃ,
καθάπερ ἡ τῶν καπήλων τέχνη τῆς τῶν αὐτοπωλῶν
D διώρισται τέχνης, καὶ τὸ βασιλικὸν γένος ἔοικεν
ἀπὸ τοῦ τῶν κηρύκων γένους ἀφωρίσθαι.

ΝΕ. ΣΩ. Πῶς;

ΞΕ. Πωληθέντα που πρότερον ἔργα ἀλλότρια
παραδεχόμενοι δεύτερον πωλοῦσι πάλιν οἱ κάπηλοι.

ΝΕ. ΣΩ. Πάνυ μὲν οὖν.

ΞΕ. Οὐκοῦν καὶ τὸ κηρυκικὸν φῦλον ἐπιταχθέντ᾽
ἀλλότρια[2] νοήματα παραδεχόμενον αὐτὸ δεύτερον
ἐπιτάττει πάλιν ἑτέροις.

ΝΕ. ΣΩ. Ἀληθέστατα.

ΞΕ. Τί οὖν; εἰς ταὐτὸν μίξομεν βασιλικὴν ἑρμη-
E νευτικῇ, κελευστικῇ, μαντικῇ, κηρυκικῇ, καὶ πολλαῖς ἑτέραις τούτων τέχναις συγγενέσιν, αἳ σύμ-

---

[1] τούτοιν τοῖν] ταύταιν ταῖν ΒΤ.
[2] ἐπιταχθὲν τἀλλότρια ΒΤ.

other the judging part, might we say we had made a fitting division?

y. soc. Yes, in my opinion.

str. And surely when men are doing anything in common it is desirable for them to agree.

y. soc. Of course it is.

str. On this point, then, so long as we ourselves are in agreement, we need not bother about the opinions of others.

y. soc. Of course not.

str. Now to which of these two classes is the kingly man to be assigned? Shall we assign him to the art of judging, as a kind of spectator, or rather to the art of commanding, inasmuch as he is a ruler?

y. soc. Rather to the latter, of course.

str. Then once more we must see whether the art of command falls into two divisions. It seems to me that it does, and I think there is much the same distinction between the kingly class and the class of heralds as between the art of men who sell what they themselves produce and that of retail dealers.

y. soc. How so?

str. Retail dealers receive and sell over again the productions of others, which have generally been sold before.

y. soc. Certainly.

str. And in like manner heralds receive the purposes of others in the form of orders, and then give the orders a second time to others.

y. soc. Very true.

str. Shall we, then, join the art of the king in the same class with the art of the interpreter, the boatswain, the prophet, the herald, and many other

17

PLATO

πασαι τό γ' ἐπιτάττειν ἔχουσιν; ἢ βούλει, καθάπερ
ᾐκάζομεν νῦν δή, καὶ τοὔνομα παρεικάσωμεν,
ἐπειδὴ καὶ σχεδὸν ἀνώνυμον ὂν τυγχάνει τὸ τῶν
αὐτεπιτακτῶν γένος, καὶ ταύτῃ ταῦτα διελώμεθα,
τὸ μὲν τῶν βασιλέων γένος εἰς τὴν αὐτεπιτακτικὴν
θέντες, τοῦ δὲ ἄλλου παντὸς ἀμελήσαντες, ὄνομα
ἕτερον αὐτοῖς παραχωρήσαντες θέσθαι τινά; τοῦ
γὰρ ἄρχοντος ἔνεκα ἡμῖν ἡ μέθοδος ἦν ἀλλ' οὐχὶ
261 τοῦ ἐναντίου.

ΝΕ. ΣΩ. Πάνυ μὲν οὖν.

5. ΞΕ. Οὐκοῦν ἐπειδὴ τοῦτο μετρίως ἀφέστηκεν
ἀπ' ἐκείνων, ἀλλοτριότητι διορισθὲν πρὸς οἰκειότητα,
τοῦτο αὐτὸ πάλιν αὖ διαιρεῖν ἀναγκαῖον, εἴ τινα
τομὴν ἔτι ἔχομεν ὑπείκουσαν ἐν τούτῳ;

ΝΕ. ΣΩ. Πάνυ γε.

ΞΕ. Καὶ μὴν φαινόμεθα ἔχειν · ἀλλ' ἐπακο-
λουθῶν σύντεμνε.

ΝΕ. ΣΩ. Πῇ;

ΞΕ. Πάντας ὁπόσους ἂν ἄρχοντας διανοηθῶμεν
ἐπιτάξει προσχρωμένους ἆρ' οὐχ εὑρήσομεν γενέ-
B σεώς τινος ἔνεκα προστάττοντας;

ΝΕ. ΣΩ. Πῶς δ' οὔ;

ΞΕ. Καὶ μὴν τά γε¹ γιγνόμενα πάντα δίχα δια-
λαβεῖν οὐ παντάπασι χαλεπόν.

ΝΕ. ΣΩ. Πῇ;

ΞΕ. Τὰ μὲν ἄψυχα αὐτῶν ἐστί που ξυμπάντων,
τὰ δ' ἔμψυχα.

ΝΕ. ΣΩ. Ναί.

ΞΕ. Τούτοις δέ γε αὐτοῖς τὸ τοῦ γνωστικοῦ μέρος
ἐπιτακτικὸν ὄν, εἴπερ βουλόμεθα τέμνειν, τεμοῦμεν.

ΝΕ. ΣΩ. Κατὰ τί;

---

¹ γε Stephanus : τε BT.

18

kindred arts, all of which involve giving orders? Or, as we just now made a comparison of functions, shall we now by comparison make a name also—since the class of those who issue orders of their own is virtually nameless — and assign kings to the science of giving orders of one's own, disregarding all the rest and leaving to someone else the task of naming them? For the object of our present quest is the ruler, not his opposite.

y. soc. Quite right.

str. Then since a reasonable distinction between this class and the rest has been made, by distinguishing the commands given as one's own or another's, shall we again divide this class, if there is in it any further line of section?

y. soc. Certainly.

str. I think there is one; please help me in making the section.

y. soc. On what line?

str. Take the case of all those whom we conceive of as rulers who give commands: shall we not find that they all issue commands for the sake of producing something?

y. soc. Of course.

str. Furthermore it is not at all difficult to divide all that is produced into two classes.

y. soc. How?

str. Of the whole class, some have life and others have no life.

y. soc. Yes.

str. And on these same lines we may, if we like, make a division of the part of intellectual science which commands.

y. soc. In what way?

ΞΕ. Τὸ μὲν ἐπὶ ταῖς τῶν ἀψύχων γενέσεσιν αὐτοῦ τάττοντες,[1] τὸ δ' ἐπὶ ταῖς τῶν[2] ἐμψύχων· καὶ πᾶν οὕτως ἤδη διαιρήσεται δίχα.

ΝΕ. ΣΩ. Παντάπασί γε.

ΞΕ. Τὸ μὲν τοίνυν αὐτῶν παραλίπωμεν, τὸ δ' ἀναλάβωμεν, ἀναλαβόντες δὲ μερισώμεθα εἰς δύο τὸ σύμπαν.

ΝΕ. ΣΩ. Λέγεις δ' αὐτοῖν ἀναληπτέον εἶναι πότερον;

ΞΕ. Πάντως που τὸ περὶ τὰ ζῷα ἐπιτακτικόν. οὐ γὰρ δὴ τό γε τῆς βασιλικῆς ἐπιστήμης ἐστί ποτε τῶν ἀψύχων ἐπιστατοῦν, οἷον ἀρχιτεκτονικόν, ἀλλὰ γενναιότερον ἐν τοῖς ζῴοις καὶ περὶ αὐτὰ ταῦτα τὴν δύναμιν ἀεὶ κεκτημένον.

ΝΕ. ΣΩ. Ὀρθῶς.

ΞΕ. Τήν γε μὴν τῶν ζῴων γένεσιν καὶ τροφὴν τὴν μέν τις ἂν ἴδοι μονοτροφίαν οὖσαν, τὴν δὲ κοινὴν τῶν ἐν ταῖς ἀγέλαις θρεμμάτων ἐπιμέλειαν.

ΝΕ. ΣΩ. Ὀρθῶς.

ΞΕ. Ἀλλ' οὐ μὴν τόν γε πολιτικὸν εὑρήσομεν ἰδιοτρόφον,[3] ὥσπερ βοηλάτην ἤ τινα ἱπποκόμον, ἀλλ' ἱπποφορβῷ τε καὶ βουφορβῷ μᾶλλον προσεοικότα.

ΝΕ. ΣΩ. Φαίνεταί γε δὴ ῥηθὲν νῦν.

ΞΕ. Πότερον οὖν τῆς ζῳοτροφίας τὴν τῶν ξυμπόλλων κοινὴν τροφὴν ἀγελαιοτροφίαν ἢ κοινοτροφικήν τινα ὀνομάζομεν;

ΝΕ. ΣΩ. Ὁπότερον ἂν ἐν τῷ λόγῳ ξυμβαίνῃ.

6. ΞΕ. Καλῶς γε, ὦ Σώκρατες· κἂν διαφυλά-

---

[1] τάσσοντες BT.
[2] ἐπὶ ταῖς τῶν D, Stephanus : ἐπὶ τῶν BT.
[3] ἰδιοτρόφον D : ἰδιότροπον BT.

STR. By assigning one part of it to the production of lifeless, the other to that of living objects; and in this way the whole will be divided into two parts.

Y. SOC. Certainly.

STR. Let us then leave one half and take up the other, and then let us divide that entire half into two parts.

Y. SOC. Which half shall we take up?

STR. That which issues commands relating to living objects, assuredly. For certainly the science of the king is not, like that of the architect, one which supervises lifeless objects; it is a nobler science, since it exercises its power among living beings and in relation to them alone.

Y. SOC. True.

STR. Now you may notice that the breeding and nurture of living beings is sometimes the nurture of a single animal and sometimes the common care of creatures in droves.

Y. SOC. True.

STR. But we shall find that the statesman is not one who tends a single creature, like the driver of a single ox or the groom who tends a horse; he has more resemblance to a man who tends a herd of cattle or a drove of horses.

Y. SOC. That seems to be true, now that you mention it.

STR. Shall we call the art of caring for many living creatures the art of tending a herd or something like community management?

Y. SOC. Whichever we happen to say.

STR. Good, Socrates! If you preserve this attitude

ξης τὸ μὴ σπουδάζειν ἐπὶ τοῖς ὀνόμασι, πλουσιώτε-
ρος εἰς τὸ γῆρας ἀναφανήσει φρονήσεως. νῦν δὲ
τοῦτο μέν, καθάπερ διακελεύει, ποιητέον· τὴν δὲ
ἀγελαιοτροφικὴν ἆρ' ἐννοεῖς πῇ τις δίδυμον ἀπο-
262 φήνας τὸ ζητούμενον ἐν διπλασίοισι¹ τὰ νῦν ἐν
τοῖς ἡμίσεσιν εἰς τότε ποιήσει ζητεῖσθαι;

ΝΕ. ΣΩ. Προθυμήσομαι. καί μοι δοκεῖ τῶν
μὲν ἀνθρώπων ἑτέρα τις εἶναι, τῶν δὲ αὖ θηρίων
ἄλλη τροφή.

ΞΕ. Παντάπασί γε προθυμότατα καὶ ἀνδρειότατα
διῄρησαι· μὴ μέντοι τοῦτό γε εἰς αὖθις κατὰ
δύναμιν πάσχωμεν.

ΝΕ. ΣΩ. Τὸ ποῖον;

ΞΕ. Μὴ σμικρὸν μόριον ἓν πρὸς μεγάλα καὶ
Β πολλὰ ἀφαιρῶμεν, μηδὲ εἴδους χωρίς· ἀλλὰ τὸ
μέρος ἅμα εἶδος ἐχέτω. κάλλιστον μὲν γὰρ ἀπὸ
τῶν ἄλλων εὐθὺς διαχωρίζειν τὸ ζητούμενον, ἂν
ὀρθῶς ἔχῃ, καθάπερ ὀλίγον σὺ πρότερον οἰηθεὶς
ἔχειν τὴν διαίρεσιν ἐπέσπευσας τὸν λόγον, ἰδὼν
ἐπ' ἀνθρώπους πορευόμενον· ἀλλὰ γάρ, ὦ φίλε,
λεπτουργεῖν οὐκ ἀσφαλές, διὰ μέσων δὲ ἀσφαλέ-
στερον ἰέναι τέμνοντας, καὶ μᾶλλον ἰδέαις ἄν τις
προστυγχάνοι. τοῦτο δὲ διαφέρει τὸ πᾶν πρὸς
C τὰς ζητήσεις.

ΝΕ. ΣΩ. Πῶς, ὦ ξένε, λέγεις τοῦτο;

ΞΕ. Πειρατέον ἔτι σαφέστερον φράζειν εὐνοίᾳ
τῆς σῆς φύσεως, ὦ Σώκρατες. ἐν τῷ μὲν οὖν
παρεστηκότι τὰ νῦν δηλῶσαι μηδὲν ἐνδεῶς ἀδύνατον·
ἐπιχειρητέον δέ τι καὶ σμικρῷ πλέον αὐτὸ προαγα-
γεῖν εἰς τὸ πρόσθεν σαφηνείας ἕνεκα.

διπλασίοισι] διπλασίοις ἢ ΒΤ.

22

of indifference to mere names, you will turn out richer in wisdom when you are old. But now we will, as you suggest, not trouble ourselves about the name; but do you see a way in which a man may show that the art of herding is twofold, and may thereby cause that which is now sought among a double number of things to be sought among half as many?

Y. SOC. I am quite willing to try. I think one kind is the care of men, the other that of beasts.

STR. You made the division with perfect willingness and courage. However, let us do our best not to fall again into your error.

Y. SOC. What error?

STR. We must not take a single small part, and set it off against many large ones, nor disregard species in making our division. On the contrary, the part must be also a species. It is a very fine thing to separate the object of our search at once from everything else, if the separation can be made correctly, and so, just now, you thought you had the right division and you hurried our discussion along, because you saw that it was leading towards man. But, my friend, it is not safe to whittle off shavings; it is safer to proceed by cutting through the middle, and in that way one is more likely to find classes. This makes all the difference in the conduct of research.

Y. SOC. What do you mean by that, Stranger?

STR. I must try to speak still more clearly, Socrates, out of regard for your capacity. Just at present it is impossible to make the matter entirely plain, but I will try to lay it before you a little more fully for the sake of clearness.

23

ΝΕ. ΣΩ. Ποῖον οὖν δὴ φράζεις διαιρουμένους ἡμᾶς οὐκ ὀρθῶς ἄρτι δρᾶν;

ΞΕ. Τοιόνδε, οἷον εἴ τις τἀνθρώπινον ἐπιχει-
D ρήσας δίχα διελέσθαι γένος διαιροῖ καθάπερ οἱ πολλοὶ τῶν ἐνθάδε διανέμουσι, τὸ μὲν Ἑλληνικὸν ὡς ἓν ἀπὸ πάντων ἀφαιροῦντες χωρίς, σύμπασι δὲ τοῖς ἄλλοις γένεσιν, ἀπείροις οὖσι καὶ ἀμίκτοις καὶ ἀσυμφώνοις πρὸς ἄλληλα, βάρβαρον μιᾷ κλήσει προσειπόντες αὐτὸ διὰ ταύτην τὴν μίαν κλῆσιν καὶ γένος ἓν αὐτὸ εἶναι προσδοκῶσιν· ἢ τὸν ἀριθμόν τις αὖ νομίζοι κατ' εἴδη δύο διαιρεῖν μυριάδα ἀποτεμνόμενος ἀπὸ πάντων, ὡς ἓν εἶδος ἀποχω-
E ρίζων, καὶ τῷ λοιπῷ δὴ παντὶ θέμενος ἓν ὄνομα διὰ τὴν κλῆσιν αὖ καὶ τοῦτ' ἀξιοῖ γένος ἐκείνου χωρὶς ἕτερον ἓν γίγνεσθαι.[1] κάλλιον δέ που καὶ μᾶλλον κατ' εἴδη καὶ δίχα διαιροῖτ' ἄν, εἰ τὸν μὲν ἀριθμὸν ἀρτίῳ καὶ περιττῷ τις τέμνοι, τὸ δὲ αὖ τῶν ἀνθρώπων γένος ἄρρενι καὶ θήλει, Λυδοὺς δὲ ἢ Φρύγας ἤ τινας ἑτέρους πρὸς ἅπαντας τάττων ἀποσχίζοι τότε, ἡνίκα ἀποροῖ γένος ἅμα καὶ μέρος
263 εὑρίσκειν ἑκάτερον τῶν σχισθέντων.

7. ΝΕ. ΣΩ. Ὀρθότατα· ἀλλὰ γὰρ τοῦτο αὐτό, ὦ ξένε, πῶς ἄν τις γένος καὶ μέρος ἐναργέστερον γνοίη, ὡς οὐ ταὐτόν ἐστον ἀλλ' ἕτερον ἀλλήλοιν;

ΞΕ. Ὦ βέλτιστε ἀνδρῶν, οὐ φαῦλον προστάττεις, Σώκρατες. ἡμεῖς μὲν καὶ νῦν μακροτέραν τοῦ δέοντος ἀπὸ τοῦ προτεθέντος λόγου πεπλανήμεθα, σὺ δὲ ἔτι πλέον ἡμᾶς κελεύεις πλανηθῆναι. νῦν μὲν οὖν, ὥσπερ εἰκός, ἐπανίωμεν πάλιν· ταῦτα δὲ

[1] ἓν γίγνεσθαι Stallbaum : ἐγγίγνεσθαι ΒΤ.

y. soc. What is it, then, that you say we did wrongly in making our division just now?

str. It was very much as if, in undertaking to divide the human race into two parts, one should make the division as most people in this country do; they separate the Hellenic race from all the rest as one, and to all the other races, which are countless in number and have no relation in blood or language to one another, they give the single name "barbarian"; then, because of this single name, they think it is a single species. Or it was as if a man should think he was dividing number into two classes by cutting off a myriad from all the other numbers, with the notion that he was making one separate class, and then should give one name to all the rest, and because of that name should think that this also formed one class distinct from the other. A better division, more truly classified and more equal, would be made by dividing number into odd and even, and the human race into male and female; as for the Lydians and Phrygians and various others they could be opposed to the rest and split off from them when it was impossible to find and separate two parts, each of which formed a class.

y. soc. Very true; but that's just the trouble, Stranger: how can we get a clearer knowledge of class and part, and see that they are not the same thing, but different?

str. Socrates, you most excellent young man, it is no small task you impose upon me. We have already strayed away from our subject more than we ought, and you wish us to wander still farther afield. So for the present let us return to our subject, as is proper; then we will go on the trail of this other

PLATO

B εἰς αὖθις κατὰ σχολὴν καθάπερ ἰχνεύοντες μέτιμεν. οὐ μὴν ἀλλὰ τοῦτό γε αὖ παντάπασι φύλαξαι, μή ποτε παρ' ἐμοῦ δόξῃς αὐτὸ ἐναργῶς διωρισμένον ἀκηκοέναι.

ΝΕ. ΣΩ. Τὸ ποῖον;

ΞΕ. Εἶδός τε καὶ μέρος ἕτερον ἀλλήλων εἶναι.

ΝΕ. ΣΩ. Τί μήν;

ΞΕ. Ὡς εἶδος μὲν ὅταν ᾖ του, καὶ μέρος αὐτὸ ἀναγκαῖον εἶναι τοῦ πράγματος ὅτουπερ ἂν εἶδος λέγηται· μέρος δὲ εἶδος[1] οὐδεμία ἀνάγκη. ταύτῃ με ἢ 'κείνῃ μᾶλλον, ὦ Σώκρατες, ἀεὶ φάθι λέγειν.

ΝΕ. ΣΩ. Ταῦτ' ἔσται.

C ΞΕ. Φράσον δή μοι τὸ μετὰ τοῦτο.

ΝΕ. ΣΩ. Ποῖον;

ΞΕ. Τὸ τῆς ἀποπλανήσεως ὁπόθεν ἡμᾶς δεῦρ' ἤγαγεν. οἶμαι μὲν γὰρ μάλιστα, ὅθεν ἐρωτηθεὶς σὺ τὴν ἀγελαιοτροφίαν ὅπῃ διαιρετέον εἶπες μάλα προθύμως δύ' εἶναι ζώων γένη, τὸ μὲν ἀνθρώπινον, ἕτερον δὲ τῶν ἄλλων ξυμπάντων θηρίων ἕν.

ΝΕ. ΣΩ. Ἀληθῆ.

ΞΕ. Καὶ ἔμοιγε δὴ τότ' ἐφάνης μέρος ἀφαιρῶν ἡγεῖσθαι καταλιπεῖν τὸ λοιπὸν αὖ πάντων γένος ἕν, D ὅτι πᾶσι ταὐτὸν ἐπονομάζειν ἔσχες ὄνομα, θηρία καλέσας.

ΝΕ. ΣΩ. Ἦν καὶ ταῦτα οὕτως.

ΞΕ. Τὸ δέ γε, ὦ πάντων ἀνδρειότατε, τάχ' ἂν εἴ που φρόνιμόν ἐστί τι ζῷον ἕτερον, οἷον δοκεῖ τὸ τῶν γεράνων, ἤ τι τοιοῦτον ἄλλο, ὃ κατὰ ταὐτὰ ἴσως διονομάζει καθάπερ καὶ σύ, γεράνους μὲν ἓν γένος ἀντιτιθὲν τοῖς ἄλλοις ζῴοις καὶ σεμνῦνον αὐτὸ ἑαυτό, τὰ δὲ ἄλλα μετὰ τῶν ἀνθρώπων ξυλλα-

[1] εἶδος] εἴδους ΒΤ.

26

matter by and by, when we have time. Only take very good care not to imagine that you ever heard me declare flatly—

Y. SOC. What?

STR. That class and part are separate from one another.

Y. SOC. But what did you say?

STR. That when there is a class of anything, it must necessarily be a part of the thing of which it is said to be a class; but there is no necessity that a part be also a class. Please always give this, rather than the other, as my doctrine.

Y. SOC. I will do so.

STR. Then please go on to the next point.

Y. SOC. What is it?

STR. That from which our present digression started. For I think it started when you were asked how the art of herding should be divided and said with great readiness that there were two kinds of living beings, the human race and a second one, a single class, comprising all the beasts.

Y. SOC. True.

STR. And it was clear to me at the time that you removed a part and then thought that the remainder was one class because you were able to call them all by the same name of beasts.

Y. SOC. That is true, too.

STR. But indeed, my most courageous young friend, perhaps, if there is any other animal capable of thought, such as the crane appears to be, or any other like creature, and it perchance gives names, just as you do, it might in its pride of self oppose cranes to all other animals, and group the rest, men included, under one head, calling them by one name,

27

PLATO

βὸν εἰς ταὐτὸ οὐδὲν ἄλλο πλὴν ἴσως θηρία προσείποι. πειραθῶμεν οὖν ἡμεῖς ἐξευλαβεῖσθαι πάνθ' ὁπόσα τοιαῦτα.

E   ΝΕ. ΣΩ. Πῶς;

ΞΕ. Μὴ πᾶν τὸ τῶν ζῴων γένος διαιρούμενοι, ἵνα ἧττον αὐτὰ πάσχωμεν.

ΝΕ. ΣΩ. Οὐδὲν γὰρ δεῖ.

ΞΕ. Καὶ γὰρ οὖν καὶ τότε ἡμαρτάνετο ταύτῃ.

ΝΕ. ΣΩ. Τί δή;

ΞΕ. Τῆς γνωστικῆς ὅσον ἐπιτακτικὸν ἡμῖν μέρος ἦν που τοῦ ζῳοτροφικοῦ γένους, ἀγελαίων μὴν ζῴων. ἦ γάρ;

ΝΕ. ΣΩ. Ναί.

ΞΕ. Διῄρητο τοίνυν ἤδη καὶ τότε ξύμπαν τὸ ζῷον 264 τῷ τιθασῷ καὶ ἀγρίῳ. τὰ μὲν γὰρ ἔχοντα τιθασεύεσθαι φύσιν ἥμερα προσείρηται, τὰ δὲ μὴ ἔχοντα ἄγρια.

ΝΕ. ΣΩ. Καλῶς.

ΞΕ. Ἦν δέ γε θηρεύομεν ἐπιστήμην, ἐν τοῖς ἡμέροις ἦν τε καὶ ἔστιν, ἐπὶ τοῖς ἀγελαίοις μὴν ζητητέα θρέμμασιν.

ΝΕ. ΣΩ. Ναί.

ΞΕ. Μὴ τοίνυν διαιρώμεθα ὥσπερ τότε πρὸς ἅπαντα ἀποβλέψαντες, μηδὲ σπεύσαντες, ἵνα δὴ B ταχὺ γενώμεθα πρὸς τῇ πολιτικῇ. πεποίηκε γὰρ ἡμᾶς καὶ νῦν παθεῖν τὸ κατὰ τὴν παροιμίαν πάθος.

ΝΕ. ΣΩ. Ποῖον;

ΞΕ. Οὐχ ἡσύχους εὖ διαιροῦντας ἠνυκέναι βραδύτερον.

28

which might very well be that of beasts. Now let us try to be on our guard against all that sort of thing.

Y. SOC. How can we guard against it?

STR. By not dividing the whole class of living beings, that so we may avoid such errors.

Y. SOC. Well, there is no need of dividing the whole.

STR. No, certainly not, for it was in that way that we fell into our former error.

Y. SOC. What do you mean?

STR. That part of intellectual science which involves giving commands was a part of our animal-tending class, with especial reference to animals in herds, was it not?

Y. SOC. Yes.

STR. Well, even at that stage of our discussion all animals had already been divided into tame and wild. For if their nature admits of domestication they are called tame; if it does not, they are called wild.

Y. SOC. Excellent.

STR. But the science we are hunting for was, and is, to be sought among tame creatures, more specifically creatures in herds.

Y. SOC. Yes.

STR. Let us, then, not make our division as we did before, with a view to all, nor in a hurry, with the idea that we may thus reach political science quickly, for that has already brought upon us the proverbial penalty.

Y. SOC. What penalty?

STR. The penalty of having made less speed, because we made too much haste and did not make our division right.

ΝΕ. ΣΩ. Καὶ καλῶς γε, ὦ ξένε, πεποίηκεν.

8. ΞΕ. Ταῦτ' ἔστω. πάλιν δ' οὖν ἐξ ἀρχῆς τὴν κοινοτροφικὴν πειρώμεθα διαιρεῖν· ἴσως γὰρ καὶ τοῦτο ὃ σὺ προθυμεῖ διαπεραινόμενος ὁ λόγος αὐτός σοι κάλλιον μηνύσει. καί μοι φράζε.

ΝΕ. ΣΩ. Ποῖον δή;

ΞΕ. Τόδε, εἴ τινων πολλάκις ἄρα διακήκοας· οὐ
C γὰρ δὴ προστυχής γε αὐτὸς οἶδ' ὅτι γέγονας ταῖς ἐν τῷ Νείλῳ τιθασείαις τῶν ἰχθύων καὶ τῶν ἐν ταῖς βασιλικαῖς λίμναις. ἐν μὲν γὰρ κρήναις τάχ' ἂν ἴσως εἴης ᾐσθημένος.

ΝΕ. ΣΩ. Πάνυ μὲν οὖν καὶ ταῦτα τεθέαμαι κἀκεῖνα πολλῶν ἀκήκοα.

ΞΕ. Καὶ μὴν χηνοβωτίας γε καὶ γερανοβωτίας, εἰ καὶ μὴ πεπλάνησαι περὶ τὰ Θετταλικὰ πεδία, πέπυσαι γοῦν καὶ πιστεύεις εἶναι.

ΝΕ. ΣΩ. Τί μήν;

D ΞΕ. Τοῦδ' ἕνεκά τοι πάντα ἠρώτησα ταῦτα, διότι τῆς τῶν ἀγελαίων τροφῆς ἔστι μὲν ἔνυδρον, ἔστι δὲ καὶ ξηροβατικόν.

ΝΕ. ΣΩ. Ἔστι γὰρ οὖν.

ΞΕ. Ἆρ' οὖν καὶ σοὶ ξυνδοκεῖ ταύτῃ δεῖν διχάζειν τὴν κοινοτροφικὴν ἐπιστήμην, ἐφ' ἑκατέρῳ τούτων τὸ μέρος αὐτῆς ἐπινέμοντας ἑκάτερον, τὸ μὲν ἕτερον ὑγροτροφικὸν ὀνομάζοντας, τὸ δ' ἕτερον ξηροτροφικόν;

ΝΕ. ΣΩ. Ἔμοιγε.

ΞΕ. Καὶ μὴν καὶ τὸ βασιλικὸν οὕτως οὐ ζη-
E τήσομεν ὁποτέρας ἐστὶ τῆς τέχνης· δῆλον γὰρ[1] παντί.

ΝΕ. ΣΩ. Πῶς δ' οὔ;

[1] γὰρ Burnet : δὴ γὰρ ΒΤ.

y. soc. And it was a good thing for us, Stranger.

str. I do not deny it. So let us begin again and try to divide the art of tending animals in common; for perhaps the information you desire so much will come to you in the ordinary course of our conversation better than by other means. Tell me—

y. soc. What?

str. Whether, as I suppose, you have often heard people speak of this,—for I know you never actually saw the preserves of fish in the Nile and in the ponds of the Persian king. But perhaps you have noticed the like in fountain-pools.

y. soc. Yes, I have often seen the fish in fountain-pools and have heard many tales of those foreign preserves.

str. And surely, even if you have not wandered over the plains of Thessaly, you have heard of goose-farms and crane-farms there and you believe that they exist.

y. soc. Yes, of course.

str. The reason why I asked you all these questions is that the rearing of flocks is in part aquatic and in part an affair of the dry land.

y. soc. Yes, that is true.

str. Then do you agree that we ought to divide the art of tending animals in common into corresponding parts, assigning one part of it to each of these two, and calling one the art of aquatic-herding and the other the art of land-herding?

y. soc. Yes, I agree.

str. And surely we shall not have to ask to which of these two arts kingship belongs, for that is clear to everyone.

y. soc. Of course.

ΞΕ. Πᾶς μὲν δὴ τό γε ξηροτροφικὸν τῆς ἀγελαιοτροφίας διέλοιτ' ἂν φῦλον.

ΝΕ. ΣΩ. Πῶς;

ΞΕ. Τῷ πτηνῷ τε καὶ πεζῷ διορισάμενος.

ΝΕ. ΣΩ. Ἀληθέστατα.

ΞΕ. Τί δέ; τὸ πολιτικὸν ἢ περὶ[1] τὸ πεζὸν
ζητητέον; ἢ οὐκ οἴει καὶ τὸν ἀφρονέστατον ὡς
ἔπος εἰπεῖν δοξάξειν οὕτως;

ΝΕ. ΣΩ. Ἔγωγε.

ΞΕ. Τὴν δὲ πεζονομικήν, καθάπερ ἄρτιον ἀριθμόν,
δεῖ τεμνομένην δίχα ἀποφαίνειν.

ΝΕ. ΣΩ. Δῆλον.

265 ΞΕ. Καὶ μὴν ἐφ' ὅ γε μέρος ὥρμηκεν ἡμῖν ὁ
λόγος, ἐπ' ἐκεῖνο δύο τινὲ καθορᾶν ὁδὼ τεταμένα
φαίνεται, τὴν μὲν θάττω, πρὸς μέγα μέρος σμικρὸν
διαιρουμένην, τὴν δέ, ὅπερ ἐν τῷ πρόσθεν ἐλέγομεν
ὅτι δεῖ μεσοτομεῖν ὡς μάλιστα, τοῦτ' ἔχουσαν
μᾶλλον, μακροτέραν γε μήν. ἔξεστιν οὖν ὁποτέραν
ἂν βουληθῶμεν, ταύτην πορευθῆναι.

ΝΕ. ΣΩ. Τί δέ; ἀμφοτέρας ἀδύνατον;

ΞΕ. Ἅμα γ', ὦ θαυμαστέ· ἐν μέρει γε μὴν
δῆλον ὅτι δυνατόν.

Β ΝΕ. ΣΩ. Ἐν μέρει τοίνυν ἔγωγε ἀμφοτέρας
αἱροῦμαι.

ΞΕ. Ῥᾴδιον, ἐπειδὴ τὸ λοιπὸν βραχύ. κατ'
ἀρχὰς μὴν καὶ μεσοῦσιν ἅμα τῆς πορείας χαλεπὸν
ἂν ἦν ἡμῖν τὸ πρόσταγμα· νῦν δ', ἐπειδὴ δοκεῖ
ταύτῃ, τὴν μακροτέραν πρότερον[2] ἴωμεν· νεαλέ-
στεροι γὰρ ὄντες ῥᾶον αὐτὴν πορευσόμεθα. τὴν δὲ
δὴ διαίρεσιν ὅρα.

ΝΕ. ΣΩ. Λέγε.

---

[1] ἢ περὶ Heindorf : ὥσπερ ΒΤ.   [2] πρότερον] προτέραν ΒΤ.

str. Anybody could doubtless make a division of the art of tending herds on land.

y. soc. What would the division be?

str. Into the tending of flying and walking animals.

y. soc. Very true.

str. And statesmanship is to be sought in connexion with walking animals, is it not? Any fool, so to speak, would believe that, don't you think?

y. soc. Of course.

str. And the art of tending animals that walk must, like an even number, be divided in half.

y. soc. Evidently.

str. And now I think I see two paths leading in that direction in which our argument has started: the quicker way, by separating a relatively small part and a larger, and the other way, which is more in accord with what we said a while ago about the need of making the division as nearly in the middle as we can, but is longer. So we can proceed by whichever of the two we wish.

y. soc. Can we not go by both?

str. Not by both at once, silly boy; but obviously we can take them in turn.

y. soc. Then I choose both in turn.

str. That is easy enough, since we have but a short distance to go. At the beginning, certainly, or middle of our journey it would have been hard to comply with your demand. But now, since this is your wish, let us go first by the longer way, for we are fresher now and shall get along on it more easily. So attend to the division.

y. soc. Go on.

33

9. ΞΕ. Τὰ πεζὰ ἡμῖν τῶν ἡμέρων, ὅσαπερ ἀγελαῖα, διῃρημένα ἐστὶ φύσει δίχα.

ΝΕ. ΣΩ. Τίνι;

ΞΕ. Τῷ τῶν μὲν τὴν γένεσιν ἄκερων εἶναι, τῶν δὲ κερασφόρον.

C   ΝΕ. ΣΩ. Φαίνεται.

ΞΕ. Τὴν δὴ πεζονομικὴν διελὼν ἀπόδος ἑκατέρῳ τῷ μέρει λόγῳ χρώμενος· ἂν γὰρ ὀνομάζειν αὐτὰ βουληθῇς, ἔσται σοι περιπεπλεγμένον μᾶλλον τοῦ δέοντος.

ΝΕ. ΣΩ. Πῶς οὖν χρὴ λέγειν;

ΞΕ. Ὧδε· τῆς πεζονομικῆς ἐπιστήμης δίχα διαιρεθείσης τὸ μόριον θάτερον ἐπὶ τῷ κερασφόρῳ[1] μέρει τῷ τῆς ἀγέλης ἐπιτετάχθαι, τὸ δὲ ἕτερον ἐπὶ τῷ τῆς ἀκεράτου.

ΝΕ. ΣΩ. Ταῦτ' ἔστω ταύτῃ λεχθέντα· πάντως D γὰρ ἱκανῶς δεδήλωται.

ΞΕ. Καὶ μὴν ὅ γε βασιλεὺς ἡμῖν αὖ καταφανὴς ὅτι κολοβὸν ἀγέλην τινὰ κεράτων νομεύει.

ΝΕ. ΣΩ. Πῶς γὰρ οὐ δῆλος;

ΞΕ. Ταύτην τοίνυν καταθραύσαντες τὸ γιγνόμενον[2] αὐτῷ πειρώμεθα ἀποδοῦναι.

ΝΕ. ΣΩ. Πάνυ γε.

ΞΕ. Πότερον οὖν βούλει τῷ σχιστῷ τε καὶ τῷ καλουμένῳ μώνυχι διαιρεῖν αὐτὴν ἢ τῇ κοινογονίᾳ τε καὶ ἰδιογονίᾳ; μανθάνεις γάρ που.

ΝΕ. ΣΩ. Τὸ ποῖον;

E   ΞΕ. Ὅτι τὸ μὲν τῶν ἵππων καὶ ὄνων πέφυκεν ἐξ ἀλλήλων γεννᾶν.

ΝΕ. ΣΩ. Ναί.

---

[1] κερασφόρῳ Τ : κεροφόρῳ Β.
[2] γιγνόμενον Cornarius : κινούμενον ΒΤW.

34

str. The tame walking animals which live in herds are divided by nature into two classes.

y. soc. How by nature?

str. Because one class is naturally without horns, and the other has horns.

y. soc. That is obvious.

str. Now divide the art of tending herds of walking animals into two parts, assigning one to each class of animals; and define the parts, for if you try to give them names, the matter will become needlessly complicated.

y. soc. How shall I speak of them then?

str. In this way: say that the science which tends herds of walking animals is divided into two parts, one of which is assigned to the horned portion of the herd, the other to the hornless portion.

y. soc. Assume that I have said that; for you have made it perfectly clear.

str. And furthermore our "king" is very clearly the herdsman of a herd devoid of horns.

y. soc. Of course; that is evident.

str. Let us then try to break up this herd and give the king the part that belongs to him.

y. soc. Very well.

str. Shall we make our division on the basis of having or not having cloven hoofs, or on that of mixing or not mixing the breed? You know what I mean.

y. soc. No. What is it?

str. Why, I mean that horses and asses can breed from each other.

y. soc. Oh yes.

ΞΕ. Τὸ δέ γε λοιπὸν ἔτι τῆς λείας ἀγέλης τῶν ἡμέρων ἀμιγὲς γένει πρὸς ἄλληλα.

ΝΕ. ΣΩ. Πῶς δ' οὔ;

ΞΕ. Τί δ'; ὁ πολιτικὸς ἆρ' ἐπιμέλειαν ἔχειν φαίνεται πότερα κοινογενοῦς φύσεως ἢ τινος ἰδιογενοῦς;

ΝΕ. ΣΩ. Δῆλον ὅτι τῆς ἀμίκτου.

ΞΕ. Ταύτην δὴ δεῖ καθάπερ τὰ ἔμπροσθεν, ὡς ἔοικεν, ἡμᾶς δίχα διαστέλλειν.

ΝΕ. ΣΩ. Δεῖ γὰρ οὖν.

266 ΞΕ. Καὶ μὴν τό γε ζῷον, ὅσον ἥμερον καὶ ἀγελαῖον, σχεδὸν πλὴν γενοῖν δυοῖν πᾶν ἤδη κατακεκερμάτισται. τὸ γὰρ τῶν κυνῶν οὐκ ἐπάξιον καταριθμεῖν γένος ὡς ἐν ἀγελαίοις θρέμμασιν.

ΝΕ. ΣΩ. Οὐ γὰρ οὖν. ἀλλὰ τίνι δὴ τὼ δύο διαιροῦμεν;

ΞΕ. Ὧιπερ καὶ δίκαιόν γε Θεαίτητόν τε καὶ σὲ διανέμειν, ἐπειδὴ καὶ γεωμετρίας ἅπτεσθον.

ΝΕ. ΣΩ. Τῷ;

ΞΕ. Τῇ διαμέτρῳ δήπου καὶ πάλιν τῇ τῆς διαμέτρου διαμέτρῳ.

ΝΕ. ΣΩ. Πῶς εἶπες;

B ΞΕ. Ἡ φύσις ἣν τὸ γένος ἡμῶν τῶν ἀνθρώπων κέκτηται, μῶν ἄλλως πως εἰς τὴν πορείαν πέφυκεν ἢ καθάπερ ἡ διάμετρος ἡ δυνάμει δίπους;

ΝΕ. ΣΩ. Οὐκ ἄλλως.

---

[1] The word "diameter" here denotes the diagonal of a square. The early Greek mathematicians worked out their arithmetical problems largely by geometrical methods (cf. *Theaetetus* 147 D ff.). The diagonal of the unit square ($\sqrt{2}$) was naturally of especial interest. It was called sometimes, as here, simply ἡ διάμετρος, sometimes, as just below, ἡ διάμετρος ἡ δυνάμει δίπους, or, more briefly, ἡ διάμετρος

sтв. But the rest of the herd of hornless tame animals cannot cross the breed.

y. soc. That is true, of course.

sтв. Well then, does the statesman appear to have charge of a kind that mixes or of one that does not mix the breed?

y. soc. Evidently of one that is unmixed.

sтв. So I suppose we must proceed as we have done heretofore and divide this into two parts.

y. soc. Yes, we must.

sтв. And yet tame gregarious animals have all, with the exception of about two species, been already divided; for dogs are not properly to be counted among gregarious creatures.

y. soc. No, they are not. But how shall we divide the two species?

sтв. As you and Theaetetus ought by rights to divide them, since you are interested in geometry.

y. soc. How do you mean?

sтв. By the diameter, of course, and again by the diameter of the square of the diameter.[1]

y. soc. What do you mean by that?

sтв. Is the nature which our human race possesses related to walking in any other way than as the diameter which is the square root of two feet?[2]

y. soc. No.

δίπους. Given a square the side of which is the unit (*i.e.* one square foot), the length of the diagonal will be $\sqrt{2}$, and the square constructed with that diagonal as its side will contain two square feet. The length of the diagonal of this square will be $\sqrt{4}=2$ feet, and its area will be four square feet.

[2] There is here a play upon words. Man, being a two-footed (δίπους) animal, is compared to the diagonal of the unit square ($\sqrt{2}$, διάμετρος δίπους).

ΞΕ. Καὶ μὴν ἥ γε τοῦ λοιποῦ γένους πάλιν ἐστὶ
κατὰ δύναμιν αὖ τῆς ἡμετέρας δυνάμεως διάμετρος,
εἴπερ δυοῖν γέ ἐστι ποδοῖν δὶς πεφυκυῖα.

ΝΕ. ΣΩ. Πῶς δ' οὐκ ἔστι; καὶ δὴ καὶ σχεδὸν
ὃ βούλει δηλοῦν μανθάνω.

ΞΕ. Πρὸς δὴ τούτοις ἕτερον αὖ τι τῶν πρὸς
γέλωτα εὐδοκιμησάντων ἄν, ὦ Σώκρατες, ἆρα καθ-
C ορῶμεν ἡμῖν γεγονὸς ἐν τοῖς διῃρημένοις;

ΝΕ. ΣΩ. Τὸ ποῖον;

ΞΕ. Τἀνθρώπινον ἡμῶν ἅμα γένος ξυνειληχὸς
καὶ ξυνδεδραμηκὸς γένει τῷ τῶν ὄντων γενναιοτάτῳ
καὶ ἅμα εὐχερεστάτῳ.

ΝΕ. ΣΩ. Καθορῶ καὶ μάλ' ἀτόπως[1] ξυμβαῖνον.

ΞΕ. Τί δ'; οὐκ εἰκὸς ὕστατα ἀφικνεῖσθαι τὰ
βραδύτατα;

ΝΕ. ΣΩ. Ναί, τοῦτό γε.

ΞΕ. Τόδε δὲ οὐκ ἐννοοῦμεν, ὡς ἔτι γελοιότερος
ὁ βασιλεὺς φαίνεται μετὰ τῆς ἀγέλης ξυνδιαθέων
καὶ ξύνδρομα πεπορευμένος τῷ τῶν ἀνδρῶν αὖ πρὸς
D τὸν εὐχερῆ βίον ἄριστα γεγυμνασμένῳ;

ΝΕ. ΣΩ. Παντάπασι μὲν οὖν.

ΞΕ. Νῦν γάρ, ὦ Σώκρατες, ἐκεῖνό ἐστι κατα-
φανὲς μᾶλλον τὸ ῥηθὲν τότ' ἐν τῇ περὶ τὸν σοφιστὴν
ζητήσει.

ΝΕ. ΣΩ. Τὸ ποῖον;

ΞΕ. Ὅτι τῇ τοιᾷδε μεθόδῳ τῶν λόγων οὔτε
σεμνοτέρου μᾶλλον ἐμέλησεν ἢ μή, τόν τε σμικρό-

---

[1] μάλ' ἀτόπως] μάλα τὸ πῶς ΒΤ.

---

[1] *i.e.* the remaining species is four-footed. Our diameter
is $\sqrt{2}$, and four is the area of the square constructed on
the diagonal of the square which has $\sqrt{2}$ as its side. All

THE STATESMAN

STR. And the nature of the remaining species, again, considered from the point of view of the square root, is the diameter of the square of our root, if it is the nature of twice two feet.[1]

Y. SOC. Of course; and now I think I almost understand what you wish to make plain.

STR. Socrates, do we see that besides this something else has turned up in these divisions of ours which would be a famous joke?

Y. SOC. No. What is it?

STR. Our human race shares the same lot and runs in the same heat as the most excellent and at the same time most easy-going race of creatures.[2]

Y. SOC. Yes, I see that; it is a very queer result.

STR. Indeed? But is it not reasonable that they arrive last, who are the slowest?

Y. SOC. Yes, that is true.

STR. And do we fail to notice this further point, that the king appears in a still more ridiculous light, running along with the herd and paired in the race with the man of all others who is most in training for a life of careless ease?[3]

Y. SOC. Certainly he does.

STR. For now, Socrates, we have shown more clearly the truth of that which we said yesterday in our search for the sophist.[4]

Y. SOC. What was it?

STR. That this method of argument pays no more heed to the noble than to the ignoble, and no less

this satirizes the tendency of contemporary thinkers to play with numbers.

[2] The animal referred to is the pig. See P. Shorey, *Classical Philology*, 1917, July, p. 308.

[3] *i.e.* the swineherd, the pig belonging to γένει εὐχερεστάτῳ.

[4] See *Sophist* 227 B.

τερον οὐδὲν ἠτίμακε πρὸ τοῦ μείζονος, ἀεὶ δὲ καθ᾽
αὑτὴν περαίνει τἀληθέστατον.

ΝΕ. ΣΩ. Ἔοικεν.

ΞΕ. Οὐκοῦν μετὰ τοῦτο, ἵνα μή με φθῇς[1] ἐρω-
τήσας, τὴν βραχυτέραν ὁδὸν ἥτις τότε ἦν ἐπὶ τὸν
Ε τοῦ βασιλέως ὅρον, αὐτός σοι πρότερον ἔλθω;

ΝΕ. ΣΩ. Σφόδρα γε.

ΞΕ. Λέγω δὴ δεῖν τότε εὐθὺς τὸ πεζὸν τῷ δίποδι
πρὸς τὸ[2] τετράπουν γένος διανεῖμαι, κατιδόντα
δὲ τἀνθρώπινον ἔτι μόνῳ τῷ πτηνῷ ξυνειληχὸς τὴν
δίποδα ἀγέλην πάλιν τῷ ψιλῷ καὶ τῷ πτεροφυεῖ
τέμνειν, τμηθείσης δὲ αὐτῆς καὶ τότ᾽ ἤδη τῆς
ἀνθρωπονομικῆς δηλωθείσης τέχνης, φέροντα τὸν
πολιτικὸν καὶ βασιλικὸν οἷον ἡνίοχον εἰς αὐτὴν ἐν-
στήσαντα, παραδοῦναι τὰς τῆς πόλεως ἡνίας ὡς
οἰκείας καὶ αὐτῷ ταύτης οὔσης τῆς ἐπιστήμης.

267   ΝΕ. ΣΩ. Καλῶς καὶ καθαπερεὶ χρέος ἀπέδω-
κάς μοι τὸν λόγον, προσθεὶς τὴν ἐκτροπὴν οἷον
τόκον καὶ ἀναπληρώσας αὐτόν.

ΙΟ.   ΞΕ. Φέρε δὴ καὶ ξυνείρωμεν ἐπανελθόντες
ἐπὶ τὴν ἀρχὴν μέχρι τῆς τελευτῆς τὸν λόγον τοῦ
ὀνόματος τῆς τοῦ πολιτικοῦ τέχνης.

ΝΕ. ΣΩ. Πάνυ μὲν οὖν.

ΞΕ. Τῆς γνωστικῆς τοίνυν ἐπιστήμης ἡμῖν ἦν
κατ᾽ ἀρχὰς μέρος ἐπιτακτικόν· τούτου δὲ ἀπεικα-
σθὲν τὸ μόριον αὐτεπιτακτικὸν[3] ἐρρήθη. ζῳοτρο-
Β φικὴ δὲ πάλιν αὐτεπιτακτικῆς οὐ τὸ σμικρότατον
τῶν γενῶν ἀπεσχίζετο· καὶ ζῳοτροφικῆς εἶδος
ἀγελαιοτροφικόν, ἀγελαιοτροφικοῦ δ᾽ αὖ πεζονομι-

---

[1] με φθῇς Stephanus e Ficino : μ᾽ ἔφθης Β : μεμφθῇς T.
[2] τὸ D, Stallbaum : om. ΒΤ.
[3] αὐτεπιτακτικὸν] αὐτεπίτακτον ΒΤ.

honour to the small than to the great, but always goes on its own way to the most perfect truth.

Y. SOC. So it seems.

STR. Then shall I now, without waiting for you to ask me, guide you of my own accord along that shorter way referred to a moment ago that leads to the definition of the king?

Y. SOC. By all means.

STR. I say, then, that we ought at that time to have divided walking animals immediately into biped and quadruped, then seeing that the human race falls into the same division with the feathered creatures and no others, we must again divide the biped class into featherless and feathered, and when that division is made and the art of herding human beings is made plain, we ought to take the statesmanlike and kingly man and place him as a sort of charioteer therein, handing over to him the reins of the state, because that is his own proper science.

Y. SOC. You have cleared up the argument finely, and as if it were a debt you were paying, you threw in the digression as interest and for good measure.

STR. Now let us go back to the beginning and join together the definition of the name of the statesman's art link by link to the end.

Y. SOC. By all means.

STR. In the first place we said that intellectual science had a part that gives commands; and a portion of this was called by a comparison the part that gives its own commands; and again the art of rearing living beings was singled out, which is by no means the smallest part of the art which gives its own commands; and a class of rearing living beings was herd-tending, and a part of this again the herding

41

κόν· τοῦ δὲ πεζονομικοῦ μάλιστα ἀπετέμνετο
τέχνη τῆς ἀκεράτου φύσεως θρεπτική. ταύτης
δ᾽ αὖ τὸ μέρος οὐκ ἔλαττον τριπλοῦν συμπλέκειν
ἀναγκαῖον, ἂν εἰς ἕν τις αὐτὸ ὄνομα ξυναγαγεῖν
βουληθῇ, γενέσεως ἀμίκτου[1] νομευτικὴν[2] ἐπιστήμην προσαγορεύων. τὸ δ᾽ ἀπὸ τούτου τμῆμα, ἐπὶ
C ποίμνη δίποδι μέρος ἀνθρωπονομικὸν ἔτι λειφθὲν
μόνον, τοῦτ᾽ αὐτό ἐστιν ἤδη τὸ ζητηθέν, ἅμα
βασιλικὸν ταὐτὸν κληθὲν καὶ πολιτικόν.

ΝΕ. ΣΩ. Παντάπασι μὲν οὖν.

ΞΕ. Ἆρά γ᾽, ὦ Σώκρατες, ἀληθῶς ἡμῖν τοῦτο
καθάπερ σὺ νῦν εἴρηκας οὕτως ἐστὶ καὶ πεπραγμέ-
νον;

ΝΕ. ΣΩ. Τὸ ποῖον δή;

ΞΕ. Τὸ παντάπασιν ἱκανῶς εἰρῆσθαι τὸ προτεθέν·
ἢ τοῦτ᾽ αὐτὸ καὶ μάλιστα ἡ ζήτησις ἐλλείπει, τὸ
τὸν λόγον εἰρῆσθαι μέν πως, οὐ μὴν παντάπασί
D γε τελέως ἀπειργάσθαι;

ΝΕ. ΣΩ. Πῶς εἶπες;

ΞΕ. Ἐγὼ νῷν πειράσομαι τοῦτ᾽ αὐτὸ ὃ διανοοῦμαι νῦν ἔτι μᾶλλον δηλῶσαι.

ΝΕ. ΣΩ. Λέγοις ἄν.

ΞΕ. Οὐκοῦν τῶν νομευτικῶν ἡμῖν πολλῶν φανει-
σῶν ἄρτι τεχνῶν μία τις ἦν ἡ πολιτικὴ καὶ μιᾶς
τινος ἀγέλης ἐπιμέλεια;

ΝΕ. ΣΩ. Ναί.

ΞΕ. Ταύτην δέ γε διώριζεν ὁ λόγος οὐχ ἵππων
εἶναι τροφὸν οὐδ᾽ ἄλλων θηρίων, ἀλλ᾽ ἀνθρώπων
κοινοτροφικὴν ἐπιστήμην.

ΝΕ. ΣΩ. Οὕτως.

---

[1] ἀμίκτου Boeckh : μικτοῦ ΒΤ.
[2] νομευτικὴν Heindorf : νομευτικῆς ΒΤ.

of walking animals ; and from the herding of walking animals the art of rearing those without horns was divided. And of this in turn one part will have to be treated as no less than threefold, if it is to be called by one comprehensive name, and it will be called (1) the science (2) of tending herds (3) which do not cross breeds. But the only possible further subdivision of this is the art of herding human beings, and this is at last what we are looking for, the single art called both kingly and statesmanlike.

y. soc. That is perfectly true.

str. And yet, Socrates, have we truly accomplished this, exactly as you have said ?

y. soc. Accomplished what ?

str. The perfectly satisfactory discussion of our subject. Or is our investigation incomplete in just this detail, that we have given a definition after a fashion, but have not perfectly completed it ?

y. soc. What do you mean ?

str. I will try to make still plainer to us both the thought which I now have in mind.

y. soc. Please do so.

str. We found just now that there were many arts of herding, and one of them was the art of statesmanship, which was the care of one particular kind of herd, did we not ?

y. soc. Yes.

str. And our argument defined this, not as the tending of horses or other beasts, but as the science of tending men in common.

y. soc. Yes, it did.

43

E   11.   ΞΕ. Τὸ δὴ τῶν νομέων πάντων διάφορον
καὶ τὸ τῶν βασιλέων θεασώμεθα.

ΝΕ. ΣΩ. Τὸ ποῖον;

ΞΕ. Εἴ τις τῶν ἄλλων τω¹ τέχνης ἄλλης ὄνομα
ἔχων κοινῇ τῆς ἀγέλης ξύντροφος εἶναί φησι καὶ
προσποιεῖται.

ΝΕ. ΣΩ. Πῶς φής;

ΞΕ. Οἷον οἱ ἔμποροι καὶ γεωργοὶ καὶ σιτουργοὶ
πάντες, καὶ πρὸς τούτοις γυμνασταὶ καὶ τὸ τῶν
ἰατρῶν γένος, οἶσθ᾽ ὅτι τοῖς περὶ τὰ ἀνθρώπινα
νομεῦσιν, οὓς πολιτικοὺς ἐκαλέσαμεν, παντάπασι
268 τῷ λόγῳ διαμάχοιντ᾽ ἂν οὗτοι σύμπαντες, ὡς
σφεῖς τῆς τροφῆς ἐπιμελοῦνται τῆς ἀνθρωπίνης,
οὐ μόνον ἀγελαίων ἀνθρώπων, ἀλλὰ καὶ τῆς τῶν
ἀρχόντων αὐτῶν;

ΝΕ. ΣΩ. Οὐκοῦν ὀρθῶς ἂν λέγοιεν;

ΞΕ. Ἴσως. καὶ τοῦτο μὲν ἐπισκεψόμεθα, τόδε
δὲ ἴσμεν, ὅτι βουκόλῳ γε οὐδεὶς ἀμφισβητήσει
περὶ τούτων οὐδενός, ἀλλ᾽ αὐτὸς τῆς ἀγέλης τροφὸς
ὁ βουφορβός, αὐτὸς ἰατρός, αὐτὸς οἷον νυμφευτὴς
B καὶ περὶ τοὺς τῶν γιγνομένων τόκους καὶ λοχείας
μόνος ἐπιστήμων τῆς μαιευτικῆς· ἔτι τοίνυν παιδιᾶς καὶ μουσικῆς ἐφ᾽ ὅσον αὐτοῦ τὰ θρέμματα
φύσει μετείληφεν, οὐκ ἄλλος κρείττων παραμυθεῖσ-
θαι καὶ κηλῶν πραΰνειν, μετά τε ὀργάνων καὶ ψιλῷ
τῷ στόματι τὴν τῆς αὐτοῦ ποίμνης ἄριστα μετα-
χειριζόμενος μουσικήν· καὶ δὴ καὶ τῶν ἄλλων
περὶ νομέων ὁ αὐτὸς τρόπος. ἦ γάρ;

ΝΕ. ΣΩ. Ὀρθότατα.

ΞΕ. Πῶς οὖν ἡμῖν ὁ λόγος ὀρθὸς φανεῖται καὶ
ἀκέραιος ὁ περὶ τοῦ βασιλέως, ὅταν αὐτὸν νομέα καὶ

¹ τῳ G : τῷ T : τὸ B.

44

str. Let us, then, observe the point of difference between kings and all other herdsmen.

y. soc. What point of difference?

str. Let us see whether anyone who is designated by the name of another art says and claims that he is fellow manager of the herd in common with any of the other kinds of herdsmen.

y. soc. What do you mean?

str. For instance, merchants, husbandmen, and all who prepare grain for use, and also gymnastic trainers and physicians would certainly all dispute with the herdsmen of humanity, whom we have called statesmen, and would assert that they themselves take care of the tending of humanity, and not the tending of the common herd only, but even that of the rulers themselves, would they not?

y. soc. And would they be right?

str. Perhaps. We will examine that matter; but this we know, that no one will ever raise such a contention against any neatherd, but the herdsman himself tends the herd, he is their physician, he is their matchmaker, and he alone knows the midwife's science of aiding at the birth of their offspring. Moreover, so far as the nature of the creatures allows them to enjoy sport or music, no one can enliven or soothe them better than he; whether with instruments or merely with his voice he performs the music best suited to his own herd; and the same applies to the other herdsmen. Is not that the case?

y. soc. You are quite right.

str. Then how can our discourse about the king be right and free from error, when we pick him out

C τροφὸν ἀγέλης ἀνθρωπίνης θῶμεν μόνον ἐκκρί-
νοντες μυρίων ἄλλων ἀμφισβητούντων;

ΝΕ. ΣΩ. Οὐδαμῶς.

ΞΕ. Οὐκοῦν ὀρθῶς ὀλίγον ἔμπροσθεν ἐφοβήθη-
μεν ὑποπτεύσαντες μὴ λέγοντες μέν τι τυγχάνοιμεν
σχῆμα βασιλικόν, οὐ μὴν ἀπειργασμένοι γε εἶμέν πω
δι᾽ ἀκριβείας τὸν πολιτικόν, ἕως ἂν τοὺς περικεχυ-
μένους αὐτῷ καὶ τῆς συννομῆς αὐτῷ ἀντιποιου-
μένους περιελόντες καὶ χωρίσαντες ἀπ᾽ ἐκείνων
καθαρὸν μόνον αὐτὸν ἀποφήνωμεν;

D ΝΕ. ΣΩ. Ὀρθότατα μὲν οὖν.

ΞΕ. Τοῦτο τοίνυν, ὦ Σώκρατες, ἡμῖν ποιητέον,
εἰ μὴ μέλλομεν[1] ἐπὶ τῷ τέλει καταισχῦναι τὸν
λόγον.

ΝΕ. ΣΩ. Ἀλλὰ μὴν οὐδαμῶς τοῦτό γε δραστέον.

12. ΞΕ. Πάλιν τοίνυν ἐξ ἄλλης ἀρχῆς δεῖ καθ᾽
ἑτέραν ὁδὸν πορευθῆναί τινα.

ΝΕ. ΣΩ. Ποίαν δή;

ΞΕ. Σχεδὸν παιδιὰν ἐγκερασαμένους· συχνῷ γὰρ
μέρει δεῖ μεγάλου μύθου προσχρήσασθαι, καὶ τὸ
λοιπὸν δή, καθάπερ ἐν τοῖς πρόσθεν, μέρος ἀεὶ
E μέρους ἀφαιρουμένους ἐπ᾽ ἄκρον ἀφικνεῖσθαι τὸ
ζητούμενον. οὐκοῦν χρή;

ΝΕ. ΣΩ. Πάνυ μὲν οὖν.

ΞΕ. Ἀλλὰ δὴ τῷ μύθῳ μου πάνυ πρόσεχε τὸν
νοῦν, καθάπερ οἱ παῖδες· πάντως οὐ πολλὰ ἐκ-
φεύγεις παιδιὰς[2] ἔτη.

ΝΕ. ΣΩ. Λέγοις ἄν.

ΞΕ. Ἦν τοίνυν καὶ ἔτι ἔσται τῶν πάλαι λεχθέν-

---

[1] μέλλομεν Ast : μέλλοιμεν ΒΤ.
[2] παιδιὰς Campbell : παιδιας ΒΤ : παιδίας Stephanus :
παιδείας al.

46

alone as herdsman and tender of the human herd,
while countless others dispute his claim?

y. soc. It cannot possibly be right.

str. We suspected a little while ago that although
we might be outlining a sort of kingly shape we had not
yet perfected an accurate portrait of the statesman,
and could not do so until, by removing those who
crowd about him and contend with him for a share
in his herdsmanship, we separated him from them
and made him stand forth alone and uncontaminated.
Was our fear justified?

y. soc. It certainly was.

str. Then we must attend to that, Socrates, if
we are not to end our argument in disgrace.

y. soc. But we certainly must not do that.

str. Then we must begin again from a new
starting-point and travel by a different road.

y. soc. By what road?

str. By one which offers us some amusement;
for there is a famous story a great part of which it
is really our duty to insert into our discussion; and
then after that we can proceed as before, by elimin-
ating part after part, and in that way reach the
ultimate object of our search. Shall we do that?

y. soc. By all means.

str. Then please pay careful attention to my
story, just as if you were a child; and anyway you
are not much too old for children's tales.

y. soc. Please tell the story.

str. Of the portents recorded in ancient tales

τῶν πολλά τε ἄλλα καὶ δὴ καὶ τὸ περὶ τὴν Ἀτρέως
τε καὶ Θυέστου λεχθεῖσαν ἔριν φάσμα. ἀκήκοας
γάρ που καὶ ἀπομνημονεύεις ὅ φασι γενέσθαι τότε.

ΝΕ. ΣΩ. Τὸ περὶ τῆς χρυσῆς ἀρνὸς ἴσως σημεῖον
φράζεις.

269   ΞΕ. Οὐδαμῶς, ἀλλὰ τὸ περὶ τῆς μεταβολῆς
δύσεώς τε καὶ ἀνατολῆς ἡλίου καὶ τῶν ἄλλων
ἄστρων, ὡς ἄρα ὅθεν μὲν ἀνατέλλει νῦν, εἰς τοῦτον
τότε τὸν τόπον ἐδύετο, ἀνέτελλε δ᾽ ἐκ τοῦ ἐναντίου,
τότε δὲ δὴ μαρτυρήσας ἄρα ὁ θεὸς Ἀτρεῖ μετέ-
βαλεν αὐτὸ ἐπὶ τὸ νῦν σχῆμα.

ΝΕ. ΣΩ. Λέγεται γὰρ οὖν δὴ καὶ τοῦτο.

ΞΕ. Καὶ μὴν αὖ καὶ τήν γε βασιλείαν ἣν ἦρξε
Κρόνος πολλῶν ἀκηκόαμεν.

B   ΝΕ. ΣΩ. Πλείστων μὲν οὖν.

ΞΕ. Τί δέ; τὸ τοὺς ἔμπροσθεν φύεσθαι γηγενεῖς
καὶ μὴ ἐξ ἀλλήλων γεννᾶσθαι;

ΝΕ. ΣΩ. Καὶ τοῦτο ἓν τῶν πάλαι λεχθέντων.

ΞΕ. Ταῦτα τοίνυν ἔστι μὲν ξύμπαντα ἐκ ταὐτοῦ
πάθους, καὶ πρὸς τούτοις ἕτερα μυρία καὶ τούτων
ἔτι θαυμαστότερα, διὰ δὲ χρόνου πλῆθος τὰ μὲν
αὐτῶν ἀπέσβηκε, τὰ δὲ διεσπαρμένα εἴρηται χωρὶς
ἕκαστα ἀπ᾽ ἀλλήλων. ὃ δ᾽ ἐστὶ πᾶσι τούτοις
C αἴτιον τὸ πάθος οὐδεὶς εἴρηκεν, νῦν δὲ δὴ λεκτέον·
εἰς γὰρ τὴν τοῦ βασιλέως ἀπόδειξιν πρέψει ῥηθέν.

---

[1] Hermes revenged upon the Pelopidae the death of his
son Myrtilus by causing a lamb with golden fleece to be
born among the flocks of Atreus. When his claim to the
succession was disputed, Atreus promised to show this
prodigy to prove that the gods were on his side. Thyestes
persuaded Aërope, the wife of Atreus, to give him the lamb,
and Atreus was in danger of losing his kingdom, had not
Zeus, who favoured his claim, made the sun and the Pleiades

many did happen and will happen again. Such an one is the portent connected with the tale of the quarrel between Atreus and Thyestes. You have doubtless heard of it and remember what is said to have taken place.

Y. SOC. You refer, I suppose, to the token of the golden lamb.[1]

STR. Oh no; I mean the change in the rising and setting of the sun and the other heavenly bodies, how in those times they used to set in the quarter where they now rise, and used to rise where they now set, but the god at the time of the quarrel, you recall, changed all that to the present system as a testimony in favour of Atreus.

Y. SOC. Yes, I've heard that, too.

STR. And again we have often heard the tale of the reign of Cronus.

Y. SOC. Yes, very often.

STR. And how about the story that the ancient folk were earthborn and not begotten of one another?

Y. SOC. That is one of the old tales, too.

STR. Well, all these stories and others still more remarkable have their source in one and the same event, but in the lapse of ages some of them have been lost and others are told in fragmentary and disconnected fashion. But no one has told the event which is the cause of them all, and so I must tell it now; for that will help us to make clear the nature of the king.

return from their setting towards their rising. This is the form of the story given in a scholium on Euripides, *Orestes*, 988, and Plato seems to have this form in mind, though variants existed. The lamb was a token (σημεῖον) of the favour of the gods, and the changed course of the sun and stars was a testimony (μαρτυρήσας) to the right of Atreus.

13. ΝΕ. ΣΩ. Κάλλιστ᾽ εἶπες, καὶ λέγε μηδὲν ἐλλείπων.

ΞΕ. Ἀκούοις ἄν. τὸ γὰρ πᾶν τόδε τοτὲ μὲν αὐτὸς ὁ θεὸς ξυμποδηγεῖ πορευόμενον καὶ συγκυκλεῖ, τοτὲ δ᾽ ἀνῆκεν, ὅταν αἱ περίοδοι τοῦ προσήκοντος αὐτῷ μέτρον εἰλήφωσιν ἤδη χρόνου, τὸ δὲ πάλιν D αὐτόματον εἰς τἀναντία περιάγεται, ζῷον ὂν καὶ φρόνησιν εἰληχὸς ἐκ τοῦ συναρμόσαντος αὐτὸ κατ᾽ ἀρχάς. τοῦτο δὲ αὐτῷ τὸ ἀνάπαλιν ἰέναι διὰ τόδ᾽ ἐξ ἀνάγκης ἔμφυτον γέγονεν.

ΝΕ. ΣΩ. Διὰ τὸ ποῖον δή;

ΞΕ. Τὸ κατὰ ταὐτὰ καὶ ὡσαύτως ἔχειν ἀεὶ καὶ ταὐτὸν εἶναι τοῖς πάντων θειοτάτοις προσήκει μόνοις, σώματος δὲ φύσις οὐ ταύτης τῆς τάξεως. ὃν δὲ οὐρανὸν καὶ κόσμον ἐπωνομάκαμεν, πολλῶν μὲν καὶ μακαρίων παρὰ τοῦ γεννήσαντος μετείληφεν, ἀτὰρ οὖν δὴ κεκοινώνηκέ γε καὶ σώματος· E ὅθεν αὐτῷ μεταβολῆς ἀμοίρῳ γίγνεσθαι διὰ παντὸς ἀδύνατον, κατὰ δύναμίν γε μὴν ὅτι μάλιστα ἐν τῷ αὐτῷ κατὰ ταὐτὰ μίαν φορὰν κινεῖται· διὸ τὴν ἀνακύκλησιν εἴληχεν, ὅτι σμικροτάτην τῆς αὑτοῦ κινήσεως παράλλαξιν. αὐτὸ δὲ ἑαυτὸ στρέφειν ἀεὶ σχεδὸν οὐδενὶ δυνατὸν πλὴν τῷ τῶν κινουμένων αὖ πάντων ἡγουμένῳ· κινεῖν δὲ τούτῳ τοτὲ μὲν ἄλλως, αὖθις δὲ ἐναντίως οὐ θέμις. ἐκ πάντων δὴ τούτων τὸν κόσμον μήτε αὐτὸν χρὴ φάναι στρέφειν ἑαυτὸν ἀεί, μήτ᾽ αὖ ὅλον ἀεὶ ὑπὸ θεοῦ στρέφεσθαι διττὰς καὶ ἐναντίας περιαγωγάς, μήτ᾽ 270 αὖ δύο τινὲ θεὼ φρονοῦντε ἑαυτοῖς ἐναντία στρέφειν αὐτόν, ἀλλ᾽ ὅπερ ἄρτι ἐρρήθη καὶ μόνον λοιπόν,

50

Y. SOC. Very good; just tell your tale and omit nothing.

STR. Listen then. During a certain period God himself goes with the universe as guide in its revolving course, but at another epoch, when the cycles have at length reached the measure of his allotted time, he lets it go, and of its own accord it turns backward in the opposite direction, since it is a living creature and is endowed with intelligence by him who fashioned it in the beginning. Now this reversal of its motion is an inevitable part of its nature for the following reason.

Y. SOC. What reason?

STR. Absolute and perpetual immutability is a property of only the most divine things of all, and body does not belong to this class. Now that which we call heaven and the universe has received from its creator many blessed qualities, but then, too, it partakes also of a bodily nature; therefore it is impossible for it to be entirely free from change; it moves, however, so far as it is able to do so, with a single motion in the same place and the same manner, and therefore it has acquired the reverse motion in a circle, because that involves the least deviation from its own motion. But to turn itself for ever is hardly possible except for the power that guides all moving things; and that this should turn now in one direction and now in the opposite direction is contrary to divine law. As the result of all this, we must not say either that the universe turns itself always, or that it is always turned by God in two opposite courses, or again that two divinities opposed to one another turn it. The only remaining alternative is what I suggested a little while ago, that

τοτὲ μὲν ὑπ' ἄλλης συμποδηγεῖσθαι θείας αἰτίας,
τὸ ζῆν πάλιν ἐπικτώμενον καὶ λαμβάνοντα ἀθανασίαν
ἐπισκευαστὴν παρὰ τοῦ δημιουργοῦ, τοτὲ δ'
ὅταν ἀνεθῇ, δι' ἑαυτοῦ[1] αὐτὸν ἰέναι, κατὰ καιρὸν
ἀφεθέντα τοιοῦτον, ὥστε ἀνάπαλιν πορεύεσθαι
πολλὰς περιόδων μυριάδας διὰ δὴ[2] τὸ μέγιστον
ὂν καὶ ἰσορροπώτατον ἐπὶ σμικροτάτου βαῖνον
ποδὸς ἰέναι.

B   ΝΕ. ΣΩ. Φαίνεται γοῦν δὴ καὶ μάλα εἰκότως
εἰρῆσθαι πάνθ' ὅσα διελήλυθας.

14.   ΞΕ. Λογισάμενοι δὴ ξυννοήσωμεν τὸ πάθος ἐκ τῶν νῦν λεχθέντων, ὃ πάντων ἔφαμεν εἶναι
τῶν θαυμαστῶν αἴτιον. ἔστι γὰρ οὖν δὴ τοῦτ' αὐτό.

ΝΕ. ΣΩ. Τὸ ποῖον;

ΞΕ. Τὸ τὴν τοῦ παντὸς φορὰν τοτὲ μὲν ἐφ' ἃ
νῦν κυκλεῖται φέρεσθαι, τοτὲ δ' ἐπὶ τἀναντία.

ΝΕ. ΣΩ. Πῶς δή;

ΞΕ. Ταύτην τὴν μεταβολὴν ἡγεῖσθαι δεῖ τῶν περὶ
τὸν οὐρανὸν γιγνομένων τροπῶν πασῶν εἶναι μεγί-
C στην καὶ τελεωτάτην τροπήν.

ΝΕ. ΣΩ. Ἔοικε γοῦν.

ΞΕ. Μεγίστας τοίνυν καὶ μεταβολὰς χρὴ νομίζειν
γίγνεσθαι τότε τοῖς ἐντὸς ἡμῖν οἰκοῦσιν αὐτοῦ.

ΝΕ. ΣΩ. Καὶ τοῦτο εἰκός.

ΞΕ. Μεταβολὰς δὲ μεγάλας καὶ πολλὰς καὶ παντοίας συμφερομένας ἆρ' οὐκ ἴσμεν τὴν τῶν ζῴων
φύσιν ὅτι χαλεπῶς ἀνέχεται;

ΝΕ. ΣΩ. Πῶς δ' οὔ;

ΞΕ. Φθοραὶ τοίνυν ἐξ ἀνάγκης τότε μέγισται
ξυμβαίνουσι τῶν τε ἄλλων ζῴων, καὶ δὴ καὶ τὸ τῶν

---

[1] ἑαυτοῦ Eusebius : ἑαυτὸν BT.
[2] δὴ Stallbaum : δὲ BT.

52

the universe is guided at one time by an extrinsic divine cause, acquiring the power of living again and receiving renewed immortality from the Creator, and at another time it is left to itself and then moves by its own motion, being left to itself at such a moment that it moves backwards through countless ages, because it is immensely large and most evenly balanced, and turns upon the smallest pivot.

y. soc. All that account of yours appears, at any rate, very reasonable.

str. Then, in the light of what has been said, let us consider and gain understanding of the event which we said was the cause of all those wonderful portents ; for it is really just this.

y. soc. Just what ?

str. The fact that at certain periods the universe has its present circular motion, and at other periods it revolves in the reverse direction.

y. soc. How was this the cause ?

str. We cannot help believing that of all the changes which take place in the heavens this reversal is the greatest and most complete.

y. soc. It certainly seems to be so.

str. Therefore we must also believe that at the same time the greatest changes come upon us who dwell within the heavens.

y. soc. That is likely too.

str. And animals cannot well endure many great and various changes at once. That is a familiar fact, is it not ?

y. soc. Of course.

str. Inevitably, then, there is at that time great destruction of animals in general, and only a small

PLATO

D ἀνθρώπων γένος ὀλίγον τι περιλείπεται· περὶ δὲ
τούτους ἄλλα τε παθήματα πολλὰ καὶ θαυμαστὰ καὶ
καινὰ ξυμπίπτει, μέγιστον δὲ τόδε καὶ ξυνεπόμενον
τῇ τοῦ παντὸς ἀνειλίξει τότε, ὅταν ἡ τῆς νῦν καθεστηκυίας ἐναντία γίγνηται τροπή.

ΝΕ. ΣΩ. Τὸ ποῖον;

ΞΕ. Ἣν ἡλικίαν ἕκαστον εἶχε τῶν ζῴων, αὕτη
πρῶτον μὲν ἔστη πάντων, καὶ ἐπαύσατο πᾶν ὅσον
ἦν θνητὸν ἐπὶ τὸ γεραίτερον ἰδεῖν πορευόμενον,
E μεταβάλλον δὲ πάλιν ἐπὶ τοὐναντίον οἷον νεώτερον
καὶ ἀπαλώτερον ἐφύετο· καὶ τῶν μὲν πρεσβυτέρων
αἱ λευκαὶ τρίχες ἐμελαίνοντο, τῶν δ᾽ αὖ γενειώντων
αἱ παρειαὶ λεαινόμεναι πάλιν ἐπὶ τὴν παρελθοῦσαν
ὥραν ἕκαστον καθίστασαν, τῶν δὲ ἡβώντων τὰ
σώματα λεαινόμενα καὶ σμικρότερα καθ᾽ ἡμέραν
καὶ νύκτα ἑκάστην γιγνόμενα πάλιν εἰς τὴν τοῦ
νεογενοῦς παιδὸς φύσιν ἀπῄει, κατά τε τὴν ψυχὴν
καὶ κατὰ τὸ σῶμα ἀφομοιούμενα· τὸ δ᾽ ἐντεῦθεν
ἤδη μαραινόμενα κομιδῇ τὸ πάμπαν ἐξηφανίζετο.
τῶν δ᾽ αὖ βιαίως τελευτώντων ἐν τῷ τότε χρόνῳ τὸ
τοῦ νεκροῦ σῶμα τὰ αὐτὰ ταῦτα πάσχον παθήματα
271 διὰ τάχους ἄδηλον ἐν ὀλίγαις ἡμέραις διεφθείρετο.

15. ΝΕ. ΣΩ. Γένεσις δὲ δὴ τίς τότ᾽ ἦν, ὦ ξένε,
ζῴων; καὶ τίνα τρόπον ἐξ ἀλλήλων ἐγεννῶντο;

ΞΕ. Δῆλον, ὦ Σώκρατες, ὅτι τὸ μὲν ἐξ ἀλλήλων
οὐκ ἦν ἐν τῇ τότε φύσει γεννώμενον, τὸ δὲ γηγενὲς

---

[1] The tale of Atreus introduces the fanciful theory of the
reversal of the revolution of the heavenly bodies, and this,
especially in an age when the stars were believed to exercise
a direct influence upon mankind and other creatures, naturally brings with it the reversal of all processes of growth.
This leads to a new birth of mankind, and the Stranger then

part of the human race survives; and the survivors have many experiences wonderful and strange, the greatest of which, a consequence of the reversal of everything at the time when the world begins to turn in the direction opposed to that of its present revolution, is this.[1]

y. soc. What is that experience?

str. First the age of all animals, whatever it was at the moment, stood still, and every mortal creature stopped growing older in appearance and then reversed its growth and became, as it were, younger and more tender; the hoary locks of the old men grew dark, and bearded cheeks grew smooth again as their possessors reverted to their earlier ages, and the bodies of young men grew smoother and smaller day by day and night by night, until they became as new-born babes, to which they were likened in mind and body; and then at last they wasted away entirely and wholly disappeared. And the bodies of those who died by violence in those times quickly underwent the same changes, were destroyed, and disappeared in a few days.

y. soc. But then, Stranger, how did animals come into existence in those days? How were they begotten of one another?

str. It is clear, Socrates, that being begotten of one another was no part of the natural order of that

briefly describes the age of innocence, the fall of man and the barbarism that follows, and the partial restoration of man through divine interposition and the gift of the various arts of civilization. Plato does not offer this as a real explanation of the existing condition of the world, but it serves, like the myths introduced in other dialogues, to present, in connexion with accepted mythology, a theory which may account for some of the facts of life.

PLATO

εἶναί ποτε γένος λεχθὲν τοῦτ' ἦν τὸ κατ' ἐκεῖνον
τὸν χρόνον ἐκ γῆς πάλιν ἀναστρεφόμενον, ἀπεμνημο-
νεύετο δὲ ὑπὸ τῶν ἡμετέρων προγόνων τῶν πρώτων,
οἳ τελευτώσῃ μὲν τῇ προτέρᾳ περιφορᾷ τὸν ἑξῆς
B χρόνον ἐγειτόνουν, τῆσδε δὲ κατ' ἀρχὰς ἐφύοντο·
τούτων γὰρ οὗτοι κήρυκες ἐγένονθ' ἡμῖν τῶν λόγων,
οἳ νῦν ὑπὸ πολλῶν οὐκ ὀρθῶς ἀπιστοῦνται. τὸ γὰρ
ἐντεῦθεν, οἶμαι, χρὴ ξυννοεῖν. ἑπόμενον[1] γάρ
ἐστι τῷ τοὺς πρεσβύτας ἐπὶ τὴν τοῦ παιδὸς ἰέναι
φύσιν, ἐκ τῶν τελευτηκότων αὖ, κειμένων δὲ ἐν γῇ,
πάλιν ἐκεῖ ξυνισταμένους καὶ ἀναβιωσκομένους,
τῇ τροπῇ[2] συνανακυκλουμένης εἰς τἀναντία τῆς
γενέσεως, καὶ γηγενεῖς δὴ κατὰ τοῦτον τὸν λόγον
C ἐξ ἀνάγκης φυομένους, οὕτως ἔχειν τοὔνομα καὶ
τὸν λόγον, ὅσους μὴ θεὸς αὐτῶν εἰς ἄλλην μοῖραν
ἐκόμισεν.

ΝΕ. ΣΩ. Κομιδῇ μὲν οὖν τοῦτό γε ἔπεται τοῖς
ἔμπροσθεν. ἀλλὰ δὴ τὸν βίον ὃν ἐπὶ τῆς Κρόνου
φῇς εἶναι δυνάμεως, πότερον ἐν ἐκείναις ἦν ταῖς
τροπαῖς ἢ ἐν ταῖσδε; τὴν μὲν γὰρ τῶν ἄστρων τε
καὶ ἡλίου μεταβολὴν δῆλον ὡς ἐν ἑκατέραις
ξυμπίπτει ταῖς τροπαῖς γίγνεσθαι.

ΞΕ. Καλῶς τῷ λόγῳ ξυμπαρηκολούθηκας. ὃ δ'
D ἤρου περὶ τοῦ πάντα αὐτόματα γίγνεσθαι τοῖς ἀνθρώποις, ἥκιστα τῆς νῦν ἐστι καθεστηκυίας φορᾶς,
ἀλλ' ἦν καὶ τοῦτο τῆς ἔμπροσθεν. τότε γὰρ αὐτῆς

---

[1] ἑπόμενον Stallbaum : ἐχόμενον BT.
[2] τῇ τροπῇ B : ἔπεσθαι τῇ τροπῇ T.

---

[1] This may refer to philosophers (*cf. Phaedo* 82 c) or,
more probably, to those who, like Menelaus, were transferred

time, but the earth-born race which, according to tradition, once existed, was the race which returned at that time out of the earth; and the memory of it was preserved by our earliest ancestors, who were born in the beginning of our period and therefore were next neighbours to the end of the previous period of the world's revolution, with no interval between. For they were to us the heralds of these stories which are nowadays unduly disbelieved by many people. For you must, I think, consider what would result. It is a natural consequence of the return of the old to childhood that those who are dead and lying in the earth take shape and come to life again, since the process of birth is reversed along with the reversal of the world's revolution; for this reason they are inevitably earth-born, and hence arises their name and the tradition about them, except those of them whom God removed to some other fate.[1]

Y. SOC. Certainly that follows from what preceded. But was the life in the reign of Cronus, which you mentioned, in that previous period of revolution or in ours? For evidently the change in the course of the stars and the sun takes place in both periods.

STR. You have followed my account very well. No, the life about which you ask, when all the fruits of the earth sprang up of their own accord for men, did not belong at all to the present period of revolution, but this also belonged to the previous one. For then, in the beginning, God ruled and

to the abode of the blessed, or, like Heracles, became gods. Such individuals would be exempt from the consequences of any subsequent reversal of the world's revolution.

57

πρῶτον τῆς κυκλήσεως ἦρχεν ἐπιμελούμενος ὅλης ὁ
θεός, ὣς δ' αὖ[1] κατὰ τόπους ταὐτὸν τοῦτο ὑπὸ θεῶν
ἀρχόντων πάντ' ἦν[2] τὰ τοῦ κόσμου μέρη διειλημμέ-
να· καὶ δὴ καὶ τὰ ζῷα κατὰ γένη καὶ ἀγέλας οἷον
νομῆς θεῖοι διειλήφεσαν δαίμονες, αὐτάρκης εἰς
πάντα ἕκαστος ἑκάστοις ὧν οἷς αὐτὸς ἔνεμεν, ὥστε
E οὔτ' ἄγριον ἦν οὐδὲν οὔτε ἀλλήλων ἐδωδαί, πόλε-
μός τε οὐκ ἐνῆν οὐδὲ στάσις τὸ παράπαν· ἀλλα θ'
ὅσα τῆς τοιαύτης ἐστὶ κατακοσμήσεως ἑπόμενα,
μυρία ἂν εἴη λέγειν. τὸ δ' οὖν τῶν ἀνθρώπων
λεχθὲν αὐτομάτου περὶ βίου διὰ τὸ τοιόνδε εἴρηται.
θεὸς ἔνεμεν αὐτοὺς αὐτὸς ἐπιστατῶν, καθάπερ νῦν
ἄνθρωποι, ζῷον ὂν ἕτερον θειότερον, ἄλλα γένη
φαυλότερα αὑτῶν νομεύουσι· νέμοντος δὲ ἐκείνου
272 πολιτεῖαί τε οὐκ ἦσαν οὐδὲ κτήσεις γυναικῶν
καὶ παίδων· ἐκ γῆς γὰρ ἀνεβιώσκοντο πάντες, οὐδὲν
μεμνημένοι τῶν πρόσθεν· ἀλλὰ τὰ μὲν τοιαῦτα
ἀπῆν πάντα, καρποὺς δὲ ἀφθόνους εἶχον ἀπό τε δέν-
δρων καὶ πολλῆς ὕλης ἄλλης, οὐχ ὑπὸ γεωργίας φυομένους, ἀλλ' αὐτομάτης ἀναδιδούσης τῆς γῆς.
γυμνοὶ δὲ καὶ ἄστρωτοι θυραυλοῦντες τὰ πολλὰ
ἐνέμοντο· τὸ γὰρ τῶν ὡρῶν αὐτοῖς ἄλυπον ἐκέκρα-
το, μαλακὰς δὲ εὐνὰς εἶχον ἀναφυομένης ἐκ γῆς
B πόας ἀφθόνου. τὸν δὴ βίον, ὦ Σώκρατες, ἀκούεις
μὲν τὸν τῶν ἐπὶ Κρόνου· τόνδε δ' ὂν[3] λόγος ἐπὶ
Διὸς εἶναι, τὸν νυνί, παρὼν αὐτὸς ᾔσθησαι· κρῖναι
δ' αὐτοῖν τὸν εὐδαιμονέστερον ἆρ' ἂν δύναιό τε καὶ
ἐθελήσειας;

ΝΕ. ΣΩ. Οὐδαμῶς.

---

[1] ὣς δ' αὖ Burnet : ὣς ‹νῦν BT.
[2] πάντ' ἦν Stallbaum : πάντῃ BT.
[3] ὂν W : ὡς BT : ὂν ὡς al.

supervised the whole revolution, and so again, in the same way, all the parts of the universe were divided by regions among gods who ruled them, and, moreover, the animals were distributed by species and flocks among inferior deities as divine shepherds, each of whom was in all respects the independent guardian of the creatures under his own care, so that no creature was wild, nor did they eat one another, and there was no war among them, nor any strife whatsoever. To tell all the other consequences of such an order of the world would be an endless task. But the reason for the story of the spontaneous life of mankind is as follows: God himself was their shepherd, watching over them, just as man, being an animal of different and more divine nature than the rest, now tends the lower species of animals. And under his care there were no states, nor did men possess wives or children; for they all came to life again out of the earth, with no recollection of their former lives. So there were no states or families, but they had fruits in plenty from the trees and other plants, which the earth furnished them of its own accord, without help from agriculture. And they lived for the most part in the open air, without clothing or bedding; for the climate was tempered for their comfort, and the abundant grass that grew up out of the earth furnished them soft couches. That, Socrates, was the life of men in the reign of Cronus; but the life of the present age, which is said to be the age of Zeus, you know by your own experience. Would you be able and willing to decide which of them is the more blessed?

y. soc. Certainly not.

ΞΕ. Βούλει δῆτα ἐγώ σοι τρόπον τινὰ διακρίνω;
ΝΕ. ΣΩ. Πάνυ μὲν οὖν.

16. ΞΕ. Εἰ μὲν τοίνυν οἱ τρόφιμοι τοῦ Κρόνου, παρούσης αὐτοῖς οὕτω πολλῆς σχολῆς καὶ δυνάμεως πρὸς τὸ μὴ μόνον ἀνθρώποις ἀλλὰ καὶ θηρίοις διὰ C λόγων δύνασθαι ξυγγίγνεσθαι, κατεχρῶντο τούτοις ξύμπασιν ἐπὶ φιλοσοφίαν, μετά τε θηρίων καὶ μετ' ἀλλήλων ὁμιλοῦντες, καὶ πυνθανόμενοι παρὰ πάσης φύσεως εἴ τινά τις ἰδίαν δύναμιν ἔχουσα ᾔσθετό τι διάφορον τῶν ἄλλων εἰς συναγυρμὸν φρονήσεως, εὔκριτον ὅτι τῶν νῦν οἱ τότε μυρίῳ πρὸς εὐδαιμονίαν διέφερον· εἰ δὲ ἐμπιμπλάμενοι σίτων ἅδην καὶ ποτῶν διελέγοντο πρὸς ἀλλήλους καὶ τὰ θηρία μύθους, οἷα δὴ καὶ τὰ νῦν περὶ αὐτῶν λέγονται, D καὶ τοῦτο, ὥς γε[1] κατὰ τὴν ἐμὴν δόξαν ἀποφήνασθαι, καὶ μάλ' εὔκριτον. ὅμως δ' οὖν ταῦτα μὲν ἀφῶμεν, ἕως ἂν ἡμῖν μηνυτής τις ἱκανὸς φανῇ, ποτέρως οἱ τότε τὰς ἐπιθυμίας εἶχον περί τε ἐπιστημῶν καὶ τῆς τῶν λόγων χρείας· οὗ δ' ἕνεκα τὸν μῦθον ἠγείραμεν, τοῦτο λεκτέον, ἵνα τὸ μετὰ τοῦτο εἰς τὸ πρόσθεν περαίνωμεν. ἐπειδὴ γὰρ πάντων τούτων χρόνος ἐτελεώθη καὶ μεταβολὴν ἔδει γίγνεσθαι καὶ δὴ καὶ τὸ γήινον ἤδη πᾶν ἀνήλωτο E γένος, πάσας ἑκάστης τῆς ψυχῆς τὰς γενέσεις ἀποδεδωκυίας, ὅσα ἦν ἑκάστῃ προσταχθὲν τοσαῦτα[2] εἰς γῆν σπέρματα πεσούσης, τότε δὴ τοῦ παντὸς ὁ μὲν κυβερνήτης, οἷον πηδαλίων οἴακος ἀφέμενος, εἰς τὴν αὑτοῦ περιωπὴν ἀπέστη, τὸν δὲ δὴ κόσμον πάλιν ἀνέστρεφεν εἱμαρμένη τε καὶ ξύμφυτος ἐπιθυμία. πάντες οὖν οἱ κατὰ τοὺς τόπους συν-

[1] ὥς γε G : ὥστε BT (in T γ is written above the τ).
[2] προσταχθὲν τοσαῦτα Eusebius : προσταχθέντας αὐτὰ BT.

STR. Shall I, then, make some sort of a judgement for you?

Y. SOC. Do so, by all means.

STR. Well, then, if the foster children of Cronus, having all this leisure and the ability to converse not only with human beings but also with beasts, made full use of all these opportunities with a view to philosophy, talking with the animals and with one another and learning from every creature that, through possession of some peculiar power he may have had in any respect beyond his fellows perceptions tending towards an increase of wisdom, it would be easy to decide that the people of those old times were immeasurably happier than those of our epoch. Or if they merely ate and drank till they were full and gossiped with each other and the animals, telling such stories as are even now told about them, in that case, too, it would, in my opinion, be very easy to reach a decision. However, let us pass those matters by, so long as there is no one capable of reporting to us what the desires of the people in those days were in regard to knowledge and the employment of speech. The reason why we revived this legend must be told, in order that we may get ahead afterwards. For when the time of all those conditions was accomplished and the change was to take place and all the earth-born race had at length been used up, since every soul had fulfilled all its births by falling into the earth as seed its prescribed number of times, then the helmsman of the universe dropped the tiller and withdrew to his place of outlook, and fate and innate desire made the earth turn backwards. So, too, all the gods who share, each in his own sphere, the rule of the

ἄρχοντες τῷ μεγίστῳ δαίμονι θεοί, γνόντες ἤδη
τὸ γιγνόμενον, ἀφίεσαν αὖ τὰ μέρη τοῦ κόσμου
273 τῆς αὐτῶν ἐπιμελείας· ὁ δὲ μεταστρεφόμενος καὶ
ξυμβάλλων, ἀρχῆς τε καὶ τελευτῆς ἐναντίαν ὁρμὴν
ὁρμηθείς, σεισμὸν πολὺν ἐν ἑαυτῷ ποιῶν ἄλλην αὖ
φθορὰν ζῴων παντοίων ἀπηργάσατο. μετὰ δὲ
ταῦτα προελθόντος ἱκανοῦ χρόνου, θορύβων τε καὶ
ταραχῆς ἤδη παυόμενος καὶ τῶν σεισμῶν γαλήνης
ἐπιλαβόμενος εἴς τε τὸν εἰωθότα δρόμον τὸν
ἑαυτοῦ κατακοσμούμενος ᾔει, ἐπιμέλειαν καὶ κράτος
B ἔχων αὐτὸς τῶν ἐν αὐτῷ τε καὶ ἑαυτοῦ, τὴν τοῦ
δημιουργοῦ καὶ πατρὸς ἀπομνημονεύων διδαχὴν εἰς
δύναμιν. κατ᾽ ἀρχὰς μὲν οὖν ἀκριβέστερον ἀπετέ-
λει, τελευτῶν δὲ ἀμβλύτερον· τούτων δὲ αὐτῷ τὸ
σωματοειδὲς τῆς συγκράσεως αἴτιον, τὸ τῆς πάλαι
ποτὲ φύσεως ξύντροφον, ὅτι πολλῆς ἦν μετέχον
ἀταξίας πρὶν εἰς τὸν νῦν κόσμον ἀφικέσθαι. παρὰ
μὲν γὰρ τοῦ συνθέντος πάντα καλὰ κέκτηται·
παρὰ δὲ τῆς ἔμπροσθεν ἕξεως, ὅσα χαλεπὰ καὶ
C ἄδικα ἐν οὐρανῷ γίγνεται, ταῦτα ἐξ ἐκείνης αὐτός
τε ἔχει καὶ τοῖς ζῴοις ἐναπεργάζεται. μετὰ μὲν
οὖν τοῦ κυβερνήτου τὰ ζῷα τρέφων ἐν αὐτῷ σμικρὰ
μὲν φλαῦρα, μεγάλα δὲ ἐνέτικτεν ἀγαθά· χωριζό-
μενος δὲ ἐκείνου τὸν ἐγγύτατα χρόνον ἀεὶ τῆς
ἀφέσεως κάλλιστα πάντα διάγει, προϊόντος δὲ τοῦ
χρόνου καὶ λήθης ἐγγιγνομένης ἐν αὐτῷ μᾶλλον καὶ
δυναστεύει τὸ τῆς παλαιᾶς ἀναρμοστίας πάθος,
D τελευτῶντος δὲ ἐξανθεῖ τοῦ χρόνου καὶ σμικρὰ μὲν
τἀγαθά, πολλὴν δὲ τὴν τῶν ἐναντίων κρᾶσιν
ἐπεγκεραννύμενος ἐπὶ διαφθορᾶς κίνδυνον αὐτοῦ τε

Supreme Spirit, promptly perceiving what was taking place, let go the parts of the world which were under their care. And as the universe was turned back and there came the shock of collision, as the beginning and the end rushed in opposite directions, it produced a great earthquake within itself and caused a new destruction of all sorts of living creatures. But after that, when a sufficient time had elapsed, there was rest now from disturbance and confusion, calm followed the earthquakes, and the world went on its own accustomed course in orderly fashion, exercising care and rule over itself and all within itself, and remembering and practising the teachings of the Creator and Father to the extent of its power, at first more accurately and at last more carelessly ; and the reason for this was the material element in its composition, because this element, which was inherent in the primeval nature, was infected with great disorder before the attainment of the existing orderly universe. For from its Composer the universe has received only good things ; but from its previous condition it retains in itself and creates in the animals all the elements of harshness and injustice which have their origin in the heavens. Now as long as the world was nurturing the animals within itself under the guidance of the Pilot, it produced little evil and great good ; but in becoming separated from him it always got on most excellently during the time immediately after it was let go, but as time went on and it grew forgetful, the ancient condition of disorder prevailed more and more and towards the end of the time reached its height, and the universe, mingling but little good with much of the opposite sort, was in danger of destruction for

ἀφικνεῖται καὶ τῶν ἐν αὑτῷ. διὸ δὴ καὶ τότ' ἤδη
θεὸς ὁ κοσμήσας αὐτόν, καθορῶν ἐν ἀπορίαις ὄντα,
κηδόμενος ἵνα μὴ χειμασθεὶς ὑπὸ ταραχῆς διαλυθεὶς
εἰς τὸν τῆς ἀνομοιότητος ἄπειρον ὄντα πόντον[1]
E δύῃ, πάλιν ἔφεδρος αὐτοῦ τῶν πηδαλίων γιγνόμενος, τὰ νοσήσαντα καὶ λυθέντα ἐν τῇ καθ' ἑαυτὸν
προτέρᾳ περιόδῳ στρέψας, κοσμεῖ τε καὶ ἐπαν-
ορθῶν ἀθάνατον αὐτὸν καὶ ἀγήρων ἀπεργάζεται.

Τοῦτο μὲν οὖν τέλος ἁπάντων εἴρηται· τὸ δ' ἐπὶ
τὴν τοῦ βασιλέως ἀπόδειξιν ἱκανὸν ἐκ τοῦ πρόσθεν
ἁπτομένοις τοῦ λόγου· στρεφθέντος γὰρ αὖ τοῦ
κόσμου τὴν ἐπὶ τὴν νῦν γένεσιν ὁδὸν τὸ τῆς ἡλικίας
αὖ πάλιν ἵστατο καὶ καινὰ τἀναντία ἀπεδίδου τοῖς
τότε. τὰ μὲν γὰρ ὑπὸ σμικρότητος ὀλίγου δέοντα
ἠφανίσθαι τῶν ζῴων ηὐξάνετο, τὰ δ' ἐκ γῆς νεογενῆ
σώματα πολιὰ[2] φύντα πάλιν ἀποθνήσκοντα εἰς γῆν
κατῄει. καὶ τἆλλά τε πάντα μετέβαλλεν, ἀπομιμού-
274 μενα καὶ ξυνακολουθοῦντα τῷ τοῦ παντὸς παθήματι, καὶ δὴ καὶ τὸ τῆς κυήσεως καὶ γεννήσεως καὶ
τροφῆς μίμημα συνείπετο τοῖς πᾶσιν ὑπ' ἀνάγκης·
οὐ γὰρ ἐξῆν ἔτ' ἐν γῇ δι' ἑτέρων συνιστάντων
φύεσθαι ζῷον, ἀλλὰ καθάπερ τῷ κόσμῳ προσ-
ετέτακτο αὐτοκράτορα εἶναι τῆς αὑτοῦ πορείας,
οὕτω δὴ κατὰ ταὐτὰ καὶ τοῖς μέρεσιν αὐτοῖς δι'
αὑτῶν, καθ' ὅσον οἷόν τ' ἦν, φύειν τε καὶ γεννᾶν
καὶ τρέφειν προσετάττετο ὑπὸ τῆς ὁμοίας ἀγωγῆς.
B Οὗ δὲ ἕνεκα ὁ λόγος ὥρμηκε πᾶς, ἐπ' αὐτῷ νῦν
ἐσμεν ἤδη. περὶ μὲν γὰρ τῶν ἄλλων θηρίων πολλὰ
ἂν καὶ μακρὰ διεξελθεῖν γίγνοιτο, ἐξ ὧν ἕκαστα
καὶ δι' ἃς αἰτίας μεταβέβληκε· περὶ δὲ ἀνθρώπων

---

[1] πόντον Simplicius, Proclus : τόπον MSS.
[2] πολιὰ W²t : πολιᾶι B : πολλὰ T : om. pr. W.

itself and those within it. Therefore at that moment God, who made the order of the universe, perceived that it was in dire trouble, and fearing that it might founder in the tempest of confusion and sink in the boundless sea of diversity, he took again his place as its helmsman, reversed whatever had become unsound and unsettled in the previous period when the world was left to itself, set the world in order, restored it and made it immortal and ageless.

So now the whole tale is told; but for our purpose of exhibiting the nature of the king it will be enough to revert to the earlier part of the story. For when the universe was turned again into the present path of generation, the age of individuals came again to a stop, and that led to new processes, the reverse of those which had gone before. For the animals which had grown so small as almost to disappear grew larger, and those newly born from the earth with hoary hair died and passed below the earth again. And all other things changed, imitating the condition of the universe and conforming to it, and so too pregnancy and birth and nurture necessarily imitated and conformed to the rest; for no living creature could any longer come into being by the union of other elements, but just as the universe was ordered to be the ruler of its own course, so in the same way the parts were ordered, so far as they could, to grow and beget and give nourishment of themselves under the same guidance.

And now we have come at last to the point for the sake of which this whole discourse was begun. For much might be said, and at great length, about the other animals, their previous forms and the causes of their several changes; but about mankind there is

65

βραχύτερα καὶ μᾶλλον προσήκοντα. τῆς γὰρ τοῦ
κεκτημένου καὶ νέμοντος ἡμᾶς δαίμονος ἀπερημω-
θέντες ἐπιμελείας, τῶν πολλῶν αὖ θηρίων, ὅσα
χαλεπὰ τὰς φύσεις ἦν, ἀπαγριωθέντων, αὐτοὶ δὲ
ἀσθενεῖς ἄνθρωποι καὶ ἀφύλακτοι γεγονότες διηρπά-
C ζοντο ὑπ' αὐτῶν, καὶ ἔτ' ἀμήχανοι καὶ ἄτεχνοι
κατὰ τοὺς πρώτους ἦσαν χρόνους, ἅτε τῆς μὲν
αὐτομάτης τροφῆς ἐπιλελοιπυίας, πορίζεσθαι δὲ
οὐκ ἐπιστάμενοί πω διὰ τὸ μηδεμίαν αὐτοὺς χρείαν
πρότερον ἀναγκάζειν. ἐκ τούτων πάντων ἐν μεγά-
λαις ἀπορίαις ἦσαν. ὅθεν δὴ τὰ πάλαι λεχθέντα
παρὰ θεῶν δῶρα ἡμῖν δεδώρηται μετ' ἀναγκαίας
διδαχῆς καὶ παιδεύσεως, πῦρ μὲν παρὰ Προμηθέως,
τέχναι δὲ παρ' Ἡφαίστου καὶ τῆς συντέχνου,
D σπέρματα δὲ αὖ καὶ φυτὰ παρ' ἄλλων[1]· καὶ πάνθ'
ὁπόσα τὸν ἀνθρώπινον βίον συγκατεσκεύακεν ἐκ
τούτων γέγονεν, ἐπειδὴ τὸ μὲν ἐκ θεῶν, ὅπερ
ἐρρήθη νῦν δή, τῆς ἐπιμελείας ἐπέλιπεν ἀνθρώπους,
δι' ἑαυτῶν δὲ ἔδει τήν τε διαγωγὴν καὶ τὴν ἐπιμέλειαν αὐτοὺς αὑτῶν ἔχειν καθάπερ ὅλος ὁ κόσμος,
ᾧ ξυμμιμούμενοι καὶ ξυνεπόμενοι τὸν ἀεὶ χρόνον
νῦν μὲν οὕτως, τότε δὲ ἐκείνως ζῶμέν τε καὶ
E φυόμεθα. καὶ τὸ μὲν δὴ τοῦ μύθου τέλος ἐχέτω,
χρήσιμον δὲ αὐτὸν ποιησόμεθα πρὸς τὸ κατιδεῖν
ὅσον ἡμάρτομεν ἀποφηνάμενοι τὸν βασιλικόν τε
καὶ πολιτικὸν ἐν τῷ πρόσθε λόγῳ.

17. ΝΕ. ΣΩ. Πῶς οὖν καὶ πόσον ἁμάρτημα
φῂς εἶναι γεγονὸς ἡμῖν;

ΞΕ. Τῇ μὲν βραχύτερον, τῇ δὲ μάλα γενναῖον καὶ
πολλῷ μεῖζον καὶ πλέον ἢ τότε.

---

[1] ἄλλων Stephanus e Ficino : ἀλλήλων BT.

less to say and it is more to our purpose. For men, deprived of the care of the deity who had possessed and tended us, since most of the beasts who were by nature unfriendly had grown fierce, and they themselves were feeble and unprotected, were ravaged by the beasts and were in the first ages still without resources or skill; the food which had formerly offered itself freely had failed them, and they did not yet know how to provide for themselves, because no necessity had hitherto compelled them. On all these accounts they were in great straits; and that is the reason why the gifts of the gods that are told of in the old traditions were given us with the needful information and instruction,—fire by Prometheus, the arts by Hephaestus and the goddess who is his fellow-artisan, seeds and plants by other deities.[1] And from these has arisen all that constitutes human life, since, as I said a moment ago, the care of the gods had failed men and they had to direct their own lives and take care of themselves, like the whole universe, which we imitate and follow through all time, being born and living now in our present manner and in that other epoch in the other manner. So, then, let our tale be finished; but we will turn it to account for opening our eyes to the great error we made in the exposition of the king and the statesman in our earlier discussion.

Y. SOC. How, then, did we err, and what is the great error you say we have committed?

STR. In one way we made a comparatively slight error, in another a very important one, much greater and more far-reaching than the first.

[1] The fellow-artisan of Hephaestus is Athena; seeds and plants are the gifts of Demeter and Dionysus.

ΝΕ. ΣΩ. Πῶς;

ΞΕ. Ὅτι μὲν ἐρωτώμενοι τὸν ἐκ τῆς νῦν περιφορᾶς καὶ γενέσεως βασιλέα καὶ πολιτικὸν τὸν ἐκ
τῆς ἐναντίας περιόδου ποιμένα τῆς τότε ἀνθρωπίνης
275 ἀγέλης εἴπομεν, καὶ ταῦτα θεὸν ἀντὶ θνητοῦ,
ταύτῃ μὲν πάμπολυ παρηνέχθημεν· ὅτι δὲ ξυμπάσης τῆς πόλεως ἄρχοντα αὐτὸν ἀπεφήναμεν, ὅντινα
δὲ τρόπον οὐ διείπομεν, ταύτῃ δὲ αὖ τὸ μὲν λεχθὲν
ἀληθές, οὐ μὴν ὅλον γε οὐδὲ σαφὲς ἐρρήθη, διὸ καὶ
βραχύτερον ἢ κατ᾽ ἐκεῖνο ἡμαρτήκαμεν.

ΝΕ. ΣΩ. Ἀληθῆ.

ΞΕ. Δεῖ τοίνυν τὸν τρόπον, ὡς ἔοικε, διορίσαντας
τῆς ἀρχῆς τῆς πόλεως οὕτω τελέως τὸν πολιτικὸν
ἡμῖν εἰρῆσθαι προσδοκᾶν.

ΝΕ. ΣΩ. Καλῶς.

B ΞΕ. Διὰ ταῦτα μὴν καὶ τὸν μῦθον παρεθέμεθα,
ἵνα ἐνδείξαιτο περὶ τῆς ἀγελαιοτροφίας μὴ μόνον ὡς
πάντες αὐτῆς ἀμφισβητοῦσι τῷ ζητουμένῳ τὰ νῦν,
ἀλλὰ κἀκεῖνον αὐτὸν ἐναργέστερον ἴδοιμεν, ὃν
προσήκει μόνον κατὰ τὸ παράδειγμα ποιμένων τε
καὶ βουκόλων τῆς[1] ἀνθρωπίνης ἐπιμέλειαν ἔχοντα
τροφῆς τούτου μόνου ἀξιωθῆναι τοῦ προσρήματος.

ΝΕ. ΣΩ. Ὀρθῶς.

ΞΕ. Οἶμαι δ᾽ ἔγωγε, ὦ Σώκρατες, τοῦτο μὲν ἔτι
C μεῖζον ἢ κατὰ βασιλέα εἶναι τὸ σχῆμα τὸ τοῦ
θείου νομέως, τοὺς δ᾽ ἐνθάδε νῦν ὄντας πολιτικοὺς
τοῖς ἀρχομένοις ὁμοίους τε εἶναι μᾶλλον πολὺ τὰς
φύσεις καὶ παραπλησιαίτερον παιδείας μετειλη-
φέναι καὶ τροφῆς.

ΝΕ. ΣΩ. Πάντως που.

[1] τῆς] τὸν BT.

THE STATESMAN

y. soc. How did we do that?

str. When we were asked about the king and the statesman of the present movement of the world and mode of generation, we told of the shepherd of the human flock in the time of the reverse movement, and he was a god, not a man, besides. That was a very great error. Then when we declared that he was ruler of the whole state, but did not fully tell in what manner he ruled, what we said was true, though it was not complete nor clear, and therefore our error was less in this case than in the other.

y. soc. True.

str. Apparently, then, we must expect a complete description of the statesman only when we have defined the manner of his rule over the state.

y. soc. Very good.

str. And this is why I introduced the myth, not only in order to show that all men compete for the care of the flock with him whom we are now seeking, but also that we may more clearly see him who alone ought to have the care of human beings as shepherds and neatherds care for their flocks and herds, and therefore alone deserves to be honoured with that appellation.

y. soc. Quite right.

str. I think, Socrates, that the form of the divine shepherd is greater than that of the king, whereas the statesmen who now exist here are by nature much more like their subjects, with whom they share much more nearly the same breeding and education.

y. soc. Certainly.

ΞΕ. Ζητητέοι[1] γε μὴν οὐδὲν ἂν εἴησαν οὔθ' ἧττον
οὔτε μᾶλλον, εἴθ' οὕτως εἴτ' ἐκείνως πεφύκασιν.

ΝΕ. ΣΩ. Πῶς γὰρ οὔ;

ΞΕ. Τῇδε[2] δὴ πάλιν ἐπανέλθωμεν. ἦν γὰρ ἔφαμεν αὐτεπιτακτικὴν μὲν εἶναι τέχνην ἐπὶ ζῴοις,
D οὐ μὴν ἰδίᾳ γε ἀλλὰ κοινῇ τὴν ἐπιμέλειαν ἔχουσαν,
καὶ προσείπομεν δὴ τότε εὐθὺς ἀγελαιοτροφικήν—
μέμνησαι γάρ;

ΝΕ. ΣΩ. Ναί.

ΞΕ. Ταύτης τοίνυν πῃ διημαρτάνομεν. τὸν γὰρ
πολιτικὸν οὐδαμοῦ συνελάβομεν οὐδ' ὠνομάσαμεν,
ἀλλ' ἡμᾶς ἔλαθε κατὰ τὴν ὀνομασίαν ἐκφυγών.

ΝΕ. ΣΩ. Πῶς;

ΞΕ. Τοῦ τὰς ἀγέλας ἑκάστας τρέφειν τοῖς μὲν
ἄλλοις που πᾶσι μέτεστι νομεῦσι, τῷ πολιτικῷ δὲ
οὐ μετὸν ἐπηνέγκαμεν τοὔνομα, δέον τῶν κοινῶν
E ἐπενεγκεῖν τι ξύμπασιν.

ΝΕ. ΣΩ. 'Αληθῆ λέγεις, εἴπερ ἐτύγχανέ γε ὄν.

ΞΕ. Πῶς δ' οὐκ ἦν τό γε θεραπεύειν που πᾶσι
κοινόν, μηδὲν διορισθείσης τροφῆς μηδέ τινος ἄλλης
πραγματείας; ἀλλ' ἤ[3] τινα ἀγελαιοκομικὴν ἢ
θεραπευτικὴν ἢ καί τινα ἐπιμελητικὴν αὐτὴν
ὀνομάσασιν ὡς κατὰ πάντων ἐξῆν περικαλύπτειν
καὶ τὸν πολιτικὸν ἅμα τοῖς ἄλλοις, ἐπειδὴ δεῖν
τοῦτ' ἐσήμαινεν ὁ λόγος.

18. ΝΕ. ΣΩ. Ὀρθῶς. ἀλλ' ἡ μετὰ τοῦτο δι-
276 αίρεσις αὖ τίνα τρόπον ἐγίγνετ' ἄν;

ΞΕ. Κατὰ ταὐτὰ καθ' ἅπερ ἔμπροσθεν διῃρούμεθα
τὴν ἀγελαιοτροφικὴν πεζοῖς τε καὶ ἁπτῆσι, καὶ
ἀμίκτοις τε καὶ ἀκεράτοις, τοῖς αὐτοῖς ἄν που

---

[1] ζητητέοι Coislin.; ζητητέον BT.
[2] τῇδε Stephanus : τί δὲ BT.

str. And yet they would have to be investigated with precisely the same care, whether their nature be like that of their subjects or like that of the divine shepherd.

y. soc. Of course.

str. Then let us go back to this point: the art which we said gave its own orders and had to do with living beings, but had charge of them not singly but in common, and which we at once called the art of the herdsman,—do you remember?

y. soc. Yes.

str. Well, it was in connexion with that, somewhere, that we made our mistake; for we never included or named the statesman; unobserved by us he slipped out of our nomenclature.

y. soc. How so?

str. All the other herdsmen have this in common that they feed their respective herds; but the statesman does not, yet we gave him the name of herdsman, when we ought to have given him one which is common to them all.

y. soc. True, if there were such a name.

str. Is not caring for herds common to them all, with no especial mention of feeding or any other activity? If we called it an art of tending herds or caring for them or managing them, as all herdsmen do, we could wrap up the statesman with the rest, since the argument showed that we ought to do so.

y. soc. Quite right; but how would the next division be made?

str. Just as we divided the art of feeding herds before by distinguishing between those that go on foot and the winged, and the unmixed breeds and the

---

³ ἀλλ' ἤ] ἄλλην T.

PLATO

τούτοις διαιρούμενοι καὶ τὴν ἀγελαιοκομικὴν τήν τε νῦν καὶ τὴν ἐπὶ Κρόνου βασιλείαν περιειληφότες ἂν ἦμεν ὁμοίως ἐν τῷ λόγῳ.

ΝΕ. ΣΩ. Φαίνεται· ζητῶ δὲ αὖ τί τὸ μετὰ τοῦτο.

ΞΕ. Δῆλον ὅτι λεχθέντος οὕτω τοῦ τῆς ἀγελαιο-
B κομικῆς ὀνόματος οὐκ ἄν ποτ' ἐγένεθ' ἡμῖν τό τινας ἀμφισβητεῖν ὡς οὐδ' ἐπιμέλεια τὸ παράπαν ἐστίν, ὥσπερ τότε δικαίως ἠμφισβητήθη μηδεμίαν εἶναι τέχνην ἐν ἡμῖν ἀξίαν τούτου τοῦ θρεπτικοῦ προσρήματος, εἰ δ' οὖν τις εἴη, πολλοῖς πρότερον αὐτῆς καὶ μᾶλλον προσήκειν ἤ τινι τῶν βασιλέων.

ΝΕ. ΣΩ. Ὀρθῶς.

ΞΕ. Ἐπιμέλεια δέ γε ἀνθρωπίνης συμπάσης κοινωνίας οὐδεμία ἂν ἐθελήσειεν ἑτέρα μᾶλλον καὶ προτέρα[1] τῆς βασιλικῆς φάναι καὶ κατὰ πάντων
C ἀνθρώπων ἀρχῆς εἶναι τέχνη.

ΝΕ. ΣΩ. Λέγεις ὀρθῶς.

ΞΕ. Μετὰ ταῦτα δέ γε, ὦ Σώκρατες, ἆρ' ἐννοοῦμεν ὅτι πρὸς αὐτῷ δὴ τῷ τέλει συχνὸν αὖ διημαρτά-νετο;

ΝΕ. ΣΩ. Τὸ ποῖον;

ΞΕ. Τόδε, ὡς ἄρ' εἰ καὶ διενοήθημεν ὅτι μάλιστα τῆς δίποδος ἀγέλης εἶναί τινα θρεπτικὴν τέχνην, οὐδέν τι μᾶλλον ἡμᾶς ἔδει βασιλικὴν αὐτὴν εὐθὺς καὶ πολιτικὴν ὡς ἀποτετελεσμένην προσαγορεύειν.

ΝΕ. ΣΩ. Τί μήν;

ΞΕ. Πρῶτον μὲν, ὃ ἐλέγομεν, τοὔνομα μετα-
D σκευωρήσασθαι, πρὸς τὴν ἐπιμέλειαν μᾶλλον προσ-αγαγόντας ἢ τὴν τροφήν, ἔπειτα ταύτην τέμνειν· οὐ γὰρ σμικρὰς ἂν ἔχοι τμήσεις ἔτι.

ΝΕ. ΣΩ. Ποίας;

---

[1] προτέρα Stallbaum : πραοτερα B : πραοτέρα T.

hornless, we might divide the art of tending herds by these same distinctions, embracing in the word both the kingship of the present time and that of the time of Cronus.

Y. SOC. Evidently; but again I wonder what the next step is.

STR. It is clear that if we had used the word "tending" herds, we should never have met with the contention that there is no caring for them at all in statesmanship, though the earlier contention was justified that there is no art in the case of human beings that deserves the name of feeding, and if there be such an art, it belongs much more to many others than to the king.

Y. SOC. Quite right.

STR. But no other art would advance a stronger claim than that of kingship to be the art of caring for the whole human community and ruling all mankind.

Y. SOC. You are right.

STR. And after all this, Socrates, do we see that another great error was committed at the very end?

Y. SOC. What was it?

STR. Why, it was this: No matter how strong our belief that there was an art of feeding the biped herd, we ought not to have called it kingship and statecraft on the spot, as if it were all quite settled.

Y. SOC. What ought we to have done, then?

STR. In the first place, as we said, we ought to have remodelled the name, making it denote care, rather than feeding, and then we ought to have divided the art, for it may still admit of not unimportant divisions.

Y. SOC. What are they?

PLATO

ΞΕ. Ἧι τε τὸν θεῖον ἄν που διειλόμεθα νομέα χωρὶς καὶ τὸν ἀνθρώπινον ἐπιμελητήν.

ΝΕ. ΣΩ. Ὀρθῶς.

ΞΕ. Αὖθις δέ γε τὴν ἀπονεμηθεῖσαν ἐπιμελητικὴν δίχα τέμνειν ἀναγκαῖον ἦν.

ΝΕ. ΣΩ. Τίνι;

ΞΕ. Τῷ βιαίῳ τε καὶ ἑκουσίῳ.

ΝΕ. ΣΩ. Τί δή;

ΞΕ. Καὶ ταύτῃ που τὸ πρότερον ἁμαρτάνοντες Ε εὐηθέστερα τοῦ δέοντος εἰς ταὐτὸν βασιλέα καὶ τύραννον ξυνέθεμεν, ἀνομοιοτάτους ὄντας αὐτούς τε καὶ τὸν τῆς ἀρχῆς ἑκατέρου τρόπον.

ΝΕ. ΣΩ. Ἀληθῆ.

ΞΕ. Νῦν δέ γε πάλιν ἐπανορθούμενοι, καθάπερ εἶπον, τὴν ἀνθρωπίνην ἐπιμελητικὴν δίχα διαιρώμεθα, τῷ βιαίῳ τε καὶ ἑκουσίῳ;

ΝΕ. ΣΩ. Πάνυ μὲν οὖν.

ΞΕ. Καὶ τὴν μέν γέ που τῶν βιαίων τυραννικήν, τὴν δὲ ἑκούσιον καὶ ἑκουσίων διπόδων ἀγελαιοκομικὴν ζῴων προσειπόντες πολιτικήν, τὸν ἔχοντα αὖ τέχνην ταύτην καὶ ἐπιμέλειαν ὄντως ὄντα βασιλέα καὶ πολιτικὸν ἀποφαινώμεθα;

277 19. ΝΕ. ΣΩ. Καὶ κινδυνεύει γε, ὦ ξένε, τελέως ἂν ἡμῖν οὕτως ἔχειν ἡ περὶ τὸν πολιτικὸν ἀπόδειξις.

ΞΕ. Καλῶς ἄν, ὦ Σώκρατες, ἡμῖν ἔχοι. δεῖ δὲ μὴ σοὶ μόνῳ ταῦτα, ἀλλὰ κἀμοὶ μετὰ σοῦ κοινῇ ξυνδοκεῖν. νῦν δὲ κατά γε τὴν ἐμὴν οὔπω φαίνεται τέλεον ὁ βασιλεὺς ἡμῖν σχῆμα ἔχειν, ἀλλὰ καθάπερ ἀνδριαντοποιοὶ παρὰ καιρὸν ἐνίοτε σπεύδοντες πλείω καὶ μείζω τοῦ δέοντος ἕκαστα τῶν ἔργων Β ἐπεμβαλλόμενοι βραδύνουσι, καὶ νῦν ἡμεῖς, ἵνα

STR. There is one by which we might have divided the divine shepherd from the human caretaker.

Y. SOC. Quite right.

STR. And again it was essential that the art of caretaking thus isolated and assigned to man be divided into two parts.

Y. SOC. On what line of division?

STR. On that of compulsory and voluntary.

Y. SOC. Why is that?

STR. Because this was about the point at which we made our mistake before; we were more simple-minded than we should have been, and we put the king and the tyrant together, whereas they and their respective modes of ruling are quite unlike.

Y. SOC. True.

STR. But now shall we, as I said, correct ourselves and divide the care of humanity into two parts, by the criterion of the compulsory and the voluntary?

Y. SOC. By all means.

STR. And if we call the art of those who use compulsion tyrannical or something of the sort and the voluntary care of voluntary bipeds political, may we not declare that he who possesses this latter art of caretaking is really the true king and statesman?

Y. SOC. Well, Stranger, it looks as though our account of the statesman were complete now.

STR. That would be a fine thing for us, Socrates. But not you alone must think so; I must think so, too, in agreement with you. As a matter of fact, however, in my opinion our figure of the king is not yet perfect, but like statue-makers who some-times in their misapplied enthusiasm make too numerous and too large additions and thus delay the completion of their several works, we too, at this

δὴ πρὸς τῷ ταχὺ καὶ μεγαλοπρεπῶς δηλώσαιμεν
τὸ τῆς ἔμπροσθεν ἁμάρτημα διεξόδου, τῷ βασιλεῖ
νομίσαντες πρέπειν μεγάλα παραδείγματα ποιεῖσθαι, θαυμαστὸν ὄγκον ἀράμενοι τοῦ μύθου, μείζονι
τοῦ δέοντος ἠναγκάσθημεν αὐτοῦ μέρει προσ-
χρήσασθαι· διὸ μακροτέραν τὴν ἀπόδειξιν πεποιή-
καμεν καὶ πάντως τῷ μύθῳ τέλος οὐκ ἐπέθεμεν,
C ἀλλ' ἀτεχνῶς ὁ λόγος ἡμῖν ὥσπερ ζῷον τὴν
ἔξωθεν μὲν περιγραφὴν ἔοικεν ἱκανῶς ἔχειν, τὴν
δὲ οἷον τοῖς φαρμάκοις καὶ τῇ συγκράσει τῶν
χρωμάτων ἐνάργειαν οὐκ ἀπειληφέναι πω. γραφῆς
δὲ καὶ συμπάσης χειρουργίας λέξει καὶ λόγῳ
δηλοῦν πᾶν ζῷον μᾶλλον πρέπει τοῖς δυναμένοις
ἕπεσθαι· τοῖς δ' ἄλλοις διὰ χειρουργιῶν.

ΝΕ. ΣΩ. Τοῦτο μὲν ὀρθῶς· ὅπη δὲ ἡμῖν οὔπω
φῂς ἱκανῶς εἰρῆσθαι δήλωσον.

D ΞΕ. Χαλεπόν, ὦ δαιμόνιε, μὴ παραδείγμασι
χρώμενον ἱκανῶς ἐνδείκνυσθαί τι τῶν μειζόνων.
κινδυνεύει γὰρ ἡμῶν ἕκαστος οἷον ὄναρ εἰδὼς
ἅπαντα πάντ' αὖ πάλιν ὥσπερ ὕπαρ ἀγνοεῖν.

ΝΕ. ΣΩ. Πῶς τοῦτ' εἶπες;

ΞΕ. Καὶ μάλ' ἀτόπως ἔοικά γε ἐν τῷ παρόντι
κινήσας τὸ περὶ τῆς ἐπιστήμης πάθος ἐν ἡμῖν.

ΝΕ. ΣΩ. Τί δή;

ΞΕ. Παραδείγματος, ὦ μακάριε, αὖ μοι καὶ τὸ
παράδειγμα αὐτὸ δεδέηκεν.

E ΝΕ. ΣΩ. Τί οὖν; λέγε μηδὲν ἐμοῦ γε ἔνεκα
ἀποκνῶν.

---

[1] *i.e.* the nature of example is to be explained below
by means of an example. The example of the letters of
the alphabet is employed also in the *Theaetetus* 202 ff.,
but the Stranger cannot properly refer to that, as he was

time, wishing to make quick progress, and also to make clear in a grand style the error of our previous course, and, moreover, fancying that the use of great illustrations was proper in the case of a king, have taken up a marvellous mass of myth and have consequently been obliged to use a greater part of it than we should. So we have made our discourse too long and after all have never made an end of the tale, but our talk, just like a picture of a living creature, seems to have a good enough outline, but not yet to have received the clearness that comes from pigments and the blending of colours. And yet it is more fitting to portray any living being by speech and argument than by painting or any handicraft whatsoever to persons who are able to follow argument; but to others it is better to do it by means of works of craftsmanship.

Y. SOC. That is true; but explain wherein you think our exposition is still deficient.

STR. It is difficult, my dear fellow, to set forth any of the greater ideas, except by the use of examples; for it would seem that each of us knows everything that he knows as if in a dream and then again, when he is as it were awake, knows nothing of it all.

Y. SOC. What do you mean by that?

STR. I seem at present in absurd fashion to have touched upon our experience in regard to knowledge.

Y. SOC. In what respect?

STR. Why, my friend, the very example I employ requires another example.[1]

Y. SOC. Indeed? What is it? Don't hesitate to tell on my account.

not present at the time. Or is this a dramatic slip on Plato's part?

PLATO

20. ΞΕ. Λεκτέον, ἐπειδὴ καὶ σύ γε ἕτοιμος ἀκολουθεῖν. τοὺς γάρ που παῖδας ἴσμεν, ὅταν ἄρτι γραμμάτων ἔμπειροι γίγνωνται —

ΝΕ. ΣΩ. Τὸ ποῖον;

ΞΕ. Ὅτι τῶν στοιχείων ἕκαστον ἐν ταῖς βραχυτάταις καὶ ῥᾴσταις τῶν συλλαβῶν ἱκανῶς διαισθάνονται, καὶ τἀληθῆ φράζειν περὶ ἐκεῖνα δυνατοὶ γίγνονται.

278 ΝΕ. ΣΩ. Πῶς γὰρ οὔ;

ΞΕ. Ταὐτὰ δέ γε ταῦτα ἐν ἄλλαις ἀμφιγνοοῦντες πάλιν δόξῃ τε ψεύδονται καὶ λόγῳ.

ΝΕ. ΣΩ. Πάνυ μὲν οὖν.

ΞΕ. Ἆρ' οὖν οὐχ ὧδε ῥᾷστον καὶ κάλλιστον ἐπάγειν αὐτοὺς ἐπὶ τὰ μήπω γιγνωσκόμενα;

ΝΕ. ΣΩ. Πῶς;

ΞΕ. Ἀνάγειν πρῶτον ἐπ' ἐκεῖνα, ἐν οἷς ταὐτὰ ταῦτα ὀρθῶς ἐδόξαζον, ἀναγαγόντας δὲ τιθέναι
B παρὰ τὰ μήπω γιγνωσκόμενα, καὶ παραβάλλοντας ἐνδεικνύναι τὴν αὐτὴν ὁμοιότητα καὶ φύσιν ἐν ἀμφοτέραις οὖσαν ταῖς συμπλοκαῖς, μέχριπερ ἂν πᾶσι τοῖς ἀγνοουμένοις τὰ δοξαζόμενα ἀληθῶς παρατιθέμενα δειχθῇ, δειχθέντα δέ, παραδείγματα οὕτω γιγνόμενα, ποιήσῃ τῶν στοιχείων πάντων ἕκαστον ἐν πάσαις ταῖς συλλαβαῖς τὸ μὲν ἕτερον ὡς τῶν ἄλλων ἕτερον ὄν, τὸ δὲ
C ταὐτὸν ὡς ταὐτὸν ἀεὶ κατὰ ταὐτὰ ἑαυτῷ προσαγορεύεσθαι.

ΝΕ. ΣΩ. Παντάπασι μὲν οὖν.

ΞΕ. Οὐκοῦν τοῦτο μὲν ἱκανῶς συνειλήφαμεν, ὅτι

---

[1] There is here a play on the words παρα-τιθέμενα δειχθῇ, δειχθέντα δέ, παρα-δείγματα. Placed beside, they are shown,

78

str. I will tell, since you on your part are prepared to listen. We know that children, when they are just getting some knowledge of letters—

y. soc. Well?

str. Recognize the several letters well enough in the short and easy syllables, and can make correct statements about them.

y. soc. Yes, of course.

str. And then again in other syllables they are in doubt about those same letters, and err in opinion and speech about them.

y. soc. Yes, certainly.

str. Would not the easiest and best way to lead them to the letters which they do not yet know be this?

y. soc. What?

str. To lead them first to those cases in which they had correct opinions about these same letters and then to lead them and set them beside the groups which they did not yet recognize and by comparing them to show that their nature is the same in both combinations alike, and to continue until the letters about which their opinions are correct have been shown in juxtaposition with all those of which they are ignorant. Being shown in this way they become examples[1] and bring it about that every letter is in all syllables always called by the same name, either by differentiation from the other letters, in case it is different, or because it is the same.

y. soc. Certainly.

str. Is this, then, a satisfactory definition, that

and being shown, they become paradigms, *i.e.* objects of comparison, *i.e.* examples.

παραδείγματός γ᾽ ἐστὶ τότε γένεσις, ὁπόταν ὂν
ταὐτὸν ἐν ἑτέρῳ διεσπασμένῳ δοξαζόμενον ὀρθῶς
καὶ συναχθὲν περὶ ἑκάτερον ὡς συνάμφω μίαν
ἀληθῆ δόξαν ἀποτελῇ;

ΝΕ. ΣΩ. Φαίνεται.

ΞΕ. Θαυμάζοιμεν ἂν οὖν, εἰ ταὐτὸν τοῦτο ἡμῶν ἡ
ψυχὴ φύσει περὶ τὰ τῶν πάντων στοιχεῖα πεπονθυῖα
D τοτὲ μὲν ὑπ᾽ ἀληθείας περὶ ἓν ἕκαστον ἔν τισι συν-
ίσταται, τοτὲ δὲ περὶ ἅπαντα ἐν ἑτέροις αὖ φέρεται,
καὶ τὰ μὲν αὐτῶν ἀμῇ γέ πῃ τῶν συγκράσεων
ὀρθῶς δοξάζει, μετατιθέμενα δ᾽ εἰς τὰς τῶν πραγμάτων μακρὰς καὶ μὴ ῥᾳδίους συλλαβὰς ταὐτὰ
ταῦτα πάλιν ἀγνοεῖ;

ΝΕ. ΣΩ. Καὶ θαυμαστόν γε οὐδέν.

ΞΕ. Πῶς γάρ, ὦ φίλε, δύναιτο ἄν τις ἀρχόμενος
ἀπὸ δόξης ψευδοῦς ἐπί τι τῆς ἀληθείας καὶ μικρὸν
E μέρος ἀφικόμενος κτήσασθαι φρόνησιν;

ΝΕ. ΣΩ. Σχεδὸν οὐδαμῶς.

ΞΕ. Οὐκοῦν ταῦτα εἰ ταύτῃ πέφυκεν, οὐδὲν δὴ
πλημμελοῖμεν ἂν ἐγώ τε καὶ σὺ πρῶτον μὲν ἐπιχει-
ρήσαντες ὅλου παραδείγματος ἰδεῖν τὴν φύσιν ἐν
σμικρῷ κατὰ μέρος ἄλλῳ παραδείγματι, μετὰ δὲ
ταῦτα μέλλοντες, ἐπὶ τὸ τοῦ βασιλέως μέγιστον ὂν
ταὐτὸν εἶδος ἀπ᾽ ἐλαττόνων φέροντές ποθεν, διὰ
παραδείγματος ἐπιχειρεῖν αὖ τὴν τῶν κατὰ πόλιν
θεραπείαν τέχνῃ γνωρίζειν, ἵνα ὕπαρ ἀντ᾽ ὀνείρατος
ἡμῖν γίγνηται;

ΝΕ. ΣΩ. Πάνυ μὲν οὖν ὀρθῶς.

279 ΞΕ. Πάλιν δὴ τὸν ἔμπροσθεν λόγον ἀναληπτέον,
ὡς ἐπειδὴ τῷ βασιλικῷ γένει τῆς περὶ τὰς πόλεις
ἐπιμελείας ἀμφισβητοῦσι μυρίοι, δεῖ δὴ πάντας
ἀποχωρίζειν τούτους καὶ μόνον ἐκεῖνον λείπειν, καὶ

an example is formed when that which is the same in some second unconnected thing is rightly conceived and compared with the first, so that the two together form one true idea?

Y. SOC. Evidently.

STR. Can we wonder, then, that our soul, whose nature involves it in the same uncertainty about the letters or elements of all things, is sometimes in some cases firmly grounded in the truth about every detail, and again in other cases is all at sea about everything, and somehow or other has correct opinions about some combinations, and then again is ignorant of the same things when they are transferred to the long and difficult syllables of life?

Y. SOC. Surely we need not wonder at that.

STR. No; for could anyone, my friend, who begins with false opinion, ever attain to even a small part of truth and acquire wisdom?

Y. SOC. No; it is hardly possible.

STR. Then if this is the case, would it be a bad thing if you and I first tried to see in another small and partial example the nature of example in general, with the intention of transferring afterwards the same figurative method from lesser things to the most exalted eminence of the king, and trying by means of an example to become acquainted in a scientific way with the management of states, in order that this may be waking knowledge for us, not dream knowledge?

Y. SOC. That is a very good idea.

STR. Then we must take up our former argument again, and since there are countless others who contend that they, rather than the royal class, have the care of states, we must accordingly remove all these

81

πρὸς τοῦτο δὴ παραδείγματος ἔφαμεν δεῖν τινος ἡμῖν.

ΝΕ. ΣΩ. Καὶ μάλα.

21. ΞΕ. Τί δῆτα παράδειγμά τις ἄν, ἔχον τὴν αὐτὴν πολιτικῇ[1] πραγματείαν, σμικρότατον παρα-
B θέμενος ἱκανῶς ἂν εὕροι τὸ ζητούμενον; βούλει πρὸς Διός, ὦ Σώκρατες, εἰ μή τι πρόχειρον ἕτερον ἔχομεν, ἀλλ' οὖν τήν γε ὑφαντικὴν προελώμεθα; καὶ ταύτην, εἰ δοκεῖ, μὴ πᾶσαν; ἀποχρήσει γὰρ ἴσως ἡ περὶ τὰ ἐκ τῶν ἐρίων ὑφάσματα· τάχα γὰρ ἂν ἡμῖν καὶ τοῦτο τὸ μέρος αὐτῆς μαρτυρήσειε προαιρεθὲν ὃ βουλόμεθα.

ΝΕ. ΣΩ. Τί γὰρ οὔ;

ΞΕ. Τί δῆτα οὔ, καθάπερ ἐν τοῖς ἔμπροσθεν τέμνοντες μέρη μερῶν ἕκαστον διῃρούμεθα, καὶ
C νῦν περὶ ὑφαντικὴν ταὐτὸν τοῦτο ἐδράσαμεν, καὶ κατὰ δύναμιν ὅτι μάλιστα διὰ βραχέων ταχὺ πάντ' ἐπελθόντες πάλιν ἤλθομεν ἐπὶ τὸ νῦν χρήσιμον;

ΝΕ. ΣΩ. Πῶς λέγεις;

ΞΕ. Αὐτὴν τὴν διέξοδον ἀπόκρισίν σοι ποιήσομαι.

ΝΕ. ΣΩ. Κάλλιστ' εἶπες.

ΞΕ. Ἔστι τοίνυν πάντα ἡμῖν ὁπόσα δημιουργοῦ-
μεν καὶ κτώμεθα, τὰ μὲν ἕνεκα τοῦ ποιεῖν τι, τὰ δὲ τοῦ μὴ πάσχειν ἀμυντήρια[2]· καὶ τῶν ἀμυντηρίων[3] τὰ μὲν ἀλεξιφάρμακα καὶ θεῖα καὶ ἀνθρώπινα, τὰ
D δὲ προβλήματα· τῶν δὲ προβλημάτων τὰ μὲν πρὸς τὸν πόλεμον ὁπλίσματα, τὰ δὲ φράγματα· καὶ τῶν φραγμάτων τὰ μὲν παραπετάσματα, τὰ δὲ πρὸς χειμῶνας καὶ καύματα ἀλεξητήρια· τῶν δὲ ἀλεξη-

---

[1] πολιτικῇ Ast : πολιτικὴν ΒΤ.
[2] ἀμυντήρια] ἀλεξιτήρια ΒΤ.
[3] ἀμυντηρίων] ἀλεξιτηρίων ΒΤ.

and isolate the king; and, as we said, to accomplish this we need an example.

Y. SOC. Certainly.

STR. What example could we apply which is very small, but has the same kind of activity as statesmanship and would enable us satisfactorily to discover that which we seek? What do you say, Socrates, if we have nothing else at hand, to taking at random the art of weaving, and, if you please, not the whole of that? For I fancy the art of weaving wool will be enough; if we choose that part only it will probably furnish us with the illustration we desire.

Y. SOC. Agreed.

STR. Then just as we divided each subject before by cutting off parts from parts, why not now apply the same process to the art of weaving and, by going through all the steps as briefly as we possibly can, arrive quickly at that which serves our present purpose?

Y. SOC. What do you mean?

STR. I will answer you by actually going through the process.

Y. SOC. Excellent!

STR. Well, then, all things which we make or acquire are for the sake of doing something or else they are for defence against suffering; and of the defensive class some are spells and antidotes, both divine and human, and some are material defences; and of the material defences some are equipment for war and some are protections; and of protections some are screens and some are defences against heat

83

τηρίων τὰ μὲν στεγάσματα, τὰ δὲ σκεπάσματα· καὶ
τῶν σκεπασμάτων ὑποπετάσματα μὲν ἄλλα, περι-
καλύμματα δὲ ἕτερα· περικαλυμμάτων δὲ τὰ μὲν
Ε ὁλόσχιστα, σύνθετα δὲ ἕτερα· τῶν δὲ συνθέτων τὰ
μὲν τρητά, τὰ δὲ ἄνευ τρήσεως συνδετά· καὶ τῶν
ἀτρήτων τὰ μὲν νεύρινα φυτῶν ἐκ γῆς, τὰ δὲ τρίχινα·
τῶν δὲ τριχίνων τὰ μὲν ὕδασι καὶ γῇ κολλητά, τὰ
δὲ αὐτὰ αὑτοῖς συνδετά. τουτοισὶ δὴ τοῖς ἐκ
τῶν ἑαυτοῖς συνδουμένων[1] ἐργασθεῖσιν ἀμυντηρίοις
καὶ σκεπάσμασι τὸ μὲν ὄνομα ἱμάτια ἐκαλέσαμεν·
τὴν δὲ τῶν ἱματίων μάλιστα ἐπιμελουμένην τέχνην,
280 ὥσπερ τότε τὴν τῆς πόλεως πολιτικὴν εἴπομεν,
οὕτω καὶ νῦν ταύτην προσείπωμεν ἀπ' αὐτοῦ τοῦ
πράγματος ἱματιουργικήν; φῶμεν δὲ καὶ ὑφαντικήν, ὅσον ἐπὶ τῇ τῶν ἱματίων ἐργασίᾳ μέγιστον ἦν
μόριον, μηδὲν διαφέρειν πλὴν ὀνόματι ταύτης τῆς
ἱματιουργικῆς, καθάπερ κἀκεῖ τότε τὴν βασιλικὴν
τῆς πολιτικῆς;

ΝΕ. ΣΩ. Ὀρθότατά γε.

ΞΕ. Τὸ μετὰ τοῦτο δὴ συλλογισώμεθα, ὅτι τὴν
ἱματίων ὑφαντικὴν οὕτω ῥηθεῖσάν τις τάχ' ἂν ἱκανῶς
Β εἰρῆσθαι δόξειε, μὴ δυνάμενος ξυννοεῖν ὅτι τῶν
μὲν ἐγγὺς ξυνεργῶν οὔπω διώρισται, πολλῶν δὲ
ἑτέρων ξυγγενῶν ἀπεμερίσθη.

ΝΕ. ΣΩ. Ποίων, εἰπέ, ξυγγενῶν;

22. ΞΕ. Οὐχ ἕσπου τοῖς λεχθεῖσιν, ὡς φαίνει·
πάλιν οὖν ἔοικεν ἐπανιτέον ἀρχόμενον ἀπὸ τελευτῆς.
εἰ γὰρ ξυννοεῖς τὴν οἰκειότητα, τὴν μὲν διετέμομεν

---

[1] ἑαυτοῖς συνδουμένων] αὑτῶν (αὐτῶν Β) συνδουμένοις ΒΤ.
84

and cold; and such defences are either shelters or coverings; and coverings are either rugs to spread under us or wrappings to wrap round us; and wrappings are either all of one piece or composed of several pieces; and of the composite garments some are stitched and others put together without stitching; and of the unstitched some are made of the fibres of plants and some are of hair; and of those made with hair some are stuck together with liquids and cement and others are fastened without any such extraneous matter. Now to these protective coverings made of materials fastened without extraneous matter we give the name of clothes; and just as we called the art statecraft which was concerned with the state, so we shall call the art concerned with clothes, from the nature of its activity, clothes-making, shall we not? And may we say further that weaving, in so far as the greatest part of it is, as we saw, concerned with the making of clothes, differs in name only from this art of clothes-making, just as in the other case the royal art differed from statecraft?

y. soc. That is perfectly correct.

str. Let us next reflect that a person might think that this description of the art of weaving was satisfactory, because he cannot understand that it has not yet been distinguished from the closely co-operative arts, though it has been separated from many other kindred arts.

y. soc. What kindred arts?

str. You do not seem to have followed what I have been saying; so I think I had better go back again and begin at the end. For if you understand what I mean by kinship, we distinguished

ἀπ' αὐτῆς νῦν δή, τὴν τῶν στρωμάτων σύνθεσιν
περιβολῇ χωρίζοντες καὶ ὑποβολῇ.

ΝΕ. ΣΩ. Μανθάνω.

C ΞΕ. Καὶ μὴν τὴν ἐκ τῶν λίνων καὶ σπάρτων
καὶ πάντων ὁπόσα φυτῶν ἄρτι νεῦρα κατὰ λόγον εἴπομεν, δημιουργίαν πᾶσαν ἀφείλομεν· τήν τ' αὖ
πιλητικὴν ἀφωρισάμεθα καὶ τὴν τρήσει καὶ ῥαφῇ
χρωμένην σύνθεσιν, ἧς ἡ πλείστη σκυτοτομική.

ΝΕ. ΣΩ. Πάνυ μὲν οὖν.

ΞΕ. Καὶ τοίνυν τὴν τῶν ὁλοσχίστων σκεπασμάτων θεραπείαν δερματουργικὴν καὶ τὰς τῶν στεγα-
σμάτων, ὅσαι τε ἐν οἰκοδομικῇ καὶ ὅλῃ τεκτονικῇ
D καὶ ἐν ἄλλαις τέχναις ῥευμάτων στεκτικαὶ γίγνονται, συμπάσας ἀφείλομεν, ὅσαι τε[1] περὶ τὰς
κλοπὰς[2] καὶ τὰς βίᾳ πράξεις διακωλυτικὰ ἔργα
παρέχονται τέχναι φραγμάτων, περί τε γένεσιν
ἐπιθηματουργίας οὖσαι καὶ τὰς τῶν θυρωμάτων
πήξεις, γομφωτικῆς ἀπονεμηθεῖσαι μόρια τέχνης·
τήν τε ὁπλοποιικὴν ἀπετεμόμεθα, μεγάλης καὶ
παντοίας τῆς προβληματουργικῆς τμῆμα οὖσαν
δυνάμεως· καὶ δὴ καὶ τὴν μαγευτικὴν τὴν περὶ τὰ
E ἀλεξιφάρμακα κατ' ἀρχὰς εὐθὺς διωρισάμεθα ξύμπασαν, καὶ λελοίπαμεν, ὡς δόξαιμεν ἄν, αὐτὴν τὴν
ζητηθεῖσαν ἀμυντικὴν χειμώνων, ἐρεοῦ προβλήμα-
τος ἐργαστικήν, ὄνομα δὲ ὑφαντικὴν λεχθεῖσαν.

ΝΕ. ΣΩ. Ἔοικε γὰρ οὖν.

ΞΕ. Ἀλλ' οὐκ ἔστι πω τέλεον, ὦ παῖ, τοῦτο λε-
λεγμένον. ὁ γὰρ ἐν ἀρχῇ τῆς τῶν ἱματίων ἐργασίας
281 ἁπτόμενος τοὐναντίον ὑφῇ δρᾶν φαίνεται.

ΝΕ. ΣΩ. Πῶς;

---

[1] τε D: om. BT.
[2] κλοπὰς] πλοκὰς ΒΤ.

from clothing something akin to it a moment ago when we separated rugs from it by the distinction between spreading under and wrapping round.

y. soc. I understand.

str. And we removed the entire manufacture of cloth made from flax and broom-cords and all that we just now called vegetable fibres; and then, too, we separated off the process of felting and the kind of joining that employs piercing and sewing, most important of which is the shoemaker's art.

y. soc. Yes, to be sure.

str. And we separated off the art of making coverings of leather in single pieces and all the arts of making shelters, which we find in house-building and carpentering in general and in other methods of protection against water, and all the arts which furnish protection against theft and acts of violence, the arts, that is to say, of making lids and constructing doors, which are regarded as parts of the joiner's art; and we cut off the armourer's art, which is a section of the great and various function of making defences; and at the very beginning we cut off the whole art of magic which is concerned with antidotes and spells, and we have left, as it would seem, just the art we were seeking, which furnishes protection from the weather, manufactures a defence of wool, and is called the art of weaving.

y. soc. That seems to be the case.

str. But, my boy, this is not yet completely stated; for the man who is engaged in the first part of the making of clothes appears to do something the opposite of weaving.

y. soc. How so?

ΞΕ. Τὸ μὲν τῆς ὑφῆς συμπλοκή τίς ἐστί που.

ΝΕ. ΣΩ. Ναί.

ΞΕ. Τὸ δέ γε τῶν συνεστώτων καὶ συμπεπιλημένων διαλυτική.

ΝΕ. ΣΩ. Τὸ ποῖον δή;

ΞΕ. Τὸ τῆς τοῦ ξαίνοντος τέχνης ἔργον. ἢ τὴν ξαντικὴν τολμήσομεν ὑφαντικὴν καὶ τὸν ξάντην ὡς ὄντα ὑφάντην καλεῖν;

ΝΕ. ΣΩ. Οὐδαμῶς.

ΞΕ. Καὶ μὴν τήν γε αὖ στήμονος ἐργαστικὴν καὶ κρόκης εἴ τις ὑφαντικὴν προσαγορεύει, παράδοξόν
B τε καὶ ψεῦδος ὄνομα λέγει.

ΝΕ. ΣΩ. Πῶς γὰρ οὔ;

ΞΕ. Τί δέ; κναφευτικὴν σύμπασαν καὶ τὴν ἀκεστικὴν πότερα μηδεμίαν ἐπιμέλειαν μηδέ τινα θεραπείαν ἐσθῆτος θῶμεν, ἢ καὶ ταύτας πάσας ὡς ὑφαντικὰς λέξομεν;

ΝΕ. ΣΩ. Οὐδαμῶς.

ΞΕ. Ἀλλὰ μὴν τῆς γε θεραπείας ἀμφισβητήσουσιν αὗται ξύμπασαι καὶ τῆς γενέσεως τῆς τῶν ἱματίων τῇ τῆς ὑφαντικῆς δυνάμει, μέγιστον μὲν μέρος ἐκείνῃ διδοῦσαι, μεγάλα δὲ καὶ σφίσιν αὐταῖς ἀπονέμουσαι.

C ΝΕ. ΣΩ. Πάνυ γε.

ΞΕ. Πρὸς τοίνυν ταύταις ἔτι τὰς τῶν ἐργαλείων δημιουργοὺς τέχνας, δι᾽ ὧν ἀποτελεῖται τὰ τῆς ὑφῆς ἔργα, δοκεῖν χρὴ τό γε¹ συναιτίας εἶναι προσποιήσασθαι παντὸς ὑφάσματος.

ΝΕ. ΣΩ. Ὀρθότατα.

ΞΕ. Πότερον οὖν ἡμῖν ὁ περὶ τῆς ὑφαντικῆς λόγος, οὗ προειλόμεθα μέρους, ἱκανῶς ἔσται διωρισμένος, ἐὰν ἄρ᾽ αὐτὴν τῶν ἐπιμελειῶν ὁπόσαι περὶ

STR. The process of weaving is, I take it, a kind of joining together.

Y. SOC. Yes.

STR. But the first part I refer to is a separation of what is combined and matted together.

Y. SOC. What do you mean?

STR. The work of the carder's art. Or shall we have the face to say that carding is weaving and the carder is a weaver?

Y. SOC. No, certainly not.

STR. And surely if we say the art of making the warp or the woof is the art of weaving, we are employing an irrational and false designation.

Y. SOC. Of course.

STR. Well then, shall we say that the whole arts of fulling and mending are no part of the care and treatment of clothes, or shall we declare that these also are entirely included in the art of weaving?

Y. SOC. By no means.

STR. But surely all these will contest the claim of the art of weaving in the matter of the treatment and the production of clothes; they will grant that the part of weaving is the most important, but will claim that their own parts are of some importance, too.

Y. SOC. Yes, certainly.

STR. Then we must believe that besides these the arts which produce the tools by means of which the works of weaving are accomplished will claim to be collaborators in every work of weaving.

Y. SOC. Quite right.

STR. Will our definition of the art of weaving (I mean the part of it we selected) be satisfactory if we say that of all the activities connected with

---

¹ γε] τε BT.

τὴν ἐρεᾶν ἐσθῆτα, εἰς τὴν καλλίστην καὶ μεγίστην
D πασῶν τιθῶμεν· ἢ λέγοιμεν μὲν ἄν τι ἀληθές, οὐ
μὴν σαφές γε οὐδὲ τέλεον, πρὶν ἂν¹ καὶ ταύτας
αὐτῆς πάσας περιέλωμεν;

ΝΕ. ΣΩ. Ὀρθῶς.

23. ΞΕ. Οὐκοῦν μετὰ ταῦτα ποιητέον ὃ λέγομεν, ἵν' ἐφεξῆς ἡμῖν ὁ λόγος ἴῃ;

ΝΕ. ΣΩ. Πῶς δ' οὔ;

ΞΕ. Πρῶτον μὲν τοίνυν δύο τέχνας οὔσας περὶ
πάντα τὰ δρώμενα θεασώμεθα.

ΝΕ. ΣΩ. Τίνας;

ΞΕ. Τὴν μὲν γενέσεως οὖσαν ξυναίτιον, τὴν δ'
αὐτὴν αἰτίαν.

ΝΕ. ΣΩ. Πῶς;

ΞΕ. Ὅσαι μὲν τὸ πρᾶγμα αὐτὸ μὴ δημιουργοῦσι,
E ταῖς δὲ δημιουργούσαις ὄργανα παρασκευάζουσιν,
ὧν μὴ παραγενομένων οὐκ ἄν ποτε ἐργασθείη τὸ
προστεταγμένον ἑκάστῃ τῶν τεχνῶν, ταύτας μὲν
ξυναιτίους, τὰς δὲ αὐτὸ τὸ πρᾶγμα ἀπεργαζομένας
αἰτίας.

ΝΕ. ΣΩ. Ἔχει γοῦν λόγον.

ΞΕ. Μετὰ τοῦτο δὴ τὰς μὲν περί τε ἀτράκτους
καὶ κερκίδας καὶ ὁπόσα ἄλλα ὄργανα τῆς περὶ τὰ
ἀμφιέσματα γενέσεως κοινωνεῖ, πάσας ξυναιτίους
εἴπωμεν, τὰς δὲ αὐτὰ θεραπευούσας καὶ δημιουρ-
γούσας αἰτίας;

ΝΕ. ΣΩ. Ὀρθότατα.

282 ΞΕ. Τῶν αἰτιῶν δὴ πλυντικὴν μὲν καὶ ἀκεστικὴν καὶ πᾶσαν τὴν περὶ ταῦτα θεραπευτικήν, πολλῆς
οὔσης τῆς κοσμητικῆς, τοὐνταῦθα αὐτῆς μόριον
εἰκὸς μάλιστα περιλαμβάνειν ὀνομάζοντας πᾶν τῇ
τέχνῃ τῇ κναφευτικῇ.

woollen clothing it is the noblest and the greatest?
Or would that, although it contains some truth, yet
lack clearness and completeness until we separate
from weaving all these other arts?

Y. SOC. You are right.

STR. Then shall our next move be to do this, that
our discussion may proceed in due order?

Y. SOC. Certainly.

STR. First, then, let us observe that there are two
arts involved in all production.

Y. SOC. What are they?

STR. The one is a contingent cause, the other
is the actual cause.

Y. SOC. What do you mean?

STR. Those arts which do not produce the actual
thing in question, but which supply to the arts
which do produce it the tools without which no art
could ever perform its prescribed work, may be
called contingent causes, and those which produce
the actual thing are causes.

Y. SOC. At any rate, that is reasonable.

STR. Next, then, shall we designate all the arts
which produce spindles, shuttles, and the various
other tools that partake in the production of clothing
as contingent causes, and those which treat and
manufacture the clothing itself as causes?

Y. SOC. Quite right.

STR. And among the causal arts we may properly
include washing and mending and all the care of
clothing in such ways; and, since the art of adornment is a wide one, we may classify them as a part
of it under the name of fulling.

---

¹ ἂν] αὖ BT.

ΝΕ. ΣΩ. Καλῶς.

ΞΕ. Καὶ μὴν ξαντική γε καὶ νηστική[1] καὶ πάντα
αὖ τὰ περὶ τὴν ποίησιν αὐτὴν τῆς ἐσθῆτος ἧς λέγομεν
μέρη, μία τίς ἐστι τέχνη τῶν ὑπὸ πάντων λεγομένων
ἡ ταλασιουργική.

B   ΝΕ. ΣΩ. Πῶς γὰρ οὔ;

ΞΕ. Τῆς δὴ ταλασιουργικῆς δύο τμήματά ἐστον,
καὶ τούτοιν ἑκάτερον ἅμα δυοῖν πεφύκατον τέχναιν
μέρη.

ΝΕ. ΣΩ. Πῶς;

ΞΕ. Τὸ μὲν ξαντικὸν καὶ τὸ τῆς κερκιστικῆς
ἥμισυ καὶ ὅσα τὰ ξυγκείμενα ἀπ' ἀλλήλων ἀφίστησι,
πᾶν τοῦτο ὡς ἓν φράζειν τῆς τε ταλασιουργίας
αὐτῆς ἐστί που, καὶ μεγάλα τινὲ κατὰ πάντα ἤμιν
ἤστην τέχνα, ἡ συγκριτική τε καὶ διακριτική.

ΝΕ. ΣΩ. Ναί.

ΞΕ. Τῆς τοίνυν διακριτικῆς ἥ τε ξαντικὴ καὶ τὰ
C νῦν δὴ ῥηθέντα ἅπαντά ἐστιν· ἡ γὰρ ἐν ἐρίοις τε
καὶ στήμοσι διακριτική, κερκίδι μὲν ἄλλον τρόπον
γιγνομένη, χερσὶ δὲ ἕτερον, ἔσχεν ὅσα ἀρτίως
ὀνόματα ἐρρήθη.

ΝΕ. ΣΩ. Πάνυ μὲν οὖν.

ΞΕ. Αὖθις δὴ πάλιν συγκριτικῆς μόριον ἅμα καὶ
ταλασιουργίας ἐν αὐτῇ γιγνόμενον λάβωμεν· ὅσα
δὲ τῆς διακριτικῆς ἦν, αὐτόθι μεθιῶμεν[2] ξύμπαντα,
δίχα τέμνοντες τὴν ταλασιουργίαν διακριτικῷ τε
καὶ συγκριτικῷ τμήματι.

ΝΕ. ΣΩ. Διῃρήσθω.

ΞΕ. Τὸ συγκριτικὸν τοίνυν αὖ σοι καὶ ταλα-

---

[1] ξαντική . . . νηστική Stephanus : ξαντικήν . . . νηστικὴν
BT.

[2] μεθιῶμεν Hermann : μετίωμεν BT.

y. soc. Good.

str. And, again, carding and spinning and all the processes concerned with the actual fabrication of the clothing under consideration, form collectively one art familiar to every one—the art of wool-working.

y. soc. Of course.

str. And wool-working comprises two divisions, and each of these is a part of two arts at once.

y. soc. How is that?

str. Carding, and one half of the use of the weaver's rod,[1] and the other crafts which separate things that are joined—all this collectively is a part of the art of wool-working; and in all things we found two great arts, that of composition and that of division.

y. soc. Yes.

str. Now carding and all the other processes just mentioned are parts of the art of division; for the art of division in wool and threads, exercised in one way with the rod and in another with the hands, has all the names just mentioned.

y. soc. Yes, certainly.

str. Then let us again take up something which is at once a part of the arts of composition and of wool-working. Let us put aside all that belongs to division, making two parts of wool-working, by applying the principles of division and of composition.

y. soc. Let us make that distinction.

str. The part which belongs at once to com-

---

[1] The weaver's rod (for the Greeks appear to have used a rod, not a comb) was used to drive the threads of the woof close together, and also to keep the threads of the warp and woof distinct (*cf. Cratylus* 388 A). All the processes here described, familiar as they were to the ancients, have been done away with, or, at least, greatly modified, in Europe and America by the modern methods of industry

PLATO

D σιουργικὸν ἅμα μόριον, ὦ Σώκρατες, διαιρετέον,
εἴπερ ἱκανῶς μέλλομεν τὴν προρρηθεῖσαν ὑφαντικὴν
αἱρήσειν.

ΝΕ. ΣΩ. Οὐκοῦν χρή.

ΞΕ. Χρὴ μὲν οὖν· καὶ λέγωμέν γε αὐτῆς τὸ μὲν
εἶναι στρεπτικόν, τὸ δὲ συμπλεκτικόν.

ΝΕ. ΣΩ. Ἆρ᾽ οὖν μανθάνω; δοκεῖς γάρ μοι τὸ
περὶ τὴν τοῦ στήμονος ἐργασίαν λέγειν στρεπτικόν.

ΞΕ. Οὐ μόνον γε, ἀλλὰ καὶ κρόκης· ἢ γένεσιν
ἄστροφόν τινα αὐτῆς εὑρήσομεν;

ΝΕ. ΣΩ. Οὐδαμῶς.

ΞΕ. Διόρισαι δὴ καὶ τούτοιν ἑκάτερον· ἴσως γὰρ
E ὁ διορισμὸς ἔγκαιρος ἄν σοι γένοιτο.

ΝΕ. ΣΩ. Πῇ;

ΞΕ. Τῇδε· τῶν περὶ ξαντικὴν ἔργων μηκυνθέν
τε καὶ σχὸν πλάτος λέγομεν εἶναι κάταγμά τι;

ΝΕ. ΣΩ. Ναί.

ΞΕ. Τούτου δὴ τὸ μὲν ἀτράκτῳ τε στραφὲν καὶ
στερεὸν νῆμα γενόμενον στήμονα μὲν φάθι τὸ νῆμα,
τὴν δὲ ἀπευθύνουσαν αὐτὸ τέχνην εἶναι στημονονη-
τικήν.

ΝΕ. ΣΩ. Ὀρθῶς.

ΞΕ. Ὅσα δέ γε αὖ τὴν μὲν συστροφὴν χαύνην
λαμβάνει, τῇ δὲ τοῦ στήμονος ἐμπλέξει πρὸς τὴν
τῆς γνάψεως ὁλκὴν ἐμμέτρως τὴν μαλακότητα
ἴσχει, ταῦτ᾽ ἄρα κρόκην μὲν τὰ νηθέντα, τὴν δὲ
ἐπιτεταγμένην αὐτοῖς εἶναι τέχνην τὴν κροκονητικὴν
283 φῶμεν.

ΝΕ. ΣΩ. Ὀρθότατα.

---

[1] *i.e.* the pull (ὁλκή) of the carder's comb was less strong
in the preparation of the threads of the woof than in that of
the threads of the warp.

94

position and to wool-working, Socrates, you must allow us to divide again, if we are to get a satisfactory concept of the aforesaid art of weaving.

y. soc. Then we must divide it.

str. Yes, we must; and let us call one part of it the art of twisting threads, and the other the art of intertwining them.

y. soc. I am not sure I understand. By the art of twisting I think you mean the making of the warp.

str. Not that only, but also the making of the woof. We shall not find that the woof is made without twisting, shall we?

y. soc. No, of course not.

str. Well, just define warp and woof; perhaps the definition would serve you well at this junction.

y. soc. How shall I do it?

str. In this way: A piece of carded wool, which is lengthened out and is wide, is said to be a lap of wool, is it not?

y. soc. Yes.

str. And if any such lap of wool is twisted with a spindle and made into a hard thread, we call the thread warp, and the art which governs this process is the art of spinning the warp.

y. soc. Right.

str. And the threads, in turn, which are more loosely twisted and have in respect to the force used in the carding a softness adapted to the interweaving with the warp we will call the woof, and the art devoted to these we will call the art of preparing the woof.[1]

y. soc. Quite right.

ΞΕ. Καὶ μὴν τό γε τῆς ὑφαντικῆς μέρος ὃ προυθέμεθα, παντί που δῆλον ἤδη. τὸ γὰρ συγκριτικῆς τῆς ἐν ταλασιουργίᾳ μόριον ὅταν εὐθυπλοκίᾳ κρόκης καὶ στήμονος ἀπεργάζηται πλέγμα, τὸ μὲν πλεχθὲν ξύμπαν ἐσθῆτα ἐρεᾶν, τὴν δὲ ἐπὶ τούτῳ τέχνην οὖσαν προσαγορεύομεν ὑφαντικήν.

ΝΕ. ΣΩ. Ὀρθότατα.

24. ΞΕ. Εἶεν· τί δή ποτε οὖν οὐκ εὐθὺς ἀπ-
B εκρινάμεθα πλεκτικὴν εἶναι κρόκης καὶ στήμονος ὑφαντικήν, ἀλλὰ περιήλθομεν ἐν κύκλῳ πάμπολλα διοριζόμενοι μάτην;

ΝΕ. ΣΩ. Οὔκουν ἔμοιγε, ὦ ξένε, μάτην οὐδὲν τῶν ῥηθέντων ἔδοξε ῥηθῆναι.

ΞΕ. Καὶ θαυμαστόν γε οὐδέν· ἀλλὰ τάχ᾽ ἄν, ὦ μακάριε, δόξειε. πρὸς δὴ τὸ νόσημα τὸ τοιοῦτον, ἂν ἄρα πολλάκις ὕστερον ἐπίῃ — θαυμαστὸν γὰρ οὐδέν —, λόγον ἄκουσόν τινα προσήκοντα περὶ
C πάντων τῶν τοιούτων ῥηθῆναι.

ΝΕ. ΣΩ. Λέγε μόνον.

ΞΕ. Πρῶτον τοίνυν ἴδωμεν[1] πᾶσαν τήν τε ὑπερβολὴν καὶ τὴν ἔλλειψιν, ἵνα κατὰ λόγον ἐπαινῶμεν καὶ ψέγωμεν τὰ μακρότερα τοῦ δέοντος ἑκάστοτε λεγόμενα καὶ τἀναντία περὶ τὰς τοιάσδε διατριβάς.

ΝΕ. ΣΩ. Οὐκοῦν χρή.

ΞΕ. Περὶ δὴ τούτων αὐτῶν ὁ λόγος ἡμῖν, οἶμαι, γιγνόμενος ὀρθῶς ἂν γίγνοιτο.

ΝΕ. ΣΩ. Τίνων;

ΞΕ. Μήκους τε πέρι καὶ βραχύτητος καὶ πάσης
D ὑπεροχῆς[2] τε καὶ ἐλλείψεως· ἡ γάρ που μετρητικὴ περὶ πάντ᾽ ἐστὶ ταῦτα.

ΝΕ. ΣΩ. Ναί.

---

[1] ἴδωμεν] εἰδῶμεν ΒΤ.

STR. So now the part of the art of weaving which we chose for our discussion is clear to pretty much every understanding; for when that part of the art of composition which is included in the art of weaving forms a web by the right intertwining of woof and warp, we call the entire web a woollen garment, and the art which directs this process we call weaving.

Y. SOC. Quite right.

STR. Very good. Then why in the world did we not say at once that weaving is the intertwining of woof and warp? Why did we beat about the bush and make a host of futile distinctions?

Y. SOC. For my part, I thought nothing that was said was futile, Stranger.

STR. And no wonder; but perhaps you might change your mind. Now to avoid any such malady, in case it should, as is not unlikely, attack you frequently hereafter, I will propose a principle of procedure which is applicable to all cases of this sort.

Y. SOC. Do so.

STR. First, then, let us scrutinize the general nature of excess and deficiency, for the sake of obtaining a rational basis for any praise or blame we may bestow upon excessive length or brevity in discussions of this kind.

Y. SOC. Yes, that is a good thing to do.

STR. Then the proper subjects for our consideration would, I fancy, be these.

Y. SOC. What?

STR. Length and shortness and excess and deficiency in general; for all of them may be regarded as the subjects of the art of measurement.

Y. SOC. Yes.

---

[2] ὑπεροχῆς] ὑπερβολῆς BTW (ὑπεροχῆς in marg. W).

ΞΕ. Διέλωμεν τοίνυν αὐτὴν δύο μέρη· δεῖ γὰρ δὴ πρὸς ὃ νῦν σπεύδοιμεν.

ΝΕ. ΣΩ. Λέγοις ἂν τὴν διαίρεσιν ὅπῃ.

ΞΕ. Τῇδε· τὸ μὲν κατὰ τὴν πρὸς ἄλληλα μεγέθους καὶ σμικρότητος κοινωνίαν, τὸ δὲ κατὰ τὴν τῆς γενέσεως ἀναγκαίαν οὐσίαν.

ΝΕ. ΣΩ. Πῶς λέγεις;

ΞΕ. Ἆρ' οὐ κατὰ φύσιν δοκεῖ σοι τὸ μεῖζον μηδενὸς ἑτέρου δεῖν μεῖζον λέγειν ἢ τοῦ ἐλάττονος, καὶ E τοὔλαττον αὖ τοῦ μείζονος ἔλαττον, ἄλλου δὲ μηδενός;

ΝΕ. ΣΩ. Ἔμοιγε.

ΞΕ. Τί δέ; τὸ τὴν τοῦ μετρίου φύσιν ὑπερβάλλον καὶ ὑπερβαλλόμενον ὑπ' αὐτῆς ἐν λόγοις εἴτε καὶ ἐν ἔργοις ἆρ' οὐκ αὖ λέξομεν ὡς ὄντως γιγνόμενον, ἐν ᾧ καὶ διαφέρουσι μάλιστα ἡμῶν οἵ τε κακοὶ καὶ οἱ ἀγαθοί;

ΝΕ. ΣΩ. Φαίνεται.

ΞΕ. Διττὰς ἄρα ταύτας οὐσίας καὶ κρίσεις τοῦ μεγάλου καὶ τοῦ σμικροῦ θετέον, ἀλλ' οὐχ ὡς ἔφαμεν ἄρτι πρὸς ἄλληλα μόνον δεῖν, ἀλλ' ὥσπερ νῦν εἴρηται μᾶλλον τὴν μὲν πρὸς ἄλληλα λεκτέον, τὴν δ' αὖ πρὸς τὸ μέτριον· οὗ δὲ ἕνεκα, μαθεῖν ἆρ' ἂν βουλοίμεθα;

ΝΕ. ΣΩ. Τί μήν;

284 ΞΕ. Εἰ πρὸς μηδὲν ἕτερον τὴν τοῦ μείζονος ἐάσει τις φύσιν ἢ πρὸς τοὔλαττον, οὐκ ἔσται ποτὲ πρὸς τὸ μέτριον· ἢ γάρ;

ΝΕ. ΣΩ. Οὕτως.

ΞΕ. Οὐκοῦν τὰς τέχνας τε αὐτὰς καὶ τἆργα αὐτῶν ξύμπαντα διολοῦμεν[1] τούτῳ τῷ λόγῳ, καὶ δὴ καὶ

---

[1] διολοῦμεν Bekker : διελοῦμεν BT.

STR. Let us, then, divide that art into two parts; that is essential for our present purpose.

Y. SOC. Please tell how to make the division.

STR. In this way: one part is concerned with relative greatness or smallness, the other with the something without which production would not be possible.

Y. SOC. What do you mean?

STR. Do you not think that, by the nature of the case, we must say that the greater is greater than the less and than nothing else, and that the less is less than the greater and than nothing else?

Y. SOC. Yes.

STR. But must we not also assert the real existence of excess beyond the standard of the mean, and of inferiority to the mean, whether in words or deeds, and is not the chief difference between good men and bad found in such excess or deficiency?

Y. SOC. That is clear.

STR. Then we must assume that there are these two kinds of great and small, and these two ways of distinguishing between them; we must not, as we did a little while ago, say that they are relative to one another only, but rather, as we have just said, that one kind is relative in that way, and the other is relative to the standard of the mean. Should we care to learn the reason for this?

Y. SOC. Of course.

STR. If we assert that the greater has no relation to anything except the less, it will never have any relation to the standard of the mean, will it?

Y. SOC. No.

STR. Will not this doctrine destroy the arts and their works one and all, and do away also with

PLATO

τὴν ζητουμένην νῦν πολιτικὴν καὶ τὴν ῥηθεῖσαν
ὑφαντικὴν ἀφανιοῦμεν; ἅπασαι γὰρ αἱ τοιαῦταί
που τὸ τοῦ μετρίου πλέον καὶ ἔλαττον οὐχ ὡς οὐκ
ὂν ἀλλ' ὡς ὂν χαλεπὸν περὶ τὰς πράξεις παραφυλάτ-
B τουσι, καὶ τούτῳ δὴ τῷ τρόπῳ τὸ μέτρον σῴζουσαι
πάντα ἀγαθὰ καὶ καλὰ ἀπεργάζονται.

ΝΕ. ΣΩ. Τί μήν;

ΞΕ. Οὐκοῦν ἂν τὴν πολιτικὴν ἀφανίσωμεν, ἄπορος
ἡμῖν ἡ μετὰ τοῦτο ἔσται ζήτησις τῆς βασιλικῆς
ἐπιστήμης;

ΝΕ. ΣΩ. Καὶ μάλα.

ΞΕ. Πότερον οὖν, καθάπερ ἐν τῷ σοφιστῇ προσ-
ηναγκάσαμεν εἶναι τὸ μὴ ὄν, ἐπειδὴ κατὰ τοῦτο[1]
διέφυγεν ἡμᾶς ὁ λόγος, οὕτω καὶ νῦν τὸ πλέον αὖ
καὶ ἔλαττον μετρητὰ προσαναγκαστέον γίγνεσθαι
C μὴ πρὸς ἄλληλα μόνον ἀλλὰ καὶ πρὸς τὴν τοῦ
μετρίου γένεσιν; οὐ γὰρ δὴ δυνατόν γε οὔτε πολιτικὸν οὔτ' ἄλλον τινὰ τῶν περὶ τὰς πράξεις ἐπιστήμονα ἀναμφισβητήτως γεγονέναι τούτου μὴ
ξυνομολογηθέντος.

ΝΕ. ΣΩ. Οὐκοῦν καὶ νῦν ὅτι μάλιστα χρὴ ταὐτὸν
ποιεῖν.

25. ΞΕ. Πλέον, ὦ Σώκρατες, ἔτι τοῦτο τὸ ἔργον
ἢ 'κεῖνο· καίτοι κἀκείνου γε μεμνήμεθα τὸ μῆκος
ὅσον ἦν· ἀλλ' ὑποτίθεσθαι μὲν τὸ τοιόνδε περὶ
αὐτῶν καὶ μάλα δίκαιον.

ΝΕ. ΣΩ. Τὸ ποῖον;

D ΞΕ. Ὡς ποτε δεήσει τοῦ νῦν λεχθέντος πρὸς τὴν
περὶ αὐτὸ τἀκριβὲς ἀπόδειξιν. ὅτι δὲ πρὸς τὰ νῦν

[1] τοῦτο] τοῦτον BT.

[1] Sophist 235.

100

statesmanship, which we are now trying to define, and with weaving, which we did define? For all these are doubtless careful about excess and deficiency in relation to the standard of the mean; they regard them not as non-existent, but as real difficulties in actual practice, and it is in this way, when they preserve the standard of the mean, that all their works are good and beautiful.

Y. SOC. Certainly.

STR. And if we do away with the art of statesmanship, our subsequent search for the kingly art will be hopeless, will it not?

Y. SOC. Certainly.

STR. Then just as in the case of the sophist [1] we forced the conclusion that not-being exists, since that was the point at which we had lost our hold of the argument, so now we must force this second conclusion, that the greater and the less are to be measured in relation, not only to one another, but also to the establishment of the standard of the mean, must we not? For if this is not admitted, neither the statesman nor any other man who has knowledge of practical affairs can be said without any doubt to exist.

Y. SOC. Then we must by all means do now the same that we did then.

STR. This, Socrates, is a still greater task than that was; and yet we remember how long that took us; but it is perfectly fair to make about them some such assumption as this.

Y. SOC. As what?

STR. That sometime we shall need this principle of the mean for the demonstration of absolute precise truth. But our belief that the demonstration

καλῶς καὶ ἱκανῶς δείκνυται, δοκεῖ μοι βοηθεῖν
μεγαλοπρεπῶς ἡμῖν οὗτος ὁ λόγος, ὡς ἄρα ἡγητέον
ὁμοίως τὰς τέχνας πάσας εἶναι, μεῖζόν τε ἅμα καὶ
ἔλαττον μετρεῖσθαι μὴ πρὸς ἄλληλα μόνον, ἀλλὰ
καὶ πρὸς τὴν τοῦ μετρίου γένεσιν. τούτου τε γὰρ
ὄντος ἐκεῖνά ἐστι, κἀκείνων οὐσῶν ἔστι καὶ τοῦτο,[1]
μὴ δὲ ὄντος ποτέρου τούτων οὐδέτερον αὐτῶν ἔσται
ποτέ.

Ε ΝΕ. ΣΩ. Τοῦτο μὲν ὀρθῶς· ἀλλὰ τί δὴ τὸ μετὰ
τοῦτο;

ΞΕ. Δῆλον ὅτι διαιροῖμεν ἂν τὴν μετρητικήν,
καθάπερ ἐρρήθη, ταύτῃ δίχα τέμνοντες, ἐν μὲν
τιθέντες αὐτῆς μόριον ξυμπάσας τέχνας ὁπόσαι τὸν
ἀριθμὸν καὶ μήκη καὶ βάθη καὶ πλάτη καὶ παχύτητας[2] πρὸς τοὐναντίον μετροῦσι· τὸ δὲ ἕτερον,
ὁπόσαι πρὸς τὸ μέτριον καὶ τὸ πρέπον καὶ τὸν
καιρὸν καὶ τὸ δέον καὶ πάνθ' ὁπόσα εἰς τὸ μέσον
ἀπῳκίσθη τῶν ἐσχάτων.

ΝΕ. ΣΩ. Καὶ μέγα γ' ἑκάτερον τμῆμα εἶπες, καὶ
πολὺ διαφέρον ἀλλήλοιν.

ΞΕ. Ὃ γὰρ ἐνίοτε, ὦ Σώκρατες, οἰόμενοι δή τι
285 σοφὸν φράζειν πολλοὶ τῶν κομψῶν λέγουσιν, ὡς
ἄρα μετρητικὴ περὶ πάντ' ἐστὶ τὰ γιγνόμενα, τοῦτ'
αὐτὸ τὸ νῦν λεχθὲν ὂν τυγχάνει. μετρήσεως μὲν
γὰρ δή τινα τρόπον πάνθ' ὁπόσα ἔντεχνα μετείληφε·
διὰ δὲ τὸ μὴ κατ' εἴδη συνειθίσθαι σκοπεῖν διαιρουμένους ταῦτά τε τοσοῦτον διαφέροντα ξυμβάλλουσιν
εὐθὺς εἰς ταὐτὸν ὅμοια νομίσαντες, καὶ τοὐναντίον
αὖ τούτου δρῶσιν ἕτερα οὐ κατὰ μέρη διαιροῦντες,

---

[1] τοῦτο] ταῦτα ΒΤ.
[2] παχύτητας Β : ταχυτῆτας Τ et al.

is for our present purpose good and sufficient is, in my opinion, magnificently supported by this argument—that we must believe that all the arts alike exist and that the greater and the less are measured in relation not only to one another but also to the establishment of the standard of the mean. For if this exists, they exist also, and if they exist, it exists also, but neither can ever exist if the other does not.

Y. SOC. That is quite right. But what comes next?

STR. We should evidently divide the science of measurement into two parts in accordance with what has been said. One part comprises all the arts which measure number, length, depth, breadth, and thickness in relation to their opposites; the other comprises those which measure them in relation to the moderate, the fitting, the opportune, the needful, and all the other standards that are situated in the mean between the extremes.

Y. SOC. Both of your divisions are extensive, and there is a great difference between them.

STR. Yes, for what many clever persons occasionally say, Socrates, fancying that it is a wise remark, namely, that the science of measurement has to do with everything, is precisely the same as what we have just said. For in a certain way all things which are in the province of art do partake of measurement; but because people are not in the habit of considering things by dividing them into classes, they hastily put these widely different relations[1] into the same category, thinking they are alike; and again they do the opposite of this when they fail to divide other things into parts. What they ought to do is this:

[1] *i.e.* relations to each other and relations to the standard of the mean.

δέον, ὅταν μὲν τὴν τῶν πολλῶν τις πρότερον αἴσθη-
B ται κοινωνίαν, μὴ προαφίστασθαι πρὶν ἂν ἐν αὐτῇ
τὰς διαφορὰς ἴδῃ πάσας ὁπόσαιπερ ἐν εἴδεσι κεῖνται,
τὰς δὲ αὖ παντοδαπὰς ἀνομοιότητας, ὅταν ἐν πλή-
θεσιν ὀφθῶσι, μὴ δυνατὸν εἶναι δυσωπούμενον
παύεσθαι, πρὶν ἂν ξύμπαντα τὰ οἰκεῖα ἐντὸς μιᾶς
ὁμοιότητος ἕρξας γένους τινὸς οὐσίᾳ περιβάληται.
ταῦτα μὲν οὖν ἱκανῶς περί τε τούτων καὶ περὶ
τῶν ἐλλείψεων καὶ ὑπερβολῶν εἰρήσθω· φυλάτ-
τωμεν δὲ μόνον ὅτι δύο γένη περὶ αὐτὰ
C ἐξεύρηται τῆς μετρητικῆς, καὶ ἃ φαμὲν αὔτ᾽ εἶναι
μεμνώμεθα.

ΝΕ. ΣΩ. Μεμνησόμεθα.

26. ΞΕ. Μετὰ τοῦτον δὴ τὸν λόγον ἕτερον
προσδεξώμεθα περὶ αὐτῶν τε τῶν ζητουμένων καὶ
περὶ πάσης τῆς ἐν τοῖς τοιοῖσδε λόγοις διατριβῆς.

ΝΕ. ΣΩ. Τὸ ποῖον;

ΞΕ. Εἴ τις ἀνέροιτο ἡμᾶς τὴν περὶ γράμματα συνουσίαν τῶν μανθανόντων, ὁπόταν τις ὁτιοῦν ὄνομα
ἐρωτηθῇ τίνων ἐστὶ γραμμάτων, πότερον αὐτῷ τότε
D φῶμεν γίγνεσθαι τὴν ζήτησιν ἑνὸς ἕνεκα μᾶλλον
τοῦ προβληθέντος ἢ τοῦ περὶ πάντα τὰ προ-
βαλλόμενα γραμματικωτέρῳ γίγνεσθαι;

ΝΕ. ΣΩ. Δῆλον ὅτι τοῦ περὶ ἅπαντα.

ΞΕ. Τί δ᾽ αὖ νῦν ἡμῖν ἡ περὶ τοῦ πολιτικοῦ ζήτησις; ἕνεκα αὐτοῦ τούτου προβέβληται μᾶλλον ἢ
τοῦ περὶ πάντα διαλεκτικωτέροις γίγνεσθαι;

ΝΕ. ΣΩ. Καὶ τοῦτο δῆλον ὅτι τοῦ περὶ πάντα.

when a person at first sees only the unity or common quality of many things, he must not give up until he sees all the differences in them, so far as they exist in classes; and conversely, when all sorts of dissimilarities are seen in a large number of objects he must find it impossible to be discouraged or to stop until he has gathered into one circle of similarity all the things which are related to each other and has included them in some sort of class on the basis of their essential nature. No more need be said, then, about this or about deficiency and excess; let us only bear carefully in mind that two kinds of measurement which apply to them have been found, and let us remember what those kinds are.

y. soc. We will remember.

str. Now that we have finished this discussion, let us take up another which concerns the actual objects of our inquiry and the conduct of such discussions in general.

y. soc. What is it?

str. Suppose we were asked the following question about a group of pupils learning their letters: "When a pupil is asked of what letters some word or other is composed, is the question asked for the sake of the one particular word before him or rather to make him more learned about all words in the lesson?"

y. soc. Clearly to make him more learned about them all.

str. And how about our own investigation of the statesman? Has it been undertaken for the sake of this particular subject or rather to make us better thinkers about all subjects?

y. soc. Clearly this also is done with a view to them all.

ΞΕ. Ἦ που τὸν τῆς ὑφαντικῆς γε λόγον αὐτῆς
ταύτης ἕνεκα θηρεύειν οὐδεὶς ἂν ἐθελήσειε νοῦν ἔχων·
ἀλλ', οἶμαι, τοὺς πλείστους λέληθεν ὅτι τοῖς μὲν τῶν
Ε ὄντων ῥᾳδίως καταμαθεῖν αἰσθηταί[1] τινες ὁμοιό-
τητες πεφύκασιν, ἃς οὐδὲν χαλεπὸν δηλοῦν, ὅταν
αὐτῶν τις βουληθῇ τῷ λόγον αἰτοῦντι περί του μὴ
μετὰ πραγμάτων ἀλλὰ χωρὶς λόγου ῥᾳδίως ἐνδεί-
ξασθαι· τοῖς δ' αὖ μεγίστοις οὖσι καὶ τιμιωτάτοις
286 οὐκ ἔστιν εἴδωλον οὐδὲν πρὸς τοὺς ἀνθρώπους
εἰργασμένον ἐναργῶς, οὗ δειχθέντος τὴν τοῦ πυνθα-
νομένου ψυχὴν ὁ βουλόμενος ἀποπληρῶσαι, πρὸς
τῶν αἰσθήσεών τινα προσαρμόττων, ἱκανῶς πληρώ-
σει. διὸ δεῖ μελετᾶν λόγον ἑκάστου δυνατὸν εἶναι
δοῦναι καὶ δέξασθαι· τὰ γὰρ ἀσώματα, κάλλιστα
ὄντα καὶ μέγιστα, λόγῳ μόνον, ἄλλῳ δὲ οὐδενὶ
σαφῶς δείκνυται, τούτων δὲ ἕνεκα πάντ' ἐστὶ τὰ
νῦν λεγόμενα. ῥᾷων δ' ἐν τοῖς ἐλάττοσιν ἡ μελέτη
Β παντὸς πέρι μᾶλλον ἢ περὶ τὰ μείζω.

ΝΕ. ΣΩ. Κάλλιστ' εἶπες.

ΞΕ. Ὧν τοίνυν χάριν ἅπανθ' ἡμῖν ταῦτ' ἐρρήθη
περὶ τούτων, μνησθῶμεν.

ΝΕ. ΣΩ. Τίνων;

ΞΕ. Ταύτης τε οὐχ ἥκιστα αὐτῆς ἕνεκα τῆς δυσχερείας ἣν περὶ τὴν μακρολογίαν τὴν περὶ τὴν
ὑφαντικὴν ἀπεδεξάμεθα δυσχερῶς, καὶ τὴν περὶ
τὴν τοῦ παντὸς ἀνείλιξιν καὶ τὴν[2] τοῦ σοφιστοῦ
περὶ τῆς τοῦ μὴ ὄντος οὐσίας, ἐννοοῦντες ὡς ἔσχε
μῆκος πλέον, καὶ ἐπὶ τούτοις δὴ πᾶσιν ἐπεπλήξαμεν
C ἡμῖν αὐτοῖς, δείσαντες μὴ περίεργα ἅμα καὶ
μακρὰ λέγοιμεν. ἵν' οὖν εἰς αὖθις μηδὲν πάσχωμεν

---

[1] αἰσθηταί Cornarius : αἰσθητικαί ΒΤ.
[2] τὴν om. ΒΤ.

STR. Of course no man of sense would wish to pursue the discussion of weaving for its own sake; but most people, it seems to me, fail to notice that some things have sensible resemblances which are easily perceived; and it is not at all difficult to show them when anyone wishes, in response to a request for an explanation of some one of them, to exhibit them easily without trouble and really without explanation. But, on the other hand, the greatest and noblest conceptions have no image wrought plainly for human vision, which he who wishes to satisfy the mind of the inquirer can apply to some one of his senses and by mere exhibition satisfy the mind. We must therefore endeavour by practice to acquire the power of giving and understanding a rational definition of each one of them; for immaterial things, which are the noblest and greatest, can be exhibited by reason only, and it is for their sake that all we are saying is said. But it is always easier to practise in small matters than in greater ones.

Y. SOC. Excellent.

STR. Let us, then, remember the reason for all that we have said about these matters.

Y. SOC. What is the reason?

STR. The reason is chiefly just that irritating impatience which we exhibited in relation to the long talk about weaving and the revolution of the universe and the sophist's long talk about the existence of not-being.[1] We felt that they were too long, and we reproached ourselves for all of them, fearing that our talk was not only long, but irrelevant. Consider, therefore, that the reason for what has just been said

---

[1] See 283 B, 277, *Sophist* 261.

τοιοῦτον, τούτων ἕνεκα πάντων τὰ πρόσθεν νῶν
εἰρῆσθαι φάθι.

ΝΕ. ΣΩ. Ταῦτ᾽ ἔσται. λέγε ἑξῆς μόνον.

ΞΕ. Λέγω τοίνυν ὅτι χρὴ δὴ μεμνημένους ἐμὲ
καὶ σὲ τῶν νῦν εἰρημένων τόν τε ψόγον ἑκάστοτε
καὶ ἔπαινον ποιεῖσθαι βραχύτητος ἅμα καὶ μήκους
ὧν ἂν ἀεὶ πέρι λέγωμεν, μὴ πρὸς ἄλληλα τὰ μήκη
κρίνοντες, ἀλλὰ κατὰ τὸ τῆς μετρητικῆς μέρος ὃ
D τότε ἔφαμεν δεῖν μεμνῆσθαι, πρὸς τὸ πρέπον.

ΝΕ. ΣΩ. Ὀρθῶς.

ΞΕ. Οὐ τοίνυν οὐδὲ πρὸς τοῦτο πάντα. οὔτε γὰρ
πρὸς τὴν ἡδονὴν μήκους ἁρμόττοντος οὐδὲν προσδεησόμεθα, πλὴν εἰ πάρεργόν τι· τό τε αὖ πρὸς τὴν τοῦ
προβληθέντος ζήτησιν, ὡς ἂν ῥᾷστα καὶ τάχιστα
εὕροιμεν, δεύτερον ἀλλ᾽ οὐ πρῶτον ὁ λόγος ἀγαπᾶν
παραγγέλλει, πολὺ δὲ μάλιστα καὶ πρῶτον τὴν
μέθοδον αὐτὴν τιμᾶν τοῦ κατ᾽ εἴδη δυνατὸν εἶναι
E διαιρεῖν, καὶ δὴ καὶ λόγον, ἄντε παμμήκης λεχθεὶς
τὸν ἀκούσαντα εὑρετικώτερον ἀπεργάζηται, τοῦτον
σπουδάζειν καὶ τῷ μήκει μηδὲν ἀγανακτεῖν, ἄντ᾽
αὖ βραχύτερος, ὡσαύτως· ἔτι δ᾽ αὖ πρὸς τούτοις
τὸν περὶ τὰς τοιάσδε συνουσίας ψέγοντα λόγων
μήκη καὶ τὰς ἐν κύκλῳ περιόδους οὐκ ἀποδεχό-
μενον, ὅτι χρὴ τὸν τοιοῦτον μὴ πάνυ ταχὺ μηδ᾽
εὐθὺς οὕτω μεθιέναι ψέξαντα μόνον ὡς μακρὰ
287 τὰ λεχθέντα, ἀλλὰ καὶ προσαποφαίνειν οἴεσθαι δεῖν
ὡς βραχύτερα ἂν γενόμενα τοὺς συνόντας ἀπηργά-
ζετο διαλεκτικωτέρους καὶ τῆς τῶν ὄντων λόγῳ
δηλώσεως εὑρετικωτέρους, τῶν δὲ ἄλλων καὶ πρὸς

is my wish to avoid any such impatience in the future.

Y. SOC. Very well. Please go on with what you have to say.

STR. What I have to say, then, is that you and I, remembering what has just been said, must praise or blame the brevity or length of our several discussions, not by comparing their various lengths with one another, but with reference to that part of the science of measurement which we said before must be borne in mind; I mean the standard of fitness.

Y. SOC. Quite right.

STR. But we must not always judge of length by fitness, either. For we shall not in the least want a length that is fitted to give pleasure, except, perhaps, as a secondary consideration; and again reason counsels us to accept fitness for the easiest and quickest completion of the inquiry in which we are engaged, not as the first, but as the second thing to be desired. By far our first and most important object should be to exalt the method itself of ability to divide by classes, and therefore, if a discourse, even though it be very long, makes the hearer better able to discover the truth, we should accept it eagerly and should not be offended by its length, or if it is short, we should judge it in the same way. And, moreover, anyone who finds fault with the length of discourses in our discussions, or objects to roundabout methods, must not merely find fault with the speeches for their length and then pass them quickly and hastily by, but he must also show that there is ground for the belief that if they had been briefer they would have made their hearers better dialecticians and quicker to discover through reason the truth of realities.

E

ἀλλ' ἄττα ψόγων καὶ ἐπαίνων μηδὲν φροντίζειν
μηδὲ τὸ παράπαν ἀκούειν δοκεῖν τῶν τοιούτων
λόγων. καὶ τούτων μὲν ἅλις, εἰ καὶ σοὶ ταύτῃ
ξυνδοκεῖ· πρὸς δὲ δὴ τὸν πολιτικὸν ἴωμεν πάλιν,
B τῆς προρρηθείσης ὑφαντικῆς αὐτῷ φέροντες τὸ
παράδειγμα.

ΝΕ. ΣΩ. Καλῶς εἶπες, καὶ ποιῶμεν ἃ λέγεις.

27. ΞΕ. Οὐκοῦν ἀπό γε τῶν πολλῶν ὁ βασιλεὺς ὅσαι ξύννομοι, μᾶλλον δὲ ἀπὸ πασῶν τῶν περὶ
τὰς ἀγέλας διακεχώρισται· λοιπαὶ δέ, φαμέν, αἱ
κατὰ πόλιν αὐτὴν τῶν τε ξυναιτίων καὶ τῶν αἰτίων,
ἃς πρώτας ἀπ' ἀλλήλων διαιρετέον.

ΝΕ. ΣΩ. Ὀρθῶς.

ΞΕ. Οἶσθ' οὖν ὅτι χαλεπὸν αὐτὰς τεμεῖν δίχα;
C τὸ δ' αἴτιον, ὡς οἶμαι, προϊοῦσιν οὐχ ἧττον ἔσται
καταφανές.

ΝΕ. ΣΩ. Οὐκοῦν χρὴ δρᾶν οὕτως.

ΞΕ. Κατὰ μέλη τοίνυν αὐτὰς οἷον ἱερεῖον διαιρώμεθα, ἐπειδὴ δίχα ἀδυνατοῦμεν. δεῖ γὰρ εἰς
τὸν ἐγγύτατα ὅτι μάλιστα τέμνειν ἀριθμὸν ἀεί.

ΝΕ. ΣΩ. Πῶς οὖν ποιῶμεν τὰ νῦν;

ΞΕ. Ὥσπερ ἔμπροσθεν, ὁπόσαι παρείχοντο ὄργανα περὶ τὴν ὑφαντικήν, πάσας δήπου[1] τότε
ἐτίθεμεν ὡς συναιτίους.

ΝΕ. ΣΩ. Ναί.

ΞΕ. Καὶ νῦν δὴ ταὐτὸν μὲν τοῦτο, ἔτι δὲ μᾶλλον
D ἢ τόθ' ἡμῖν ποιητέον. ὅσαι γὰρ σμικρὸν ἢ μέγα τι
δημιουργοῦσι κατὰ πόλιν ὄργανον, θετέον ἁπάσας
ταύτας ὡς οὔσας συναιτίους. ἄνευ γὰρ τούτων οὐκ
ἄν ποτε γένοιτο πόλις οὐδὲ πολιτική, τούτων δ'
αὖ βασιλικῆς ἔργον τέχνης οὐδέν που θήσομεν.

---

[1] δήπου] δέ που B : που T.

About other people and the praise or blame they direct towards other qualities in discourse, we need not be concerned; we need not even appear to hear them. But enough of this, if you feel about it as I do; so let us go back to the statesman and apply to him the example of weaving that we spoke of a while ago.

Y. SOC. Very well; let us do so.

STR. The art of the king, then, has been separated from most of the kindred arts, or rather from all the arts that have to do with herds. There remain, however, the arts that have to do with the state itself. These are both causes and contingent causes, and our first duty is to separate them from one another.

Y. SOC. Quite right.

STR. It is not easy to divide them into halves, you know. But I think the reason will nevertheless be clear as we go on.

Y. SOC. Then we had better divide in another way.

STR. Let us divide them, then, like an animal that is sacrificed, by joints, since we cannot bisect them; for we must always divide into a number of parts as near two as possible

Y. SOC. How shall we do it in the present instance?

STR. Just as in the previous case, you know, we classed all the arts which furnished tools for weaving as contingent causes.

Y. SOC. Yes.

STR. So now we must do the same thing, but it is even more imperative. For all the arts which furnish any implement, great or small, for the state, must be classed as contingent causes; for without them neither state nor statesmanship could ever exist, and yet I do not suppose we shall reckon any of them as the work of the kingly art.

ΝΕ. ΣΩ. Οὐ γάρ.

ΞΕ. Καὶ μὲν δὴ χαλεπὸν ἐπιχειροῦμεν δρᾶν ἀπο-
χωρίζοντες τοῦτο ἀπὸ τῶν ἄλλων τὸ γένος· ὅ τι
γὰρ οὖν τῶν ὄντων ἔστιν ὡς[1] ἑνός γέ τινος ὄργανον
εἰπόντα δοκεῖν εἰρηκέναι τι πιθανόν. ὅμως δὲ ἔτε-
Ε ρον αὖ τῶν ἐν πόλει κτημάτων εἴπωμεν τόδε.

ΝΕ. ΣΩ. Τὸ ποῖον;

ΞΕ. Ὡς οὐκ ἔστι ταύτην τὴν δύναμιν ἔχον. οὐ
γὰρ ἐπὶ γενέσεως αἰτίᾳ πήγνυται,[2] καθάπερ ὄργανον, ἀλλ' ἕνεκα τοῦ δημιουργηθέντος σωτηρίας.

ΝΕ. ΣΩ. Τὸ ποῖον;

ΞΕ. Τοῦτο ὃ δὴ ξηροῖς καὶ ὑγροῖς καὶ ἐμπύροις
καὶ ἀπύροις παντοδαπὸν εἶδος ἐργασθὲν ἀγγεῖον[3]
μιᾷ κλήσει προσφθεγγόμεθα, καὶ μάλα γε συχνὸν
εἶδος καὶ τῇ ζητουμένῃ γε, ὡς οἶμαι, προσῆκον
288 οὐδὲν ἀτεχνῶς ἐπιστήμῃ.

ΝΕ. ΣΩ. Πῶς γὰρ οὔ;

ΞΕ. Τούτων δὴ τρίτον ἕτερον εἶδος κτημάτων
πάμπολυ κατοπτέον πεζὸν καὶ ἔνυδρον καὶ πολυ-
πλανὲς καὶ ἀπλανὲς καὶ τίμιον καὶ ἄτιμον, ἓν δὲ
ὄνομα ἔχον, διότι πᾶν ἕνεκά τινος ἐφέδρας ἐστί,
θᾶκος ἀεί τινι γιγνόμενον.

ΝΕ. ΣΩ. Τὸ ποῖον;

ΞΕ. Ὄχημα αὐτό που λέγομεν, οὐ πάνυ πολιτικῆς
ἔργον, ἀλλὰ μᾶλλον πολὺ τεκτονικῆς καὶ κεραμικῆς
καὶ χαλκοτυπικῆς.

ΝΕ. ΣΩ. Μανθάνω.

Β 28. ΞΕ. Τί δὲ τέταρτον; ἆρ' ἕτερον εἶναι

---

[1] ἔστιν ὡς Campbell : ὡς ἔστιν Β : ὡς ἔστιν Τ : ἔστιν Hermann.
[2] αἰτίᾳ πήγνυται Bekker : αἰτίαι πήγνυνται ΒΤ.
[3] ἀγγεῖον Hermann : ἀγγεῖον δ δὴ ΒΤ.

y. soc. No.

str. We shall certainly be undertaking a hard task in separating this class from the rest; for it might be said that everything that exists is the instrument of something or other, and the statement seems plausible. But there are possessions of another kind in the state, about which I wish to say something.

y. soc. What do you wish to say?

str. That they do not possess this instrumental function. For they are not, like tools or instruments, made for the purpose of being causes of production, but exist for the preservation of that which has been produced.

y. soc. What is this class of possessions?

str. That very various class which is made with dry and wet materials and such as are wrought by fire and without fire; it is called collectively the class of receptacles; it is a very large class and has, so far as I can see, nothing at all to do with the art we are studying.

y. soc. No, of course not.

str. And there is a third very large class of possessions to be noticed, differing from these; it is found on land and on water, it wanders about and is stationary, it is honourable and without honour, but it has one name, because the whole class is always a seat for some one and exists to be sat upon.

y. soc. What is it?

str. We call it a vehicle, and it certainly is not at all the work of statesmanship, but much rather that of the arts of carpentry, pottery and bronze-working.

y. soc. I understand.

str. And is there a fourth class? Shall we say

τούτων λεκτέον, ἐν ᾧ τὰ πλεῖστά ἐστι τῶν πάλαι ῥηθέντων, ἐσθής τε ξύμπασα καὶ τῶν ὅπλων τὸ πολὺ καὶ τείχη πάντα θ᾽[1] ὅσα γήινα περιβλήματα καὶ λίθινα, καὶ μυρία ἕτερα; προβολῆς δὲ ἕνεκα ξυμπάντων αὐτῶν εἰργασμένων δικαιότατ᾽ ἂν ὅλον προσαγορεύοιτο πρόβλημα, καὶ πολλῷ μᾶλλον τέχνης οἰκοδομικῆς ἔργον καὶ ὑφαντικῆς τὸ πλεῖστον νομίζοιτ᾽ ἂν ὀρθότερον ἢ πολιτικῆς.

ΝΕ. ΣΩ. Πάνυ μὲν οὖν.

C   ΞΕ. Πέμπτον δὲ ἆρ᾽ ἂν ἐθέλοιμεν τὸ περὶ τὸν κόσμον καὶ γραφικὴν θεῖναι καὶ ὅσα ταύτῃ προσχρώμενα καὶ μουσικῇ μιμήματα τελεῖται, πρὸς τὰς ἡδονὰς μόνον ἡμῶν ἀπειργασμένα, δικαίως δ᾽ ἂν ὀνόματι περιληφθέντα ἑνί;

ΝΕ. ΣΩ. Ποίῳ;

ΞΕ. Παίγνιόν πού τι λέγεται.

ΝΕ. ΣΩ. Τί μήν;

ΞΕ. Τοῦτο τοίνυν τούτοις ἓν ὄνομα ἅπασι πρέψει προσαγορευθέν· οὐ γὰρ σπουδῆς οὐδὲν αὐτῶν χάριν, ἀλλὰ παιδιᾶς ἕνεκα πάντα δρᾶται.

D   ΝΕ. ΣΩ. Καὶ τοῦτο σχεδὸν ἔτι μανθάνω.

ΞΕ. Τὸ δὲ πᾶσι τούτοις σώματα παρέχον, ἐξ ὧν καὶ ἐν οἷς δημιουργοῦσιν ὁπόσαι τῶν τεχνῶν νῦν εἴρηνται, παντοδαπὸν εἶδος πολλῶν ἑτέρων τεχνῶν ἔκγονον ὄν, ἆρ᾽ οὐχ ἕκτον θήσομεν;

ΝΕ. ΣΩ. Τὸ ποῖον δὴ λέγεις;

ΞΕ. Χρυσόν τε καὶ ἄργυρον καὶ πάνθ᾽ ὁπόσα μεταλλεύεται καὶ ὅσα δρυοτομικὴ καὶ κουρὰ ξύμπασα τέμνουσα παρέχει τεκτονικῇ καὶ πλεκτικῇ· καὶ ἔτι φλοιστικὴ φυτῶν τε καὶ ἐμψύχων δέρματα E σωμάτων περιαιροῦσα σκυτοτομική, καὶ ὅσαι

―――――――――
[1] θ᾽] δ᾽ ΒΤ.

114

that there is one, differing from those three, one to which most of the things we have mentioned belong —all clothing, most arms, all circuit walls of earth or of stone, and countless other things? And since they are all made for defence, they may most rightly be called by the collective name of defence, and this may much more properly be considered for the most part the work of the art of building or of weaving than of statesmanship.

Y. SOC. Certainly.

STR. And should we care to make a fifth class, of ornamentation and painting and all the imitations created by the use of painting and music solely for our pleasure and properly included under one name?

Y. SOC. What is its name?

STR. It is called by some such name as plaything.

Y. SOC. To be sure.

STR. So this one name will properly be applied to all the members of this class; for none of them is practised for any serious purpose, but all of them merely for play.

Y. SOC. I understand that pretty well, too.

STR. And shall we not make a sixth class of that which furnishes to all these the materials of which and in which all the arts we have mentioned fashion their works, a very various class, the offspring of many other arts?

Y. SOC. What do you mean?

STR. Gold and silver and all the products of the mines and all the materials which tree-felling and wood-cutting in general cut and provide for carpentry and basket-weaving; and then, too, the art of stripping the bark from plants and the leather-worker's art which takes off the skins of animals, and

PLATO

περὶ τὰ τοιαῦτα εἰσιν τέχναι, καὶ φελλῶν καὶ βύβλων καὶ δεσμῶν ἐργαστικαὶ παρέσχον δημιουργεῖν σύνθετα ἐκ μὴ συντιθεμένων εἴδη γενῶν. ἓν δὲ αὐτὸ προσαγορεύομεν πᾶν τὸ πρωτογενὲς ἀνθρώποις κτῆμα καὶ ἀξύνθετον καὶ βασιλικῆς ἐπιστήμης οὐδαμῶς ἔργον ὄν.

ΝΕ. ΣΩ. Καλῶς.

ΞΕ. Τὴν δὴ τῆς τροφῆς κτῆσιν, καὶ ὅσα εἰς τὸ σῶμα ξυγκαταμιγνύμενα ἑαυτῶν μέρεσι μέρη σώματος εἰς τὸ θεραπεῦσαί τινα δύναμιν εἴληχε, 289 λεκτέον ἕβδομον ὀνομάσαντας αὐτὸ ξύμπαν ἡμῶν εἶναι τροφόν, εἰ μή τι κάλλιον ἔχομεν ἄλλο θέσθαι· γεωργικῇ δὲ καὶ θηρευτικῇ καὶ γυμναστικῇ καὶ ἰατρικῇ καὶ μαγειρικῇ πᾶν ὑποτιθέντες ὀρθότερον ἀποδώσομεν ἢ τῇ πολιτικῇ.

ΝΕ. ΣΩ. Πῶς γὰρ οὔ;

29. ΞΕ. Σχεδὸν τοίνυν ὅσα ἔχεται κτήσεως, πλὴν τῶν ἡμέρων ζώων, ἐν τούτοις ἑπτὰ οἶμαι γένεσιν εἰρῆσθαι. σκόπει δέ· ἦν γὰρ δικαιότατα μὲν ἂν τεθὲν κατ' ἀρχὰς τὸ πρωτογενὲς εἶδος, μετὰ
B δὲ τοῦτο ὄργανον, ἀγγεῖον, ὄχημα, πρόβλημα, παίγνιον, θρέμμα. ἃ[1] παραλείπομεν δέ, εἴ τι μὴ μέγα λέληθεν, εἴς τι τούτων δυνατὸν ἁρμόττειν, οἷον ἡ τοῦ νομίσματος ἰδέα καὶ σφραγίδων καὶ παντὸς χαρακτῆρος. γένος τε γὰρ ἐν αὐτοῖς ταῦτα οὐδὲν ἔχει μέγα ξύννομον, ἀλλὰ τὰ μὲν εἰς κόσμον, τὰ δὲ εἰς ὄργανα βίᾳ μέν, ὅμως δὲ πάντως ἑλκόμενα συμφωνήσει. τὰ δὲ περὶ ζώων κτῆσιν τῶν ἡμέρων,
C πλὴν δούλων, ἡ πρότερον ἀγελαιοτροφικὴ διαμερισθεῖσα πάντα εἰληφυῖα ἀναφαίνεται.

ΝΕ. ΣΩ. Πάνυ μὲν οὖν.

[1] ἃ add. Madvig.

116

all the other arts which have to do with such matters, and those that make corks and paper and cords and enable us to manufacture composite classes of things from kinds that are not composite. We call all this, as one class, the primary and simple possession of man, and it is in no way the work of the kingly science.

Y. SOC. Good.

STR. And property in food and all the things which, mingling parts of themselves with parts of the body, have any function of keeping it in health, we may say is the seventh class, and we will call it collectively our nourishment, unless we have some better name to give it. All this we can assign to the arts of husbandry, hunting, gymnastics, medicine, and cooking more properly than to that of statesmanship.

Y. SOC. Of course.

STR. Now I think I have in these seven classes mentioned nearly all kinds of property except tame animals. See: there was the primary possession, which ought in justice to have been placed first, and after this the instrument, receptacle, vehicle, defence, plaything, nourishment. Whatever we have omitted, if some unimportant thing has been overlooked, can find its place in one of those classes; for instance, the group of coins, seals, and stamps, for there is not among these any kinship such as to form a large class, but some of them can be made to fit into the class of ornaments, others into that of instruments, though the classification is somewhat forced. All property in tame animals, except slaves, is included in the art of herding, which has already been divided into parts.

Y. SOC. Yes; quite true.

ΞΕ. Τὸ δὲ δὴ δούλων καὶ πάντων ὑπηρετῶν λοιπόν, ἐν οἷς που καὶ μαντεύομαι τοὺς περὶ αὐτὸ τὸ
πλέγμα ἀμφισβητοῦντας τῷ βασιλεῖ καταφανεῖς
γενήσεσθαι, καθάπερ τοῖς ὑφάνταις τότε τοὺς περὶ
τὸ νήθειν τε καὶ ξαίνειν καὶ ὅσα ἄλλα εἴπομεν. οἱ
δὲ ἄλλοι πάντες, ὡς συναίτιοι λεχθέντες, ἅμα τοῖς
ἔργοις τοῖς νῦν δὴ ῥηθεῖσιν ἀνήλωνται καὶ ἀπεχωρί-
D σθησαν ἀπὸ βασιλικῆς τε καὶ πολιτικῆς πράξεως.

ΝΕ. ΣΩ. Ἐοίκασι γοῦν.

ΞΕ. Ἴθι δὴ σκεψώμεθα τοὺς λοιποὺς προσελθόν-
τες ἐγγύθεν, ἵν᾽ αὐτοὺς εἰδῶμεν βεβαιότερον.

ΝΕ. ΣΩ. Οὐκοῦν χρή.

ΞΕ. Τοὺς μὲν δὴ μεγίστους ὑπηρέτας, ὡς ἐνθένδε
ἰδεῖν, τοὐναντίον ἔχοντας εὑρίσκομεν οἷς ὑπωπτεύ-
σαμεν ἐπιτήδευμα καὶ πάθος.

ΝΕ. ΣΩ. Τίνας;

ΞΕ. Τοὺς ὠνητούς τε καὶ τῷ τρόπῳ τούτῳ κτη-
τούς· οὓς ἀναμφισβητήτως δούλους ἔχομεν εἰπεῖν,
Ε ἥκιστα βασιλικῆς μεταποιουμένους τέχνης.

ΝΕ. ΣΩ. Πῶς δ᾽ οὔ;

ΞΕ. Τί δέ; τῶν ἐλευθέρων ὅσοι τοῖς νῦν δὴ ῥηθεῖσιν εἰς ὑπηρετικὴν ἑκόντες αὑτοὺς τάττουσι, τά
τε γεωργίας καὶ τὰ τῶν ἄλλων τεχνῶν ἔργα διακομί-
ζοντες ἐπ᾽ ἀλλήλους καὶ ἀνισοῦντες, οἱ μὲν κατ᾽
ἀγοράς, οἱ δὲ πόλιν ἐκ πόλεως ἀλλάττοντες κατὰ
θάλατταν καὶ πεζῇ, νόμισμά τε πρὸς τὰ ἄλλα καὶ
αὐτὸ πρὸς αὐτὸ διαμείβοντες, οὓς ἀργυραμοιβούς
290 τε καὶ ἐμπόρους καὶ ναυκλήρους καὶ καπήλους ἐπωνομάκαμεν, μῶν τῆς πολιτικῆς ἀμφισβητήσουσί τι;

ΝΕ. ΣΩ. Τάχ᾽ ἂν ἴσως τῆς γε τῶν ἐμπορευτικῶν.

STR. There remains the class of slaves and servants in general, and here I prophesy that we shall find those who set up claims against the king for the very fabric of his art, just as the spinners and carders and the rest of whom we spoke advanced claims against the weavers a while ago. All the others, whom we called contingent causes, have been removed along with the works we just mentioned and have been separated from the activity of the king and the statesman.

Y. SOC. That seems to be the case, at least.

STR. Come then, let us step up and look from close at hand at those who are left, that so we may know them more surely.

Y. SOC. Yes, that is what we should do.

STR. We shall find, then, that the greatest servants, when seen from near at hand, are in conduct and condition the opposite of that which we suspected.

Y. SOC. Who are they?

STR. The bought servants, acquired by purchase, whom we can without question call slaves. They make no claim to any share in the kingly art.

Y. SOC. Certainly not.

STR. How about those free men who put themselves voluntarily in the position of servants of those whom we mentioned before? I mean the men who carry about and distribute among one another the productions of husbandry and the other arts, whether in the domestic market-places or by travelling from city to city by land or sea, exchanging money for wares or money for money, the men whom we call brokers, merchants, shipmasters, and peddlers; do they lay any claim to statesmanship?

Y. SOC. Possibly to commercial statesmanship.

ΞΕ. Ἀλλ' οὐ μήν, οὕς γε ὁρῶμεν μισθωτοὺς καὶ θῆτας πᾶσιν ἑτοιμότατα ὑπηρετοῦντας, μή ποτε βασιλικῆς μεταποιουμένους εὕρωμεν.

ΝΕ. ΣΩ. Πῶς γάρ;

ΞΕ. Τί δὲ ἄρα τοὺς τὰ τοιάδε διακονοῦντας ἡμῖν ἑκάστοτε;

ΝΕ. ΣΩ. Τὰ ποῖα εἶπες καὶ τίνας;

B   ΞΕ. Ὧν τὸ κηρυκικὸν ἔθνος, ὅσοι τε περὶ γράμματα σοφοὶ γίγνονται πολλάκις ὑπηρετήσαντες, καὶ πόλλ' ἄττα ἕτερα περὶ τὰς ἀρχὰς διαπονεῖσθαί τινες ἕτεροι πάνδεινοι, τί τούτους αὖ λέξομεν;

ΝΕ. ΣΩ. Ὅπερ εἶπες νῦν, ὑπηρέτας, ἀλλ' οὐκ αὐτοὺς ἐν ταῖς πόλεσιν ἄρχοντας.

ΞΕ. Ἀλλ' οὐ μήν, οἶμαί γε, ἐνύπνιον ἰδὼν εἶπον ταύτῃ πῃ φανήσεσθαι τοὺς διαφερόντως ἀμφισβητοῦντας τῆς πολιτικῆς. καίτοι σφόδρα γε ἄτοπον
C ἂν εἶναι δόξειε τὸ ζητεῖν τούτους ἐν ὑπηρετικῇ μοίρᾳ τινί.

ΝΕ. ΣΩ. Κομιδῇ μὲν οὖν.

ΞΕ. Ἔτι δὴ προσμίξωμεν ἐγγύτερον ἐπὶ τοὺς μήπω βεβασανισμένους. εἰσὶ δὲ οἵ τε περὶ μαντικὴν ἔχοντές τινος ἐπιστήμης διάκονον μόριον· ἑρμηνευταὶ γάρ που νομίζονται παρὰ θεῶν ἀνθρώποις.

ΝΕ. ΣΩ. Ναί.

ΞΕ. Καὶ μὴν καὶ τὸ τῶν ἱερέων αὖ γένος, ὡς τὸ νόμιμόν φησι, παρὰ μὲν ἡμῶν δωρεὰς θεοῖς διὰ θυσιῶν ἐπιστῆμόν ἐστι κατὰ νοῦν ἐκείνοις δωρεῖσθαι,
D παρὰ δὲ ἐκείνων ἡμῖν εὐχαῖς κτῆσιν ἀγαθῶν αἰτήσασθαι· ταῦτα δὲ διακόνου τέχνης ἐστί που μόρια ἀμφότερα.

ΝΕ. ΣΩ. Φαίνεται γοῦν.

30.   ΞΕ. Ἤδη τοίνυν μοι δοκοῦμεν οἷόν γέ τινος

STR. But certainly we shall never find labourers, whom we see only too glad to serve anybody for hire, claiming a share in the kingly art.

Y. SOC. Certainly not.

STR. But there are people who perform services of another kind. How about them?

Y. SOC. What services and what men do you mean?

STR. The class of heralds and those who become by long practice skilled as clerks and other clever men who perform various services in connexion with public offices. What shall we call them?

Y. SOC. What you called the others, servants; they are not themselves rulers in the states.

STR. But surely it was no dream that made me say we should find somewhere in this region those who more than others lay claim to the art of statesmanship; and yet it would be utterly absurd to look for them in any servile position.

Y. SOC. Certainly.

STR. But let us draw a little closer still to those whom we have not yet examined. There are men who have to do with divination and possess a portion of a certain menial science; for they are supposed to be interpreters of the gods to men.

Y. SOC. Yes.

STR. And then, too, the priests, according to law and custom, know how to give the gods, by means of sacrifices, the gifts that please them from us and by prayers to ask for us the gain of good things from them; now these are both part of a servant's art.

Y. SOC. At least they seem to be so.

STR. At last, then, I think we are, as it were,

ἴχνους ἐφ' ὃ πορευόμεθα προσάπτεσθαι. τὸ γὰρ
δὴ τῶν ἱερέων σχῆμα καὶ τὸ τῶν μάντεων εὖ μάλα
φρονήματος πληροῦται καὶ δόξαν σεμνὴν λαμβάνει
διὰ τὸ μέγεθος τῶν ἐγχειρημάτων, ὥστε περὶ μὲν
Αἴγυπτον οὐδ' ἔξεστι βασιλέα χωρὶς ἱερατικῆς
E ἄρχειν, ἀλλ' ἐὰν ἄρα καὶ τύχῃ πρότερον ἐξ ἄλλου
γένους βιασάμενος, ὕστερον ἀναγκαῖον εἰς τοῦτο
εἰστελεῖσθαι αὐτὸν τὸ γένος· ἔτι δὲ καὶ τῶν
Ἑλλήνων πολλαχοῦ ταῖς μεγίσταις ἀρχαῖς τὰ μέγιστα τῶν περὶ τὰ τοιαῦτα θύματα εὕροι τις ἂν
προσταττόμενα θύειν. καὶ δὴ καὶ παρ' ὑμῖν οὐχ
ἥκιστα δῆλον ὃ λέγω· τῷ γὰρ λαχόντι βασιλεῖ
φασι τῇδε τὰ σεμνότατα καὶ μάλιστα πάτρια τῶν
ἀρχαίων θυσιῶν ἀποδεδόσθαι.

ΝΕ. ΣΩ. Καὶ πάνυ γε.

291 ΞΕ. Τούτους τε τοίνυν τοὺς κληρωτοὺς βασιλέας
ἅμα καὶ ἱερέας, καὶ ὑπηρέτας αὐτῶν καί τινα ἕτερον
πάμπολυν ὄχλον σκεπτέον, ὃς ἄρτι κατάδηλος νῦν
ἡμῖν γέγονεν ἀποχωρισθέντων τῶν ἔμπροσθεν.

ΝΕ. ΣΩ. Τίνας δ' αὐτοὺς καὶ λέγεις;

ΞΕ. Καὶ μάλα τινὰς ἀτόπους.

ΝΕ. ΣΩ. Τί δή;

ΞΕ. Πάμφυλόν τι γένος αὐτῶν, ὥς γε ἄρτι σκο-
πουμένῳ φαίνεται. πολλοὶ μὲν γὰρ λέουσι τῶν
ἀνδρῶν εἴξασι καὶ Κενταύροις καὶ τοιούτοισιν ἑτέ-
B ροις, πάμπολλοι δὲ Σατύροις καὶ τοῖς ἀσθενέσι
καὶ πολυτρόποις θηρίοις· ταχὺ δὲ μεταλλάττουσι
τάς τε ἰδέας καὶ τὴν δύναμιν εἰς ἀλλήλους. καὶ
μέντοι μοι νῦν, ὦ Σώκρατες, ἄρτι δοκῶ κατανενοη-
κέναι τοὺς ἄνδρας.

ΝΕ. ΣΩ. Λέγοις ἄν· ἔοικας γὰρ ἄτοπόν τι καθορᾶν.

on the track of our quarry. For the bearing of the priests and prophets is indeed full of pride, and they win high esteem because of the magnitude of their undertakings. In Egypt, for example, no king can rule without being a priest, and if he happens to have forced his way to the throne from some other class, he must enroll himself in the class of priests afterwards; and among the Greeks, too, you would find that in many states the performance of the greatest public sacrifices is a duty imposed upon the highest officials. Yes, among you Athenians this is very plain, for they say the holiest and most national of the ancient sacrifices are performed by the man whom the lot has chosen to be the King.[1]

Y. SOC. Yes, certainly.

STR. We must, then, examine these elected kings and priests and their assistants, and also another very large crowd of people which has just come in sight now that the others are out of the way.

Y. SOC. Who are these people?

STR. A very queer lot.

Y. SOC. How so?

STR. They are of very mixed race, at least they seem so now, when I can just see them. For many of them are like lions and centaurs and other fierce creatures, and very many are like satyrs and the weak and cunning beasts; and they make quick exchanges of forms and qualities with one another. Ah, but now, Socrates, I think I have just made out who they are.

Y. SOC. Tell me; for you seem to have caught sight of something strange.

---

[1] The second in order of the nine annual archons.

PLATO

ΞΕ. Ναί· τὸ γὰρ ἄτοπον ἐξ ἀγνοίας πᾶσι συμβαίνει. καὶ γὰρ δὴ καὶ νῦν αὐτὸς τοῦτο ἔπαθον·
ἐξαίφνης ἠμφεγνόησα κατιδὼν τὸν περὶ τὰ τῶν
C πόλεων πράγματα χορόν.

ΝΕ. ΣΩ. Ποῖον;

ΞΕ. Τὸν πάντων τῶν σοφιστῶν μέγιστον γόητα
καὶ ταύτης τῆς τέχνης ἐμπειρότατον· ὃν ἀπὸ τῶν
ὄντως ὄντων πολιτικῶν καὶ βασιλικῶν καίπερ
παγχάλεπον ὄντα ἀφαιρεῖν ἀφαιρετέον, εἰ μέλλομεν
ἰδεῖν ἐναργῶς τὸ ζητούμενον.

ΝΕ. ΣΩ. Ἀλλὰ μὴν τοῦτό γε οὐκ ἀνετέον.

ΞΕ. Οὔκουν δὴ κατά γε τὴν ἐμήν. καί μοι φράζε
τόδε.

ΝΕ. ΣΩ. Τὸ ποῖον;

31. ΞΕ. Ἆρ' οὐ μοναρχία τῶν πολιτικῶν ἡμῖν
D ἀρχῶν ἐστι μία;

ΝΕ. ΣΩ. Ναί.

ΞΕ. Καὶ μετὰ μοναρχίαν εἴποι τις ἄν, οἶμαι, τὴν
ὑπὸ τῶν ὀλίγων δυναστείαν.

ΝΕ. ΣΩ. Πῶς δ' οὔ;

ΞΕ. Τρίτον δὲ σχῆμα πολιτείας οὐχ ἡ τοῦ πλήθους ἀρχή, δημοκρατία τοὔνομα κληθεῖσα;

ΝΕ. ΣΩ. Καὶ[1] πάνυ γε.

ΞΕ. Τρεῖς δ' οὖσαι μῶν οὐ πέντε τρόπον τινὰ
γίγνονται, δύο ἐξ ἑαυτῶν ἄλλα πρὸς αὐταῖς ὀνόματα
τίκτουσαι;

ΝΕ. ΣΩ. Ποῖα δή;

E ΞΕ. Πρὸς τὸ βίαιόν που καὶ ἑκούσιον ἀποσκο-
ποῦντες νῦν καὶ πενίαν καὶ πλοῦτον καὶ νόμον καὶ
ἀνομίαν ἐν αὐταῖς γιγνόμενα διπλῆν ἑκατέραν τοῖν
δυοῖν διαιροῦντες μοναρχίαν μὲν προσαγορεύουσιν

[1] καὶ om. B.

124

str. Yes, for ignorance makes things seem strange to everybody. That was what happened to me just now; when I suddenly caught sight of them I did not recognize the troop of those who busy themselves with the affairs of the state.

y. soc. What troop?

str. That which of all the sophists is the greatest charlatan and most practised in charlatanry. This, although it is a hard thing to do, must be separated from the band of really statesmanlike and kingly men, if we are to get a clear view of the object of our search.

y. soc. But we certainly cannot give that up.

str. No, of course not. I agree to that. And now please answer a question.

y. soc. What is it?

str. We agree that monarchy is one of the forms of government, do we not?

y. soc. Yes.

str. And after monarchy one might, I should say, mention the rule of the few.

y. soc. Yes, of course.

str. And a third form of government is the rule of the multitude, called democracy, is it not?

y. soc. Yes, certainly.

str. Do not these three become after a fashion five, producing out of themselves two additional names?

y. soc. What names?

str. People nowadays are likely to take into consideration enforced subjection and voluntary obedience, poverty and wealth, law and lawlessness as they occur in governments, and so they divide two of the forms we mentioned, giving to the two

ὡς δύο παρεχομένην εἴδη δυοῖν ὀνόμασι, τυραννίδι, τὸ δὲ βασιλικῇ.

ΝΕ. ΣΩ. Τί μήν;

ΞΕ. Τὴν δὲ ὑπὸ ὀλίγων γε ἑκάστοτε κρατηθεῖσαν πόλιν ἀριστοκρατίᾳ καὶ ὀλιγαρχίᾳ.

ΝΕ. ΣΩ. Καὶ πάνυ γε.

ΞΕ. Δημοκρατίας γε μήν, ἐάντ᾽ οὖν βιαίως ἐάντε 292 ἑκουσίως τῶν τὰς οὐσίας ἐχόντων τὸ πλῆθος ἄρχῃ, καὶ ἐάντε τοὺς νόμους ἀκριβῶς φυλάττον ἐάντε μή, πάντως τοὔνομα οὐδεὶς αὐτῆς εἴωθε μεταλλάττειν.

ΝΕ. ΣΩ. Ἀληθῆ.

ΞΕ. Τί οὖν; οἰόμεθά τινα τούτων τῶν πολιτειῶν ὀρθὴν εἶναι τούτοις τοῖς ὅροις ὁρισθεῖσαν, ἑνὶ καὶ ὀλίγοις καὶ πολλοῖς, καὶ πλούτῳ καὶ πενίᾳ, καὶ τῷ βιαίῳ καὶ ἑκουσίῳ, καὶ μετὰ γραμμάτων καὶ ἄνευ νόμων ξυμβαίνουσαν γίγνεσθαι;

ΝΕ. ΣΩ. Τί γὰρ δὴ καὶ κωλύει;

B ΞΕ. Σκόπει δὴ σαφέστερον τῇδε ἑπόμενος.

ΝΕ. ΣΩ. Πῇ;

ΞΕ. Τῷ ῥηθέντι κατὰ πρώτας πότερον ἐμμενοῦμεν ἢ διαφωνήσομεν;

ΝΕ. ΣΩ. Τῷ δὴ ποίῳ λέγεις;

ΞΕ. Τὴν βασιλικὴν ἀρχὴν τῶν ἐπιστημῶν εἶναί τινα ἔφαμεν, οἶμαι.

ΝΕ. ΣΩ. Ναί.

ΞΕ. Καὶ τούτων γε οὐχ ἁπασῶν, ἀλλὰ κριτικὴν δήπου τινὰ καὶ ἐπιστατικὴν ἐκ τῶν ἄλλων προειλόμεθα.

ΝΕ. ΣΩ. Ναί.

ΞΕ. Κἀκ τῆς ἐπιστατικῆς τὴν μὲν ἐπ᾽ ἀψύχοις C ἔργοις, τὴν δὲ ἐπὶ ζῴοις· καὶ κατὰ τοῦτον δὴ τὸν

aspects of monarchy the two names tyranny and royalty.

Y. SOC. Certainly.

STR. And the state that is ruled by the few is called, as the case may be, aristocracy or oligarchy.

Y. SOC. To be sure.

STR. In the case of democracy, however, whether the multitude rule those who have property by violence or with their willing consent, and whether the laws are carefully observed or not, no one ever habitually changes the name.

Y. SOC. True.

STR. Now then, do we believe that any of these forms of government which are defined by the distinctions between the one, the few, and the many, or wealth and poverty, or violence and willingness, or written constitution and absence of laws, is a right one?

Y. SOC. I don't see why not.

STR. Look a bit more closely along the line I am going to point out.

Y. SOC. What is it?

STR. Shall we abide by what we said in the beginning, or dissent from it?

Y. SOC. To what do you refer?

STR. We said, I believe, that royal power was one of the sciences.

Y. SOC. Yes.

STR. And not only a science, but we selected it from the rest as a science of judgement and command.

Y. SOC. Yes.

STR. And from the science of command we distinguished one part which rules inanimate works, and one which rules living beings; and so we have gone

τρόπον μερίζοντες δεῦρ᾽ ἀεὶ προεληλύθαμεν, ἐπιστήμης οὐκ ἐπιλανθανόμενοι, τὸ δ᾽ ἥτις[1] οὐχ ἱκανῶς
πω[2] δυνάμενοι διακριβώσασθαι.

ΝΕ. ΣΩ. Λέγεις ὀρθῶς.

ΞΕ. Τοῦτ᾽ αὐτὸ τοίνυν ἆρ᾽ ἐννοοῦμεν, ὅτι τὸν
ὅρον οὐκ ὀλίγους οὐδὲ πολλούς, οὐδὲ τὸ ἑκούσιον,
οὐδὲ τὸ ἀκούσιον, οὐδὲ πενίαν οὐδὲ πλοῦτον γίγνεσθαι περὶ αὐτῶν χρεών, ἀλλά τινα ἐπιστήμην, εἴπερ
ἀκολουθήσομεν τοῖς πρόσθεν;

D 32. ΝΕ. ΣΩ. Ἀλλὰ μὴν τοῦτό γε ἀδύνατον
μὴ ποιεῖν.

ΞΕ. Ἐξ ἀνάγκης δὴ νῦν τοῦτο οὕτω σκεπτέον,
ἐν τίνι ποτὲ τούτων ἐπιστήμη ξυμβαίνει γίγνεσθαι
περὶ ἀνθρώπων ἀρχῆς, σχεδὸν τῆς χαλεπωτάτης καὶ
μεγίστης κτήσασθαι. δεῖ γὰρ ἰδεῖν αὐτήν, ἵνα
θεασώμεθα τίνας ἀφαιρετέον ἀπὸ τοῦ φρονίμου
βασιλέως, οἳ προσποιοῦνται μὲν εἶναι πολιτικοὶ καὶ
πείθουσι πολλούς, εἰσὶ δὲ οὐδαμῶς.

ΝΕ. ΣΩ. Δεῖ γὰρ δὴ ποιεῖν τοῦτο, ὡς ὁ λόγος
ἡμῖν προείρηκεν.

E ΞΕ. Μῶν οὖν δοκεῖ πλῆθός γε ἐν πόλει ταύτην
τὴν ἐπιστήμην δυνατὸν εἶναι κτήσασθαι;

ΝΕ. ΣΩ. Καὶ πῶς;

ΞΕ. Ἀλλ᾽ ἆρα ἐν χιλιάνδρῳ πόλει δυνατὸν
ἑκατόν τινας ἢ καὶ πεντήκοντα αὐτὴν ἱκανῶς
κτήσασθαι;

ΝΕ. ΣΩ. Ῥᾴστη μέντ᾽ ἂν οὕτω γ᾽ εἴη πασῶν τῶν
τεχνῶν· ἴσμεν γὰρ ὅτι χιλίων ἀνδρῶν ἄκροι
πεττευταὶ τοσοῦτοι πρὸς τοὺς ἐν τοῖς ἄλλοις
Ἕλλησιν οὐκ ἂν γένοιντό ποτε, μή τι δὴ
βασιλεῖς γε. δεῖ γὰρ δὴ τόν γε τὴν βασιλικὴν

---

[1] ἥτις] ἦν τις B : ἥν τις T.   [2] πω] πως BT : που vulg.

on dividing in this manner to the present moment, never forgetting that it is a science, but as yet unable to state with sufficient accuracy what science it is.

Y. SOC. You are right.

STR. Then is this our understanding, that the distinction between forms of government ought not to be found in the words few or many, or voluntary or unwilling, or wealth or poverty, but some science must be the distinguishing feature, if we are to be consistent with our previous statement?

Y. SOC. Yes, indeed; it cannot be otherwise.

STR. Necessarily, then, our present duty is to inquire in which, if any, of these forms of government is engendered the science of ruling men, which is about the greatest of sciences and the most difficult to acquire. We must discover that in order to see what men are to be distinguished from the wise king—men, I mean, who pretend to be, and make many believe that they are, statesmen, but are really not such at all.

Y. SOC. Yes, we must do this; that is implied in what was said before.

STR. Does it seem at all possible that a multitude in a state could acquire this science?

Y. SOC. By no means.

STR. But in a state of one thousand men could perhaps a hundred or as many as fifty acquire it adequately?

Y. SOC. No, in that case this would be the easiest of all the arts; for we know that a city of a thousand men could never produce that number of finished draught-players in comparison with those in other Greek cities, still less so many kings. For the man

ἔχοντα ἐπιστήμην, ἄν τ᾽ ἄρχῃ καὶ ἐὰν μή,
293 κατὰ τὸν ἔμπροσθεν λόγον ὅμως βασιλικὸν προσαγορεύεσθαι.

ΞΕ. Καλῶς ἀπεμνημόνευσας. ἑπόμενον δέ, οἶμαι,
τούτῳ τὴν μὲν ὀρθὴν ἀρχὴν περὶ ἕνα τινὰ καὶ δύο
καὶ παντάπασιν ὀλίγους δεῖ ζητεῖν, ὅταν ὀρθὴ γίγνηται.

ΝΕ. ΣΩ. Τί μήν;

ΞΕ. Τούτους δέ γε, ἐάντε ἑκόντων ἐάντε ἀκόντων
ἄρχωσιν, ἐάντε κατὰ γράμματα ἐάντε ἄνευ γραμμάτων, καὶ ἐὰν πλουτοῦντες ἢ πενόμενοι, νομιστέον,
ὥσπερ νῦν ἡγούμεθα, κατὰ τέχνην ἡντινοῦν ἀρχὴν
Β ἄρχοντας. τοὺς ἰατροὺς δὲ οὐχ ἥκιστα νενομίκα-
μεν, ἐάντε ἑκόντας ἐάντε ἄκοντας ἡμᾶς ἰῶνται,
τέμνοντες ἢ καίοντες ἤ τινα ἄλλην ἀλγηδόνα
προσάπτοντες, καὶ ἐὰν κατὰ γράμματα ἢ χωρὶς
γραμμάτων, καὶ ἐὰν πένητες ὄντες ἢ πλούσιοι,
πάντως οὐδὲν ἧττον ἰατρούς φαμεν, ἔωσπερ ἂν ἐπι-
στατοῦντες τέχνῃ, καθαίροντες εἴτε ἄλλως ἰσχναί-
νοντες εἴτε καὶ αὐξάνοντες, ἂν μόνον ἐπ᾽ ἀγαθῷ
τῷ τῶν σωμάτων, βελτίω ποιοῦντες ἐκ χειρόνων,
C σῴζωσιν οἱ θεραπεύοντες ἕκαστοι τὰ θεραπευό-
μενα· ταύτῃ θήσομεν, ὡς οἶμαι, καὶ οὐκ ἄλλῃ,
τοῦτον ὅρον ὀρθὸν εἶναι μόνον ἰατρικῆς καὶ ἄλλης
ἡστινοσοῦν ἀρχῆς.

ΝΕ. ΣΩ. Κομιδῇ μὲν οὖν.

33. ΞΕ. Ἀναγκαῖον δὴ καὶ πολιτειῶν, ὡς
ἔοικε, ταύτην διαφερόντως ὀρθὴν εἶναι καὶ μόνην
πολιτείαν, ἐν ᾗ τις ἂν εὑρίσκοι τοὺς ἄρχοντας ἀληθῶς

who possesses the kingly science, whether he rule or not, must be called kingly, as our previous argument showed.

str. You did well to remind me. And in agreement with this, we must, I suppose, look for the right kind of rule in one or two or very few men, whenever such right rule occurs.

y. soc. Certainly.

str. And these men, whether they rule over willing or unwilling subjects, with or without written laws, and whether they are rich or poor, must, according to our present opinion, be supposed to exercise their rule in accordance with some art or science. And physicians offer a particularly good example of this point of view. Whether they cure us against our will or with our will, by cutting us or burning us or causing us pain in any other way, and whether they do it by written rules or without them, and whether they are rich or poor, we call them physicians just the same, so long as they exercise authority by art or science, purging us or reducing us in some other way, or even adding to our weight, provided only that they who treat their patients treat them for the benefit of their health and preserve them by making them better than they were. In this way and no other, in my opinion, shall we determine this to be the only right definition of the rule of the physician or of any other rule whatsoever.

y. soc. Very true.

str. It is, then, a necessary consequence that among forms of government that one is preeminently right and is the only real government, in which the rulers are found to be truly possessed

ἐπιστήμονας καὶ οὐ δοκοῦντας μόνον, ἐάντε κατὰ
νόμους ἐάντε ἄνευ νόμων ἄρχωσι, καὶ ἑκόντων ἢ
D ἰκόντων, καὶ πενόμενοι ἢ πλουτοῦντες, τούτων
ὑπολογιστέον οὐδὲν οὐδαμῶς εἶναι κατ' οὐδεμίαν
ὀρθότητα.

ΝΕ. ΣΩ. Καλῶς.

ΞΕ. Καὶ ἐάντε γε ἀποκτιννύντες τινὰς ἢ καὶ ἐκ-
βάλλοντες καθαίρωσιν ἐπ' ἀγαθῷ τὴν πόλιν, εἴτε καὶ
ἀποικίας οἷον σμήνη μελιττῶν ἐκπέμποντές ποι
σμικροτέραν ποιῶσιν, ἤ τινας ἐπεισαγόμενοί ποθεν
ἄλλους ἔξωθεν πολίτας ποιοῦντες αὐτὴν αὔξωσιν,
ἕωσπερ ἂν ἐπιστήμῃ καὶ τῷ δικαίῳ προσχρώμενοι
σῴζοντες ἐκ χείρονος βελτίω ποιῶσι κατὰ δύναμιν,
E ταύτην τότε καὶ κατὰ τοὺς τοιούτους ὅρους ἡμῖν
μόνην ὀρθὴν πολιτείαν εἶναι ῥητέον· ὅσας δὲ ἄλλας
λέγομεν, οὐ γνησίας οὐδ' ὄντως οὔσας λεκτέον, ἀλλὰ
μεμιμημένας ταύτην, ἃς μὲν ὡς[1] εὐνόμους λέγομεν,
ἐπὶ τὰ καλλίω, τὰς δὲ ἄλλας ἐπὶ τὰ αἰσχίονα μεμιμῆ-
σθαι.

ΝΕ. ΣΩ. Τὰ μὲν ἄλλα, ὦ ξένε, μετρίως ἔοικεν
εἰρῆσθαι· τὸ δὲ καὶ ἄνευ νόμων δεῖν ἄρχειν χαλεπώτερον ἀκούειν ἐρρήθη.

ΞΕ. Σμικρόν γε ἔφθης με ἐρόμενος, ὦ Σώκρατες.
294 ἔμελλον γάρ σε διερωτήσειν ταῦτα πότερον ἀπο-
δέχει πάντα, ἤ τι καὶ δυσχεραίνεις τῶν λεχθέντων·
νῦν δὲ ἤδη φανερόν, ὅτι τοῦτο βουλησόμεθα τὸ
περὶ τῆς τῶν ἄνευ νόμων ἀρχόντων ὀρθότητος
διελθεῖν ἡμᾶς.

ΝΕ. ΣΩ. Πῶς γὰρ οὔ;

ΞΕ. Τρόπον μέντοι τινὰ δῆλον ὅτι τῆς βασιλικῆς
ἐστιν ἡ νομοθετική· τὸ δ' ἄριστον οὐ τοὺς νόμους

---

[1] ἃς μὲν ὡς Stallbaum : ἀσμένως B : ασμένως T.

of science, not merely to seem to possess it, whether they rule by law or without law, whether their subjects are willing or unwilling, and whether they themselves are rich or poor—none of these things can be at all taken into account on any right method.

y. soc. Excellent.

str. And whether they purge the state for its good by killing or banishing some of the citizens, or make it smaller by sending out colonies somewhere, as bees swarm from the hive, or bring in citizens from elsewhere to make it larger, so long as they act in accordance with science and justice and preserve and benefit it by making it better than it was, so far as is possible, that must at that time and by such characteristics be declared to be the only right form of government. All other forms must be considered not as legitimate or really existent, but as imitating this; those states which are said to be well governed imitate it better, and the others worse.

y. soc. Everything else that you have said seems reasonable; but that government should be carried on without laws is a hard saying.

str. You got ahead of me a little with your question, Socrates; for I was just going to ask whether you accepted all I have said, or were displeased with anything. But now it is clear that we shall have to discuss the question of the propriety of government without laws.

y. soc. Of course we shall.

str. In a sense, however, it is clear that lawmaking belongs to the science of kingship; but the best thing is not that the laws be in power, but that

ἐστὶν ἰσχύειν, ἀλλὰ ἄνδρα τὸν μετὰ φρονήσεως
βασιλικόν. οἶσθ' ὅπῃ;

ΝΕ. ΣΩ. Πῇ δὴ λέγεις;

ΞΕ. Ὅτι νόμος οὐκ ἄν ποτε δύναιτο τό τε ἄρι-
B στον καὶ τὸ δικαιότατον ἀκριβῶς ἅμα πᾶσιν περι-
λαβὼν τὸ βέλτιστον ἐπιτάττειν· αἱ γὰρ ἀνομοιό-
τητες τῶν τε ἀνθρώπων καὶ τῶν πράξεων καὶ τὸ[1]
μηδέποτε μηδέν, ὡς ἔπος εἰπεῖν, ἡσυχίαν ἄγειν
τῶν ἀνθρωπίνων οὐδὲν ἐῶσιν ἁπλοῦν ἐν οὐδενὶ περὶ
ἁπάντων καὶ ἐπὶ πάντα τὸν χρόνον ἀποφαίνεσθαι
τέχνην οὐδ' ἡντινοῦν. ταῦτα δὴ συγχωροῦμέν που;

ΝΕ. ΣΩ. Τί μήν;

ΞΕ. Τὸν δέ γε νόμον ὁρῶμεν σχεδὸν ἐπ' αὐτὸ
τοῦτο ξυντείνοντα, ὥσπερ τινὰ ἄνθρωπον αὐθάδη
C καὶ ἀμαθῆ καὶ μηδένα μηδὲν ἐῶντα ποιεῖν παρὰ τὴν
ἑαυτοῦ τάξιν, μηδ' ἐπερωτᾶν μηδένα, μηδ' ἄν τι
νέον ἄρα τῳ ξυμβαίνῃ βέλτιον παρὰ τὸν λόγον ὃν
αὐτὸς ἐπέταξεν.

ΝΕ. ΣΩ. Ἀληθῆ· ποιεῖ γὰρ ἀτεχνῶς, καθάπερ
εἴρηκας νῦν, ὁ νόμος ἡμῖν ἑκάστοις.

ΞΕ. Οὐκοῦν ἀδύνατον εὖ ἔχειν πρὸς τὰ μηδέποτε
ἁπλᾶ τὸ διὰ παντὸς γιγνόμενον ἁπλοῦν;

ΝΕ. ΣΩ. Κινδυνεύει.

34. ΞΕ. Διὰ τί δή ποτ' οὖν ἀναγκαῖον νομοθετεῖν,
ἐπειδήπερ οὐκ ὀρθότατον ὁ νόμος; ἀνευρετέον
D τούτου τὴν αἰτίαν.

ΝΕ. ΣΩ. Τί μήν;

ΞΕ. Οὐκοῦν καὶ παρ' ὑμῖν εἰσί τινες οἷαι καὶ
ἐν ἄλλαις πόλεσιν ἀθρόων ἀνθρώπων ἀσκήσεις, εἴτε
πρὸς δρόμον εἴτε πρὸς ἄλλο τι, φιλονεικίας ἕνεκα;

ΝΕ. ΣΩ. Καὶ πάνυ γε πολλαί.

---

[1] τὸ] τοῦ BT.

the man who is wise and of kingly nature be ruler.
Do you see why?

Y. SOC. Why is it?

STR. Because law could never, by determining
exactly what is noblest and most just for one and
all, enjoin upon them that which is best; for the
differences of men and of actions and the fact that
nothing, I may say, in human life is ever at rest,
forbid any science whatsoever to promulgate any
simple rule for everything and for all time. We
agree to that, I suppose?

Y. SOC. Yes, of course.

STR. But we see that law aims at pretty nearly
this very thing, like a stubborn and ignorant man
who allows no one to do anything contrary to his
command, or even to ask a question, not even if
something new occurs to some one, which is better
than the rule he has himself ordained.

Y. SOC. True; the law treats each and all of us
exactly as you describe.

STR. So that which is persistently simple is in-
applicable to things which are never simple?

Y. SOC. I suppose so.

STR. Why in the world, then, is it necessary to
make laws, since law is not the most perfect right?
We must ask the reason for this.

Y. SOC. Yes, of course.

STR. Well, there are here at Athens, as in other
cities, classes for practice in athletics to prepare for
contests in running or the like, are there not?

Y. SOC. Yes, a great many of them.

135

ΞΕ. Φέρε νῦν ἀναλάβωμεν πάλιν μνήμῃ τὰς τῶν τέχνῃ γυμναζόντων ἐπιτάξεις ἐν ταῖς τοιαύταις ἀρχαῖς.

ΝΕ. ΣΩ. Τὸ ποῖον;

ΞΕ. Ὅτι λεπτουργεῖν οὐκ ἐγχωρεῖν ἡγοῦνται καθ᾽ ἕνα ἕκαστον, τῷ σώματι τὸ προσῆκον ἑκάστῳ

E προστάττοντες, ἀλλὰ παχύτερον οἴονται δεῖν ὡς ἐπὶ τὸ πολὺ καὶ ἐπὶ πολλοὺς τὴν τοῦ λυσιτελοῦντος τοῖς σώμασι ποιεῖσθαι τάξιν.

ΝΕ. ΣΩ. Καλῶς.

ΞΕ. Διὸ δή γε καὶ ἴσους πόνους νῦν διδόντες ἀθρό-οις ἅμα μὲν ἐξορμῶσιν, ἅμα δὲ καὶ καταπαύουσι δρόμου καὶ πάλης καὶ πάντων τῶν κατὰ τὰ σώματα πόνων.

ΝΕ. ΣΩ. Ἔστι ταῦτα.

ΞΕ. Καὶ τὸν νομοθέτην τοίνυν ἡγώμεθα, τὸν ταῖσιν ἀγέλαις ἐπιστατήσοντα τοῦ δικαίου πέρι καὶ

295 τῶν πρὸς ἀλλήλους ξυμβολαίων, μή ποθ᾽ ἱκανὸν γενήσεσθαι πᾶσιν ἀθρόοις προστάττοντα ἀκριβῶς ἑνὶ ἑκάστῳ τὸ προσῆκον ἀποδιδόναι.

ΝΕ. ΣΩ. Τὸ γοῦν εἰκός.

ΞΕ. Ἀλλὰ τὸ τοῖς πολλοῖς γε, οἶμαι, καὶ ὡς ἐπὶ τὸ πολὺ καί πως οὑτωσὶ παχυτέρως ἑκάστοις τὸν νόμον θήσει,[1] καὶ ἐν γράμμασιν ἀποδιδοὺς καὶ ἐν ἀγραμμάτοις, πατρίοις δὲ ἔθεσι νομοθετῶν.

ΝΕ. ΣΩ. Ὀρθῶς.

ΞΕ. Ὀρθῶς μέντοι. πῶς γὰρ ἄν τις ἱκανὸς γένοιτ᾽ ἄν ποτε, ὦ Σώκρατες, ὥστε διὰ βίου ἀεὶ

B παρακαθήμενος ἑκάστῳ δι᾽ ἀκριβείας προστάττειν τὸ προσῆκον; ἐπεὶ τοῦτ᾽ ἂν δυνατὸς ὤν, ὡς οἶμαι, τῶν τὴν βασιλικὴν ὁστισοῦν ὄντως ἐπιστήμην

---

[1] θήσει] θήσειν ΒΤ.

136

str. Now let us recall to mind the orders given by the professional trainers when they are in charge of such classes.

y. soc. What do you mean?

str. They think they cannot go into details in individual cases and order what is best for each person's physique; they think they must employ a rougher method and give a general rule which will be good for the physique of the majority.

y. soc. Good.

str. And therefore they nowadays assign equal exercise to whole classes; they make them begin at the same time and stop at the same time, whether they run or wrestle or practise any other kind of bodily exercise.

y. soc. That is true.

str. And so we must believe that the law-maker who is to watch over the herds and maintain justice and the obligation of contracts, will never be able by making laws for all collectively, to provide exactly that which is proper for each individual.

y. soc. Probably not, at any rate.

str. But he will, I fancy, legislate for the majority and in a general way only roughly for individuals, whether he issues written laws or his enactments follow the unwritten traditional customs.

y. soc. Quite right.

str. Yes, quite right. For how could anyone, Socrates, sit beside each person all his life and tell him exactly what is proper for him to do? Certainly anyone who really possessed the kingly science, if he were able to do this, would hardly, I imagine,

PLATO

εἰληφότων σχολῇ ποτ' ἂν ἑαυτῷ θεῖτ' ἐμποδίσματα
γράφων τοὺς λεχθέντας τούτους νόμους.

ΝΕ. ΣΩ. Ἐκ τῶν νῦν γοῦν, ὦ ξένε, εἰρημένων.

ΞΕ. Μᾶλλον δέ γε, ὦ βέλτιστε, ἐκ τῶν μελλόντων
ῥηθήσεσθαι.

ΝΕ. ΣΩ. Τίνων δή;

ΞΕ. Τῶν τοιῶνδε. εἴπωμεν γὰρ δὴ πρός γε ἡμᾶς
C αὐτούς, ἰατρὸν μέλλοντα ἢ καί τινα γυμναστικὸν ἀπο-
δημεῖν καὶ ἀπέσεσθαι τῶν θεραπευομένων συχνόν,
ὡς οἴοιτο, χρόνον, μὴ μνημονεύσειν οἰηθέντα τὰ προσταχθέντα τοὺς γυμναζομένους ἢ τοὺς κάμνοντας,
ὑπομνήματα γράφειν ἂν ἐθέλειν αὐτοῖς, ἢ πῶς;

ΝΕ. ΣΩ. Οὕτως.

ΞΕ. Τί δ' εἰ[1] παρὰ δόξαν ἐλάττω χρόνον ἀποδη-
μήσας ἔλθοι πάλιν; ἆρ' οὐκ ἂν παρ' ἐκεῖνα τὰ γράμματα τολμήσειεν ἄλλα ὑποθέσθαι, ξυμβαινόντων
D ἄλλων βελτιόνων τοῖς κάμνουσι διὰ πνεύματα ἤ
τι καὶ ἄλλο παρὰ τὴν ἐλπίδα τῶν ἐκ Διὸς ἑτέρως
πως τῶν εἰωθότων γενόμενα, καρτερῶν δ' ἂν ἡγοῖτο
δεῖν μὴ ἐκβαίνειν τὰ ἀρχαῖά ποτε νομοθετηθέντα
μήτε αὐτὸν προστάττοντα ἄλλα μήτε τὸν κάμνοντα
ἕτερα τολμῶντα παρὰ τὰ γραφέντα δρᾶν, ὡς ταῦτα
ὄντα ἰατρικὰ καὶ ὑγιεινά, τὰ δὲ ἑτέρως γιγνόμενα
νοσώδη τε καὶ οὐκ ἔντεχνα· ἢ πᾶν τὸ τοιοῦτον ἔν
γε ἐπιστήμῃ ξυμβαῖνον καὶ ἀληθεῖ τέχνῃ περὶ
E ἅπαντα παντάπασι γέλως ἂν ὁ μέγιστος γίγνοιτο
τῶν τοιούτων νομοθετημάτων;

ΝΕ. ΣΩ. Παντάπασι μὲν οὖν.

ΞΕ. Τῷ δὲ τὰ δίκαια δὴ καὶ ἄδικα καὶ καλὰ καὶ
αἰσχρὰ καὶ ἀγαθὰ καὶ κακὰ γράψαντι καὶ ἄγραφα
νομοθετήσαντι ταῖς τῶν ἀνθρώπων ἀγέλαις, ὁπόσαι

---

[1] δ' εἰ] δαὶ εἰ T: δὴ B.

138

ever put obstacles in his own way by writing what we call laws.

Y. SOC. No, at least not according to what has just been said.

STR. Or rather, my friend, not according to what is going to be said.

Y. SOC. What is that?

STR. Something of this sort: Let us suppose that a physician or a gymnastic trainer is going away and expects to be a long time absent from his patients or pupils; if he thinks they will not remember his instructions, he would want to write them down, would he not?

Y. SOC. Yes.

STR. What if he should come back again after a briefer absence than he expected? Would he not venture to substitute other rules for those written instructions if others happened to be better for his patients, because the winds or something else had, by act of God, changed unexpectedly from their usual course? Would he persist in the opinion that no one must transgress the old laws, neither he himself by enacting new ones nor his patient by venturing to do anything contrary to the written rules, under the conviction that these laws were medicinal and healthful and anything else was unhealthful and unscientific? If anything of that sort occurred in the realm of science and true art, would not any such regulations on any subject assuredly arouse the greatest ridicule?

Y. SOC. Most assuredly.

STR. But he who has made written or unwritten laws about the just and unjust, the honourable and disgraceful, the good and the bad for the herds

139

κατὰ πόλιν ἐν ἑκάσταις νομεύονται κατὰ τοὺς τῶν
γραψάντων νόμους, ἂν ὁ μετὰ τέχνης γράψας ἤ τις
ἕτερος ὅμοιος ἀφίκηται, μὴ ἐξέστω δὴ παρὰ ταῦτα
296 ἕτερα προστάττειν; ἢ καὶ τοῦτο τὸ ἀπόρρημα
οὐδὲν ἧττον ἂν ἐκείνου τῇ ἀληθείᾳ γελοῖον φαίνοιτο;

ΝΕ. ΣΩ. Τί μήν;

35. ΞΕ. Οἶσθ' οὖν ἐπὶ τῷ τοιούτῳ λόγον τὸν
παρὰ τῶν πολλῶν λεγόμενον;

ΝΕ. ΣΩ. Οὐκ ἐννοῶ νῦν γ' οὕτως.

ΞΕ. Καὶ μὴν εὐπρεπής. φασὶ γὰρ δὴ δεῖν, εἴ τις
γιγνώσκει παρὰ τοὺς τῶν ἔμπροσθεν βελτίους
νόμους, νομοθετεῖν τὴν ἑαυτοῦ πόλιν ἕκαστον πεί-
σαντα, ἄλλως δὲ μή.

ΝΕ. ΣΩ. Τί οὖν; οὐκ ὀρθῶς;

B   ΞΕ. Ἴσως. ἂν δ' οὖν μὴ πείθων τις βιάζηται τὸ
βέλτιον, ἀπόκριναι, τί τοὔνομα τῆς βίας ἔσται; μὴ
μέντοι πω, περὶ δὲ τῶν ἔμπροσθεν πρότερον.

ΝΕ. ΣΩ. Ποῖον δὴ λέγεις;

ΞΕ. Ἄν τις ἄρα μὴ πείθων τὸν ἰατρευόμενον,
ἔχων δὲ ὀρθῶς τὴν τέχνην, παρὰ τὰ γεγραμμένα τὸ
βέλτιον ἀναγκάζῃ δρᾶν παῖδα ἤ τινα ἄνδρα ἢ καὶ
γυναῖκα, τί τοὔνομα τῆς βίας ἔσται ταύτης; ἆρ' οὐ
πᾶν μᾶλλον ἢ τὸ παρὰ τὴν τέχνην λεγόμενον ἁμάρ-
C τημα τὸ νοσῶδες; καὶ πάντα ὀρθῶς εἰπεῖν ἔστι
πρότερον τῷ βιασθέντι περὶ τὸ τοιοῦτον, πλὴν ὅτι
νοσώδη καὶ ἄτεχνα πέπονθεν ὑπὸ τῶν βιασαμένων
ἰατρῶν;

ΝΕ. ΣΩ. Ἀληθέστατα λέγεις.

ΞΕ. Τί δὲ ἡμῖν δὴ τὸ παρὰ τὴν πολιτικὴν τέχνην

140

of men that are tended in their several cities in accordance with the laws of the law-makers, is not to be permitted to give other laws contrary to those, if the scientific law-maker, or another like him, should come! Would not such a prohibition appear in truth as ridiculous as the other?

y. soc. It certainly would.

str. Do you know what people in general say about such a case?

y. soc. I don't recall it just now off-hand.

str. Yes, it is very plausible; for they say that if anyone has anything better than the old laws to offer, he must first persuade the state, and then he may make his laws, but not otherwise.

y. soc. And is that not right?

str. Perhaps. But suppose a man does not use persuasion, but makes an improvement by force. What is this force to be called? Answer me—or, no, not yet; first answer in reference to what we were talking of before.

y. soc. What do you mean?

str. Suppose a physician who has right knowledge of his profession does not persuade, but forces, his patient, whether man, woman, or child, to do the better thing, though it be contrary to the written precepts, what will such violence be called? The last name in the world to call it would be "unscientific and baneful error," as the phrase is, would it not? And the patient so forced might rightly say anything else rather than that he had been treated in a baneful or unscientific way by the physicians who used force upon him.

y. soc. Very true.

str. But what can we call the unscientific error

ἁμάρτημα λεγόμενόν ἐστιν; ἆρ' οὐ τὸ αἰσχρὸν καὶ κακὸν καὶ ἄδικον;

ΝΕ. ΣΩ. Παντάπασί γε.

ΞΕ. Τῶν δὴ βιασθέντων παρὰ τὰ γεγραμμένα καὶ πάτρια δρᾶν ἕτερα δικαιότερα καὶ ἀμείνω καὶ
D καλλίω τῶν ἔμπροσθεν, φέρε, τὸν τῶν τοιούτων αὖ ψόγον περὶ τῆς τοιαύτης βίας, ἆρ', εἰ μέλλει μὴ καταγελαστότατος εἶναι πάντων, πάντα αὐτῷ μᾶλλον λεκτέον ἑκάστοτε, πλὴν ὡς αἰσχρὰ καὶ ἄδικα καὶ κακὰ πεπόνθασιν οἱ βιασθέντες ὑπὸ τῶν βιασαμένων;

ΝΕ. ΣΩ. Ἀληθέστατα λέγεις.

ΞΕ. Ἀλλ' ἆρα ἐὰν μὲν πλούσιος ὁ βιασάμενος ᾖ, δίκαια, ἂν δ' ἄρα πένης, ἄδικα τὰ βιασθέντα ἐστίν; ἢ κἂν πείσας κἂν μὴ πείσας τις, πλούσιος ἢ πένης,
E ἢ κατὰ γράμματα ἢ παρὰ γράμματα, δρᾷ ξύμφορα,[1] τοῦτον δεῖ καὶ περὶ ταῦτα τὸν ὅρον εἶναι τόν γε ἀληθινώτατον ὀρθῆς πόλεως διοικήσεως, ὃν ὁ σοφὸς καὶ ἀγαθὸς ἀνὴρ διοικήσει τὸ τῶν ἀρχομένων; ὥσπερ ὁ κυβερνήτης τὸ τῆς νεὼς καὶ ναυτῶν ἀεὶ ξυμφέρον
297 παραφυλάττων, οὐ γράμματα τιθεὶς ἀλλὰ τὴν τέχνην νόμον παρεχόμενος, σῴζει τοὺς συνναύτας, οὕτω καὶ κατὰ τὸν αὐτὸν τρόπον τοῦτον παρὰ τῶν οὕτως ἄρχειν δυναμένων ὀρθὴ γίγνοιτ' ἂν πολιτεία, τὴν τῆς τέχνης ῥώμην τῶν νόμων παρεχομένων κρείττω; καὶ πάντα ποιοῦσι τοῖς ἔμφροσιν ἄρχουσιν οὐκ ἔστιν ἁμάρτημα, μέχριπερ ἂν ἓν μέγα φυλάττωσι, τὸ
B μετὰ νοῦ καὶ τέχνης δικαιότατον ἀεὶ διανέμοντες τοῖς ἐν τῇ πόλει σῴζειν τε αὐτοὺς οἷοί τε ὦσι καὶ ἀμείνους ἐκ χειρόνων ἀποτελεῖν κατὰ τὸ δυνατόν;

---

[1] δρᾷ ξύμφορα Cornarius : δρᾷ μὴ ξύμφορα ἢ ξύμφορα mss.

in the field of statesmanship? Is it not baseness and evil and injustice?

y. soc. Certainly.

str. Now if people are forced, contrary to the written laws and inherited traditions, to do what is juster and nobler and better than what they did before, tell me, will not anyone who blames such use of force, unless he is to be most utterly ridiculous, always say anything or everything rather than that those who have been so forced have suffered base and unjust and evil treatment at the hands of those who forced them?

y. soc. Very true.

str. But would the violence be just if he who uses it is rich, and unjust if he is poor? Or if a man, whether rich or poor, by persuasion or by other means, in accordance with written laws or contrary to them, does what is for the good of the people, must not this be the truest criterion of right government, in accordance with which the wise and good man will govern the affairs of his subjects? Just as the captain of a ship keeps watch for what is at any moment for the good of the vessel and the sailors, not by writing rules, but by making his science his law, and thus preserves his fellow voyagers, so may not a right government be established in the same way by men who could rule by this principle, making science more powerful than the laws? And whatever the wise rulers do, they can commit no error, so long as they maintain one great principle and by always dispensing absolute justice to them with wisdom and science are able to preserve the citizens and make them better than they were, so far as that is possible. Is not this true?

143

PLATO

ΝΕ. ΣΩ. Οὐκ ἔστ᾽ ἀντειπεῖν παρά γε ἃ νῦν εἴρηται.

ΞΕ. Καὶ μὴν πρὸς ἐκεῖνα οὐδὲ ἀντιρρητέον.

36. ΝΕ. ΣΩ. Τὰ ποῖα εἶπες;

ΞΕ. Ὡς οὐκ ἄν ποτε πλῆθος οὐδ᾽ ὡντινωνοῦν τὴν τοιαύτην λαβὸν ἐπιστήμην οἷόν τ᾽ ἂν γένοιτο C μετὰ νοῦ διοικεῖν πόλιν, ἀλλὰ περὶ σμικρόν τι καὶ ὀλίγον καὶ τὸ ἕν ἐστι ζητητέον τὴν μίαν ἐκείνην πολιτείαν τὴν ὀρθήν, τὰς δ᾽ ἄλλας μιμήματα θετέον, ὥσπερ καὶ ὀλίγον πρότερον ἐρρήθη, τὰς μὲν ἐπὶ τὰ καλλίονα, τὰς δὲ ἐπὶ τὰ αἰσχίω μιμουμένας ταύτην.

ΝΕ. ΣΩ. Πῶς τί τοῦτ᾽ εἴρηκας; οὐδὲ γὰρ ἄρτι δῆθεν κατέμαθον τὸ περὶ τῶν μιμημάτων.

ΞΕ. Καὶ μὴν οὐ φαῦλόν γε, ἂν κινήσας τις τοῦτον τὸν λόγον αὐτοῦ καταβάλῃ καὶ μὴ διελθὼν ἐνδείξηται D τὸ νῦν γιγνόμενον ἁμάρτημα περὶ αὐτό.

ΝΕ. ΣΩ. Ποῖον δή;

ΞΕ. Τοιόνδε τι δεῖ γε ζητεῖν, οὐ πάνυ ξύνηθες οὐδὲ ῥάδιον ἰδεῖν· ὅμως μὴν πειρώμεθα λαβεῖν αὐτό. φέρε γάρ· ὀρθῆς ἡμῖν μόνης οὔσης ταύτης τῆς πολιτείας, ἣν εἰρήκαμεν, οἶσθ᾽ ὅτι τὰς ἄλλας δεῖ τοῖς ταύτης συγγράμμασι χρωμένας οὕτω σῴζεσθαι, δρώσας τὸ νῦν ἐπαινούμενον, καίπερ οὐκ ὀρθότατον ὄν;

ΝΕ. ΣΩ. Τὸ ποῖον;

ΞΕ. Τὸ παρὰ τοὺς νόμους μηδὲν μηδένα τολμᾶν ποιεῖν τῶν ἐν τῇ πόλει, τὸν τολμῶντα δὲ θανάτῳ E ζημιοῦσθαι καὶ πᾶσι τοῖς ἐσχάτοις. καὶ τοῦτ᾽ ἔστιν ὀρθότατα καὶ κάλλιστ᾽ ἔχον ὡς δεύτερον, ἐπειδὰν τὸ πρῶτόν τις μεταθῇ τὸ νῦν δὴ ῥηθέν·

y. soc. There is no denying the truth of what you have just said.

str. And those other statements cannot be denied, either.

y. soc. What statements?

str. That no great number of men, whoever they may be, could ever acquire political science and be able to administer a state with wisdom, but our one right form of government must be sought in some small number or one person, and all other forms are merely, as we said before, more or less successful imitations of that.

y. soc. What do you mean by that? I did not understand about the imitations a little while ago, either.

str. And yet it is quite a serious matter if after stirring up this question we drop it and do not go on and show the error which is committed in relation to it nowadays.

y. soc. What is the error?

str. I will tell you what we must investigate; it is not at all familiar or easy to see, but let us try to grasp it nevertheless. Tell me this: Assuming that the form of government we have described is the only right form, don't you see that the other forms must employ its written laws if they are to be preserved by doing that which is approved of nowadays, although it is not perfectly right?

y. soc. What is not perfectly right?

str. That no citizen shall dare to do anything contrary to the laws, and that he who does shall be punished by death and the most extreme penalties. And this is perfectly right and good as a second choice, as soon as you depart from the first form of

PLATO

ᾧ δὲ τρόπῳ γεγονός ἐστι τοῦτο ὃ δὴ δεύτερον
ἐφήσαμεν, διαπερανώμεθα. ἦ γάρ;

ΝΕ. ΣΩ. Πάνυ μὲν οὖν.

37. ΞΕ. Εἰς δὴ τὰς εἰκόνας ἐπανίωμεν πάλιν,
αἷς ἀναγκαῖον ἀπεικάζειν ἀεὶ τοὺς βασιλικοὺς
ἄρχοντας.

ΝΕ. ΣΩ. Ποίας;

ΞΕ. Τὸν γενναῖον κυβερνήτην καὶ τὸν ἑτέρων
πολλῶν ἀντάξιον ἰατρόν. κατίδωμεν γὰρ δή τι
σχῆμα ἐν τούτοις αὐτοῖς πλασάμενοι.

ΝΕ. ΣΩ. Ποῖόν τι;

298 ΞΕ. Τοιόνδε οἷον εἰ πάντες περὶ αὐτῶν διανοηθεῖμεν, ὅτι δεινότατα ὑπ' αὐτῶν πάσχομεν. ὃν μὲν
γὰρ ἂν ἐθελήσωσιν ἡμῶν τούτων ἑκάτεροι σῴζειν,
ὁμοίως δὴ σῴζουσιν, ὃν δ' ἂν λωβᾶσθαι βουληθῶσι,
λωβῶνται τέμνοντες καὶ καίοντες καὶ προστάττοντες ἀναλώματα φέρειν παρ' ἑαυτοὺς οἷον φόρους,
ὧν σμικρὰ μὲν εἰς τὸν κάμνοντα καὶ οὐδὲν ἀναλί-
σκουσι, τοῖς δ' ἄλλοις αὐτοί τε καὶ οἱ οἰκέται χρῶνται·
B καὶ δὴ καὶ τελευτῶντες ἢ παρὰ ξυγγενῶν ἢ παρά
τινων ἐχθρῶν τοῦ κάμνοντος χρήματα μισθὸν
λαμβάνοντες ἀποκτιννύασιν. οἵ τ' αὖ κυβερνῆται
μυρία ἕτερα τοιαῦτα ἐργάζονται, καταλείποντές[1] τε
ἔκ τινος ἐπιβουλῆς ἐν ταῖς ἀναγωγαῖς ἐρήμους,
καὶ σφάλματα ποιοῦντες ἐν τοῖς πελάγεσιν ἐκβάλ-
λουσιν εἰς τὴν θάλατταν, καὶ ἕτερα κακουργοῦσιν.
εἰ δὴ ταῦτα διανοηθέντες βουλευσαίμεθα περὶ αὐτῶν

[1] καταλείποντες codd. Paris. BCH : καταλιπόντες BT.

---

[1] *Cf.* Homer, *Iliad*, xii. 514 ἰητρὸς γὰρ ἀνὴρ πολλῶν ἀντάξιος
ἄλλων. The image of the physician was used above, 293.
The image of the captain (for the Greek κυβερνήτης had an

146

deliberated about them and decided that we would no longer allow either of these arts to rule without control over slaves or free men, but that we would call an assembly either of all the people or of the rich only, and that anyone, whether he were engaged in some other form of skilled labour or were without any special qualifications, should be free to offer an opinion about navigation and diseases, how drugs and surgical or medical instruments should be applied to the patients, and how ships and nautical instruments should be used for navigation and in meeting dangers, not only those of winds and sea that affect the voyage itself, but also those met in encounters with pirates, and if battles have to be fought between ships of war; and that whatever the majority decided about these matters, whether any physicians or ship captains or merely unskilled persons took part in the deliberations, should be inscribed upon tablets and slabs or in some instances should be adopted as unwritten ancestral customs, and that henceforth forever navigation and the care of the sick should be conducted in accordance with these provisions.

y. soc. That is a most absurd state of things that you have described.

str. And suppose that rulers of the people are set up annually, whether from the rich or from the whole people, on the principle that whoever is chosen by lot should rule, and that these rulers exercise their authority in commanding the ships or treating the sick in accordance with the written rules.

y. soc. That is still harder to imagine.

str. Now consider what comes next. When the year of office has passed for each set of rulers, there

PLATO

τὸς ἐξέλθῃ, δεήσει δικαστήρια καθίσαντας[1] ἀνδρῶν,
299 ἢ τῶν πλουσίων ἐκ προκρίσεως ἢ ξύμπαντος αὖ
τοῦ δήμου τοὺς λαχόντας, εἰς τούτους εἰσάγειν τοὺς
ἄρξαντας καὶ εὐθύνειν, κατηγορεῖν δὲ τὸν βουλόμενον ὡς οὐ κατὰ τὰ γράμματα τὸν ἐνιαυτὸν ἐκυ-
βέρνησε τὰς ναῦς οὐδὲ κατὰ τὰ παλαιὰ τῶν προγόνων ἔθη· τὰ αὐτὰ δὲ ταῦτα καὶ περὶ τῶν τοὺς
κάμνοντας ἰωμένων· ὧν δ' ἂν καταψηφισθῇ τιμᾶν
ὅ τι χρὴ παθεῖν αὐτῶν τινας ἢ ἀποτίνειν.

ΝΕ. ΣΩ. Οὐκοῦν ὅ γ' ἐθέλων καὶ ἑκὼν ἐν τοῖς
B τοιούτοις ἄρχειν δικαιότατ' ἂν ὁτιοῦν πάσχοι καὶ
ἀποτίνοι.

ΞΕ. Καὶ τοίνυν ἔτι δεήσει θέσθαι νόμον ἐπὶ πᾶσι
τούτοις, ἄν τις κυβερνητικὴν καὶ τὸ ναυτικὸν ἢ τὸ
ὑγιεινὸν καὶ ἰατρικῆς ἀλήθειαν περὶ πνεύματά τε καὶ
θερμὰ καὶ ψυχρὰ ζητῶν φαίνηται παρὰ τὰ γράμματα
καὶ σοφιζόμενος ὁτιοῦν περὶ τὰ τοιαῦτα, πρῶτον
μὲν μήτε ἰατρικὸν αὐτὸν μήτε κυβερνητικὸν ὀνομάζειν ἀλλὰ μετεωρολόγον, ἀδολέσχην τινὰ σοφιστήν,
εἶθ' ὡς διαφθείροντα ἄλλους νεωτέρους καὶ ἀνα-
C πείθοντα ἐπιτίθεσθαι κυβερνητικῇ καὶ ἰατρικῇ μὴ
κατὰ νόμους, ἀλλ' αὐτοκράτορας ἄρχειν τῶν πλοίων
καὶ τῶν νοσούντων, γραψάμενον εἰσάγειν τὸν βουλόμενον οἷς ἔξεστιν εἰς δή τι δικαστήριον· ἂν δὲ
παρὰ τοὺς νόμους καὶ τὰ γεγραμμένα δόξῃ πείθειν
εἴτε νέους εἴτε πρεσβύτας, κολάζειν τοῖς ἐσχάτοις.

---

[1] καθίσαντας D : καθήσαντας B : καθιστάντας T.

---

[1] This passage obviously refers to the trial of Socrates.
The word μετέωρα was used by those who made all sorts of
general accusations against Socrates (see *Apology,* 18 B,
19 B, with its reference to the *Clouds* of Aristophanes), and
the reference of the words διαφθείροντα ἄλλους νεωτέρους to
the accusation brought against him by Miletus, Anytus,

will have to be sessions of courts in which the judges are chosen by lot either from a selected list of the rich or from the whole people, and the rulers will have to be brought before these courts and examined as to their conduct in office, and anyone who pleases can bring against the captains an accusation for failure to command the ships during the year in accordance with the written laws or the ancestral customs, and similarly against the physicians for their treatment of the sick; and if any of them is found guilty, the court shall decide what his punishment or his fine shall be.

y. soc. Surely anyone who consents voluntarily to hold office under such conditions would richly deserve any penalty or fine that might be imposed.

str. And then, in addition to all this, there will have to be a law that if anyone is found to be investigating the art of pilotage or navigation or the subject of health and true medical doctrine about winds and things hot and cold, contrary to the written rules, or to be indulging in any speculation whatsoever on such matters, he shall in the first place not be called a physician or a ship captain, but a star-gazer,[1] a kind of loquacious sophist, and secondly anyone who is properly qualified may bring an accusation against him and hale him into court for corrupting the young and persuading them to essay the arts of navigation and medicine in opposition to the laws and to govern the ships and the sick according to their own will; and if he is found to be so persuading either young or old contrary to the laws and written rules, he shall suffer

and Lycon (*Apology* 24 c φησὶ γὰρ δὴ τοὺς νέους ἀδικεῖν με διαφθείροντα) is perfectly plain.

οὐδὲν γὰρ δεῖν τῶν νόμων εἶναι σοφώτερον· οὐδένα
γὰρ ἀγνοεῖν τό τε ἰατρικὸν καὶ τὸ ὑγιεινὸν οὐδὲ
τὸ κυβερνητικὸν καὶ ναυτικόν· ἐξεῖναι γὰρ τῷ
D βουλομένῳ μανθάνειν γεγραμμένα καὶ πάτρια ἔθη
κείμενα. ταῦτα δὴ περί τε ταύτας τὰς ἐπιστήμας
εἰ γίγνοιτο οὕτως ὡς λέγομεν, ὦ Σώκρατες, καὶ
στρατηγικῆς καὶ ξυμπάσης ἡστινοσοῦν θηρευτικῆς
καὶ γραφικῆς ἢ ξυμπάσης μέρος ὁτιοῦν μιμητικῆς
καὶ τεκτονικῆς καὶ ξυνόλης ὁποιασοῦν σκευουργίας
ἢ καὶ γεωργίας καὶ τῆς περὶ τὰ φυτὰ ξυνόλης τέχνης,
ἢ καί τινα ἱπποφορβίαν αὖ κατὰ συγγράμματα
θεασαίμεθα γιγνομένην ἢ ξύμπασαν ἀγελαιοκομικὴν
ἢ μαντικὴν ἢ πᾶν ὅ τι μέρος διακονικὴ περιείληφεν,
E ἢ πεττείαν ἢ ξύμπασαν ἀριθμητικὴν ψιλὴν εἴτε
ἐπίπεδον εἴτε ἐν βάθεσιν εἴτε ἐν τάχεσιν[1] οὖσάν
που,—περὶ ἅπαντα ταῦτα οὕτω πραττόμενα τί
ποτ' ἂν φανείη, κατὰ συγγράμματα γιγνόμενα καὶ
μὴ κατὰ τέχνην;

ΝΕ. ΣΩ. Δῆλον ὅτι πᾶσαί τε[2] αἱ τέχναι παντελῶς
ἂν ἀπόλοινθ' ἡμῖν, καὶ οὐδὲ εἰς αὖθις γένοιντ' ἄν
ποτε διὰ τὸν ἀποκωλύοντα τοῦτον ζητεῖν νόμον·
ὥστε ὁ βίος, ὢν καὶ νῦν χαλεπός, εἰς τὸν χρόνον
300 ἐκεῖνον ἀβίωτος γίγνοιτ' ἂν τὸ παράπαν.

39. ΞΕ. Τί δὲ τόδε; εἰ κατὰ συγγράμματα
μὲν ἀναγκάζοιμεν ἕκαστον γίγνεσθαι τῶν εἰρημένων
καὶ τοῖς συγγράμμασιν ἡμῶν ἐπιστατεῖν τὸν
χειροτονηθέντα ἢ λαχόντα ἐκ τύχης, οὗτος δὲ μηδὲν
φροντίζων τῶν γραμμάτων ἢ κέρδους ἕνεκά[3] τινος
ἢ χάριτος ἰδίας παρὰ ταῦτα ἐπιχειροῖ δρᾶν ἕτερα,
μηδὲν γιγνώσκων, ἆρα οὐ τοῦ κακοῦ τοῦ πρόσθεν
μεῖζον ἂν ἔτι τοῦτο γίγνοιτο κακόν;

---

[1] τάχεσιν] πάχεσιν al.   [2] τε om. B.   [3] ἕνεκέν ΒΤ.

the most extreme penalties. Nothing, they say, ought to be wiser than the laws; for no one is ignorant of medicine and the laws of health or of the pilot's art and navigation, since anyone who pleases can learn the existing written rules and ancestral customs. Now if these regulations which I speak of were to be applied to these sciences, Socrates, and to strategy and every part of the entire art of hunting and to painting or every kind of imitation and to carpentry including every kind of utensil-making, or even to husbandry and all the art that is concerned with plants, or if we were to see an art of horse-breeding conducted by written rules, or herdsmanship in general or prophecy or everything that is included in the art of serving, or draught-playing or the whole science of number, whether arithmetic or plane geometry or solid geometry or problems of motion—what would you think of carrying on all these in such a way, by written rules and not by knowledge?

y. soc. Clearly all the arts would be utterly ruined, nor could they ever rise again, through the operation of the law prohibiting investigation; and so life, which is hard enough now, would then become absolutely unendurable.

str. Here is a further point. If we ordained that each of the aforesaid arts must be carried on by written rules and that the observance of our written rules be under the charge of the man who is elected or chosen by lot, but he should disregard the written rules and for the sake of some gain or to do a favour to some one should try to act contrary to them, without possessing any knowledge, would not this be a greater evil than the former?

ΝΕ. ΣΩ. Ἀληθέστατά γε.

Β   ΞΕ. Παρὰ γὰρ οἶμαι τοὺς νόμους τοὺς ἐκ πείρας πολλῆς κειμένους καί τινων ξυμβούλων ἕκαστα χαριέντως ξυμβουλευσάντων καὶ πεισάντων θέσθαι τὸ πλῆθος, ὁ παρὰ ταῦτα τολμῶν δρᾶν, ἁμαρτήματος ἁμάρτημα πολλαπλάσιον ἀπεργαζόμενος, ἀνατρέποι πᾶσαν ἂν πρᾶξιν ἔτι μειζόνως τῶν ξυγγραμμάτων.

ΝΕ. ΣΩ. Πῶς δ' οὐ μέλλει;

ΞΕ. Διὰ ταῦτα δὴ τοῖς περὶ ὁτουοῦν νόμους καὶ
C ξυγγράμματα τιθεμένοις δεύτερος πλοῦς τὸ παρὰ ταῦτα μήτε ἕνα μήτε πλῆθος μηδὲν μηδέποτε ἐᾶν δρᾶν μηδ' ὁτιοῦν.

ΝΕ. ΣΩ. Ὀρθῶς.

ΞΕ. Οὐκοῦν μιμήματα μὲν ἂν ἑκάστων ταῦτα εἴη τῆς ἀληθείας, τὰ παρὰ τῶν εἰδότων εἰς δύναμιν εἶναι γεγραμμένα;

ΝΕ. ΣΩ. Πῶς δ' οὔ;

ΞΕ. Καὶ μὴν τόν γε εἰδότα ἔφαμεν, τὸν ὄντως πολιτικόν, εἰ μεμνήμεθα, ποιήσειν τῇ τέχνῃ πολλὰ εἰς τὴν αὑτοῦ πρᾶξιν τῶν γραμμάτων οὐδὲν φροντίζοντα, ὁπόταν ἄλλ' αὑτῷ βελτίω δόξῃ παρὰ τὰ
D γεγραμμένα ὑφ' αὑτοῦ καὶ ἐπεσταλμένα ἀποῦσί τισιν.

ΝΕ. ΣΩ. Ἔφαμεν γάρ.

ΞΕ. Οὐκοῦν ἀνὴρ ὁστισοῦν εἷς ἢ πλῆθος ὁτιοῦν, οἷς ἂν νόμοι κείμενοι τυγχάνωσι, παρὰ ταῦτα ὅ τι ἂν ἐπιχειρήσωσι ποιεῖν ὡς βέλτιον ἕτερον ὄν, ταὐτὸν δρῶσι κατὰ δύναμιν ὅπερ ὁ ἀληθινὸς ἐκεῖνος;

ΝΕ. ΣΩ. Πάνυ μὲν οὖν.

ΞΕ. Ἆρ' οὖν εἰ μὲν ἀνεπιστήμονες ὄντες τὸ τοιοῦ-

---

[1] See 295 E.

y. soc. Most assuredly.

str. Since the laws are made after long experience and after commissioners of some kind have carefully considered each detail with delicate skill and have persuaded the people to pass them, anyone, I fancy, who ventured to violate them would be involved in error many times greater than the first, and would cause even greater ruin than the written laws to all kinds of transactions.

y. soc. Of course he would.

str. Therefore the next best course for those who make laws or written rules about anything whatsoever is to prohibit any violation of them whatsoever, either by one person or by a greater number.

y. soc. Right.

str. These laws, then, written by men who know in so far as knowledge is possible, are imitations in each instance of some part of truth?

y. soc. Of course.

str. And yet we said, if we remember, that the man of knowledge, the real statesman, would by his art make many changes in his practice without regard to his writings, when he thought another course was better though it violated the rules he had written and sent to his absent subjects.[1]

y. soc. Yes, we did say that.

str. But is it not true that any man or any number of men whatsoever who have written laws, if they undertake to make any change in those laws, thinking it is an improvement, are doing, to the best of their ability, the same thing which our true statesman does?

y. soc. Certainly.

str. If, then, they were to do this without science,

τον δρῶεν, μιμεῖσθαι μὲν ἂν ἐπιχειροῖεν τὸ ἀληθές,
E μιμοῖντ᾽ ἂν μέντοι πᾶν κακῶς¹· εἰ δ᾽ ἔντεχνοι,
τοῦτο οὐκ ἔστιν ἔτι μίμημα, ἀλλ᾽ αὐτὸ τὸ ἀληθέστατον ἐκεῖνο;

ΝΕ. ΣΩ. Πάντως που.

ΞΕ. Καὶ μὴν ἔμπροσθέν γε ὡμολογημένον ἡμῖν
κεῖται μηδὲν πλῆθος μηδ᾽ ἡντινοῦν δυνατὸν εἶναι
λαβεῖν τέχνην.

ΝΕ. ΣΩ. Κεῖται γὰρ οὖν.

ΞΕ. Οὐκοῦν εἰ μὲν ἔστι βασιλική τις τέχνη, τὸ
τῶν πλουσίων πλῆθος καὶ ὁ ξύμπας δῆμος οὐκ ἄν
ποτε λάβοι τὴν πολιτικὴν ταύτην ἐπιστήμην.

ΝΕ. ΣΩ. Πῶς γὰρ ἄν;

ΞΕ. Δεῖ δὴ τὰς τοιαύτας γε, ὡς ἔοικε, πολιτείας,
εἰ μέλλουσι καλῶς τὴν ἀληθινὴν ἐκείνην τὴν τοῦ
301 ἑνὸς μετὰ τέχνης ἄρχοντος πολιτείαν εἰς δύναμιν
μιμήσεσθαι, μηδέποτε κειμένων αὐτοῖς τῶν νόμων
μηδὲν ποιεῖν παρὰ τὰ γεγραμμένα καὶ πάτρια ἔθη.

ΝΕ. ΣΩ. Κάλλιστ᾽ εἴρηκας.

ΞΕ. Ὅταν ἄρα οἱ πλούσιοι ταύτην μιμῶνται, τότε
ἀριστοκρατίαν καλοῦμεν τὴν τοιαύτην πολιτείαν·
ὁπόταν δὲ τῶν νόμων μὴ φροντίζωσιν, ὀλιγαρχίαν.

ΝΕ. ΣΩ. Κινδυνεύει.

ΞΕ. Καὶ μὴν ὁπόταν αὖθις εἰς ἄρχῃ κατὰ νόμους,
B μιμούμενος τὸν ἐπιστήμονα, βασιλέα καλοῦμεν, οὐ
διορίζοντες ὀνόματι τὸν μετ᾽ ἐπιστήμης ἢ δόξης
κατὰ νόμους μοναρχοῦντα.

ΝΕ. ΣΩ. Κινδυνεύομεν.

ΞΕ. Οὐκοῦν κἄν τις ἄρα ἐπιστήμων ὄντως ὢν
εἷς ἄρχῃ, πάντως τό γε ὄνομα ταὐτὸν βασιλεὺς καὶ
οὐδὲν ἕτερον προσρηθήσεται· δι᾽ ἃ² δὴ τὰ πέντε

¹ πᾶν κακῶς] πανκακῶς B : πᾶν · κακῶς T : πανκάκως Burnet.

156

they would be trying to imitate reality, they would, however, imitate badly in every case; but if they were scientific, then it would no longer be imitation, but the actual perfect reality of which we spoke?

Y. SOC. Yes, assuredly.

STR. And yet we agreed definitely a while ago that no multitude is able to acquire any art whatsoever.

Y. SOC. Yes, that is definitely agreed.

STR. Then if there is a kingly[1] art, neither the collective body of the wealthy nor the whole people could ever acquire this science of statesmanship.

Y. SOC. No; certainly not.

STR. Such states, then, it seems, if they are to imitate well, so far as possible, that true form of government—by a single ruler who rules with science —must never do anything in contravention of their existing written laws and ancestral customs.

Y. SOC. You are quite right.

STR. Then whenever the rich imitate this government, we call such a state an aristocracy; and when they disregard the laws, we call it an oligarchy.

Y. SOC. Yes, I think we do.

STR. And again, when one man rules according to laws and imitates the scientific ruler, we call him a king, making no distinction in name between the single ruler who rules by science and him who rules by opinion if they both rule in accordance with laws.

Y. SOC. Yes, I think we do.

STR. Accordingly, if one man who is really scientific rules, he will assuredly be called by the same name, king, and by no other; and so the five names of what

[1] See 292 E.

---

[2] δι' ἅ] διὰ BT.

ὀνόματα τῶν νῦν λεγομένων πολιτειῶν ἓν μόνον
γέγονεν.

ΝΕ. ΣΩ. Ἔοικε γοῦν.

ΞΕ. Τί δ', ὅταν μήτε κατὰ νόμους μήτε κατὰ ἔθη
πράττῃ τις εἷς ἄρχων, προσποιῆται δὲ ὥσπερ ὁ ἐπι-
C στήμων ὡς ἄρα παρὰ τὰ γεγραμμένα τό γε βέλτιστον ποιητέον, ᾖ δέ τις ἐπιθυμία καὶ ἄγνοια τούτου
τοῦ μιμήματος ἡγουμένη, μῶν οὐ τότε τὸν τοιοῦτον
ἕκαστον τύραννον κλητέον;

ΝΕ. ΣΩ. Τί μήν;

40. ΞΕ. Οὕτω δὴ τύραννός τε γέγονε, φαμέν,
καὶ βασιλεὺς καὶ ὀλιγαρχία καὶ ἀριστοκρατία καὶ
δημοκρατία, δυσχερανάντων τῶν ἀνθρώπων τὸν
ἕνα ἐκεῖνον μόναρχον, καὶ ἀπιστησάντων μηδένα
τῆς τοιαύτης ἀρχῆς ἄξιον ἂν γενέσθαι ποτέ, ὥστε
D ἐθέλειν καὶ δυνατὸν εἶναι μετ' ἀρετῆς καὶ ἐπιστήμης
ἄρχοντα τὰ δίκαια καὶ ὅσια διανέμειν ὀρθῶς πᾶσι,
λωβᾶσθαι δὲ καὶ ἀποκτιννύναι καὶ κακοῦν ὃν ἂν
βουληθῇ ἑκάστοτε ἡμῶν· ἐπεὶ γενόμενόν γ' ἂν οἷον
λέγομεν ἀγαπᾶσθαί τε ἂν καὶ οἰκεῖν διακυβερνῶντα
εὐδαιμόνως ὀρθὴν ἀκριβῶς μόνον πολιτείαν

ΝΕ. ΣΩ. Πῶς δ' οὔ;

ΞΕ. Νῦν δέ γε ὁπότε οὐκ ἔστι γιγνόμενος, ὡς
δή φαμεν, ἐν ταῖς πόλεσι βασιλεὺς οἷος ἐν σμήνεσιν
E ἐμφύεται, τό τε σῶμα εὐθὺς καὶ τὴν ψυχὴν
διαφέρων εἷς, δεῖ δὴ συνελθόντας ξυγγράμματα
γράφειν, ὡς ἔοικε, μεταθέοντας τὰ τῆς ἀληθεστάτης
πολιτείας ἴχνη.

[1] What are called five distinct forms of government are
resolved into one—the one right form of which all others are
imitations (297 c). This is to be sought in some small
number or one person (*ibid.*). We have found it in the
really scientific monarchy, and the other so-called forms of

are now called the forms of government have become only one.[1]

Y. SOC. So it seems, at least.

STR. But when a single ruler acts in accordance with neither laws nor customs, but claims, in imitation of the scientific ruler, that whatever is best must be done, even though it be contrary to the written laws, and this imitation is inspired by desire and ignorance, is not such a ruler to be called in every instance a tyrant?

Y. SOC. Certainly.

STR. Thus, we say, the tyrant has arisen, and the king and oligarchy and aristocracy and democracy, because men are not contented with that one perfect ruler, and do not believe that there could ever be any one worthy of such power or willing and able by ruling with virtue and knowledge to dispense justice and equity rightly to all, but that he will harm and kill and injure any one of us whom he chooses on any occasion, since they admit that if such a man as we describe should really arise, he would be welcomed and would continue to dwell among them, directing to their weal as sole ruler a perfectly right form of government.

Y. SOC. Certainly.

STR. But, as the case now stands, since, as we claim, no king is produced in our states who is, like the ruler of the bees in their hives, by birth pre-eminently fitted from the beginning in body and mind, we are obliged, as it seems, to follow in the track of the perfect and true form of government by coming together and making written laws.

government, being merely imitations of this, require no names of their own.

ΝΕ. ΣΩ. Κινδυνεύει.

ΞΕ. Θαυμάζομεν δῆτα, ὦ Σώκρατες, ἐν ταῖς τοιαύταις πολιτείαις ὅσα ξυμβαίνει γίγνεσθαι κακὰ καὶ
ὅσα ξυμβήσεται, τοιαύτης τῆς κρηπῖδος ὑποκειμέ-
νης αὐταῖς, τῆς κατὰ γράμματα καὶ ἔθη μὴ μετὰ
ἐπιστήμης πραττούσης τὰς πράξεις, ᾗ[1] ἑτέρᾳ
302 προσχρωμένη παντὶ κατάδηλος ὡς πάντ' ἂν δι-
ολέσειε τὰ ταύτῃ γιγνόμενα; ἢ ἐκεῖνο ἡμῖν θαυμα-
στέον μᾶλλον, ὡς ἰσχυρόν τι πόλις ἐστὶ φύσει;
πάσχουσαι γὰρ δὴ τοιαῦτα αἱ πόλεις νῦν χρόνον
ἀπέραντον, ὅμως ἔνιαί τινες αὐτῶν μόνιμοί τέ εἰσι
καὶ οὐκ ἀνατρέπονται· πολλαὶ μὴν ἐνίοτε καὶ καθάπερ πλοῖα καταδυόμεναι διόλλυνται καὶ διολώλασι
καὶ ἔτι διολοῦνται διὰ τὴν τῶν κυβερνητῶν καὶ
ναυτῶν μοχθηρίαν τῶν περὶ τὰ μέγιστα μεγίστην
Β ἄγνοιαν εἰληφότων, οἳ περὶ τὰ πολιτικὰ κατ'
οὐδὲν γιγνώσκοντες ἡγοῦνται κατὰ πάντα σαφέστατα πασῶν ἐπιστημῶν ταύτην εἰληφέναι.

ΝΕ. ΣΩ. Ἀληθέστατα.

41. ΞΕ. Τίς οὖν δὴ τῶν οὐκ ὀρθῶν πολιτειῶν
τούτων ἥκιστα χαλεπὴ συζῆν, πασῶν χαλεπῶν
οὐσῶν, καὶ τίς βαρυτάτη, δεῖ τι κατιδεῖν ἡμᾶς,
καίπερ πρός γε τὸ νῦν προτεθὲν ἡμῖν πάρεργον
λεγόμενον; οὐ μὴν ἀλλ' εἴς γε τὸ ὅλον ἴσως ἅπανθ'
ἕνεκα τοῦ τοιούτου πάντες δρῶμεν χάριν.

ΝΕ. ΣΩ. Δεῖ· πῶς δ' οὔ;

C ΞΕ. Τὴν αὐτὴν τοίνυν φάθι τριῶν οὐσῶν χαλε-
πὴν διαφερόντως γίγνεσθαι καὶ ῥᾴστην.[2]

ΝΕ. ΣΩ. Πῶς φῄς;

ΞΕ. Οὐκ ἄλλως, πλὴν μοναρχίαν φημὶ καὶ ὀλίγων

---

[1] ᾗ add. Stephanus e Ficino.
[2] διαφερόντως ἅμα καὶ ῥᾴστην γίγνεσθαι Τ.

THE STATESMAN

Y. SOC. Yes, I suppose we are.

STR. Can we wonder, then, Socrates, at all the evils that arise and are destined to arise in such kinds of government, when they are based upon such a foundation, and must conduct their affairs in accordance with written laws and with customs, without knowledge? For every one can see that any other art built upon such a foundation would ruin all its works that are so produced. Ought we not rather to wonder at the stability that inheres in the state? For states have laboured under such conditions for countless ages, nevertheless some of them are lasting and are not overthrown. Many, to be sure, like ships that founder at sea, are destroyed, have been destroyed, and will be destroyed hereafter, through the worthlessness of their captains and crews who have the greatest ignorance of the greatest things, men who have no knowledge of statesmanship, but think they have in every respect most perfect knowledge of this above all other sciences.

Y. SOC. Very true.

STR. Is it, then, our duty to see which of these not right forms of government is the least difficult to live with, though all are difficult, and which is the most oppressive, although this is somewhat aside from the subject we had proposed for ourselves? On the whole, however, perhaps all of us have some such motive in mind in all that we are doing.

Y. SOC. Yes, it is our duty, of course.

STR. Well then, you may say that of the three forms, the same is both the hardest and the easiest.

Y. SOC. What do you mean?

STR. Just this: I mean that there are three forms of government, as we said at the beginning of the

ἀρχὴν καὶ πολλῶν, εἶναι τρεῖς ταύτας ἡμῖν λεγομένας τοῦ νῦν ἐπικεχυμένου λόγου κατ' ἀρχάς.

ΝΕ. ΣΩ. Ἦσαν γὰρ οὖν.

ΞΕ. Ταύτας τοίνυν δίχα τέμνοντες μίαν ἑκάστην
ἐξ ποιῶμεν, τὴν ὀρθὴν χωρὶς ἀποκρίναντες τούτων
ἑβδόμην.

ΝΕ. ΣΩ. Πῶς;

D   ΞΕ. Ἐκ μὲν τῆς μοναρχίας βασιλικὴν καὶ τυραννικήν, ἐκ δ' αὖ τῶν μὴ πολλῶν τήν τε εὐώνυμον
ἔφαμεν εἶναι ἀριστοκρατίαν καὶ ὀλιγαρχίαν· ἐκ δ'
αὖ τῶν πολλῶν τότε μὲν ἁπλῆν ἐπονομάζοντες
ἐτίθεμεν δημοκρατίαν, νῦν δὲ αὖ καὶ ταύτην ἡμῖν
θετέον ἐστὶ διπλῆν.

ΝΕ. ΣΩ. Πῶς δή; καὶ τίνι διαιροῦντες ταύτην;

ΞΕ. Οὐδὲν διαφέροντι τῶν ἄλλων, οὐδ' εἰ τοὔνομα ἤδη διπλοῦν ἐστι ταύτης· ἀλλὰ τό γε κατὰ
E νόμους ἄρχειν καὶ παρανόμως ἔστι καὶ ταύτῃ καὶ
ταῖς ἄλλαις.

ΝΕ. ΣΩ. Ἔστι γὰρ οὖν.

ΞΕ. Τότε μὲν τοίνυν τὴν ὀρθὴν ζητοῦσι τοῦτο τὸ
τμῆμα οὐκ ἦν χρήσιμον, ὡς ἐν τοῖς πρόσθεν ἀπεδεί-
ξαμεν· ἐπειδὴ δὲ ἐξείλομεν ἐκείνην, τὰς δ' ἄλλας
ἔθεμεν ἀναγκαίας, ἐν ταύταις δὴ τὸ παράνομον καὶ
ἔννομον ἑκάστην διχοτομεῖ τούτων.

ΝΕ. ΣΩ. Ἔοικε τούτου νῦν ῥηθέντος τοῦ λόγου.

ΞΕ. Μοναρχία τοίνυν ζευχθεῖσα μὲν ἐν γράμμασιν
ἀγαθοῖς, οὓς νόμους λέγομεν, ἀρίστη πασῶν τῶν ἕξ·
ἄνομος δὲ χαλεπὴ καὶ βαρυτάτη ξυνοικῆσαι.

---

[1] The name is said to be twofold in meaning, probably
because it was applied in cases in which there was a
regularly constituted popular government and also in cases
of mob rule.

discussion which has now flowed in upon us—monarchy, the rule of the few, and the rule of the many.

Y. SOC. Yes, there were those three.

STR. Let us, then, by dividing each of these into two parts, make six, and by distinguishing the right government from these, a seventh.

Y. SOC. How shall we make the division?

STR. We said that monarchy comprised royalty and tyranny, and the rule of the few comprised aristocracy, which has a name of good omen, and oligarchy; but to the rule of the many we gave then only a single name, democracy; now, however, that also must be divided.

Y. SOC. How? On what principle shall we divide that?

STR. On the same that we used for the others, though the name of this form is already twofold in meaning.[1] At any rate, the distinction between ruling according to law and without law applies alike to this and the rest.

Y. SOC. Yes, it does.

STR. Before, when we were in search of the right government, this division was of no use, as we showed at the time; but now that we have set that apart and have decided that the others are the only available forms of government, the principle of lawfulness and lawlessness bisects each of them.

Y. SOC. So it seems, from what has been said.

STR. Monarchy, then, when bound by good written rules, which we call laws, is the best of all the six; but without law it is hard and most oppressive to live with.

PLATO

303   ΝΕ. ΣΩ. Κινδυνεύει.

ΞΕ. Τὴν δέ γε τῶν μὴ πολλῶν, ὥσπερ ἑνὸς καὶ πλήθους τὸ ὀλίγον μέσον, οὕτως ἡγησώμεθα μέσην ἐπ' ἀμφότερα· τὴν δ' αὖ τοῦ πλήθους κατὰ πάντα ἀσθενῆ καὶ μηδὲν μήτε ἀγαθὸν μήτε κακὸν μέγα δυναμένην ὡς πρὸς τὰς ἄλλας διὰ τὸ τὰς ἀρχὰς ἐν ταύτῃ διανενεμῆσθαι κατὰ σμικρὰ εἰς πολλούς. διὸ γέγονε πασῶν μὲν νομίμων τῶν πολιτειῶν οὐσῶν τούτων χειρίστη, παρανόμων δ' οὐσῶν
B ξυμπασῶν βελτίστη· καὶ ἀκολάστων μὲν πασῶν οὐσῶν ἐν δημοκρατίᾳ νικᾷ¹ ζῆν, κοσμίων δ' οὐσῶν ἥκιστα ἐν ταύτῃ βιωτέον, ἐν τῇ πρώτῃ δὲ πολὺ πρῶτόν τε καὶ ἄριστον, πλὴν τῆς ἑβδόμης· πασῶν γὰρ ἐκείνην γε ἐκκριτέον, οἷον θεὸν ἐξ ἀνθρώπων, ἐκ τῶν ἄλλων πολιτειῶν.

ΝΕ. ΣΩ. Φαίνεται τοῦθ' οὕτω γίγνεσθαί τε καὶ ξυμβαίνειν, καὶ ποιητέον ᾗπερ λέγεις.

ΞΕ. Οὐκοῦν δὴ καὶ τοὺς κοινωνοὺς τούτων τῶν πολιτειῶν πασῶν πλὴν τῆς ἐπιστήμονος ἀφαιρετέον
C ὡς οὐκ ὄντας πολιτικοὺς ἀλλὰ στασιαστικούς, καὶ εἰδώλων μεγίστων προστάτας ὄντας καὶ αὐτοὺς εἶναι τοιούτους, μεγίστους δὲ ὄντας μιμητὰς καὶ γόητας μεγίστους γίγνεσθαι τῶν σοφιστῶν σοφιστάς.

¹ νικᾷ] νικαη B: νικᾶν T.

---

[1] The concentration of power in the hands of one man makes monarchy most efficient, but, since no human monarch is perfect, monarchy must be regulated by laws. Its efficiency makes it under such conditions the best government to live under. But without restraint of law monarchy becomes tyranny—the worst kind of oppression. Oligarchy occupies a position intermediate between

164

y. soc. I fancy it is.

str. But just as few is intermediate between one and a multitude, so the government of the few must be considered intermediate, both in good and in evil. But the government of the multitude is weak in all respects and able to do nothing great, either good or bad, when compared with the other forms of government, because in this the powers of government are distributed in small shares among many men; therefore of all these governments when they are lawful, this is the worst, and when they are all lawless it is the best; and if they are all without restraint, life is most desirable in a democracy, but if they are orderly, that is the worst to live in; but life in the first kind of state is by far the first and best, with the exception of the seventh, for that must be set apart from all the others, as God is set apart from men.[1]

y. soc. That statement appears to be true to the facts, and we must do as you say.

str. Then those who participate in all those governments—with the exception of the scientific one—are to be eliminated as not being statesmen, but partisans; and since they preside over the greatest counterfeits, they are themselves counterfeits, and since they are the greatest of imitators and cheats, they are the greatest of all sophists.

monarchy and democracy—less efficient than the one and more efficient than the other, because power is distributed among a small number of persons—and is, therefore, when lawful less good, and when lawless less bad, than monarchy. Democracy, in turn, since power is too greatly subdivided, is inefficient, either for good or evil, and is, therefore, when lawful less good, and when lawless less bad, than either of the others.

ΝΕ. ΣΩ. Κινδυνεύει τοῦτο εἰς τοὺς πολιτικοὺς λεγομένους περιεστράφθαι¹ τὸ ῥῆμα ὀρθότατα.

ΞΕ. Εἶεν· τοῦτο μὲν ἀτεχνῶς ἡμῖν ὥσπερ δρᾶμα, καθάπερ ἐρρήθη νῦν δὴ Κενταυρικὸν ὁρᾶσθαι καὶ Σατυρικόν τινα θίασον, ὃν δὴ χωριστέον ἀπὸ D πολιτικῆς εἴη τέχνης· νῦν δ' οὕτω πάνυ μόγις ἐχωρίσθη.

ΝΕ. ΣΩ. Φαίνεται.

ΞΕ. Τούτου δέ γ' ἕτερον ἔτι χαλεπώτερον λείπεται τῷ ξυγγενές θ' ὁμοῦ τ' εἶναι μᾶλλον τῷ βασιλικῷ γένει καὶ δυσκαταμαθητότερον· καί μοι φαινόμεθα τοῖς τὸν χρυσὸν καθαίρουσι πάθος ὅμοιον πεπονθέναι.

ΝΕ. ΣΩ. Πῶς;

ΞΕ. Γῆν που καὶ λίθους καὶ πόλλ' ἄττα ἕτερα ἀποκρίνουσι κἀκεῖνοι πρῶτον² οἱ δημιουργοί· E μετὰ δὲ ταῦτα λείπεται ξυμμεμιγμένα τὰ ξυγγενῆ τοῦ χρυσοῦ τίμια καὶ πυρὶ μόνον ἀφαιρετά, χαλκὸς καὶ ἄργυρος, ἔστι δ' ὅτε καὶ ἀδάμας, ἃ³ μετὰ βασάνων ταῖς ἑψήσεσι μόγις ἀφαιρεθέντα τὸν λεγόμενον ἀκήρατον χρυσὸν εἴασεν ἡμᾶς ἰδεῖν αὐτὸν μόνον ἐφ' ἑαυτοῦ.

ΝΕ. ΣΩ. Λέγεται γὰρ οὖν δὴ ταῦτα οὕτω γίγνεσθαι.

42. ΞΕ. Κατὰ τὸν αὐτὸν τοίνυν λόγον ἔοικε καὶ νῦν ἡμῖν τὰ μὲν ἕτερα καὶ ὁπόσα ἀλλότρια καὶ τὰ μὴ φίλα πολιτικῆς ἐπιστήμης ἀποκεχωρίσθαι, λείπεσθαι δὲ τὰ τίμια καὶ ξυγγενῆ. τούτων δ' ἐστί 304 που στρατηγία καὶ δικαστικὴ καὶ ὅση βασιλικῇ κοινωνοῦσα ῥητορεία πείθουσα τὸ δίκαιον ξυν-

---

¹ περιεστρέφθαι ΒΤ.
² πρότερον Β.   ³ ἃ add. Stephanus e Ficino.

y. soc. This term "sophist" seems to have come round quite rightly to the so-called statesmen.

str. Well, this part has been exactly like a play. Just as we remarked a moment ago,[1] a festive troop of centaurs or satyrs was coming into view, which we had to separate from the art of statesmanship; and now we have succeeded in doing this, though it has been very difficult.

y. soc. So it seems.

str. But another group remains, which is still more difficult to separate, because it is more closely akin to the kingly class and is also harder to recognize. I think we are in somewhat the same position as refiners of gold.

y. soc. How so?

str. Why, the refiners first remove earth and stones and all that sort of thing; and after that there remain the precious substances which are mixed with the gold and akin to it and can be removed only by fire—copper and silver and sometimes adamant.[2] These are removed by the difficult processes of smelting and tests, leaving before our eyes what is called unalloyed gold in all its purity.

y. soc. Yes, that is said, at least, to be the process.

str. By the same method I think all that is different and alien and incompatible has now been eliminated by us from the science of statesmanship, and what is precious and akin to it is left. Herein are included the arts of the general and of the judge and that kind of oratory which partakes of the kingly art because it persuades men to justice and

[1] 291 A.

[2] Plato, *Timaeus* 59 B, defines adamant as χρυσοῦ ὄζος, "a branch of gold." It was, then, a substance akin to gold. Platinum has been suggested.

διακυβερνᾷ τὰς ἐν ταῖς πόλεσι πράξεις· ἃ δὴ τίνι
τρόπῳ ῥᾷστά τις ἀπομερίζων δείξει γυμνὸν καὶ
μόνον ἐκεῖνον καθ᾽ αὑτὸν τὸν ζητούμενον ὑφ᾽ ἡμῶν;

ΝΕ. ΣΩ. Δῆλον ὅτι τοῦτό πῃ δρᾶν πειρατέον.

ΞΕ. Πείρας μὲν τοίνυν ἕνεκα φανερὸς ἔσται· διὰ
δὲ μουσικῆς αὐτὸν ἐγχειρητέον δηλῶσαι. καί μοι
λέγε.

ΝΕ. ΣΩ. Τὸ ποῖον;

B   ΞΕ. Μουσικῆς ἔστι πού τις ἡμῖν μάθησις, καὶ
ὅλως τῶν περὶ χειροτεχνίας ἐπιστημῶν;

ΝΕ. ΣΩ. Ἔστιν.

ΞΕ. Τί δὲ τόδ᾽ αὖ[1]; τούτων ἡντινοῦν εἴτε δεῖ
μανθάνειν ἡμᾶς εἴτε μή, πότερα φήσομεν ἐπιστήμην
αὖ καὶ ταύτην εἶναί τινα περὶ αὐτὰ ταῦτα, ἢ πῶς;

ΝΕ. ΣΩ. Οὕτως, εἶναι φήσομεν.

ΞΕ. Οὐκοῦν ἑτέραν ὁμολογήσομεν ἐκείνων εἶναι
ταύτην;

ΝΕ. ΣΩ. Ναί.

ΞΕ. Πότερα δ᾽ αὐτῶν οὐδεμίαν ἄρχειν δεῖν ἄλλην
C ἄλλης, ἢ ἐκείνας ταύτης, ἢ ταύτην δεῖν ἐπιτρο-
πεύουσαν ἄρχειν ξυμπασῶν τῶν ἄλλων;

ΝΕ. ΣΩ. Ταύτην ἐκείνων.

ΞΕ. Τὴν[2] εἰ δεῖ μανθάνειν ἢ μὴ τῆς μανθανομένης
καὶ διδασκούσης ἄρα σύ γ᾽ ἀποφαίνει δεῖν ἡμῖν
ἄρχειν;

ΝΕ. ΣΩ. Σφόδρα γε.

ΞΕ. Καὶ τὴν εἰ δεῖ πείθειν ἄρα ἢ μὴ τῆς δυνα-
μένης πείθειν;

ΝΕ. ΣΩ. Πῶς δ᾽ οὔ;

---

[1] δὲ τόδ᾽ αὖ Ast: δὲ τὸ δ᾽ αὖ BT.
[2] τὴν om. BT (and give εἰ . . . μὴ to young Socrates):
corr. Stallbaum.

thereby helps to steer the ship of state. Now in what way shall we most easily eliminate these and show him whom we seek alone by himself and undisguised?

Y. soc. Clearly we must do this somehow.

str. Then if it is a question of trying, he will be shown. But I think we had better try to disclose him by means of music. Please answer my question.

Y. soc. What is it?

str. Shall we agree that there is such a thing as learning music and the sciences of handicraft in general?

Y. soc. There is.

str. And how about this? Shall we say that there is another science connected with those, which tells whether we ought or ought not to learn any one of them?

Y. soc. Yes, we shall say that there is.

str. And shall we agree that this is different from those?

Y. soc. Yes.

str. And shall we say that none of them ought to have control of any other, or that those sciences should control this one, or that this should control and rule all the others?

Y. soc. This should control those others.

str. You mean that the science which decides whether we ought to learn or not should control the science which is learnt or teaches?

Y. soc. Emphatically.

str. And the science which decides whether to persuade or not should control that which can persuade?

Y. soc. Certainly.

ΞΕ. Εἶεν· τίνι τὸ πειστικὸν οὖν ἀποδώσομεν
ἐπιστήμῃ πλήθους τε καὶ ὄχλου διὰ μυθολογίας
D ἀλλὰ μὴ διὰ διδαχῆς;

ΝΕ. ΣΩ. Φανερόν, οἶμαι, καὶ τοῦτο ῥητορικῇ
δοτέον ὄν.

ΞΕ. Τὸ δ᾽ εἴτε διὰ πειθοῦς εἴτε καὶ διά τινος
βίας δεῖ πράττειν πρός τινας ὁτιοῦν ἢ καὶ τὸ παράπαν ἡσυχίαν¹ ἔχειν, τοῦτ᾽ αὖ ποίᾳ προσθήσομεν ἐπιστήμῃ;

ΝΕ. ΣΩ. Τῇ τῆς πειστικῆς ἀρχούσῃ καὶ λεκτικῆς.

ΞΕ. Εἴη δὲ ἂν οὐκ ἄλλη τις, ὡς οἶμαι, πλὴν ἡ
τοῦ πολιτικοῦ δύναμις.

ΝΕ. ΣΩ. Κάλλιστ᾽ εἴρηκας.

ΞΕ. Καὶ τοῦτο μὲν ἔοικε ταχὺ κεχωρίσθαι πολι-
E τικῆς τὸ ῥητορικόν, ὡς ἕτερον εἶδος ὄν, ὑπηρετοῦν
μὴν ταύτῃ.

ΝΕ. ΣΩ. Ναί.

43. ΞΕ. Τί δὲ περὶ τῆς τοιᾶσδ᾽ αὖ δυνάμεως
διανοητέον;

ΝΕ. ΣΩ. Ποίας;

ΞΕ. Τῆς ὡς πολεμητέον ἑκάστοις οἷς ἂν προελώμεθα πολεμεῖν, εἴτε αὐτὴν ἄτεχνον εἴτε ἔντεχνον
ἐροῦμεν;

ΝΕ. ΣΩ. Καὶ πῶς ἂν ἄτεχνον διανοηθεῖμεν, ἥν
γε ἡ στρατηγικὴ καὶ πᾶσα ἡ πολεμικὴ πρᾶξις
πράττει;

ΞΕ. Τὴν δ᾽ εἴτε πολεμητέον εἴτε διὰ φιλίας ἀπαλ-
λακτέον οἵαν τε καὶ ἐπιστήμονα διαβουλεύσασθαι,
ταύτης ἑτέραν ὑπολάβωμεν ἢ τὴν αὐτὴν ταύτῃ;

ΝΕ. ΣΩ. Τοῖς πρόσθεν ἀναγκαῖον ἑπομένοισιν
ἑτέραν.

---

¹ ἡσυχίαν add. Hermann.

STR. Well, then, to what science shall we assign the power of persuading a multitude or a mob by telling edifying stories, not by teaching?

Y. SOC. It is, I think, clear that this must be added to rhetoric.

STR. But the power of deciding whether some action, no matter what, should be taken, either by persuasion or by some exercise of force, in relation to any person, or whether to take no action at all—to what science is that to be assigned?

Y. SOC. To the science which controls the sciences of persuasion and speech.

STR. And that would, I think, be no other than the function of the statesman.

Y. SOC. A most excellent conclusion.

STR. So rhetoric also seems to have been quickly separated from statesmanship [1] as a different species, subservient to the other.

Y. SOC. Yes.

STR. Here is another function or power; what are we to think about it?

Y. SOC. What is it?

STR. The power of determining how war shall be waged against those upon whom we have declared war, whether we are to call this a science or not a science?

Y. SOC. How could we think it is not a science, when generalship and all military activity practise it?

STR. And the power which is able and knows how to deliberate and decide whether to make war or peace, shall we assume that it is the same as this or different?

Y. SOC. If we are consistent, we must assume that it is different.

[1] *Cf.* 303 c.

PLATO

305 ΞΕ. Οὐκοῦν ἄρχουσαν ταύτης αὐτὴν ἀποφανού-
μεθα, εἴπερ τοῖς ἔμπροσθέν γε ὑποληψόμεθα ὁμοίως;

ΝΕ. ΣΩ. Φημί.

ΞΕ. Τίν᾽ οὖν ποτε καὶ ἐπιχειρήσομεν οὕτω δεινῆς
καὶ μεγάλης τέχνης ξυμπάσης τῆς πολεμικῆς δεσπό-
τιν ἀποφαίνεσθαι πλήν γε δὴ τὴν ὄντως οὖσαν
βασιλικήν;

ΝΕ. ΣΩ. Οὐδεμίαν ἄλλην.

ΞΕ. Οὐκ ἄρα πολιτικήν γε θήσομεν, ὑπηρετικὴν
οὖσαν, τὴν τῶν στρατηγῶν ἐπιστήμην.

ΝΕ. ΣΩ. Οὐκ εἰκός.

B ΞΕ. Ἴθι δή, καὶ τὴν τῶν δικαστῶν τῶν ὀρθῶς
δικαζόντων θεασώμεθα δύναμιν.

ΝΕ. ΣΩ. Πάνυ μὲν οὖν.

ΞΕ. Ἆρ᾽ οὖν ἐπὶ πλέον τι δύναται τοῦ περὶ τὰ
ξυμβόλαια, πάνθ᾽ ὁπόσα κεῖται νόμιμα παρὰ νομοθέτου βασιλέως παραλαβοῦσα, κρίνειν εἰς ἐκεῖνα
σκοποῦσα τά τε δίκαια ταχθέντα εἶναι καὶ ἄδικα,
τὴν αὑτῆς ἰδίαν ἀρετὴν παρεχομένη τοῦ μήθ᾽ ὑπό
τινων δώρων μήθ᾽ ὑπὸ φόβων μήτε οἴκτων μήθ᾽
C ὑπό τινος ἄλλης ἔχθρας μηδὲ φιλίας ἡττηθεῖσα
παρὰ τὴν τοῦ νομοθέτου τάξιν ἐθέλειν ἂν τὰ ἀλλήλων
ἐγκλήματα διαιρεῖν;

ΝΕ. ΣΩ. Οὔκ, ἀλλὰ σχεδὸν ὅσον εἴρηκας ταύτης
ἐστὶ τῆς δυνάμεως ἔργον.

ΞΕ. Καὶ τὴν τῶν δικαστῶν ἄρα ῥώμην ἀνευρίσκο-
μεν οὐ βασιλικὴν οὖσαν ἀλλὰ νόμων φύλακα καὶ
ὑπηρέτιν ἐκείνης.

ΝΕ. ΣΩ. Ἔοικέ γε.

ΞΕ. Τόδε δὴ κατανοητέον ἰδόντι συναπάσας τὰς
ἐπιστήμας αἳ εἴρηνται, ὅτι πολιτική γε αὐτῶν
οὐδεμία ἀνεφάνη. τὴν γὰρ ὄντως οὖσαν βασιλικὴν

172

STR. Shall we, then, assume that it controls the other, if we are to agree with our views in the former examples?

Y. SOC. Yes.

STR. And what other art shall we make bold to declare is mistress of that great and terrible art, the art of war as a whole, except the truly kingly art?

Y. SOC. No other.

STR. We shall, then, not call the art of the generals statesmanship, since it is subservient.

Y. SOC. No; that would not be reasonable.

STR. Now let us examine the function of the righteous judges.

Y. SOC. Certainly.

STR. Has it any power beyond that of judging men's contracts with one another, pronouncing them right or wrong by the standard of the existing laws which it has received from the king and law-giver, showing its own peculiar virtue in that it is not so perverted by any bribes, or fears, or pity, or enmity, or friendship, as ever to consent to decide the lawsuits of men with each other contrary to the enactments of the law-giver?

Y. SOC. No; the business of this power is about as you have described it.

STR. Then we find that the strength of judges is not kingly, but is guardian of laws and a servant of the kingly power.

Y. SOC. So it appears.

STR. The consideration of all these arts which have been mentioned leads to the conclusion that none of them is the art of the statesman. For the

D οὐκ αὐτὴν δεῖ πράττειν, ἀλλ' ἄρχειν τῶν δυναμένων πράττειν, γιγνώσκουσαν τὴν ἀρχήν τε καὶ ὁρμὴν τῶν μεγίστων ἐν ταῖς πόλεσιν ἐγκαιρίας τε πέρι καὶ ἀκαιρίας, τὰς δ' ἄλλας τὰ προσταχθέντα δρᾶν.

ΝΕ. ΣΩ. Ὀρθῶς.

ΞΕ. Διὰ ταῦτα ἄρα ἃς μὲν ἄρτι διεληλύθαμεν οὔτε ἀλλήλων οὔθ' αὑτῶν ἄρχουσαι, περὶ δέ τινα ἰδίαν αὑτῆς οὖσα ἑκάστη πρᾶξιν κατὰ τὴν ἰδιότητα τῶν πράξεων τοὔνομα δικαίως εἴληφεν ἴδιον.

E ΝΕ. ΣΩ. Εἴξασι γοῦν.

ΞΕ. Τὴν δὲ πασῶν τε τούτων ἄρχουσαν καὶ τῶν νόμων καὶ ξυμπάντων τῶν κατὰ πόλιν ἐπιμελουμένην καὶ πάντα ξυνυφαίνουσαν ὀρθότατα, τοῦ κοινοῦ τῇ κλήσει περιλαβόντες τὴν δύναμιν αὐτῆς, προσαγορεύοιμεν δικαιότατ' ἄν, ὡς ἔοικε, πολιτικήν.

ΝΕ. ΣΩ. Παντάπασι μὲν οὖν.

44. ΞΕ. Οὐκοῦν δὴ καὶ κατὰ τὸ τῆς ὑφαντικῆς παράδειγμα βουλοίμεθ' ἂν ἐπεξελθεῖν αὐτὴν νῦν, ὅτε καὶ πάντα τὰ γένη τὰ κατὰ πόλιν δῆλα ἡμῖν γέγονεν;

ΝΕ. ΣΩ. Καὶ σφόδρα γε.

ΞΕ. Τὴν δὴ βασιλικὴν συμπλοκήν, ὡς ἔοικε, 306 λεκτέον, ποία τ' ἐστὶ καὶ τίνι τρόπῳ συμπλέκουσα ποῖον ἡμῖν ὕφασμα ἀποδίδωσιν.

ΝΕ. ΣΩ. Δῆλον.

ΞΕ. Ἦ χαλεπὸν ἐνδείξασθαι πρᾶγμα ἀναγκαῖον ἄρα γέγονεν, ὡς φαίνεται.

ΝΕ. ΣΩ. Πάντως γε μὴν ῥητέον.

ΞΕ. Τὸ γὰρ ἀρετῆς μέρος ἀρετῆς εἴδει διάφορον

---

[1] See 287-290, 303-305.

art that is truly kingly ought not to act itself, but should rule over the arts that have the power of action; it should decide upon the right or wrong time for the initiation of the most important measures in the state, and the other arts should perform its behests.

y. soc. Right.

str. Therefore those arts which we have just described, as they control neither one another nor themselves, but have each its own peculiar sphere of action, are quite properly called by special names corresponding to those special actions.

y. soc. That appears, at least, to be the case.

str. But the art which holds sway over them all and watches over the laws and all things in the state, weaving them all most perfectly together, we may, I think, by giving to its function a designation which indicates its power over the community, with full propriety call "statecraft."

y. soc. Most assuredly.

str. Shall we then proceed to discuss it after the model supplied by weaving,[1] now that all the classes in the state have been made plain to us?

y. soc. By all means.

str. Then the kingly process of weaving must be described, its nature, the manner in which it combines the threads, and the kind of web it produces.

y. soc. Evidently.

str. It has, apparently, become necessary, after all, to explain a difficult matter.

y. soc. But certainly the explanation must be made.

str. It is difficult, for the assertion that one part of virtue is in a way at variance with another sort

εἶναί τινα τρόπον τοῖς περὶ λόγους ἀμφισβητικοῖς
καὶ μάλ᾽ εὐεπίθετον πρὸς τὰς τῶν πολλῶν δόξας.

ΝΕ. ΣΩ. Οὐκ ἔμαθον.

ΞΕ. Ἀλλ᾽ ὧδε πάλιν. ἀνδρείαν γὰρ οἶμαί σε
B ἡγεῖσθαι μέρος ἓν ἀρετῆς ἡμῖν εἶναι.

ΝΕ. ΣΩ. Πάνυ γε.

ΞΕ. Καὶ μὴν σωφροσύνην γε ἀνδρείας μὲν ἕτερον,
ἓν δ᾽ οὖν καὶ τοῦτο μόριον ἧς κἀκεῖνο.

ΝΕ. ΣΩ. Ναί.

ΞΕ. Τούτων δὴ πέρι θαυμαστόν τινα λόγον ἀποφαίνεσθαι τολμητέον.

ΝΕ. ΣΩ. Ποῖον;

ΞΕ. Ὡς ἐστὸν κατὰ δή τινα τρόπον εὖ μάλα πρὸς
ἀλλήλας ἔχθραν καὶ στάσιν ἐναντίαν ἔχοντε[1] ἐν
πολλοῖς τῶν ὄντων.

ΝΕ. ΣΩ. Πῶς λέγεις;

ΞΕ. Οὐκ εἰωθότα λόγον οὐδαμῶς· πάντα γὰρ
C οὖν δὴ ἀλλήλοις τά γε τῆς ἀρετῆς μόρια λέγεταί
που φίλια.

ΝΕ. ΣΩ. Ναί.

ΞΕ. Σκοπῶμεν δὴ προσσχόντες τὸν νοῦν εὖ μάλα,
πότερον οὕτως ἁπλοῦν ἐστι τοῦτο, ἢ παντὸς μᾶλλον
αὐτῶν ἔχον διαφορὰν τοῖς ξυγγενέσιν ἔς τι[2];

ΝΕ. ΣΩ. Ναί, λέγοις ἂν πῇ σκεπτέον.

ΞΕ. Ἐν τοῖς ξύμπασι χρὴ ζητεῖν ὅσα καλὰ μὲν
λέγομεν, εἰς δύο δ᾽ αὐτὰ τίθεμεν ἐναντία ἀλλήλων
εἴδη.

---

[1] ἔχοντε] ἔχετον BT : corr. Stallbaum.
[2] ἔς τι Campbell : ἐστι T : ἐστίν B : ἔστι τι Heindorf.

---

[1] The word ἀνδρεία has a much wider meaning than the
English "courage." Like the Latin *virtus* it embraces all

of virtue may very easily be assailed by those who appeal to popular opinion in contentious arguments.

Y. SOC. I do not understand.

STR. I will say it again in another way. I suppose you believe that courage [1] is one part of virtue.

Y. SOC. Certainly.

STR. And, of course, that self-restraint is different from courage, but is also a part of virtue of which courage is a part.

Y. SOC. Yes.

STR. Now I must venture to utter a strange doctrine about them.

Y. SOC. What is it?

STR. That, in a way, they are in a condition of great hostility and opposition to each other in many beings.

Y. SOC. What do you mean?

STR. Something quite unusual; for, you know, all the parts of virtue are usually said to be friendly to one another.

Y. SOC. Yes.

STR. Now shall we pay careful attention and see whether this is so simple, or, quite the contrary, there is in some respects a variance between them and their kin?

Y. SOC. Yes; please tell how we shall investigate the question.

STR. Among all the parts we must look for those which we call excellent but place in two opposite classes.

qualities which are desirable in a perfect man, especially the more active and positive virtues. When applied to one particular kind of virtue it is applied to courage, but throughout this discussion it is used in the wider sense, for which there is no single English equivalent.

177

ΝΕ. ΣΩ. Λέγ᾽ ἔτι σαφέστερον.

ΞΕ. Ὀξύτητα καὶ τάχος, εἴτε κατὰ σώματα εἴτε
D ἐν ψυχαῖς εἴτε κατὰ φωνῆς φοράν, εἴτε αὐτῶν
τούτων εἴτ᾽ ἐν εἰδώλοις ὄντων, ὁπόσα μουσικὴ
μιμουμένη καὶ ἔτι γραφικὴ μιμήματα παρέχεται,
τούτων τινὸς ἐπαινέτης εἴτε αὐτὸς πώποτε γέγονας
εἴτε ἄλλου παρὼν ἐπαινοῦντος ἤσθησαι;

ΝΕ. ΣΩ. Τί μήν;

ΞΕ. Ἦ καὶ μνήμην ἔχεις ὅντινα τρόπον αὐτὸ δρῶσιν ἐν ἑκάστοις τούτων;

ΝΕ. ΣΩ. Οὐδαμῶς.

ΞΕ. Ἆρ᾽ οὖν δυνατὸς αὐτὸ ἂν γενοίμην, ὥσπερ
καὶ διανοοῦμαι, διὰ λόγων ἐνδείξασθαί σοι;

E ΝΕ. ΣΩ. Τί δ᾽ οὔ;

ΞΕ. Ῥάδιον ἔοικας ἡγεῖσθαι τὸ τοιοῦτον· σκο-
πώμεθα δ᾽ οὖν αὐτὸ ἐν τοῖς ὑπεναντίοις γένεσι.
τῶν γὰρ δὴ πράξεων ἐν πολλαῖς καὶ πολλάκις
ἑκάστοτε τάχος καὶ σφοδρότητα καὶ ὀξύτητα δια-
νοήσεώς τε καὶ σώματος, ἔτι δὲ καὶ φωνῆς, ὅταν
ἀγασθῶμεν, λέγομεν αὐτὸ ἐπαινοῦντες μιᾷ χρώμενοι
προσρήσει τῇ τῆς ἀνδρείας.

ΝΕ. ΣΩ. Πῶς;

ΞΕ. Ὀξὺ καὶ ἀνδρεῖον πρῶτόν πού φαμεν, καὶ
ταχὺ καὶ ἀνδρικόν, καὶ σφοδρὸν ὡσαύτως· καὶ
πάντως ἐπιφέροντες τοὔνομα ὃ λέγω κοινὸν πάσαις
ταῖς φύσεσι ταύταις ἐπαινοῦμεν αὐτάς.

ΝΕ. ΣΩ. Ναί.

ΞΕ. Τί δέ; τὸ τῆς ἠρεμαίας αὖ γενέσεως εἶδος ἆρ᾽
307 οὐ πολλάκις ἐπηνέκαμεν ἐν πολλαῖς τῶν πράξεων;

ΝΕ. ΣΩ. Καὶ σφόδρα γε.

ΞΕ. Μῶν οὖν οὐ τἀναντία λέγοντες ἢ περὶ ἐκείνων τοῦτο φθεγγόμεθα;

178

Y. SOC. Say more clearly what you mean.

STR. Acuteness and quickness, whether in body or soul or vocal utterance, whether they are real or exist in such likenesses as music and graphic art produce in imitation of them—have you never yourself praised one of them or heard them praised by others?

Y. SOC. Yes, of course.

STR. And do you remember in what way they praise them as occasion offers?

Y. SOC. Not in the least.

STR. I wonder if I can express to you in words what I have in mind.

Y. SOC. Why not?

STR. You seem to think that is an easy thing to do. However, let us consider the matter as it appears in the opposite classes. For example, when we admire, as we frequently do in many actions, quickness and energy and acuteness of mind or body or even of voice, we express our praise of them by one word, courage.

Y. SOC. How so?

STR. We say acute and courageous in the first instance, also quick and courageous, and energetic and courageous; and when we apply this word as a common term applicable to all persons and actions of this class, we praise them.

Y. SOC. Yes, we do.

STR. But do we not also praise the gentle type of movement in many actions?

Y. SOC. We do, decidedly.

STR. And in doing so, do we not say the opposite of what we said about the other class?

179

PLATO

ΝΕ. ΣΩ. Πῶς;

ΞΕ. Ὡς ἡσυχαῖά πού φαμεν ἑκάστοτε καὶ σωφρο-
νικά, περί τε διάνοιαν πραττόμενα ἀγασθέντες καὶ
κατὰ τὰς πράξεις αὖ βραδέα καὶ μαλακά, καὶ ἔτι
περὶ φωνὰς γιγνόμενα λεῖα καὶ βαρέα, καὶ πᾶσαν
ῥυθμικὴν κίνησιν καὶ ὅλην μοῦσαν ἐν καιρῷ βραδυ-
Β τῆτι προσχρωμένην, οὐ τὸ τῆς ἀνδρείας ἀλλὰ τὸ
τῆς κοσμιότητος ὄνομα ἐπιφέρομεν αὐτοῖς ξύμπασιν.

ΝΕ. ΣΩ. Ἀληθέστατα.

ΞΕ. Καὶ μὴν ὁπόταν αὖ γε ἀμφότερα γίγνηται
ταῦτα ἡμῖν ἄκαιρα,[1] μεταβάλλοντες ἑκάτερα αὐτῶν
ψέγομεν ἐπὶ τἀναντία πάλιν ἀπονέμοντες τοῖς
ὀνόμασιν.

ΝΕ. ΣΩ. Πῶς;

ΞΕ. Ὀξύτερα μὲν αὐτὰ γιγνόμενα τοῦ καιροῦ καὶ
θάττω καὶ σκληρότερα φαινόμενα[2] ὑβριστικὰ καὶ
μανικὰ λέγοντες, τὰ δὲ βαρύτερα καὶ βραδύτερα
C καὶ μαλακώτερα δειλὰ καὶ βλακικά· καὶ σχεδὸν
ὡς τὸ πολὺ ταῦτά τε καὶ τὴν σώφρονα φύσιν καὶ
τὴν ἀνδρείαν τὴν τῶν ἐναντίων, οἷον πολεμίαν[3]
διαλαχούσας στάσιν ἰδέας, οὔτ' ἀλλήλαις μιγνυμένας
ἐφευρίσκομεν ἐν ταῖς περὶ τὰ τοιαῦτα πράξεσιν, ἔτι
τε τοὺς ἐν ταῖς ψυχαῖς αὐτὰς ἴσχοντας διαφερομέ-
νους ἀλλήλοις ὀψόμεθα ἐὰν μεταδιώκωμεν.

45. ΝΕ. ΣΩ. Ποῦ δὴ[4] λέγεις;

ΞΕ. Ἐν πᾶσί τε δὴ τούτοις οἷς νῦν εἴπομεν, ὡς
D εἰκός τε ἐν ἑτέροις πολλοῖς. κατὰ γὰρ οἶμαι τὴν
αὐτῶν ἑκατέροις ξυγγένειαν τὰ μὲν ἐπαινοῦντες ὡς

---

[1] ἄκαιρα Stephanus e Ficino : ἀκέραια ΒΤ.
[2] καὶ after φαινόμενα add. ΒΤ.
[3] πολεμίαν Campbell : πολεμίας ΒΤ.
[4] ποῦ δὴ] σπουδῆι Β : σπουδῆ Τ.

180

y. soc. How is that?

str. We are always saying " How quiet! " and " How restrained! " when we are admiring the workings of the mind, and again we speak of actions as slow and gentle, of the voice as smooth and deep, and of every rhythmic motion and of music in general as having appropriate slowness; and we apply to them all the term which signifies, not courage, but decorum.

y. soc. Very true.

str. And again, on the other hand, when these two classes seem to us out of place, we change our attitude and blame them each in turn; then we use the terms in the opposite sense.

y. soc. How is that?

str. Why, whatsoever is sharper than the occasion warrants, or seems to be too quick or too hard, is called violent or mad, and whatever is too heavy or slow or gentle, is called cowardly and sluggish; and almost always we find that the restraint of one class of qualities and the courage of the opposite class, like two parties arrayed in hostility to each other, do not mix with each other in the actions that are concerned with such qualities. Moreover, if we pursue the inquiry, we shall see that the men who have these qualities in their souls are at variance with one another.

y. soc. In what do you mean that they are at variance?

str. In all those points which we just mentioned, and probably in many others. For men who are akin to each class, I imagine, praise some qualities as

οἰκεῖα σφέτερα,[1] τὰ δὲ τῶν διαφόρων ψέγοντες ὡς
ἀλλότρια, πολλὴν εἰς ἔχθραν ἀλλήλοις καὶ πολλῶν
πέρι καθίστανται.

ΝΕ. ΣΩ. Κινδυνεύουσιν.

ΞΕ. Παιδιὰ[2] τοίνυν αὕτη γέ τις ἡ διαφορὰ τούτων
ἐστὶ τῶν εἰδῶν· περὶ δὲ τὰ μέγιστα νόσος ξυμβαίνει
πασῶν ἐχθίστη γίγνεσθαι ταῖς πόλεσιν.

ΝΕ. ΣΩ. Περὶ δὴ ποῖα φῇς;

Ε   ΞΕ. Περὶ ὅλην, ὥς γε εἰκός, τὴν τοῦ ζῆν παρα-
σκευήν. οἱ μὲν γὰρ δὴ διαφερόντως ὄντες κόσμιοι
τὸν ἥσυχον ἀεὶ βίον ἕτοιμοι ζῆν, αὐτοὶ καθ᾽ αὑτοὺς
μόνοι τὰ σφέτερα αὐτῶν πράττοντες, οἴκοι τε αὖ
πρὸς ἅπαντας οὕτως ὁμιλοῦντες, καὶ πρὸς τὰς
ἔξωθεν πόλεις ὡσαύτως ἕτοιμοι πάντα ὄντες τρόπον
τινὰ ἄγειν εἰρήνην· καὶ διὰ τὸν ἔρωτα δὴ τοῦτον
ἀκαιρότερον ὄντα ἢ χρή, ὅταν ἃ βούλωνται[3] πράττω-
σιν, ἔλαθον αὐτοί τε ἀπολέμως ἴσχοντες καὶ τοὺς
νέους ὡσαύτως διατιθέντες, ὄντες τε ἀεὶ τῶν
ἐπιτιθεμένων, ἐξ ὧν οὐκ ἐν πολλοῖς ἔτεσιν αὐτοὶ
308 καὶ παῖδες καὶ ξύμπασα ἡ πόλις ἀντ᾽ ἐλευθέρων
πολλάκις ἔλαθον αὑτοὺς γενόμενοι δοῦλοι.

ΝΕ. ΣΩ. Χαλεπὸν εἶπες καὶ δεινὸν πάθος.

ΞΕ. Τί δ᾽ οἱ πρὸς τὴν ἀνδρείαν μᾶλλον ῥέποντες;
ἆρ᾽ οὐκ ἐπὶ πόλεμον ἀεί τινα τὰς αὑτῶν ξυντείνοντες
πόλεις διὰ τὴν τοῦ τοιούτου βίου σφοδροτέραν τοῦ
δέοντος ἐπιθυμίαν εἰς ἔχθραν πολλοῖς καὶ δυνατοῖς
καταστάντες ἢ πάμπαν διώλεσαν ἢ δούλας αὖ καὶ
ὑποχειρίους τοῖς ἐχθροῖς ὑπέθεσαν τὰς αὑτῶν πατρί-
δας;

Β   ΝΕ. ΣΩ. Ἔστι καὶ ταῦτα.

---

[1] σφέτερα] ἐφ᾽ ἕτερα ΒΤ.   [2] παιδιὰ] παιδεία ΒΤ.
[3] βούλωνται ΒΤ.

their own and find fault with those of their opposites as alien to themselves, and thus great enmity arises between them on many grounds.

y. soc. Yes, that is likely to be the case.

str. Now this opposition of these two classes is mere child's-play; but when it affects the most important matters it becomes a most detestable disease in the state.

y. soc. What matters does it affect?

str. The whole course of life, in all probability. For those who are especially decorous are ready to live always a quiet and retired life and to mind their own business; this is the manner of their intercourse with every one at home, and they are equally ready at all times to keep peace in some way or other with foreign states. And because of this desire of theirs, which is often inopportune and excessive, when they have their own way they quite unconsciously become unwarlike, and they make the young men unwarlike also; they are at the mercy of aggressors; and thus in a few years they and their children and the whole state often pass by imperceptible degrees from freedom to slavery.

y. soc. That is a hard and terrible experience.

str. But how about those who incline towards courage? Do they not constantly urge their countries to war, because of their excessive desire for a warlike life? Do they not involve them in hostilities with many powerful opponents and either utterly destroy their native lands or enslave and subject them to their foes?

y. soc. Yes, that is true, too.

ΞΕ. Πῶς οὖν μὴ φῶμεν ἐν τούτοις ἀμφότερα ταῦτα τὰ γένη πολλὴν πρὸς ἄλληλα ἀεὶ καὶ τὴν μεγίστην ἴσχειν ἔχθραν καὶ στάσιν;

ΝΕ. ΣΩ. Οὐδαμῶς ὡς οὐ φήσομεν.

ΞΕ. Οὐκοῦν ὅπερ ἐπεσκοπούμεν κατ' ἀρχάς ἀνηυρήκαμεν, ὅτι μόρια ἀρετῆς οὐ σμικρὰ ἀλλήλοις διαφέρεσθον φύσει καὶ δὴ καὶ τοὺς ἴσχοντας δρᾶτον τὸ αὐτὸ τοῦτο;

ΝΕ. ΣΩ. Κινδυνεύετον.

ΞΕ. Τόδε τοίνυν αὖ λάβωμεν.

ΝΕ. ΣΩ. Τὸ ποῖον;

C 46. ΞΕ. Εἴ τίς που τῶν συνθετικῶν ἐπιστημῶν πρᾶγμα ὁτιοῦν τῶν αὑτῆς ἔργων, κἂν εἰ τὸ φαυλότατον, ἑκοῦσα ἐκ μοχθηρῶν καὶ χρηστῶν τινων ξυνίστησιν, ἢ πᾶσα ἐπιστήμη πανταχοῦ τὰ μὲν μοχθηρὰ εἰς δύναμιν ἀποβάλλει, τὰ δ' ἐπιτήδεια καὶ τὰ χρηστὰ ἔλαβεν, ἐκ τούτων δὲ καὶ ὁμοίων καὶ ἀνομοίων ὄντων, πάντα εἰς ἓν αὐτὰ ξυνάγουσα, μίαν τινὰ δύναμιν καὶ ἰδέαν δημιουργεῖ.

ΝΕ. ΣΩ. Τί μήν;

ΞΕ. Οὐδ' ἄρα ἡ κατὰ φύσιν ἀληθῶς οὖσα ἡμῖν
D πολιτικὴ μή ποτε ἐκ χρηστῶν καὶ κακῶν ἀνθρώπων ἑκοῦσα εἶναι συστήσηται πόλιν τινά, ἀλλ' εὔδηλον ὅτι παιδιᾷ πρῶτον βασανιεῖ, μετὰ δὲ τὴν βάσανον αὖ τοῖς δυναμένοις παιδεύειν καὶ ὑπηρετεῖν πρὸς τοῦτο αὐτὸ παραδώσει, προστάττουσα καὶ ἐπιστατοῦσα αὐτή, καθάπερ ὑφαντικὴ τοῖς τε ξαίνουσι καὶ τοῖς τἆλλα προπαρασκευάζουσιν ὅσα πρὸς τὴν πλέξιν αὐτῆς ξυμπαρακολουθοῦσα προστάττει καὶ
E ἐπιστατεῖ, τοιαῦτα ἑκάστοις ἐνδεικνῦσα τὰ ἔργα ἀποτελεῖν, οἷα ἂν ἐπιτήδεια ἡγῆται πρὸς τὴν αὑτῆς εἶναι ξυμπλοκήν.

184

STR. Then in these examples how can we deny that these two classes are always filled with the greatest hostility and opposition to one another?

Y. SOC. We certainly cannot deny it.

STR. Have we not, then, found just what we had in view in the beginning, that important parts of virtue are by nature at variance with one another and also that the persons who possess them exhibit the same opposition?

Y. SOC. Yes, I suppose that is true.

STR. Let us then take up another question.

Y. SOC. What question?

STR. Whether any constructive science voluntarily composes any, even the most worthless, of its works out of good and bad materials, or every science invariably rejects the bad, so far as possible, taking only the materials which are good and fitting, out of which, whether they be like or unlike, it gathers all elements together and produces one form or value.

Y. SOC. The latter, of course.

STR. Then neither will the true natural art of statecraft ever voluntarily compose a state of good and bad men; but obviously it will first test them in play, and after the test will entrust them in turn to those who are able to teach and help them to attain the end in view; it will itself give orders and exercise supervision, just as the art of weaving constantly commands and supervises the carders and others who prepare the materials for its web, directing each person to do the tasks which it thinks are requisite for its fabric.

ΝΕ. ΣΩ. Πάνυ μὲν οὖν.

ΞΕ. Ταὐτὸν δή μοι τοῦθ' ἡ βασιλικὴ φαίνεται πᾶσι τοῖς κατὰ νόμον παιδευταῖς καὶ τροφεῦσι, τὴν τῆς ἐπιστατικῆς αὐτὴ δύναμιν ἔχουσα, οὐκ ἐπιτρέψειν ἀσκεῖν ὅ τι μή τις πρὸς τὴν αὐτῆς ξύγκρασιν ἀπεργαζόμενος ἦθός τι πρέπον ἀποτελεῖ, ταῦτα δὲ μόνα παρακελεύεσθαι παιδεύειν· καὶ τοὺς μὲν μὴ δυναμένους κοινωνεῖν ἤθους ἀνδρείου καὶ σώφρονος ὅσα τε ἄλλα ἐστὶ τείνοντα πρὸς ἀρετήν, ἀλλ' εἰς 309 ἀθεότητα καὶ ὕβριν καὶ ἀδικίαν ὑπὸ κακῆς βίᾳ φύσεως ἀπωθουμένους,[1] θανάτοις τε ἐκβάλλει καὶ φυγαῖς καὶ ταῖς μεγίσταις κολάζουσα ἀτιμίαις.

ΝΕ. ΣΩ. Λέγεται γοῦν πως οὕτως.

ΞΕ. Τοὺς δ' ἐν ἀμαθίᾳ τ' αὖ καὶ ταπεινότητι πολλῇ κυλινδουμένους εἰς τὸ δουλικὸν ὑποζεύγνυσι γένος.

ΝΕ. ΣΩ. Ὀρθότατα.

ΞΕ. Τοὺς λοιποὺς τοίνυν, ὅσων αἱ φύσεις ἐπὶ τὸ γενναῖον ἱκαναὶ παιδείας τυγχάνουσαι καθίστασθαι Β καὶ δέξασθαι μετὰ τέχνης ξύμμιξιν πρὸς ἀλλήλας, τούτων τὰς μὲν ἐπὶ τὴν ἀνδρείαν μᾶλλον ξυντεινούσας, οἷον στημονοφυὲς νομίσας[2] αὐτῶν εἶναι τὸ στερεὸν ἦθος, τὰς δὲ ἐπὶ τὸ κόσμιον πίονί τε καὶ μαλακῷ καὶ κατὰ τὴν εἰκόνα κροκώδει διανήματι[3] προσχρωμένας, ἐναντία δὲ τεινούσας ἀλλήλαις, πειρᾶται τοιόνδε τινὰ τρόπον ξυνδεῖν καὶ ξυμπλέκειν.

ΝΕ. ΣΩ. Ποῖον δή;

C ΞΕ. Πρῶτον μὲν κατὰ τὸ ξυγγενὲς τὸ ἀειγενὲς ὂν τῆς ψυχῆς αὐτῶν μέρος θείῳ ξυναρμοσαμένη

---

[1] ἀπωθουμένους Stallbaum : ἀπωθούμενα ΒΤ.
[2] νομίσας ΒΤ : corr. Heusde.

y. soc. Certainly.

str. In the same way I think the kingly art, keeping for itself the function of supervision, will not allow the duly appointed teachers and foster fathers to give any training, unless they can thereby produce characters suitable to the constitution it is creating, but in these things only it exhorts them to give instruction. And those men who have no capacity for courage and self-restraint and the other qualities which tend towards virtue, but by the force of an evil nature are carried away into godlessness, violence, and injustice, it removes by inflicting upon them the punishments of death and exile and deprivation of the most important civic rights.

y. soc. That is about what people say, at any rate.

str. And those in turn who wallow in ignorance and craven humility it places under the yoke of slavery.

y. soc. Quite right.

str. As for the rest of the people, those whose natures are capable, if they get education, of being made into something fine and noble and of uniting with each other as art requires, the kingly art takes those natures which tend more towards courage, considering that their character is sturdier, like the warp in weaving, and those which incline towards decorum, for these, to continue the simile, are spun thick and soft like the threads of the woof, and tries to combine these natures of opposite tendencies and weave them together in the following manner.

y. soc. In what manner?

str. First it binds the eternal part of their souls with a divine bond, to which that part is akin, and

---

³ διανήματι Cornarius: διανθήματι BT.

PLATO

δεσμῷ, μετὰ δὲ τὸ θεῖον τὸ ζωογενὲς αὐτῶν αὖθις ἀνθρωπίνοις.

ΝΕ. ΣΩ. Πῶς τοῦτ' εἶπες αὖ;

47. ΞΕ. Τὴν τῶν καλῶν καὶ δικαίων πέρι καὶ ἀγαθῶν καὶ τῶν τούτοις ἐναντίων ὄντως οὖσαν ἀληθῆ δόξαν μετὰ βεβαιώσεως, ὁπόταν ἐν ταῖς ψυχαῖς ἐγγίγνηται, θείαν φημὶ ἐν δαιμονίῳ γίγνεσθαι γένει.

ΝΕ. ΣΩ. Πρέπει γοῦν οὕτως.

ΞΕ. Τὸν δὴ πολιτικὸν καὶ τὸν ἀγαθὸν νομοθέτην
D ἆρ' ἴσμεν ὅτι προσήκει μόνον δυνατὸν εἶναι τῇ τῆς βασιλικῆς μούσῃ τοῦτο αὐτὸ ἐμποιεῖν τοῖς ὀρθῶς μεταλαβοῦσι παιδείας, οὓς ἐλέγομεν νῦν δή;

ΝΕ. ΣΩ. Τὸ γοῦν εἰκός.

ΞΕ. Ὃς δ' ἂν δρᾶν γε, ὦ Σώκρατες, ἀδυνατῇ τὸ τοιοῦτον, μηδέποτε τοῖς νῦν ζητουμένοις ὀνόμασιν αὐτὸν προσαγορεύωμεν.

ΝΕ. ΣΩ. Ὀρθότατα.

ΞΕ. Τί οὖν; ἀνδρεία ψυχὴ λαμβανομένη τῆς τοιαύτης ἀληθείας ἆρ' οὐχ ἡμεροῦται καὶ τῶν δι-
E καίων μάλιστα οὕτω κοινωνεῖν ἂν ἐθελήσειεν, μὴ μεταλαβοῦσα δὲ ἀποκλίνει μᾶλλον πρὸς θηριώδη τινὰ φύσιν;

ΝΕ. ΣΩ. Πῶς δ' οὔ;

ΞΕ. Τί δέ; τὸ τῆς κοσμίας φύσεως ἆρ' οὐ τούτων μὲν μεταλαβὸν τῶν δοξῶν ὄντως σῶφρον καὶ φρόνιμον, ὥς γε ἐν πολιτείᾳ, γίγνεται, μὴ κοινωνῆσαν δὲ ὧν λέγομεν ἐπονείδιστόν τινα εὐηθείας δικαιότατα λαμβάνει φήμην;

ΝΕ. ΣΩ. Πάνυ μὲν οὖν.

ΞΕ. Οὐκοῦν ξυμπλοκὴν καὶ δεσμὸν τοῦτον τοῖς μὲν κακοῖς πρὸς σφᾶς αὐτοὺς καὶ τοῖς ἀγαθοῖς πρὸς τοὺς κακοὺς μηδέποτε μόνιμον φῶμεν γίγνεσθαι,

after the divine it binds the animal part of them with human bonds.

Y. soc. Again I ask What do you mean?

str. I mean that really true and assured opinion about honour, justice, goodness and their opposites is divine, and when it arises in men's souls, it arises in a godlike race.

Y. soc. That would be fitting, at any rate.

str. Do we not know, then, that the statesman and good law-giver is the only one to whom the power properly belongs, by the inspiration of the kingly art, to implant this true opinion in those who have rightly received education, those of whom we were just now speaking?

Y. soc. Well, probably.

str. And let us never, Socrates, call him who has not such power by the names we are now examining.

Y. soc. Quite right.

str. Now is not a courageous soul, when it lays hold upon such truth, made gentle, and would it not then be most ready to partake of justice? And without it, does it not incline more towards brutality?

Y. soc. Yes, of course.

str. And again if the decorous nature partakes of these opinions, does it not become truly self-restrained and wise, so far as the state is concerned, and if it lacks participation in such qualities, does it not very justly receive the shameful epithet of simpleton?

Y. soc. Certainly.

str. Then can we say that such interweaving and binding together of the bad with the bad or of the good with the bad ever becomes enduring, or that

189

μηδέ τινα ἐπιστήμην αὐτῷ σπουδῇ πρὸς τοὺς τοιούτους ἂν χρῆσθαί ποτε;

ΝΕ. ΣΩ. Πῶς γάρ;

310 ΞΕ. Τοῖς δ' εὐγενέσι γενομένοις τε¹ ἐξ ἀρχῆς
ἤθεσι θρεφθεῖσί τε κατὰ φύσιν μόνοις διὰ νόμων
ἐμφύεσθαι, καὶ ἐπὶ τούτοις δὴ τοῦτ' εἶναι τέχνῃ
φάρμακον, καὶ καθάπερ εἴπομεν τοῦτον θειότερον
εἶναι τὸν ξύνδεσμον ἀρετῆς μερῶν φύσεως ἀνομοίων
καὶ ἐπὶ τἀναντία φερομένων.

ΝΕ. ΣΩ. Ἀληθέστατα.

ΞΕ. Τοὺς μὲν λοιπούς, ὄντας ἀνθρωπίνους δε-
σμούς, ὑπάρχοντος τούτου τοῦ θείου σχεδὸν οὐδὲν
χαλεπὸν οὔτε ἐννοεῖν οὔτε ἐννοήσαντα ἀποτελεῖν.

Β ΝΕ. ΣΩ. Πῶς δή, καὶ τίνας;

ΞΕ. Τοὺς τῶν ἐπιγαμιῶν καὶ παίδων κοινωνήσεων
καὶ τῶν περὶ τὰς ἰδίας ἐκδόσεις καὶ γάμους. οἱ γὰρ
πολλοὶ τὰ περὶ ταῦτα οὐκ ὀρθῶς ξυνδοῦνται πρὸς
τὴν τῶν παίδων γέννησιν.

ΝΕ. ΣΩ. Τί δή;

ΞΕ. Τὰ μὲν πλούτου καὶ δυνάμεως ἐν τοῖς τοιούτοις διώγματα τί καί τις ἂν ὡς ἄξια λόγου σπου-
δάζοι μεμφόμενος;

ΝΕ. ΣΩ. Οὐδέν.

48. ΞΕ. Μᾶλλον δέ γε δίκαιον τῶν περὶ τὰ
C γένη ποιουμένων ἐπιμέλειαν τούτων πέρι λέγειν, εἴ
τι μὴ κατὰ τρόπον πράττουσιν.

ΝΕ. ΣΩ. Εἰκὸς γὰρ οὖν.

---

¹ τε] γ' Β: γε (and γενομένοις after ἐξ ἀρχῆς) Τ.

---

¹ More or less equivalent to naturalization. It apparently
means the adoption into one state of children born to

190

any science would ever seriously make use of it in uniting such persons?

Y. soc. Of course not.

str. But we may say that in those only who were of noble nature from their birth and have been nurtured as befits such natures it is implanted by the laws, and for them this is the medicine prescribed by science, and, as we said before, this bond which unites unlike and divergent parts of virtue is more divine.

Y. soc. Very true.

str. The remaining bonds, moreover, being human, are not very difficult to devise or, after one has devised them, to create, when once this divine bond exists.

Y. soc. How so? And what are the bonds?

str. Those made between states concerning intermarriages and the sharing of children by adoption,[1] and those relating to portionings and marriages within the state. For most people make such bonds without proper regard to the procreation of children.

Y. soc. How is that?

str. The pursuit of wealth or power in connexion with matrimony—but why should anyone ever take the trouble to blame it, as though it were worth arguing about?

Y. soc. There is no reason for doing so.

str. We have better cause, however, to speak our minds about those whose chief care is the family, in case their conduct is not what it should be.

Y. soc. Yes; very likely.

citizens of another. This was not, as a rule, practised in the Greek city states, but Plato here seems to recommend it.

PLATO

ΞΕ. Πράττουσι μὲν δὴ οὐδὲ ἐξ ἑνὸς ὀρθοῦ λόγου, τὴν ἐν τῷ παραχρῆμα διώκοντες ῥᾳστώνην καὶ τῷ τοὺς μὲν προσομοίους αὑτοῖς ἀσπάζεσθαι, τοὺς δ' ἀνομοίους μὴ στέργειν, πλεῖστον τῇ δυσχερείᾳ μέρος ἀπονέμοντες.

ΝΕ. ΣΩ. Πῶς;

ΞΕ. Οἱ μέν που κόσμιοι τὸ σφέτερον αὑτῶν ἦθος ζητοῦσι, καὶ κατὰ δύναμιν γαμοῦσί τε παρὰ τούτων καὶ τὰς ἐκδιδομένας παρ' αὑτῶν εἰς τούτους D ἐκπέμπουσι πάλιν· ὡς δ' αὕτως τὸ περὶ τὴν ἀνδρείαν γένος δρᾷ, τὴν αὑτοῦ μεταδιῶκον φύσιν, δέον ποιεῖν ἀμφότερα τὰ γένη τούτων τοὐναντίον ἅπαν.

ΝΕ. ΣΩ. Πῶς, καὶ διὰ τί;

ΞΕ. Διότι πέφυκεν ἀνδρεία τε ἐν πολλαῖς γενέσεσιν ἄμικτος γεννωμένη σώφρονι φύσει κατὰ μὲν ἀρχὰς ἀκμάζειν ῥώμῃ, τελευτῶσα δὲ ἐξανθεῖν παντάπασι μανίαις.

ΝΕ. ΣΩ. Εἰκός.

ΞΕ. Ἡ δὲ αἰδοῦς γε αὖ λίαν πλήρης ψυχὴ καὶ E ἀκέραστος τόλμης ἀνδρείας, ἐπὶ δὲ γενεὰς πολλὰς οὕτω γεννηθεῖσα, νωθεστέρα φύεσθαι τοῦ καιροῦ καὶ ἀποτελευτῶσα δὴ παντάπασιν ἀναπηροῦσθαι.

ΝΕ. ΣΩ. Καὶ τοῦτο εἰκὸς οὕτω ξυμβαίνειν.

ΞΕ. Τούτους δὴ τοὺς δεσμοὺς ἔλεγον ὅτι χαλεπὸν οὐδὲν ξυνδεῖν ὑπάρξαντος τοῦ περὶ τὰ καλὰ καὶ ἀγαθὰ μίαν ἔχειν ἀμφότερα τὰ γένη δόξαν. τοῦτο γὰρ ἓν καὶ ὅλον ἐστὶ βασιλικῆς ξυνυφάνσεως ἔργον, μηδέποτε ἐᾶν ἀφίστασθαι σώφρονα ἀπὸ τῶν ἀνδρείων ἤθη, ξυγκερκίζοντα δὲ ὁμοδοξίαις καὶ τιμαῖς καὶ ἀτιμίαις καὶ δόξαις καὶ ὁμηρειῶν ἐκδόσεσιν εἰς ἀλλήλους, λεῖον καὶ τὸ λεγόμενον εὐήτριον ὕφασμα

STR. The fact is, they act on no right theory at all; they seek their ease for the moment; welcoming gladly those who are like themselves, and finding those who are unlike them unendurable, they give the greatest weight to their feeling of dislike.

Y. SOC. How so?

STR. The decorous people seek for characters like their own; so far as they can they marry wives of that sort and in turn give their daughters in marriage to men of that sort; and the courageous do the same, eagerly seeking natures of their own kind, whereas both classes ought to do quite the opposite.

Y. SOC. How so, and why?

STR. Because in the nature of things courage, if propagated through many generations with no admixture of a self-restrained nature, though at first it is strong and flourishing, in the end blossoms forth in utter madness.

Y. SOC. That is likely.

STR. But the soul, on the other hand, that is too full of modesty and contains no alloy of courage or boldness, after many generations of the same kind becomes too sluggish and finally is utterly crippled.

Y. SOC. That also is likely to happen.

STR. It was these bonds, then, that I said there was no difficulty in creating, provided that both classes have one and the same opinion about the honourable and the good. For indeed the whole business of the kingly weaving is comprised in this and this alone,—in never allowing the self-restrained characters to be separated from the courageous, but in weaving them together by common beliefs and honours and dishonours and opinions and interchanges of pledges, thus making of them a smooth and, as

311 ξυνάγοντα ἐξ αὐτῶν, τὰς ἐν ταῖς πόλεσιν ἀρχὰς
ἀεὶ κοινῇ τούτοις ἐπιτρέπειν.

ΝΕ. ΣΩ. Πῶς;

ΞΕ. Οὗ μὲν ἂν ἑνὸς ἄρχοντος χρεία ξυμβαίνῃ,
τὸν ταῦτα ἀμφότερα ἔχοντα αἱρούμενον ἐπιστάτην·
οὗ δ' ἂν πλειόνων, τούτων μέρος ἑκατέρων ξυμμιγ-
νύντα. τὰ μὲν γὰρ σωφρόνων ἀρχόντων ἤθη
σφόδρα μὲν εὐλαβῆ καὶ δίκαια καὶ σωτήρια,
δριμύτητος δὲ καί τινος ἰταμότητος ὀξείας καὶ
πρακτικῆς ἐνδεῖται.

ΝΕ. ΣΩ. Δοκεῖ γοῦν δὴ καὶ τάδε.

B ΞΕ. Τὰ δ' ἀνδρεῖά γε αὖ πρὸς μὲν τὸ δίκαιον
καὶ εὐλαβὲς ἐκείνων ἐπιδεέστερα, τὸ δ' ἐν ταῖς
πράξεσι ἰταμὸν[1] διαφερόντως ἴσχει. πάντα δὲ
καλῶς γίγνεσθαι τὰ περὶ τὰς πόλεις ἰδίᾳ καὶ δημοσίᾳ
τούτοιν μὴ παραγενομένοιν ἀμφοῖν ἀδύνατον.

ΝΕ. ΣΩ. Πῶς γὰρ οὔ;

ΞΕ. Τοῦτο δὴ τέλος ὑφάσματος εὐθυπλοκίᾳ συμ-
πλακὲν[2] γίγνεσθαι φῶμεν πολιτικῆς πράξεως τὸ
τῶν ἀνδρείων καὶ σωφρόνων ἀνθρώπων ἦθος,
C ὁπόταν ὁμονοίᾳ καὶ φιλίᾳ κοινὸν ξυναγαγοῦσα
αὐτῶν τὸν βίον ἡ βασιλικὴ τέχνη, πάντωνμεγαλο-
πρεπέστατον ὑφασμάτων καὶ ἄριστον ἀποτελέσασα[3]
τούς τ' ἄλλους ἐν ταῖς πόλεσι πάντας δούλους καὶ
ἐλευθέρους ἀμπίσχουσα, συνέχῃ τούτῳ τῷ πλέγματι,
καὶ καθ' ὅσον εὐδαίμονι προσήκει γίγνεσθαι πόλει
τούτου μηδαμῇ μηδὲν ἐλλείπουσα ἄρχῃ τε καὶ
ἐπιστατῇ.

ΝΕ. ΣΩ. Κάλλιστα αὖ τὸν βασιλικὸν ἀπετέλεσας
ἄνδρα ἡμῖν, ὦ ξένε, καὶ τὸν πολιτικόν.

---

[1] ἰταμὸν Ast: τὸ μὲν ΒΤ.   [2] συμπλέκειν Β: ξυμπλεκὲν Τ.
[3] ἀποτελέσασα Ast: ἀποτελέσασα ὥστ' εἶναι κοινόν mss.

we say, well-woven fabric, and then entrusting to them in common for ever the offices of the state.

Y. SOC. How is that to be done?

STR. When one official is needed, by choosing a president who possesses both qualities; and when a board is desired, by combining men of each class. For the characters of self-restrained officials are exceedingly careful and just and conservative, but they lack keenness and a certain quick and active boldness.

Y. SOC. That also seems, at least, to be true.

STR. The courageous natures, on the other hand, are deficient in justice and caution in comparison with the former, but excel in boldness of action; and unless both these qualities are present it is impossible for a state to be entirely prosperous in public and private matters.

Y. SOC. Yes, certainly.

STR. This, then, is the end, let us declare, of the web of the statesman's activity, the direct inter-weaving of the characters of restrained and courageous men, when the kingly science has drawn them together by friendship and community of sentiment into a common life, and having perfected the most glorious and the best of all textures, clothes with it all the inhabitants of the state, both slaves and freemen, holds them together by this fabric, and omitting nothing which ought to belong to a happy state, rules and watches over them.

Y. SOC. You have given us, Stranger, a most complete and admirable treatment of the king and the statesman.

PHILEBUS

INTRODUCTION TO THE *PHILEBUS*

THE object of the *Philebus* is the determination of "the good." Philebus, a totally unknown person whose name serves as the title of the dialogue, is represented as a thinker of the hedonistic school. He has, apparently, been lecturing or taking part in a discussion, but has withdrawn on account of weariness. He speaks only a few short sentences in the whole dialogue. Protarchus, son of the wealthy Callias, serves to give the form of dialogue to the discourse, but his personality is not even outlined, and his remarks are as colourless as are those of the younger Socrates in *The Statesman*. Even Socrates himself, as in *The Sophist, The Statesman*, and other dialogues of approximately the same date, shows little personality: he is merely the mouthpiece of the doctrine.

This dialogue, like *The Sophist* and *The Statesman*, contains a preliminary illustration of method; for the discussion of sounds in speech (17 ff.) serves the same purpose as the "angler" in *The Sophist* and the "art of weaving" in *The Statesman*. The *Philebus* seems to be slightly later in date than the other two dialogues.

In opposition to the assertion ascribed to Philebus, that pleasure is the good, Socrates seems at first prepared to maintain (with Eucleides and the Cynics)

199

that knowledge is the good, but presently announces his suspicion that some third competitor will be awarded the first place, and that even the second place will not be held by pleasure. It is soon agreed that a mixture of knowledge and pleasure is necessary for the most desirable life. The discussion is carried on in great measure by means of classification or division, which is here founded on the principles (derived from Pythagorean sources) of the Limited and the Unlimited. Pleasure and pain, and everything which is capable of degrees of intensity, belong to the class of the Unlimited, whereas number, measure, and knowledge belong to that of the Limited, which is regarded as essentially superior.

The composition of the mixture which is necessary for the most perfect life is discussed in detail. This involves a description and condemnation of excess in the most intense pleasures and an interesting analysis of the mixture of pain and pleasure in anger, pity, revenge, and other emotions as they affect us in theatrical representations or in real life. The pleasures of scientific knowledge are said to be absolutely pure and unmixed, therefore truer than all mixed pleasures and preferable to them. Again, pleasure being, according to certain hedonists, a process or Becoming, is found to be on that account inferior to knowledge, which is a state or Being. The discussion of kinds of knowledge (55 c ff.) includes (55 e) the distinction between scientific knowledge, based on arithmetic, measuring, and weighing, and such knowledge as rests upon the mere schooling of the senses.

In the end the order in which possessions may be called good is established as follows: (1) measure,

moderation, fitness, and the like ; (2) proportion, beauty, perfection, and their kin ; (3) mind and wisdom ; (4) sciences, arts, and true opinions ; (5) pure pleasures.

This dialogue, though it lacks the dramatic qualities which make many of Plato's works take rank among the most charming products of all literature, and in spite of certain inconsistencies and even defects of reasoning—for instance, the confusion between goodness and a good thing (55 B) or the insistence upon the existence of false pleasures, though the epithet " false " belongs really to opinion, not to the pleasures themselves—is an interesting and instructive presentation of an important subject. It also exhibits clearly one side, at least, of Plato's development at a time which must be somewhat after the middle of his career.

Annotated editions of the *Philebus* are by Charles Badham (London, 1855 and 1878) and E. Poste (Oxford University Press, 1860).

ΦΙΛΗΒΟΣ

[Η ΠΕΡΙ ΗΔΟΝΗΣ, ΗΘΙΚΟΣ]

TA TOT ΔΙΑΛΟΓΟΥ ΠΡΟΣΩΠΑ

ΣΩΚΡΑΤΗΣ, ΠΡΩΤΑΡΧΟΣ, ΦΙΛΗΒΟΣ

1. ΣΩ. Ὅρα δή, Πρώταρχε, τίνα λόγον μέλλεις παρὰ Φιλήβου δέχεσθαι νυνὶ καὶ πρὸς τίνα τὸν[1] παρ' ἡμῖν ἀμφισβητεῖν, ἐὰν μή σοι κατὰ νοῦν B ᾖ λεγόμενος. βούλει συγκεφαλαιωσώμεθα ἑκάτερον;

ΠΡΩ. Πάνυ μὲν οὖν.

ΣΩ. Φίληβος μὲν τοίνυν ἀγαθὸν εἶναί φησι τὸ χαίρειν πᾶσι ζῴοις καὶ τὴν ἡδονὴν καὶ τέρψιν, καὶ ὅσα τοῦ γένους ἐστὶ τούτου σύμφωνα· τὸ δὲ παρ' ἡμῶν ἀμφισβήτημά ἐστι μὴ ταῦτα, ἀλλὰ τὸ φρονεῖν καὶ τὸ νοεῖν καὶ τὸ μεμνῆσθαι καὶ τὰ τούτων αὖ ξυγγενῆ, δόξαν τε ὀρθὴν καὶ ἀληθεῖς C λογισμούς, τῆς γε ἡδονῆς ἀμείνω καὶ λῴω γίγνεσθαι ξύμπασιν ὅσαπερ αὐτῶν δυνατὰ μεταλαβεῖν· δυνατοῖς δὲ μετασχεῖν ὠφελιμώτατον ἁπάντων εἶναι πᾶσι τοῖς οὖσί τε καὶ ἐσομένοις. μῶν οὐχ οὕτω πως λέγομεν, ὦ Φίληβε, ἑκάτεροι;

ΦΙ. Πάντων μὲν οὖν μάλιστα, ὦ Σώκρατες.

---

[1] τὸν Schleiermacher: τῶν BT.

202

PHILEBUS

[OR ON PLEASURE, ETHICAL]

CHARACTERS
SOCRATES, PROTARCHUS, PHILEBUS

soc. Observe, then, Protarchus, what the doctrine is which you are now to accept from Philebus, and what our doctrine is, against which you are to argue, if you do not agree with it. Shall we make a brief statement of each of them?

PRO. By all means.

soc. Very well: Philebus says that to all living beings enjoyment and pleasure and gaiety and whatever accords with that sort of thing are a good; whereas our contention is that not these, but wisdom and thought and memory and their kindred, right opinion and true reasonings, are better and more excellent than pleasure for all who are capable of taking part in them, and that for all those now existing or to come who can partake of them they are the most advantageous of all things. Those are pretty nearly the two doctrines we maintain, are they not, Philebus?

PHI. Yes, Socrates, exactly.

ΣΩ. Δέχει δὴ τοῦτον τὸν νῦν διδόμενον, ὦ Πρώταρχε, λόγον;

ΠΡΩ. Ἀνάγκη δέχεσθαι· Φίληβος γὰρ ἡμῖν ὁ καλὸς ἀπείρηκεν.

ΣΩ. Δεῖ δὴ περὶ αὐτῶν τρόπῳ παντὶ τἀληθές πῃ περανθῆναι;

D   ΠΡΩ. Δεῖ γὰρ οὖν.

2. ΣΩ. Ἴθι δή, πρὸς τούτοις διομολογησώμεθα καὶ τόδε.

ΠΡΩ. Τὸ ποῖον;

ΣΩ. Ὡς νῦν ἡμῶν ἑκάτερος ἕξιν ψυχῆς καὶ διάθεσιν ἀποφαίνειν τινὰ ἐπιχειρήσει τὴν δυναμένην ἀνθρώποις πᾶσι τὸν βίον εὐδαίμονα παρέχειν. ἆρ᾽ οὐχ οὕτως;

ΠΡΩ. Οὕτω μὲν οὖν.

ΣΩ. Οὐκοῦν ὑμεῖς μὲν τὴν τοῦ χαίρειν, ἡμεῖς δ᾽ αὖ τὴν τοῦ φρονεῖν;

ΠΡΩ. Ἔστι ταῦτα.

ΣΩ. Τί δ᾽, ἂν ἄλλη τις κρείττων τούτων φανῇ;
E μῶν οὐκ, ἂν μὲν ἡδονῇ[1] μᾶλλον φαίνηται ξυγγενής, ἡττώμεθα μὲν ἀμφότεροι τοῦ ταῦτα ἔχοντος
12 βεβαίως βίου, κρατεῖ δὲ ὁ τῆς ἡδονῆς τὸν τῆς φρονήσεως;

ΠΡΩ. Ναί.

ΣΩ. Ἂν δέ γε φρονήσει, νικᾷ μὲν φρόνησις τὴν ἡδονήν, ἡ δὲ ἡττᾶται; ταῦθ᾽ οὕτως ὁμολογούμενά φατε, ἢ πῶς;

ΠΡΩ. Ἐμοὶ γοῦν δοκεῖ.

ΣΩ. Τί δὲ Φιλήβῳ; τί φῄς;

ΦΙ. Ἐμοὶ μὲν πάντως νικᾶν ἡδονὴ δοκεῖ καὶ δόξει· σὺ δέ, Πρώταρχε, αὐτὸς γνώσει.

[1] ἡδονῇ] ἡδονὴ BT.

soc. And do you, Protarchus, accept this doctrine which is now committed to you?

pro. I must accept it; for our handsome Philebus has withdrawn.

soc. And must the truth about these doctrines be attained by every possible means?

pro. Yes, it must.

soc. Then let us further agree to this:

pro. To what?

soc. That each of us will next try to prove clearly that it is a condition and disposition of the soul which can make life happy for all human beings. Is not that what we are going to do?

pro. It is.

soc. Then you will show that it is the condition of pleasure, and I that it is that of wisdom?

pro. True.

soc. What if some other life be found superior to these two? Then if that life is found to be more akin to pleasure, both of us are defeated, are we not, by the life which has firm possession of this superiority, but the life of pleasure is victor over the life of wisdom.

pro. Yes.

soc. But if it is more akin to wisdom, then wisdom is victorious and pleasure is vanquished? Do you agree to that? Or what do you say?

pro. Yes, I at least am satisfied with that.

soc. But how about you, Philebus? What do you say?

phi. I think and always shall think that pleasure is the victor. But you, Protarchus, will make your own decision.

ΠΡΩ. Παραδούς, ὦ Φίληβε, ἡμῖν τὸν λόγον οὐκ ἂν ἔτι κύριος εἴης τῆς πρὸς Σωκράτη ὁμολογίας ἢ καὶ τοὐναντίον.

Β ΦΙ. Ἀληθῆ λέγεις· ἀλλὰ γὰρ ἀφοσιοῦμαι καὶ μαρτύρομαι νῦν αὐτὴν τὴν θεόν.

ΠΡΩ. Καὶ ἡμεῖς σοι τούτων γε αὐτῶν συμμάρτυρες ἂν εἶμεν,[1] ὡς ταῦτα ἔλεγες ἃ λέγεις. ἀλλὰ δὴ τὰ μετὰ ταῦτα ἑξῆς, ὦ Σώκρατες, ὅμως καὶ μετὰ Φιλήβου ἑκόντος ἢ ὅπως ἂν ἐθέλῃ, πειρώμεθα περαίνειν.

3. ΣΩ. Πειρατέον, ἀπ' αὐτῆς δὲ τῆς θεοῦ, ἣν ὅδε Ἀφροδίτην μὲν λέγεσθαί φησι, τὸ δ' ἀληθέστατον αὐτῆς ὄνομα Ἡδονὴν εἶναι.

ΠΡΩ. Ὀρθότατα.

C ΣΩ. Τὸ δ' ἐμὸν δέος, ὦ Πρώταρχε, ἀεὶ πρὸς τὰ τῶν θεῶν ὀνόματα οὐκ ἔστι κατ' ἄνθρωπον, ἀλλὰ πέρα τοῦ μεγίστου φόβου. καὶ νῦν τὴν μὲν Ἀφροδίτην, ὅπῃ ἐκείνῃ φίλον, ταύτῃ προσαγορεύω· τὴν δὲ ἡδονὴν οἶδα ὡς ἔστι ποικίλον, καὶ ὅπερ εἶπον, ἀπ' ἐκείνης ἡμᾶς ἀρχομένους ἐνθυμεῖσθαι δεῖ καὶ σκοπεῖν ἥντινα φύσιν ἔχει. ἔστι γάρ, ἀκούειν μὲν οὕτως ἁπλῶς, ἕν τι, μορφὰς δὲ δήπου παντοίας εἴληφε καί τινα τρόπον ἀνομοίους ἀλλήλαις. ἰδὲ γάρ· ἥδεσθαι μέν φαμεν

D τὸν ἀκολασταίνοντα ἄνθρωπον, ἥδεσθαι δὲ καὶ τὸν σωφρονοῦντα αὐτῷ τῷ σωφρονεῖν· ἥδεσθαι δ' αὖ καὶ τὸν ἀνοηταίνοντα καὶ ἀνοήτων δοξῶν καὶ ἐλπίδων μεστόν, ἥδεσθαι δ' αὖ καὶ τὸν φρονοῦντα αὐτῷ τῷ φρονεῖν·[2] καὶ τούτων τῶν ἡδονῶν ἑκατέρας πῶς ἄν τις ὁμοίας ἀλλήλαις εἶναι λέγων οὐκ ἀνόητος φαίνοιτο ἐνδίκως;

[1] εἶμεν corr. Ven. 189: ἦμεν ΒΤ.

PRO. Since you entrusted the argument to me, Philebus, you can no longer dictate whether to make the agreement with Socrates or not.

PHI. True; and for that reason I wash my hands of it and now call upon the goddess [1] herself to witness that I do so.

PRO. And we also will bear witness to these words of yours. But all the same, Socrates, Philebus may agree or do as he likes, let us try to finish our argument in due order.

SOC. We must try, and let us begin with the very goddess who Philebus says is spoken of as Aphrodite but is most truly named Pleasure.

PRO. Quite right.

SOC. My awe, Protarchus, in respect to the names of the gods is always beyond the greatest human fear. And now I call Aphrodite by that name which is agreeable to her; but pleasure I know has various aspects, and since, as I said, we are to begin with her, we must consider and examine what her nature is. For, when you just simply hear her name, she is only one thing, but surely she takes on all sorts of shapes which are even, in a way, unlike each other. For instance, we say that the man who lives without restraint has pleasure, and that the self-restrained man takes pleasure in his very self-restraint; and again that the fool who is full of foolish opinions and hopes is pleased, and also that the wise man takes pleasure in his very wisdom. And would not any person who said these two kinds of pleasure were like each other be rightly regarded as a fool?

---

[1] The goddess of Pleasure, Ἡδονή personified.

[2] φρονοῦντα . . φρονεῖν T: σωφρονοῦντα . . σωφρονεῖν B.

ΠΡΩ. Εἰσὶ μὲν γὰρ ἀπ' ἐναντίων, ὦ Σώκρατες, αὗται πραγμάτων, οὐ μὴν αὐταί γε ἀλλήλαις ἐναν-
E τίαι. πῶς γὰρ ἡδονή γε ἡδονῇ οὐχ¹ ὁμοιότατον ἂν εἴη, τοῦτο αὐτὸ ἑαυτῷ, πάντων χρημάτων;

ΣΩ. Καὶ γὰρ χρῶμα, ὦ δαιμόνιε, χρώματι· κατά γε αὐτὸ τοῦτο οὐδὲν διοίσει τὸ χρῶμα εἶναι πᾶν, τό γε μὴν μέλαν τῷ λευκῷ πάντες γιγνώσκομεν ὡς πρὸς τῷ διάφορον εἶναι καὶ ἐναντιώτατον ὂν τυγχάνει· καὶ δὴ καὶ σχῆμα σχήματι κατὰ ταὐτόν· γένει μέν ἐστι πᾶν ἕν, τὰ δὲ μέρη τοῖς μέρεσιν αὐτοῦ τὰ μὲν ἐναντιώτατα ἀλλήλοις,
13 τὰ δὲ διαφορότητα ἔχοντα μυρίαν που τυγχάνει· καὶ πόλλ' ἕτερα οὕτως ἔχονθ' εὑρήσομεν· ὥστε τούτῳ γε τῷ λόγῳ μὴ πίστευε, τῷ πάντα τὰ ἐναντιώτατα ἓν ποιοῦντι. φοβοῦμαι δέ μή τινας ἡδονὰς ἡδοναῖς εὑρήσομεν ἐναντίας.

ΠΡΩ. Ἴσως· ἀλλὰ τί τοῦθ' ἡμῶν βλάψει τὸν λόγον;

ΣΩ. Ὅτι προσαγορεύεις αὐτὰ ἀνόμοια ὄντα ἑτέρῳ, φήσομεν, ὀνόματι. λέγεις γὰρ ἀγαθὰ πάντα εἶναι τὰ ἡδέα. τὸ μὲν οὖν μὴ οὐχ ἡδέα
B εἶναι τὰ ἡδέα λόγος οὐδεὶς ἀμφισβητεῖ· κακὰ δ' ὄντα αὐτῶν τὰ πολλὰ καὶ ἀγαθὰ δέ, ὡς ἡμεῖς φαμέν, ὅμως πάντα σὺ προσαγορεύεις ἀγαθά αὐτά, ὁμολογῶν ἀνόμοια εἶναι, τῷ λόγῳ εἴ τίς σε προσαναγκάζοι. τί οὖν δὴ ταὐτὸν ἐν ταῖς κακαῖς ὁμοίως καὶ ἐν ἀγαθαῖς ἐνὸν πάσας ἡδονὰς ἀγαθὸν εἶναι προσαγορεύεις;

ΠΡΩ. Πῶς λέγεις, ὦ Σώκρατες; οἴει γάρ τινα συγχωρήσεσθαι, θέμενον ἡδονὴν εἶναι τἀγαθόν,

¹ οὐχ Badham: μὴ οὐχ BT.

208

PRO. No, Socrates, for though they spring from opposite sources, they are not in themselves opposed to one another; for how can pleasure help being of all things most like pleasure, that is, like itself?

SOC. Yes, my friend, and colour is like colour; in so far as every one of them is a colour they will all be the same, yet we all recognize that black is not only different from white, but is its exact opposite. And so, too, figure is like figure; they are all one in kind; but the parts of the kind are in some instances absolutely opposed to each other, and in other cases there is endless variety of difference; and we can find many other examples of such relations. Do not, therefore, rely upon this argument, which makes all the most absolute opposites identical. I am afraid we shall find some pleasures the opposites of other pleasures.

PRO. Perhaps; but why will that injure my contention?

SOC. Because I shall say that, although they are unlike, you apply to them a different designation. For you say that all pleasant things are good. Now no argument contends that pleasant things are not pleasant; but whereas most of them are bad and only some are good, as we assert, nevertheless you call them all good, though you confess, if forced to it by argument, that they are unlike. Now what is the identical element which exists in the good and bad pleasures alike and makes you call them all a good?

PRO. What do you mean, Socrates? Do you suppose anyone who asserts that the good is pleasure

εἶτα ἀνέξεσθαί σου λέγοντος τὰς μὲν εἶναί τινας
C ἀγαθὰς ἡδονάς, τὰς δέ τινας ἑτέρας αὐτῶν κακάς;

ΣΩ. Ἀλλ' οὖν ἀνομοίους γε φήσεις αὐτὰς ἀλλήλαις εἶναι καί τινας ἐναντίας.

ΠΡΩ. Οὔτι καθ' ὅσον γε ἡδοναί.

ΣΩ. Πάλιν εἰς τὸν αὐτὸν φερόμεθα λόγον, ὦ
Πρώταρχε, οὐδ' ἄρα ἡδονὴν ἡδονῆς διάφορον,
ἀλλὰ πάσας ὁμοίας εἶναι φήσομεν, καὶ τὰ παρα-
δείγματα ἡμᾶς τὰ νῦν δὴ λεχθέντα οὐδὲν τιτρώσκει,
πεισόμεθα[1] δὲ καὶ ἐροῦμεν ἅπερ οἱ πάντων φαυ-
D λότατοί τε καὶ περὶ λόγους ἅμα νέοι.

ΠΡΩ. Τὰ ποῖα δὴ λέγεις;

ΣΩ. Ὅτι σὲ μιμούμενος ἐγὼ καὶ ἀμυνόμενος
ἐὰν τολμῶ λέγειν ὡς τὸ ἀνομοιότατόν ἐστι τῷ
ἀνομοιοτάτῳ πάντων ὁμοιότατον, ἕξω τὰ αὐτὰ
σοὶ λέγειν, καὶ φανούμεθά γε νεώτεροι τοῦ δέοντος,
καὶ ὁ λόγος ἡμῖν ἐκπεσὼν οἰχήσεται. πάλιν οὖν
αὐτὸν ἀνακρουώμεθα, καὶ τάχ' ἂν ἰόντες[2] εἰς τὰς
ὁμοίας ἴσως ἄν πως ἀλλήλοις συγχωρήσαιμεν.

E   ΠΡΩ. Λέγε πῶς;

4. ΣΩ. Ἐμὲ θὲς ὑπὸ σοῦ πάλιν ἐρωτώμενον,
ὦ Πρώταρχε.

ΠΡΩ. Τὸ ποῖον δή;

ΣΩ. Φρόνησίς τε καὶ ἐπιστήμη καὶ νοῦς καὶ
πάνθ' ὁπόσα δὴ κατ' ἀρχὰς ἐγὼ θέμενος εἶπον
ἀγαθά, διερωτώμενος ὅ τι ποτ' ἐστὶν ἀγαθόν,
ἆρ' οὐ ταὐτὸν πείσονται τοῦτο ὅπερ ὁ σὸς λόγος;

ΠΡΩ. Πῶς;

ΣΩ. Πολλαί τε αἱ ξυνάπασαι ἐπιστῆμαι δόξουσιν
εἶναι καὶ ἀνόμοιοί τινες αὐτῶν ἀλλήλαις· εἰ δὲ
14 καὶ ἐναντίαι πῃ γίγνονταί τινες, ἆρα ἄξιος ἂν

---

[1] πεισόμεθα Badham: πειρόμεθα B: πειρασόμεθα T.

will concede, or will endure to hear you say, that some pleasures are good and others bad?

soc. But you will concede that they are unlike and in some instances opposed to each other.

pro. Not in so far as they are pleasures.

soc. Here we are again at the same old argument, Protarchus, and we shall presently assert that one pleasure is not different from another, but all pleasures are alike, and the examples just cited do not affect us at all, but we shall behave and talk just like the most worthless and inexperienced reasoners.

pro. In what way do you mean?

soc Why, if I have the face to imitate you and to defend myself by saying that the utterly unlike is most completely like that which is most utterly unlike it, I can say the same things you said, and we shall prove ourselves to be excessively inexperienced, and our argument will be shipwrecked and lost. Let us, then, back her out, and perhaps if we start fair again we may come to an agreement.

pro. How? Tell me.

soc. Assume, Protarchus, that I am questioned in turn by you.

pro. What question do I ask?

soc. Whether wisdom and knowledge and intellect and all the things which I said at first were good, when you asked me what is good, will not have the same fate as this argument of yours.

pro. How is that?

soc. It will appear that the forms of knowledge collectively are many and some of them are unlike each other; but if some of them turn out to be actually opposites, should I be fit to engage in

---

² ἂν ἰόντες Ven. 189: ἀνιόντες BT.

εἴην τοῦ διαλέγεσθαι νῦν, εἰ φοβηθεὶς τοῦτο
αὐτὸ μηδεμίαν ἀνόμοιον φαίην ἐπιστήμην ἐπιστήμῃ γίγνεσθαι, κἄπειθ' ἡμῖν οὕτως ὁ λόγος
ὥσπερ μῦθος ἀπολόμενος οἴχοιτο, αὐτοὶ δὲ σῳζοί-
μεθα ἐπί τινος ἀλογίας;

ΠΡΩ. Ἀλλ' οὐ μὴν δεῖ τοῦτο γενέσθαι, πλὴν
τοῦ σωθῆναι. τό γε μὴν μοι ἴσον τοῦ σοῦ τε
καὶ ἐμοῦ λόγου ἀρέσκει· πολλαὶ μὲν ἡδοναὶ καὶ
ἀνόμοιοι γιγνέσθων,[1] πολλαὶ δὲ ἐπιστῆμαι καὶ
διάφοροι.

B   ΣΩ. Τὴν τοίνυν διαφορότητα, ὦ Πρώταρχε,
τοῦ ἀγαθοῦ τοῦ τ' ἐμοῦ καὶ τοῦ σοῦ μὴ ἀπο-
κρυπτόμενοι, κατατιθέντες δὲ εἰς τὸ μέσον, τολ-
μῶμεν, ἄν πη ἐλεγχόμενοι μηνύσωσι, πότερον
ἡδονὴν τἀγαθὸν δεῖ λέγειν ἢ φρόνησιν ἤ τι τρίτον
ἄλλο εἶναι. νῦν γὰρ οὐ δήπου πρός γε αὐτὸ
τοῦτο[2] φιλονεικοῦμεν, ὅπως ἁγὼ[3] τίθεμαι, ταῦτ'
ἔσται τὰ νικῶντα, ἢ ταῦθ' ἃ σύ, τῷ δ' ἀληθεστάτῳ
δεῖ που συμμαχεῖν ἡμᾶς ἄμφω.

ΠΡΩ. Δεῖ γὰρ οὖν.

5. ΣΩ. Τοῦτον τοίνυν τὸν λόγον ἔτι μᾶλλον
C δι' ὁμολογίας βεβαιωσώμεθα.

ΠΡΩ. Τὸν ποῖον δή;

ΣΩ. Τὸν πᾶσι παρέχοντα ἀνθρώποις πράγματα
ἑκούσί τε καὶ ἄκουσιν ἐνίοις καὶ ἐνίοτε.

ΠΡΩ. Λέγε σαφέστερον.

ΣΩ. Τὸν νῦν δὴ παραπεσόντα λέγω, φύσει πως
πεφυκότα θαυμαστόν. ἐν γὰρ δὴ τὰ πολλὰ
εἶναι καὶ τὸ ἓν πολλὰ θαυμαστὸν λεχθέν, καὶ
ῥᾴδιον ἀμφισβητῆσαι τῷ τούτων ὁποτερονοῦν
τιθεμένῳ.

----

[1] γιγνέσθων] γίγνεσθον BT.

dialectics now if, through fear of just that, I should say that no form of knowledge is unlike any other, and then, as a consequence, our argument should vanish and be lost, like a tale that is told, and we ourselves should be saved by clinging to some irrational notion ?

PRO. No, that must never be, except the part about our being saved. However, I like the equal treatment of your doctrine and mine. Let us grant that pleasures are many and unlike and that the forms of knowledge are many and different.

SOC. With no concealment, then, Protarchus, of the difference between my good and yours, but with fair and open acknowledgement of it, let us be bold and see if perchance on examination they will tell us whether we should say that pleasure is the good, or wisdom, or some other third principle. For surely the object of our present controversy is not to gain the victory for my assertions or yours, but both of us must fight for the most perfect truth.

PRO. Yes, we must.

SOC. Then let us establish this principle still more firmly by means of an agreement.

PRO. What principle ?

SOC. The principle which gives trouble to all men, to some of them sometimes against their will.

PRO. Speak more plainly.

SOC. I mean the principle which came in our way just now ; its nature is quite marvellous. For the assertions that one is many and many are one are marvellous, and it is easy to dispute with anyone who makes either of them.

---

² τοῦτο corr. Coisl.: τοῦτο δ BT.
³ ἀγὼ] ἄγω B: ἀ 'γὼ T.

ΠΡΩ. Ἀρ᾽ οὖν λέγεις, ὅταν τις ἐμὲ φῇ Πρώτ-
D αρχον ἕνα γεγονότα φύσει πολλοὺς εἶναι πάλιν
τοὺς ἐμὲ καὶ ἐναντίους ἀλλήλοις, μέγαν καὶ σμικρὸν τιθέμενος καὶ βαρὺν καὶ κοῦφον τὸν αὐτὸν
καὶ ἄλλα μυρία;

ΣΩ. Σὺ μέν, ὦ Πρώταρχε, εἴρηκας τὰ δε-
δημευμένα τῶν θαυμαστῶν περὶ τὸ ἓν καὶ πολλά,
συγκεχωρημένα δὲ ὡς ἔπος εἰπεῖν ὑπὸ πάντων
ἤδη μὴ δεῖν τῶν τοιούτων ἅπτεσθαι, παιδαριώδη
καὶ ῥᾴδια καὶ σφόδρα τοῖς λόγοις ἐμπόδια ὑπο-
λαμβανόντων γίγνεσθαι, ἐπεὶ μηδὲ τὰ τοιάδε,
E ὅταν τις ἑκάστου τὰ μέλη τε καὶ ἅμα μέρη διελὼν
τῷ λόγῳ, πάντα ταῦτα τὸ ἓν ἐκεῖνο εἶναι δι-
ομολογησάμενος, ἐλέγχῃ καταγελῶν ὅτι τέρατα
διηνάγκασται φάναι, τό τε ἓν ὡς πολλά ἐστι
καὶ ἄπειρα, καὶ τὰ πολλὰ ὡς ἓν μόνον.

ΠΡΩ. Σὺ δὲ δὴ ποῖα, ὦ Σώκρατες, ἕτερα λέγεις,
ἃ μήπω συγκεχωρημένα δεδήμευται περὶ τὸν
αὐτὸν τοῦτον λόγον;

15 ΣΩ. Ὁπόταν, ὦ παῖ, τὸ ἓν μὴ τῶν γιγνομένων
τε καὶ ἀπολλυμένων τις τιθῆται, καθάπερ ἀρτίως
ἡμεῖς εἴπομεν. ἐνταυθοῖ μὲν γὰρ καὶ τὸ τοιοῦτον
ἕν, ὅπερ εἴπομεν νῦν δή, συγκεχώρηται τὸ μὴ
δεῖν ἐλέγχειν· ὅταν δέ τις ἕνα ἄνθρωπον ἐπιχειρῇ
τίθεσθαι καὶ βοῦν ἕνα καὶ τὸ καλὸν ἓν καὶ τὸ
ἀγαθὸν ἕν, περὶ τούτων τῶν ἑνάδων καὶ τῶν
τοιούτων ἡ πολλὴ σπουδὴ μετὰ διαιρέσεως ἀμφι-
σβήτησις γίγνεται.

ΠΡΩ. Πῶς;

B ΣΩ. Πρῶτον μὲν εἴ τινας δεῖ τοιαύτας εἶναι
μονάδας ὑπολαμβάνειν ἀληθῶς οὔσας· εἶτα πῶς
αὖ ταύτας, μίαν ἑκάστην οὖσαν ἀεὶ τὴν αὐτὴν

PRO. You mean when a person says that I, Protarchus, am by nature one and that there are also many of me which are opposites of each other, asserting that I, the same Protarchus, am great and small and heavy and light and countless other things?

SOC. Those wonders concerning the one and the many which you have mentioned, Protarchus, are common property, and almost everybody is agreed that they ought to be disregarded because they are childish and easy and great hindrances to speculation; and this sort of thing also should be disregarded, when a man in his discussion divides the members and likewise the parts of anything, acknowledges that they all collectively are that one thing, and then mockingly refutes himself because he has been compelled to declare miracles—that the one is many and infinite and the many only one.

PRO. But what other wonders do you mean, Socrates, in relation to this same principle, which are not yet common property and generally acknowledged?

SOC. I mean, my boy, when a person postulates unity which is not the unity of one of the things which come into being and perish, as in the examples we had just now. For in cases of a unity of that sort, as I just said, it is agreed that refutation is needless. But when the assertion is made that man is one, or ox is one, or beauty is one, or the good is one, the intense interest in these and similar unities becomes disagreement and controversy.

PRO. How is that?

SOC. The first question is whether we should believe that such unities really exist; the second, how these unities, each of which is one, always the same,

καὶ μήτε γένεσιν μήτε ὄλεθρον προσδεχομένην,
ὅμως εἶναι βεβαιότατα μίαν ταύτην· μετὰ δὲ
τοῦτ' ἐν τοῖς γιγνομένοις αὖ καὶ ἀπείροις εἴτε
διεσπασμένην καὶ πολλὰ γεγονυῖαν θετέον, εἴθ'
ὅλην αὐτὴν αὑτῆς χωρίς, ὃ δὴ πάντων ἀδυνα-
τώτατον φαίνοιτ' ἄν, ταὐτὸν καὶ ἓν ἅμα ἐν ἑνί
τε καὶ πολλοῖς γίγνεσθαι. ταῦτ' ἔστι τὰ περὶ
C τὰ τοιαῦτα ἓν καὶ πολλά, ἀλλ' οὐκ ἐκεῖνα, ὦ
Πρώταρχε, ἁπάσης ἀπορίας αἴτια μὴ καλῶς
ὁμολογηθέντα καὶ εὐπορίας αὖ¹ καλῶς.

ΠΡΩ. Οὐκοῦν χρὴ τοῦθ' ἡμᾶς, ὦ Σώκρατες,
ἐν τῷ νῦν πρῶτον διαπονήσασθαι;

ΣΩ. Ὡς γοῦν ἐγὼ φαίην ἄν.

ΠΡΩ. Καὶ πάντας τοίνυν ἡμᾶς ὑπόλαβε συγχω-
ρεῖν σοι τούσδε τὰ τοιαῦτα· Φίληβον δ' ἴσως
κράτιστον ἐν τῷ νῦν ἐπερωτῶντα μὴ κινεῖν εὖ
κείμενον.

D 6. ΣΩ. Εἶεν· πόθεν οὖν τις ταύτης ἄρξηται
πολλῆς οὔσης καὶ παντοίας περὶ τὰ ἀμφισβη-
τούμενα μάχης; ἆρ' ἐνθένδε;

ΠΡΩ. Πόθεν;²

ΣΩ. Φαμέν που ταὐτὸν ἓν καὶ πολλὰ ὑπὸ λόγων
γιγνόμενα περιτρέχειν πάντῃ καθ' ἕκαστον τῶν
λεγομένων ἀεὶ καὶ πάλαι καὶ νῦν. καὶ τοῦτο
οὔτε μὴ παύσηταί ποτε οὔτε ἤρξατο νῦν, ἀλλ'
ἔστι τὸ τοιοῦτον, ὡς ἐμοὶ φαίνεται, τῶν λόγων
αὐτῶν ἀθάνατόν τι καὶ ἀγήρων πάθος ἐν ἡμῖν·
ὁ δὲ πρῶτον αὐτοῦ γευσάμενος ἑκάστοτε τῶν
E νέων, ἡσθεὶς ὥς τινα σοφίας εὑρηκὼς θησαυρόν,
ὑφ' ἡδονῆς ἐνθουσιᾷ τε καὶ πάντα κινεῖ λόγον

---

¹ ἂν αὖ ΒΤ: ἂν bracketed by Badham.
² ἐνθένδε πόθεν assigned to Socrates ΒΤ.

and admitting neither generation nor destruction, can nevertheless be permanently this one unity; and the third, how in the infinite number of things which come into being this unity, whether we are to assume that it is dispersed and has become many, or that it is entirely separated from itself—which would seem to be the most impossible notion of all—being the same and one, is to be at the same time in one and in many. These are the questions, Protarchus, about this kind of one and many, not those others, which cause the utmost perplexity, if ill solved, and are, if well solved, of the greatest assistance.

PRO. Then is it now, Socrates, our first duty to thresh this matter out?

SOC. Yes, that is what I should say.

PRO. You may assume, then, that we are all willing to agree with you about that; and perhaps it is best not to ask Philebus any questions; let sleeping dogs lie.

SOC. Very well; then where shall we begin this great and vastly complicated battle about the matters at issue? Shall we start at this point?

PRO. At what point?

SOC. We say that one and many are identified by reason, and always, both now and in the past, circulate everywhere in every thought that is uttered. This is no new thing and will never cease; it is, in my opinion, a quality within us which will never die or grow old, and which belongs to reason itself as such. And any young man, when he first has an inkling of this, is delighted, thinking he has found a treasure of wisdom; his joy fills him with enthusiasm; he joyously sets every possible argument in motion, some-

ἄσμενος, τοτὲ μὲν ἐπὶ θάτερα κυκλῶν καὶ συμφύρων
εἰς ἕν, τοτὲ δὲ πάλιν ἀνειλίττων καὶ διαμερίζων,
εἰς ἀπορίαν αὑτὸν μὲν πρῶτον καὶ μάλιστα κατα-
βάλλων, δεύτερον δ᾽ ἀεὶ τὸν ἐχόμενον, ἄντε νεώ-
τερος ἄντε πρεσβύτερος ἄντε ἧλιξ ὢν τυγχάνῃ,
16 φειδόμενος οὔτε πατρὸς οὔτε μητρὸς οὔτε ἄλλου
τῶν ἀκουόντων οὐδενός, ὀλίγου δὲ καὶ τῶν ἄλλων
ζῴων, οὐ μόνον τῶν ἀνθρώπων, ἐπεὶ βαρβάρων
γε οὐδενὸς ἂν φείσαιτο, εἴπερ μόνον ἑρμηνέα
ποθὲν ἔχοι.

ΠΡΩ. Ἆρ᾽, ὦ Σώκρατες, οὐχ ὁρᾷς ἡμῶν τὸ
πλῆθος, ὅτι νέοι πάντες ἐσμέν, καὶ οὐ φοβεῖ μή
σοι μετὰ Φιλήβου ξυνεπιθώμεθα, ἐὰν ἡμᾶς λοι-
δορῇς; ὅμως δέ—μανθάνομεν γὰρ ὃ λέγεις—εἴ
τις τρόπος ἔστι καὶ μηχανὴ τὴν μὲν τοιαύτην
ταραχὴν ἡμῖν ἔξω τοῦ λόγου εὐμενῶς πως ἀπ-
B ελθεῖν, ὁδὸν δέ τινα καλλίω ταύτης ἐπὶ τὸν λόγον
ἀνευρεῖν, σύ τε προθυμοῦ τοῦτο καὶ ἡμεῖς συν-
ακολουθήσομεν εἰς δύναμιν· οὐ γὰρ σμικρὸς ὁ
παρὼν λόγος, ὦ Σώκρατες.

ΣΩ. Οὐ γὰρ οὖν, ὦ παῖδες, ὥς φησιν ὑμᾶς
προσαγορεύων Φίληβος. οὐ μὴν ἔστι καλλίων
ὁδὸς οὐδ᾽ ἂν γένοιτο, ἧς ἐγὼ ἐραστὴς μέν εἰμι
ἀεί, πολλάκις δέ με ἤδη διαφυγοῦσα ἔρημον καὶ
ἄπορον κατέστησεν.

ΠΡΩ. Τίς αὕτη; λεγέσθω μόνον.

C ΣΩ. Ἣν δηλῶσαι μὲν οὐ πάνυ χαλεπόν, χρῆ-
σθαι δὲ παγχάλεπον· πάντα γὰρ ὅσα τέχνης
ἐχόμενα ἀνηυρέθη[1] πώποτε, διὰ ταύτης φανερὰ
γέγονε. σκόπει δὲ ἣν λέγω.

ΠΡΩ. Λέγε μόνον.

ΣΩ. Θεῶν μὲν εἰς ἀνθρώπους δόσις, ὥς γε

218

times in one direction, rolling things up and kneading them into one, and sometimes again unrolling and dividing them ; he gets himself into a muddle first and foremost, then anyone who happens to be near him, whether he be younger or older or of his own age ; he spares neither father nor mother nor any other human being who can hear, and hardly even the lower animals, for he would certainly not spare a foreigner,[1] if he could get an interpreter anywhere.

PRO. Socrates, do you not see how many we are and that we are all young men ? Are you not afraid that we shall join with Philebus and attack you, if you revile us ? However—for we understand your meaning—if there is any way or means of removing this confusion gently from our discussion and finding some better road than this to bring us towards the goal of our argument, kindly lead on, and we will do our best to follow ; for our present discussion, Socrates, is no trifling matter.

SOC. No, it is not, boys, as Philebus calls you ; and there certainly is no better road, nor can there ever be, than that which I have always loved, though it has often deserted me, leaving me lonely and forlorn.

PRO. What is the road ? Only tell us.

SOC. One which is easy to point out, but very difficult to follow ; for through it all the inventions of art have been brought to light. See ; this is the road I mean.

PRO. Go on ; what is it ?

SOC. A gift of gods to men, as I believe, was

[1] Apparently foreigners are considered among the lower animals.

---

[1] ἀνηυρέθη] ἀνευρεθῆ B: ἂν εὑρεθῆ T.

καταφαίνεται ἐμοί, ποθὲν ἐκ θεῶν ἐρρίφη διά τινος
Προμηθέως ἅμα φανοτάτῳ τινὶ πυρί· καὶ οἱ μὲν
παλαιοί, κρείττονες ἡμῶν καὶ ἐγγυτέρω θεῶν
οἰκοῦντες, ταύτην φήμην παρέδοσαν, ὡς ἐξ ἑνὸς
μὲν καὶ[1] πολλῶν ὄντων τῶν ἀεὶ λεγομένων
εἶναι, πέρας δὲ καὶ ἀπειρίαν ἐν αὑτοῖς ξύμφυτον
ἐχόντων. δεῖν οὖν ἡμᾶς τούτων οὕτω διακε-
D κοσμημένων ἀεὶ μίαν ἰδέαν περὶ παντὸς ἑκάστοτε
θεμένους ζητεῖν—εὑρήσειν γὰρ ἐνοῦσαν—ἐὰν οὖν
μεταλάβωμεν, μετὰ μίαν δύο, εἴ πως εἰσί, σκοπεῖν, εἰ δὲ μή, τρεῖς ἤ τινα ἄλλον ἀριθμόν, καὶ
τῶν ἓν ἐκείνων ἕκαστον πάλιν ὡσαύτως, μέχριπερ
ἂν τὸ κατ' ἀρχὰς ἓν μὴ ὅτι ἓν καὶ πολλὰ καὶ
ἄπειρά ἐστι μόνον ἴδῃ τις, ἀλλὰ καὶ ὁπόσα· τὴν
δὲ τοῦ ἀπείρου ἰδέαν πρὸς τὸ πλῆθος μὴ προσ-
φέρειν πρὶν ἄν τις τὸν ἀριθμὸν αὐτοῦ πάντα κατίδῃ
E τὸν μεταξὺ τοῦ ἀπείρου τε καὶ τοῦ ἑνός· τότε δ'
ἤδη τὸ ἓν ἕκαστον τῶν πάντων εἰς τὸ ἄπειρον
μεθέντα χαίρειν ἐᾶν. οἱ μὲν οὖν θεοί, ὅπερ εἶπον,
οὕτως ἡμῖν παρέδοσαν σκοπεῖν καὶ μανθάνειν
καὶ διδάσκειν ἀλλήλους· οἱ δὲ νῦν τῶν ἀνθρώπων
17 σοφοὶ ἓν μέν, ὅπως ἂν τύχωσι, καὶ πολλὰ θᾶττον
καὶ βραδύτερον ποιοῦσι τοῦ δέοντος, μετὰ δὲ τὸ
ἓν ἄπειρα εὐθύς· τὰ δὲ μέσα αὐτοὺς ἐκφεύγει,
οἷς διακεχώρισται τό τε διαλεκτικῶς πάλιν καὶ
τὸ ἐριστικῶς ἡμᾶς ποιεῖσθαι πρὸς ἀλλήλους τοὺς
λόγους.

7. ΠΡΩ. Τὰ μέν πως, ὦ Σώκρατες, δοκῶ σου
μανθάνειν, τὰ δὲ ἔτι σαφέστερον δέομαι ἃ λέγεις
ἀκοῦσαι.

ΣΩ. Σαφὲς μήν, ὦ Πρώταρχε, ἐστὶν ἐν τοῖς

―――――
[1] καὶ T: καὶ ἐκ B.

tossed down from some divine source through the agency of a Prometheus together with a gleaming fire ; and the ancients, who were better than we and lived nearer the gods, handed down the tradition that all the things which are ever said to exist are sprung from one and many and have inherent in them the finite and the infinite. This being the way in which these things are arranged, we must always assume that there is in every case one idea of everything and must look for it—for we shall find that it is there—and if we get a grasp of this, we must look next for two, if there be two, and if not, for three or some other number ; and again we must treat each of those units in the same way, until we can see not only that the original unit is one and many and infinite, but just how many it is. And we must not apply the idea of infinite to plurality until we have a view of its whole number between infinity and one ; then, and not before, we may let each unit of everything pass on unhindered into infinity. The gods, then, as I said, handed down to us this mode of investigating, learning, and teaching one another ; but the wise men of the present day make the one and the many too quickly or too slowly, in haphazard fashion, and they put infinity immediately after unity ; they disregard all that lies between them, and this it is which distinguishes between the dialectic and the disputatious methods of discussion.

PRO. I think I understand you in part, Socrates, but I need a clearer statement of some things.

SOC. Surely my meaning, Protarchus, is made clear

γράμμασιν ὃ λέγω, καὶ λάμβανε αὐτὸ ἐν τούτοις
B οἷσπερ καὶ πεπαίδευσαι.

ΠΡΩ. Πῶς;

ΣΩ. Φωνὴ μὲν ἡμῖν ἐστί που μία διὰ τοῦ στό-
ματος ἰοῦσα, καὶ ἄπειρος αὖ πλήθει, πάντων τε καὶ
ἑκάστου.

ΠΡΩ. Τί μήν;

ΣΩ. Καὶ οὐδὲν ἑτέρῳ γε τούτων ἐσμέν πω
σοφοί, οὔτε ὅτι τὸ ἄπειρον αὐτῆς ἴσμεν οὔθ' ὅτι
τὸ ἕν· ἀλλ' ὅτι πόσα τ' ἐστὶ καὶ ὁποῖα, τοῦτό ἐστι
τὸ γραμματικὸν ἕκαστον ποιοῦν ἡμῶν.

ΠΡΩ. Ἀληθέστατα.

ΣΩ. Καὶ μὴν καὶ τὸ μουσικὸν ὃ τυγχάνει ποιοῦν,
τοῦτ' ἔστι ταὐτόν.

ΠΡΩ. Πῶς;

C ΣΩ. Φωνὴ μέν που καὶ τὸ κατ' ἐκείνην τὴν
τέχνην ἐστὶ μία ἐν αὐτῇ.

ΠΡΩ. Πῶς δ' οὔ;

ΣΩ. Δύο δὲ θῶμεν βαρὺ καὶ ὀξύ, καὶ τρίτον
ὁμότονον. ἢ πῶς;

ΠΡΩ. Οὕτως.

ΣΩ. Ἀλλ' οὔπω σοφὸς ἂν εἴης τὴν μουσικὴν
εἰδὼς ταῦτα μόνα, μὴ δὲ εἰδὼς ὥς γ' ἔπος εἰπεῖν
εἰς ταῦτα οὐδενὸς ἄξιος ἔσει.

ΠΡΩ. Οὐ γὰρ οὖν.

ΣΩ. Ἀλλ', ὦ φίλε, ἐπειδὰν λάβῃς τὰ διαστήματα
ὁπόσα ἐστὶ τὸν ἀριθμὸν τῆς φωνῆς ὀξύτητός τε
πέρι καὶ βαρύτητος, καὶ ὁποῖα, καὶ τοὺς ὅρους
D τῶν διαστημάτων, καὶ τὰ ἐκ τούτων ὅσα συ-
στήματα γέγονεν, ἃ κατιδόντες οἱ πρόσθεν παρέδοσαν ἡμῖν τοῖς ἑπομένοις ἐκείνοις καλεῖν αὐτὰ

in the letters of the alphabet, which you were taught as a child; so learn it from them.

PRO. How?

SOC. Sound, which passes out through the mouth of each and all of us, is one, and yet again it is infinite in number.

PRO. Yes, to be sure.

SOC. And one of us is no wiser than the other merely for knowing that it is infinite or that it is one; but that which makes each of us a grammarian is the knowledge of the number and nature of sounds.

PRO. Very true.

SOC. And it is this same knowledge which makes the musician.

PRO. How is that?

SOC. Sound is one in the art of music also, so far as that art is concerned.

PRO. Of course.

SOC. And we may say that there are two sounds, low and high, and a third, which is the intermediate, may we not?

PRO. Yes.

SOC. But knowledge of these facts would not suffice to make you a musician, although ignorance of them would make you, if I may say so, quite worthless in respect to music.

PRO. Certainly.

SOC. But, my friend, when you have grasped the number and quality of the intervals of the voice in respect to high and low pitch, and the limits of the intervals, and all the combinations derived from them, which the men of former times discovered and handed down to us, their successors, with the traditional

PLATO

ἁρμονίας, ἔν τε ταῖς κινήσεσιν αὖ τοῦ σώματος
ἕτερα τοιαῦτα ἐνόντα πάθη γιγνόμενα, ἃ δὴ δι'
ἀριθμῶν μετρηθέντα δεῖν αὖ φασὶ ῥυθμοὺς καὶ
μέτρα ἐπονομάζειν, καὶ ἅμα ἐννοεῖν ὡς οὕτω
δεῖ περὶ παντὸς ἑνὸς καὶ πολλῶν σκοπεῖν· ὅταν
γὰρ αὐτά¹ τε λάβῃς οὕτω, τότε ἐγένου σοφός,
E ὅταν τε ἄλλο τῶν ὄντων ἕν² ὁτιοῦν ταύτῃ σκοπού-
μενος ἕλῃς, οὕτως ἔμφρων περὶ τοῦτο γέγονας·
τὸ δ' ἄπειρόν σε ἑκάστων καὶ ἐν ἑκάστοις πλῆθος
ἄπειρον ἑκάστοτε ποιεῖ τοῦ φρονεῖν καὶ οὐκ
ἐλλόγιμον οὐδ' ἐνάριθμον, ἅτ' οὐκ εἰς ἀριθμὸν
οὐδένα ἐν οὐδενὶ πώποτε ἀπιδόντα.

8. πρω. Κάλλιστα, ὦ Φίληβε, ἔμοιγε τὰ νῦν
λεγόμενα εἰρηκέναι φαίνεται Σωκράτης.

Φι. Καὶ ἐμοὶ ταῦτά γε αὐτά· ἀλλὰ τί δή ποτε
18 πρὸς ἡμᾶς ὁ λόγος οὗτος νῦν εἴρηται καὶ τί ποτε
βουλόμενος;

Σω. Ὀρθῶς μέντοι ταῦθ' ἡμᾶς, ὦ Πρώταρχε,
ἠρώτηκε Φίληβος.

πρω. Πάνυ μὲν οὖν, καὶ ἀποκρίνου γε αὐτῷ.

Σω. Δράσω ταῦτα διελθὼν σμικρὸν ἔτι περὶ
αὐτῶν τούτων. ὥσπερ γὰρ ἓν ὁτιοῦν εἴ τίς
ποτε λάβοι, τοῦτον, ὥς φαμεν, οὐκ ἐπ' ἀπείρου
φύσιν δεῖ βλέπειν εὐθὺς ἀλλ' ἐπί τινα ἀριθμόν,
οὕτω καὶ τὸ ἐναντίον ὅταν τις τὸ ἄπειρον ἀναγκα-
B ζῇ πρῶτον λαμβάνειν, μὴ ἐπὶ τὸ ἓν εὐθὺς ἀλλ'³
ἀριθμὸν αὖ τινὰ πλῆθος ἕκαστον ἔχοντά τι κατα-
νοεῖν, τελευτᾶν τε ἐκ πάντων εἰς ἕν. πάλιν δὲ ἐν
τοῖς γράμμασι τὸ νῦν λεγόμενον λάβωμεν.

---

¹ αὐτά TG: ταῦτά BT.
² ὄντων ἕν Wohlrab: ἓν B: ὄντων T.
³ ἀλλ' Liebhold: ἀλλ' ἐπ' BT.

224

name of harmonies, and also the corresponding effects in the movements of the body, which they say are measured by numbers and must be called rhythms and measures—and they say that we must also understand that every one and many should be considered in this way—when you have thus grasped the facts, you have become a musician, and when by considering it in this way you have obtained a grasp of any other unity of all those which exist, you have become wise in respect to that unity. But the infinite number of individuals and the infinite number in each of them makes you in every instance indefinite in thought and of no account and not to be considered among the wise, so long as you have never fixed your eye upon any definite number in anything.

PRO. I think, Philebus, that what Socrates has said is excellent.

PHI. So do I; it is excellent in itself, but why has he said it now to us, and what purpose is there in it?

SOC. Protarchus, that is a very proper question which Philebus has asked us.

PRO. Certainly it is, so please answer it.

SOC. I will, when I have said a little more on just this subject. For if a person begins with some unity or other, he must, as I was saying, not turn immediately to infinity, but to some definite number; now just so, conversely, when he has to take the infinite first, he must not turn immediately to the one, but must think of some number which possesses in each case some plurality, and must end by passing from all to one. Let us revert to the letters of the alphabet to illustrate this.

225

ΠΡΩ. Πῶς;

ΣΩ. Ἐπειδὴ φωνὴν ἄπειρον κατενόησεν εἴτε
τις θεὸς εἴτε καὶ θεῖος ἄνθρωπος, ὡς λόγος ἐν
Αἰγύπτῳ Θεύθ τινα τοῦτον γενέσθαι λέγων, ὃς
πρῶτος τὰ φωνήεντα ἐν τῷ ἀπείρῳ κατενόησεν
οὐχ ἓν ὄντα ἀλλὰ πλείω, καὶ πάλιν ἕτερα φωνῆς
C μὲν οὔ, φθόγγου δὲ μετέχοντά τινος, ἀριθμὸν
δέ τινα καὶ τούτων εἶναι· τρίτον δὲ εἶδος γραμμάτων διεστήσατο τὰ νῦν λεγόμενα ἄφωνα ἡμῖν·
τὸ μετὰ τοῦτο διῄρει τά τε ἄφθογγα καὶ ἄφωνα
μέχρι ἑνὸς ἑκάστου, καὶ τὰ φωνήεντα καὶ τὰ
μέσα κατὰ τὸν αὐτὸν τρόπον, ἕως ἀριθμὸν αὐτῶν
λαβὼν ἑνί τε ἑκάστῳ καὶ ξύμπασι στοιχεῖον
ἐπωνόμασε· καθορῶν δὲ ὡς οὐδεὶς ἡμῶν οὐδ᾽ ἂν
ἓν αὐτὸ καθ᾽ αὑτὸ ἄνευ πάντων αὐτῶν μάθοι,
τοῦτον τὸν δεσμὸν αὖ λογισάμενος ὡς ὄντα ἕνα καὶ
D πάντα ταῦτα[1] ἕν πως ποιοῦντα μίαν ἐπ᾽ αὐτοῖς ὡς
οὖσαν γραμματικὴν τέχνην ἐπεφθέγξατο προσειπών.

ΦΙ. Ταῦτ᾽ ἔτι σαφέστερον ἐκείνων αὐτά γε
πρὸς ἄλληλα, ὦ Πρώταρχε, ἔμαθον· τὸ δ᾽ αὐτό
μοι τοῦ λόγου νῦν τε καὶ σμικρὸν ἔμπροσθεν
ἐλλείπεται.

ΣΩ. Μῶν, ὦ Φίληβε, τὸ τί πρὸς ἔπος αὖ ταῦτ᾽
ἐστίν;

ΦΙ. Ναί, τοῦτ᾽ ἔστιν ὃ πάλαι ζητοῦμεν ἐγώ τε
καὶ Πρώταρχος.

ΣΩ. Ἦ μὴν ἐπ᾽ αὐτῷ γε ἤδη γεγονότες ζητεῖτε,
E ὡς φής, πάλαι;

ΦΙ. Πῶς;

9. ΣΩ. Ἆρ᾽ οὐ περὶ φρονήσεως ἦν καὶ ἡδονῆς
ἡμῖν ἐξ ἀρχῆς ὁ λόγος, ὁπότερον αὐτοῖν αἱρετέον;

---

[1] πάντα ταῦτα] πάντα τὰ ταῦτα Β : ταῦτα πάντα Τ.

PRO. How?

SOC. When some one, whether god or godlike man, —there is an Egyptian story that his name was Theuth—observed that sound was infinite, he was the first to notice that the vowel sounds in that infinity were not one, but many, and again that there were other elements which were not vowels but did have a sonant quality, and that these also had a definite number; and he distinguished a third kind of letters which we now call mutes. Then he divided the mutes until he distinguished each individual one, and he treated the vowels and semivowels in the same way, until he knew the number of them and gave to each and all the name of letters. Perceiving, however, that none of us could learn any one of them alone by itself without learning them all, and considering that this was a common bond which made them in a way all one, he assigned to them all a single science and called it grammar.

PHI. I understand that more clearly than the earlier statement, Protarchus, so far as the reciprocal relations of the one and the many are concerned, but I still feel the same lack as a little while ago.

SOC. Do you mean, Philebus, that you do not see what this has to do with the question?

PHI. Yes; that is what Protarchus and I have been trying to discover for a long time.

SOC. Really, have you been trying, as you say, for a long time to discover it, when it was close to you all the while?

PHI. How is that?

SOC. Was not our discussion from the beginning about wisdom and pleasure and which of them is preferable?

ΦΙ. Πῶς γὰρ οὔ;

ΣΩ. Καὶ μὴν ἕν γε ἑκάτερον αὐτοῖν εἶναί φαμεν.

ΦΙ. Πάνυ μὲν οὖν.

ΣΩ. Τοῦτ' αὐτὸ τοίνυν ἡμᾶς ὁ πρόσθεν λόγος ἀπαιτεῖ, πῶς ἔστιν ἓν καὶ πολλὰ αὐτῶν ἑκάτερον, καὶ πῶς μὴ ἄπειρα εὐθύς, ἀλλά τινά ποτε ἀριθμὸν ἑκάτερον ἔμπροσθεν κέκτηται τοῦ ἄπειρα αὐτῶν[1] ἕκαστα γεγονέναι;

19 ΠΡΩ. Οὐκ εἰς φαῦλόν γε ἐρώτημα, ὦ Φίληβε, οὐκ οἶδ' ὅντινα τρόπον κύκλῳ πως περιαγαγὼν ἡμᾶς ἐμβέβληκε Σωκράτης. καὶ σκόπει δή, πότερος ἡμῶν ἀποκρινεῖται τὸ νῦν ἐρωτώμενον. ἴσως δὴ γελοῖον τὸ ἐμὲ τοῦ λόγου διάδοχον παντελῶς ὑποστάντα διὰ τὸ μὴ δύνασθαι τὸ νῦν ἐρωτηθὲν ἀποκρίνασθαι σοὶ πάλιν τοῦτο προστάττειν· γελοιότερον δ' οἶμαι πολὺ τὸ μηδέτερον Β ἡμῶν δύνασθαι. σκόπει δή, τί δράσομεν. εἴδη γάρ μοι δοκεῖ νῦν ἐρωτᾶν ἡδονῆς ἡμᾶς Σωκράτης, εἴτ' ἔστιν εἴτε μή, καὶ ὁπόσα ἐστὶ καὶ ὁποῖα τῆς τ' αὖ φρονήσεως πέρι κατὰ ταὐτὰ ὡσαύτως.

ΣΩ. Ἀληθέστατα λέγεις, ὦ παῖ Καλλίου· μὴ γὰρ δυνάμενοι τοῦτο κατὰ παντὸς ἑνὸς καὶ ὁμοίου καὶ ταὐτοῦ δρᾶν καὶ τοῦ ἐναντίου, ὡς ὁ παρελθὼν λόγος ἐμήνυσεν, οὐδεὶς εἰς οὐδὲν οὐδενὸς ἂν ἡμῶν οὐδέποτε γένοιτο ἄξιος.

C ΠΡΩ. Σχεδὸν ἔοικεν οὕτως, ὦ Σώκρατες, ἔχειν. ἀλλὰ καλὸν μὲν τὸ ξύμπαντα γιγνώσκειν τῷ σώφρονι, δεύτερος δ' εἶναι πλοῦς δοκεῖ μὴ λανθάνειν αὐτὸν αὐτόν. τί δή μοι τοῦτο εἴρηται τὰ νῦν, ἐγώ σοι φράσω. σὺ τήνδε ἡμῖν τὴν συνουσίαν, ὦ Σώκρατες, ἐπέδωκας πᾶσι καὶ σεαυτὸν

---

[1] αὐτὸν T: αὐτὸν B.

PHI. Yes, of course.

soc. And surely we say that each of them is one.

PHI. Certainly.

soc. This, then, is precisely the question which the previous discussion puts to us : How is each of them one and many, and how is it that they are not immediately infinite, but each possesses a definite number, before the individual phenomena become infinite ?

PRO. Philebus, somehow or other Socrates has led us round and plunged us into a serious question. Consider which of us shall answer it. Perhaps it is ridiculous that I, after taking your place in entire charge of the argument, should ask you to come back and answer this question because I cannot do so, but I think it would be still more ridiculous if neither of us could answer. Consider, then, what we are to do. For I think Socrates is asking us whether there are or are not kinds of pleasure, how many kinds there are, and what their nature is, and the same of wisdom.

soc. You are quite right, son of Callias ; for, as our previous discussion showed, unless we can do this in the case of every unity, every like, every same, and their opposites, none of us can ever be of any use in anything.

PRO. That, Socrates, seems pretty likely to be true. However, it is splendid for the wise man to know everything, but the next best thing, it seems, is not to be ignorant of himself. I will tell you why I say that at this moment. You, Socrates, have granted to all of us this conversation and your co-operation

πρὸς τὸ διελέσθαι τί τῶν ἀνθρωπίνων κτημάτων
ἄριστον. Φιλήβου γὰρ εἰπόντος ἡδονὴν καὶ τέρψιν καὶ χαρὰν καὶ πάνθ' ὁπόσα τοιαῦτ' ἐστί, σὺ
πρὸς αὐτὰ ἀντεῖπες ὡς οὐ ταῦτα ἀλλ' ἐκεῖνά
D ἐστιν, ἃ πολλάκις ἡμᾶς αὐτοὺς ἀναμιμνήσκομεν
ἑκόντες, ὀρθῶς δρῶντες, ἵν' ἐν μνήμῃ παρακείμενα
ἑκάτερα βασανίζηται. φῂς δ', ὡς ἔοικε, σὺ
τὸ προσρηθησόμενον ὀρθῶς ἄμεινον ἡδονῆς γε
ἀγαθὸν εἶναι νοῦν, ἐπιστήμην, σύνεσιν, τέχνην
καὶ πάντα αὖ τὰ τούτων ξυγγενῆ, ἃ¹ κτᾶσθαι
δεῖν, ἀλλ' οὐχὶ ἐκεῖνα. τούτων δὴ μετ' ἀμφι-
σβητήσεως ἑκατέρων λεχθέντων ἡμεῖς σοι μετὰ
παιδιᾶς ἠπειλήσαμεν ὡς οὐκ ἀφήσομεν οἴκαδέ σε
E πρὶν ἂν τούτων τῶν λόγων πέρας ἱκανὸν γένηταί
τι διορισθέντων. σὺ δὲ συνεχώρησας καὶ ἔδωκας
εἰς ταῦθ' ἡμῖν σαυτόν, ἡμεῖς δὲ δὴ λέγομεν,
καθάπερ οἱ παῖδες, ὅτι τῶν ὀρθῶς δοθέντων
ἀφαίρεσις οὐκ ἔστι· παῦσαι δὴ τὸν τρόπον ἡμῖν
ἁπάντων τοῦτον ἐπὶ τὰ νῦν λεγόμενα.

ΣΩ. Τίνα λέγεις;

20 ΠΡΩ. Εἰς ἀπορίαν ἐμβάλλων καὶ ἀνερωτῶν ὧν
μὴ δυναίμεθ' ἂν ἱκανὴν ἀπόκρισιν ἐν τῷ παρόντι
διδόναι σοι. μὴ γὰρ οἰώμεθα τέλος ἡμῖν εἶναι
τῶν νῦν τὴν πάντων ἡμῶν ἀπορίαν, ἀλλ' εἰ δρᾶν
τοῦθ' ἡμεῖς ἀδυνατοῦμεν, σοὶ δραστέον· ὑπέσχου
γάρ. βουλεύου δὴ πρὸς ταῦτα αὐτὸς πότερον
ἡδονῆς εἴδη σοι καὶ ἐπιστήμης διαιρετέον ἢ καὶ
ἐατέον, εἴ πῃ καθ' ἕτερόν τινα τρόπον οἷός τ'
εἶ καὶ βούλει δηλῶσαί πως ἄλλως τὰ νῦν ἀμφισβη-
τούμενα παρ' ἡμῖν.

B ΣΩ. Δεινὸν μὲν τοίνυν ἔτι προσδοκᾶν οὐδὲν
δεῖ τὸν² ἐμέ, ἐπειδὴ τοῦθ' οὕτως εἶπες· τὸ γὰρ

for the purpose of determining what is the best of human possessions. For when Philebus said it was pleasure and gaiety and enjoyment and all that sort of thing, you objected and said it was not those things, but another sort, and we very properly keep reminding ourselves voluntarily of this, in order that both claims may be present in our memory for examination. You, as it appears, assert that the good which is rightly to be called better than pleasure is mind, knowledge, intelligence, art, and all their kin; you say we ought to acquire these, not that other sort. When those two claims were made and an argument arose, we playfully threatened that we would not let you go home until the discussion was brought to some satisfactory conclusion. You agreed and put yourself at our disposal for that purpose. Now, we say that, as children put it, you cannot take back a gift once fairly given. So cease this way of meeting all that we say.

soc. What way do you mean?

pro. I mean puzzling us and asking questions to which we cannot at the moment give a satisfactory answer. Let us not imagine that the end of our present discussion is a mere puzzling of us all, but if we cannot answer, you must do so; for you gave us a promise. Consider, therefore, whether you yourself must distinguish the kinds of pleasure and knowledge or will let that go, in case you are able and willing to make clear in some other way the matters now at issue among us.

soc. I need no longer anticipate anything terrible, since you put it in that way; for the words " in

---

[1] ἂ Ven. 189: om. BT.   [2] δεῖ τὸν] δεῖτον BT.

εἰ βούλει ῥηθὲν λύει πάντα φόβον ἑκάστων πέρι. πρὸς δὲ αὖ τούτοις[1] μνήμην τινὰ δοκεῖ τίς μοι δεδωκέναι θεῶν ἡμῖν.

ΠΡΩ. Πῶς δὴ καὶ τίνων;

10. ΣΩ. Λόγων ποτέ τινων πάλαι ἀκούσας ὄναρ ἢ καὶ ἐγρηγορὼς νῦν ἐννοῶ περί τε ἡδονῆς καὶ φρονήσεως, ὡς οὐδέτερον αὐτοῖν ἐστι τἀγαθόν, ἀλλ' ἄλλο τι τρίτον, ἕτερον μὲν τούτων, ἄμεινον C δὲ ἀμφοῖν. καίτοι τοῦτό γε ἂν[2] ἐναργῶς ἡμῖν φανῇ νῦν, ἀπήλλακται μὲν ἡδονὴ τοῦ νικᾶν· τὸ γὰρ ἀγαθὸν οὐκ ἂν ἔτι ταὐτὸν αὐτῇ γίγνοιτο. ἢ πῶς;

ΠΡΩ. Οὕτως.

ΣΩ. Τῶν δέ γε εἰς τὴν διαίρεσιν εἰδῶν ἡδονῆς οὐδὲν ἔτι προσδεησόμεθα κατ' ἐμὴν δόξαν. προϊὸν δ' ἔτι σαφέστερον δείξει.

ΠΡΩ. Κάλλιστ' εἰπὼν οὕτω καὶ διαπέραινε.

ΣΩ. Σμίκρ' ἄττα τοίνυν ἔμπροσθεν ἔτι διομολογησώμεθα.

ΠΡΩ. Τὰ ποῖα;

ΣΩ. Τὴν τἀγαθοῦ μοῖραν πότερον ἀνάγκη τέ-D λεον ἢ μὴ τέλεον εἶναι,

ΠΡΩ. Πάντων δήπου τελεώτατον, ὦ Σώκρατες.

ΣΩ. Τί δέ; ἱκανὸν τἀγαθόν;

ΠΡΩ. Πῶς γὰρ οὔ; καὶ πάντων γε εἰς τοῦτο διαφέρειν τῶν ὄντων.

ΣΩ. Τόδε γε μήν, ὡς οἶμαι, περὶ αὐτοῦ ἀναγκαιότατον εἶναι λέγειν, ὡς πᾶν τὸ γιγνῶσκον αὐτὸ θηρεύει καὶ ἐφίεται βουλόμενον ἑλεῖν καὶ περὶ

---

[1] αὖ τούτοις t: αὖ τοῖς B: αὐτοῖς Τ.
[2] καίτοι τοῦτό γε ἂν Badham: καὶ τοιοῦτό γε ἂν B: καὶ τοι οὕτω γε ἂν in margin B[2]: καίτοι τοῦτο ἐὰν Τ.

case you are willing" relieve me of all fear. And besides, I think some god has given me a vague recollection.

PRO. How is that, and what is the recollection about?

SOC. I remember now having heard long ago in a dream, or perhaps when I was awake, some talk about pleasure and wisdom to the effect that neither of the two is the good, but some third thing, different from them and better than both. However, if this be now clearly proved to us, pleasure is deprived of victory; for the good would no longer be identical with it. Is not that true?

PRO. It is.

SOC. And we shall have, in my opinion, no longer any need of distinguishing the kinds of pleasure. But the progress of the discussion will make that still clearer.

PRO. Excellent! Just go on as you have begun.

SOC. First, then, let us agree on some further small points.

PRO. What are they?

SOC. Is the nature of the good necessarily perfect or imperfect?

PRO. The most perfect of all things, surely, Socrates.

SOC. Well, and is the good sufficient?

PRO. Of course; so that it surpasses all other things in sufficiency.

SOC. And nothing, I should say, is more certain about it than that every intelligent being pursues it, desires it, wishes to catch and get possession of it,

αὐτό[1] κτήσασθαι, καὶ τῶν ἄλλων οὐδὲν φροντίζει πλὴν τῶν ἀποτελουμένων ἅμα ἀγαθοῖς.

ΠΡΩ. Οὐκ ἔστι τούτοις ἀντειπεῖν.

Ε ΣΩ. Σκοπῶμεν δὴ καὶ κρίνωμεν τόν τε ἡδονῆς καὶ τὸν φρονήσεως βίον ἰδόντες χωρίς.

ΠΡΩ. Πῶς εἶπες;

ΣΩ. Μήτε ἐν τῷ τῆς ἡδονῆς ἐνέστω φρόνησις μήτ' ἐν τῷ τῆς φρονήσεως ἡδονή. δεῖ γάρ, εἴπερ πότερον αὐτῶν ἐστὶ τἀγαθόν, μηδὲν μηδενὸς ἔτι προσδεῖσθαι· δεόμενον δ' ἂν φανῇ πότερον,
21 οὐκ ἔστι που τοῦτ' ἔτι τὸ ὄντως ἡμῖν ἀγαθόν.

ΠΡΩ. Πῶς γὰρ ἄν;

ΣΩ. Οὐκοῦν ἐν σοὶ πειρώμεθα βασανίζοντες ταῦτα;

ΠΡΩ. Πάνυ μὲν οὖν.

ΣΩ. Ἀποκρίνου δή.

ΠΡΩ. Λέγε.

ΣΩ. Δέξαι'[2] ἄν, Πρώταρχε, σὺ ζῆν τὸν βίον ἅπαντα ἡδόμενος ἡδονὰς τὰς μεγίστας;

ΠΡΩ. Τί δ' οὔ;

ΣΩ. Ἆρ' οὖν ἔτι τινὸς ἄν σοι προσδεῖν ἡγοῖο, εἰ τοῦτ' ἔχεις παντελῶς;

ΠΡΩ. Οὐδαμῶς.

ΣΩ. Ὅρα δή, τοῦ φρονεῖν καὶ τοῦ νοεῖν καὶ
Β λογίζεσθαι τὰ δέοντα, καὶ ὅσα τούτων ἀδελφά, μῶν μὴ δέοι'[3] ἄν τι;

ΠΡΩ. Καὶ τί; πάντα γὰρ ἔχοιμ' ἄν που τὸ χαίρειν ἔχων.

ΣΩ. Οὐκοῦν οὕτω ζῶν ἀεὶ μὲν διὰ βίου ταῖς μεγίσταις ἡδοναῖς χαίροις ἄν;

---

[1] αὐτὸ] αὐτὸ BT.   [2] δέξαι'] δέξαι BT : δέξαιο vulg.
[3] μὴ δέοι' ἄν Klitsch : μηδὲ ὁρᾶν BT.

and has no interest in anything in which the good is not included.

PRO. There is no denying that.

SOC. Let us, then, look at the life of pleasure and the life of wisdom separately and consider and judge them.

PRO. How do you mean?

SOC. Let there be no wisdom in the life of pleasure and no pleasure in the life of wisdom. For if either of them is the good, it cannot have need of anything else, and if either be found to need anything, we can no longer regard it as our true good.

PRO. No, of course not.

SOC. Shall we then undertake to test them through you?

PRO. By all means.

SOC. Then answer.

PRO. Ask.

SOC. Would you, Protarchus, be willing to live your whole life in the enjoyment of the greatest pleasures?

PRO. Of course I should.

SOC. Would you think you needed anything further, if you were in complete possession of that enjoyment?

PRO. Certainly not.

SOC. But consider whether you would not have some need of wisdom and intelligence and power of calculating your wants and the like.

PRO. Why should I? If I have enjoyment, I have everything.

SOC. Then living thus you would enjoy the greatest pleasures all your life?

ΠΡΩ. Τί δ' οὔ;

ΣΩ. Νοῦν δέ γε καὶ μνήμην καὶ ἐπιστήμην καὶ δόξαν μὴ κεκτημένος ἀληθῆ, πρῶτον μὲν τοῦτο αὐτό, εἰ χαίρεις ἢ μὴ χαίρεις, ἀνάγκη δήπου σε ἀγνοεῖν, κενόν γε ὄντα πάσης φρονήσεως;

ΠΡΩ. Ἀνάγκη.

C ΣΩ. Καὶ μὴν ὡσαύτως μνήμην μὴ κεκτημένον ἀνάγκη δή που μηδ' ὅτι ποτὲ ἔχαιρες μεμνῆσθαι, τῆς τ' ἐν τῷ παραχρῆμα ἡδονῆς προσπιπτούσης μηδ' ἡντινοῦν μνήμην ὑπομένειν· δόξαν δ' αὖ μὴ κεκτημένον ἀληθῆ μὴ δοξάζειν χαίρειν χαίροντα, λογισμοῦ δὲ στερόμενον μηδ' εἰς τὸν ἔπειτα χρόνον ὡς χαιρήσεις δυνατὸν εἶναι λογίζεσθαι, ζῆν δὲ οὐκ ἀνθρώπου βίον, ἀλλά τινος πλεύμονος ἢ τῶν ὅσα θαλάττια μετ' ὀστρεΐνων D ἔμψυχά ἐστι σωμάτων. ἔστι ταῦτα, ἢ παρὰ ταῦτα ἔχομεν ἄλλως πως διανοηθῆναι;

ΠΡΩ. Καὶ πῶς;

ΣΩ. Ἆρ' οὖν αἱρετὸς ἡμῖν βίος ὁ τοιοῦτος;

ΠΡΩ. Εἰς ἀφασίαν παντάπασί με, ὦ Σώκρατες, οὗτος ὁ λόγος ἐμβέβληκε τὰ νῦν.

ΣΩ. Μήπω τοίνυν μαλθακιζώμεθα, τὸν δὲ τοῦ νοῦ μεταλαβόντες αὖ βίον ἴδωμεν.

11. ΠΡΩ. Τὸν[1] ποῖον δὴ λέγεις;

ΣΩ. Εἴ τις δέξαιτ' ἂν αὖ ζῆν ἡμῶν φρόνησιν μὲν καὶ νοῦν καὶ ἐπιστήμην καὶ μνήμην πᾶσαν E πάντων κεκτημένος, ἡδονῆς δὲ μετέχων μήτε μέγα μήτε σμικρόν, μηδ' αὖ λύπης, ἀλλὰ τὸ παράπαν ἀπαθὴς πάντων τῶν τοιούτων.

ΠΡΩ. Οὐδέτερος ὁ βίος, ὦ Σώκρατες, ἔμοιγε τούτων αἱρετός, οὐδ' ἄλλῳ μή ποτε, ὡς ἐγῷμαι, φανῇ.

---

[1] τὸν T: om. B.

pro. Yes; why not?

soc. But if you did not possess mind or memory or knowledge or true opinion, in the first place, you would not know whether you were enjoying your pleasures or not. That must be true, since you are utterly devoid of intellect, must it not?

pro. Yes, it must.

soc. And likewise, if you had no memory you could not even remember that you ever did enjoy pleasure, and no recollection whatever of present pleasure could remain with you; if you had no true opinion you could not think you were enjoying pleasure at the time when you were enjoying it, and if you were without power of calculation you would not be able to calculate that you would enjoy it in the future; your life would not be that of a man, but of a mollusc or some other shell-fish like the oyster. Is that true, or can we imagine any other result?

pro. We certainly cannot.

soc. And can we choose such a life?

pro. This argument, Socrates, has made me utterly speechless for the present.

soc. Well, let us not give in yet. Let us take up the life of mind and scrutinize that in turn.

pro. What sort of life do you mean?

soc. I ask whether anyone would be willing to live possessing wisdom and mind and knowledge and perfect memory of all things, but having no share, great or small, in pleasure, or in pain, for that matter, but being utterly unaffected by everything of that sort.

pro. Neither of the two lives can ever appear desirable to me, Socrates, or, I think, to anyone else.

22 ΣΩ. Τί δ' ὁ ξυναμφότερος, ὦ Πρώταρχε, ἐξ
ἀμφοῖν συμμιχθεὶς κοινὸς γενόμενος;

ΠΡΩ. Ἡδονῆς λέγεις καὶ νοῦ καὶ φρονήσεως;

ΣΩ. Οὕτω καὶ τῶν τοιούτων λέγω ἔγωγε.[1]

ΠΡΩ. Πᾶς δήπου τοῦτόν γε αἱρήσεται πρότερον ἢ 'κείνων ὁποτερονοῦν, καὶ πρὸς τούτοις οὐχ
ὁ μέν, ὁ δ' οὔ.

ΣΩ. Μανθάνομεν οὖν ὅ τι νῦν ἡμῖν ἐστὶ τὸ
ξυμβαῖνον ἐν τοῖς παροῦσι λόγοις;

ΠΡΩ. Πάνυ μὲν οὖν, ὅτι γε τρεῖς μὲν βίοι προὐ-
B τέθησαν, τοῖν δυοῖν δ' οὐδέτερος ἱκανὸς οὐδὲ
αἱρετὸς οὔτε ἀνθρώπων οὔτε ζῴων οὐδενί.

ΣΩ. Μῶν οὖν οὐκ ἤδη τούτων γε πέρι δῆλον
ὡς οὐδέτερος αὐτῶν εἶχε τἀγαθόν; ἦν γὰρ ἂν
ἱκανὸς καὶ τέλεος καὶ πᾶσι φυτοῖς καὶ ζῴοις
αἱρετός, οἷσπερ δυνατὸν ἦν οὕτως ἀεὶ διὰ βίου
ζῆν· εἰ δέ τις ἄλλα ἡρεῖθ' ἡμῶν, παρὰ φύσιν ἂν
τὴν τοῦ ἀληθῶς αἱρετοῦ ἐλάμβανεν ἄκων ἐξ
ἀγνοίας ἤ τινος ἀνάγκης οὐκ εὐδαίμονος.

ΠΡΩ. Ἔοικε γοῦν ταῦθ' οὕτως ἔχειν.

C ΣΩ. Ὡς μὲν τοίνυν τήν γε Φιλήβου θεὸν οὐ
δεῖ διανοεῖσθαι ταὐτὸν καὶ τἀγαθόν, ἱκανῶς
εἰρῆσθαί μοι δοκεῖ.

ΦΙ. Οὐδὲ γὰρ ὁ σὸς νοῦς, ὦ Σώκρατες, ἔστι
τἀγαθόν, ἀλλ' ἕξει που ταὐτὰ ἐγκλήματα.

ΣΩ. Τάχ' ἄν, ὦ Φίληβε, ὅ γ' ἐμός· οὐ μέντοι
τόν γε ἀληθινὸν ἅμα καὶ θεῖον οἶμαι νοῦν,
ἀλλ' ἄλλως πως ἔχειν. τῶν μὲν οὖν νικητηρίων
πρὸς τὸν κοινὸν βίον οὐκ ἀμφισβητῶ πω ὑπὲρ
νοῦ, τῶν δὲ δὴ δευτερείων ὁρᾶν καὶ σκοπεῖν χρὴ
D πέρι τί δράσομεν. τάχα γὰρ ἂν τοῦ κοινοῦ τούτου

---

[1] ἔγωγε om. BT: add. in marg. T.

soc. How about the combined life, Protarchus, made up by a union of the two ?

pro. You mean a union of pleasure with mind or wisdom ?

soc. Yes, I mean a union of such elements.

pro. Every one will prefer this life to either of the two others—yes, every single person without exception.

soc. Then do we understand the consequences of what we are now saying ?

pro. Certainly. Three lives have been proposed, and of two of them neither is sufficient or desirable for man or any other living being.

soc. Then is it not already clear that neither of these two contained the good ? For if it did contain the good, it would be sufficient and perfect, and such as to be chosen by all living creatures which would be able to live thus all their lives ; and if any of us chose anything else, he would be choosing contrary to the nature of the truly desirable, not of his own free will, but from ignorance or some unfortunate necessity.

pro. That seems at any rate to be true.

soc. And so I think we have sufficiently proved that Philebus's divinity is not to be considered identical with the good.

phi. But neither is your " mind " the good, Socrates ; it will be open to the same objections.

soc. My mind, perhaps, Philebus ; but not so, I believe, the true mind, which is also divine ; that is different. I do not as yet claim for mind the victory over the combined life, but we must look and see what is to be done about the second place ; for each of us might perhaps put forward a

βίου αἰτιώμεθ᾽ ἂν ἑκάτερος ὁ μὲν τὸν νοῦν αἴτιον,
ὁ δ᾽ ἡδονὴν εἶναι, καὶ οὕτω τὸ μὲν ἀγαθὸν τούτων
ἀμφοτέρων οὐδέτερον ἂν εἴη, τάχα δ᾽ ἂν αἴτιόν
τις ὑπολάβοι πότερον αὐτῶν εἶναι. τούτου δὴ
πέρι καὶ μᾶλλον ἔτι πρὸς Φίληβον διαμαχοίμην
ἂν ὡς ἐν τῷ μικτῷ τούτῳ βίῳ, ὅ τι ποτ᾽ ἔστι
τοῦτο ὃ λαβὼν ὁ βίος οὗτος γέγονεν αἱρετὸς ἅμα
καὶ ἀγαθός, οὐχ ἡδονὴ ἀλλὰ νοῦς τούτῳ ξυγγενέστερον καὶ ὁμοιότερόν ἐστι, καὶ κατὰ τοῦτον
E τὸν λόγον οὔτ᾽ ἂν τῶν πρωτείων οὐδ᾽ αὖ τῶν
δευτερείων ἡδονὴ μετὸν ἀληθῶς ἄν ποτε λέγοιτο·
πορρωτέρω δέ ἐστι τῶν τριτείων, εἴ τι τῷ ἐμῷ
νῷ δεῖ πιστεύειν ἡμᾶς τὰ νῦν.

ΠΡΩ. Ἀλλὰ μήν, ὦ Σώκρατες, ἔμοιγε δοκεῖ
νῦν μὲν ἡδονή σοι πεπτωκέναι καθαπερεὶ πλη-
γεῖσα ὑπὸ τῶν νῦν δὴ λόγων· τῶν γὰρ νικητηρίων
23 πέρι μαχομένη κεῖται. τὸν δὲ νοῦν, ὡς ἔοικε,
λεκτέον ὡς ἐμφρόνως οὐκ ἀντεποιεῖτο τῶν νικη-
τηρίων· τὰ γὰρ αὐτὰ ἔπαθεν ἄν. τῶν δὲ δὴ
δευτερείων στερηθεῖσα ἡδονὴ παντάπασιν ἄν τινα
καὶ ἀτιμίαν σχοίη πρὸς τῶν αὑτῆς ἐραστῶν· οὐδὲ
γὰρ ἐκείνοις ἔτ᾽ ἂν ὁμοίως φαίνοιτο καλή.

ΣΩ. Τί οὖν; οὐκ ἄμεινον αὐτὴν ἐᾶν ἤδη καὶ
μὴ τὴν ἀκριβεστάτην αὐτῇ προσφέροντα βάσανον
καὶ ἐξελέγχοντα λυπεῖν;

ΠΡΩ. Οὐδὲν λέγεις, ὦ Σώκρατες.

B ΣΩ. Ἆρ᾽ ὅτι τὸ ἀδύνατον εἶπον, λυπεῖν ἡδονήν;

ΠΡΩ. Οὐ μόνον γε, ἀλλ᾽ ὅτι καὶ ἀγνοεῖς ὡς
οὐδείς πώ σε ἡμῶν μεθήσει πρὶν ἂν εἰς τέλος
ἐπεξέλθῃς τούτων τῷ λόγῳ.

ΣΩ. Βαβαὶ ἄρα, ὦ Πρώταρχε, συχνοῦ μὲν

claim, one that mind is the cause of this combined
life, the other that pleasure is the cause ; and thus
neither of these two would be the good, but one or
the other of them might be regarded as the cause
of the good. On this point I might keep up the
fight all the more against Philebus and contend that
in this mixed life it is mind that is more akin and
more similar than pleasure to that, whatever it may
be, which makes it both desirable and good ; and
from this point of view pleasure could advance no
true claim to the first or even the second place. It
is farther behind than the third place, if my mind is
at all to be trusted at present.

PRO. Certainly, Socrates, it seems to me that
pleasure has fought for the victory and has fallen
in this bout, knocked down by your words. And
we can only say, as it seems, that mind was wise
in not laying claim to the victory ; for it would
have met with the same fate. Now pleasure, if she
were to lose the second prize, would be deeply
humiliated in the eyes of her lovers ; for she would
no longer appear even to them so lovely as before.

SOC. Well, then, is it not better to leave her now
and not to pain her by testing her to the utmost and
proving her in the wrong ?

PRO. Nonsense, Socrates !

SOC. Nonsense because I spoke of paining pleasure,
and that is impossible ?

PRO. Not only that, but because you do not understand that not one of us will let you go yet until
you have finished the argument about these matters.

SOC. Whew, Protarchus ! Then we have a long

PLATO

λόγου τοῦ λοιποῦ, σχεδὸν δὲ οὐδὲ ῥᾳδίου πάνυ
τι νῦν. καὶ γὰρ δὴ φαίνεται δεῖν ἄλλης μηχανῆς
ἐπὶ τὰ δευτερεῖα ὑπὲρ νοῦ πορευόμενον, οἷον
βέλη ἔχειν ἕτερα τῶν ἔμπροσθεν λόγων· ἔστι δὲ
ἴσως ἔνια καὶ ταῦτά.[1] οὐκοῦν χρή;

ΠΡΩ. Πῶς γὰρ οὔ;

12. ΣΩ. Τὴν δέ γε ἀρχὴν αὐτοῦ διευλαβεῖσθαι
C πειρώμεθα τιθέμενοι.

ΠΡΩ. Ποίαν δὴ λέγεις;

ΣΩ. Πάντα τὰ νῦν ὄντα ἐν τῷ παντὶ διχῇ δια-
λάβωμεν, μᾶλλον δ', εἰ βούλει, τριχῇ.

ΠΡΩ. Καθ' ὅ τι, φράζοις ἄν.

ΣΩ. Λάβωμεν ἄττα τῶν νῦν δὴ λόγων.

ΠΡΩ. Ποῖα;

ΣΩ. Τὸν θεὸν ἐλέγομέν που τὸ μὲν ἄπειρον
δεῖξαι τῶν ὄντων, τὸ δὲ πέρας;

ΠΡΩ. Πάνυ μὲν οὖν.

ΣΩ. Τούτω[2] δὴ τῶν εἰδῶν τὰ δύο τιθώμεθα,
τὸ δὲ τρίτον ἐξ ἀμφοῖν τούτοιν ἕν τι συμμισγό-
D μενον. εἰμὶ δ', ὡς ἔοικεν, ἐγὼ γελοῖός τις
ἄνθρωπος[3] κατ' εἴδη διιστὰς καὶ συναριθμούμενος.

ΠΡΩ. Τί φής, ὠγαθέ;

ΣΩ. Τετάρτου μοι γένους αὖ προσδεῖν φαίνεται.

ΠΡΩ. Λέγε τίνος.

ΣΩ. Τῆς ξυμμίξεως τούτων πρὸς ἄλληλα τὴν
αἰτίαν ὅρα, καὶ τίθει μοι πρὸς τρισὶν ἐκείνοις
τέταρτον τοῦτο.

ΠΡΩ. Μῶν οὖν σοι καὶ πέμπτου προσδεήσει
διάκρισίν τινος δυναμένου;

ΣΩ. Τάχ' ἄν· οὐ μὴν οἶμαί γε ἐν τῷ νῦν· ἐὰν

[1] ταῦτα BT.   [2] τούτω Stallbaum: τούτων BT.
[3] τις ἄνθρωπος Badham: τις ἱκανὸς B: τις ἱκανῶς T.
242

discussion before us, and not an easy one, either, this time. For in going ahead to fight mind's battle for the second place, I think I need a new contrivance—other weapons, as it were, than those of our previous discussion, though perhaps some of the old ones will serve. Must I then go on?

PRO. Of course you must.

SOC. Then let us try to be careful in making our beginning.

PRO. What kind of a beginning do you mean?

SOC. Let us divide all things that now exist in the universe into two, or rather, if you please, three classes.

PRO. Please tell us on what principle you would divide them.

SOC. Let us take some of the subjects of our present discussion.

PRO. What subjects?

SOC. We said that God revealed in the universe two elements, the infinite and the finite, did we not?

PRO. Certainly.

SOC. Let us, then, assume these as two of our classes, and a third, made by combining these two. But I cut a ridiculous figure, it seems, when I attempt a division into classes and an enumeration.

PRO. What do you mean, my friend?

SOC. I think we need a fourth class besides.

PRO. Tell us what it is.

SOC. Note the cause of the combination of those two and assume that as the fourth in addition to the previous three.

PRO. And then will you not need a fifth, which has the power of separation?

SOC. Perhaps; but not at present, I think. How-

243

Ε δέ τι δέῃ, συγγνώσει πού μοι σὺ μεταδιώκοντι
πέμπτον.¹

ΠΡΩ. Τί μήν;

ΣΩ. Πρῶτον μὲν δὴ τῶν τεττάρων τὰ τρία
διελόμενοι, τὰ δύο τούτων πειρώμεθα, πολλὰ
ἑκάτερον ἐσχισμένον καὶ διεσπασμένον ἰδόντες,
εἰς ἓν πάλιν ἑκάτερον συναγαγόντες, νοῆσαι πῇ
ποτε ἦν αὐτῶν ἓν καὶ πολλὰ ἑκάτερον.

ΠΡΩ. Εἴ μοι σαφέστερον ἔτι περὶ αὐτῶν εἴποις,
τάχ᾽ ἂν ἑποίμην.

24 ΣΩ. Λέγω τοίνυν τὰ δύο ἃ προτίθεμαι ταῦτ᾽
εἶναι ἅπερ νῦν δή, τὸ μὲν ἄπειρον, τὸ δὲ πέρας
ἔχον· ὅτι δὲ τρόπον τινὰ τὸ ἄπειρον πολλά ἐστι,
πειράσομαι φράζειν· τὸ δὲ πέρας ἔχον ἡμᾶς
περιμενέτω.

ΠΡΩ. Μένει.

ΣΩ. Σκέψαι δή. χαλεπὸν μὲν γὰρ καὶ ἀμφισβη-
τήσιμον ὃ κελεύω σε σκοπεῖν, ὅμως δὲ σκόπει.
θερμοτέρου καὶ ψυχροτέρου πέρι πρῶτον ὅρα
πέρας εἴ ποτέ τι νοήσαις ἄν, ἢ τὸ μᾶλλόν τε καὶ
ἧττον ἐν αὐτοῖς οἰκοῦντε² τοῖς γένεσιν, ἔωσπερ
Β ἂν ἐνοικῆτον, τέλος οὐκ ἂν ἐπιτρεψαίτην γίγνε-
σθαι· γενομένης γὰρ τελευτῆς καὶ αὐτὼ τετελευ-
τήκατον.

ΠΡΩ. Ἀληθέστατα λέγεις.

ΣΩ. Ἀεὶ δέ γε, φαμέν, ἔν τε τῷ θερμοτέρῳ καὶ
ψυχροτέρῳ τὸ μᾶλλόν τε καὶ ἧττον ἔνι.

ΠΡΩ. Καὶ μάλα.

ΣΩ. Ἀεὶ τοίνυν ὁ λόγος ἡμῖν σημαίνει τούτω
μὴ τέλος ἔχειν· ἀτελῆ δ᾽ ὄντε δήπου παντάπασιν
ἀπείρω γίγνεσθον.

ΠΡΩ. Καὶ σφόδρα γε, ὦ Σώκρατες.

ever, if we do need a fifth, you will pardon me for going after it.

PRO. Of course.

SOC. First, then, let us take three of the four and, as we see that two of these are split up and scattered each one into many, let us try, by collecting each of them again into one, to learn how each of them was both one and many.

PRO. If you could tell me more clearly about them, I might be able to follow you.

SOC. I mean, then, that the two which I select are the same which I mentioned before, the infinite and the finite. I will try to show that the infinite is, in a certain sense, many ; the finite can wait.

PRO. Yes.

SOC. Consider then. What I ask you to consider is difficult and debatable ; but consider it all the same. In the first place, take hotter and colder and see whether you can conceive any limit of them, or whether the more and less which dwell in their very nature do not, so long as they continue to dwell therein, preclude the possibility of any end ; for if there were any end of them, the more and less would themselves be ended.

PRO. Very true.

SOC. But always, we affirm, in the hotter and colder there is the more and less.

PRO. Certainly.

SOC. Always, then, the argument shows that these two have no end ; and being endless, they are of course infinite.

PRO. Most emphatically, Socrates.

---

¹ πέμπτον βίον BT : βίον bracketed by Schanz.
² οἰκοῦντε sec. Coisl. : οἰκοῦν BT.

ΣΩ. Ἀλλ᾽ εὖ γε, ὦ φίλε Πρώταρχε, ὑπέλαβες
C καὶ ἀνέμνησας ὅτι καὶ τὸ σφόδρα τοῦτο, ὃ σὺ νῦν
ἐφθέγξω, καὶ τό γε ἠρέμα τὴν αὐτὴν δύναμιν
ἔχετον τῷ μᾶλλόν τε καὶ ἧττον. ὅπου γὰρ ἂν
ἐνῆτον, οὐκ ἐᾶτον εἶναι ποσὸν ἕκαστον, ἀλλ᾽
ἀεὶ σφοδρότερον ἡσυχαιτέρου καὶ τοὐναντίον ἑκάσταις πράξεσιν ἐμποιοῦντε τὸ πλέον καὶ τὸ ἔλαττον
ἀπεργάζεσθον, τὸ δὲ ποσὸν ἀφανίζετον. ὃ γὰρ
ἐλέχθη νῦν δή, μὴ ἀφανίσαντε τὸ ποσόν, ἀλλ᾽
ἐάσαντε αὐτό τε καὶ τὸ μέτριον ἐν τῇ τοῦ μᾶλλον
D καὶ ἧττον καὶ σφόδρα καὶ ἠρέμα ἕδρᾳ ἐγγενέσθαι,
αὐτὰ ἔρρει ταῦτα ἐκ τῆς αὐτῶν χώρας ἐν ᾗ ἐνῆν.
οὐ γὰρ ἔτι θερμότερον οὐδὲ ψυχρότερον εἴτην[1]
ἂν λαβόντε τὸ ποσόν· προχωρεῖ γὰρ καὶ οὐ
μένει τό τε θερμότερον ἀεὶ καὶ τὸ ψυχρότερον
ὡσαύτως, τὸ δὲ ποσὸν ἔστη καὶ προϊὸν ἐπαύσατο·
κατὰ δὴ τοῦτον τὸν λόγον ἄπειρον γίγνοιτ᾽ ἂν τὸ
θερμότερον καὶ τοὐναντίον ἅμα.

ΠΡΩ. Φαίνεται γοῦν, ὦ Σώκρατες· ἔστι δ᾽,
ὅπερ εἶπες, οὐ ῥᾴδια ταῦτα συνέπεσθαι· τὸ δὲ
E εἰς αὖθίς τε καὶ αὖθις ἴσως λεχθέντα τόν τε ἐρω-
τῶντα καὶ τὸν ἐρωτώμενον ἱκανῶς ἂν ξυμφω-
νοῦντας ἀποφήναιεν.

ΣΩ. Ἀλλ᾽ εὖ μὲν λέγεις, καὶ πειρατέον οὕτω
ποιεῖν. νῦν μέντοι ἄθρει τῆς τοῦ ἀπείρου φύσεως
εἰ τοῦτο δεξόμεθα σημεῖον, ἵνα μὴ πάντ᾽ ἐπεξ-
ιόντες μηκύνωμεν.

ΠΡΩ. Τὸ ποῖον δὴ λέγεις;

ΣΩ. Ὁπόσ᾽ ἂν ἡμῖν φαίνηται μᾶλλόν τε καὶ
ἧττον γιγνόμενα καὶ τὸ σφόδρα καὶ ἠρέμα δεχό-
25 μενα καὶ τὸ λίαν καὶ ὅσα τοιαῦτα πάντα, εἰς τὸ

---

[1] εἴτην Τ: ἔστην Β: ἥτην vulg.

soc. I am glad you responded, my dear Protarchus, and reminded me that the word " emphatically " which you have just used, and the word " gently " have the same force as " more " and " less." For wherever they are present, they do not allow any definite quantity to exist ; they always introduce in every instance a comparison—more emphatic than that which is quieter, or *vice versa*—and thus they create the relation of more and less, thereby doing away with fixed quantity. For, as I said just now, if they did not abolish quantity, but allowed it and measure to make their appearance in the abode of the more and less, the emphatically and gently, those latter would be banished from their own proper place. When once they had accepted definite quantity, they would no longer be hotter or colder ; for hotter and colder are always progressing and never stationary ; but quantity is at rest and does not progress. By this reasoning hotter and its opposite are shown to be infinite.

pro. That appears to be the case, Socrates ; but, as you said, these subjects are not easy to follow. Perhaps, however, continued repetition might lead to a satisfactory agreement between the questioner and him who is questioned.

soc. That is a good suggestion, and I must try to carry it out. However, to avoid waste of time in discussing all the individual examples, see if we can accept this as a designation of the infinite.

pro. Accept what ?

soc. All things which appear to us to become more or less, or to admit of emphatic and gentle and excessive and the like, are to be put in the class of

τοῦ ἀπείρου γένος ὡς εἰς ἓν δεῖ πάντα ταῦτα
τιθέναι, κατὰ τὸν ἔμπροσθεν λόγον ὃν ἔφαμεν
ὅσα διέσπασται καὶ διέσχισται συναγαγόντας χρῆ-
ναι κατὰ δύναμιν μίαν ἐπισημαίνεσθαί τινα φύσιν,
εἰ μέμνησαι.

ΠΡΩ. Μέμνημαι.

ΣΩ. Οὐκοῦν τὰ μὴ δεχόμενα ταῦτα, τούτων
δὲ τὰ ἐναντία πάντα δεχόμενα, πρῶτον μὲν τὸ
ἴσον καὶ ἰσότητα, μετὰ δὲ τὸ ἴσον τὸ διπλάσιον
καὶ πᾶν ὅτιπερ ἂν πρὸς ἀριθμὸν ἀριθμὸς ἢ μέτρον
B ᾖ πρὸς μέτρον, ταῦτα ξύμπαντα εἰς τὸ πέρας
ἀπολογιζόμενοι καλῶς ἂν δοκοῖμεν δρᾶν τοῦτο.
ἢ πῶς σὺ φῄς;

ΠΡΩ. Κάλλιστά γε, ὦ Σώκρατες.

13. ΣΩ. Εἶεν· τὸ δὲ τρίτον τὸ μικτὸν ἐκ τούτοιν ἀμφοῖν τίνα ἰδέαν φήσομεν ἔχειν;

ΠΡΩ. Σοὶ καὶ ἐμοὶ φράσεις, ὡς οἶμαι.

ΣΩ. Θεὸς μὲν οὖν, ἄνπερ γε ἐμαῖς εὐχαῖς ἐπή-
κοος γίγνηταί τις θεῶν.

ΠΡΩ. Εὔχου δὴ καὶ σκόπει.

ΣΩ. Σκοπῶ· καί μοι δοκεῖ τις, ὦ Πρώταρχε,
αὐτῶν φίλος ἡμῖν νῦν δὴ γεγονέναι.

C ΠΡΩ. Πῶς λέγεις τοῦτο καὶ τίνι τεκμηρίῳ χρῇ;

ΣΩ. Φράσω δῆλον ὅτι. σὺ δέ μοι συνακο-
λούθησον τῷ λόγῳ.

ΠΡΩ. Λέγε μόνον.

ΣΩ. Θερμότερον ἐφθεγγόμεθα νῦν δή πού τι
καὶ ψυχρότερον. ἢ γάρ;

ΠΡΩ. Ναί.

ΣΩ. Πρόσθες δὴ ξηρότερον καὶ ὑγρότερον αὐτοῖς
καὶ πλέον καὶ ἔλαττον καὶ θᾶττον καὶ βραδύτερον
καὶ μεῖζον καὶ σμικρότερον καὶ ὁπόσα ἐν τῷ
248

the infinite as their unity, in accordance with what we said a while ago, if you remember, that we ought to collect all things that are scattered and split up and impress upon them to the best of our ability the seal of some single nature.

PRO. I remember.

SOC. And the things which do not admit of more and less and the like, but do admit of all that is opposed to them—first equality and the equal, then the double, and anything which is a definite number or measure in relation to such a number or measure —all these might properly be assigned to the class of the finite. What do you say to that?

PRO. Excellent, Socrates.

SOC. Well, what shall we say is the nature of the third class, made by combining these two?

PRO. You will tell me, I fancy, by answering your own question.

SOC. Nay, a god will do so, if any god will give ear to my prayers.

PRO. Pray, then, and watch.

SOC. I am watching; and I think, Protarchus, one of the gods has this moment been gracious unto me.

PRO. What do you mean, and what evidence have you?

SOC. I will tell you, of course. Just follow what I say.

PRO. Say on.

SOC. We spoke just now of hotter and colder, did we not?

PRO. Yes.

SOC. Add to them drier and wetter, more and less, quicker and slower, greater and smaller, and all that

πρόσθεν τῆς τὸ μᾶλλόν τε καὶ ἧττον δεχομένης
ἐτίθεμεν εἰς ἓν φύσεως.

D ΠΡΩ. Τῆς τοῦ ἀπείρου λέγεις;

ΣΩ. Ναί. συμμίγνυ δέ γε εἰς αὐτὴν τὸ μετὰ
ταῦτα τὴν αὖ τοῦ[1] πέρατος γένναν.

ΠΡΩ. Ποίαν;

ΣΩ. Ἣν καὶ νῦν δή, δέον ἡμᾶς καθάπερ τὴν
τοῦ ἀπείρου συνηγάγομεν εἰς ἕν, οὕτω καὶ τὴν
τοῦ περατοειδοῦς συναγαγεῖν, οὐ συνηγάγομεν.
ἀλλ᾽ ἴσως καὶ νῦν ταὐτὸν δράσει, εἰ[2] τούτων
ἀμφοτέρων συναγομένων καταφανὴς κἀκείνη γε-
νήσεται.

ΠΡΩ. Ποίαν καὶ πῶς λέγεις;

ΣΩ. Τὴν τοῦ ἴσου καὶ διπλασίου, καὶ ὁπόση
E παύει πρὸς ἄλληλα τἀναντία διαφόρως ἔχοντα,
σύμμετρα δὲ καὶ σύμφωνα ἐνθεῖσα ἀριθμὸν ἀπεργάζεται.

ΠΡΩ. Μανθάνω· φαίνει γάρ μοι λέγειν, μιγνὺς
ταῦτα γενέσεις τινὰς ἐφ᾽ ἑκάστων αὐτῶν συμβαί-
νειν.

ΣΩ. Ὀρθῶς γὰρ φαίνομαι.

ΠΡΩ. Λέγε τοίνυν.

ΣΩ. Ἆρ᾽ οὐκ ἐν μὲν νόσοις ἡ τούτων ὀρθὴ
κοινωνία τὴν ὑγιείας φύσιν ἐγέννησεν;

26 ΠΡΩ. Παντάπασι μὲν οὖν.

ΣΩ. Ἐν δὲ ὀξεῖ καὶ βαρεῖ καὶ ταχεῖ καὶ βραδεῖ,
ἀπείροις οὖσιν, ἆρ᾽ οὐ ταὐτὰ ἐγγιγνόμενα ταῦτα
ἅμα πέρας τε ἀπειργάσατο καὶ μουσικὴν ξύμπασαν
τελεώτατα ξυνεστήσατο;

ΠΡΩ. Κάλλιστά γε.

ΣΩ. Καὶ μὴν ἔν γε χειμῶσι καὶ πνίγεσιν ἐγγενόμενα[3] τὸ μὲν πολὺ λίαν καὶ ἄπειρον ἀφ-

250

we assigned before to the class which unites more and less.

PRO. You mean the class of the infinite?

SOC. Yes. Mix with that the second class, the offspring of the limit.

PRO. What class do you mean?

SOC. The class of the finite, which we ought just now to have reduced to unity, as we did that of the infinite. We have not done that, but perhaps we shall even now accomplish the same end, if these two are both unified and then the third class is revealed.

PRO. What third class, and what do you mean?

SOC. The class of the equal and double and everything which puts an end to the differences between opposites and makes them commensurable and harmonious by the introduction of number.

PRO. I understand. I think you mean that by mixture of these elements certain results are produced in each instance.

SOC. Yes, you are right.

PRO. Go on.

SOC. In cases of illness, does not the proper combination of these elements produce health?

PRO. Certainly.

SOC. And in the acute and the grave, the quick and the slow, which are unlimited, the addition of these same elements creates a limit and establishes the whole art of music in all its perfection, does it not?

PRO. Excellent.

SOC. And again in the case of cold and hot weather, the introduction of these elements removes the excess

---

¹ αὖ τοῦ Coisl.: αὐτοῦ BT.   ² δράσει εἰ Vahlen: δράσει BT.
³ ἐγγενόμενα B: ἐγγενομένη TG.

εἵλετο, τὸ δὲ ἔμμετρον καὶ ἅμα σύμμετρον
ἀπειργάσατο.

ΠΡΩ. Τί μήν;

ΣΩ. Οὐκοῦν ἐκ τούτων ὧραί τε καὶ ὅσα καλὰ
B πάντα ἡμῖν γέγονε, τῶν τε ἀπείρων καὶ τῶν
πέρας ἐχόντων συμμιχθέντων;

ΠΡΩ. Πῶς δ' οὔ;

ΣΩ. Καὶ ἄλλα γε δὴ μυρία ἐπιλείπω λέγων,
οἷον μεθ' ὑγιείας κάλλος καὶ ἰσχύν, καὶ ἐν ψυχαῖς
αὖ πάμπολλα ἕτερα καὶ πάγκαλα. ὕβριν γάρ που
καὶ ξύμπασαν πάντων πονηρί⟨αν⟩ αὕτη κατιδοῦσα
ἡ θεός, ὦ καλὲ Φίληβε, πέρας οὔτε ἡδονῶν
οὐδὲν οὔτε πλησμονῶν ἐνὸν ἐν αὐτοῖς, νόμον καὶ
τάξιν πέρας ἔχοντ'[1] ἔθετο· καὶ σὺ μὲν ἀπο-
C κναῖσαι φὴς[2] αὐτήν, ἐγὼ δὲ τοὐναντίον ἀποσῶσαι
λέγω. σοὶ δέ, ὦ Πρώταρχε, πῶς φαίνεται;

ΠΡΩ. Καὶ μάλα, ὦ Σώκρατες, ἔμοιγε κατὰ νοῦν.

ΣΩ. Οὐκοῦν τὰ μὲν δὴ τρία ταῦτα εἴρηκα, εἰ
ξυννοεῖς.

ΠΡΩ. 'Αλλ' οἶμαι κατανοεῖν· ἓν μὲν γάρ μοι
δοκεῖς τὸ ἄπειρον λέγειν, ἓν δὲ καὶ δεύτερον τὸ
πέρας ἐν τοῖς οὖσι· τρίτον δὲ οὐ σφόδρα κατέχω
τί βούλει φράζειν.

ΣΩ. Τὸ γὰρ πλῆθός σε, ὦ θαυμάσιε, ἐξέπληξε
τῆς τοῦ τρίτου γενέσεως· καίτοι πολλά γε καὶ τὸ
D ἄπειρον παρέσχετο γένη, ὅμως δ' ἐπισφραγισθέντα
τῷ τοῦ μᾶλλον καὶ ἐναντίου γένει ἓν ἐφάνη.

---

[1] ἔχοντ' T: ἐχόντων B.
[2] ἀποκναῖσαι φὴς Kidd. misc. Porson, p. 265; ἀποκναῖς ἔφης BT.

---

[1] This goddess may be Μουσική (in which case ἐγγενομένη,
the reading of T and G, would be preferable to ἐγγενόμενα
above), not music in the restricted modern sense, but the

and indefiniteness and creates moderation and harmony.

PRO. Assuredly.

SOC. And thence arise the seasons and all the beauties of our world, by mixture of the infinite with the finite ?

PRO. Of course.

SOC. There are countless other things which I pass over, such as health, beauty, and strength of the body and the many glorious beauties of the soul. For this goddess,[1] my fair Philebus, beholding the violence and universal wickedness which prevailed, since there was no limit of pleasures or of indulgence in them, established law and order, which contain a limit. You say she did harm ; I say, on the contrary, she brought salvation. What do you think, Protarchus ?

PRO. What you say, Socrates, pleases me greatly.

SOC. I have spoken of these three classes, you observe.

PRO. Yes, I believe I understand ; I think you mean that the infinite is one class and the finite is another class among existing things ; but what you wish to designate as the third class, I do not comprehend very well.

SOC. No, because the multitude which springs up in the third class overpowers you ; and yet the infinite also comprised many classes, nevertheless, since they were sealed with the seal of the more and less, they were seen to be of one class.

spirit of numbers and measure which underlies all music, and all the beauties of the world ; or the goddess may be mentioned here in reference (and opposition) to the goddess Pleasure (12 B) ; she is the nameless deity who makes Pleasure and all others conform to her rules.

ΠΡΩ. Ἀληθῆ.

ΣΩ. Καὶ μὴν τό γε πέρας οὔτε πολλὰ εἶχεν, οὔτ᾽ ἐδυσκολαίνομεν ὡς οὐκ ἦν ἓν φύσει.

ΠΡΩ. Πῶς γὰρ ἄν;

ΣΩ. Οὐδαμῶς. ἀλλὰ τρίτον φάθι με λέγειν, ἓν τοῦτο τιθέντα τὸ τούτων ἔκγονον ἅπαν, γένεσιν εἰς οὐσίαν ἐκ τῶν μετὰ τοῦ πέρατος ἀπειργασμένων μέτρων.

ΠΡΩ. Ἔμαθον.

E   14. ΣΩ. Ἀλλὰ δὴ πρὸς τρισὶ τέταρτόν τι τότε ἔφαμεν εἶναι γένος σκεπτέον· κοινὴ δ᾽ ἡ σκέψις. ὅρα γάρ, εἴ σοι δοκεῖ ἀναγκαῖον εἶναι πάντα τὰ γιγνόμενα διά τινα αἰτίαν γίγνεσθαι.

ΠΡΩ. Ἔμοιγε· πῶς γὰρ ἂν χωρὶς τούτου γίγνοιτο;

ΣΩ. Οὐκοῦν ἡ τοῦ ποιοῦντος φύσις οὐδὲν πλὴν ὀνόματι τῆς αἰτίας διαφέρει, τὸ δὲ ποιοῦν καὶ τὸ αἴτιον ὀρθῶς ἂν εἴη λεγόμενον ἕν;

ΠΡΩ. Ὀρθῶς.

27   ΣΩ. Καὶ μὴν τό γε ποιούμενον αὖ καὶ τὸ γιγνόμενον οὐδὲν πλὴν ὀνόματι, καθάπερ τὸ νῦν δή, διαφέρον εὑρήσομεν. ἢ πῶς;

ΠΡΩ. Οὕτως.

ΣΩ. Ἆρ᾽ οὖν ἡγεῖται μὲν τὸ ποιοῦν ἀεὶ κατὰ φύσιν, τὸ δὲ ποιούμενον ἐπακολουθεῖ γιγνόμενον ἐκείνῳ;

ΠΡΩ. Πάνυ γε.

ΣΩ. Ἄλλο ἄρα καὶ οὐ ταὐτὸν αἰτία τ᾽ ἐστὶ καὶ τὸ δουλεῦον εἰς γένεσιν αἰτίᾳ.

ΠΡΩ. Τί μήν;

PRO. True.

SOC. And the finite, again, did not contain many classes, nor were we disturbed about its natural unity.

PRO. Of course not.

SOC. No, not at all. And as to the third class, understand that I mean every offspring of these two which comes into being as a result of the measures created by the co-operation of the finite.

PRO. I understand.

SOC. But we said there was, in addition to three classes, a fourth to be investigated. Let us do that together. See whether you think that everything which comes into being must necessarily come into being through a cause.

PRO. Yes, I do ; for how could it come into being apart from a cause ?

SOC. Does not the nature of that which makes or creates differ only in name from the cause, and may not the creative agent and the cause be properly considered one ?

PRO. Yes.

SOC. And, again, we shall find that, on the same principle, that which is made or created differs in name only from that which comes into being, shall we not ?

PRO. We shall.

SOC. And the creative agent always naturally leads, and that which is created follows after it as it comes into being ?

PRO. Certainly.

SOC. Then the cause and that which is the servant of the cause for the purpose of generation are not the same.

PRO. Of course not.

ΣΩ. Οὐκοῦν τὰ μὲν γιγνόμενα καὶ ἐξ ὧν γίγνεται πάντα τὰ τρία παρέσχετο ἡμῖν γένη;

ΠΡΩ. Καὶ μάλα.

B ΣΩ. Τὸ δὲ δὴ πάντα ταῦτα δημιουργοῦν λέγομεν τέταρτον, τὴν αἰτίαν, ὡς ἱκανῶς ἕτερον ἐκείνων δεδηλωμένον;

ΠΡΩ. Ἕτερον γὰρ οὖν.

ΣΩ. Ὀρθῶς μὴν ἔχει, διωρισμένων τῶν τεττάρων ἑνὸς ἑκάστου μνήμης ἕνεκα ἐφεξῆς αὐτὰ καταριθμήσασθαι.

ΠΡΩ. Τί μήν;

ΣΩ. Πρῶτον μὲν τοίνυν ἄπειρον λέγω, δεύτερον δὲ πέρας, ἔπειτ' ἐκ τούτων τρίτον μικτὴν καὶ γεγενημένην οὐσίαν· τὴν δὲ τῆς μίξεως αἰτίαν καὶ γενέσεως C τετάρτην λέγων ἆρα μὴ πλημμελοίην ἄν τι;

ΠΡΩ. Καὶ πῶς;

ΣΩ. Φέρε δή, τὸ μετὰ τοῦθ' ἡμῖν τίς ὁ λόγος, καὶ τί ποτε βουληθέντες εἰς ταῦτα ἀφικόμεθα; ἆρ' οὐ τόδε ἦν; δευτερεῖα ἐζητοῦμεν πότερον ἡδονῆς γίγνοιτ' ἂν ἢ φρονήσεως. οὐχ οὕτως ἦν;

ΠΡΩ. Οὕτω μὲν οὖν.

ΣΩ. Ἆρ' οὖν ἴσως[1] νῦν, ἐπειδὴ ταῦτα οὕτω διειλόμεθα, κάλλιον ἂν καὶ τὴν κρίσιν ἐπιτελεσαίμεθα πρώτου πέρι καὶ δευτέρου, περὶ ὧν δὴ τὸ πρῶτον ἠμφισβητήσαμεν;

ΠΡΩ. Ἴσως.

D ΣΩ. Ἴθι δή· νικῶντα μὲν ἔθεμέν που τὸν μικτὸν βίον ἡδονῆς τε καὶ φρονήσεως. ἦν οὕτως;

ΠΡΩ. Ἦν.

ΣΩ. Οὐκοῦν τοῦτον μὲν τὸν βίον ὁρῶμέν που τίς τέ ἐστι καὶ ὁποίου γένους;

[1] ἴσως Stallbaum: ὡς BT.

soc. Did not the things which come into being and the things out of which they come into being furnish us all the three classes?

pro. Certainly.

soc. And that which produces all these, the cause, we call the fourth, as it has been satisfactorily shown to be distinct from the others?

pro. Yes, it is distinct.

soc. It is, then, proper, now that we have distinguished the four, to make sure that we remember them separately by enumerating them in order.

pro. Yes, certainly.

soc. The first, then, I call infinite, the second limit or finite, and the third something generated by a mixture of these two. And should I be making any mistake if I called the cause of this mixture and creation the fourth?

pro. Certainly not.

soc. Now what is the next step in our argument, and what was our purpose in coming to the point we have reached? Was it not this? We were trying to find out whether the second place belonged to pleasure or to wisdom, were we not?

pro. Yes, we were.

soc. And may we not, perhaps, now that we have finished with these points, be better able to come to a decision about the first and second places, which was the original subject of our discussion?

pro. Perhaps.

soc. Well then; we decided that the mixed life of pleasure and wisdom was the victor, did we not?

pro. Yes.

soc. And do we not see what kind of life this is, and to what class it belongs?

ΠΡΩ. Πῶς γὰρ οὔ;

ΣΩ. Καὶ μέρος γ' αὐτὸν φήσομεν εἶναι τοῦ τρίτου, οἶμαι, γένους· οὐ γὰρ δυοῖν τινοῖν ἐστὶ μικτὸν ἐκεῖνο,[1] ἀλλὰ ξυμπάντων τῶν ἀπείρων ὑπὸ τοῦ πέρατος δεδεμένων, ὥστε ὀρθῶς ὁ νικηφόρος οὗτος βίος μέρος ἐκείνου γίγνοιτ' ἄν.

ΠΡΩ. Ὀρθότατα μὲν οὖν.

E 15. ΣΩ. Εἶεν· τί δὲ ὁ σός, ὦ Φίληβε, ἡδὺς καὶ ἄμικτος ὤν; ἐν τίνι γένει τῶν εἰρημένων λεγόμενος ὀρθῶς ἄν ποτε λέγοιτο; ὧδε δ' ἀπόκριναί μοι πρὶν ἀποφήνασθαι.

ΦΙ. Λέγε μόνον.

ΣΩ. Ἡδονὴ καὶ λύπη πέρας ἔχετον, ἢ τῶν τὸ μᾶλλόν τε καὶ ἧττον δεχομένων ἐστόν;

ΦΙ. Ναί, τῶν τὸ μᾶλλον, ὦ Σώκρατες· οὐ γὰρ ἂν ἡδονὴ πᾶν ἀγαθὸν ἦν, εἰ μὴ ἄπειρον ἐτύγχανε πεφυκὸς καὶ πλήθει καὶ τῷ μᾶλλον.

28 ΣΩ. Οὐδέ γ' ἄν, ὦ Φίληβε, λύπη πᾶν κακόν· ὥστ' ἄλλο τι νῷν σκεπτέον ἢ τὴν τοῦ ἀπείρου φύσιν, ὡς παρέχεταί τι μέρος ταῖς ἡδοναῖς ἀγαθοῦ. τοῦτο[2] δή σοι τῶν ἀπεράντων γε γένους ἔστων·[3] φρόνησιν δὲ καὶ ἐπιστήμην καὶ νοῦν εἰς τί ποτε τῶν προειρημένων, ὦ Πρώταρχέ τε καὶ Φίληβε, νῦν θέντες οὐκ ἂν ἀσεβοῖμεν; οὐ γάρ μοι δοκεῖ σμικρὸς ἡμῖν εἶναι ὁ κίνδυνος κατορθώσασι καὶ μὴ περὶ τὸ νῦν ἐρωτώμενον.

B ΦΙ. Σεμνύνεις γάρ, ὦ Σώκρατες, τὸν σεαυτοῦ θεόν.

ΣΩ. Καὶ γὰρ σύ, ὦ ἑταῖρε, τὴν σαυτοῦ· τὸ δ' ἐρωτώμενον ὅμως ἡμῖν λεκτέον.

---

[1] μικτὸν ἐκεῖνο Schütz: μικτὸς ἐκεῖνος BT: om. Jackson.
[2] τούτῳ Burnet: τούτων BT: τοῦτο Ven. 189.

PRO. Of course we do.

SOC. We shall say that it belongs to the third class; for that class is not formed by mixture of any two things, but of all the things which belong to the infinite, bound by the finite; and therefore this victorious life would rightly be considered a part of this class.

PRO. Quite rightly.

SOC. Well then, what of your life, Philebus, of unmixed pleasure? In which of the aforesaid classes may it properly be said to belong? But before you tell me, please answer this question.

PHI. Ask your question.

SOC. Have pleasure and pain a limit, or are they among the things which admit of more and less?

PHI. Yes, they are among those which admit of the more, Socrates; for pleasure would not be absolute good if it were not infinite in number and degree.

SOC. Nor would pain, Philebus, be absolute evil; so it is not the infinite which supplies any element of good in pleasure; we must look for something else. Well, I grant you that pleasure and pain are in the class of the infinite; but to which of the aforesaid classes, Protarchus and Philebus, can we now without irreverence assign wisdom, knowledge, and mind? I think we must find the right answer to this question, for our danger is great if we fail.

PHI. Oh Socrates, you exalt your own god.

SOC. And you your goddess, my friend. But the question calls for an answer, all the same.

---

[3] γε γένους ἔστων Burnet: γεγενὸς ἔστω BT.

PLATO

πρω. Ὀρθῶς τοι λέγει Σωκράτης, ὦ Φίληβε, καὶ αὐτῷ πειστέον.

ΦΙ. Οὐκοῦν ὑπὲρ ἐμοῦ σύ, Πρώταρχε, προῄρησαι λέγειν;

πρω. Πάνυ γε· νῦν μέντοι σχεδὸν ἀπορῶ, καὶ δέομαί γε, ὦ Σώκρατες, αὐτόν σε ἡμῖν γενέσθαι προφήτην, ἵνα μηδὲν ἡμεῖς σοι περὶ τὸν ἀγωνιστὴν ἐξαμαρτάνοντες παρὰ μέλος φθεγξώμεθά τι.

C ΣΩ. Πειστέον, ὦ Πρώταρχε· οὐδὲ γὰρ χαλεπὸν οὐδὲν ἐπιτάττεις· ἀλλ᾽ ὄντως σε ἐγώ, καθάπερ εἶπε Φίληβος, σεμνύνων ἐν τῷ παίζειν ἐθορύβησα, νοῦν καὶ ἐπιστήμην ἐρόμενος ὁποίου γένους εἶεν;

πρω. Παντάπασί γε, ὦ Σώκρατες.

ΣΩ. Ἀλλὰ μὴν ῥᾴδιον. πάντες γὰρ συμφωνοῦσιν οἱ σοφοί, ἑαυτοὺς ὄντως σεμνύνοντες, ὡς νοῦς ἐστι βασιλεὺς ἡμῖν οὐρανοῦ τε καὶ γῆς. καὶ ἴσως εὖ λέγουσι. διὰ μακροτέρων δ᾽, εἰ βούλει, τὴν σκέψιν αὐτοῦ τοῦ γένους ποιησώμεθα.

D πρω. Λέγ᾽ ὅπως βούλει, μηδὲν μῆκος ἡμῖν ὑπολογιζόμενος, ὦ Σώκρατες, ὡς οὐκ ἀπεχθησόμενος.

16. ΣΩ. Καλῶς εἶπες. ἀρξώμεθα δέ πως ὧδε ἐπανερωτῶντες.

πρω. Πῶς;

ΣΩ. Πότερον, ὦ Πρώταρχε, τὰ ξύμπαντα καὶ τόδε τὸ καλούμενον ὅλον ἐπιτροπεύειν φῶμεν τὴν τοῦ ἀλόγου καὶ εἰκῇ δύναμιν καὶ τὸ ὅπῃ ἔτυχεν, ἢ τἀναντία, καθάπερ οἱ πρόσθεν ἡμῶν ἔλεγον, νοῦν καὶ φρόνησίν τινα θαυμαστὴν συντάττουσαν διακυβερνᾶν;

E πρω. Οὐδὲν τῶν αὐτῶν, ὦ θαυμάσιε Σώκρατες. ὃ μὲν γὰρ σὺ νῦν λέγεις, οὐδ᾽ ὅσιον εἶναί μοι
260

PRO. Socrates is right, Philebus; you ought to do as he asks.

PHI. Did you not, Protarchus, elect to reply in my place?

PRO. Yes; but now I am somewhat at a loss, and I ask you, Socrates, to be our spokesman yourself, that we may not select the wrong representative and so say something improper.

SOC. I must do as you ask, Protarchus; and it is not difficult. But did I really, as Philebus said, embarrass you by playfully exalting my god, when I asked to what class mind and knowledge should be assigned?

PRO. You certainly did, Socrates.

SOC. Yet the answer is easy; for all philosophers agree—whereby they really exalt themselves—that mind is king of heaven and earth. Perhaps they are right. But let us, if you please, investigate the question of its class more at length.

PRO. Speak just as you like, Socrates. Do not consider length, so far as we are concerned; you cannot bore us.

SOC. Good. Then let us begin by asking a question.

PRO. What is the question?

SOC. Shall we say, Protarchus, that all things and this which is called the universe are governed by an irrational and fortuitous power and mere chance, or, on the contrary, as our forefathers said, are ordered and directed by mind and a marvellous wisdom?

PRO. The two points of view have nothing in common, my wonderful Socrates. For what you are now saying seems to me actually impious. But

φαίνεται· τὸ δὲ νοῦν πάντα διακοσμεῖν αὐτὰ
φάναι καὶ τῆς ὄψεως τοῦ κόσμου καὶ ἡλίου καὶ
σελήνης καὶ ἀστέρων καὶ πάσης τῆς περιφορᾶς
ἄξιον, καὶ οὐκ ἄλλως ἔγωγ' ἄν ποτε περὶ αὐτῶν
εἴποιμι οὐδ' ἂν δοξάσαιμι.

ΣΩ. Βούλει δῆτά τι καὶ ἡμεῖς τοῖς ἔμπροσθεν
ὁμολογούμενον ξυμφήσωμεν, ὡς ταῦθ' οὕτως ἔχει,
29 καὶ μὴ μόνον οἰώμεθα δεῖν τἀλλότρια ἄνευ κινδύ-
νου λέγειν, ἀλλὰ καὶ συγκινδυνεύωμεν καὶ μετ-
έχωμεν τοῦ ψόγου, ὅταν ἀνὴρ δεινὸς φῇ ταῦτα
μὴ οὕτως ἀλλ' ἀτάκτως ἔχειν;

ΠΡΩ. Πῶς γὰρ οὐκ ἂν βουλοίμην;

ΣΩ. Ἴθι δή, τὸν ἐπιόντα περὶ τούτων νῦν ἡμῖν
λόγον ἄθρει.

ΠΡΩ. Λέγε μόνον.

ΣΩ. Τὰ περὶ τὴν τῶν σωμάτων φύσιν ἁπάντων
τῶν ζῴων, πῦρ καὶ ὕδωρ καὶ πνεῦμα καθορῶμέν
που καὶ γῆν, καθάπερ οἱ χειμαζόμενοί φασιν,
B ἐνόντα ἐν τῇ συστάσει.

ΠΡΩ. Καὶ μάλα· χειμαζόμεθα γὰρ ὄντως ὑπ'
ἀπορίας ἐν τοῖς νῦν λόγοις.

ΣΩ. Φέρε δή, περὶ ἑκάστου τῶν παρ' ἡμῖν
λαβὲ τὸ τοιόνδε.

ΠΡΩ. Ποῖον;

ΣΩ. Ὅτι σμικρόν τε τούτων ἕκαστον παρ' ἡμῖν
ἔνεστι καὶ φαῦλον καὶ οὐδαμῇ οὐδαμῶς εἰλικρινὲς
ὂν καὶ τὴν δύναμιν οὐκ ἀξίαν τῆς φύσεως ἔχον·
ἐν ἑνὶ δὲ λαβὼν περὶ πάντων νόει ταὐτόν. οἷον
πῦρ ἔστι μέν που παρ' ἡμῖν, ἔστι δ' ἐν τῷ παντί.

ΠΡΩ. Τί μήν;

C ΣΩ. Οὐκοῦν σμικρὸν μέν τι τὸ παρ' ἡμῖν καὶ
ἀσθενὲς καὶ φαῦλον, τὸ δ' ἐν τῷ παντὶ πλήθει τε

the assertion that mind orders all things is worthy
of the aspect of the world, of sun, moon, stars, and
the whole revolving universe ; I can never say or
think anything else about it.

soc. Do you, then, think we should assent to this
and agree in the doctrine of our predecessors, not
merely intending to repeat the words of others, with
no risk to ourselves, but ready to share with them in
the risk and the blame, if any clever man declares
that this world is not thus ordered, but is without
order ?

pro. Yes, of course I do.

soc. Then observe the argument that now comes
against us.

pro. Go on.

soc. We see the elements which belong to the
natures of all living beings, fire, water, air, and
earth—or, as the storm-tossed mariners say, land
in sight—in the constitution of the universe.

pro. Certainly ; and we are truly storm-tossed
in the puzzling cross-currents of this discussion.

soc. Well, here is a point for you to consider in
relation to each of these elements as it exists in us.

pro. What is the point ?

soc. Each element in us is small and poor and in
no way pure at all or endowed with the power which
is worthy of its nature. Take one example and
apply it to all. Fire, for instance, exists in us and
also in the universe.

pro. Of course.

soc. And that which is in us is small, weak, and
poor, but that which is in the universe is marvellous

θαυμαστὸν καὶ κάλλει καὶ πάσῃ δυνάμει τῇ περὶ
τὸ πῦρ οὔσῃ.

ΠΡΩ. Καὶ μάλα ἀληθὲς ὃ λέγεις.

ΣΩ. Τί δέ; τρέφεται καὶ γίγνεται ἐκ τούτου
καὶ ἄρχεται τὸ τοῦ παντὸς πῦρ ὑπὸ τοῦ παρ᾽
ἡμῖν πυρός, ἢ τοὐναντίον ὑπ᾽ ἐκείνου τό τ᾽ ἐμὸν καὶ
τὸ σὸν καὶ τὸ τῶν ἄλλων ζῴων ἅπαντ᾽ ἴσχει ταῦτα;

ΠΡΩ. Τοῦτο μὲν οὐδ᾽ ἀποκρίσεως ἄξιον ἐρωτᾷς.

D ΣΩ. Ὀρθῶς· ταὐτὰ γὰρ ἐρεῖς, οἶμαι, περί τε
τῆς ἐν τοῖς ζῴοις γῆς τῆς ἐνθάδε καὶ τῆς ἐν τῷ
παντί, καὶ τῶν ἄλλων δὴ πάντων ὅσων ἠρώτησα
ὀλίγον ἔμπροσθεν οὕτως ἀποκρινεῖ.

ΠΡΩ. Τίς γὰρ ἀποκρινόμενος ἄλλως ὑγιαίνων
ἄν ποτε φανείη;

ΣΩ. Σχεδὸν οὐδ᾽ ὁστισοῦν· ἀλλὰ τὸ μετὰ τοῦτο
ἑξῆς ἕπου. πάντα γὰρ ἡμεῖς ταῦτα τὰ νῦν δὴ
λεχθέντα ἆρ᾽ οὐκ εἰς ἓν συγκείμενα ἰδόντες ἐπωνο-
μάσαμεν σῶμα;

ΠΡΩ. Τί μήν;

E ΣΩ. Ταὐτὸν δὴ λαβὲ καὶ περὶ τοῦδε ὃν κόσμον
λέγομεν· τὸν[1] αὐτὸν γὰρ τρόπον ἂν εἴη που
σῶμα, σύνθετον ὂν ἐκ τῶν αὐτῶν.

ΠΡΩ. Ὀρθότατα λέγεις.

ΣΩ. Πότερον οὖν ἐκ τούτου τοῦ σώματος ὅλως
τὸ παρ᾽ ἡμῖν σῶμα ἢ ἐκ τοῦ παρ᾽ ἡμῖν τοῦτο
τρέφεταί τε καὶ ὅσα νῦν δὴ περὶ αὐτῶν εἴπομεν
εἴληφέ τε καὶ ἔχει;

ΠΡΩ. Καὶ τοῦθ᾽ ἕτερον, ὦ Σώκρατες, οὐκ
ἄξιον ἐρωτήσεως.

30 ΣΩ. Τί δέ; τόδε ἆρα ἄξιον; ἢ πῶς ἐρεῖς;

ΠΡΩ. Λέγε τὸ ποῖον.

----

[1] τὸν Badham : διὰ τὸν BT.

in quantity, beauty, and every power which belongs to fire.

PRO. What you say is very true.

SOC. Well, is the fire of the universe nourished, originated, and ruled by the fire within us, or, on the contrary, does my fire, and yours, and that of all living beings derive nourishment and all that from the universal fire ?

PRO. That question does not even deserve an answer.

SOC. True ; and you will, I fancy, say the same of the earth which is in us living creatures and that which is in the universe, and concerning all the other elements about which I asked a moment ago your answer will be the same.

PRO. Yes. Who could answer otherwise without being called a lunatic ?

SOC. Nobody, I fancy. Now follow the next step. When we see that all the aforesaid elements are gathered together into a unit, do we not call them a body ?

PRO. Of course.

SOC. Apply the same line of thought to that which we call the universe. It would likewise be a body, being composed of the same elements.

PRO. Quite right.

SOC. Does our body derive, obtain, and possess from that body, or that body from ours, nourishment and everything else that we mentioned just now ?

PRO. That, Socrates, is another question not worth asking.

SOC. Well, is this next one worth asking ? What will you say to it ?

PRO. What is it ?

ΣΩ. Τὸ παρ' ἡμῖν σῶμα ἆρ' οὐ ψυχὴν φήσομεν ἔχειν;

ΠΡΩ. Δῆλον ὅτι φήσομεν.

ΣΩ. Πόθεν, ὦ φίλε Πρώταρχε, λαβόν, εἴπερ μὴ τό γε τοῦ παντὸς σῶμα ἔμψυχον ὂν ἐτύγχανε, ταὐτά γε ἔχον τούτῳ καὶ ἔτι πάντῃ καλλίονα;

ΠΡΩ. Δῆλον ὡς οὐδαμόθεν ἄλλοθεν, ὦ Σώκρατες.

ΣΩ. Οὐ γάρ που δοκοῦμέν γε, ὦ Πρώταρχε, τὰ τέτταρα ἐκεῖνα, πέρας καὶ ἄπειρον καὶ κοινὸν
B καὶ τὸ τῆς αἰτίας γένος ἐν ἅπασι τέταρτον ἐνόν, τοῦτο ἐν μὲν τοῖς παρ' ἡμῖν ψυχήν τε παρέχον καὶ σωμασκίαν[1] ἐμποιοῦν καὶ πταίσαντος σώματος ἰατρικὴν καὶ ἐν ἄλλοις ἄλλα συντιθὲν καὶ ἀκούμενον πᾶσαν καὶ παντοίαν σοφίαν ἐπικαλεῖσθαι, τῶν δ' αὐτῶν τούτων ὄντων ἐν ὅλῳ τε οὐρανῷ καὶ κατὰ μεγάλα μέρη, καὶ προσέτι καλῶν καὶ εἰλικρινῶν, ἐν τούτοις δ' οὐκ ἄρα μεμηχανῆσθαι τὴν τῶν καλλίστων καὶ τιμιωτάτων φύσιν.

C ΠΡΩ. Ἀλλ' οὐδαμῶς τοῦτό γ' ἂν λόγον ἔχοι.

ΣΩ. Οὐκοῦν εἰ μὴ τοῦτο, μετ' ἐκείνου τοῦ λόγου ἂν ἑπόμενοι βέλτιον λέγοιμεν ὡς ἔστιν, ἃ πολλάκις εἰρήκαμεν, ἄπειρόν τε ἐν τῷ παντὶ πολύ, καὶ πέρας ἱκανόν, καί τις ἐπ' αὐτοῖς αἰτία οὐ φαύλη, κοσμοῦσά τε καὶ συντάττουσα ἐνιαυτούς τε καὶ ὥρας καὶ μῆνας, σοφία καὶ νοῦς λεγομένη δικαιότατ' ἄν.

ΠΡΩ. Δικαιότατα δῆτα.

ΣΩ. Σοφία μὴν καὶ νοῦς ἄνευ ψυχῆς οὐκ ἄν ποτε γενοίσθην.

ΠΡΩ. Οὐ γὰρ οὖν.

ΣΩ. Οὐκοῦν ἐν μὲν τῇ τοῦ Διὸς ἐρεῖς φύσει
D βασιλικὴν μὲν ψυχήν, βασιλικὸν δὲ νοῦν ἐγγί-

soc. Shall we not say that our body has a soul ?

pro. Clearly we shall.

soc. Where did it get it, Protarchus, unless the body of the universe had a soul, since that body has the same elements as ours, only in every way superior ?

pro. Clearly it could get it from no other source.

soc. No ; for we surely do not believe, Protarchus, that of those four elements, the finite, the infinite, the combination, and the element of cause which exists in all things, this last, which gives to our bodies souls and the art of physical exercise¹ and medical treatment when the body is ill, and which is in general a composing and healing power, is called the sum of all wisdom, and yet, while these same elements exist in the entire heaven and in great parts thereof, and are, moreover, fair and pure, there is no means of including among them that nature which is the fairest and most precious of all.

pro. Certainly there would be no sense in that.

soc. Then if that is not the case, it would be better to follow the other line of thought and say, as we have often said, that there is in the universe a plentiful infinite and a sufficient limit, and in addition a by no means feeble cause which orders and arranges years and seasons and months, and may most justly be called wisdom and mind.

pro. Yes, most justly.

soc. Surely reason and mind could never come into being without soul.

pro. No, never.

soc. Then in the nature of Zeus you would say that a kingly soul and a kingly mind were implanted

---

¹ σωμασκίαν Eustathius: σῶμα σκιὰν BT.

γνεσθαι διὰ τὴν τῆς αἰτίας δύναμιν, ἐν δὲ ἄλλοις
ἄλλα καλά, καθ᾽ ὅ τι φίλον ἑκάστοις λέγεσθαι.

ΠΡΩ. Μάλα γε.

ΣΩ. Τοῦτον δὴ τὸν λόγον ἡμᾶς μή τι μάτην
δόξῃς, ὦ Πρώταρχε, εἰρηκέναι, ἀλλ᾽ ἔστι τοῖς
μὲν πάλαι ἀποφηναμένοις ὡς ἀεὶ τοῦ παντὸς νοῦς
ἄρχει ξύμμαχος ἐκείνοις.

ΠΡΩ. Ἔστι γὰρ οὖν.

ΣΩ. Τῇ δέ γε ἐμῇ ζητήσει πεπορικὼς ἀπό-
E κρισιν, ὅτι νοῦς ἐστι γένους[1] τοῦ πάντων αἰτίου
λεχθέντος τῶν τεττάρων ὧν[2] ἦν ἡμῖν ἓν τοῦτο.[3]
ἔχεις γὰρ δήπου νῦν ἡμῶν ἤδη τὴν ἀπόκρισιν.

ΠΡΩ. Ἔχω καὶ μάλα ἱκανῶς· καίτοι με ἀπο-
κρινάμενος ἔλαθες.

ΣΩ. Ἀνάπαυλα γάρ, ὦ Πρώταρχε, τῆς σπουδῆς
γίγνεται ἐνίοτε ἡ παιδιά.

ΠΡΩ. Καλῶς[4] εἶπες.

ΣΩ. Νοῦς δήπου,[5] ὦ ἑταῖρε, οὗ μὲν γένους
31 ἐστὶ καὶ τίνα ποτὲ δύναμιν κέκτηται, σχεδὸν
ἐπιεικῶς ἡμῖν τὰ νῦν δεδήλωται.

ΠΡΩ. Πάνυ μὲν οὖν.

ΣΩ. Καὶ μὴν ἡδονῆς γε ὡσαύτως πάλαι τὸ
γένος ἐφάνη.

ΠΡΩ. Καὶ μάλα.

ΣΩ. Μεμνώμεθα δὴ καὶ ταῦτα περὶ ἀμφοῖν,
ὅτι νοῦς μὲν αἰτίας ἦν ξυγγενὴς καὶ τούτου σχεδὸν
τοῦ γένους, ἡδονὴ δὲ ἄπειρός τε αὐτὴ καὶ τοῦ
μήτε ἀρχὴν μήτε μέσα μήτε τέλος ἐν αὑτῷ ἀφ᾽
ἑαυτοῦ ἔχοντος μηδὲ ἕξοντός ποτε γένους.

---

[1] γένους Bekker: γένους τῆς ΒΤ.
[2] ὧν om. ΒΤ: add. in marg. Τ.
[3] τῶν τεττάρων . . τοῦτο bracketed by Badham.

through the power of the cause, and in other deities other noble qualities from which they derive their favourite epithets.

PRO. Certainly.

SOC. Now do not imagine, Protarchus, that this is mere idle talk of mine ; it confirms the utterances of those who declared of old [1] that mind always rules the universe.

PRO. Yes, certainly.

SOC. And to my question it has furnished the reply that mind belongs to that one of our four classes which was called the cause of all. Now, you see, you have at last my answer.

PRO. Yes, and a very sufficient one ; and yet you answered without my knowing it.

SOC. Yes, Protarchus, for sometimes a joke is a restful change from serious talk.

PRO. You are right.

SOC. We have now, then, my friend, pretty clearly shown to what class mind belongs and what power it possesses.

PRO. Certainly.

SOC. And likewise the class of pleasure was made clear some time ago.

PRO. Yes, it was.

SOC. Let us, then, remember concerning both of them that mind was akin to cause and belonged more or less to that class, and that pleasure was itself infinite and belonged to the class which, in and by itself, has not and never will have either beginning or middle or end.

---

[1] Anaxagoras and probably some now unknown precursors.

[4] καλῶς T : καὶ καλῶς B.
[5] νοῦς δήπου Bekker : νῦν δήπου T : νῦν δὴ νοῦς B.

K   269

Β ΠΡΩ. Μεμνησόμεθα· πῶς γὰρ οὔ;

17. ΣΩ. Δεῖ δὴ τὸ μετὰ τοῦτο, ἐν ᾧ τέ ἐστιν ἑκάτερον αὐτοῖν καὶ διὰ τί πάθος γίγνεσθον ὁπόταν γίγνησθον ἰδεῖν ἡμᾶς· πρῶτον τὴν ἡδονήν· ὥσπερ τὸ γένος αὐτῆς πρότερον ἐβασανίσαμεν, οὕτω καὶ ταῦτα πρότερα. λύπης δ᾽ αὖ χωρὶς τὴν ἡδονὴν οὐκ ἄν ποτε δυναίμεθα ἱκανῶς βασανίσαι.

ΠΡΩ. Ἀλλ᾽ εἰ ταύτῃ χρὴ πορεύεσθαι, ταύτῃ πορευώμεθα.

ΣΩ. Ἆρ᾽ οὖν σοὶ καθάπερ ἐμοὶ φαίνεται τῆς γενέσεως αὐτῶν πέρι;

C ΠΡΩ. Τὸ ποῖον;

ΣΩ. Ἐν τῷ κοινῷ μοι γένει ἅμα φαίνεσθον λύπη τε καὶ ἡδονὴ γίγνεσθαι κατὰ φύσιν.

ΠΡΩ. Κοινὸν δέ γε, ὦ φίλε Σώκρατες, ὑπομίμνησκε ἡμᾶς τί ποτε τῶν προειρημένων βούλει δηλοῦν.

ΣΩ. Ἔσται ταῦτ᾽ εἰς δύναμιν, ὦ θαυμάσιε.

ΠΡΩ. Καλῶς εἶπες.

ΣΩ. Κοινὸν τοίνυν ὑπακούωμεν ὃ δὴ τῶν τεττάρων τρίτον ἐλέγομεν.

ΠΡΩ. Ὃ μετὰ τὸ ἄπειρον καὶ πέρας ἔλεγες, ἐν ᾧ καὶ ὑγίειαν, οἶμαι δὲ καὶ ἁρμονίαν, ἐτίθεσο;

D ΣΩ. Κάλλιστ᾽ εἶπες. τὸν νοῦν δὲ ὅτι μάλιστ᾽ ἤδη πρόσεχε.

ΠΡΩ. Λέγε μόνον.

ΣΩ. Λέγω τοίνυν τῆς ἁρμονίας μὲν λυομένης ἡμῖν ἐν τοῖς ζῴοις ἅμα λύσιν τῆς φύσεως καὶ γένεσιν ἀλγηδόνων ἐν τῷ τότε γίγνεσθαι χρόνῳ.

ΠΡΩ. Πάνυ λέγεις εἰκός.

ΣΩ. Πάλιν δὲ ἁρμοττομένης τε καὶ εἰς τὴν αὑτῆς φύσιν ἀπιούσης ἡδονὴν γίγνεσθαι λεκτέον,

270

PRO. We will remember that, of course.

SOC. Our next task is to see in what and by means of what feeling each of them comes into being whenever they do come into being. We will take pleasure first and discuss these questions in relation to pleasure, as we examined its class first. But we cannot examine pleasure successfully apart from pain.

PRO. If that is our proper path, let us follow it.

SOC. Do you agree with us about the origin of pleasure?

PRO. What do you think it is?

SOC. I think pain and pleasure naturally originate in the combined class.

PRO. Please, my dear Socrates, remind us which of the aforesaid classes you mean by the combined class.

SOC. I will do so, as well as I can, my brilliant friend.

PRO. Thank you.

SOC. By combined class, then, let us understand that which we said was the third of the four.

PRO. The one you mentioned after the infinite and the finite, and in which you put health and also, I believe, harmony?

SOC. You are quite right. Now please pay very close attention.

PRO. I will. Say on.

SOC. I say, then, that when, in us living beings, harmony is broken up, a disruption of nature and a generation of pain also take place at the same moment.

PRO. What you say is very likely.

SOC. But if harmony is recomposed and returns to its own nature, then I say that pleasure is generated,

εἰ δεῖ δι' ὀλίγων περὶ μεγίστων ὅτι τάχιστα
ῥηθῆναι.

Ε ΠΡΩ. Οἶμαι μέν σε ὀρθῶς λέγειν, ὦ Σώκρατες,
ἐμφανέστερον δὲ ἔτι ταὐτὰ ταῦτα πειρώμεθα
λέγειν.

ΣΩ. Οὐκοῦν τὰ δημόσιά που καὶ περιφανῆ
ῥᾷστον συννοεῖν;

ΠΡΩ. Ποῖα;

ΣΩ. Πείνη μέν που λύσις καὶ λύπη;

ΠΡΩ. Ναί.

ΣΩ. Ἐδωδὴ δέ, πλήρωσις γιγνομένη πάλιν,
ἡδονή;

ΠΡΩ. Ναί.

ΣΩ. Δίψος δ' αὖ φθορὰ καὶ λύπη,[1] ἡ δὲ τοῦ
32 ὑγροῦ πάλιν τὸ ξηρανθὲν πληροῦσα δύναμις ἡδονή·
διάκρισις δέ γ' αὖ καὶ διάλυσις ἡ παρὰ φύσιν,
τοῦ πνίγους πάθη, λύπη, κατὰ φύσιν δὲ[2] πάλιν
ἀπόδοσίς τε καὶ ψῦξις ἡδονή.

ΠΡΩ. Πάνυ μὲν οὖν.

ΣΩ. Καὶ ῥίγους ἡ μὲν παρὰ φύσιν τοῦ ζῴου
τῆς ὑγρότητος πῆξις λύπη· πάλιν δ' εἰς ταὐτὸν
ἀπιόντων καὶ διακρινομένων ἡ κατὰ φύσιν ὁδὸς
ἡδονή. καὶ ἑνὶ λόγῳ σκόπει εἴ σοι μέτριος
ὁ λόγος ὃς ἂν φῇ τὸ ἐκ τοῦ[3] ἀπείρου καὶ πέρατος
Β κατὰ φύσιν ἔμψυχον γεγονὸς εἶδος, ὅπερ ἔλεγον
ἐν τῷ πρόσθεν, ὅταν μὲν τοῦτο φθείρηται, τὴν
μὲν φθορὰν λύπην εἶναι, τὴν δ' εἰς τὴν αὐτῶν
οὐσίαν ὁδόν, ταύτην δ' αὖ πάλιν τὴν ἀναχώρησιν
πάντων ἡδονήν.

ΠΡΩ. Ἔστω· δοκεῖ γάρ μοι τύπον γέ τινα ἔχειν.

---

[1] λύπη καὶ λύσις (λῦσις Β) ΒΤ Stobaeus: bracketed by
Schleiermacher.

if I may speak in the fewest and briefest words about matters of the highest import.

PRO. I think you are right, Socrates; but let us try to be more explicit.

SOC. It is easiest to understand common and obvious examples, is it not?

PRO. What examples?

SOC. Is hunger a kind of breaking up and a pain?

PRO. Yes.

SOC. And eating, which is a filling up again, is a pleasure?

PRO. Yes.

SOC. Thirst again is a destruction and a pain, but the filling with moisture of that which was dried up is a pleasure. Then, too, the unnatural dissolution and disintegration we experience through heat are a pain, but the natural restoration and cooling are a pleasure.

PRO. Certainly.

SOC. And the unnatural hardening of the moisture in an animal through cold is pain; but the natural course of the elements returning to their place and separating is a pleasure. See, in short, if you think it is a reasonable statement that whenever in the class of living beings, which, as I said before, arises out of the natural union of the infinite and the finite, that union is destroyed, the destruction is pain, and the passage and return of all things to their own nature is pleasure.

PRO. Let us accept that; for it seems to me to be true in its general lines.

---

[2] δὲ Stobaeus: δὴ BT: δ' ἡ Heusde.
[3] τοῦ Stallbaum: τῆς BT.

ΣΩ. Τοῦτο μὲν τοίνυν ἓν εἶδος τιθώμεθα λύπης τε καὶ ἡδονῆς ἐν τούτοις τοῖς πάθεσιν ἑκατέροις;

ΠΡΩ. Κείσθω.

18. ΣΩ. Τίθει τοίνυν αὐτῆς τῆς ψυχῆς κατὰ C τὸ τούτων τῶν παθημάτων προσδόκημα τὸ μὲν πρὸ τῶν ἡδέων ἐλπιζόμενον ἡδὺ καὶ θαρραλέον, τὸ δὲ πρὸ τῶν λυπηρῶν φοβερὸν καὶ ἀλγεινόν.

ΠΡΩ. Ἔστι γὰρ οὖν τοῦθ' ἡδονῆς καὶ λύπης ἕτερον εἶδος, τὸ χωρὶς τοῦ σώματος αὐτῆς τῆς ψυχῆς διὰ προσδοκίας γιγνόμενον.

ΣΩ. Ὀρθῶς ὑπέλαβες. ἐν γὰρ τούτοις οἶμαι, κατά γε τὴν ἐμὴν δόξαν, εἰλικρινέσι τε ἑκατέροις γιγνομένοις, ὡς δοκεῖ, καὶ ἀμίκτοις λύπης τε καὶ ἡδονῆς, ἐμφανὲς ἔσεσθαι τὸ περὶ τὴν ἡδονήν, D πότερον ὅλον ἐστὶ τὸ γένος ἀσπαστόν, ἢ τοῦτο μὲν ἑτέρῳ τινὶ τῶν προειρημένων δοτέον ἡμῖν γενῶν, ἡδονῇ δὲ καὶ λύπῃ, καθάπερ θερμῷ καὶ ψυχρῷ καὶ πᾶσι τοῖς τοιούτοις, τοτὲ μὲν ἀσπαστέον αὐτά, τοτὲ δὲ οὐκ ἀσπαστέον, ὡς ἀγαθὰ μὲν οὐκ ὄντα, ἐνίοτε δὲ καὶ ἔνια δεχόμενα τὴν τῶν ἀγαθῶν ἔστιν ὅτε φύσιν.

ΠΡΩ. Ὀρθότατα λέγεις, ὅτι ταύτῃ πῃ δεῖ δια-θηρευθῆναι[1] τὸ νῦν μεταδιωκόμενον.

ΣΩ. Πρῶτον μὲν τοίνυν τόδε ξυνίδωμεν· ὡς E εἴπερ ὄντως ἔστι τὸ λεγόμενον, διαφθειρομένων μὲν αὐτῶν ἀλγηδών, ἀνασῳζομένων δὲ ἡδονή, τῶν μήτε διαφθειρομένων μήτε ἀνασῳζομένων ἐννοήσωμεν πέρι, τίνα ποτὲ ἕξιν δεῖ τότε ἐν ἑκάστοις εἶναι τοῖς ζῴοις, ὅταν οὕτως ἴσχῃ. σφόδρα δὲ προσέχων τὸν νοῦν εἰπέ· ἆρα οὐ πᾶσα

---

[1] διαθηρευθῆναι Stephanus: διαπορευθῆναι ΒΤ: διαπορηθῆναι Solomon.

274

soc. Then we may assume this as one kind of pain and pleasure arising severally under the conditions I have described ?

pro. Let that be assumed.

soc. Now assume within the soul itself the anticipation of these conditions, the sweet and cheering hope of pleasant things to come, the fearful and woful expectation of painful things to come.

pro. Yes, indeed, this is another kind of pleasure and pain, which belongs to the soul itself, apart from the body, and arises through expectation.

soc. You are right. I think that in these two kinds, both of which are, in my opinion, pure, and not formed by mixture of pain and pleasure, the truth about pleasure will be made manifest, whether the entire class is to be desired or such desirability is rather to be attributed to some other class among those we have mentioned, whereas pleasure and pain, like heat, cold, and other such things, are sometimes desirable and sometimes undesirable, because they are not good in themselves, though some of them sometimes admit on occasion the nature of the good.

pro. You are quite right in saying that we must track our quarry on this trail.

soc. First, then, let us agree on this point : If it is true, as we said, that destruction is pain and restoration is pleasure, let us consider the case of living beings in which neither destruction nor restoration is going on, and what their state is under such conditions. Fix your mind on my question : Must

ἀνάγκη πᾶν ἐν τῷ τότε χρόνῳ ζῷον μήτε τι
λυπεῖσθαι μήτε ἥδεσθαι μήτε μέγα μήτε σμικρόν;

ΠΡΩ. Ἀνάγκη μὲν οὖν.

ΣΩ. Οὐκοῦν ἔστι τις τρίτη ἡμῶν ἡ τοιαύτη
33 διάθεσις παρά τε τὴν τοῦ χαίροντος καὶ παρὰ τὴν
τοῦ λυπουμένου;

ΠΡΩ. Τί μήν;

ΣΩ. Ἄγε δὴ τοίνυν, ταύτης προθυμοῦ μεμνῆσθαι. πρὸς γὰρ τὴν τῆς ἡδονῆς κρίσιν οὐ σμικρὸν
μεμνῆσθαι ταύτην ἔσθ' ἡμῖν ἢ μή. βραχὺ δέ
τι περὶ αὐτῆς, εἰ βούλει, διαπεράνωμεν.

ΠΡΩ. Λέγε ποῖον.

ΣΩ. Τὸν[1] τοῦ φρονεῖν βίον[2] οἶσθ' ὡς τοῦτον
τὸν τρόπον οὐδὲν ἀποκωλύει ζῆν.

B ΠΡΩ. Τὸν τοῦ μὴ χαίρειν μηδὲ λυπεῖσθαι λέγεις;

ΣΩ. Ἐρρήθη γάρ που τότε ἐν τῇ παραβολῇ τῶν
βίων μηδὲν δεῖν μήτε μέγα μήτε σμικρὸν χαίρειν
τῷ τὸν τοῦ νοεῖν καὶ φρονεῖν βίον ἑλομένῳ.

ΠΡΩ. Καὶ μάλα οὕτως ἐρρήθη.

ΣΩ. Οὐκοῦν οὕτως ἂν ἐκείνῳ γε ὑπάρχοι· καὶ
ἴσως οὐδὲν ἄτοπον, εἰ πάντων τῶν βίων ἐστὶ
θειότατος.

ΠΡΩ. Οὔκουν εἰκός γε οὔτε χαίρειν θεοὺς οὔτε
τὸ ἐναντίον.

ΣΩ. Πάνυ μὲν οὖν οὐκ εἰκός· ἄσχημον γοῦν
αὐτῶν ἑκάτερον γιγνόμενόν ἐστιν. ἀλλὰ δὴ τοῦτο
C μὲν ἔτι καὶ εἰς αὖθις ἐπισκεψώμεθα, ἐὰν πρὸς
λόγον τι ᾖ, καὶ τῷ νῷ πρὸς τὰ δευτερεῖα, ἐὰν
μὴ πρὸς τὰ πρωτεῖα δυνώμεθα προσθεῖναι, προσθήσομεν.

ΠΡΩ. Ὀρθότατα λέγεις.

<hr />

[1] τὸν Badham: τῷ τὸν BT.

not every living being under those conditions necessarily be devoid of any feeling of pain or pleasure, great or small ?

PRO. Yes, necessarily.

SOC. Have we, then, a third condition, besides those of feeling pleasure and pain ?

PRO. Certainly.

SOC. Well then, do your best to bear it in mind ; for remembering or forgetting it will make a great difference in our judgement of pleasure. And I should like, if you do not object, to speak briefly about it.

PRO. Pray do so.

SOC. You know that there is nothing to hinder a man from living the life of wisdom in this manner.

PRO. You mean without feeling pleasure or pain ?

SOC. Yes, for it was said, you know, in our comparison of the lives that he who chose the life of mind and wisdom was to have no feeling of pleasure, great or small.

PRO. Yes, surely, that was said.

SOC. Such a man, then, would have such a life ; and perhaps it is not unreasonable, if that is the most divine of lives.

PRO. Certainly it is not likely that gods feel either joy or its opposite.

SOC. No, it is very unlikely ; for either is unseemly for them. But let us reserve the discussion of that point for another time, if it is appropriate, and we will give mind credit for it in contending for the second place, if we cannot count it for the first.

PRO. Quite right.

---

² βίον Badham : ἑλομένῳ βίον BT. Probably inserted here from the passage just below.

19. ΣΩ. Καὶ μὴν τό γε ἕτερον εἶδος τῶν ἡδονῶν, ὃ τῆς ψυχῆς αὐτῆς ἔφαμεν εἶναι, διὰ μνήμης πᾶν ἐστι γεγονός.

ΠΡΩ. Πῶς;

ΣΩ. Μνήμην, ὡς ἔοικεν, ὅ τι ποτ' ἔστι πρότερον ἀναληπτέον, καὶ κινδυνεύει πάλιν ἔτι πρότερον αἴσθησιν μνήμης, εἰ μέλλει τὰ περὶ ταῦθ' ἡμῖν κατὰ τρόπον φανερά πῃ γενήσεσθαι.

D ΠΡΩ. Πῶς φής;

ΣΩ. Θὲς τῶν περὶ τὸ σῶμα ἡμῶν ἑκάστοτε παθημάτων τὰ μὲν ἐν τῷ σώματι κατασβεννύμενα πρὶν ἐπὶ τὴν ψυχὴν διεξελθεῖν ἀπαθῆ ἐκείνην ἐάσαντα, τὰ δὲ δι' ἀμφοῖν ἰόντα καί τινα ὥσπερ σεισμὸν ἐντιθέντα ἴδιόν τε καὶ κοινὸν ἑκατέρῳ.

ΠΡΩ. Κείσθω.

ΣΩ. Τὰ μὲν δὴ μὴ δι' ἀμφοῖν ἰόντα ἐὰν τὴν ψυχὴν ἡμῶν φῶμεν λανθάνειν, τὰ δὲ δι' ἀμφοῖν μὴ λανθάνειν, ἆρ' ὀρθότατα ἐροῦμεν;

E ΠΡΩ. Πῶς γὰρ οὔ;

ΣΩ. Τὸ τοίνυν λεληθέναι μηδαμῶς ὑπολάβῃς ὡς λέγω λήθης ἐνταῦθά που γένεσιν· ἔστι γὰρ λήθη μνήμης ἔξοδος, ἡ δ' ἐν τῷ λεγομένῳ νῦν οὔπω γέγονε· τοῦ δὴ μήτε ὄντος μήτε γεγονότος πω[1] γίγνεσθαι φάναι τινὰ ἀποβολὴν ἄτοπον. ἢ γάρ;

ΠΡΩ. Τί μήν;

ΣΩ. Τὰ τοίνυν ὀνόματα μετάβαλε μόνον.

ΠΡΩ. Πῶς;

ΣΩ. Ἀντὶ μὲν τοῦ λεληθέναι τὴν ψυχήν, ὅταν ἀπαθὴς αὕτη γίγνηται τῶν σεισμῶν τῶν τοῦ
34 σώματος, ἣν νῦν λήθην καλεῖς, ἀναισθησίαν ἐπονόμασον.

soc. Now the other class of pleasure, which we said was an affair of the soul alone, originates entirely in memory.

pro. How is that?

soc. We must, apparently, first take up memory, and perception even before memory, if these matters are to be made clear to us properly.

pro. What do you mean?

soc. Assume that some of the affections of our body are extinguished in the body before they reach the soul, leaving the soul unaffected, and that other affections permeate both body and soul and cause a vibration in both conjointly and in each individually.

pro. Let us assume that.

soc. Shall we be right in saying that the soul forgets those which do not permeate both, and does not forget those which do?

pro. Yes, certainly.

soc. Do not in the least imagine that when I speak of forgetting I mean that forgetfulness arises in this case; for forgetfulness is the departure of memory, and in the case under consideration memory has not yet come into being; now it is absurd to speak of the loss of that which does not exist and has not yet come into being, is it not?

pro. Certainly.

soc. Then just change the terms.

pro. How?

soc. Instead of saying that the soul forgets, when it is unaffected by the vibrations of the body, apply the term want of perception to that which you are now calling forgetfulness.

---

¹ πω Stobaeus: πῶς B: πως T.

ΠΡΩ. Ἔμαθον.

ΣΩ. Τὸ δ' ἐν ἑνὶ πάθει τὴν ψυχὴν καὶ τὸ σῶμα
κοινῇ γιγνόμενον κοινῇ καὶ κινεῖσθαι, ταύτην δ'
αὖ τὴν κίνησιν ὀνομάζων αἴσθησιν οὐκ ἀπὸ τρόπου
φθέγγοι' ἄν.

ΠΡΩ. Ἀληθέστατα λέγεις.

ΣΩ. Οὐκοῦν ἤδη μανθάνομεν ὃ βουλόμεθα καλεῖν τὴν αἴσθησιν;

ΠΡΩ. Τί μήν;

ΣΩ. Σωτηρίαν τοίνυν αἰσθήσεως τὴν μνήμην
λέγων ὀρθῶς ἄν τις λέγοι κατά γε τὴν ἐμὴν δόξαν.

B ΠΡΩ. Ὀρθῶς γὰρ οὖν.

ΣΩ. Μνήμης δὲ ἀνάμνησιν ἆρ' οὐ διαφέρουσαν
λέγομεν;

ΠΡΩ. Ἴσως.

ΣΩ. Ἆρ' οὖν οὐ τόδε;

ΠΡΩ. Τὸ ποῖον;

ΣΩ. Ὅταν ἃ μετὰ τοῦ σώματος ἔπασχέν ποθ'
ἡ[1] ψυχή, ταῦτ' ἄνευ τοῦ σώματος αὐτὴ ἐν ἑαυτῇ
ὅτι μάλιστα ἀναλαμβάνῃ, τότε ἀναμιμνήσκεσθαί
που λέγομεν. ἦ γάρ;

ΠΡΩ. Πάνυ μὲν οὖν.

ΣΩ. Καὶ μὴν καὶ ὅταν ἀπολέσασα μνήμην εἴτε
αἰσθήσεως εἴτ' αὖ μαθήματος αὖθις ταύτην ἀν-
C απολήσῃ πάλιν αὐτὴ ἐν ἑαυτῇ, καὶ ταῦτα ξύμπαντα
ἀναμνήσεις[2] που λέγομεν.

ΠΡΩ. Ὀρθῶς λέγεις.

ΣΩ. Οὗ δὴ χάριν ἅπαντ' εἴρηται ταῦτα, ἔστι
τόδε.

ΠΡΩ. Τὸ ποῖον;

ΣΩ. Ἵνα ἤδη[3] τὴν τῆς ψυχῆς ἡδονὴν χωρὶς
σώματος ὅτι μάλιστα καὶ ἐναργέστατα λάβοιμεν,

PRO. I understand.

SOC. And the union of soul and body in one common affection and one common motion you may properly call perception.

PRO. Very true.

SOC. Then do we now understand what we mean by perception?

PRO. Certainly.

SOC. I think, then, that memory may rightly be defined as the preservation of perception.

PRO. Quite rightly.

SOC. But do we not say that memory differs from recollection?

PRO. Perhaps.

SOC. And is this the difference?

PRO. What?

SOC. When the soul alone by itself, apart from the body, recalls completely any experience it has had in company with the body, we say that it recollects, do we not?

PRO. Certainly.

SOC. And again when the soul has lost the memory of a perception or of something it has learned and then alone by itself regains this, we call everything of that kind recollection.

PRO. You are right.

SOC. Now my reason for saying all this is——

PRO. What?

SOC. That henceforth we may comprehend as completely and clearly as possible the pleasure of

---

¹ πόθ' ἡ T: πάθη B.

² ἀναμνήσεις καὶ μνήμας BT: καὶ μνήμας bracketed by Gloël.

³ ἤδη Hermann: μὴ BT: πῇ Schütz.

PLATO

καὶ ἅμα ἐπιθυμίαν· διὰ γὰρ τούτων πως ταῦτα
ἀμφότερα ἔοικε δηλοῦσθαι.

20. ΠΡΩ. Λέγωμεν τοίνυν, ὦ Σώκρατες, ἤδη
τὸ μετὰ ταῦτα.

ΣΩ. Πολλά γε περὶ γένεσιν ἡδονῆς καὶ πᾶσαν
D τὴν μορφὴν αὐτῆς ἀναγκαῖον, ὡς ἔοικε, λέγοντας
σκοπεῖν. καὶ γὰρ νῦν πρότερον ἔτι φαίνεται
ληπτέον ἐπιθυμίαν εἶναι, τί ποτ' ἔστι καὶ ποῦ
γίγνεται.

ΠΡΩ. Σκοπῶμεν τοίνυν· οὐδὲν γὰρ ἀπολοῦμεν.

ΣΩ. Ἀπολοῦμεν μὲν οὖν, καὶ ταῦτά γε, ὦ
Πρώταρχε, εὑρόντες ὃ νῦν ζητοῦμεν, ἀπολοῦμεν[1]
τὴν περὶ αὐτὰ ταῦτα ἀπορίαν.

ΠΡΩ. Ὀρθῶς ἡμύνω· τὸ δ' ἐφεξῆς τούτοις
πειρώμεθα λέγειν.

ΣΩ. Οὐκοῦν νῦν δὴ πείνην τε καὶ δίψος καὶ
E πόλλ' ἕτερα τοιαῦτα ἔφαμεν εἶναί τινας ἐπιθυμίας;

ΠΡΩ. Σφόδρα γε.

ΣΩ. Πρὸς τί ποτε ἄρα ταὐτὸν βλέψαντες οὕτω
πολὺ διαφέροντα ταῦθ' ἑνὶ προσαγορεύομεν ὀνόματι;

ΠΡΩ. Μὰ Δί' οὐ ῥᾴδιον ἴσως εἰπεῖν, ὦ Σώκρατες, ἀλλ' ὅμως λεκτέον.

ΣΩ. Ἐκεῖθεν δὴ ἐκ τῶν αὐτῶν πάλιν ἀναλάβωμεν.

ΠΡΩ. Πόθεν δή;

ΣΩ. Διψῇ που λέγομεν ἑκάστοτέ τι;

ΠΡΩ. Πῶς δ' οὔ;

ΣΩ. Τοῦτο δέ γ' ἐστὶ κενοῦται;

ΠΡΩ. Τί μήν;

ΣΩ. Ἆρ' οὖν τὸ δίψος ἐστὶν ἐπιθυμία;

ΠΡΩ. Ναί, πώματός γε.

the soul, and likewise its desire, apart from the body; for both of these appear to be made plain by what has been said about memory and recollection.

PRO. Let us, then, Socrates, discuss the next point.

SOC. We must, it seems, consider many things in relation to the origin and general aspect of pleasure; but now I think our first task is to take up the nature and origin of desire.

PRO. Then let us examine that; for we shall not lose anything.

SOC. Oh yes, Protarchus, we shall lose a great deal! When we find what we are seeking we shall lose our perplexity about these very questions.

PRO. That is a fair counter; but let us try to take up the next point.

SOC. Did we not say just now that hunger, thirst, and the like were desires?

PRO. They are, decidedly.

SOC. What sort of identity have we in view when we call these, which are so different, by one name?

PRO. By Zeus, Socrates, that question may not be easy to answer, yet it must be answered.

SOC. Let us, then, begin again at that point with the same examples.

PRO. At what point?

SOC. We say of a thing on any particular occasion, "it's thirsty," do we not?

PRO. Of course.

SOC. And that means being empty?

PRO. Certainly.

SOC. And is thirst, then, a desire?

PRO. Yes, of drink.

---

¹ ἀπολοῦμεν B: om. T.

35 ΣΩ. Πώματος, ἢ πληρώσεως πώματος;

ΠΡΩ. Οἶμαι μὲν πληρώσεως.

ΣΩ. Ὁ κενούμενος ἡμῶν ἄρα, ὡς ἔοικεν, ἐπιθυμεῖ τῶν ἐναντίων ἢ πάσχει· κενούμενος γὰρ ἐρᾷ πληροῦσθαι.

ΠΡΩ. Σαφέστατά γε.

ΣΩ. Τί οὖν; ὁ τὸ πρῶτον κενούμενος ἔστιν ὁπόθεν εἴτ' αἰσθήσει πληρώσεως ἐφάπτοιτ' ἂν εἴτε μνήμῃ, τούτου ὃ μήτ' ἐν τῷ νῦν χρόνῳ πάσχει μήτ' ἐν τῷ πρόσθε πώποτ' ἔπαθεν;

ΠΡΩ. Καὶ πῶς;

B ΣΩ. Ἀλλὰ μὴν ὅ γ' ἐπιθυμῶν τινὸς ἐπιθυμεῖ, φαμέν.

ΠΡΩ. Πῶς γὰρ οὔ;

ΣΩ. Οὐκ ἄρα ὅ γε πάσχει, τούτου ἐπιθυμεῖ. διψῇ γάρ, τοῦτο δὲ κένωσις· ὁ δὲ ἐπιθυμεῖ πληρώσεως.

ΠΡΩ. Ναί.

ΣΩ. Πληρώσεώς γ' ἄρα πῄ τι τῶν τοῦ διψῶντος ἂν ἐφάπτοιτο.

ΠΡΩ. Ἀναγκαῖον.

ΣΩ. Τὸ μὲν δὴ σῶμα ἀδύνατον· κενοῦται γάρ που.

ΠΡΩ. Ναί.

ΣΩ. Τὴν ψυχὴν ἄρα τῆς πληρώσεως ἐφάπτεσθαι
C λοιπόν, τῇ μνήμῃ δῆλον ὅτι· τῷ γὰρ ἂν ἔτ' ἄλλῳ ἐφάψαιτο;

ΠΡΩ. Σχεδὸν οὐδενί.

21. ΣΩ. Μανθάνομεν οὖν ὃ συμβέβηχ' ἡμῖν ἐκ τούτων τῶν λόγων;

ΠΡΩ. Τὸ ποῖον;

ΣΩ. Σώματος ἐπιθυμίαν οὔ φησιν ἡμῖν οὗτος ὁ λόγος γίγνεσθαι.

ΠΡΩ. Πῶς;

soc. Of drink, or of being filled with drink ?

pro. Of being filled, I suppose.

soc. The man, then, who is empty desires, as it appears, the opposite of what he feels ; for, being empty, he longs to be filled.

pro. That is very plain.

soc. Well then, is there any source from which a man who is empty at first can gain a comprehension, whether by perception or by memory, of fulness, a thing which he does not feel at the time and has never felt before ?

pro. It cannot be done.

soc. And yet he who desires, desires something, we say.

pro. Of course.

soc. And he does not desire that which he feels ; for he is thirsty, and that is emptiness, but he desires fulness.

pro. Yes.

soc. Then somehow some part of him who is thirsty can apprehend fulness.

pro. Yes, obviously.

soc. But it cannot be the body, for that is empty.

pro. True.

soc. The only remaining possibility is that the soul apprehends it, which it must do by means of memory ; for what other means could it employ ?

pro. No other, I should say.

soc. And do we understand the consequences of this argument ?

pro. What are the consequences ?

soc. This argument declares that we have no bodily desire.

pro. How so ?

ΣΩ. Ὅτι τοῖς ἐκείνου παθήμασιν ἐναντίαν ἀεὶ παντὸς ζῴου μηνύει τὴν ἐπιχείρησιν.

ΠΡΩ. Καὶ μάλα.

ΣΩ. Ἡ δ᾽ ὁρμή γε ἐπὶ τοὐναντίον ἄγουσα ἢ τὰ παθήματα δηλοῖ που μνήμην οὖσαν τῶν τοῖς παθήμασιν ἐναντίων.

ΠΡΩ. Πάνυ γε.

D ΣΩ. Τὴν ἄρα ἐπάγουσαν ἐπὶ τὰ ἐπιθυμούμενα ἀποδείξας μνήμην ὁ λόγος ψυχῆς ξύμπασαν τήν τε ὁρμὴν καὶ ἐπιθυμίαν καὶ τὴν ἀρχὴν τοῦ ζῴου παντὸς ἀπέφηνεν.

ΠΡΩ. Ὀρθότατα.

ΣΩ. Διψῆν ἄρα ἡμῶν τὸ σῶμα ἢ πεινῆν ἤ τι τῶν τοιούτων πάσχειν οὐδαμῇ ὁ λόγος αἱρεῖ.

ΠΡΩ. Ἀληθέστατα.

ΣΩ. Ἔτι δὴ καὶ τόδε περὶ ταὐτὰ ταῦτα κατανοήσωμεν. βίου γὰρ εἶδός τί μοι φαίνεται βούλεσθαι δηλοῦν ὁ λόγος ἡμῖν ἐν τούτοις αὐτοῖς.

E ΠΡΩ. Ἐν τίσι καὶ ποίου περὶ βίου φράζεις;

ΣΩ. Ἐν τῷ πληροῦσθαι καὶ κενοῦσθαι καὶ πᾶσιν ὅσα περὶ σωτηρίαν τέ ἐστι τῶν ζῴων καὶ τὴν φθοράν, καὶ εἴ τις τούτων ἐν ἑκατέρῳ γιγνόμενος ἡμῶν ἀλγεῖ, τοτὲ[1] δὲ χαίρει κατὰ τὰς μεταβολάς.

ΠΡΩ. Ἔστι ταῦτα.

ΣΩ. Τί δ᾽ ὅταν ἐν μέσῳ τούτων γίγνηται;

ΠΡΩ. Πῶς ἐν μέσῳ;

ΣΩ. Διὰ μὲν τὸ πάθος ἀλγῇ, μεμνῆται δὲ τῶν ἡδέων, ὧν[2] γενομένων παύοιτ᾽ ἂν τῆς ἀλγηδόνος,

---

[1] τοτὲ Stallbaum: τότε BT.
[2] ὧν add. corr. Ven. 189: om. BT.

soc. Because it shows that the endeavour of every living being is always towards the opposite of the actual conditions of the body.

pro. Yes, certainly.

soc. And the impulse which leads towards the opposite of those conditions shows that there is a memory of the opposite of the conditions.

pro. Certainly.

soc. And the argument, by showing that memory is that which leads us towards the objects of desire, has proved that all the impulse, the desire, and the ruling principle in every living being are of the soul.

pro. Quite right.

soc. So the argument denies utterly that the body hungers or thirsts or has any such affection.

pro. Very true.

soc. Let us consider a further point in connexion with those very affections. For I think the purpose of the argument is to point out to us a state of life existing in them.

pro. Of what sort of life are you speaking, and in what affections does it exist?

soc. In the affections of fulness and emptiness and all which pertain to the preservation and destruction of living beings, and I am thinking that if we fall into one of these we feel pain, which is followed by joy when we change to the other.

pro. That is true.

soc. And what if a man is between the two?

pro. How between them?

soc. Because of his condition, he is suffering, but he remembers the pleasures the coming of which would bring him an end of his pain; as yet, however,

287

πληρῶται δὲ μήπω· τί τότε; φῶμεν ἢ μὴ φῶμεν
36 αὐτὸν ἐν μέσῳ τῶν παθημάτων εἶναι;

ΠΡΩ. Φῶμεν μὲν οὖν.

ΣΩ. Πότερον ἀλγοῦνθ' ὅλως ἢ χαίροντα;

ΠΡΩ. Μὰ Δί', ἀλλὰ διπλῇ τινὶ λύπῃ λυπού-
μενον, κατὰ μὲν τὸ σῶμα ἐν τῷ παθήματι, κατὰ δὲ
τὴν ψυχὴν προσδοκίας τινὶ πόθῳ.

ΣΩ. Πῶς, ὦ Πρώταρχε, τὸ διπλοῦν τῆς λύπης
εἶπες; ἆρ' οὐκ ἔστι μὲν ὅτε τις ἡμῶν κενούμενος
B ἐν ἐλπίδι φανερᾷ τοῦ πληρωθήσεσθαι καθέστηκε,
τοτὲ τοὐναντίον ἀνελπίστως ἔχει;

ΠΡΩ. Καὶ μάλα γε.

ΣΩ. Μῶν οὖν οὐχὶ ἐλπίζων μὲν πληρωθήσεσθαι
τῷ μεμνῆσθαι δοκεῖ σοι χαίρειν, ἅμα δὲ κενούμενος
ἐν τούτοις τοῖς χρόνοις ἀλγεῖν;

ΠΡΩ. Ἀνάγκη.

ΣΩ. Τότ' ἄρα ἄνθρωπος καὶ τἆλλα ζῷα λυπεῖταί
τε ἅμα καὶ χαίρει.

ΠΡΩ. Κινδυνεύει.

ΣΩ. Τί δ' ὅταν ἀνελπίστως ἔχῃ κενούμενος
τεύξεσθαι πληρώσεως; ἆρ' οὐ τότε τὸ διπλοῦν
γίγνοιτ' ἂν περὶ τὰς λύπας πάθος, ὃ σὺ νῦν δὴ
C κατιδὼν ᾠήθης ἁπλῶς εἶναι διπλοῦν;

ΠΡΩ. Ἀληθέστατα, ὦ Σώκρατες.

ΣΩ. Ταύτῃ δὴ τῇ σκέψει τούτων τῶν παθημάτων
τόδε χρησώμεθα.

ΠΡΩ. Τὸ ποῖον;

ΣΩ. Πότερον ἀληθεῖς ταύτας τὰς λύπας τε καὶ
ἡδονὰς ἢ ψευδεῖς εἶναι λέξομεν; ἢ τὰς μέν τινας
ἀληθεῖς, τὰς δ' οὔ;

ΠΡΩ. Πῶς δ', ὦ Σώκρατες, ἂν εἶεν ψευδεῖς
ἡδοναὶ ἢ λῦπαι;

he does not possess them. Well then, shall we say that he is between the affections, or not?

PRO. Let us say so.

SOC. Shall we say that he is wholly pained or wholly pleased?

PRO. No, by Zeus, but he is afflicted with a twofold pain; he suffers in body from his sensation, and in soul from expectation and longing.

SOC. How could you, Protarchus, speak of twofold pain? Is not an empty man sometimes possessed of a sure hope of being filled, and sometimes, on the contrary, quite hopeless?

PRO. Certainly.

SOC. And do you not think that when he has a hope of being filled he takes pleasure in his memory, and yet at the same time, since he is at the moment empty, suffers pain?

PRO. It cannot be otherwise.

SOC. At such a time, then, a man, or any other animal, has both pain and pleasure at once.

PRO. Yes, I suppose so.

SOC. And when an empty man is without hope of being filled, what then? Is not that the time when the twofold feeling of pain would arise, which you just now observed and thought the pain simply was twofold?

PRO. Very true, Socrates.

SOC. Let us make use of our examination of those affections for a particular purpose.

PRO. For what purpose?

SOC. Shall we say that those pleasures and pains are true or false, or that some are true and others not so?

PRO. But, Socrates, how can there be false pleasures or pains?

ΣΩ. Πῶς δέ, ὦ Πρώταρχε, φόβοι ἂν ἀληθεῖς ἢ
ψευδεῖς, ἢ προσδοκίαι ἀληθεῖς ἢ μή, ἢ δόξαι ἀληθεῖς
ἢ ψευδεῖς;

D ΠΡΩ. Δόξας μὲν ἔγωγ᾽ ἄν που συγχωροίην, τὰ
δ᾽ ἕτερα ταῦτ᾽ οὐκ ἄν.

ΣΩ. Πῶς φής; λόγον μέντοι τινὰ κινδυνεύομεν
οὐ πάνυ σμικρὸν ἐπεγείρειν.

ΠΡΩ. Ἀληθῆ λέγεις.

ΣΩ. Ἀλλ᾽ εἰ πρὸς τὰ παρεληλυθότα, ὦ παῖ
᾽κείνου τἀνδρός, προσήκοντα, τοῦτο σκεπτέον.

ΠΡΩ. Ἴσως τοῦτό γε.

ΣΩ. Χαίρειν τοίνυν δεῖ λέγειν τοῖς ἄλλοις μήκεσιν
ἢ καὶ ὁτῳοῦν τῶν παρὰ τὸ προσῆκον λεγομένων.

ΠΡΩ. Ὀρθῶς.

E ΣΩ. Λέγε δή μοι· θαῦμα γὰρ ἐμέ γ᾽ ἔχει διὰ
τέλους ἀεὶ περὶ τὰ αὐτὰ ἃ νῦν δὴ προυθέμεθα ἀπο-
ρήματα.

ΠΡΩ. Πῶς δὴ φής;

ΣΩ. Ψευδεῖς, αἱ δ᾽ ἀληθεῖς οὐκ εἰσὶν ἡδοναί;

ΠΡΩ. Πῶς γὰρ ἄν;

ΣΩ. Οὔτε δὴ ὄναρ οὔθ᾽ ὕπαρ, ὡς φής,[1] οὔτ᾽ ἐν
μανίαις οὔτ᾽ ἐν παραφροσύναις[2] οὐδεὶς ἔσθ᾽ ὅστις
ποτὲ δοκεῖ μὲν χαίρειν, χαίρει δὲ οὐδαμῶς, οὐδ᾽
αὖ δοκεῖ μὲν λυπεῖσθαι, λυπεῖται δ᾽ οὔ.

ΠΡΩ. Πάνθ᾽ οὕτω ταῦτ᾽, ὦ Σώκρατες, ἔχειν
πάντες ὑπειλήφαμεν.

ΣΩ. Ἆρ᾽ οὖν ὀρθῶς; ἢ σκεπτέον εἴτ᾽ ὀρθῶς εἴτε
μὴ ταῦτα λέγεται;

37 22. ΠΡΩ. Σκεπτέον, ὥς γ᾽ ἐγὼ φαίην ἄν.

---

[1] φής Stallbaum: φής, ἔστιν ΒΤ.
[2] παραφροσύναις Β, from πάσαις ἀφροσύναις: πάσαις ἀφροσύναις Τ.

soc. But, Protarchus, how can there be true and false fears, or true and false expectations, or true and false opinions ?

pro. Opinions I would grant you, but not the rest.

soc. What ? I am afraid we are starting a very considerable discussion.

pro. You are right.

soc. And yet we must consider, thou son of that man,[1] whether the discussion is relevant to what has gone before.

pro. Yes, no doubt.

soc. We must dismiss everything else, tedious or otherwise, that is irrelevant.

pro. Right.

soc. Now tell me ; for I am always utterly amazed by the same questions we were just proposing.

pro. What do you mean ?

soc. Are not some pleasures false and others true ?

pro. How could that be ?

soc. Then, as you maintain, nobody, either sleeping or waking or insane or deranged, ever thinks he feels pleasure when he does not feel it, and never, on the other hand, thinks he suffers pain when he does not suffer it ?

pro. We have, Socrates, always believed that all this is as you suggest.

soc. But is the belief correct ? Shall we consider whether it is so or not ?

pro. I should say we ought to consider that.

[1] " Son of that man " may mean " son of Philebus," in so far as Protarchus is a pupil of Philebus, or (so Bury) " son of Gorgias," the orator and teacher (cf. 58 b), or the father of Protarchus may be referred to by the pronoun, possibly because Socrates does not at the moment recall his name or because he wishes to imply that he was a man of mark.

ΣΩ. Διορισώμεθα δὴ σαφέστερον ἔτι τὸ νῦν δὴ
λεγόμενον ἡδονῆς τε πέρι καὶ δόξης. ἔστι γάρ
πού τι δοξάζειν ἡμῖν;

ΠΡΩ. Ναί.

ΣΩ. Καὶ ἥδεσθαι;

ΠΡΩ. Ναί.

ΣΩ. Καὶ μὴν καὶ τὸ δοξαζόμενόν ἐστί τι;

ΠΡΩ. Πῶς δ' οὔ;

ΣΩ. Καὶ τό γε ᾧ τὸ ἡδόμενον ἥδεται;

ΠΡΩ. Καὶ πάνυ γε.

ΣΩ. Οὐκοῦν τὸ δοξάζον, ἄντε ὀρθῶς ἄντε μὴ
ὀρθῶς δοξάζῃ, τό γε δοξάζειν ὄντως οὐδέποτ' ἀπόλ-
λυσιν.

B   ΠΡΩ. Πῶς γὰρ ἄν;

ΣΩ. Οὐκοῦν καὶ τὸ ἡδόμενον, ἄντε ὀρθῶς ἄντε
μὴ ὀρθῶς ἥδηται, τό γε ὄντως ἥδεσθαι δῆλον ὡς
οὐδέποτε ἀπολεῖ.

ΠΡΩ. Ναί, καὶ τοῦθ' οὕτως ἔχει.

ΣΩ. Ὅτῳ[1] ποτὲ οὖν δὴ τρόπῳ δόξα ψευδής τε καὶ
ἀληθὴς ἡμῖν φιλεῖ γίγνεσθαι, τὸ δὲ τῆς ἡδονῆς
μόνον ἀληθές, δοξάζειν δ' ὄντως καὶ χαίρειν ἀμφότερα ὁμοίως εἴληχεν[2] σκεπτέον.[3]

ΠΡΩ. Σκεπτέον.

ΣΩ. Ἆρ' ὅτι δόξῃ μὲν ἐπιγίγνεσθον ψεῦδός τε
C καὶ ἀληθές, καὶ ἐγένετο οὐ μόνον δόξα διὰ ταῦτα
ἀλλὰ καὶ ποιά τις ἑκατέρα, σκεπτέον φῂς τοῦτ'
εἶναι;

ΠΡΩ. Ναί.

ΣΩ. Πρὸς δέ γε τούτοις, εἰ καὶ τὸ παράπαν

---

[1] ὅτῳ BT : τῷ t vulg.
[2] εἴληχε Stallbaum : εἴληφεν BT.
[3] σκεπτέον add. Baiter.

soc. Then let us analyse still more clearly what we were just now saying about pleasure and opinion. There is a faculty of having an opinion, is there not ?

pro. Yes.

soc. And of feeling pleasure ?

pro. Yes.

soc. And there is an object of opinion ?

pro. Of course.

soc. And something by which that which feels pleasure is pleased ?

pro. Certainly.

soc. And that which has opinion, whether right or wrong, never loses its function of really having opinion ?

pro. Of course not.

soc. And that which feels pleasure, whether rightly or wrongly, will clearly never lose its function of really feeling pleasure ?

pro. Yes, that is true, too.

soc. Then we must consider how it is that opinion is both true and false and pleasure only true, though the holding of opinion and the feeling of pleasure are equally real.

pro. Yes, so we must.

soc. You mean that we must consider this question because falsehood and truth are added as attributes to opinion, and thereby it becomes not merely opinion, but opinion of a certain quality in each instance ?

pro. Yes.

soc. And furthermore, we must reach an agreement on the question whether, even if some things

ἡμῖν τὰ μέν ἐστι ποῖ᾽ ἄττα, ἡδονὴ δὲ καὶ λύπη μόνον
ἅπερ ἐστί, ποιώ τινε¹ δὲ οὐ γίγνεσθον, καὶ ταῦθ᾽ ἡμῖν
διομολογητέον.

ΠΡΩ. Δῆλον.

ΣΩ. Ἀλλ᾽ οὐδὲν τοῦτό γε χαλεπὸν ἰδεῖν, ὅτι
καὶ ποιώ τινε. πάλαι γὰρ εἴπομεν ὅτι μεγάλαι τε
καὶ σμικραὶ καὶ σφόδρα ἑκάτεραι γίγνονται, λῦπαί
D τε καὶ ἡδοναί.

ΠΡΩ. Παντάπασι μὲν οὖν.

ΣΩ. Ἂν δέ γε πονηρία τούτων, ὦ Πρώταρχε,
προσγίγνηταί τινι, πονηρὰν μὲν φήσομεν οὕτω γίγνεσθαι δόξαν, πονηρὰν δὲ καὶ ἡδονήν;

ΠΡΩ. Ἀλλὰ τί μήν, ὦ Σώκρατες;

ΣΩ. Τί δ᾽, ἂν ὀρθότης ἢ τοὐναντίον ὀρθότητι
τινὶ τούτων προσγίγνηται; μῶν οὐκ ὀρθὴν μὲν
δόξαν ἐροῦμεν, ἂν ὀρθότητα ἴσχῃ, ταὐτὸν δὲ ἡδονήν;

ΠΡΩ. Ἀναγκαῖον.

E ΣΩ. Ἂν δέ γε ἁμαρτανόμενον τὸ δοξαζόμενον
ᾖ, τὴν δόξαν τότε ἁμαρτάνουσάν γε οὐκ ὀρθὴν
ὁμολογητέον οὐδ᾽ ὀρθῶς δοξάζουσαν;

ΠΡΩ. Πῶς γὰρ ἄν;

ΣΩ. Τί δ᾽, ἂν αὖ λύπην ἤ τινα ἡδονὴν περὶ τὸ
ἐφ᾽ ᾧ λυπεῖται ἢ τοὐναντίον ἁμαρτάνουσαν ἐφ-
ορῶμεν, ὀρθὴν ἢ χρηστὴν ἤ τι τῶν καλῶν ὀνομάτων
αὐτῇ προσθήσομεν;

ΠΡΩ. Ἀλλ᾽ οὐχ οἷόν τε, εἴπερ ἁμαρτήσεταί γε
ἡδονή.

ΣΩ. Καὶ μὴν ἔοικέ γε ἡδονὴ πολλάκις οὐ μετὰ
δόξης ὀρθῆς ἀλλὰ μετὰ ψεύδους ἡμῖν γίγνεσθαι.

ΠΡΩ. Πῶς γὰρ οὔ; καὶ τὴν μὲν δόξαν γε, ὦ
38 Σώκρατες, ἐν τῷ τοιούτῳ καὶ τότε λέγομεν² ψευδῆ,
τὴν δ᾽ ἡδονὴν αὐτὴν οὐδεὶς ἄν ποτε προσείποι ψευδῆ.

have qualities, pleasure and pain are not merely
what they are, without qualities or attributes.

PRO. Evidently we must.

SOC. But it is easy enough to see that they have
qualities. For we said a long time ago that both
pains and pleasures are great and small and intense.

PRO. Yes, certainly.

SOC. And if badness becomes an attribute of any
of these, Protarchus, shall we say that the opinion
or the pleasure thereby becomes bad?

PRO. Why certainly, Socrates.

SOC. And what if rightness or its opposite becomes
an attribute of one of them? Shall we not say that
the opinion is right, if it has rightness, and the
pleasure likewise?

PRO. Obviously.

SOC. And if that which is opined is mistaken,
must we not agree that the opinion, since it is at
the moment making a mistake, is not right or rightly
opining?

PRO. Of course.

SOC. And what if we see a pain or a pleasure
making a mistake in respect of that by which the
pain or pleasure is caused? Shall we give it the
attribute of right or good or any of the words which
denote excellence?

PRO. That is impossible if the pleasure is mistaken.

SOC. And certainly pleasure often seems to come
to us in connexion with false, not true, opinion.

PRO. Of course it does; and in such a case,
Socrates, we call the opinion false; but nobody
would ever call the actual pleasure false.

---

[1] ποιώ τινε t: ποιῶν τινε T: ποιων· τινε B.
[2] λέγομεν Stallbaum: ἐλέγομεν BT.

ΣΩ. Ἀλλὰ προθύμως ἀμύνεις τῷ τῆς ἡδονῆς, ὦ
Πρώταρχε, λόγῳ τὰ νῦν.

ΠΡΩ. Οὐδέν γε, ἀλλ' ἅπερ ἀκούω λέγω.

ΣΩ. Διαφέρει δ' ἡμῖν οὐδέν, ὦ ἑταῖρε, ἡ μετὰ
δόξης τε ὀρθῆς καὶ μετ' ἐπιστήμης ἡδονὴ τῆς μετὰ
τοῦ ψεύδους καὶ ἀγνοίας[1] πολλάκις ἑκάστοις ἡμῶν
ἐγγιγνομένης;

B ΠΡΩ. Εἰκὸς γοῦν μὴ σμικρὸν διαφέρειν.

23. ΣΩ. Τῆς δὴ διαφορᾶς αὐτοῖν ἐπὶ θεωρίαν
ἔλθωμεν.

ΠΡΩ. Ἄγε ὅπῃ σοι φαίνεται.

ΣΩ. Τῇδε δὴ ἄγω.

ΠΡΩ. Πῇ;

ΣΩ. Δόξα, φαμέν, ἡμῖν ἔστι μὲν ψευδής, ἔστι
δὲ καὶ ἀληθής;

ΠΡΩ. Ἔστιν.

ΣΩ. Ἕπεται μὴν ταύταις, ὃ νῦν δὴ ἐλέγομεν,
ἡδονὴ καὶ λύπη πολλάκις, ἀληθεῖ καὶ ψευδεῖ δόξῃ
λέγω.

ΠΡΩ. Πάνυ γε.

ΣΩ. Οὐκοῦν ἐκ μνήμης τε καὶ αἰσθήσεως δόξα
C ἡμῖν καὶ τὸ διαδοξάζειν ἐγχειρεῖν γίγνεθ'[2] ἑκάστοτε;

ΠΡΩ. Καὶ μάλα.

ΣΩ. Ἆρ' οὖν ἡμᾶς ὧδε περὶ ταῦτα ἀναγκαῖον
ἡγούμεθα ἴσχειν;

ΠΡΩ. Πῶς;

ΣΩ. Πολλάκις ἰδόντι τινὶ πόρρωθεν μὴ πάνυ
σαφῶς τὰ καθορώμενα ξυμβαίνειν βούλεσθαι κρίνειν φαίης ἂν ταῦθ' ἅπερ ὁρᾷ;

ΠΡΩ. Φαίην ἄν.

ΣΩ. Οὐκοῦν τὸ μετὰ τοῦτο αὐτὸς αὑτὸν οὗτος
ἀνέροιτ' ἂν ὧδε;

PHILEBUS

soc. You are an eager advocate of the case of pleasure just now, Protarchus.

pro. Oh no, I merely say what I hear.

soc. Is there no difference, my friend, between the pleasure which is connected with right opinion and knowledge and that which often comes to each of us with falsehood and ignorance?

pro. There is likely to be a great difference.

soc. Then let us proceed to the contemplation of the difference between them.

pro. Lead on as you think best.

soc. Then this is the way I lead.

pro. What way?

soc. Do we agree that there is such a thing as false opinion and also as true opinion?

pro. There is.

soc. And, as we were saying just now, pleasure and pain often follow them—I mean true and false opinion.

pro. Certainly.

soc. And do not opinion and the power of forming an opinion always come to us from memory and perception?

pro. Certainly.

soc. Do we, then, believe that our relation to these faculties is somewhat as follows?

pro. How?

soc. Would you say that often when a man sees things at a distance and not very clearly, he wishes to distinguish between the things which he sees?

pro. Yes, I should say so.

soc. Next, then, would he not ask himself——

---

¹ ἀγνοίας Cornarius: ἀνοίας BT.
² γίγνεθ' Vat.: γίγνεσθ' B: γίγνεται T.

ΠΡΩ. Πῶς;

ΣΩ. Τί ποτε ἄρα ἔστι τὸ παρὰ τὴν πέτραν τοῦθ'
D ἑστάναι φανταζόμενον ὑπό τινι δένδρῳ; ταῦτ'
εἰπεῖν ἄν τις πρὸς ἑαυτὸν δοκεῖ σοι,[1] τοιαῦτα ἄττα
κατιδὼν φαντασθέντα αὑτῷ ποτέ;

ΠΡΩ. Τί μήν;

ΣΩ. Ἆρ' οὖν μετὰ ταῦτα ὁ τοιοῦτος ὡς ἀποκρινόμενος ἂν πρὸς αὑτὸν εἴποι τοῦτο, ὡς ἔστιν
ἄνθρωπος, ἐπιτυχῶς εἰπών;

ΠΡΩ. Καὶ πάνυ γε.

ΣΩ. Καὶ παρενεχθείς γ' αὖ τάχ' ἂν ὡς ἔστι τινῶν
ποιμένων ἔργον τὸ καθορώμενον ἄγαλμα προσείποι.

ΠΡΩ. Μάλα γε.

E ΣΩ. Κἂν μέν τίς γ' αὑτῷ παρῇ, τά τε πρὸς
αὑτὸν ῥηθέντα ἐντείνας εἰς φωνὴν πρὸς τὸν παρόντα
αὐτὰ ταῦτ' ἂν πάλιν φθέγξαιτο, καὶ λόγος δὴ
γέγονεν οὕτως ὃ τότε δόξαν ἐκαλοῦμεν;

ΠΡΩ. Τί μήν;

ΣΩ. Ἂν δ' ἄρα μόνος ᾖ τοῦτο ταὐτὸν πρὸς
αὑτὸν[2] διανοούμενος, ἐνίοτε καὶ πλείω χρόνον
ἔχων ἐν αὑτῷ πορεύεται.

ΠΡΩ. Πάνυ μὲν οὖν.

ΣΩ. Τί οὖν; ἆρα σοὶ φαίνεται τὸ περὶ τούτων
γιγνόμενον ὅπερ ἐμοί;

ΠΡΩ. Τὸ ποῖον;

ΣΩ. Δοκεῖ μοι τότε ἡμῶν ἡ ψυχὴ βιβλίῳ τινὶ
προσεοικέναι.

ΠΡΩ. Πῶς;

39 ΣΩ. Ἡ μνήμη ταῖς αἰσθήσεσι ξυμπίπτουσα εἰς
ταὐτὸν κἀκεῖνα ἃ περὶ ταῦτά ἐστι τὰ παθήματα φαί-
νονταί μοι σχεδὸν οἷον γράφειν ἡμῶν ἐν ταῖς ψυχαῖς
τότε λόγους· καὶ ὅταν μὲν ἀληθῆ γράψῃ τοῦτο τὸ

PRO. What ?

SOC. " What is that which is visible standing beside
the rock under a tree ? " Do you not think a man
might ask himself such a question if he saw such
objects presented to his view ?

PRO. To be sure.

SOC. And after that our gazer might reply to
himself correctly " It is a man " ?

PRO. Certainly.

SOC. Or, again, perhaps he might be misled into
the belief that it was a work of some shepherds, and
then he would call the thing which he saw an image.

PRO. Yes, indeed.

SOC. And if some one is with him, he might
repeat aloud to his companion what he had said to
himself, and thus that which we called an opinion
now becomes a statement ?

PRO. Certainly.

SOC. But if he is alone when he has this thought,
he sometimes carries it about in his mind for a long
time.

PRO. Undoubtedly.

SOC. Well, is your view about what takes place in
such cases the same as mine ?

PRO. What is yours ?

SOC. I think the soul at such a time is like a book.

PRO. How is that ?

SOC. Memory unites with the senses, and they and
the feelings which are connected with them seem to
me almost to write words in our souls ; and when
the feeling in question writes the truth, true opinions

---

¹ δοκεῖ σοι Coisl.: δοκῇ σοι T : δοκήσοι B.
² αὐτὸν] αὐτὸν T : αὐτὸ B.

πάθημα, δόξα τε ἀληθὴς καὶ λόγοι ἀπ᾽ αὐτοῦ ξυμ-
βαίνουσιν ἀληθεῖς ἐν ἡμῖν γιγνόμενοι· ψευδῆ δ᾽
ὅταν ὁ τοιοῦτος παρ᾽ ἡμῖν γραμματεὺς γράψῃ,
τἀναντία τοῖς ἀληθέσιν ἀπέβη.

Β ΠΡΩ. Πάνυ μὲν οὖν δοκεῖ μοι, κα ιἀποδέχομαι
τὰ ῥηθέντα οὕτως.

ΣΩ. Ἀποδέχου δὴ καὶ ἕτερον δημιουργὸν ἡμῶν
ἐν ταῖς ψυχαῖς ἐν τῷ τότε χρόνῳ γιγνόμενον.

ΠΡΩ. Τίνα;

ΣΩ. Ζωγράφον, ὃς μετὰ τὸν γραμματιστὴν τῶν
λεγομένων εἰκόνας ἐν τῇ ψυχῇ τούτων γράφει.

ΠΡΩ. Πῶς δὴ τοῦτον αὖ καὶ πότε λέγομεν;

ΣΩ. Ὅταν ἀπ᾽ ὄψεως ἤ τινος ἄλλης αἰσθήσεως
τὰ τότε δοξαζόμενα καὶ λεγόμενα ἀπαγαγών τις τὰς
τῶν δοξασθέντων καὶ λεχθέντων εἰκόνας ἐν αὑτῷ

C ὁρᾷ πως. ἢ τοῦτο οὐκ ἔστι γιγνόμενον παρ᾽ ἡμῖν;

ΠΡΩ. Σφόδρα μὲν οὖν.

ΣΩ. Οὐκοῦν αἱ μὲν τῶν ἀληθῶν δοξῶν καὶ λόγων εἰκόνες ἀληθεῖς, αἱ δὲ τῶν ψευδῶν ψευδεῖς;

ΠΡΩ. Παντάπασιν.

ΣΩ. Εἰ δὴ ταῦτ᾽ ὀρθῶς εἰρήκαμεν, ἔτι καὶ τόδε
ἐπὶ τούτοις σκεψώμεθα.

ΠΡΩ. Τὸ ποῖον;

ΣΩ. Εἰ περὶ μὲν τῶν ὄντων καὶ τῶν γεγονότων
ταῦτα ἡμῖν οὕτω πάσχειν ἀναγκαῖον, περὶ δὲ τῶν
μελλόντων οὔ;

ΠΡΩ. Περὶ ἁπάντων μὲν οὖν τῶν χρόνων ὡσαύτως.

D ΣΩ. Οὐκοῦν αἵ γε διὰ τῆς ψυχῆς αὐτῆς ἡδοναὶ
καὶ λῦπαι ἐλέχθησαν ἐν τοῖς πρόσθεν ὡς πρὸ τῶν
διὰ τοῦ σώματος ἡδονῶν καὶ λυπῶν προγίγνοιντ᾽[1] ἄν,
ὥσθ᾽ ἡμῖν ξυμβαίνει τὸ προχαίρειν τε καὶ προλυ-
πεῖσθαι περὶ τὸν μέλλοντα χρόνον εἶναι γιγνόμενον;

and true statements are produced in us; but when the writer within us writes falsehoods, the resulting opinions and statements are the opposite of true.

PRO. That is my view completely, and I accept it as stated.

SOC. Then accept also the presence of another workman in our souls at such a time.

PRO. What workman?

SOC. A painter, who paints in our souls pictures to illustrate the words which the writer has written.

PRO. But how do we say he does this, and when?

SOC. When a man receives from sight or some other sense the opinions and utterances of the moment and afterwards beholds in his own mind the images of those opinions and utterances. That happens to us often enough, does it not?

PRO. It certainly does.

SOC. And the images of the true opinions are true, and those of the false are false?

PRO. Assuredly.

SOC. Then if we are right about that, let us consider a further question.

PRO. What is it?

SOC. Whether this is an inevitable experience in relation to the present and the past, but not in relation to the future.

PRO. It is in the same relation to all kinds of time.

SOC. Was it not said a while ago that the pleasures and pains which belong to the soul alone might come before the pleasures and pains of the body, so that we have the pleasure and pain of anticipation, which relate to the future?

---

¹ προγίγνοιντ' recc.: προγίγνοιτ' BT.

ΠΡΩ. Ἀληθέστατα.

ΣΩ. Πότερον οὖν τὰ γράμματά τε καὶ ζωγραφήματα, ἃ σμικρῷ πρότερον ἐτίθεμεν ἐν ἡμῖν γίγνεσθαι, περὶ μὲν τὸν γεγονότα καὶ τὸν παρόντα
Ε χρόνον ἐστί, περὶ δὲ τὸν μέλλοντα οὐκ ἔστιν;

ΠΡΩ. Σφόδρα γε.

ΣΩ. Ἆρα σφόδρα λέγεις, ὅτι πάντ' ἐστὶ ταῦτα ἐλπίδες εἰς τὸν ἔπειτα χρόνον οὖσαι, ἡμεῖς δ' αὖ διὰ παντὸς τοῦ βίου ἀεὶ γέμομεν ἐλπίδων;

ΠΡΩ. Παντάπασι μὲν οὖν.

24. ΣΩ. Ἄγε δή, πρὸς τοῖς νῦν εἰρημένοις καὶ τόδε ἀπόκριναι.

ΠΡΩ. Τὸ ποῖον;

ΣΩ. Δίκαιος ἀνὴρ καὶ εὐσεβὴς καὶ ἀγαθὸς πάντως ἆρ' οὐ θεοφιλής ἐστιν;

ΠΡΩ. Τί μήν;

ΣΩ. Τί δέ; ἄδικός τε καὶ παντάπασι κακὸς ἆρ'
40 οὐ τοὐναντίον ἐκείνῳ;

ΠΡΩ. Πῶς δ' οὔ;

ΣΩ. Πολλῶν μὴν ἐλπίδων, ὡς ἐλέγομεν ἄρτι, πᾶς ἄνθρωπος γέμει;

ΠΡΩ. Τί δ' οὔ;

ΣΩ. Λόγοι μήν εἰσιν ἐν ἑκάστοις ἡμῶν, ἃς ἐλπίδας ὀνομάζομεν;

ΠΡΩ. Ναί.

ΣΩ. Καὶ δὴ καὶ τὰ φαντάσματα ἐζωγραφημένα· καί τις ὁρᾷ πολλάκις ἑαυτῷ χρυσὸν γιγνόμενον ἄφθονον καὶ ἐπ' αὐτῷ πολλὰς ἡδονάς· καὶ δὴ καὶ ἐνεζωγραφημένον αὐτὸν ἐφ' αὑτῷ χαίροντα σφόδρα καθορᾷ.

Β ΠΡΩ. Τί δ' οὔ;

ΣΩ. Τούτων οὖν πότερα φῶμεν τοῖς μὲν ἀγαθοῖς

PRO. Very true.

SOC. Do the writings and pictures, then, which we imagined a little while ago to exist within us, relate to the past and present, but not to the future?

PRO. To the future especially.

SOC. Do you say "to the future especially" because they are all hopes relating to the future and we are always filled with hopes all our lives?

PRO. Precisely.

SOC. Well, here is a further question for you to answer.

PRO. What is it?

SOC. A just, pious, and good man is surely a friend of the gods, is he not?

PRO. Certainly.

SOC. And an unjust and thoroughly bad man is the reverse?

PRO. Of course.

SOC. But, as we were just now saying, every man is full of many hopes?

PRO. Yes, to be sure.

SOC. And there are in all of us written words which we call hopes?

PRO. Yes.

SOC. And also the images painted there; and often a man sees an abundance of gold coming into his possession, and in its train many pleasures; and he even sees a picture of himself enjoying himself immensely.

PRO. Yes, certainly.

SOC. Shall we or shall we not say that of these

ὡς τὸ πολὺ τὰ γεγραμμένα παρατίθεσθαι ἀληθῆ διὰ
τὸ θεοφιλεῖς εἶναι, τοῖς δὲ κακοῖς ὡς αὖ τὸ¹ πολὺ
τοὐναντίον, ἢ μὴ φῶμεν;

ΠΡΩ. Καὶ μάλα φατέον.

ΣΩ. Οὐκοῦν καὶ τοῖς κακοῖς ἡδοναί γε οὐδὲν
ἧττον πάρεισιν ἐζωγραφημέναι, ψευδεῖς δὲ αὗταί
που.

ΠΡΩ. Τί μήν;

C ΣΩ. Ψευδέσιν ἄρα ἡδοναῖς τὰ πολλὰ οἱ πονη-
ροὶ χαίρουσιν, οἱ δ' ἀγαθοὶ τῶν ἀνθρώπων ἀληθέσιν.

ΠΡΩ. Ἀναγκαιότατα λέγεις.

ΣΩ. Εἰσὶ δὴ κατὰ τοὺς νῦν λόγους ψευδεῖς ἐν
ταῖς τῶν ἀνθρώπων ψυχαῖς ἡδοναί, μεμιμημέναι
μέντοι τὰς ἀληθεῖς ἐπὶ τὰ γελοιότερα· καὶ λῦπαι
δὲ ὡσαύτως.

ΠΡΩ. Εἰσίν.

ΣΩ. Οὐκοῦν ἦν δοξάζειν μὲν ὄντως ἀεὶ τῷ τὸ
παράπαν δοξάζοντι, μὴ ἐπ' οὖσι² δὲ μηδὲ ἐπὶ
γεγονόσι² μηδ' ἐπ' ἐσομένοις² ἐνίοτε.

ΠΡΩ. Πάνυ γε.

D ΣΩ. Καὶ ταῦτά γε ἦν, οἶμαι, τὰ ἀπεργαζόμενα
δόξαν ψευδῆ τότε καὶ τὸ ψευδῶς δοξάζειν. ἦ γάρ;

ΠΡΩ. Ναί.

ΣΩ. Τί οὖν; οὐκ ἀνταποδοτέον ταῖς λύπαις
τε καὶ ἡδοναῖς τὴν τούτων ἀντίστροφον ἕξιν ἐν
ἐκείνοις;

ΠΡΩ. Πῶς;

ΣΩ. Ὡς ἦν μὲν χαίρειν ὄντως ἀεὶ τῷ τὸ παράπαν ὁπωσοῦν καὶ εἰκῇ χαίροντι, μὴ μέντοι ἐπὶ τοῖς
οὖσι μηδ' ἐπὶ τοῖς γεγονόσιν ἐνίοτε, πολλάκις δὲ

____

¹ αὖ ⟨τὸ⟩ Stallbaum: αὖ BT.
² BT read ἐπούσι, ἐπιγεγονόσι, and ἐπεσομένοις.

pictures those are for the most part true which are
presented to the good, because they are friends of
the gods, whereas those presented to the bad are for
the most part false ?

PRO. Surely we must say that.

SOC. Then the bad also, no less than the good,
have pleasures painted in their souls, but they are
false pleasures.

PRO. Yes, surely.

SOC. Then the bad rejoice for the most part in
the false, and the good in true pleasures.

PRO. That is inevitably true.

SOC. According to our present view, then, there
are false pleasures in the souls of men, imitations or
caricatures of the true pleasures ; and pains likewise.

PRO. There are.

SOC. We saw, you remember, that he who had an
opinion at all always really had an opinion, but it
was sometimes not based upon realities, whether
present, past, or future.

PRO. Certainly.

SOC. And this it was, I believe, which created false
opinion and the holding of false opinions, was it not ?

PRO. Yes.

SOC. Very well, must we not also grant that
pleasure and pain stand in the same relation to
realities ?

PRO. What do you mean ?

SOC. I mean that he who feels pleasure at all in
any way or manner always really feels pleasure, but
it is sometimes not based upon realities, whether
present or past, and often, perhaps most frequently,

καὶ ἴσως πλειστάκις ἐπὶ τοῖς μηδὲ μέλλουσί ποτε
γενήσεσθαι.

Ε ΠΡΩ. Καὶ ταῦθ' οὕτως ἀναγκαῖον, ὦ Σώκρατες, ἔχειν.

ΣΩ. Οὐκοῦν ὁ αὐτὸς λόγος ἂν εἴη περὶ φόβων
τε καὶ θυμῶν καὶ πάντων τῶν τοιούτων, ὡς ἔστι
καὶ ψευδῆ πάντα τὰ τοιαῦτα ἐνίοτε;

ΠΡΩ. Πάνυ μὲν οὖν.

ΣΩ. Τί δέ; πονηρὰς δόξας καὶ χρηστὰς[1] ἄλλως
ἢ ψευδεῖς γιγνομένας ἔχομεν εἰπεῖν;

ΠΡΩ. Οὐκ ἄλλως.

ΣΩ. Οὐδ' ἡδονάς γ', οἶμαι, κατανοοῦμεν ὡς ἄλλον
41 τινὰ τρόπον εἰσὶ πονηραὶ πλὴν τῷ ψευδεῖς εἶναι.

ΠΡΩ. Πάνυ μὲν οὖν τοὐναντίον, ὦ Σώκρατες,
εἴρηκας. σχεδὸν γὰρ τῷ ψεύδει μὲν οὐ πάνυ
πονηρὰς ἄν τις λύπας τε καὶ ἡδονὰς θείη, μεγάλῃ
δὲ ἄλλῃ καὶ πολλῇ συμπιπτούσας πονηρίᾳ.

ΣΩ. Τὰς μὲν τοίνυν πονηρὰς ἡδονὰς καὶ διὰ
πονηρίαν οὔσας τοιαύτας ὀλίγον ὕστερον ἐροῦμεν,
ἂν ἔτι δοκῇ νῷν· τὰς δὲ ψευδεῖς κατ' ἄλλον τρόπον
ἐν ἡμῖν πολλὰς καὶ πολλάκις ἐνούσας τε καὶ ἐγγιγνο-
Β μένας λεκτέον. τούτῳ γὰρ ἴσως χρησόμεθα πρὸς
τὰς κρίσεις.

ΠΡΩ. Πῶς γὰρ οὔκ; εἴπερ γε εἰσίν.

ΣΩ. Ἀλλ', ὦ Πρώταρχε, εἰσὶ κατά γε τὴν ἐμήν.
τοῦτο δὲ τὸ δόγμα ἕως ἂν κέηται παρ' ἡμῖν, ἀδύνατον ἀνέλεγκτον δήπου γίγνεσθαι.

ΠΡΩ. Καλῶς.

25. ΣΩ. Περιστώμεθα[2] δὴ καθάπερ ἀθληταὶ
πρὸς τοῦτον αὖ τὸν λόγον.

---

[1] καὶ χρηστὰς BT: formerly bracketed by Stallbaum:
κἀχρήστους Apelt.

upon things which will never even be realities in the future.

PRO. This also, Socrates, must inevitably be the case.

SOC. And the same may be said of fear and anger and all that sort of thing—that they are all sometimes false ?

PRO. Certainly.

SOC. Well, can we say that opinions become bad or good except as they become false ?

PRO. No.

SOC. And we understand, I believe, that pleasures also are not bad except by being false.

PRO. No ; you have said quite the reverse of the truth, Socrates ; for no one would be at all likely to call pains and pleasures bad because they are false, but because they are involved in another great and manifold evil.

SOC. Then of the evil pleasures which are such because of evil we will speak a little later, if we still care to do so ; but of the false pleasures we must prove in another way that they exist and come into existence in us often and in great numbers ; for this may help us to reach our decisions.

PRO. Yes, of course ; that is, if such pleasures exist.

SOC. But they do exist, Protarchus, in my opinion ; however, until we have established the truth of this opinion, it cannot be unquestioned.

PRO. Good.

SOC. Then let us, like athletes, approach and grapple with this new argument.

---

² περιστώμεθα B : προσιστώμεθα T.

ΠΡΩ. Ἴωμεν.

ΣΩ. Ἀλλὰ μὴν εἴπομεν, εἴπερ μεμνήμεθα, ὀλίγον
C ἐν τοῖς πρόσθεν, ὡς ὅταν αἱ λεγόμεναι ἐπιθυμίαι
ἐν ἡμῖν ὦσι, δίχα ἄρα τότε τὸ σῶμα καὶ χωρὶς τῆς
ψυχῆς τοῖς παθήμασι διείληπται.

ΠΡΩ. Μεμνήμεθα, καὶ προερρήθη ταῦτα.

ΣΩ. Οὐκοῦν τὸ μὲν ἐπιθυμοῦν ἦν ἡ ψυχὴ τῶν
τοῦ σώματος ἐναντίων ἕξεων, τὸ δὲ τὴν ἀλγηδόνα ἤ
τινα διὰ πάθος ἡδονὴν τὸ σῶμα ἦν τὸ παρεχόμενον;

ΠΡΩ. Ἦν γὰρ οὖν.

ΣΩ. Συλλογίζου δὴ τὸ γιγνόμενον ἐν τούτοις.

ΠΡΩ. Λέγε.

D ΣΩ. Γίγνεται τοίνυν, ὁπόταν ᾖ ταῦτα, ἅμα
παρακεῖσθαι λύπας τε καὶ ἡδονάς, καὶ τούτων
αἰσθήσεις ἅμα παρ' ἀλλήλας ἐναντίων οὐσῶν
γίγνεσθαι, ὃ καὶ νῦν δὴ ἐφάνη.

ΠΡΩ. Φαίνεται γοῦν.

ΣΩ. Οὐκοῦν καὶ τόδε εἴρηται καὶ συνωμολογη-
μένον ἡμῖν ἔμπροσθεν κεῖται;

ΠΡΩ. Τὸ ποῖον;

ΣΩ. Ὡς τὸ μᾶλλόν τε καὶ ἧττον ἄμφω τούτω
δέχεσθον, λύπη τε καὶ ἡδονή, καὶ ὅτι τῶν ἀπείρων εἴτην.

ΠΡΩ. Εἴρηται. τί μήν;

ΣΩ. Τίς οὖν μηχανὴ ταῦτ' ὀρθῶς κρίνεσθαι;

E ΠΡΩ. Πῇ δὴ καὶ πῶς;

ΣΩ. Εἰ τὸ βούλημα ἡμῖν τῆς κρίσεως τούτων
ἐν τοιούτοις τισὶ διαγνῶναι βούλεται ἑκάστοτε τίς
τούτων πρὸς ἀλλήλας μείζων καὶ τίς ἐλάττων καὶ
τίς μᾶλλον καὶ τίς σφοδροτέρα, λύπη τε πρὸς
ἡδονὴν καὶ λύπη πρὸς λύπην καὶ ἡδονὴ πρὸς
ἡδονήν.

pro. Let us do so.

soc. We said, you may remember, a little while ago, that when desires, as they are called, exist in us, the body is apart from and separate from the soul in that it has feelings.

pro. I remember ; that was said.

soc. And was not the soul that which desired the opposites of the conditions of the body and the body that which caused pleasure or pain because of feeling ?

pro. Yes, that was the case.

soc. Then draw the conclusion as to what takes place in these circumstances.

pro. Go on.

soc. What takes place is this : in these circumstances pleasures and pains exist at the same time and the sensations of opposite pleasures and pains are present side by side simultaneously, as was made clear just now.

pro. Yes, that is clear.

soc. And have we not also said and agreed and settled something further ?

pro. What ?

soc. That both pleasure and pain admit of the more and less and are of the class of the infinite.

pro. Yes, we have said that, certainly.

soc. Then what means is there of judging rightly of this ?

pro. How and in what way do you mean ?

soc. I mean to ask whether the purpose of our judgement of these matters in such circumstances is to recognize in each instance which of these elements is greater or smaller or more intense, comparing pain with pleasure, pain with pain, and pleasure with pleasure.

ΠΡΩ. Ἀλλ' ἔστι ταῦτά τε τοιαῦτα καὶ ἡ βούλησις τῆς κρίσεως αὕτη.

ΣΩ. Τί οὖν; ἐν μὲν ὄψει τὸ πόρρωθεν καὶ
42 ἐγγύθεν ὁρᾶν τὰ μεγέθη τὴν ἀλήθειαν ἀφανίζει καὶ ψευδῆ ποιεῖ δοξάζειν, ἐν λύπαις δ' ἄρα καὶ ἡδοναῖς οὐκ ἔστι ταὐτὸν τοῦτο γιγνόμενον;

ΠΡΩ. Πολὺ μὲν οὖν μᾶλλον, ὦ Σώκρατες.

ΣΩ. Ἐναντίον δὴ τὸ νῦν τῷ σμικρὸν ἔμπροσθεν γέγονεν.

ΠΡΩ. Τὸ ποῖον λέγεις;

ΣΩ. Τότε μὲν αἱ δόξαι ψευδεῖς τε καὶ ἀληθεῖς αὗται γιγνόμεναι τὰς λύπας τε καὶ ἡδονὰς ἅμα τοῦ παρ' αὑταῖς[1] παθήματος ἀνεπίμπλασαν.

B ΠΡΩ. Ἀληθέστατα.

ΣΩ. Νῦν δέ γε αὗται[2] διὰ τὸ πόρρωθέν τε καὶ ἐγγύθεν ἑκάστοτε μεταβαλλόμεναι θεωρεῖσθαι, καὶ ἅμα τιθέμεναι παρ' ἀλλήλας, αἱ μὲν ἡδοναὶ παρὰ τὸ λυπηρὸν μείζους φαίνονται καὶ σφοδρότεραι, λῦπαι δ' αὖ διὰ τὸ παρ' ἡδονὰς τοὐναντίον ἐκείναις.

ΠΡΩ. Ἀνάγκη γίγνεσθαι τὰ τοιαῦτα διὰ ταῦτα.

ΣΩ. Οὐκοῦν ὅσῳ μείζους τῶν οὐσῶν ἑκάτεραι καὶ ἐλάττους φαίνονται, τοῦτο ἀποτεμόμενος ἑκατέρων[3] τὸ φαινόμενον ἀλλ' οὐκ ὄν, οὔτε αὐτὸ ὀρθῶς
C φαινόμενον ἐρεῖς, οὐδ' αὖ ποτὲ τὸ ἐπὶ τούτῳ[4] μέρος τῆς ἡδονῆς καὶ λύπης γιγνόμενον ὀρθόν τε καὶ ἀληθὲς τολμήσεις λέγειν.

ΠΡΩ. Οὐ γὰρ οὖν.

ΣΩ. Τούτων τοίνυν ἑξῆς ὀψόμεθα ἐὰν τῇδε

---

[1] αὑταῖς BT : αὑτοὺς Coisl.
[2] αὗται] αὑταὶ BT.
[3] ἑκατέρων Schleiermacher : ἑκάτερον BT.
[4] τούτῳ BT : τοῦτο vulg.

PRO. Certainly there are such differences, and that is the purpose of our judgement.

SOC. Well then, in the case of sight, seeing things from too near at hand or from too great a distance obscures their real sizes and causes us to have false opinions ; and does not this same thing happen in the case of pains and pleasures ?

PRO. Yes, Socrates, even much more than in the case of sight.

SOC. Then our present conclusion is the opposite of what we said a little while ago.

PRO. To what do you refer ?

SOC. A while ago these opinions, being false or true, imbued the pains and pleasures with their own condition of truth or falsehood.

PRO. Very true.

SOC. But now, because they are seen at various and changing distances and are compared with one another, the pleasures themselves appear greater and more intense by comparison with the pains, and the pains in turn, through comparison with the pleasures, vary inversely as they.

PRO. That is inevitable for the reasons you have given.

SOC. They both, then, appear greater and less than the reality. Now if you abstract from both of them this apparent, but unreal, excess or inferiority, you cannot say that its appearance is true, nor again can you have the face to affirm that the part of pleasure or pain which corresponds to this is true or real.

PRO. No, I cannot.

SOC. Next, then, we will see whether we may not

ἀπαντῶμεν ἡδονὰς καὶ λύπας ψευδεῖς ἔτι μᾶλλον ἢ
ταύτας φαινομένας τε καὶ οὔσας ἐν τοῖς ζῴοις.

ΠΡΩ. Ποίας δὴ καὶ πῶς λέγεις;

26. ΣΩ. Εἴρηταί που πολλάκις ὅτι τῆς φύσεως ἑκάστων διαφθειρομένης μὲν συγκρίσεσι καὶ
D διακρίσεσι καὶ πληρώσεσι καὶ κενώσεσι καί τισιν
αὔξαις καὶ φθίσεσι λῦπαί τε καὶ ἀλγηδόνες καὶ ὀδύ-
ναι καὶ πάνθ' ὁπόσα τοιαῦτ' ὀνόματ' ἔχει ξυμβαίνει
γιγνόμενα.

ΠΡΩ. Ναί, ταῦτα εἴρηται πολλάκις.

ΣΩ. Εἰς δέ γε τὴν αὑτῶν φύσιν ὅταν καθιστῆ-
ται, ταύτην αὖ τὴν κατάστασιν ἡδονὴν ἀπεδεξάμεθα
παρ' ἡμῶν αὐτῶν.

ΠΡΩ. Ὀρθῶς.

ΣΩ. Τί δ', ὅταν περὶ τὸ σῶμα μηδὲν τούτων
γιγνόμενον ἡμῶν ᾖ;

ΠΡΩ. Πότε δὲ τοῦτ' ἂν γένοιτο, ὦ Σώκρατες;

E ΣΩ. Οὐδὲν πρὸς λόγον ἐστίν, ὦ Πρώταρχε, ὃ
σὺ νῦν ἤρου τὸ ἐρώτημα.

ΠΡΩ. Τί δή;

ΣΩ. Διότι τὴν ἐμὴν ἐρώτησιν οὐ κωλύεις με[1]
διερέσθαι σε πάλιν.

ΠΡΩ. Ποίαν;

ΣΩ. Εἰ δ' οὖν μὴ γίγνοιτο, ὦ Πρώταρχε, φήσω,
τὸ τοιοῦτον, τί ποτε ἀναγκαῖον ἐξ αὐτοῦ συμβαί-
νειν ἡμῖν;

ΠΡΩ. Μὴ κινουμένου τοῦ σώματος ἐφ' ἑκάτερα φῇς;

ΣΩ. Οὕτως.

ΠΡΩ. Δῆλον δὴ τοῦτό γε, ὦ Σώκρατες, ὡς
οὔτε ἡδονὴ γίγνοιτ' ἂν ἐν τῷ τοιούτῳ ποτὲ οὔτ' ἄν
τις λύπη.

312

in another direction come upon pleasures and pains still more false than these appearing and existing in living beings.

PRO. What pleasures and what method do you mean?

SOC. It has been said many times that pains and woes and aches and everything that is called by names of that sort are caused when nature in any instance is corrupted through combinations and dissolutions, fillings and emptyings, increases and diminutions.

PRO. Yes, that has been said many times.

SOC. And we agreed that when things are restored to their natural condition, that restoration is pleasure.

PRO. Right.

SOC. But when neither of these changes takes place in the body, what then?

PRO. When could that be the case, Socrates?

SOC. That question of yours is not to the point, Protarchus.

PRO. Why not?

SOC. Because you do not prevent my asking my own question again.[1]

PRO. What question?

SOC. Why, Protarchus, I may say, granting that such a condition does not arise, what would be the necessary result if it did?

PRO. You mean if the body is not changed in either direction?

SOC. Yes.

PRO. It is clear, Socrates, that in that case there would never be either pleasure or pain.

---

[1] κωλύεις με Burnet: κωλύει ἐμὲ B: κωλύσεις με T.

PLATO

43 ΣΩ. Κάλλιστ' εἶπες. ἀλλὰ γάρ, οἶμαι, τόδε λέγεις, ὡς ἀεί τι τούτων ἀναγκαῖον ἡμῖν ξυμβαίνειν, ὡς οἱ σοφοί φασιν· ἀεὶ γὰρ ἅπαντα ἄνω τε καὶ κάτω ῥεῖ.

ΠΡΩ. Λέγουσι γὰρ οὖν, καὶ δοκοῦσί γε οὐ φαύλως λέγειν.

ΣΩ. Πῶς γὰρ ἂν μὴ φαυλοί γε ὄντες; ἀλλὰ γὰρ ὑπεκστῆναι τὸν λόγον ἐπιφερόμενον τοῦτον βούλομαι. τῇδ' οὖν διανοοῦμαι φεύγειν, καὶ σύ μοι ξύμφευγε.

ΠΡΩ. Λέγε ὅπῃ.

ΣΩ. Ταῦτα μὲν τοίνυν οὕτως ἔστω, φῶμεν πρὸς B τούτους. σὺ δ' ἀπόκριναι· πότερον ἀεὶ πάντα, ὁπόσα πάσχει τι τῶν ἐμψύχων, ταῦτ' αἰσθάνεται τὸ πάσχον, καὶ οὔτ' αὐξανόμενοι λανθάνομεν ἡμᾶς αὐτοὺς οὔτε τι τῶν τοιούτων οὐδὲν πάσχοντες, ἢ πᾶν τοὐναντίον;

ΠΡΩ. Ἅπαν δήπου τοὐναντίον.[1] ὀλίγου γὰρ τά γε τοιαῦτα λέληθε πάνθ' ἡμᾶς.[2]

ΣΩ. Οὐ τοίνυν καλῶς ἡμῖν εἴρηται τὸ νῦν δὴ ῥηθέν, ὡς αἱ μεταβολαὶ κάτω τε καὶ ἄνω γιγνόμεναι λύπας τε καὶ ἡδονὰς ἀπεργάζονται.

ΠΡΩ. Τί μήν;

C ΣΩ. Ὧδ' ἔσται κάλλιον καὶ ἀνεπιληπτότερον τὸ λεγόμενον.

ΠΡΩ. Πῶς;

ΣΩ. Ὡς αἱ μὲν μεγάλαι μεταβολαὶ λύπας τε καὶ ἡδονὰς ποιοῦσιν ἡμῖν, αἱ δ' αὖ μέτριαί τε καὶ σμικραὶ τὸ παράπαν οὐδέτερα τούτων.

ΠΡΩ. Ὀρθότερον οὕτως ἢ 'κείνως, ὦ Σώκρατες.

---

[1] ἅπαν δήπου τοὐναντίον add. in marg. T: om. BT.
[2] ἡμᾶς add. vulg.

soc. Excellent. But you believe, I fancy, that some such change must always be taking place in us, as the philosophers[1] say; for all things are always flowing and shifting.

pro. Yes, that is what they say, and I think their theory is important.

soc. Of course it is, in view of their own importance. But I should like to avoid this argument which is rushing at us. I am going to run away; come along and escape with me.

pro. What is your way of escape?

soc. " We grant you all this " let us say to them. But answer me this, Protarchus, are we and all other living beings always conscious of everything that happens to us—of our growth and all that sort of thing—or is the truth quite the reverse of that?

pro. Quite the reverse, surely; for we are almost entirely unconscious of everything of that sort.

soc. Then we were not right in saying just now that the fluctuations and changes cause pains and pleasures.

pro. No, certainly not.

soc. A better and more unassailable statement would be this.

pro. What?

soc. That the great changes cause pains and pleasures in us, but the moderate and small ones cause no pains or pleasures at all.

pro. That is more correct than the other statement, Socrates.

[1] Heracleitus and his followers.

315

ΣΩ. Οὐκοῦν εἰ ταῦτα οὕτω, πάλιν ὁ νῦν δὴ ῥηθεὶς βίος ἂν ἥκοι.

ΠΡΩ. Ποῖος;

ΣΩ. Ὃν ἄλυπόν τε καὶ ἄνευ χαρμονῶν ἔφαμεν εἶναι.

ΠΡΩ. Ἀληθέστατα λέγεις.

ΣΩ. Ἐκ δὴ τούτων τιθῶμεν τριττοὺς ἡμῖν βίους, ἵνα μὲν ἡδύν, τὸν δ' αὖ λυπηρόν, τὸν δ' ἕνα μηδέτερα. ἢ πῶς ἂν φαίης σὺ περὶ τούτων;

ΠΡΩ. Οὐκ ἄλλως ἔγωγε ἢ ταύτῃ, τρεῖς εἶναι τοὺς βίους.

ΣΩ. Οὐκοῦν οὐκ ἂν εἴη τὸ μὴ λυπεῖσθαί ποτε ταὐτὸν τῷ χαίρειν;

ΠΡΩ. Πῶς γὰρ ἄν;

ΣΩ. Ὁπόταν οὖν ἀκούσῃς ὡς ἥδιστον πάντων ἐστὶν ἀλύπως διατελεῖν τὸν βίον ἅπαντα, τί τόθ' ὑπολαμβάνεις λέγειν τὸν τοιοῦτον;

ΠΡΩ. Ἡδὺ λέγειν φαίνεται ἔμοιγε οὗτος τὸ μὴ λυπεῖσθαι.

ΣΩ. Τριῶν ὄντων οὖν ἡμῖν, ὧντινων βούλει, τίθει, καλλίοσιν ἵνα ὀνόμασι χρώμεθα, τὸ μὲν χρυσόν, τὸ δ' ἄργυρον, τρίτον δὲ τὸ¹ μηδέτερα τούτων.

ΠΡΩ. Κεῖται.

ΣΩ. Τὸ δὴ μηδέτερα τούτων ἔσθ' ἡμῖν ὅπως θάτερα γένοιτ' ἄν, χρυσὸς ἢ ἄργυρος;

ΠΡΩ. Καὶ πῶς ἄν;

ΣΩ. Οὐδ' ἄρα ὁ μέσος βίος ἡδὺς ἢ λυπηρὸς λεγόμενος ὀρθῶς ἄν ποτε οὔτ' εἰ δοξάζοι τις, δοξάζοιτο, οὔτ' εἰ λέγοι, λεχθείη, κατά γε τὸν ὀρθὸν λόγον.

ΠΡΩ. Πῶς γὰρ ἄν;

¹ τὸ T: om. B.

soc. But if that is the case, the life of which we spoke just now would come back again.

pro. What life?

soc. The life which we said was painless and without joys.

pro. Very true.

soc. Let us, therefore, assume three lives, one pleasant, one painful, and one neither of the two; or do you disagree?

pro. No, I agree to this, that there are the three lives.

soc. Then freedom from pain would not be identical with pleasure?

pro. Certainly not.

soc. When you hear anyone say that the pleasantest of all things is to live all one's life without pain, what do you understand him to mean?

pro. I think he means that freedom from pain is pleasure.

soc. Now let us assume that we have three things; no matter what they are, but let us use fine names and call one gold, another silver, and the third neither of the two.

pro. Agreed.

soc. Now can that which is neither become either gold or silver?

pro. Certainly not.

soc. Neither can that middle life of which we spoke ever be rightly considered in opinion or called in speech pleasant or painful, at any rate by those who reason correctly.

pro. No, certainly not.

ΣΩ. Ἀλλὰ μήν, ὦ ἑταῖρε, λεγόντων γε ταῦτα
44 καὶ δοξαζόντων αἰσθανόμεθα.

ΠΡΩ. Καὶ μάλα.

ΣΩ. Πότερον οὖν καὶ χαίρειν οἴονται τότε ὅταν
μὴ λυπῶνται;

ΠΡΩ. Φασὶ γοῦν.

ΣΩ. Οὐκοῦν οἴονται τότε χαίρειν· οὐ γὰρ ἂν
ἔλεγόν που.

ΠΡΩ. Κινδυνεύει.

ΣΩ. Ψευδῆ γε μὴν δοξάζουσι περὶ τοῦ χαίρειν,
εἴπερ χωρὶς τοῦ μὴ λυπεῖσθαι καὶ τοῦ χαίρειν ἡ
φύσις ἑκατέρου.

ΠΡΩ. Καὶ μὴν χωρίς γε ἦν.

ΣΩ. Πότερον οὖν αἱρώμεθα παρ᾽ ἡμῖν ταῦτ᾽
B εἶναι, καθάπερ ἄρτι, τρία, ἢ δύο μόνα, λύπην μὲν
κακὸν τοῖς ἀνθρώποις, τὴν δ᾽ ἀπαλλαγὴν τῶν λυπῶν,
αὐτὸ τοῦτο ἀγαθὸν ὄν, ἡδὺ προσαγορεύεσθαι;

27. ΠΡΩ. Πῶς δὴ νῦν τοῦτο, ὦ Σώκρατες,
ἐρωτώμεθα ὑφ᾽ ἡμῶν αὐτῶν; οὐ γὰρ μανθάνω.

ΣΩ. Ὄντως γὰρ τοὺς πολεμίους Φιλήβου τοῦδε,
ὦ Πρώταρχε, οὐ μανθάνεις;

ΠΡΩ. Λέγεις δὲ αὐτοὺς τίνας;

ΣΩ. Καὶ μάλα δεινοὺς λεγομένους τὰ περὶ φύσιν,
οἳ τὸ παράπαν ἡδονὰς οὔ φασιν εἶναι.

ΠΡΩ. Τί μήν;

C ΣΩ. Λυπῶν ταύτας εἶναι πάσας ἀποφυγάς, ἃς
νῦν οἱ περὶ Φίληβον ἡδονὰς ἐπονομάζουσιν.

ΠΡΩ. Τούτοις οὖν ἡμᾶς πότερα πείθεσθαι ξυμ-
βουλεύεις, ἢ πῶς, ὦ Σώκρατες;

ΣΩ. Οὔκ, ἀλλ᾽ ὥσπερ μάντεσι προσχρῆσθαί τισι,
μαντευομένοις οὐ τέχνῃ ἀλλά τινι δυσχερείᾳ φύσεως
οὐκ ἀγεννοῦς λίαν μεμισηκότων τὴν τῆς ἡδονῆς δύ-

318

soc. But surely, my friend, we are aware of persons who call it and consider it so.

pro. Certainly.

soc. Do they, then, think they feel pleasure whenever they are not in pain ?

pro. That is what they say.

soc. Then they do think they feel pleasure at such times ; for otherwise they would not say so.

pro. Most likely.

soc. Certainly, then, they have a false opinion about pleasure, if there is an essential difference between feeling pleasure and not feeling pain.

pro. And we certainly found that difference.

soc. Then shall we adopt the view that there are, as we said just now, three states, or that there are only two—pain, which is an evil to mankind, and freedom from pain, which is of itself a good and is called pleasure ?

pro. Why do we ask ourselves that question now, Socrates ? I do not understand.

soc. No, Protarchus, for you certainly do not understand about the enemies of our friend Philebus.

pro. Whom do you mean ?

soc. Certain men who are said to be master thinkers about nature, and who deny the existence of pleasures altogether.

pro. Is it possible ?

soc. They say that what Philebus and his school call pleasures are all merely refuges from pain.

pro. Do you recommend that we adopt their view, Socrates ?

soc. No, but that we make use of them as seers who divine the truth, not by acquired skill, but by some innate and not ignoble repugnance which makes

ναμιν καὶ νενομικότων οὐδὲν ὑγιές, ὥστε καὶ αὐτὸ
τοῦτο αὐτῆς τὸ ἐπαγωγὸν γοήτευμα, ἀλλ' οὐχ ἡδο-
D νήν,[1] εἶναι. τούτοις μὲν οὖν ταῦτα ἂν προσχρήσαιο,
σκεψάμενος ἔτι καὶ τὰ ἄλλα αὐτῶν δυσχεράσματα·
μετὰ δὲ ταῦτα αἵ γέ μοι δοκοῦσιν ἡδοναὶ ἀληθεῖς
εἶναι πεύσει, ἵνα ἐξ ἀμφοῖν τοῖν λόγοιν σκεψάμενοι
τὴν δύναμιν αὐτῆς παραθώμεθα πρὸς τὴν κρίσιν.

ΠΡΩ. Ὀρθῶς λέγεις.

ΣΩ. Μεταδιώκωμεν δὴ τούτους, ὥσπερ ξυμμά-
χους, κατὰ τὸ τῆς δυσχερείας αὐτῶν ἴχνος. οἶμαι
γὰρ τοιόνδε τι λέγειν αὐτούς, ἀρχομένους ποθὲν
E ἄνωθεν, ὡς εἰ βουληθεῖμεν ὁτουοῦν εἴδους τὴν
φύσιν ἰδεῖν, οἷον τὴν τοῦ σκληροῦ, πότερον εἰς τὰ
σκληρότατα ἀποβλέποντες οὕτως ἂν μᾶλλον συννοή-
σαιμεν ἢ πρὸς τὰ πολλοστὰ σκληρότητι; δεῖ δή
σε, ὦ Πρώταρχε, καθάπερ ἐμοί, καὶ τούτοις τοῖς
δυσχερέσιν ἀποκρίνεσθαι.

ΠΡΩ. Πάνυ μὲν οὖν, καὶ λέγω γε αὐτοῖς ὅτι
πρὸς τὰ πρῶτα μεγέθει.

ΣΩ. Οὐκοῦν εἰ καὶ τὸ τῆς ἡδονῆς γένος ἰδεῖν
ἥντινά ποτε ἔχει φύσιν βουληθεῖμεν, οὐκ εἰς τὰς
45 πολλοστὰς ἡδονὰς ἀποβλεπτέον, ἀλλ' εἰς τὰς ἀκρο-
τάτας καὶ σφοδροτάτας λεγομένας.

ΠΡΩ. Πᾶς ἄν σοι ταύτῃ συγχωροίη τὰ νῦν.

ΣΩ. Ἆρ' οὖν, αἱ πρόχειροί γε αἵπερ καὶ μέγισται τῶν ἡδονῶν, ὃ λέγομεν πολλάκις, αἱ περὶ τὸ
σῶμά εἰσιν αὗται;

ΠΡΩ. Πῶς γὰρ οὔ;

ΣΩ. Πότερον οὖν καὶ[2] μείζους εἰσὶ καὶ γίγνονται
περὶ τοὺς κάμνοντας ἐν ταῖς νόσοις ἢ περὶ τοὺς

---

[1] ἡδονήν recc. : ἡδονή ΒΤ.
[2] καί Τ : om. Β.

them hate the power of pleasure and think it so
utterly unsound that its very attractiveness is mere
trickery, not pleasure. You may make use of them
in this way, considering also their other expressions
of dislike ; and after that you shall learn of the
pleasures which seem to me to be true, in order that
we may consider the power of pleasure from both
points of view and form our judgement by comparing
them.

PRO. You are right.

SOC. Let us, then, consider these men as allies
and follow them in the track of their dislike. I
fancy their method would be to begin somewhere
further back and ask whether, if we wished to
discover the nature of any class—take the hard, for
instance—we should be more likely to learn it by
looking at the hardest things or at the least hard.
Now you, Protarchus, must reply to them as you
have been replying to me.

PRO. By all means, and I say to them that we
should look at the greatest things.

SOC. Then if we wished to discover what the
nature of pleasure is, we should look, not at the
smallest pleasures, but at those which are considered
most extreme and intense.

PRO. Every one would agree to that now.

SOC. And the commonest and greatest pleasures
are, as we have often said, those connected with the
body, are they not ?

PRO. Certainly.

SOC. Are they greater, then, and do they become
greater in those who are ill or in those who are in

ὑγιαίνοντας; εὐλαβηθῶμεν δέ, μὴ προπετῶς ἀπο-
κρινόμενοι πταίσωμέν πῃ.   τάχα γὰρ ἴσως φαῖμεν
B ἂν περὶ ὑγιαίνοντας.

ΠΡΩ.   Εἰκός γε.

ΣΩ.   Τί δ'; οὐχ αὗται τῶν ἡδονῶν ὑπερβάλλου-
σιν, ὧν ἂν καὶ ἐπιθυμίαι μέγισται προγίγνωνται[1];

ΠΡΩ.   Τοῦτο μὲν ἀληθές.

ΣΩ.   Ἀλλ' οὐχ οἱ πυρέττοντες καὶ ἐν τοιούτοις
νοσήμασιν ἐχόμενοι μᾶλλον διψῶσι καὶ ῥιγοῦσι καὶ
πάντα, ὁπόσα διὰ τοῦ σώματος εἰώθασι πάσχειν,
μᾶλλόν τ' ἐνδείᾳ ξυγγίγνονται καὶ ἀποπληρουμένων
μείζους ἡδονὰς ἴσχουσιν; ἢ τοῦτο οὐ φήσομεν
ἀληθὲς εἶναι;

C ΠΡΩ.   Πάνυ μὲν οὖν νῦν ῥηθὲν φαίνεται.

ΣΩ.   Τί οὖν; ὀρθῶς ἂν φαινοίμεθα λέγοντες ὡς
εἴ τις τὰς μεγίστας ἡδονὰς ἰδεῖν βούλοιτο, οὐκ εἰς
ὑγίειαν ἀλλ' εἰς νόσον ἰόντας δεῖ σκοπεῖν; ὅρα δέ,
μή με ἡγῇ[2] διανοούμενον ἐρωτᾶν σε εἰ πλείω
χαίρουσιν οἱ σφόδρα νοσοῦντες τῶν ὑγιαινόντων,
ἀλλ' οἴου μέγεθός με ζητεῖν ἡδονῆς, καὶ τὸ σφόδρα
περὶ τοῦ τοιούτου ποῦ ποτε γίγνεται ἑκάστοτε.
νοῆσαι γὰρ δεῖν φαμὲν ἥντινα φύσιν ἔχει καὶ τίνα
D λέγουσιν οἱ φάσκοντες μηδ' εἶναι τὸ παράπαν αὐτήν.

ΠΡΩ.   Ἀλλὰ σχεδὸν ἕπομαι τῷ λόγῳ σου.

28. ΣΩ.   Τάχα, ὦ Πρώταρχε, οὐχ ἧττον δείξεις.
ἀπόκριναι[3] γάρ· ἐν ὕβρει μείζους ἡδονάς—οὐ
πλείους λέγω, τῷ σφόδρα δὲ καὶ τῷ μᾶλλον ὑπερ-
εχούσας—ὁρᾷς ἢ ἐν τῷ σώφρονι βίῳ; λέγε δὲ
προσέχων τὸν νοῦν.

---

[1] προγίγνωνται Stephanus : προσγίγνονται BT.
[2] ἡγῇ] ἡγεῖ BT.
[3] ἀπόκριναι Schleiermacher : ἀποκρινεῖ BT.

health ? Let us take care not to answer hastily and fall into error. Perhaps we might say they are greater in those who are in health.

PRO. That is reasonable.

SOC. Yes, but are not those pleasures the greatest which gratify the greatest desires ?

PRO. That is true.

SOC. But do not people who are in a fever, or in similar diseases, feel more intensely thirst and cold and other bodily sufferings which they usually have; and do they not feel greater want, followed by greater pleasure when their want is satisfied ? Is this true, or not ?

PRO. Now that you have said it, it certainly appears to be true.

SOC. Then should we appear to be right in saying that if we wished to discover the greatest pleasures we should have to look, not at health, but at disease ? Now do not imagine that I mean to ask you whether those who are very ill have more pleasures than those who are well, but assume that I am asking about the greatness of pleasure, and where the greatest intensity of such feeling normally occurs. For we say that it is our task to discover the nature of pleasure and what those who deny its existence altogether say that it is.[1]

PRO. I think I understand you.

SOC. Presently, Protarchus, you will show that more clearly, for I want you to answer a question. Do you see greater pleasures—I do not mean greater in number, but greater in intensity and degree—in riotous living or in a life of self-restraint ? Be careful about your reply.

[1] This paradox means " what those say it is who deny that it is really pleasure."

ΠΡΩ. Ἀλλ' ἔμαθον ὃ λέγεις, καὶ πολὺ τὸ διαφέρον ὁρῶ. τοὺς μὲν γὰρ σώφρονάς που καὶ ὁ
παροιμιαζόμενος ἐπίσχει λόγος ἑκάστοτε, ὁ τὸ
Ε ' μηδὲν ἄγαν ' παρακελευόμενος, ᾧ πείθονται· τὸ
δὲ τῶν ἀφρόνων τε καὶ ὑβριστῶν μέχρι μανίας ἡ
σφοδρὰ ἡδονὴ κατέχοντας περιβοήτους ἀπεργάζεται.

ΣΩ. Καλῶς· καὶ εἴ γε ταῦθ' οὕτως ἔχει, δῆλον
ὡς ἔν τινι πονηρίᾳ ψυχῆς καὶ τοῦ σώματος, ἀλλ' οὐκ
ἐν ἀρετῇ μέγισται μὲν ἡδοναί, μέγισται δὲ καὶ λῦπαι
γίγνονται.

ΠΡΩ. Πάνυ μὲν οὖν.

ΣΩ. Οὐκοῦν τούτων τινὰς προελόμενον δεῖ σκοπεῖσθαι τίνα ποτὲ τρόπον ἐχούσας ἐλέγομεν αὐτὰς
εἶναι μεγίστας.

46 ΠΡΩ. Ἀνάγκη.

ΣΩ. Σκόπει δὴ τὰς τῶν τοιῶνδε νοσημάτων ἡδονάς, τίνα ποτὲ ἔχουσι τρόπον.

ΠΡΩ. Ποίων;

ΣΩ. Τὰς τῶν ἀσχημόνων, ἃς οὓς εἴπομεν δυσ-
χερεῖς μισοῦσι παντελῶς.

ΠΡΩ. Ποίας;

ΣΩ. Οἷον τὰς τῆς ψώρας ἰάσεις τῷ τρίβειν, καὶ
ὅσα τοιαῦτα, οὐκ ἄλλης δεόμενα φαρμάξεως· τοῦτο
γὰρ δὴ τὸ πάθος ἡμῖν, ὦ πρὸς θεῶν, τί ποτε φῶμεν
ἐγγίγνεσθαι; πότερον ἡδονὴν ἢ λύπην;

ΠΡΩ. Σύμμικτον τοῦτό γ' ἄρ', ὦ Σώκρατες, ἔοικε
γίγνεσθαί τι κακόν.

Β ΣΩ. Οὐ μὲν δὴ Φιλήβου γε ἕνεκα παρεθέμην
τὸν λόγον· ἀλλ' ἄνευ τούτων, ὦ Πρώταρχε, τῶν
ἡδονῶν καὶ τῶν ταύταις ἑπομένων, ἂν μὴ κατ-
ορθῶσι, σχεδὸν οὐκ ἄν ποτε δυναίμεθα διακρίνασθαι
τὸ νῦν ζητούμενον.

PRO. I understand you, and I see that there is a great difference. For the self-restrained are always held in check by the advice of the proverbial expression "nothing too much," which guides their actions; but intense pleasure holds sway over the foolish and dissolute even to the point of madness and makes them notorious.

SOC. Good; and if that is true, it is clear that the greatest pleasures and the greatest pains originate in some depravity of soul and body, not in virtue.

PRO. Certainly.

SOC. Then we must select some of these pleasures and see what there is about them which made us say that they are the greatest.

PRO. Yes, we must.

SOC. Now see what there is about the pleasures which are related to certain diseases.

PRO. What diseases?

SOC. Repulsive diseases which the philosophers of dislike whom we mentioned utterly abominate.

PRO. What are the pleasures?

SOC. For instance, the relief of the itch and the like by scratching, no other treatment being required. For in Heaven's name what shall we say the feeling is which we have in this case? Is it pleasure or pain?

PRO. I think, Socrates, it is a mixed evil.

SOC. I did not introduce this question on Philebus' account; but unless we consider these pleasures and those that follow in their train, Protarchus, we can probably never settle the point at issue.

ΠΡΩ. Οὐκοῦν ἰτέον ἐπὶ τὰς τούτων ξυγγενεῖς.

ΣΩ. Τὰς ἐν τῇ μίξει κοινωνούσας λέγεις;

ΠΡΩ. Πάνυ μὲν οὖν.

ΣΩ. Εἰσὶ τοίνυν μίξεις αἱ μὲν κατὰ τὸ σῶμα ἐν αὐτοῖς τοῖς σώμασιν, αἱ δ' αὐτῆς τῆς ψυχῆς ἐν τῇ C ψυχῇ· τὰς δ' αὖ τῆς ψυχῆς καὶ τοῦ σώματος ἀνευρήσομεν λύπας ἡδοναῖς μιχθείσας τοτὲ μὲν ἡδονὰς τὰ ξυναμφότερα, τοτὲ δὲ λύπας ἐπικαλουμένας.

ΠΡΩ. Πῶς;

ΣΩ. Ὁπόταν ἐν τῇ καταστάσει τις ἢ τῇ διαφθορᾷ τἀναντία ἅμα πάθη πάσχῃ, ποτὲ ῥιγῶν θέρηται καὶ θερμαινόμενος ἐνίοτε ψύχηται, ζητῶν, οἶμαι, τὸ μὲν ἔχειν, τοῦ δ' ἀπαλλάττεσθαι, τὸ δὴ λεγόμενον πικρῷ γλυκὺ μεμιγμένον, μετὰ δυσαπαλλακτίας D παρόν, ἀγανάκτησιν καὶ ὕστερον σύντασιν ἀγρίαν ποιεῖ.

ΠΡΩ. Καὶ μάλ' ἀληθὲς τὸ νῦν λεγόμενον.

ΣΩ. Οὐκοῦν αἱ τοιαῦται μίξεις αἱ μὲν ἐξ ἴσων εἰσὶ λυπῶν τε καὶ ἡδονῶν, αἱ δ' ἐκ τῶν ἑτέρων πλειόνων;

ΠΡΩ. Πῶς γὰρ οὔ;

ΣΩ. Λέγε δὴ τὰς μέν, ὅταν πλείους λῦπαι τῶν ἡδονῶν γίγνωνται—τὰς τῆς ψώρας λεγομένας νῦν δὴ ταύτας εἶναι καὶ τὰς τῶν γαργαλισμῶν—ὁπόταν ἐντὸς τὸ ζέον ᾖ καὶ τὸ φλεγμαῖνον, τῇ τρίψει δὲ καὶ E τῇ κνήσει[1] μὴ ἐφικνῆταί τις, τὰ δ' ἐπιπολῆς μόνον διαχέῃ, τοτὲ φέροντες εἰς πῦρ αὐτὰ καὶ εἰς τοὐναντίον, ἀπορίαις μεταβάλλοντες ἐνίοτε ἀμηχάνους ἡδονάς, τοτὲ δὲ τοὐναντίον τοῖς ἐντὸς πρὸς τὰ τῶν[2] ἔξω λύπας ἡδοναῖς ξυγκερασθείσας, εἰς ὁπότερ' ἂν

---

[1] κνήσει Heusde: κινήσει BT.
[2] πρὸς τὰ τῶν Wohlrab: προστάττων B: πρὸς τὰς τῶν T.

PRO. Then we must attack this family of pleasures.

SOC. You mean those which are mixed?

PRO. Certainly.

SOC. Some mixtures are concerned with the body and are in the body only, and some belong only to the soul and are in the soul; and we shall also find some mingled pains and pleasures belonging both to the soul and to the body, and these are sometimes called pleasures, sometimes pains.

PRO. How so?

SOC. Whenever, in the process of restoration or destruction, anyone has two opposite feelings, as we sometimes are cold, but are growing warm, or are hot, but are growing cold, the desire of having the one and being free from the other, the mixture of bitter and sweet, as they say, joined with the difficulty in getting rid of the bitter, produces impatience and, later, wild excitement.

PRO. What you say is perfectly true.

SOC. And such mixtures sometimes consist of equal pains and pleasures and sometimes contain more of one or the other, do they not?

PRO. Of course.

SOC. In the case of the mixtures in which the pains are more than the pleasures—say the itch, which we mentioned just now, or tickling—when the burning inflammation is within and is not reached by the rubbing and scratching, which separate only such mixtures as are on the surface, sometimes by bringing the affected parts to the fire or to something cold we change from wretchedness to inexpressible pleasures, and sometimes the opposition between the internal and the external produces a mixture of pains and pleasures, whichever happens to preponderate;

ρέψῃ, παρέσχοντο τῷ τὰ συγκεκριμένα βίᾳ διαχεῖν
47 ἢ τὰ διακεκριμένα συγχεῖν καὶ ὁμοῦ λύπας ἡδοναῖς
παρατιθέναι.

ΠΡΩ. Ἀληθέστατα.

ΣΩ. Οὐκοῦν ὁπόταν αὖ πλείων ἡδονὴ κατὰ τὰ[1]
τοιαῦτα πάντα ξυμμιχθῇ, τὸ μὲν ὑπομεμιγμένον τῆς
λύπης γαργαλίζει τε καὶ ἠρέμα ἀγανακτεῖν ποιεῖ, τὸ
δ' αὖ τῆς ἡδονῆς πολὺ πλέον ἐγκεχυμένον συντείνει
τε καὶ ἐνίοτε πηδᾶν ποιεῖ, καὶ παντοῖα μὲν χρώματα, παντοῖα δὲ σχήματα, παντοῖα δὲ πνεύματα
ἀπεργαζόμενον[2] πᾶσαν ἔκπληξιν καὶ βοὰς μετ'
ἀφροσύνης ἐνεργάζεται;

B   ΠΡΩ. Μάλα γε.

ΣΩ. Καὶ λέγειν τε, ὦ ἑταῖρε, αὑτόν τε περὶ
ἑαυτοῦ ποιεῖ καὶ ἄλλον ὡς ταύταις ταῖς ἡδοναῖς
τερπόμενος οἷον ἀποθνήσκει· καὶ ταύτας γε δὴ
παντάπασιν ἀεὶ μεταδιώκει τοσούτῳ μᾶλλον ὅσῳ
ἂν ἀκολαστότερός τε καὶ ἀφρονέστερος ὢν τυγχάνῃ,
καὶ καλεῖ δὴ μεγίστας ταύτας, καὶ τὸν ἐν αὐταῖς
ὅτι μάλιστ' ἀεὶ[3] ζῶντα εὐδαιμονέστατον κατ-
αριθμεῖται.

ΠΡΩ. Πάντα, ὦ Σώκρατες, τὰ συμβαίνοντα πρὸς
C τῶν πολλῶν ἀνθρώπων εἰς δόξαν διεπέρανας.

ΣΩ. Περί γε τῶν ἡδονῶν, ὦ Πρώταρχε, τῶν ἐν
τοῖς κοινοῖς παθήμασιν αὐτοῦ τοῦ σώματος τῶν
ἐπιπολῆς τε καὶ ἐντὸς κερασθέντων· περὶ δέ γ' ὧν[4]
ψυχὴ[5] σώματι τἀναντία ξυμβάλλεται, λύπην τε
ἅμα πρὸς ἡδονὴν καὶ ἡδονὴν πρὸς λύπην, ὥστ' εἰς
μίαν ἀμφότερα κρᾶσιν ἰέναι, ταῦτα ἔμπροσθεν μὲν
διήλθομεν, ὡς, ὁπόταν[6] κενῶται, πληρώσεως

---

[1] τὰ add. Par. 1809 : om. BT.
[2] ἀπεργαζόμενον Buttmann : ἀπεργαζόμενα BT.

this is the result of the forcible separation of combined elements, or the combination of those that were separate, and the concomitant juxtaposition of pains and pleasures.

PRO. Very true.

SOC. And when the pleasure is the predominant element in the mixture, the slight tincture of pain tickles a man and makes him mildly impatient, or again an excessive proportion of pleasure excites him and sometimes even makes him leap for joy; it produces in him all sorts of colours, attitudes, and pantings, and even causes great amazement and foolish shouting, does it not?

PRO. Certainly.

SOC. And it makes him say of himself, and others say of him, that he is pleased to death with these delights, and the more unrestrained and foolish he is, the more he always gives himself up to the pursuit of these pleasures; he calls them the greatest of all things and counts that man the happiest who lives most entirely in the enjoyment of them.

PRO. Socrates, you have described admirably what happens in the case of most people.

SOC. That may be, Protarchus, so far as concerns purely bodily pleasures in which internal and external sensations unite; but concerning the pleasures in which the soul and the body contribute opposite elements, each adding pain or pleasure to the other's pleasure or pain, so that both unite in a single mixture—concerning these I said before that when a man is empty he desires to be filled, and rejoices

3 μάλιστ' ἀεὶ T: μάλιστα εἰ B.
4 γ' ὦν Badham; τῶν BT.   5 ψυχὴ Burnet: ἐν ψυχῇ BT.
6 ὁπόταν Wohlrab: ὁπόταν αὖ BT.

ἐπιθυμεῖ, καὶ ἐλπίζων μὲν χαίρει, κενούμενος δὲ
ἀλγεῖ, ταῦτα δὲ τότε μὲν οὐκ ἐμαρτυράμεθα, νῦν δὲ
D λέγομεν ὡς ψυχῆς πρὸς σῶμα διαφερομένης ἐν
πᾶσι τούτοις πλήθει ἀμηχάνοις οὖσι μῖξις μία
λύπης τε καὶ ἡδονῆς ξυμπίπτει γενομένη.

ΠΡΩ. Κινδυνεύεις ὀρθότατα λέγειν.

29. ΣΩ. Ἔτι τοίνυν ἡμῖν τῶν μίξεων λύπης
τε καὶ ἡδονῆς λοιπὴ μία.

ΠΡΩ. Ποία, φής;

ΣΩ. Ἣν αὐτὴν τὴν ψυχὴν αὐτῇ πολλάκις λαμβάνειν σύγκρασιν ἔφαμεν.

ΠΡΩ. Πῶς οὖν δὴ τοῦτ' αὐτὸ λέγομεν;

E ΣΩ. Ὀργὴν καὶ φόβον καὶ πόθον καὶ θρῆνον
καὶ ἔρωτα καὶ ζῆλον καὶ φθόνον καὶ ὅσα τοιαῦτα,
ἆρ' οὐκ αὐτῆς τῆς ψυχῆς τίθεσαι ταύτας λύπας
τινάς;

ΠΡΩ. Ἔγωγε.

ΣΩ. Οὐκοῦν αὐτὰς ἡδονῶν μεστὰς εὑρήσομεν
ἀμηχάνων; ἢ δεόμεθα ὑπομιμνήσκεσθαι τὸ

ὅς τ'[1] ἐφέηκε πολύφρονά περ χαλεπῆναι,[2]
ὅς τε[3] πολὺ γλυκίων μέλιτος καταλειβομένοιο,

48 καὶ τὰς ἐν τοῖς θρήνοις καὶ πόθοις[4] ἡδονὰς ἐν
λύπαις οὔσας ἀναμεμιγμένας;

ΠΡΩ. Οὔκ, ἀλλ' οὕτω ταῦτά γε καὶ οὐκ ἄλλως
ἂν ξυμβαίνοι γιγνόμενα.

ΣΩ. Καὶ μὴν καὶ τάς γε τραγικὰς θεωρήσεις,
ὅταν ἅμα χαίροντες κλάωσι, μέμνησαι;

ΠΡΩ. Τί δ' οὔ;

ΣΩ. Τὴν δ' ἐν ταῖς κωμῳδίαις διάθεσιν ἡμῶν
τῆς ψυχῆς, ἆρ' οἶσθ' ὡς ἔστι κἀν τούτοις μῖξις
λύπης τε καὶ ἡδονῆς;

in his expectation, but is pained by his emptiness, and now I add, what I did not say at that time, that in all these cases, which are innumerable, of opposition between soul and body, there is one single mixture of pain and pleasure.

PRO. I believe you are quite right.

SOC. One further mixture of pain and pleasure is left.

PRO. What is it?

SOC. That mixture of its own feelings which we said the soul often experiences.

PRO. And what do we call this?

SOC. Do you not regard anger, fear, yearning, mourning, love, jealousy, envy, and the like as pains of the soul and the soul only?

PRO. I do.

SOC. And shall we not find them full of ineffable pleasures? Or must I remind you of the anger

> Which stirs a man, though very wise, to wrath,
> And sweeter is than honey from the comb,

and of the pleasures mixed with pains, which we find in mournings and longings?

PRO. No, you need not remind me; those things occur just as you suggest.

SOC. And you remember, too, how people enjoy weeping at tragedies?

PRO. Yes, certainly.

SOC. And are you aware of the condition of the soul at comedies, how there also we have a mixture of pain and pleasure?

---

¹ ὅς τ' Homer (*Iliad* xviii. 109): ὥστε BT.
² τὸ ὥστ' ἐφέηκεν τοῖς θυμοῖς καὶ ταῖς ὀργαῖς τὸ πολύφρονά περ χαλεπῆναι BT: τοῖς . . τὸ del. Fischer.
³ ὅς τε Homer (*Iliad* xviii. 110): ὥστε BT.
⁴ πόθοις Par. 1812 in marg.: πότοις BT.

ΠΡΩ. Οὐ πάνυ κατανοῶ.

Β ΣΩ. Παντάπασι γὰρ οὐ ῥᾴδιον, ὦ Πρώταρχε,
ἐν τούτῳ ξυννοεῖν τὸ τοιοῦτον ἑκάστοτε πάθος.

ΠΡΩ. Οὔκουν ὥς γ᾽ ἔοικεν ἐμοί.

ΣΩ. Λάβωμέν γε μὴν αὐτὸ τοσούτῳ μᾶλλον,
ὅσῳ σκοτεινότερόν ἐστιν, ἵνα καὶ ἐν ἄλλοις ῥᾷον
καταμαθεῖν τις οἷός τ᾽ ᾖ μῖξιν λύπης τε καὶ ἡδονῆς.

ΠΡΩ. Λέγοις ἄν.

ΣΩ. Τό τοι νῦν δὴ ῥηθὲν ὄνομα φθόνου πότερα
λύπην τινὰ ψυχῆς θήσεις, ἢ πῶς;

ΠΡΩ. Οὕτως.

ΣΩ. Ἀλλὰ μὴν ὁ φθονῶν γε ἐπὶ κακοῖς τοῖς
τῶν πέλας ἡδόμενος ἀναφανήσεται.

C ΠΡΩ. Σφόδρα γε.

ΣΩ. Κακὸν μὴν ἄγνοια[1] καὶ ἣν δὴ λέγομεν
ἀβελτέραν ἕξιν.

ΠΡΩ. Τί μήν;

ΣΩ. Ἐκ δὴ τούτων ἰδὲ τὸ γελοῖον ἥντινα φύσιν ἔχει.

ΠΡΩ. Λέγε μόνον.

ΣΩ. Ἔστι δὴ πονηρία μέν τις τὸ κεφάλαιον,
ἕξεώς τινος ἐπίκλην λεγομένη· τῆς δ᾽ αὖ πάσης
πονηρίας ἐστὶ τοὐναντίον πάθος ἔχον ἢ τὸ λεγόμενον ὑπὸ τῶν ἐν Δελφοῖς γραμμάτων.

ΠΡΩ. Τὸ " γνῶθι σαυτὸν " λέγεις, ὦ Σώκρατες;

D ΣΩ. Ἔγωγε. τοὐναντίον μὴν ἐκείνῳ δῆλον ὅτι
τὸ μηδαμῇ γιγνώσκειν αὑτὸν λεγόμενον ὑπὸ τοῦ
γράμματος ἂν εἴη.

ΠΡΩ. Τί μήν;

ΣΩ. Ὦ Πρώταρχε, πειρῶ δὲ αὐτὸ τοῦτο τριχῇ
τέμνειν.

---

[1] ἄγνοια Cornarius : ἄνοια ΒΤ.

332

PRO. I do not quite understand.

soc. Indeed it is by no means easy, Protarchus, to understand such a condition under those circumstances.

PRO. No ; at least I do not find it so.

soc. Well, then, let us take this under consideration, all the more because of its obscurity ; then we can more readily understand the mixture of pain and pleasure in other cases.

PRO. Please go on.

soc. Would you say that envy, which was mentioned just now, was a pain of the soul, or not ?

PRO. I say it is.

soc. But certainly we see the envious man rejoicing in the misfortunes of his neighbours.

PRO. Yes, very much so.

soc. Surely ignorance is an evil, as is also what we call stupidity.

PRO. Surely.

soc. Next, then, consider the nature of the ridiculous.

PRO. Please proceed.

soc. The ridiculous is in its main aspect a kind of vice which gives its name to a condition ; and it is that part of vice in general which involves the opposite of the condition mentioned in the inscription at Delphi.

PRO. You mean " Know thyself," Socrates ?

soc. Yes ; and the opposite of that, in the language of the inscription, would evidently be not to know oneself at all.

PRO. Of course.

soc. Protarchus, try to divide this into three.

M   333

ΠΡΩ. Πῇ φῄς; οὐ γὰρ μὴ δυνατὸς ὦ.

ΣΩ. Λέγεις δὴ δεῖν ἐμὲ τοῦτο διελέσθαι τὰ νῦν;

ΠΡΩ. Λέγω, καὶ δέομαί γε πρὸς τῷ λέγειν.

ΣΩ. Ἆρ᾽ οὖν οὐ τῶν ἀγνοούντων αὑτοὺς κατὰ τρία ἀνάγκη τοῦτο τὸ πάθος πάσχειν ἕκαστον;

ΠΡΩ. Πῶς;

ΣΩ. Πρῶτον μὲν κατὰ χρήματα, δοξάζειν εἶναι
E πλουσιώτερον ἢ κατὰ τὴν αὑτῶν οὐσίαν.

ΠΡΩ. Πολλοὶ γοῦν εἰσὶ τὸ τοιοῦτον πάθος ἔχοντες.

ΣΩ. Πλείους δέ γε οἱ μείζους καὶ καλλίους αὑτοὺς δοξάζουσι, καὶ πάντα ὅσα κατὰ τὸ σῶμα εἶναι διαφερόντως τῆς οὔσης αὐτοῖς ἀληθείας.

ΠΡΩ. Πάνυ γε.

ΣΩ. Πολὺ δὲ πλεῖστοί γε, οἶμαι, περὶ τὸ τρίτον εἶδος τὸ τῶν ἐν ταῖς ψυχαῖς[1] διημαρτήκασιν, ἀρετὴν[2] δοξάζοντες βελτίους ἑαυτούς, οὐκ ὄντες.

ΠΡΩ. Σφόδρα μὲν οὖν.

49 ΣΩ. Τῶν ἀρετῶν δ᾽ ἆρ᾽ οὐ σοφίας πέρι τὸ πλῆθος πάντως ἀντεχόμενον μεστὸν ἐρίδων καὶ δοξοσοφίας ἐστὶ ψευδοῦς[3];

ΠΡΩ. Πῶς δ᾽ οὔ;

ΣΩ. Κακὸν μὲν δὴ πᾶν ἄν τις τὸ τοιοῦτον εἰπὼν ὀρθῶς ἂν εἴποι πάθος.

ΠΡΩ. Σφόδρα γε.

ΣΩ. Τοῦτο τοίνυν ἔτι διαιρετέον, ὦ Πρώταρχε, δίχα, εἰ μέλλομεν τὸν παιδικὸν ἰδόντες φθόνον ἄτοπον ἡδονῆς καὶ λύπης ὄψεσθαι μῖξιν. πῶς οὖν

---

[1] τὸ τῶν ἐν ταῖς ψυχαῖς Badham : τούτων ἐν ταῖς ψυχαῖς B Stobaeus : ἐν ταῖς ψυχαῖς τούτων T.
[2] ἀρετὴν various sources : ἀρετῆς BT : ἀρετῇ Stobaeus.
[3] ψευδοῦς] ψεύδους BT.

PRO. How do you mean? I am afraid I can never do it.

SOC. Then you say that I must now make the division?

PRO. Yes, I say so, and I beg you to do so, besides.

SOC. Must not all those who do not know themselves be affected by their condition in one of three ways?

PRO. How is that?

SOC. First in regard to wealth; such a man thinks he is richer than he is.

PRO. Certainly a good many are affected in that way.

SOC. And there are still more who think they are taller and handsomer than they are and that they possess better physical qualities in general than is the case.

PRO. Certainly.

SOC. But by far the greatest number, I fancy, err in the third way, about the qualities of the soul, thinking that they excel in virtue when they do not.

PRO. Yes, most decidedly.

SOC. And of all the virtues, is not wisdom the one to which people in general lay claim, thereby filling themselves with strife and false conceit of wisdom?

PRO. Yes, to be sure.

SOC. And we should surely be right in calling all that an evil condition.

PRO. Very much so.

SOC. Then this must further be divided into two parts, if we are to gain insight into childish envy with its absurd mixture of pleasure and pain. " How

335

τέμνομεν δίχα, λέγεις;[1] πάντες[2] ὁπόσοι ταύτην
B τὴν ψευδῆ δόξαν περὶ ἑαυτῶν ἀνοήτως δοξάζουσι,
καθάπερ ἁπάντων ἀνθρώπων, καὶ τούτων ἀναγκαιότατον ἕπεσθαι τοῖς μὲν ῥώμην αὐτῶν καὶ δύναμιν,
τοῖς δέ, οἶμαι, τοὐναντίον.

ΠΡΩ. Ἀνάγκη.

ΣΩ. Ταύτῃ τοίνυν δίελε, καὶ ὅσοι μὲν αὐτῶν
εἰσὶ μετ᾽ ἀσθενείας τοιοῦτοι καὶ ἀδύνατοι καταγελώ-
μενοι τιμωρεῖσθαι, γελοίους τούτους φάσκων εἶναι
τἀληθῆ φθέγξει· τοὺς δὲ δυνατοὺς τιμωρεῖσθαι καὶ
ἰσχυροὺς φοβεροὺς[3] καὶ ἐχθροὺς προσαγορεύων
C ὀρθότατον τούτων σαυτῷ λόγον ἀποδώσεις. ἄγνοια[4]
γὰρ ἡ μὲν τῶν ἰσχυρῶν ἐχθρά τε καὶ αἰσχρά—
βλαβερὰ γὰρ καὶ τοῖς πέλας αὐτή[5] τε καὶ ὅσαι
εἰκόνες αὐτῆς εἰσίν—ἡ δ᾽ ἀσθενὴς ἡμῖν τὴν τῶν
γελοίων εἴληχε τάξιν τε[6] καὶ[7] φύσιν.

ΠΡΩ. Ὀρθότατα λέγεις. ἀλλὰ γὰρ ἡ τῶν ἡδονῶν καὶ λυπῶν μῖξις ἐν τούτοις οὔπω μοι καταφανής.

ΣΩ. Τὴν τοίνυν τοῦ φθόνου λαβὲ δύναμιν
πρῶτον.

ΠΡΩ. Λέγε μόνον.

D ΣΩ. Λύπη τις ἄδικός ἐστί που καὶ ἡδονή;

ΠΡΩ. Τοῦτο μὲν ἀνάγκη.

ΣΩ. Οὐκοῦν ἐπὶ μὲν τοῖς τῶν ἐχθρῶν κακοῖς
οὔτ᾽ ἄδικον οὔτε φθονερόν ἐστι τὸ χαίρειν;

ΠΡΩ. Τί μήν;

ΣΩ. Τὰ δέ γε τῶν φίλων ὁρῶντας ἔστιν ὅτε
κακὰ μὴ λυπεῖσθαι, χαίρειν δέ, ἆρ᾽ οὐκ ἄδικόν ἐστιν;

ΠΡΩ. Πῶς δ᾽ οὔ;

[1] πῶς . . λέγεις; given to Socrates T (after λέγεις t adds ναί
above the line): to Protarchus B.
[2] πάντες κέ. to Socrates Stallbaum: to Protarchus BT.
[3] ἰσχυροὺς φοβεροὺς Vahlen: φοβεροὺς καὶ ἰσχυροὺς BT.

shall we divide it," do you say? All who have this
false and foolish conceit of themselves fall, like the
rest of mankind, into two classes : some necessarily
have strength and power, others, as I believe, the
reverse.

PRO. Yes, necessarily.

SOC. Make the division, then, on that principle ;
those of them who have this false conceit and are
weak and unable to revenge themselves when they
are laughed at you may truly call ridiculous, but
those who are strong and able to revenge themselves you will define most correctly to yourself by
calling them powerful, terrible, and hateful, for
ignorance in the powerful is hateful and infamous—
since whether real or feigned it injures their neighbours—but ignorance in the weak appears to us as
naturally ridiculous.

PRO. Quite right. But the mixture of pleasure
and pain in all this is not yet clear to me.

SOC. First, then, take up the nature of envy.

PRO. Go on.

SOC. Is envy a kind of unrighteous pain and also
a pleasure ?

PRO. Undoubtedly.

SOC. But it is neither wrong nor envious to rejoice
in the misfortunes of our enemies, is it ?

PRO. No, of course not.

SOC. But when people sometimes see the misfortunes of their friends and rejoice instead of
grieving, is not that wrong ?

PRO. Of course it is.

---

⁴ ἄγνοια Cornarius : ἄνοια BT.
⁵ αὐτή Heusde : αὕτη BT.
⁶ τε] γε B.   ⁷ τάξιν . . καὶ om. T.

ΣΩ. Οὐκοῦν τὴν ἄγνοιαν[1] εἴπομεν ὅτι κακὸν πᾶσιν;

ΠΡΩ. Ὀρθῶς.

ΣΩ. Τὴν οὖν τῶν φίλων δοξοσοφίαν καὶ δοξο-
E καλίαν καὶ ὅσα νῦν δὴ διήλθομεν, ἐν τρισὶ λέγοντες εἴδεσι γίγνεσθαι, γελοῖα μὲν ὁπόσα ἀσθενῆ, μισητὰ δ᾽ ὁπόσα ἐρρωμένα, φῶμεν[2] ἢ μὴ φῶμεν ὅπερ εἶπον ἄρτι, τὴν τῶν φίλων ἕξιν ταύτην ὅταν ἔχῃ τις τὴν ἀβλαβῆ τοῖς ἄλλοις γελοίαν εἶναι;

ΠΡΩ. Πάνυ γε.

ΣΩ. Κακὸν δ᾽ οὐχ ὁμολογοῦμεν αὐτὴν ἄγνοιάν[1] γε οὖσαν εἶναι;

ΠΡΩ. Σφόδρα γε.

ΣΩ. Χαίρομεν δὲ ἢ λυπούμεθα, ὅταν ἐπ᾽ αὐτῇ γελῶμεν;

50 ΠΡΩ. Δῆλον ὅτι χαίρομεν.

ΣΩ. Ἡδονὴν δὲ ἐπὶ τοῖς τῶν φίλων κακοῖς, οὐ φθόνον ἔφαμεν εἶναι τὸν τοῦτο ἀπεργαζόμενον;

ΠΡΩ. Ἀνάγκη.

ΣΩ. Γελῶντας ἄρα ἡμᾶς ἐπὶ τοῖς τῶν φίλων γελοίοις φησὶν ὁ λόγος, κεραννύντας ἡδονὴν αὖ φθόνῳ, λύπῃ τὴν ἡδονὴν ξυγκεραννύναι· τὸν γὰρ φθόνον ὡμολογῆσθαι λύπην τῆς ψυχῆς ἡμῖν πάλαι, τὸ δὲ γελᾶν ἡδονήν, ἅμα γίγνεσθαι δὲ τούτω[3] ἐν τούτοις τοῖς χρόνοις.

ΠΡΩ. Ἀληθῆ.

B ΣΩ. Μηνύει δὴ νῦν ὁ λόγος ἡμῖν ἐν θρήνοις τε καὶ ἐν τραγῳδίαις καὶ κωμῳδίαις,[4] μὴ τοῖς

---

[1] ἄγνοιαν Cornarius: ἄνοιαν BT.
[2] φῶμεν corr. Ven. 189: om. BT.
[3] τούτω Badham: τοῦτο BT.
[4] καὶ κωμῳδίαις add. Hermann.

soc. And we said that ignorance was an evil to every one, did we not?

pro. True.

soc. Then the false conceits of our friends concerning their wisdom, their beauty, and their other qualities which we mentioned just now, saying that they belong to three classes, are ridiculous when they are weak, but hateful when they are powerful. Shall we, or shall we not, affirm that, as I said just now, this state of mind when possessed in its harmless form by any of our friends, is ridiculous in the eyes of others?

pro. Certainly it is ridiculous.

soc. And do we not agree that ignorance is in itself a misfortune?

pro. Yes, a great one.

soc. And do we feel pleasure or pain when we laugh at it?

pro. Pleasure, evidently.

soc. Did we not say that pleasure in the misfortunes of friends was caused by envy?

pro. There can be no other cause.

soc. Then our argument declares that when we laugh at the ridiculous qualities of our friends, we mix pleasure with pain, since we mix it with envy; for we have agreed all along that envy is a pain of the soul, and that laughter is a pleasure, yet these two are present at the same time on such occasions.

pro. True.

soc. So now our argument shows that in mournings and tragedies and comedies, not merely on the

δράμασι μόνον ἀλλὰ καὶ τῇ τοῦ βίου ξυμπάσῃ
τραγῳδίᾳ καὶ κωμῳδίᾳ, λύπας ἡδοναῖς ἅμα κε-
ράννυσθαι, καὶ ἐν ἄλλοις δὴ μυρίοις.

ΠΡΩ. Ἀδύνατον μὴ ὁμολογεῖν ταῦτα, ὦ Σώκρατες, εἰ καί τις φιλονεικοῖ πάνυ πρὸς τἀναντία.

30. ΣΩ. Ὀργὴν μὴν καὶ πόθον καὶ θρῆνον
καὶ φόβον καὶ ἔρωτα καὶ ζῆλον καὶ φθόνον προυθέ-
C μεθα καὶ ὁπόσα τοιαῦτα, ἐν οἷς ἔφαμεν εὑρήσειν
μιγνύμενα τὰ νῦν πολλάκις λεγόμενα. ἦ γάρ;

ΠΡΩ. Ναί.

ΣΩ. Μανθάνομεν οὖν ὅτι θρήνου πέρι καὶ φθόνου καὶ ὀργῆς πάντα ἐστὶ τὰ νῦν δὴ διαπερανθέντα;

ΠΡΩ. Πῶς γὰρ οὐ μανθάνομεν;

ΣΩ. Οὐκοῦν πολλὰ ἔτι τὰ λοιπά;

ΠΡΩ. Καὶ πάνυ γε.

ΣΩ. Διὰ δὴ τί μάλισθ' ὑπολαμβάνεις με δεῖξαί
σοι τὴν ἐν τῇ κωμῳδίᾳ μῖξιν; ἆρ' οὐ πίστεως χάριν,
D ὅτι τήν γε ἐν τοῖς φόβοις καὶ ἔρωσι καὶ τοῖς ἄλλοις
ῥᾴδιον κρᾶσιν ἐπιδεῖξαι· λαβόντα δὲ τοῦτο παρὰ
σαυτῷ ἀφεῖναί με μηκέτι ἐπ' ἐκεῖνα ἰόντα δεῖν μη-
κύνειν τοὺς λόγους, ἀλλ' ἁπλῶς λαβεῖν τοῦτο, ὅτι
καὶ σῶμα ἄνευ ψυχῆς καὶ ψυχὴ ἄνευ σώματος καὶ
κοινῇ μετ' ἀλλήλων ἐν τοῖς παθήμασι μεστά ἐστι
συγκεκραμένης ἡδονῆς λύπαις; νῦν οὖν λέγε, πότερα
ἀφίῃς με ἢ μέσας ποιήσεις νύκτας; εἰπὼν δὲ
σμικρὰ οἶμαί σου τεύξεσθαι μεθεῖναί με· τούτων
E γὰρ ἁπάντων αὔριον ἐθελήσω σοι λόγον δοῦναι, τὰ

stage, but in all the tragedy and comedy of life, and in countless other ways, pain is mixed with pleasure.

PRO. It is impossible not to agree with that, Socrates, even though one be most eager to maintain the opposite opinion.

SOC. Again we mentioned anger, yearning, mourning, love, jealousy, envy, and the like, as conditions in which we should find a mixture of the two elements we have now often named, did we not?

PRO. Yes.

SOC. And we understand that all the details I have been describing just now are concerned only with sorrow and envy and anger?

PRO. Of course we understand that.

SOC. Then there are still many others of those conditions left for us to discuss.

PRO. Yes, very many.

SOC. Now why do you particularly suppose I pointed out to you the mixture of pain and pleasure in comedy? Was it not for the sake of convincing you, because it is easy to show the mixture in love and fear and the rest, and because I thought that when you had made this example your own, you would relieve me from the necessity of discussing those other conditions in detail, and would simply accept the fact that in the affections of the body apart from the soul, of the soul apart from the body, and of the two in common, there are plentiful mixtures of pain and pleasure? So tell me; will you let me off, or will you keep on till midnight? But I think I need say only a few words to induce you to let me off. I will agree to give you an account of all these matters to-morrow, but now I wish to steer

νῦν δὲ ἐπὶ τὰ λοιπὰ βούλομαι στέλλεσθαι πρὸς τὴν
κρίσιν ἣν Φίληβος ἐπιτάττει.

ΠΡΩ. Καλῶς εἶπες, ὦ Σώκρατες· ἀλλ' ὅσα
λοιπὰ ἡμῖν διέξελθε ὅπῃ σοι φίλον.

31. ΣΩ. Κατὰ φύσιν τοίνυν μετὰ τὰς μιχθείσας
ἡδονὰς ὑπὸ δή τινος ἀνάγκης ἐπὶ τὰς ἀμίκτους
πορευοίμεθ' ἂν ἐν τῷ μέρει.

51 ΠΡΩ. Κάλλιστ' εἶπες.

ΣΩ. Ἐγὼ δὴ πειράσομαι μεταβαλὼν σημαίνειν
ἡμῖν αὐτάς. τοῖς γὰρ φάσκουσι λυπῶν εἶναι
παῦλαν πάσας τὰς ἡδονὰς οὐ πάνυ πως πείθομαι,
ἀλλ' ὅπερ εἶπον, μάρτυσι καταχρῶμαι πρὸς τὸ
τινὰς ἡδονὰς εἶναι δοκούσας, οὔσας δ' οὐδαμῶς,
καὶ μεγάλας ἑτέρας τινὰς ἅμα καὶ πολλὰς φαντα-
σθείσας, εἶναι δ' αὐτὰς συμπεφυρμένας ὁμοῦ λύπαις
τε καὶ ἀναπαύσεσιν ὀδυνῶν τῶν μεγίστων περί τε
σώματος καὶ ψυχῆς ἀπορίας.

B ΠΡΩ. Ἀληθεῖς δ' αὖ τίνας, ὦ Σώκρατες, ὑπο-
λαμβάνων ὀρθῶς τις διανοοῖτ' ἄν;

ΣΩ. Τὰς περί τε τὰ καλὰ λεγόμενα χρώματα
καὶ περὶ τὰ σχήματα καὶ τῶν ὀσμῶν τὰς πλείστας
καὶ τὰς τῶν φθόγγων καὶ ὅσα τὰς ἐνδείας ἀναισθή-
τους ἔχοντα καὶ ἀλύπους τὰς πληρώσεις αἰσθητὰς
καὶ ἡδείας καθαρὰς λυπῶν παραδίδωσιν.

ΠΡΩ. Πῶς δὴ ταῦτα, ὦ Σώκρατες, αὖ λέγομεν
οὕτως;

ΣΩ. Πάνυ μὲν οὖν οὐκ εὐθὺς δῆλά ἐστιν ἃ
C λέγω, πειρατέον μὴν δηλοῦν. σχημάτων τε γὰρ
κάλλος[1] οὐχ ὅπερ ἂν ὑπολάβοιεν οἱ πολλοὶ πειρῶμαι
νῦν λέγειν, οἷον[2] ζῴων ἤ τινων ζωγραφημάτων, ἀλλ'

---

[1] κάλλος T: καλῶς B: κάλλους vulg.
[2] οἷον T: ἤ B.

my bark towards the remaining points that are needful for the judgement which Philebus demands.

PRO. Good, Socrates; just finish what remains in any way you please.

SOC. Then after the mixed pleasures we should naturally and almost of necessity proceed in turn to the unmixed.

PRO. Very good.

SOC. So I will turn to them and try to explain them; for I do not in the least agree with those who say that all pleasures are merely surcease from pain, but, as I said, I use them as witnesses to prove that some pleasures are apparent, but not in any way real, and that there are others which appear to be both great and numerous, but are really mixed up with pains and with cessations of the greatest pains and distresses of body and soul.

PRO. But what pleasures, Socrates, may rightly be considered true?

SOC. Those arising from what are called beautiful colours, or from forms, most of those that arise from odours and sounds, in short all those the want of which is unfelt and painless, whereas the satisfaction furnished by them is felt by the senses, pleasant, and unmixed with pain.

PRO. Once more, Socrates, what do you mean by this?

SOC. My meaning is certainly not clear at the first glance, and I must try to make it so. For when I say beauty of form, I am trying to express, not what most people would understand by the words, such as the beauty of animals or of paintings,

εὐθύ τι λέγω, φησὶν ὁ λόγος, καὶ περιφερὲς καὶ ἀπὸ
τούτων δὴ τά τε τοῖς τόρνοις γιγνόμενα ἐπίπεδά τε
καὶ στερεὰ καὶ τὰ τοῖς κανόσι καὶ γωνίαις, εἴ μου
μανθάνεις.   ταῦτα γὰρ οὐκ εἶναι πρός τι καλὰ
λέγω, καθάπερ ἄλλα, ἀλλ' ἀεὶ καλὰ καθ' αὑτὰ
D πεφυκέναι καί τινας ἡδονὰς οἰκείας ἔχειν, οὐδὲν
ταῖς τῶν κνήσεων[1] προσφερεῖς· καὶ χρώματα δὴ
τοῦτον τὸν τύπον ἔχοντα καλὰ καὶ ἡδονάς.   ἀλλ'
ἆρα μανθάνομεν, ἢ πῶς;

ΠΡΩ. Πειρῶμαι μέν, ὦ Σώκρατες· πειράθητι δὲ
καὶ σὺ σαφέστερον ἔτι λέγειν.

ΣΩ. Λέγω δὴ ἠχὰς[2] τῶν φθόγγων τὰς λείας καὶ
λαμπρὰς τὰς ἕν τι καθαρὸν ἱείσας[3] μέλος, οὐ πρὸς
ἕτερον καλὰς ἀλλ' αὑτὰς καθ' αὑτὰς εἶναι, καὶ τούτων ξυμφύτους ἡδονὰς ἑπομένας.

ΠΡΩ. Ἔστι γὰρ οὖν καὶ τοῦτο.

E ΣΩ. Τὸ δὲ περὶ τὰς ὀσμὰς ἧττον μὲν τούτων
θεῖον γένος ἡδονῶν· τὸ δὲ μὴ συμμεμῖχθαι ἐν
αὐταῖς ἀναγκαίους λύπας, καὶ ὅπη τοῦτο καὶ ἐν
ὅτῳ τυγχάνει γεγονὸς ἡμῖν, τοῦτ' ἐκείνοις τίθημι
ἀντίστροφον ἅπαν.   ἀλλ', εἰ κατανοεῖς, ταῦτα
εἴδη δύο ὧν λέγομεν[4] ἡδονῶν.

ΠΡΩ. Κατανοῶ.

52 ΣΩ. Ἔτι δὴ τοίνυν τούτοις προσθῶμεν τὰς
περὶ τὰ μαθήματα ἡδονάς, εἰ ἄρα δοκοῦσιν ἡμῖν
αὗται πείνας μὲν μὴ ἔχειν τοῦ μανθάνειν μηδὲ διὰ
μαθημάτων πείνην ἀλγηδόνας ἐξ ἀρχῆς γιγνομένας.

ΠΡΩ. Ἀλλ' οὕτω ξυνδοκεῖ.

---

[1] κνήσεων Heusde: κινήσεων BT.
[2] ἠχὰς Bury: τὰς BT.
[3] ἱείσας (sic) T: ἰούσας (sic) B.
[4] ὧν λέγομεν Jackson: λεγομένων BT.

but I mean, says the argument, the straight line and the circle and the plane and solid figures formed from these by turning-lathes and rulers and patterns of angles; perhaps you understand. For I assert that the beauty of these is not relative, like that of other things, but they are always absolutely beautiful by nature and have peculiar pleasures in no way subject to comparison with the pleasures of scratching; and there are colours which possess beauty and pleasures of this character. Do you understand?

PRO. I am trying to do so, Socrates; and I hope you also will try to make your meaning still clearer.

SOC. I mean that those sounds which are smooth and clear and send forth a single pure note are beautiful, not relatively, but absolutely, and that there are pleasures which pertain to these by nature and result from them.

PRO. Yes, that also is true.

SOC. The pleasures of smell are a less divine class; but they have no necessary pains mixed with them, and wherever and in whatever we find this freedom from pain, I regard it always as a mark of similarity to those other pleasures. These, then, are two classes of the pleasures of which I am speaking. Do you understand me?

PRO. I understand.

SOC. And further let us add to these the pleasures of knowledge, if they appear to us not to have hunger for knowledge or pangs of such hunger as their source.

PRO. I agree to that.

ΣΩ. Τί δέ; μαθημάτων πληρωθεῖσιν[1] ἐὰν ὕστερον
ἀποβολαὶ διὰ τῆς λήθης γίγνωνται, καθορᾷς τινὰς ἐν
αὐταῖς ἀλγηδόνας;

ΠΡΩ. Οὔ τι φύσει γε, ἀλλ' ἔν τισι λογισμοῖς τοῦ
B παθήματος,[2] ὅταν τις στερηθεὶς λυπηθῇ διὰ τὴν
χρείαν.

ΣΩ. Καὶ μήν, ὦ μακάριε, νῦν γε ἡμεῖς αὐτὰ τὰ
τῆς φύσεως μόνον παθήματα χωρὶς τοῦ λογισμοῦ
διαπεραίνομεν.

ΠΡΩ. Ἀληθῆ τοίνυν λέγεις ὅτι χωρὶς λύπης
ἡμῖν λήθη γίγνεται ἑκάστοτε ἐν τοῖς μαθήμασιν.

ΣΩ. Ταύτας τοίνυν τὰς τῶν μαθημάτων ἡδονὰς
ἀμίκτους τε εἶναι λύπαις ῥητέον καὶ οὐδαμῶς τῶν
πολλῶν ἀνθρώπων ἀλλὰ τῶν σφόδρα ὀλίγων.

ΠΡΩ. Πῶς γὰρ οὐ ῥητέον;

C 32. ΣΩ. Οὐκοῦν ὅτε μετρίως ἤδη διακεκρίμεθα
χωρὶς τάς τε καθαρὰς ἡδονὰς καὶ τὰς σχεδὸν
ἀκαθάρτους ὀρθῶς ἂν λεχθείσας, προσθῶμεν τῷ
λόγῳ ταῖς μὲν σφοδραῖς ἡδοναῖς ἀμετρίαν, ταῖς δὲ
μὴ τοὐναντίον ἐμμετρίαν· καὶ τὰς[3] τὸ μέγα καὶ τὸ
σφοδρὸν αὖ δεχομένας[4] καὶ πολλάκις καὶ ὀλιγάκις
γιγνομένας τοιαύτας[5] τοῦ ἀπείρου γε ἐκείνου καὶ
ἧττον καὶ μᾶλλον διά τε σώματος καὶ ψυχῆς φερο-
D μένου θῶμεν[6] αὐτὰς[7] εἶναι γένους, τὰς δὲ μὴ τῶν
ἐμμέτρων.

ΠΡΩ. Ὀρθότατα λέγεις, ὦ Σώκρατες.

ΣΩ. Ἔτι τοίνυν πρὸς τούτοις μετὰ ταῦτα τόδε
αὐτῶν διαθεατέον.[8]

ΠΡΩ. Τὸ ποῖον;

---

[1] πληρωθεῖσιν Schütz: πληρωθεισῶν BT.
[2] παθήματος Gt: μαθήματος BT.
[3] τὰς add. Stallbaum.

soc. Well, if men are full of knowledge and then lose it through forgetfulness, do you see any pains in the losses?

pro. Not by their inherent nature, but sometimes there is pain in reflecting on the event, when a man who has lost knowledge is pained by the lack of it.

soc. True, my dear fellow, but just at present we are recounting natural feelings only, not reflection.

pro. Then you are right in saying that we feel no pain in the loss of knowledge.

soc. Then we may say that these pleasures of knowledge are unmixed with pain and are felt not by the many but only by very few.

pro. Yes, certainly.

soc. And now that we have fairly well separated the pure pleasures and those which may be pretty correctly called impure, let us add the further statement that the intense pleasures are without measure and those of the opposite sort have measure; those which admit of greatness and intensity and are often or seldom great or intense we shall assign to the class of the infinite, which circulates more or less freely through the body and soul alike, and the others we shall assign to the class of the limited.

pro. Quite right, Socrates.

soc. There is still another question about them to be considered.

pro. What is it?

---

⁴ δεχομένας add. Stallbaum (Ficinus).
⁵ τοιαύτας τῆς BT: τῆς bracketed by Stallbaum (Stephanus).
⁶ θῶμεν Stallbaum: προσθῶμεν BT.
⁷ αὐτὰς corr. Ven. 189: αὐταῖς BT.
⁸ διαθεατέον corr. Ven. 159: διαθετέον BT.

ΣΩ. Τί ποτε χρὴ φάναι πρὸς ἀλήθειαν εἶναι; τὸ καθαρόν τε καὶ εἰλικρινὲς ἢ τὸ σφόδρα τε καὶ τὸ πολὺ καὶ τὸ μέγα καὶ τὸ ἱκανόν;

ΠΡΩ. Τί ποτ' ἄρα, ὦ Σώκρατες, ἐρωτᾷς βουλόμενος;

ΣΩ. Μηδέν, ὦ Πρώταρχε, ἐπιλείπειν ἐλέγχων Ε ἡδονῆς τε καὶ ἐπιστήμης, εἰ τὸ μὲν ἄρ' αὐτῶν ἑκατέρου καθαρόν ἐστι, τὸ δ' οὐ καθαρόν, ἵνα καθαρὸν ἑκάτερον ἰὸν εἰς τὴν κρίσιν ἐμοὶ καὶ σοὶ καὶ ξυνάπασι τοῖσδε ῥᾴω παρέχῃ τὴν κρίσιν.

ΠΡΩ. Ὀρθότατα.

ΣΩ. Ἴθι δή, περὶ πάντων ὅσα καθαρὰ γένη λέγομεν, οὑτωσὶ διανοηθῶμεν· προελόμενοι πρῶτον αὐτῶν ἕν τι σκοπῶμεν.

53 ΠΡΩ. Τί οὖν προελώμεθα;

ΣΩ. Τὸ λευκὸν ἐν τοῖς πρῶτον, εἰ βο λει, θεασώμεθα γένος.

ΠΡΩ. Πάνυ μὲν οὖν.

ΣΩ. Πῶς οὖν ἂν λευκοῦ καὶ τίς καθαρότης ἡμῖν εἴη; πότερα τὸ μέγιστόν τε καὶ πλεῖστον ἢ τὸ ἀκρατέστατον, ἐν ᾧ χρώματος μηδεμία μοῖρα ἄλλη μηδενὸς ἐνείη;

ΠΡΩ. Δῆλον ὅτι τὸ μάλιστα εἰλικρινὲς ὄν.

ΣΩ. Ὀρθῶς. ἆρ' οὖν οὐ τοῦτο ἀληθέστατον, ὦ Πρώταρχε, καὶ ἅμα δὴ κάλλιστον τῶν λευκῶν Β πάντων θήσομεν, ἀλλ' οὐ τὸ πλεῖστον οὐδὲ τὸ μέγιστον;

ΠΡΩ. Ὀρθότατά γε.

ΣΩ. Σμικρὸν ἄρα καθαρὸν λευκὸν μεμιγμένου πολλοῦ λευκοῦ λευκότερον ἅμα καὶ κάλλιον καὶ ἀληθέστερον ἐὰν φῶμεν γίγνεσθαι, παντάπασιν ἐροῦμεν ὀρθῶς.

soc. What kind of thing is most closely related to truth? The pure and unadulterated, or the violent, the widespread, the great, and the sufficient?

pro. What is your object, Socrates, in asking that question?

soc. My object, Protarchus, is to leave no gap in my test of pleasure and knowledge, if some part of each of them is pure and some part impure, in order that each of them may offer itself for judgement in a condition of purity, and thus make the judgement easier for you and me and all our audience.

pro. Quite right.

soc. Very well, let us adopt that point of view towards all the classes which we call pure. First let us select one of them and examine it.

pro. Which shall we select?

soc. Let us first, if agreeable to you, consider whiteness.

pro. By all means.

soc. How can we have purity in whiteness, and what purity? Is it the greatest and most widespread, or the most unmixed, that in which there is no trace of any other colour?

pro. Clearly it is the most unadulterated.

soc. Right. Shall we not, then, Protarchus, declare that this, and not the most numerous or the greatest, is both the truest and the most beautiful of all whitenesses?

pro. Quite right.

soc. Then we shall be perfectly right in saying that a little pure white is whiter and more beautiful and truer than a great deal of mixed white.

ΠΡΩ. Ὀρθότατα μὲν οὖν.

ΣΩ. Τί οὖν; οὐ δή που πολλῶν δεησόμεθα παραδειγμάτων τοιούτων ἐπὶ τὸν τῆς ἡδονῆς πέρι λόγον, ἀλλ' ἀρκεῖ νοεῖν ἡμῖν αὐτόθεν ὡς ἄρα καὶ ξύμπασα C ἡδονὴ σμικρὰ μεγάλης καὶ ὀλίγη πολλῆς, καθαρὰ λύπης, ἡδίων καὶ ἀληθεστέρα καὶ καλλίων γίγνοιτ' ἄν.

ΠΡΩ. Σφόδρα μὲν οὖν, καὶ τό γε παράδειγμα ἱκανόν.

ΣΩ. Τί δὲ τὸ τοιόνδε; ἆρα περὶ ἡδονῆς οὐκ ἀκηκόαμεν ὡς ἀεὶ γένεσίς ἐστιν, οὐσία δὲ οὐκ ἔστι τὸ παράπαν ἡδονῆς; κομψοὶ γὰρ δή τινες αὖ τοῦτον τὸν λόγον ἐπιχειροῦσι μηνύειν ἡμῖν, οἷς δεῖ χάριν ἔχειν.

ΠΡΩ. Τί δή;

ΣΩ. Διαπερανοῦμαί σοι τοῦτ' αὐτὸ ἐπανερωτῶν, D ὦ Πρώταρχε φίλε.

ΠΡΩ. Λέγε καὶ ἐρώτα μόνον.

33. ΣΩ. Ἔστον δή τινε δύο, τὸ μὲν αὐτὸ καθ' αὑτό, τὸ δὲ ἀεὶ ἐφιέμενον ἄλλου.

ΠΡΩ. Πῶς τούτω καὶ τίνε λέγεις;

ΣΩ. Τὸ μὲν σεμνότατον ἀεὶ πεφυκός, τὸ δ' ἐλλιπὲς ἐκείνου.

ΠΡΩ. Λέγ' ἔτι σαφέστερον.

ΣΩ. Παιδικά που καλὰ καὶ ἀγαθὰ τεθεωρήκαμεν ἅμα καὶ ἐραστὰς ἀνδρείους αὐτῶν.

ΠΡΩ. Σφόδρα γε.

ΣΩ. Τούτοις τοίνυν ἐοικότα δυοῖν οὖσι δύ' ἄλλα E ζήτει κατὰ πάνθ' ὅσα λέγομεν εἶναι.

ΠΡΩ. Τὸ τρίτον ἔτ' ἐρῶ;[1] λέγε σαφέστερον, ὦ Σώκρατες, ὅ τι λέγεις.

PRO. Perfectly right.

SOC. Well then, we shall have no need of many such examples in our discussion of pleasure; we see well enough from this one that any pleasure, however small or infrequent, if uncontaminated with pain, is pleasanter and more beautiful than a great or often repeated pleasure without purity.

PRO. Most certainly; and the example is sufficient.

SOC. Here is another point. Have we not often heard it said of pleasure that it is always a process or generation and that there is no state or existence of pleasure? There are some clever people who try to prove this theory to us, and we ought to be grateful to them.

PRO. Well, what then?

SOC. I will explain this whole matter, Protarchus, by asking questions.

PRO. Go on; ask your questions.

SOC. There are two parts of existence, the one self-existent, the other always desiring something else.

PRO. What do you mean? What are these two?

SOC. The one is by nature more imposing, the other inferior.

PRO. Speak still more plainly.

SOC. We have seen beloved boys who are fair and good, and brave lovers of them.

PRO. Yes, no doubt of it.

SOC. Try to find another pair like these in all the relations we are speaking of.[1]

PRO. Must I say it a third time? Please tell your meaning more plainly, Socrates.

---

[1] τὸ τρίτον ἔτ' ἐρῶ; Badham: τὸ τρίτον ἑτέρῳ BT, giving the words to Socrates.

PLATO

ΣΩ. Οὐδέν τι ποικίλον, ὦ Πρώταρχε· ἀλλ᾽ ὁ λόγος ἐρεσχηλεῖ νῷν, λέγει δ᾽ ὅτι τὸ μὲν ἕνεκά του τῶν ὄντων ἔστ᾽ ἀεί, τὸ δ᾽ οὗ χάριν ἑκάστοτε τὸ τινὸς ἕνεκα γιγνόμενον ἀεὶ γίγνεται.

ΠΡΩ. Μόγις ἔμαθον διὰ τὸ πολλάκις λεχθῆναι.

ΣΩ. Τάχα δ᾽ ἴσως, ὦ παῖ, μᾶλλον μαθησόμεθα
54 προελθόντος τοῦ λόγου.

ΠΡΩ. Τί γὰρ οὔ;

ΣΩ. Δύο δὴ τάδε ἕτερα λάβωμεν.

ΠΡΩ. Ποῖα;

ΣΩ. Ἕν μέν τι γένεσιν πάντων, τὴν δὲ οὐσίαν ἕτερον ἕν.

ΠΡΩ. Δύο ἀποδέχομαί σου ταῦτα, οὐσίαν καὶ γένεσιν.

ΣΩ. Ὀρθότατα. πότερον οὖν τούτων ἕνεκα ποτέρου, τὴν γένεσιν οὐσίας ἕνεκα φῶμεν ἢ τὴν οὐσίαν εἶναι γενέσεως ἕνεκα;

ΠΡΩ. Τοῦτο ὃ προσαγορεύεται οὐσία εἰ γενέσεως ἕνεκα τοῦτ᾽ ἔστιν ὅπερ ἐστί, νῦν πυνθάνει;

ΣΩ. Φαίνομαι.

B ΠΡΩ. Πρὸς θεῶν ἆρ᾽[1] ἐπανερωτᾷς με τοιόνδε[2] τι; λέγ᾽, ὦ[3] Πρώταρχε, μοί, πότερα πλοίων ναυ- πηγίαν ἕνεκα φῂς γίγνεσθαι μᾶλλον ἢ πλοῖα ἕνεκα ναυπηγίας, καὶ πάνθ᾽ ὁπόσα τοιαῦτ᾽ ἐστί;[2]

ΣΩ. Λέγω τοῦτ᾽ αὐτό, ὦ Πρώταρχε.

ΠΡΩ. Τί οὖν οὐκ αὐτὸς ἀπεκρίνω σαυτῷ, ὦ Σώ- κρατες;

ΣΩ. Οὐδὲν ὅ τι οὔ· σὺ μέντοι τοῦ λόγου συμ- μέτεχε.

---

[1] ἆρ᾽ Badham: ἆρ᾽ ἂν BT.
[2] τοιόνδε . . ἐστίν; given to Protarchus Badham: to Socrates BT.

352

soc. It is no riddle, Protarchus; the talk is merely jesting with us and means that one part of existences always exists for the sake of something, and the other part is that for the sake of which the former is always coming into being.

pro. I can hardly understand after all your repetition.

soc. Perhaps, my boy, you will understand better as the discussion proceeds.

pro. I hope so.

soc. Let us take another pair.

pro. What are they?

soc. One is the generation of all things (the process of coming into being), the other is existence or being.

pro. I accept your two, generation and being.

soc. Quite right. Now which of these shall we say is for the sake of the other, generation for the sake of being, or being for the sake of generation?

pro. You are now asking whether that which is called being is what it is for the sake of generation?

soc. Yes, plainly.

pro. For Heaven's sake, is this the kind of question you keep asking me, "Tell me, Protarchus, whether you think shipbuilding is for the sake of ships, or ships for the sake of shipbuilding," and all that sort of thing?

soc. Yes, that is just what I mean, Protarchus.

pro. Then why did you not answer it yourself, Socrates?

soc. There is no reason why I should not; but I want you to take part in the discussion.

---

³ λέγ' ὦ Badham: λέγω ὦ BT.

ΠΡΩ. Πάνυ μὲν οὖν.

ΣΩ. Φημὶ δὴ γενέσεως μὲν ἕνεκα φάρμακά τε
C καὶ πάντα ὄργανα καὶ πᾶσαν ὕλην παρατίθεσθαι
πᾶσιν, ἑκάστην δὲ γένεσιν ἄλλην ἄλλης οὐσίας τινὸς
ἑκάστης ἕνεκα γίγνεσθαι, ξύμπασαν δὲ γένεσιν οὐσίας
ἕνεκα γίγνεσθαι ξυμπάσης.

ΠΡΩ. Σαφέστατα μὲν οὖν.

ΣΩ. Οὐκοῦν ἡδονή γε, εἴπερ γένεσίς ἐστιν,
ἕνεκά τινος οὐσίας ἐξ ἀνάγκης γίγνοιτ' ἄν.

ΠΡΩ. Τί μήν;

ΣΩ. Τό γε μὴν οὗ ἕνεκα τὸ ἕνεκά του γιγνόμενον ἀεὶ γίγνοιτ' ἄν, ἐν τῇ τοῦ ἀγαθοῦ μοίρᾳ ἐκεῖνό
ἐστι· τὸ δὲ τινὸς ἕνεκα γιγνόμενον εἰς ἄλλην, ὦ
ἄριστε, μοῖραν θετέον.

D ΠΡΩ. Ἀναγκαιότατον.

ΣΩ. Ἆρ' οὖν ἡδονή γε εἴπερ γένεσίς ἐστιν, εἰς
ἄλλην ἢ τὴν τοῦ ἀγαθοῦ μοῖραν αὐτὴν τιθέντες
ὀρθῶς θήσομεν;

ΠΡΩ. Ὀρθότατα μὲν οὖν.

ΣΩ. Οὐκοῦν ὅπερ ἀρχόμενος εἶπον τούτου τοῦ
λόγου, τῷ μηνύσαντι τῆς ἡδονῆς πέρι τὸ γένεσιν μέν,
οὐσίαν δὲ μηδ' ἡντινοῦν αὐτῆς εἶναι, χάριν ἔχειν δεῖ·
δῆλον γὰρ ὅτι οὗτος τῶν φασκόντων ἡδονὴν ἀγαθὸν
εἶναι καταγελᾷ.

ΠΡΩ. Σφόδρα γε.

ΣΩ. Καὶ μὴν ὁ[1] αὐτὸς οὗτος ἑκάστοτε καὶ τῶν
E ἐν ταῖς γενέσεσιν ἀποτελουμένων καταγελάσεται.

ΠΡΩ. Πῶς δὴ καὶ ποίων λέγεις;

ΣΩ. Τῶν ὅσοι ἐξιώμενοι ἢ πείνην ἢ δίψαν ἤ τι
τῶν τοιούτων, ὅσα γένεσις ἐξιᾶται, χαίρουσι διὰ τὴν

---

[1] ὁ add. Bekker.

PRO. Certainly.

SOC. I say that drugs and all sorts of instruments and materials are always employed for the sake of production or generation, but that every instance of generation is for the sake of some being or other, and generation in general is for the sake of being in general.

PRO. That is very clear.

SOC. Then pleasure, if it is a form of generation, would be generated for the sake of some form of being.

PRO. Of course.

SOC. Now surely that for the sake of which anything is generated is in the class of the good, and that which is generated for the sake of something else, my friend, must be placed in another class.

PRO. Most undeniably.

SOC. Then if pleasure is a form of generation, we shall be right in placing it in a class other than that of the good, shall we not?

PRO. Quite right.

SOC. Then, as I said when we began to discuss this point, we ought to be grateful to him who pointed out that there is only a generation, but no existence, of pleasure; for he is clearly making a laughing-stock of those who assert that pleasure is a good.

PRO. Yes, most emphatically.

SOC. And he will also surely make a laughing-stock of all those who find their highest end in forms of generation.

PRO. How is that, and to whom do you refer?

SOC. To those who, when cured of hunger or thirst or any of the troubles which are cured by generation,

γένεσιν ἅτε ἡδονῆς οὔσης αὐτῆς, καί φασι ζῆν οὐκ ἂν δέξασθαι μὴ διψῶντές τε καὶ πεινῶντες καὶ τἆλλα ἅ τις ἂν εἴποι πάντα τὰ ἑπόμενα τοῖς τοιούτοις παθήμασι μὴ πάσχοντες.

55 ΠΡΩ. Ἐοίκασι γοῦν.

ΣΩ. Οὐκοῦν τῷ γίγνεσθαί γε τοὐναντίον ἅπαντες τὸ φθείρεσθαι φαῖμεν ἄν;

ΠΡΩ. Ἀναγκαῖον.

ΣΩ. Τὴν δὴ φθορὰν καὶ γένεσιν αἱροῖτ' ἄν τις τοῦθ' αἱρούμενος, ἀλλ' οὐ τὸν τρίτον ἐκεῖνον βίον, τὸν ἐν ᾧ μήτε χαίρειν μήτε λυπεῖσθαι, φρονεῖν δ' ἦν δυνατὸν ὡς οἷόν τε καθαρώτατα.

ΠΡΩ. Πολλή τις, ὡς ἔοικεν, ὦ Σώκρατες, ἀλογία συμβαίνει γίγνεσθαι, ἐάν τις τὴν ἡδονὴν ὡς ἀγαθὸν ἡμῖν τιθῆται.

ΣΩ. Πολλή, ἐπεὶ καὶ τῇδε ἔτι λέγωμεν.

ΠΡΩ. Πῇ;

B ΣΩ. Πῶς οὐκ ἄλογόν ἐστι μηδὲν ἀγαθὸν εἶναι μηδὲ καλὸν μήτ' ἐν σώμασι μήτ' ἐν πολλοῖς ἄλλοις πλὴν ἐν ψυχῇ, καὶ ἐνταῦθα ἡδονὴν μόνον, ἀνδρείαν δὲ ἢ σωφροσύνην ἢ νοῦν ἤ τι τῶν ἄλλων ὅσα ἀγαθὰ εἴληχε ψυχή, μηδὲν τοιοῦτον εἶναι; πρὸς τούτοις δὲ ἔτι τὸν μὴ χαίροντα, ἀλγοῦντα δέ, ἀναγκάζεσθαι φάναι κακὸν εἶναι τότε ὅταν ἀλγῇ, κἂν ᾖ ἄριστος πάντων, καὶ τὸν χαίροντα αὖ, ὅσῳ μᾶλλον χαίρει, C τότε ὅταν χαίρῃ, τοσούτῳ διαφέρειν πρὸς ἀρετήν;

ΠΡΩ. Πάντ' ἐστὶ ταῦτα, ὦ Σώκρατες, ὡς δυνατὸν ἀλογώτατα.

34. ΣΩ. Μὴ τοίνυν ἡδονῆς μὲν πάντως ἐξέτασιν πᾶσαν ἐπιχειρῶμεν ποιήσασθαι, νοῦ δὲ καὶ ἐπιστήμης οἷον φειδόμενοι σφόδρα φανῶμεν· γενναίως δέ, εἴ πή τι σαθρὸν ἔχει, πᾶν περικρούωμεν, ὡς¹ ὅτι

356

are pleased because of the generation, as if it were pleasure, and say that they would not wish to live without thirst and hunger and the like, if they could not experience the feelings which follow after them.

PRO. That seems to be their view.

SOC. We should all agree that the opposite of generation is destruction, should we not?

PRO. Inevitably.

SOC. And he who chooses as they do would be choosing destruction and generation, not that third life in which there was neither pleasure nor pain, but only the purest possible thought.

PRO. It is a great absurdity, as it appears, Socrates, to tell us that pleasure is a good.

SOC. Yes, a great absurdity, and let us go still further.

PRO. How?

SOC. Is it not absurd to say that there is nothing good in the body or many other things, but only in the soul, and that in the soul the only good is pleasure, and that courage and self-restraint and understanding and all the other good things of the soul are nothing of the sort; and beyond all this to be obliged to say that he who is not feeling pleasure, and is feeling pain, is bad when he feels pain, though he be the best of men, and that he who feels pleasure is, when he feels pleasure, the more excellent in virtue the greater the pleasure he feels?

PRO. All that, Socrates, is the height of absurdity.

SOC. Now let us not undertake to subject pleasure to every possible test and then be found to give mind and knowledge very gentle treatment. Let us rather strike them boldly everywhere to see if

---

¹ ὡς Apelt: ἕως BT.

καθαρώτατόν ἐστ' αὐτῶν φύσει, τοῦτο κατιδόντες
εἰς τὴν κρίσιν χρώμεθα τὴν κοινὴν τοῖς τε[1] τούτων
καὶ τοῖς τῆς ἡδονῆς μέρεσιν ἀληθεστάτοις.

ΠΡΩ. Ὀρθῶς.

D ΣΩ. Οὐκοῦν ἡμῖν τὸ μέν, οἶμαι, δημιουργικόν
ἐστι τῆς περὶ τὰ μαθήματα ἐπιστήμης, τὸ δὲ περὶ
παιδείαν καὶ τροφήν. ἢ πῶς;

ΠΡΩ. Οὕτως.

ΣΩ. Ἐν δὴ ταῖς χειροτεχνικαῖς διανοηθῶμεν
πρῶτα εἰ τὸ μὲν ἐπιστήμης αὐτῶν μᾶλλον ἐχόμενον, τὸ δὲ ἧττον ἔνι, καὶ δεῖ τὰ μὲν ὡς καθαρώτατα
νομίζειν, τὰ δ' ὡς ἀκαθαρτότερα.

ΠΡΩ. Οὐκοῦν χρή.

ΣΩ. Τὰς τοίνυν ἡγεμονικὰς διαληπτέον ἑκάστων
αὐτῶν χωρίς;

ΠΡΩ. Ποίας καὶ πῶς;

E ΣΩ. Οἷον πασῶν που τεχνῶν ἄν τις ἀριθμητικὴν χωρίζῃ καὶ μετρητικὴν καὶ στατικήν, ὡς ἔπος
εἰπεῖν, φαῦλον τὸ καταλειπόμενον ἑκάστης ἂν
γίγνοιτο.

ΠΡΩ. Φαῦλον μὲν δή.

ΣΩ. Τὸ γοῦν μετὰ ταῦτ' εἰκάζειν λείποιτ' ἂν
καὶ τὰς αἰσθήσεις καταμελετᾶν ἐμπειρίᾳ καί τινι
τριβῇ, ταῖς τῆς στοχαστικῆς προσχρωμένους δυνά-
56 μεσιν ἃς πολλοὶ τέχνας ἐπονομάζουσι, μελέτῃ καὶ
πόνῳ τὴν ῥώμην ἀπειργασμένας.

ΠΡΩ. Ἀναγκαιότατα λέγεις.

ΣΩ. Οὐκοῦν μεστὴ μέν που μουσικὴ πρῶτον, τὸ
ξύμφωνον ἁρμόττουσα οὐ μέτρῳ ἀλλὰ μελέτης
στοχασμῷ· καὶ ξύμπασα αὐτῆς αὐλητική, τὸ μέτρον
ἑκάστης χορδῆς τῷ στοχάζεσθαι φερομένης θη-

[1] τοῖς τε t: τῆς τε BT.

their metal rings unsound at any point ; so we shall find out what is by nature purest in them, and then we can make use of the truest elements of these and of pleasure to form our judgement of both.

PRO. Right.

SOC. Well, then, one part of knowledge is productive, the other has to do with education and support. Is that true ?

PRO. It is.

SOC. Let us first consider whether in the manual arts one part is more allied to knowledge, and the other less, and the one should be regarded as purest, the other as less pure.

PRO. Yes, we ought to consider that.

SOC. And should the ruling elements of each of them be separated and distinguished from the rest ?

PRO. What are they, and how can they be separated ?

SOC. For example, if arithmetic and the sciences of measurement and weighing were taken away from all arts, what was left of any of them would be, so to speak, pretty worthless.

PRO. Yes, pretty worthless.

SOC. All that would be left for us would be to conjecture and to drill the perceptions by practice and experience, with the additional use of the powers of guessing, which are commonly called arts and acquire their efficacy by practice and toil.

PRO. That is undeniable.

SOC. Take music first ; it is full of this ; it attains harmony by guesswork based on practice, not by measurement ; and flute music throughout tries to find the pitch of each note as it is produced by guess,

ρέουσα, ὥστε πολὺ μεμιγμένον ἔχειν τὸ μὴ σαφές, σμικρὸν δὲ τὸ βέβαιον.

ΠΡΩ. Ἀληθέστατα.

Β ΣΩ. Καὶ μὴν ἰατρικήν τε καὶ γεωργίαν καὶ κυβερνητικὴν καὶ στρατηγικὴν ὡσαύτως εὑρήσομεν ἐχούσας.

ΠΡΩ. Καὶ πάνυ γε.

ΣΩ. Τεκτονικὴν δέ γε, οἶμαι, πλείστοις μέτροις τε καὶ ὀργάνοις χρωμένην τὰ πολλὴν ἀκρίβειαν αὐτῇ πορίζοντα τεχνικωτέραν τῶν πολλῶν ἐπιστημῶν παρέχεται.

ΠΡΩ. Πῇ;

ΣΩ. Κατά τε ναυπηγίαν καὶ κατ᾽ οἰκοδομίαν καὶ ἐν πολλοῖς ἄλλοις τῆς ξυλουργικῆς. κανόνι γάρ, οἶμαι, καὶ τόρνῳ χρῆται καὶ διαβήτῃ καὶ στάθμῃ

C καὶ τινι προσαγωγίῳ¹ κεκομψευμένῳ.

ΠΡΩ. Καὶ πάνυ γε, ὦ Σώκρατες, ὀρθῶς λέγεις.

ΣΩ. Θῶμεν τοίνυν διχῇ τὰς λεγομένας τέχνας, τὰς μὲν μουσικῇ ξυνεπομένας ἐν τοῖς ἔργοις ἐλάττονος ἀκριβείας μετισχούσας, τὰς δὲ τεκτονικῇ πλείονος.

ΠΡΩ. Κείσθω.

ΣΩ. Τούτων δὲ ταύτας ἀκριβεστάτας εἶναι τέχνας, ἃς νῦν δὴ πρώτας εἴπομεν.

ΠΡΩ. Ἀριθμητικὴν φαίνει μοι λέγειν καὶ ὅσας μετὰ ταύτης τέχνας ἐφθέγξω νῦν δή.

D ΣΩ. Πάνυ μὲν οὖν. ἀλλ᾽, ὦ Πρώταρχε, ἆρ᾽ οὐ διττὰς αὖ καὶ ταύτας λεκτέον; ἢ πῶς;

ΠΡΩ. Ποίας δὴ λέγεις;

ΣΩ. Ἀριθμητικὴν πρῶτον ἆρ᾽ οὐκ ἄλλην μέν τινα τὴν τῶν πολλῶν φατέον, ἄλλην δ᾽ αὖ τὴν τῶν φιλοσοφούντων;

so that the amount of uncertainty mixed up in it is great, and the amount of certainty small.

PRO. Very true.

SOC. And we shall find that medicine and agriculture and piloting and generalship are all in the same case.

PRO. Certainly.

SOC. But the art of building, I believe, employs the greatest number of measures and instruments which give it great accuracy and make it more scientific than most arts.

PRO. In what way ?

SOC. In shipbuilding and house-building, and many other branches of wood-working. For the artisan uses a rule, I imagine, a lathe, compasses, a chalk-line, and an ingenious instrument called a vice.

PRO. Certainly, Socrates ; you are right.

SOC. Let us, then, divide the arts, as they are called, into two kinds, those which resemble music, and have less accuracy in their works, and those which, like building, are more exact.

PRO. Agreed.

SOC. And of these the most exact are the arts which I just now mentioned first.

PRO. I think you mean arithmetic and the other arts you mentioned with it just now.

SOC. Certainly. But, Protarchus, ought not these to be divided into two kinds ? What do you say ?

PRO. What kinds ?

SOC. Are there not two kinds of arithmetic, that of the people and that of philosophers ?

---

[1] προσαγωγίῳ rec. t Hesychius Suidas : προσαγωγείῳ B : προαγωγίῳ T.

ΠΡΩ. Πῇ ποτὲ διορισάμενος οὖν ἄλλην, τὴν δὲ ἄλλην θείη τις ἂν ἀριθμητικήν;

ΣΩ. Οὐ σμικρὸς ὅρος, ὦ Πρώταρχε. οἱ μὲν γάρ που μονάδας ἀνίσους καταριθμοῦνται τῶν περὶ Ε ἀριθμόν, οἷον στρατόπεδα δύο καὶ βοῦς δύο καὶ δύο τὰ σμικρότατα ἢ καὶ τὰ πάντων μέγιστα· οἱ δ' οὐκ ἄν ποτε αὐτοῖς συνακολουθήσειαν, εἰ μὴ μονάδα μονάδος ἑκάστης τῶν μυρίων μηδεμίαν ἄλλην ἄλλης διαφέρουσάν τις θήσει.

ΠΡΩ. Καὶ μάλα εὖ λέγεις οὐ σμικρὰν διαφορὰν τῶν περὶ ἀριθμὸν τευταζόντων, ὥστε λόγον ἔχειν δύο αὐτὰς εἶναι.

ΣΩ. Τί δέ; λογιστικὴ καὶ μετρητικὴ ἡ[1] κατὰ τεκτονικὴν καὶ κατ' ἐμπορικὴν τῆς κατὰ φιλο-
57 σοφίαν γεωμετρίας τε καὶ λογισμῶν καταμελετω-μένων—πότερον ὡς μία ἑκατέρα λεκτέον ἢ δύο τιθῶμεν;

ΠΡΩ. Τῇ πρόσθεν ἑπόμενος ἔγωγ' ἂν δύο κατὰ τὴν ἐμὴν ψῆφον τιθείην ἑκατέραν τούτων.

ΣΩ. Ὀρθῶς. οὗ δ' ἕνεκα ταῦτα προηνεγκάμεθα εἰς τὸ μέσον, ἆρα ἐννοεῖς;

ΠΡΩ. Ἴσως, ἀλλὰ σὲ βουλοίμην ἂν ἀποφήνασθαι τὸ νῦν ἐρωτώμενον.

ΣΩ. Δοκεῖ τοίνυν ἔμοιγε οὗτος ὁ λόγος, οὐχ ἧττον ἢ ὅτε λέγειν αὐτὸν ἠρχόμεθα, ταῖς ἡδοναῖς Β ζητῶν ἀντίστροφον ἐνταῦθα προβεβληκέναι, σκο-πῶν ἆρά ἐστί τις ἑτέρας ἄλλη καθαρωτέρα ἐπιστή-μης ἐπιστήμη, καθάπερ ἡδονῆς ἡδονή.

ΠΡΩ. Καὶ μάλα σαφὲς τοῦτό γε, ὅτι ταῦθ' ἕνεκα τούτων ἐπικεχείρηκεν.

35. ΣΩ. Τί οὖν; ἆρ' οὐκ ἐν μὲν τοῖς ἔμπρο-

―――――
[1] ἡ add. corr. Ven. 189: om. BT.

PRO. How can one kind of arithmetic be distinguished from the other?

SOC. The distinction is no small one, Protarchus. For some arithmeticians reckon unequal units, for instance, two armies and two oxen and two very small or incomparably large units; whereas others refuse to agree with them unless each of countless units is declared to differ not at all from each and every other unit.

PRO. You are certainly quite right in saying that there is a great difference between the devotees of arithmetic, so it is reasonable to assume that it is of two kinds.

SOC. And how about the arts of reckoning and measuring as they are used in building and in trade when compared with philosophical geometry and elaborate computations—shall we speak of each of these as one or as two?

PRO. On the analogy of the previous example, I should say that each of them was two.

SOC. Right. But do you understand why I introduced this subject?

PRO. Perhaps; but I wish you would give the answer to your question.

SOC. This discussion of ours is now, I think, no less than when we began it, seeking a counterpart of pleasure, and therefore it has introduced the present subject and is considering whether there is one kind of knowledge purer than another, as one pleasure is purer than another.

PRO. That is very clear; it was evidently introduced with that object.

SOC. Well, had not the discussion already found

σθεν ἐπ᾽ ἄλλοις ἄλλην τέχνην οὖσαν ἀνηυρήκειν[1]
σαφεστέραν καὶ ἀσαφεστέραν ἄλλην ἄλλης;

ΠΡΩ. Πάνυ μὲν οὖν.

ΣΩ. Ἐν τούτοις δὲ ἆρ᾽ οὔ τινα τέχνην ὡς ὁμώ-
νυμον φθεγξάμενος, εἰς δόξαν καταστήσας ὡς μιᾶς,
C πάλιν ὡς δυοῖν ἐπανερωτᾷ τούτοιν αὐτοῖν τὸ σαφὲς
καὶ τὸ καθαρὸν περὶ ταῦτα πότερον ἢ τῶν φιλοσοφούντων ἢ μὴ φιλοσοφούντων ἀκριβέστερον ἔχει;

ΠΡΩ. Καὶ μάλα δοκεῖ μοι τοῦτο διερωτᾶν.

ΣΩ. Τίν᾽ οὖν, ὦ Πρώταρχε, αὐτῷ δίδομεν ἀπόκρισιν;

ΠΡΩ. Ὦ Σώκρατες, εἰς θαυμαστὸν διαφορᾶς
μέγεθος εἰς σαφήνειαν προεληλύθαμεν ἐπιστημῶν.

ΣΩ. Οὐκοῦν ἀποκρινούμεθα ῥᾷον;

ΠΡΩ. Τί μήν; καὶ εἰρήσθω γε ὅτι πολὺ μὲν
αὗται τῶν ἄλλων τεχνῶν διαφέρουσι, τούτων δ᾽
D αὐτῶν αἱ περὶ τὴν τῶν ὄντως φιλοσοφούντων
ὁρμὴν ἀμήχανον ἀκριβείᾳ τε καὶ ἀληθείᾳ περὶ μέτρα
τε καὶ ἀριθμοὺς διαφέρουσιν.

ΣΩ. Ἔστω ταῦτα κατὰ σέ, καὶ σοὶ δὴ πιστεύοντες
θαρροῦντες ἀποκρινόμεθα τοῖς δεινοῖς περὶ λόγων
ὁλκήν—

ΠΡΩ. Τὸ ποῖον;

ΣΩ. Ὡς εἰσὶ δύο ἀριθμητικαὶ καὶ δύο μετρητικαὶ
καὶ ταύταις[2] ἄλλαι τοιαῦται συνεπόμεναι συχναί, τὴν
διδυμότητα ἔχουσαι ταύτην, ὀνόματος δὲ ἑνὸς κεκοι-
νωμέναι.

E ΠΡΩ. Διδῶμεν τύχῃ ἀγαθῇ τούτοις οὓς φῂς δεινοὺς εἶναι ταύτην τὴν ἀπόκρισιν, ὦ Σώκρατες.

---

[1] ἀνηυρήκειν Burnet (ἀνηυρήκει corr. Ven. 189): ἀνευρίσκειν
BT.
[2] καὶ δύο μετρητικαὶ ταύταις B : καὶ ταύταις T.

in what preceded that the various arts had various purposes and various degrees of exactness ?

PRO. Certainly.

SOC. And after having given an art a single name in what has preceded, thereby making us think that it was a single art, does not the discussion now assume that the same art is two and ask whether the art of the philosophers or that of the non-philosophers possesses the higher degree of clearness and purity ?

PRO. Yes, I think that is just the question it asks.

SOC. Then what reply shall we make, Protarchus ?

PRO. Socrates, we have found a marvellously great difference in the clearness of different kinds of knowledge.

SOC. That will make the reply easier, will it not ?

PRO. Yes, to be sure ; and let our reply be this, that the arithmetical and metrical arts far surpass the others and that of these the arts which are stirred by the impulse of the true philosophers are immeasurably superior in accuracy and truth about measures and numbers.

SOC. We accept that as our judgement, and relying upon you we make this confident reply to those who are clever in straining arguments——

PRO. What reply ?

SOC. That there are two arts of arithmetic and two of measuring, and many other arts which, like these, are twofold in this way, but possess a single name in common.

PRO. Let us give this answer, Socrates, to those who you say are clever ; I hope we shall have luck with it.

PLATO

ΣΩ. Ταύτας οὖν λέγομεν ἐπιστήμας ἀκριβεῖς μάλιστα εἶναι;

ΠΡΩ. Πάνυ μὲν οὖν.

ΣΩ. Ἀλλ' ἡμᾶς, ὦ Πρώταρχε, ἀναίνοιτ' ἂν ἡ τοῦ διαλέγεσθαι δύναμις, εἴ τινα πρὸ αὐτῆς ἄλλην κρίναιμεν.

58 ΠΡΩ. Τίνα δὲ ταύτην αὖ δεῖ λέγειν;

ΣΩ. Δῆλον ὅτι ἡ[1] πᾶς ἂν[2] τήν γε νῦν λεγομένην γνοίη. τὴν γὰρ περὶ τὸ ὄν καὶ τὸ ὄντως καὶ τὸ κατὰ ταὐτὸν ἀεὶ πεφυκὸς πάντως ἔγωγε οἶμαι ἡγεῖσθαι ξύμπαντας ὅσοις νοῦ καὶ σμικρὸν προσήρτηται μακρῷ ἀληθεστάτην εἶναι γνῶσιν· σὺ δὲ τί; πῶς τοῦτο, ὦ Πρώταρχε, διακρίνοις ἄν;

ΠΡΩ. Ἤκουον μὲν ἔγωγε, ὦ Σώκρατες, ἑκάστοτε Γοργίου πολλάκις ὡς ἡ τοῦ πείθειν πολὺ διαφέροι πασῶν τεχνῶν· πάντα γὰρ ὑφ' αὑτῇ
B δοῦλα δι' ἑκόντων ἀλλ' οὐ διὰ βίας ποιοῖτο, καὶ μακρῷ ἀρίστη πασῶν εἴη τῶν τεχνῶν· νῦν δ' οὔτε σοὶ οὔτε δὴ ἐκείνῳ βουλοίμην ἂν ἐναντία τίθεσθαι.

ΣΩ. Τὰ ὅπλα μοι δοκεῖς βουληθεὶς εἰπεῖν αἰσχυνθεὶς ἀπολιπεῖν.

ΠΡΩ. Ἔστω νῦν ταῦτα ταύτῃ ὅπῃ σοι δοκεῖ.

ΣΩ. Ἆρ' οὖν αἴτιος ἐγὼ τοῦ μὴ καλῶς ὑπολαβεῖν σε;

ΠΡΩ. Τὸ ποῖον;

ΣΩ. Οὐκ, ὦ φίλε Πρώταρχε, τοῦτο ἔγωγε ἐζήτουν πω, τίς τέχνη ἢ τίς ἐπιστήμη πασῶν διαφέρει
C τῷ μεγίστη καὶ ἀρίστη καὶ πλεῖστα ὠφελοῦσα ἡμᾶς, ἀλλὰ τίς ποτε τὸ σαφὲς καὶ τἀκριβὲς καὶ τὸ ἀληθέστατον ἐπισκοπεῖ, κἂν εἰ σμικρὰ καὶ σμικρὰ ὀνινᾶσα,[3] τοῦτ' ἔστιν ὃ νῦν δὴ ζητοῦμεν. ἀλλ' ὅρα· οὐδὲ

soc. These, then, we say, are the most exact arts or sciences ?

pro. Certainly.

soc. But the art of dialectic would spurn us, Protarchus, if we should judge that any other art is preferable to her.

pro. But what is the art to which this name belongs ?

soc. Clearly anybody can recognize the art I mean ; for I am confident that all men who have any intellect whatsoever believe that the knowledge which has to do with being, reality, and eternal immutability is the truest kind of knowledge. What do you think, Protarchus ?

pro. I have often heard Gorgias constantly maintain that the art of persuasion surpasses all others ; for this, he said, makes all things subject to itself, not by force, but by their free will, and is by far the best of all arts ; so now I hardly like to oppose either him or you.

soc. It seems to me that you wanted to speak and threw down your arms out of modesty.

pro. Very well ; have it as you like.

soc. Is it my fault that you have misunderstood ?

pro. Misunderstood what ?

soc. My question, dear Protarchus, was not as yet what art or science surpasses all others by being the greatest and best and most useful to us : what I am trying to find out at present is which art, however little and of little use, has the greatest regard for clearness, exactness, and truth. See ; you will not

---

¹ ὅτιὴ Thompson: ὅτιη B: ὅτι ἢ T.
² πᾶς ἂν Madvig: πᾶσαν BT.
³ ὀνινᾶσα Bekker: ὀνήνασα B: ὀνίνασα T.

γὰρ ἀπεχθήσει Γοργίᾳ, τῇ μὲν ἐκείνου ὑπάρχειν
τέχνῃ διδοὺς πρὸς χρείαν τοῖς ἀνθρώποις κρατεῖν,
ᾗ δ' εἶπον ἐγὼ νῦν πραγματείᾳ, καθάπερ τοῦ λευκοῦ
πέρι τότε ἔλεγον, κἂν εἰ σμικρόν, καθαρὸν δ' εἴη, τοῦ
D πολλοῦ καὶ μὴ τοιούτου διαφέρειν τούτῳ γ' αὐτῷ
τῷ ἀληθεστάτῳ, καὶ νῦν δὴ σφόδρα διανοηθέντες
καὶ ἱκανῶς διαλογισάμενοι, μήτ' εἴς τινας ὠφελείας
ἐπιστημῶν βλέψαντες μήτε τινὰς εὐδοκιμίας, ἀλλ'
εἴ τις πέφυκε τῆς ψυχῆς ἡμῶν δύναμις ἐρᾶν τε τοῦ
ἀληθοῦς καὶ πάντα ἕνεκα τούτου πράττειν, ταύτην
εἴπωμεν διεξερευνησάμενοι, τὸ καθαρὸν νοῦ τε καὶ
φρονήσεως, εἰ ταύτην μάλιστα ἐκ τῶν εἰκότων
ἐκτῆσθαι φαῖμεν ἂν ἤ τινα ἑτέραν ταύτης κυριω-
E τέραν ἡμῖν ζητητέον.

ΠΡΩ. Ἀλλὰ σκοπῶ, καὶ χαλεπόν, οἶμαι, συγχω-
ρῆσαί τινα ἄλλην ἐπιστήμην ἢ τέχνην τῆς ἀληθείας
ἀντέχεσθαι μᾶλλον ἢ ταύτην.

ΣΩ. Ἆρ' οὖν ἐννοήσας τὸ τοιόνδε εἴρηκας ὃ
λέγεις νῦν, ὡς αἱ πολλαὶ τέχναι, καὶ ὅσοι[1] περὶ
59 ταῦτα πεπόνηνται, πρῶτον μὲν δόξαις χρῶνται καὶ
τὰ περὶ δόξας ζητοῦσι συντεταμένως[2]; εἴ τε καὶ περὶ
φύσεως ἡγεῖταί τις ζητεῖν, οἶσθ' ὅτι τὰ περὶ τὸν
κόσμον τόνδε, ὅπῃ τε γέγονεν καὶ ὅπῃ πάσχει τι
καὶ ὅπῃ ποιεῖ, ταῦτα ζητεῖ διὰ βίου; φαῖμεν ἂν
ταῦτα, ἢ πῶς;

ΠΡΩ. Οὕτως.

ΣΩ. Οὐκοῦν οὐ περὶ τὰ ὄντα ἀεί, περὶ δὲ τὰ
γιγνόμενα καὶ γενησόμενα καὶ γεγονότα ἡμῶν ὁ
τοιοῦτος ἀνῄρηται τὸν πόνον;

---

[1] ὅσοι Ast: ὅσαι BT.
[2] συντεταμένως corr. Ven. 189: συντεταγμένως B: ξυντεταγ-
μένως T.

make Gorgias angry if you grant that his art is superior for the practical needs of men, but say that the study of which I spoke is superior in the matter of the most perfect truth, just as I said in speaking about the white that if it was small and pure it was superior to that which was great but impure. Now, therefore, with careful thought and due consideration, paying attention neither to the usefulness nor to the reputation of any arts or sciences, but to that faculty of our souls, if such there be, which by its nature loves the truth and does all things for the sake of the truth, let us examine this faculty and say whether it is most likely to possess mind and intelligence in the greatest purity, or we must look for some other faculty which has more valid claims.

PRO. I am considering, and I think it is difficult to concede that any other science or art cleaves more closely to truth than this.

SOC. In saying that, did you bear in mind that the arts in general, and the men who devote themselves to them, make use of opinion and persistently investigate things which have to do with opinion? And even if they think they are studying nature, they are spending their lives in the study of the things of this world, the manner of their production, their action, and the forces to which they are subjected. Is not that true?

PRO. Yes, it is.

SOC. Such thinkers, then, toil to discover, not eternal verities, but transient productions of the present, the future, or the past?

369

ΠΡΩ. Ἀληθέστατα.

ΣΩ. Τούτων οὖν τι σαφὲς ἂν φαῖμεν τῇ ἀκριβε-
B στάτῃ ἀληθείᾳ γίγνεσθαι, ὧν μήτε ἔσχε μηδὲν
πώποτε κατὰ ταὐτὰ μήθ᾽ ἕξει μήτε εἰς τὸ νῦν παρὸν
ἔχει;

ΠΡΩ. Καὶ πῶς;

ΣΩ. Περὶ οὖν τὰ μὴ κεκτημένα βεβαιότητα μηδ᾽
ἡντινοῦν πῶς ἄν ποτε βέβαιον γίγνοιθ᾽ ἡμῖν καὶ
ὁτιοῦν;

ΠΡΩ. Οἶμαι μὲν οὐδαμῶς.

ΣΩ. Οὐδ᾽ ἄρα νοῦς οὐδέ τις ἐπιστήμη περὶ αὐτά
ἐστι τὸ ἀληθέστατον ἔχουσα.

ΠΡΩ. Οὔκουν εἰκός γε.

36. ΣΩ. Τὸν μὲν δὴ σὲ καὶ ἐμὲ καὶ Γοργίαν
καὶ Φίληβον χρὴ συχνὰ χαίρειν ἐᾶν, τόδε δὲ δια-
C μαρτύρασθαι τῷ λόγῳ.

ΠΡΩ. Τὸ ποῖον;

ΣΩ. Ὡς ἢ¹ περὶ ἐκεῖνα ἔσθ᾽ ἡμῖν τό τε βέβαιον
καὶ τὸ καθαρὸν καὶ τὸ ἀληθὲς καὶ ὃ δὴ λέγομεν
εἰλικρινές, περὶ τὰ ἀεὶ κατὰ τὰ αὐτὰ ὡσαύτως
ἀμικτότατα ἔχοντα, ἢ² ἐκείνων ὅτι μάλιστά
ἐστι ξυγγενές· τὰ δ᾽ ἄλλα πάντα δεύτερά τε καὶ
ὕστερα λεκτέον.

ΠΡΩ. Ἀληθέστατα λέγεις.

ΣΩ. Τὰ δὴ τῶν ὀνομάτων περὶ τὰ τοιαῦτα κάλλιστα ἆρ᾽ οὐ τοῖς καλλίστοις δικαιότατον ἀπονέμειν;

ΠΡΩ. Εἰκός γε.

D ΣΩ. Οὐκοῦν νοῦς ἐστι καὶ φρόνησις, ἅ γ᾽ ἄν τις
τιμήσειε μάλιστα ὀνόματα;

¹ ἢ Stephanus : ἡ BT.
² ἢ δεύτερος BT (δευτέρως corr. Ven. 189) : δεύτερος bracketed
by Hermann.

PRO. Perfectly true.

SOC. And can we say that any of these things becomes certain, if tested by the touchstone of strictest truth, since none of them ever was, will be, or is in the same state?

PRO. Of course not.

SOC. How can we gain anything fixed whatsoever about things which have no fixedness whatsoever?

PRO. In no way, as it seems to me.

SOC. Then no mind or science which is occupied with them possesses the most perfect truth.

PRO. No, it naturally does not.

SOC. Then we must dismiss the thought of you and me and Gorgias and Philebus, and make this solemn declaration on the part of our argument.

PRO. What is the solemn declaration?

SOC. That fixed and pure and true and what we call unalloyed knowledge has to do with the things which are eternally the same without change or mixture, or with that which is most akin to them; and all other things are to be regarded as secondary and inferior.

PRO. Very true.

SOC. And of the names applied to such matters, it would be fairest to give the finest names to the finest things, would it not?

PRO. That is reasonable.

SOC. Are not mind, then, and wisdom the names which we should honour most?

ΠΡΩ. Ναί.

ΣΩ. Ταῦτ᾽ ἄρα ἐν ταῖς περὶ τὸ ὂν ὄντως ἐννοίαις ἔστιν ἀπηκριβωμένα ὀρθῶς κείμενα καλεῖσθαι.

ΠΡΩ. Πάνυ μὲν οὖν.

ΣΩ. Καὶ μὴν ἅ γε εἰς τὴν κρίσιν ἐγὼ τότε παρεσχόμην, οὐκ ἄλλ᾽ ἐστὶν ἢ ταῦτα τὰ ὀνόματα.

ΠΡΩ. Τί μήν, ὦ Σώκρατες;

ΣΩ. Εἶεν· τὸ μὲν δὴ φρονήσεώς τε καὶ ἡδονῆς E πέρι πρὸς τὴν ἀλλήλων μῖξιν εἴ τις φαίη καθαπερεὶ δημιουργοῖς ἡμῖν ἐξ ὧν ἢ ἐν οἷς δεῖ δημιουργεῖν τι, παρακεῖσθαι, καλῶς ἂν τῷ λόγῳ ἀπεικάζοι.

ΠΡΩ. Καὶ μάλα.

ΣΩ. Τὸ δὴ μετὰ ταῦτα ἆρ᾽ οὐ μιγνύναι ἐπιχειρητέον;

ΠΡΩ. Τί μήν;

ΣΩ. Οὐκοῦν τάδε προειποῦσι καὶ ἀναμνήσασιν ἡμᾶς αὐτοὺς ὀρθότερον ἂν ἔχοι;

ΠΡΩ. Τὰ ποῖα;

ΣΩ. Ἃ καὶ πρότερον ἐμνήσθημεν· εὖ δ᾽ ἡ παροιμία δοκεῖ ἔχειν, τὸ καὶ δὶς καὶ τρὶς τό γε καλῶς 60 ἔχον ἐπαναπολεῖν τῷ λόγῳ δεῖν.

ΠΡΩ. Τί μήν;

ΣΩ. Φέρε δὴ πρὸς Διός· οἶμαι γὰρ οὑτωσί πως τὰ τότε λεχθέντα ῥηθῆναι.

ΠΡΩ. Πῶς;

ΣΩ. Φίληβός φησι τὴν ἡδονὴν σκοπὸν ὀρθὸν πᾶσι ζῴοις γεγονέναι καὶ δεῖν πάντας τούτου στοχάζεσθαι, καὶ δὴ καὶ τἀγαθὸν τοῦτ᾽ αὐτὸ εἶναι ξύμπασι, καὶ δύο ὀνόματα, ἀγαθὸν καὶ ἡδύ, ἑνί τινι καὶ φύσει μιᾷ τούτω ὀρθῶς τεθέντ᾽[1] ἔχειν· Σωκρά-

---

[1] τούτω ὀρθῶς τεθέντ᾽ Heindorf: τοῦτο ὀρθῶς τιθέν ΒΤ.

PRO. Yes.

SOC. Then these names are applied most accurately and correctly to cases of contemplation of true being.

PRO. Certainly.

SOC. And these are precisely the names which I brought forward in the first place as parties to our suit.

PRO. Yes, of course they are, Socrates.

SOC. Very well. As to the mixture of wisdom and pleasure, if anyone were to say that we are like artisans, with the materials before us from which to create our work, the simile would be a good one.

PRO. Certainly.

SOC. And is it, then, our next task to try to make the mixture?

PRO. Surely.

SOC. Would it not be better first to repeat certain things and recall them to our minds?

PRO. What things?

SOC. Those which we mentioned before. I think the proverb " we ought to repeat twice and even three times that which is good " is an excellent one.

PRO. Surely.

SOC. Well then, in God's name; I think this is the gist of our discussion.

PRO. What is it?

SOC. Philebus says that pleasure is the true goal of every living being and that all ought to aim at it, and that therefore this is also the good for all, and the two designations " good " and " pleasant " are properly and essentially one; Socrates, however,

B της δ' ἕν[1] μὲν οὔ φησι τοῦτ' εἶναι, δύο δὲ καθάπερ
τὰ ὀνόματα, καὶ τό τε ἀγαθὸν καὶ τὸ ἡδὺ διάφορον
ἀλλήλων φύσιν ἔχειν, μᾶλλον δὲ μέτοχον εἶναι
τῆς τοῦ ἀγαθοῦ μοίρας τὴν φρόνησιν ἢ τὴν ἡδονήν.
οὐ ταῦτ' ἔστιν τε καὶ ἦν τὰ τότε λεγόμενα, ὦ
Πρώταρχε;

ΠΡΩ. Σφόδρα μὲν οὖν.

ΣΩ. Οὐκοῦν καὶ τόδε καὶ τότε καὶ νῦν ἡμῖν ἂν
ξυνομολογοῖτο;

ΠΡΩ. Τὸ ποῖον;

ΣΩ. Τὴν τἀγαθοῦ διαφέρειν φύσιν τῷδε τῶν
ἄλλων.

C ΠΡΩ. Τίνι;

ΣΩ. Ὧι παρείη τοῦτ' ἀεὶ τῶν ζῴων διὰ τέλους
πάντως καὶ πάντῃ, μηδενὸς ἑτέρου ποτὲ ἔτι προσδεῖσθαι, τὸ δὲ ἱκανὸν τελεώτατον ἔχειν. οὐχ
οὕτως;

ΠΡΩ. Οὕτω μὲν οὖν.

ΣΩ. Οὐκοῦν τῷ λόγῳ ἐπειράθημεν χωρὶς ἑκάτερον ἑκατέρου θέντες εἰς τὸν βίον ἑκάστων,
ἄμικτον μὲν ἡδονὴν φρονήσει, φρόνησιν δὲ ὡσαύτως
ἡδονῆς μηδὲ τὸ σμικρότατον ἔχουσαν;

ΠΡΩ. Ἦν ταῦτα.

D ΣΩ. Μῶν οὖν ἡμῖν αὐτῶν τότε πότερον ἱκανὸν
ἔδοξεν εἶναί τῳ;

ΠΡΩ. Καὶ πῶς;

37. ΣΩ. Εἰ δέ γε παρηνέχθημέν τι τότε, νῦν
ὁστισοῦν ἐπαναλαβὼν ὀρθότερον εἰπάτω, μνήμην
καὶ φρόνησιν καὶ ἐπιστήμην καὶ ἀληθῆ δόξαν τῆς
αὐτῆς ἰδέας τιθέμενος καὶ σκοπῶν εἴ τις ἄνευ
τούτων δέξαιτ' ἂν οἱ καὶ ὁτιοῦν εἶναι ἢ καὶ γίγνεσθαι,

[1] ἕν Badham: πρῶτον BT.

says that they are not one, but two in fact as in name, that the good and the pleasant differ from one another in nature, and that wisdom's share in the good is greater than pleasure's. Is not and was not that what was said, Protarchus?

PRO. Yes, certainly.

SOC. And furthermore, is not and was not this a point of agreement among us?

PRO. What?

SOC. That the nature of the good differs from all else in this respect.

PRO. In what respect?

SOC. That whatever living being possesses the good always, altogether, and in all ways, has no further need of anything, but is perfectly sufficient. We agreed to that?

PRO. We did.

SOC. And then we tried in thought to separate each from the other and apply them to individual lives, pleasure unmixed with wisdom and likewise wisdom which had not the slightest alloy of pleasure?

PRO. Yes.

SOC. And did we think then that either of them would be sufficient for any one?

PRO. By no means.

SOC. And if we made any mistake at that time, let any one now take up the question again. Assuming that memory, wisdom, knowledge, and true opinion belong to the same class, let him ask whether anyone would wish to have or acquire anything whatsoever without these not to speak of pleasure,

μὴ ὅτι δή γε ἡδονὴν εἴθ' ὡς πλείστην εἴθ' ὡς σφο-
δροτάτην, ἣν μήτε ἀληθῶς δοξάζοι χαίρειν μήτε τὸ
E παράπαν γιγνώσκοι τί ποτε πέπονθε πάθος μήτ'
αὖ μνήμην τοῦ πάθους μηδ' ὁντινοῦν χρόνον ἔχοι.
ταὐτὰ δὲ λεγέτω[1] καὶ περὶ φρονήσεως, εἴ τις ἄνευ
πάσης ἡδονῆς καὶ τῆς βραχυτάτης δέξαιτ' ἂν
φρόνησιν ἔχειν μᾶλλον ἢ μετά τινων ἡδονῶν ἢ
πάσας ἡδονὰς χωρὶς φρονήσεως μᾶλλον ἢ μετὰ
φρονήσεως αὖ τινός.

ΠΡΩ. Οὐκ ἔστιν, ὦ Σώκρατες, ἀλλ' οὐδὲν δεῖ
ταῦτά γε πολλάκις ἐπερωτᾶν.

61 ΣΩ. Οὐκοῦν τό γε τέλεον καὶ πᾶσιν αἱρετὸν
καὶ τὸ παντάπασιν ἀγαθὸν οὐδέτερον ἂν τούτων εἴη;

ΠΡΩ. Πῶς γὰρ ἄν;

ΣΩ. Τὸ τοίνυν ἀγαθὸν ἤτοι σαφῶς ἢ καί τινα
τύπον αὐτοῦ ληπτέον, ἵν', ὅπερ ἐλέγομεν, δευτερεῖα
ὅτῳ δώσομεν ἔχωμεν.

ΠΡΩ. Ὀρθότατα λέγεις.

ΣΩ. Οὐκοῦν ὁδὸν μέν τινα ἐπὶ τἀγαθὸν εἰλήφαμεν;

ΠΡΩ. Τίνα;

ΣΩ. Καθάπερ εἴ τίς τινα ἄνθρωπον ζητῶν τὴν
B οἴκησιν πρῶτον ὀρθῶς ἵν' οἰκεῖ πύθοιτο αὐτοῦ,
μέγα τι δή που πρὸς τὴν εὕρεσιν ἂν ἔχοι τοῦ ζητου-
μένου.

ΠΡΩ. Πῶς δ' οὔ;

ΣΩ. Καὶ νῦν δή τις λόγος ἐμήνυσεν ἡμῖν, ὥσπερ
καὶ κατ' ἀρχάς, μὴ ζητεῖν ἐν τῷ ἀμίκτῳ βίῳ τἀγαθὸν
ἀλλ' ἐν τῷ μικτῷ.

ΠΡΩ. Πάνυ γε.

ΣΩ. Ἐλπὶς μὴν πλείων ἐν τῷ μιχθέντι καλῶς
τὸ ζητούμενον ἔσεσθαι φανερώτερον ἢ ἐν τῷ μή;

___
[1] λεγέτω Vahlen: λέγω B: λέγε T.

be it never so abundant or intense, if he could have no true opinion that he is pleased, no knowledge whatsoever of what he has felt, and not even the slightest memory of the feeling. And let him ask in the same way about wisdom, whether anyone would wish to have wisdom without any, even the slightest, pleasure rather than with some pleasures, or all pleasures without wisdom rather than with some wisdom.

PRO. That is impossible, Socrates; it is useless to ask the same question over and over again.

SOC. Then the perfect, that which is to be desired by all and is altogether good, is neither of these?

PRO. Certainly not.

SOC. We must, then, gain a clear conception of the good, or at least an outline of it, that we may, as we said, know to what the second place is to be assigned.

PRO. Quite right.

SOC. And have we not found a road which leads to the good?

PRO. What road?

SOC. If you were looking for a particular man and first found out correctly where he lived, you would have made great progress towards finding him whom you sought.

PRO. Yes, certainly.

SOC. And just now we received an indication, as we did in the beginning, that we must seek the good, not in the unmixed, but in the mixed life.

PRO. Certainly.

SOC. Surely there is greater hope that the object of our search will be clearly present in the well mixed life than in the life which is not well mixed?

ΠΡΩ. Πολύ γε.

ΣΩ. Τοῖς δὴ θεοῖς, ὦ Πρώταρχε, εὐχόμενοι
C κεραννύωμεν, εἴτε Διόνυσος εἴτε Ἥφαιστος εἴθ᾽
ὅστις θεῶν ταύτην τὴν τιμὴν εἴληχε τῆς συγκράσεως.

ΠΡΩ. Πάνυ μὲν οὖν.

ΣΩ. Καὶ μὴν καθάπερ ἡμῖν οἰνοχόοις τισὶ παρ-
εστᾶσι κρῆναι· μέλιτος μὲν ἂν ἀπεικάζοι τις τὴν
τῆς ἡδονῆς, τὴν δὲ τῆς φρονήσεως νηφαντικὴν
καὶ ἄοινον αὐστηροῦ καὶ ὑγιεινοῦ τινος ὕδατος, ἃς
προθυμητέον ὡς κάλλιστα συμμιγνύναι.

ΠΡΩ. Πῶς γὰρ οὔ;

D ΣΩ. Φέρε δὴ πρότερον· ἆρα πᾶσαν ἡδονὴν
πάσῃ φρονήσει μιγνύντες τοῦ καλῶς ἂν μάλιστα ἐπι-
τύχοιμεν;

ΠΡΩ. Ἴσως.

ΣΩ. Ἀλλ᾽ οὐκ ἀσφαλές. ᾗ δὲ ἀκινδυνότερον ἂν
μιγνύοιμεν, δόξαν μοι δοκῶ τινὰ ἀποφήνασθαι ἄν.

ΠΡΩ. Λέγε τίνα.

ΣΩ. Ἦν ἡμῖν ἡδονή τε ἀληθῶς, ὡς οἰόμεθα,
μᾶλλον ἑτέρας ἄλλη καὶ δὴ καὶ τέχνη τέχνης ἀκρι-
βεστέρα;

ΠΡΩ. Πῶς γὰρ οὔ;

ΣΩ. Καὶ ἐπιστήμη δὴ ἐπιστήμης διάφορος, ἡ
μὲν ἐπὶ τὰ γιγνόμενα καὶ ἀπολλύμενα ἀποβλέπουσα,
E ἡ δὲ ἐπὶ τὰ μήτε γιγνόμενα μήτε ἀπολλύμενα,
κατὰ ταὐτὰ δὲ καὶ ὡσαύτως ὄντα ἀεί. ταύτην
εἰς τὸ ἀληθὲς ἐπισκοπούμενοι ἡγησάμεθα ἐκείνης
ἀληθεστέραν εἶναι.

ΠΡΩ. Πάνυ μὲν οὖν ὀρθῶς.

ΣΩ. Οὐκοῦν εἰ τἀληθέστατα τμήματα ἑκατέρας
ἴδοιμεν πρῶτον συμμίξαντες, ἆρα ἱκανὰ ταῦτα
συγκεκραμένα τὸν ἀγαπητότατον βίον ἀπεργα-

PRO. Far greater.

SOC. Let us make the mixture, Protarchus, with a prayer to the gods, to Dionysus or Hephaestus, or whoever he be who presides over the mixing.

PRO. By all means.

SOC. We are like wine-pourers, and beside us are fountains—that of pleasure may be likened to a fount of honey, and the sober, wineless fount of wisdom to one of pure, health-giving water—of which we must do our best to mix as well as possible.

PRO. Certainly we must.

SOC. Before we make the mixture, tell me : should we be most likely to succeed by mixing all pleasure with all wisdom ?

PRO. Perhaps.

SOC. But that is not safe ; and I think I can offer a plan by which we can make our mixture with less risk.

PRO. What is it ?

SOC. We found, I believe, that one pleasure was greater than another and one art more exact than another ?

PRO. Certainly.

SOC. And knowledge was of two kinds, one turning its eyes towards transitory things, the other towards things which neither come into being nor pass away, but are the same and immutable for ever. Considering them with a view to truth, we judged that the latter was truer than the former.

PRO. That is quite right.

SOC. Then what if we first mix the truest sections of each and see whether, when mixed together, they are capable of giving us the most adorable life,

σάμενα παρέχειν ἡμῖν, ἤ τινος ἔτι προσδεόμεθα καὶ
τῶν μὴ τοιούτων;

62   ΠΡΩ. Ἐμοὶ γοῦν δοκε δρᾶν οὕτως.

38. ΣΩ. Ἔστω δή τις ἡμῖν φρονῶν ἄνθρωπος
αὐτῆς περὶ δικαιοσύνης, ὅ τι ἔστιν, καὶ λόγον ἔχων
ἑπόμενον τῷ νοεῖν, καὶ δὴ καὶ περὶ τῶν ἄλλων
ἁπάντων τῶν ὄντων ὡσαύτως διανοούμενος.

ΠΡΩ. Ἔστω γὰρ οὖν.

ΣΩ. Ἆρ᾽ οὖν οὗτος ἱκανῶς ἐπιστήμης ἕξει,
κύκλου μὲν καὶ σφαίρας αὐτῆς τῆς θείας τὸν λόγον
ἔχων, τὴν δὲ ἀνθρωπίνην ταύτην σφαῖραν καὶ τοὺς
κύκλους τούτους ἀγνοῶν, καὶ χρώμενος ἐν οἰκοδομίᾳ
B καὶ τοῖς ἄλλοις ὁμοίως κανόσι καὶ τοῖς κύκλοις;

ΠΡΩ. Γελοίαν διάθεσιν ἡμῶν, ὦ Σώκρατες, ἐν
ταῖς θείαις οὖσαν μόνον ἐπιστήμαις λέγομεν.

ΣΩ. Πῶς φής; ἢ τοῦ ψευδοῦς κανόνος ἅμα καὶ
τοῦ κύκλου τὴν οὐ βέβαιον οὐδὲ καθαρὰν τέχνην
ἐμβλητέον κοινῇ καὶ συγκρατέον;

ΠΡΩ. Ἀναγκαῖον γάρ, εἰ μέλλει τις ἡμῶν καὶ
τὴν ὁδὸν ἑκάστοτε ἐξευρήσειν οἴκαδε.

ΣΩ. Ἦ καὶ μουσικήν, ἣν ὀλίγον ἔμπροσθεν
C ἔφαμεν στοχάσεώς τε καὶ μιμήσεως μεστὴν οὖσαν
καθαρότητος ἐνδεῖν;

ΠΡΩ. Ἀναγκαῖον φαίνεται ἔμοιγε, εἴπερ γε ἡμῶν
ὁ βίος ἔσται καὶ ὁπωσοῦν ποτὲ βίος.

ΣΩ. Βούλει δῆτα, ὥσπερ θυρωρὸς ὑπ᾽ ὄχλου
τις ὠθούμενος καὶ βιαζόμενος, ἡττηθεὶς ἀναπετάσας
τὰς θύρας ἀφῶ πάσας τὰς ἐπιστήμας εἰσρεῖν καὶ
μίγνυσθαι ὁμοῦ καθαρᾷ τὴν ἐνδεεστέραν;

D   ΠΡΩ. Οὔκουν ἔγωγε οἶδα, ὦ Σώκρατες, ὅ τι τις
ἂν βλάπτοιτο πάσας λαβὼν τὰς ἄλλας ἐπιστήμας,
ἔχων τὰς πρώτας.

or whether we still need something more and different?

PRO. I think that is what we should do.

SOC. Let us assume, then, a man who possesses wisdom about the nature of justice itself, and reason in accordance with his wisdom, and has the same kind of knowledge of all other things.

PRO. Agreed.

SOC. Now will this man have sufficient knowledge, if he is master of the theory of the divine circle and sphere, but is ignorant of our human sphere and human circles, even when he uses these and other kinds of rules or patterns in building houses?

PRO. We call that a ridiculous state of intellect in a man, Socrates, which is concerned only with divine knowledge.

SOC. What? Do you mean to say that the uncertain and impure art of the false rule and circle is to be put into our mixture?

PRO. Yes, that is inevitable, if any man is ever to find his own way home.

SOC. And must we add music, which we said a little while ago was full of guesswork and imitation and lacked purity?

PRO. Yes, I think we must, if our life is to be life at all.

SOC. Shall I, then, like a doorkeeper who is pushed and hustled by a mob, give up, open the door, and let all the kinds of knowledge stream in, the impure mingling with the pure?

PRO. I do not know, Socrates, what harm it can do a man to take in all the other kinds of knowledge if he has the first.

ΣΩ. Μεθιῶ δὴ τὰς ξυμπάσας ῥεῖν εἰς τὴν τῆς
Ὁμήρου καὶ μάλα ποιητικῆς μισγαγκείας ὑποδοχήν;

ΠΡΩ. Πάνυ μὲν οὖν.

39. ΣΩ. Μεθεῖνται· καὶ πάλιν ἐπὶ τὴν τῶν
ἡδονῶν πηγὴν ἰτέον. ὡς γὰρ διενοήθημεν αὐτὰς
μιγνῦναι, τὰ τῶν ἀληθῶν μόρια πρῶτον, οὐκ
ἐξεγένεθ᾽[1] ἡμῖν, ἀλλὰ διὰ τὸ πᾶσαν ἀγαπᾶν ἐπιστή-
Ε μην εἰς ταὐτὸν μεθεῖμεν ἀθρόας καὶ πρόσθεν τῶν
ἡδονῶν.

ΠΡΩ. Ἀληθέστατα λέγεις.

ΣΩ. Ὥρα δὴ βουλεύεσθαι νῶν καὶ περὶ τῶν
ἡδονῶν, πότερα καὶ ταύτας πάσας ἀθρόας ἀφετέον
ἢ καὶ τούτων πρώτας μεθετέον ἡμῖν ὅσαι ἀληθεῖς.

ΠΡΩ. Πολύ τι διαφέρει πρός γε ἀσφάλειαν πρώτας τὰς ἀληθεῖς ἀφεῖναι.

ΣΩ. Μεθείσθων δή. τί δὲ μετὰ ταῦτα; ἆρ᾽ οὐκ
εἰ μέν τινες ἀναγκαῖαι, καθάπερ ἐκεῖ, ξυμμικτέον
καὶ ταύτας;

ΠΡΩ. Τί δ᾽ οὔ; τάς γε ἀναγκαίας δήπουθεν.

63 ΣΩ. Εἰ δέ γε καί, καθάπερ τὰς τέχνας πάσας
ἀβλαβές τε καὶ ὠφέλιμον ἦν ἐπίστασθαι διὰ βίου,
καὶ νῦν δὴ ταῦτα λέγομεν[2] περὶ τῶν ἡδονῶν, εἴπερ
πάσας ἡδονὰς ἥδεσθαι διὰ βίου συμφέρον τε ἡμῖν
ἐστι καὶ ἀβλαβὲς ἅπασι, πάσας συγκρατέον.

ΠΡΩ. Πῶς οὖν δὴ περὶ αὐτῶν τούτων λέγωμεν[3];
καὶ πῶς ποιῶμεν;

ΣΩ. Οὐχ ἡμᾶς, ὦ Πρώταρχε, διερωτᾶν χρή, τὰς
ἡδονὰς δὲ αὐτὰς καὶ τὰς φρονήσεις διαπυνθανομένους
Β τὸ τοιόνδε ἀλλήλων πέρι.

---

[1] ἐξεγένεθ᾽ Stallbaum: ἐξεγενήθη BT.
[2] λέγομεν corr. Ven. 189: λέγωμεν BT.
[3] λέγωμεν Ven. 189: λέγομεν BT.

soc. Shall I, then, let them all flow into what Homer [1] very poetically calls the mingling of the vales ?

pro. Certainly.

soc. They are let in ; and now we must turn again to the spring of pleasure. For our original plan for making the mixture, by taking first the true parts, did not succeed ; because of our love of knowledge, we let all kinds of knowledge in together before pleasure.

pro. Very true.

soc. So now it is time for us to consider about pleasures also, whether these, too, shall be all let loose together, or we shall let only the true ones loose at first.

pro. It is much safer to let loose the true first.

soc. We will let them loose, then. But what next ? If there are any necessary pleasures, as there were kinds of knowledge, must we not mix them with the true ?

pro. Of course ; the necessary pleasures must certainly be added.

soc. And as we said it was harmless and useful to know all the arts throughout our life, if we now say the same of pleasures—that is, if it is advantageous and harmless for us to enjoy all pleasures throughout life—they must all form part of the mixture.

pro. What shall we say about these pleasures, and what shall we do ?

soc. There is no use in asking us, Protarchus ; we must ask the pleasures and the arts and sciences themselves about one another.

[1] *Iliad* iv. 453.

ΠΡΩ. Τὸ ποῖον;

ΣΩ. "Ὦ φίλαι,[1] εἴτε ἡδονὰς ὑμᾶς[2] χρὴ προσαγορεύειν εἴτε ἄλλῳ ὁτῳοῦν ὀνόματι, μῶν οὐκ ἂν δέξαισθε[3] οἰκεῖν μετὰ φρονήσεως πάσης ἢ χωρὶς τοῦ φρονεῖν;" οἶμαι μὲν πρὸς ταῦτα τόδ' αὐτὰς ἀναγκαιότατον εἶναι λέγειν.

ΠΡΩ. Τὸ ποῖον;

ΣΩ. Ὅτι καθάπερ ἔμπροσθεν ἐρρήθη, "τὸ μόνον καὶ ἔρημον εἰλικρινὲς εἶναί τι γένος οὔτε πάνυ τι δυνατὸν οὔτ' ὠφέλιμον· πάντων γε μὴν ἡγούμεθα C γενῶν ἄριστον ἓν ἀνθ' ἑνὸς συνοικεῖν ἡμῖν τὸ τοῦ γιγνώσκειν τἆλλά τε πάντα καὶ αὐτὴν[4] ἡμῶν τελέως εἰς δύναμιν ἑκάστην."

ΠΡΩ. "Καὶ καλῶς γε εἰρήκατε τὰ νῦν," φήσομεν.

ΣΩ. Ὀρθῶς. πάλιν τοίνυν μετὰ τοῦτο τὴν φρόνησιν καὶ τὸν νοῦν ἀνερωτητέον· "ἆρ' ἡδονῶν τι προσδεῖσθε[5] ἐν τῇ συγκράσει;" φαῖμεν ἂν αὖ τὸν νοῦν τε καὶ τὴν φρόνησιν ἀνερωτῶντες. "ποίων," φαῖεν ἂν ἴσως, "ἡδονῶν;"

ΠΡΩ. Εἰκός.

D ΣΩ. Ὁ δέ γ' ἡμέτερος λόγος μετὰ τοῦτ' ἐστὶν ὅδε. "πρὸς ταῖς ἀληθέσιν ἐκείναις ἡδοναῖς," φήσομεν, "ἆρ' ἔτι προσδεῖσθ' ὑμῖν τὰς μεγίστας ἡδονὰς συνοίκους εἶναι καὶ τὰς σφοδροτάτας;" "καὶ πῶς, ὦ Σώκρατες," ἴσως φαῖεν ἄν, "αἵ γ' ἐμποδίσματά τε μυρία ἡμῖν ἔχουσι, τὰς ψυχὰς ἐν αἷς οἰκοῦμεν ταράττουσαι διὰ μανικὰς ἡδονάς, καὶ γίγνεσθαί τε ἡμᾶς τὴν ἀρχὴν οὐκ ἐῶσι, τά τε E γιγνόμενα ἡμῶν τέκνα ὡς τὸ πολύ, δι' ἀμέλειαν

---

[1] φίλαι corr. Ven. 189: φίλε BT.
[2] ὑμᾶς recc. t: ἡμᾶς BT.
[3] δέξαισθε corr. Vat.: δέξασθαι T: δέξεσθαι B.

PRO. What shall we ask them ?

SOC. " Dear ones—whether you should be called pleasures or by any other name—would you choose to dwell with all wisdom, or with none at all ? " I think only one reply is possible.

PRO. What is it ?

SOC. What we said before : " For any class to be alone, solitary, and unalloyed is neither altogether possible nor is it profitable ; but of all classes, comparing them one with another, we think the best to live with is the knowledge of all other things and, so far as is possible, the perfect knowledge of our individual selves."

PRO. " Your reply is excellent," we shall tell them.

SOC. Right. And next we must turn to wisdom and mind, and question them. We shall ask them, " Do you want any further pleasures in the mixture ? " And they might reply, " What pleasures ? "

PRO. Quite likely.

SOC. Then we should go on to say : " In addition to those true pleasures, do you want the greatest and most intense pleasures also to dwell with you ? " " How can we want them, Socrates," they might perhaps say, " since they contain countless hindrances for us, inasmuch as they disturb with maddening pleasures the souls of men in which we dwell, thereby preventing us from being born at all, and utterly destroying for the most part, through the carelessness and forgetfulness which they engender,

---

4 αὖ τὴν (τὴν B) before αὐτὴν bracketed by Wohlrab.
5 προσδεῖσθε] προσδεῖσθαι BT.

PLATO

λήθην ἐμποιοῦσαι, παντάπασι διαφθείρουσιν; ἀλλ'
ἃς¹ τε ἡδονὰς ἀληθεῖς καὶ καθαρὰς² εἶπες, σχεδὸν
οἰκείας ἡμῖν νόμιζε, καὶ πρὸς ταύταις τὰς μεθ'
ὑγιείας καὶ τοῦ σωφρονεῖν, καὶ δὴ καὶ ξυμπάσης
ἀρετῆς ὁπόσαι καθάπερ θεοῦ ὀπαδοὶ γιγνόμεναι
αὐτῇ συνακολουθοῦσι πάντη, ταύτας μίγνυ· τὰς³ δ'
ἀεὶ μετ' ἀφροσύνης καὶ τῆς ἄλλης κακίας ἑπομένας
πολλή που ἀλογία τῷ νῷ μιγνύναι τὸν βουλόμενον
ὅτι καλλίστην ἰδόντα καὶ ἀστασιαστοτάτην μῖξιν καὶ
κρᾶσιν, ἐν ταύτῃ μαθεῖν πειρᾶσθαι τί ποτε ἔν τε
64 ἀνθρώπῳ καὶ τῷ παντὶ πέφυκεν ἀγαθὸν καὶ τίνα
ἰδέαν αὐτὴν εἶναί ποτε μαντευτέον.'' ἆρ' οὐκ
ἐμφρόνως ταῦτα καὶ ἔχοντος ἑαυτὸν τὸν νοῦν φήσομεν ὑπέρ τε αὑτοῦ καὶ μνήμης καὶ δόξης ὀρθῆς
ἀποκρίνασθαι τὰ νῦν ῥηθέντα;

ΠΡΩ. Παντάπασι μὲν οὖν.

ΣΩ. Ἀλλὰ μὴν καὶ τόδε γε ἀναγκαῖον, καὶ οὐκ
ἄλλως ἄν ποτε γένοιτο οὐδ' ἂν ἕν.

B ΠΡΩ. Τὸ ποῖον;

ΣΩ. Ὧι μὴ μίξομεν ἀλήθειαν, οὐκ ἄν ποτε τοῦτο
ἀληθῶς γίγνοιτο οὐδ' ἂν γενόμενον εἴη.

ΠΡΩ. Πῶς γὰρ ἄν;

40. ΣΩ. Οὐδαμῶς. ἀλλ' εἴ τινος ἔτι προσδεῖ
τῇ συγκράσει ταύτῃ, λέγετε σύ τε καὶ Φίληβος.
ἐμοὶ μὲν γὰρ καθαπερεὶ κόσμος τις ἀσώματος
ἄρξων καλῶς ἐμψύχου σώματος ὁ νῦν λόγος ἀπειργάσθαι φαίνεται.

ΠΡΩ. Καὶ ἐμοὶ τοίνυν, ὦ Σώκρατες, οὕτω λέγε
δεδόχθαι.

---

¹ ἀλλ' ἃς Hermann : ἄλλας B : ἄλλας T.
² καθαρὰς Hermann : καθαρὰς ἃς BT.
³ μίγνυ τὰς Heusde : μιγνύντας BT.

those of our children which are born? But the true and pure pleasures, of which you spoke, you must consider almost our own by nature, and also those which are united with health and self-restraint, and furthermore all those which are handmaids of virtue in general and follow everywhere in its train as if it were a god,—add these to the mixture; but as for the pleasures which follow after folly and all baseness, it would be very senseless for anyone who desires to discover the most beautiful and most restful mixture or compound, and to try to learn which of its elements is good in man and the universe, and what we should divine its nature to be, to mix these with mind." Shall we not say that this reply which mind has now made for itself and memory and right opinion is wise and reasonable?

PRO. Certainly.

SOC. But another addition is surely necessary, without which nothing whatsoever can ever come into being.

PRO. What is it?

SOC. That in which there is no admixture of truth can never truly come into being or exist.

PRO. No, of course not.

SOC. No. But if anything is still wanting in our mixture, you and Philebus must speak of it. For to me it seems that our argument is now completed, as it were an incorporeal order which shall rule nobly a living body.

PRO. And you may say, Socrates, that I am of the same opinion.

PLATO

C ΣΩ. Ἆρ᾽ οὖν ἐπὶ μὲν τοῖς τοῦ ἀγαθοῦ νῦν ἤδη προθύροις καὶ τῆς οἰκήσεως ἐφεστάναι τῆς τοῦ τοιούτου λέγοντες ἴσως ὀρθῶς ἄν τινα τρόπον φαῖμεν;

ΠΡΩ. Ἐμοὶ γοῦν δοκεῖ.

ΣΩ. Τί δῆτα ἐν τῇ ξυμμίξει τιμιώτατον ἅμα καὶ μάλιστ᾽ αἴτιον εἶναι δόξειεν ἂν ἡμῖν τοῦ πᾶσι γεγονέναι προσφιλῆ τὴν τοιαύτην διάθεσιν; τοῦτο γὰρ ἰδόντες μετὰ τοῦτ᾽ ἐπισκεψόμεθα εἴθ᾽ ἡδονῇ εἴτε τῷ νῷ προσφυέστερον[1] καὶ οἰκειότερον ἐν τῷ παντὶ ξυνέστηκεν.

D ΠΡΩ. Ὀρθῶς· τοῦτο γὰρ εἰς τὴν κρίσιν ἡμῖν ἐστὶ συμφορώτατον.

ΣΩ. Καὶ μὴν καὶ ξυμπάσης γε μίξεως οὐ χαλεπὸν ἰδεῖν τὴν αἰτίαν δι᾽ ἣν ἢ παντὸς ἀξία γίγνεται ἡτισοῦν ἢ τὸ παράπαν οὐδενός.

ΠΡΩ. Πῶς λέγεις;

ΣΩ. Οὐδείς που τοῦτο ἀνθρώπων ἀγνοεῖ.

ΠΡΩ. Τὸ ποῖον;

ΣΩ. Ὅτι μέτρου καὶ τῆς συμμέτρου φύσεως μὴ τυχοῦσα ἡτισοῦν καὶ ὁπωσοῦν σύγκρασις πᾶσα ἐξ ἀνάγκης ἀπόλλυσι τά τε κεραννύμενα καὶ πρώτην E αὑτήν· οὐδὲ γὰρ κρᾶσις, ἀλλά τις ἄκρατος συμπεφορημένη ἀληθῶς ἡ τοιαύτη γίγνεται ἑκάστοτε ὄντως τοῖς κεκτημένοις ξυμφορά.

ΠΡΩ. Ἀληθέστατα.

ΣΩ. Νῦν δὴ καταπέφευγεν ἡμῖν ἡ τοῦ ἀγαθοῦ δύναμις εἰς τὴν τοῦ καλοῦ φύσιν. μετριότης γὰρ καὶ συμμετρία κάλλος δήπου καὶ ἀρετὴ πανταχοῦ ξυμβαίνει γίγνεσθαι.

ΠΡΩ. Πάνυ μὲν οὖν.

[1] προσφυέστερον Heusde : προσφυές τε BT.

388

soc. And if we were to say that we are now in the vestibule of the good and of the dwelling of the good, should we not be speaking the truth after a fashion?

pro. I certainly think so.

soc. What element, then, of the mixture would appear to us to be the most precious and also the chief cause why such a state is beloved of all? When we have discovered this, we will then consider whether it is more closely attached and more akin to pleasure or to mind in the universe.

pro. Right; for that is most serviceable to us in forming our judgement.

soc. And it is quite easy to see the cause which makes any mixture whatsoever either of the highest value or of none at all.

pro. What do you mean?

soc. Why, everybody knows that.

pro. Knows what?

soc. That any compound, however made, which lacks measure and proportion, must necessarily destroy its components and first of all itself; for it is in truth no compound, but an uncompounded jumble, and is always a misfortune to those who possess it.

pro. Perfectly true.

soc. So now the power of the good has taken refuge in the nature of the beautiful; for measure and proportion are everywhere identified with beauty and virtue.

pro. Certainly.

PLATO

ΣΩ. Καὶ μὴν ἀλήθειάν γε ἔφαμεν αὐτοῖς ἐν τῇ κράσει μεμῖχθαι.

ΠΡΩ. Πάνυ γε.

ΣΩ. Οὐκοῦν εἰ μὴ μιᾷ δυνάμεθα ἰδέᾳ τὸ ἀγα-
65 θὸν θηρεῦσαι, σὺν τρισὶ λαβόντες, κάλλει καὶ ξυμ-
μετρίᾳ καὶ ἀληθείᾳ, λέγωμεν ὡς τοῦτο οἷον ἓν
ὀρθότατ᾽ ἂν αἰτιασαίμεθ᾽ ἂν τῶν ἐν τῇ συμμίξει,
καὶ διὰ τοῦτο ὡς ἀγαθὸν ὂν τοιαύτην αὐτὴν γεγονέναι.

ΠΡΩ. Ὀρθότατα μὲν οὖν.

41. ΣΩ. Ἤδη τοίνυν, ὦ Πρώταρχε, ἱκανὸς
ἡμῖν γένοιτ᾽ ἂν ὁστισοῦν κριτὴς ἡδονῆς τε πέρι
B καὶ φρονήσεως, ὁπότερον αὐτοῖν τοῦ ἀρίστου ξυγ-
γενέστερόν τε καὶ τιμιώτερον ἐν ἀνθρώποις τέ
ἐστι καὶ θεοῖς.

ΠΡΩ. Δῆλον μέν, ὅμως δ᾽ οὖν τῷ λόγῳ ἐπεξελθεῖν βέλτιον.

ΣΩ. Καθ᾽ ἓν ἕκαστον τοίνυν τῶν τριῶν πρὸς
τὴν ἡδονὴν καὶ τὸν νοῦν κρίνωμεν. δεῖ γὰρ ἰδεῖν,
ποτέρῳ ὡς[1] μᾶλλον ξυγγενὲς ἕκαστον αὐτῶν ἀπο-
νεμοῦμεν.

ΠΡΩ. Κάλλους καὶ ἀληθείας καὶ μετριότητος
πέρι λέγεις;

ΣΩ. Ναί. πρῶτον δέ γε ἀληθείας λαβοῦ, ὦ
Πρώταρχε· καὶ λαβόμενος, βλέψας εἰς τρία, νοῦν
C καὶ ἀλήθειαν καὶ ἡδονήν, πολὺν ἐπισχὼν χρόνον
ἀπόκριναι σαυτῷ πότερον ἡδονὴ ξυγγενέστερον ἢ
νοῦς ἀληθείᾳ.

ΠΡΩ. Τί δὲ χρόνου δεῖ; πολὺ γάρ, οἶμαι, διαφέρετον. ἡδονὴ μὲν γὰρ ἁπάντων ἀλαζονίστατον,
ὡς δὲ λόγος, καὶ ἐν ταῖς ἡδοναῖς ταῖς περὶ τὰ-

[1] ὡς add. Burnet after Badham.

390

soc. We said that truth also was mingled with them in the compound.

pro. Certainly.

soc. Then if we cannot catch the good with the aid of one idea, let us run it down with three—beauty, proportion, and truth, and let us say that these, considered as one, may more properly than all other components of the mixture be regarded as the cause, and that through the goodness of these the mixture itself has been made good.

pro. Quite right.

soc. So now, Protarchus, any one would be able to judge about pleasure and wisdom, and to decide which of them is more akin to the highest good and of greater value among men and gods.

pro. That is clear ; but still it is better to carry on the discussion to the end.

soc. Let us, then, judge each of the three separately in its relation to pleasure and mind ; for it is our duty to see to which of the two we shall assign each of them as more akin.

pro. You refer to beauty, truth, and measure ?

soc. Yes. Take truth first, Protarchus ; take it and look at the three—mind, truth, and pleasure ; take plenty of time, and answer to yourself whether pleasure or mind is more akin to truth.

pro. Why take time ? For the difference, to my mind, is great. For pleasure is the greatest of impostors, and the story goes that in the pleasures of

φροδίσια, αἳ δὴ μέγισται δοκοῦσιν εἶναι, καὶ τὸ
ἐπιορκεῖν συγγνώμην εἴληφε παρὰ θεῶν, ὡς καθάπερ παίδων τῶν ἡδονῶν νοῦν οὐδὲ τὸν ὀλίγιστον
D κεκτημένων· νοῦς δὲ ἤτοι ταὐτὸν καὶ ἀλήθειά
ἐστιν ἢ πάντων ὁμοιότατόν τε καὶ ἀληθέστατον.

ΣΩ. Οὐκοῦν τὸ μετὰ τοῦτο τὴν μετριότητα ὡσαύτως σκέψαι, πότερον ἡδονὴ φρονήσεως ἢ φρόνησις ἡδονῆς πλείω κέκτηται.

ΠΡΩ. Εὔσκεπτόν γε καὶ ταύτην σκέψιν προβέ-
βληκας. οἶμαι γὰρ ἡδονῆς μὲν καὶ περιχαρείας
οὐδὲν τῶν ὄντων πεφυκὸς ἀμετρώτερον εὑρεῖν ἄν
τινα, νοῦ δὲ καὶ ἐπιστήμης ἐμμετρώτερον οὐδ᾽ ἂν ἕν
ποτε.

E ΣΩ. Καλῶς εἴρηκας. ὅμως δ᾽ ἔτι λέγε τὸ
τρίτον. νοῦς ἡμῖν κάλλους μετείληφε πλεῖον ἢ
τὸ τῆς ἡδονῆς γένος, ὥστε εἶναι καλλίω νοῦν ἡδονῆς,
ἢ τοὐναντίον;

ΠΡΩ. Ἀλλ᾽[1] οὖν φρόνησιν μὲν καὶ νοῦν, ὦ
Σώκρατες, οὐδεὶς πώποτε οὔθ᾽ ὕπαρ οὔτ᾽ ὄναρ
αἰσχρὸν οὔτε εἶδεν οὔτε ἐπενόησεν οὐδαμῇ οὐδαμῶς
οὔτε γιγνόμενον οὔτε ὄντα οὔτε ἐσόμενον.

ΣΩ. Ὀρθῶς.

ΠΡΩ. Ἡδονὰς δέ γέ που, καὶ ταῦτα σχεδὸν τὰς
μεγίστας, ὅταν ἴδωμεν ἡδόμενον ὁντινοῦν, ἢ τὸ γελοῖον ἐπ᾽ αὐταῖς ἢ τὸ πάντων αἴσχιστον ἑπόμενον
66 ὁρῶντες αὐτοί τε αἰσχυνόμεθα καὶ ἀφανίζοντες
κρύπτομεν ὅτι μάλιστα, νυκτὶ πάντα τὰ τοιαῦτα
διδόντες, ὡς φῶς οὐ δέον ὁρᾶν αὐτά.

ΣΩ. Πάντῃ δὴ φήσεις, ὦ Πρώταρχε, ὑπό τε
ἀγγέλων πέμπων καὶ παροῦσι φράζων, ὡς ἡδονὴ
κτῆμα οὐκ ἔστι πρῶτον οὐδ᾽ αὖ δεύτερον, ἀλλὰ

---

[1] ἀλλ᾽ Stallbaum: ἄρ᾽ T Stobaeus: ἄρ᾽ B.

love, which are said to be the greatest, perjury is even pardoned by the gods, as if the pleasures were like children, utterly devoid of all sense. But mind is either identical with truth or of all things most like it and truest.

soc. Next, then, consider measure in the same way, and see whether pleasure possesses more of it than wisdom, or wisdom than pleasure.

pro. That also is an easy thing to consider. For I think nothing in the world could be found more immoderate than pleasure and its transports, and nothing more in harmony with measure than mind and knowledge.

soc. You are right. However, go on and tell about the third. Has mind or pleasure the greater share in beauty, so that mind is fairer than pleasure, or the other way round ?

pro. But Socrates, no one, either asleep or awake, ever saw or knew wisdom or mind to be or become unseemly at any time or in any way whatsoever, now or in the future.

soc. Right.

pro. But pleasures, and the greatest pleasures at that, when we see any one enjoying them and observe the ridiculous or utterly disgraceful element which accompanies them, fill us with a sense of shame ; we put them out of sight and hide them, so far as possible ; we confine everything of that sort to the night time, as unfit for the sight of day.

soc. Then you will proclaim everywhere, Protarchus, by messengers to the absent and by speech to those present, that pleasure is not the first of possessions, nor even the second, but first the eternal

πρῶτον μέν πῃ περὶ μέτρον καὶ τὸ μέτριον καὶ καίριον καὶ πάντα ὁπόσα χρὴ τοιαῦτα νομίζειν, τὴν ἀΐδιον ἡρῆσθαι φύσιν.[1]

ΠΡΩ. Φαίνεται γοῦν ἐκ τῶν νῦν λεγομένων.

Β ΣΩ. Δεύτερον μὴν περὶ τὸ σύμμετρον καὶ καλὸν καὶ τὸ τέλεον καὶ ἱκανὸν καὶ πάνθ' ὁπόσα τῆς γενεᾶς αὖ ταύτης ἐστίν.

ΠΡΩ. Ἔοικε γοῦν.

ΣΩ. Τὸ τοίνυν τρίτον, ὡς ἡ ἐμὴ μαντεία, νοῦν καὶ φρόνησιν τιθεὶς οὐκ ἂν μέγα τι τῆς ἀληθείας παρεξέλθοις.

ΠΡΩ. Ἴσως.

ΣΩ. Ἆρ' οὖν οὐ τέταρτα, ἃ τῆς ψυχῆς αὐτῆς ἔθεμεν, ἐπιστήμας τε καὶ τέχνας καὶ δόξας ὀρθὰς Ϲ λεχθείσας, ταῦτ' εἶναι τὰ πρὸς τοῖς τρισὶ τέταρτα, εἴπερ τοῦ ἀγαθοῦ γέ ἐστι μᾶλλον τῆς[2] ἡδονῆς ξυγγενῆ;

ΠΡΩ. Τάχ' ἄν.

ΣΩ. Πέμπτας τοίνυν, ἃς ἡδονὰς ἔθεμεν ἀλύπους ὁρισάμενοι, καθαρὰς ἐπονομάσαντες τῆς ψυχῆς αὐτῆς, ἐπιστήμαις,[3] τὰς[4] δὲ αἰσθήσεσιν ἑπομένας;

ΠΡΩ. Ἴσως.

ΣΩ. "Ἕκτῃ δ' ἐν γενεᾷ," φησὶν Ὀρφεύς, "καταπαύσατε κόσμον ἀοιδῆς·" ἀτὰρ κινδυνεύει καὶ ὁ ἡμέτερος λόγος ἐν ἕκτῃ καταπεπαυμένος εἶναι Ɗ κρίσει. τὸ δὴ μετὰ ταῦθ' ἡμῖν οὐδὲν λοιπὸν πλὴν ὥσπερ κεφαλὴν ἀποδοῦναι τοῖς εἰρημένοις.

ΠΡΩ. Οὐκοῦν χρή.

42. ΣΩ. Ἴθι δή, τὸ τρίτον τῷ σωτῆρι τὸν αὐτὸν διαμαρτυράμενοι λόγον ἐπεξέλθωμεν.

---

[1] ἡρῆσθαι Stobaeus : ἡρῆσθαι B : εἰρῆσθαι φάσιν T : εἰρῆσθαι φύσιν vulg. : ηὑρῆσθαι φύσιν Badham.

nature has chosen measure, moderation, fitness, and all which is to be considered similar to these.

PRO. That appears to result from what has now been said.

SOC. Second, then, comes proportion, beauty, perfection, sufficiency, and all that belongs to that class.

PRO. Yes, so it appears.

SOC. And if you count mind and wisdom as the third, you will, I prophesy, not wander far from the truth.

PRO. That may be.

SOC. And will you not put those properties fourth which we said belonged especially to the soul—sciences, arts, and true opinions they are called—and say that these come after the first three, and are fourth, since they are more akin than pleasure to the good ?

PRO. Perhaps.

SOC. And fifth, those pleasures which we separated and classed as painless, which we called pure pleasures of the soul itself, those which accompany knowledge and, sometimes, perceptions ?

PRO. May be.

SOC. " But with the sixth generation," says Orpheus, " cease the rhythmic song." It seems that our discussion, too, is likely to cease with the sixth decision. So after this nothing remains for us but to give our discussion a sort of head.

PRO. Yes, that should be done.

SOC. Come then, let us for the third time call the same argument to witness before Zeus the saviour, and proceed.

---

² τῆς Stallbaum : ἢ τῆς BT.
³ ἐπιστήμαις corr. Ven. 189 : ἐπιστήμας BT.
⁴ τὰς Badham : ταῖς BT.

ΠΡΩ. Ποῖον δή;

ΣΩ. Φίληβος τἀγαθὸν ἐτίθετο ἡμῖν ἡδονὴν εἶναι πᾶσαν καὶ παντελῆ.

ΠΡΩ. Τὸ τρίτον, ὦ Σώκρατες, ὡς ἔοικας, ἔλεγες ἀρτίως τὸν ἐξ ἀρχῆς ἐπαναλαβεῖν δεῖν λόγον.

Ε ΣΩ. Ναί, τὸ δέ γε μετὰ τοῦτο ἀκούωμεν. ἐγὼ γὰρ δὴ κατιδὼν ἅπερ νῦν δὴ διελήλυθα, καὶ δυσχεράνας τὸν Φιλήβου λόγον οὐ μόνον ἀλλὰ καὶ ἄλλων πολλάκις μυρίων, εἶπον ὡς ἡδονῆς γε νοῦς εἴη μακρῷ βέλτιόν τε καὶ ἄμεινον τῷ τῶν ἀνθρώπων βίῳ.

ΠΡΩ. ῏Ην ταῦτα.

ΣΩ. Ὑποπτεύων δέ γε καὶ ἄλλα εἶναι πολλὰ εἶπον ὡς εἰ φανείη τι τούτοιν ἀμφοῖν βέλτιον, ὑπὲρ τῶν δευτερείων νῷ πρὸς ἡδονὴν ξυνδιαμαχοίμην, ἡδονὴ δὲ καὶ δευτερείων στερήσοιτο.

67 ΠΡΩ. Εἶπες γὰρ οὖν.

ΣΩ. Καὶ μετὰ ταῦτά γε πάντων ἱκανώτατα τούτοιν οὐδέτερον ἱκανὸν ἐφάνη.

ΠΡΩ. Ἀληθέστατα.

ΣΩ. Οὐκοῦν παντάπασιν ἐν τούτῳ τῷ λόγῳ καὶ νοῦς ἀπήλλακτο καὶ ἡδονὴ μή τοι τἀγαθόν γε αὐτὸ μηδ᾽ ἕτερον αὐτοῖν εἶναι, στερομένοιν[1] αὐταρκείας καὶ τῆς τοῦ ἱκανοῦ καὶ τελέου δυνάμεως;

ΠΡΩ. Ὀρθότατα.

ΣΩ. Φανέντος δέ γε ἄλλου τρίτου κρείττονος τούτοιν ἑκατέρου, μυρίῳ γ᾽ αὖ νοῦς ἡδονῆς οἰκειότερον καὶ προσφυέστερον πέφανται νῦν τῇ τοῦ νικῶντος ἰδέᾳ.

ΠΡΩ. Πῶς γὰρ οὔ;

---

[1] στερομένοιν corr. Ven. 189: στερομένον BT.

pro. What argument?

soc. Philebus declared that pleasure was entirely and in all respects the good.

pro. Apparently, Socrates, when you said " the third time " just now, you meant that we must take up our argument again from the beginning.

soc. Yes; but let us hear what follows. For I, perceiving the truths which I have now been detailing, and annoyed by the theory held not only by Philebus but by many thousands of others, said that mind was a far better and more excellent thing for human life than pleasure.

pro. True.

soc. But suspecting that there were many other things to be considered, I said that if anything should be found better than these two, I should support mind against pleasure in the struggle for the second place, and even the second place would be lost by pleasure.

pro. Yes, that is what you said.

soc. And next it was most sufficiently proved that each of these two was insufficient.

pro. Very true.

soc. In this argument, then, both mind and pleasure were set aside; neither of them is the absolute good, since they are devoid of self-sufficiency, adequacy, and perfection?

pro. Quite right.

soc. And on the appearance of a third competitor, better than either of these, mind is now found to be ten thousand times more akin than pleasure to the victor.

pro. Certainly.

ΣΩ. Οὐκοῦν πέμπτον κατὰ τὴν κρίσιν, ἣν νῦν ὁ λόγος ἀπεφήνατο, γίγνοιτ᾽ ἂν ἡ τῆς ἡδονῆς δύναμις.

ΠΡΩ. Ἔοικεν.

B   ΣΩ. Πρῶτον δέ γε οὐδ᾽ ἂν οἱ πάντες βόες τε καὶ ἵπποι καὶ τἆλλα ξύμπαντα θηρία φῶσι τῷ τὸ χαίρειν διώκειν· οἷς πιστεύοντες, ὥσπερ μάντεις ὄρνισιν, οἱ πολλοὶ κρίνουσι τὰς ἡδονὰς εἰς τὸ ζῆν ἡμῖν εὖ κρατίστας εἶναι, καὶ τοὺς θηρίων ἔρωτας[1] οἴονται κυρίους εἶναι μάρτυρας μᾶλλον ἢ τοὺς τῶν ἐν μούσῃ φιλοσόφῳ μεμαντευμένων ἑκάστοτε λόγων.

ΠΡΩ. Ἀληθέστατα, ὦ Σώκρατες, εἰρῆσθαί σοι νῦν ἤδη φαμὲν ἅπαντες.

ΣΩ. Οὐκοῦν καὶ ἀφίετέ με;

ΠΡΩ. Σμικρὸν ἔτι τὸ λοιπόν, ὦ Σώκρατες· οὐ γὰρ δήπου σύ γε ἀπερεῖς πρότερος ἡμῶν· ὑπομνήσω δέ σε τὰ λειπόμενα.

      [1] ἔρωτας t : ἐρῶντας BT.

soc. Then, according to the judgement which has now been given by our discussion, the power of pleasure would be fifth.

pro. So it seems.

soc. But not first, even if all the cattle and horses and other beasts in the world, in their pursuit of enjoyment, so assert. Trusting in them, as augurs trust in birds, the many judge that pleasures are the greatest blessings in life, and they imagine that the lusts of beasts are better witnesses than are the aspirations and thoughts inspired by the philosophic muse.

pro. Socrates, we all now declare that what you have said is perfectly true.

soc. Then you will let me go?

pro. There is still a little left, Socrates. I am sure you will not give up before we do, and I will remind you of what remains.

ION

INTRODUCTION TO THE *ION*

THIS graceful little piece is remarkable not only for the evidence it affords of the popularity and procedure of Homeric recitals in the fifth and fourth centuries, or again, for its brilliant witness to Plato's skill in characterization, but also for its insistence—implied rather than expressed—on the doctrine that no art, however warmly accepted and encouraged by the multitude, can be of real worth unless it is based on some systematic knowledge ; and that the common claim of successful artists to be useful servants of the public is probably a dangerous delusion. The " rhapsode," Ion of Ephesus, appears before us in the two capacities of reciter and expositor of Homer. His profession, which bore in its name the suggestion of " song-stitching," was probably developed from extempore performances of epic poets in their own person, when they strung verses or groups of verses together in a continuous chant : the rhapsode was able to recite from memory the most interesting or moving narratives in the great epics, and this practice came to be known by the general name of " rhapsody." The rhapsode's profession was distinguished and lucrative. We read here of the golden crowns he wore, his audience of more than twenty thousand persons (535 D), and his pecuniary reward for successfully stirring their

emotions (535 E). Isocrates (*Paneg.* 74 A, B) speaks of the importance of such recitals for keeping alive the national feeling of valour against the barbarians ; and we read (Xenophon, *Sympos.* 3. 6) of one person at least who used to hear rhapsodes almost every day, and thus preserved his memory of the whole of the *Iliad* and the *Odyssey*, which he had learnt by heart as a boy. These solemn recitals of the rhapsodes at great national festivals were both a sign and a support of the immense popularity of the Homeric poems ; the rhapsodes' art corresponded to that of the actors in dramatic and to that of the minstrels in lyric performances. But besides these public recitals they gave lectures on the subject matter of the poems to classes of those who hoped to acquire some practical knowledge from their interpretations and disquisitions ; and on this side of their profession they closely resembled the sophists. It is this educative work of the rhapsode which interests Plato. He is bent on criticizing the whole system—or rather, the unsystematic tradition —of Greek education ; and he seeks to show that the rhapsode's pretensions to any particular knowledge of human affairs are absurd, and further, that even his great success in impassioned recitation is a matter not of studied art, but of divine " possession "— something divorced from reason, and a possible danger to the truth. The irrational nature of Ion's skill is illustrated by the striking comparison of the magnet, which transmits an attractive force through a series of iron rings. In the same way, the divine inspiration, originating from the Muse, passes to the poet, from him to the rhapsode, and from him again to the audience. Performer and hearer alike are

held and swayed, like any frenzied bacchanal, by
something unreasonable, unaccountable, and over-
mastering. Ion does not like this theory—that he
must be out of his mind when he exercises his famous
fascination—but he is eventually trapped into a
reluctant acceptance of it. For he cannot stand the
Socratic testing of his scientific knowledge, and
prefers to rest on his mysterious " afflatus." What
he would like best would be to give a regular lecture
on the beauties of Homer (536 D); but Socrates puts
him off with a few questions which expose the
scantiness of his knowledge, and only allows him to
show off his wonderful memory by quoting a few
passages of the poet. Yet Socrates' tone towards
him throughout is friendly and restrained. Plato
was ever aware of the mighty influence of the poets
upon himself as well as upon the mass of his country-
men, and there is regret no less than respect in his
voice when he bids them depart from his ideal state
(*Rep.* iii. 398).

The supposed time of the conversation with Ion is
the last year or two of the Peloponnesian War (*cf.*
541 D, note). There is a useful edition of the dialogue
by St. George Stock (Clarendon Press, 1909).

ΙΩΝ

[Η ΠΕΡΙ ΙΛΙΑΔΟΣ, ΠΕΙΡΑΣΤΙΚΟΣ]

ΤΑ ΤΟΥ ΔΙΑΛΟΓΟΥ ΠΡΟΣΩΠΑ

ΣΩΚΡΑΤΗΣ, ΙΩΝ

St. I
p. 530

ΣΩ. Τὸν Ἴωνα χαίρειν. πόθεν τὰ νῦν ἡμῖν ἐπιδεδήμηκας; ἢ οἴκοθεν ἐξ Ἐφέσου;

ΙΩΝ. Οὐδαμῶς, ὦ Σώκρατες, ἀλλ' ἐξ Ἐπιδαύρου ἐκ τῶν Ἀσκληπιείων.

ΣΩ. Μῶν καὶ ῥαψῳδῶν ἀγῶνα τιθέασι τῷ θεῷ οἱ Ἐπιδαύριοι;

ΙΩΝ. Πάνυ γε, καὶ τῆς ἄλλης γε μουσικῆς.

ΣΩ. Τί οὖν; ἠγωνίζου τι ἡμῖν; καὶ πῶς τι ἠγωνίσω;

ΙΩΝ. Τὰ πρῶτα τῶν ἄθλων ἠνεγκάμεθα, ὦ Σώκρατες.

B ΣΩ. Εὖ λέγεις· ἄγε δὴ ὅπως καὶ τὰ Παναθήναια νικήσομεν.

ΙΩΝ. Ἀλλ' ἔσται ταῦτα, ἐὰν θεὸς ἐθέλῃ.

ΣΩ. Καὶ μὴν πολλάκις γε ἐζήλωσα ὑμᾶς τοὺς ῥαψῳδούς, ὦ Ἴων, τῆς τέχνης· τὸ γὰρ ἅμα μὲν τὸ σῶμα κεκοσμῆσθαι ἀεὶ πρέπον ὑμῶν εἶναι τῇ

---

[1] " Music " with the Greeks included poetry.

ION

[or ON THE *ILIAD* : tentative]

CHARACTERS

SOCRATES, ION

soc. Welcome, Ion. Where have you come from now, to pay us this visit? From your home in Ephesus?

ION. No, no, Socrates; from Epidaurus and the festival there of Asclepius.

soc. Do you mean to say that the Epidaurians honour the god with a contest of rhapsodes also?

ION. Certainly, and of music [1] in general.

soc. Why then, you were competing in some contest, were you? And how went your competition?

ION. We carried off the first prize, Socrates.

soc. Well done: so now, mind that we win too at the Panathenaea.[2]

ION. Why, so we shall, God willing.

soc. I must say I have often envied you rhapsodes, Ion, for your art: for besides that it is fitting to your art that your person should be adorned and that

---

[2] The Athenian festival of the Great Panathenaea was held every fourth year, and the Small Panathenaea probably every year, about July.

τέχνῃ καὶ ὡς καλλίστοις φαίνεσθαι, ἅμα δὲ ἀναγκαῖον εἶναι ἔν τε ἄλλοις ποιηταῖς διατρίβειν
πολλοῖς καὶ ἀγαθοῖς καὶ δὴ καὶ μάλιστα ἐν Ὁμήρῳ,
τῷ ἀρίστῳ καὶ θειοτάτῳ τῶν ποιητῶν, καὶ τὴν
C τούτου διάνοιαν ἐκμανθάνειν, μὴ μόνον τὰ ἔπη,
ζηλωτόν ἐστιν. οὐ γὰρ ἂν γένοιτό ποτε ἀγαθὸς
ῥαψῳδός, εἰ μὴ συνείη τὰ λεγόμενα ὑπὸ τοῦ
ποιητοῦ. τὸν γὰρ ῥαψῳδὸν ἑρμηνέα δεῖ τοῦ
ποιητοῦ τῆς διανοίας γίγνεσθαι τοῖς ἀκούουσι·
τοῦτο δὲ καλῶς ποιεῖν μὴ γιγνώσκοντα ὅ τι λέγει
ὁ ποιητὴς ἀδύνατον. ταῦτα οὖν πάντα ἄξια
ζηλοῦσθαι.

ΙΩΝ. Ἀληθῆ λέγεις, ὦ Σώκρατες· ἐμοὶ γοῦν
τοῦτο πλεῖστον ἔργον παρέσχε τῆς τέχνης, καὶ
οἶμαι κάλλιστα ἀνθρώπων λέγειν περὶ Ὁμήρου,
D ὡς οὔτε Μητρόδωρος ὁ Λαμψακηνὸς οὔτε Στησίμ-
βροτος ὁ Θάσιος οὔτε Γλαύκων οὔτε ἄλλος οὐδεὶς
τῶν πώποτε γενομένων ἔσχεν εἰπεῖν οὕτω πολλὰς
καὶ καλὰς διανοίας περὶ Ὁμήρου, ὅσας ἐγώ.

ΣΩ. Εὖ λέγεις, ὦ Ἴων· δῆλον γὰρ ὅτι οὐ φθο-
νήσεις μοι ἐπιδεῖξαι.

ΙΩΝ. Καὶ μὴν ἄξιόν γε ἀκοῦσαι, ὦ Σώκρατες, ὡς
εὖ κεκόσμηκα τὸν Ὅμηρον· ὥστε οἶμαι ὑπὸ
Ὁμηριδῶν ἄξιος εἶναι χρυσῷ στεφάνῳ στεφανω-
θῆναι.

ΣΩ. Καὶ μὴν ἐγὼ ἔτι ποιήσομαι σχολὴν ἀκροά-

---

[1] A friend of the philosopher Anaxagoras who wrote
allegorical interpretations of Homer in the first part of the
fifth century B.C.

you should look as handsome as possible, the necessity of being conversant with a number of good poets, and especially with Homer, the best and divinest poet of all, and of apprehending his thought and not merely learning off his words, is a matter for envy; since a man can never be a good rhapsode without understanding what the poet says. For the rhapsode ought to make himself an interpreter of the poet's thought to his audience; and to do this properly without knowing what the poet means is impossible. So one cannot but envy all this.

ION. What you say is true, Socrates: I at any rate have found this the most laborious part of my art; and I consider I speak about Homer better than anybody, for neither Metrodorus[1] of Lampsacus, nor Stesimbrotus[2] of Thasos, nor Glaucon,[3] nor any one that the world has ever seen, had so many and such fine comments to offer on Homer as I have.

SOC. That is good news, Ion; for obviously you will not grudge me an exhibition of them.

ION. And indeed it is worth hearing, Socrates, how well I have embellished Homer; so that I think I deserve to be crowned with a golden crown by the Homeridae.[4]

SOC. Yes, and I must find myself leisure some time

[2] A rhapsode, interpreter of Homer, and historian who lived in the time of Cimon and Pericles.

[3] Perhaps the Homeric commentator mentioned by Aristotle, *Poet.* 25. 16.

[4] There was a society or clan in Chios called Homeridae (" sons of Homer "), but the name seems to be used here and elsewhere in Plato for any persons specially devoted to Homer's poetry. See Jebb, *Homer*, p. 78.

531 σασθαί σου· νῦν δέ μοι τοσόνδε ἀπόκριναι· πότερον
περὶ Ὁμήρου μόνον δεινὸς εἶ ἢ καὶ περὶ Ἡσιόδου
καὶ Ἀρχιλόχου;

ΙΩΝ. Οὐδαμῶς, ἀλλὰ περὶ Ὁμήρου μόνον· ἱκανὸν
γάρ μοι δοκεῖ εἶναι.

ΣΩ. Ἔστι δὲ περὶ ὅτου Ὅμηρός τε καὶ Ἡσίοδος
ταὐτὰ λέγετον;

ΙΩΝ. Οἶμαι ἔγωγε καὶ πολλά.

ΣΩ. Πότερον οὖν περὶ τούτων κάλλιον ἂν ἐξηγήσαιο ἃ Ὅμηρος λέγει ἢ ἃ Ἡσίοδος;

ΙΩΝ. Ὁμοίως ἂν περί γε τούτων, ὦ Σώκρατες,
περὶ ὧν ταὐτὰ λέγουσιν.

B ΣΩ. Τί δέ, ὧν πέρι μὴ ταὐτὰ λέγουσιν; οἷον
περὶ μαντικῆς λέγει τι Ὅμηρός τε καὶ Ἡσίοδος.

ΙΩΝ. Πάνυ γε.

ΣΩ. Τί οὖν; ὅσα τε ὁμοίως καὶ ὅσα διαφόρως
περὶ μαντικῆς λέγετον τὼ ποιητὰ τούτω, πότερον
σὺ κάλλιον ἂν ἐξηγήσαιο ἢ τῶν μάντεών τις τῶν
ἀγαθῶν;

ΙΩΝ. Τῶν μάντεων.

ΣΩ. Εἰ δὲ σὺ ἦσθα μάντις, οὐκ, εἴπερ περὶ τῶν
ὁμοίως λεγομένων οἷός τ᾽ ἦσθα ἐξηγήσασθαι, καὶ
περὶ τῶν διαφόρως λεγομένων ἠπίστω ἂν ἐξηγεῖσθαι;

ΙΩΝ. Δῆλον ὅτι.

ΣΩ. Τί οὖν ποτε περὶ μὲν Ὁμήρου δεινὸς εἶ,
C περὶ δὲ Ἡσιόδου οὔ, οὐδὲ τῶν ἄλλων ποιητῶν;
ἢ Ὅμηρος περὶ ἄλλων τινῶν λέγει ἢ ὧνπερ
σύμπαντες οἱ ἄλλοι ποιηταί; οὐ περὶ πολέμου
τε τὰ πολλὰ διελήλυθε καὶ περὶ ὁμιλιῶν πρὸς
ἀλλήλους ἀνθρώπων ἀγαθῶν τε καὶ κακῶν καὶ
ἰδιωτῶν καὶ δημιουργῶν, καὶ περὶ θεῶν πρὸς

to listen to you ; but for the moment, please answer this little question : are you skilled in Homer only, or in Hesiod and Archilochus as well ?

ION. No, no, only in Homer ; for that seems to me quite enough.

SOC. And is there anything on which Homer and Hesiod both say the same ?

ION. Yes, I think there are many such cases.

SOC. Then in those cases would you expound better what Homer says than what Hesiod says ?

ION. I should do it equally well in those cases, Socrates, where they say the same.

SOC. But what of those where they do not say the same ? For example, about the seer's art, on which both Homer and Hesiod say something.

ION. Quite so.

SOC. Well then, would you, or one of the good seers, expound better what these two poets say, not only alike but differently, about the seer's art ?

ION. One of the seers.

SOC. And if you were a seer, would you not, with an ability to expound what they say in agreement, know also how to expound the points on which they differ ?

ION. Of course.

SOC. Then how is it that you are skilled in Homer, and not in Hesiod or the other poets ? Does Homer speak of any other than the very things that all the other poets speak of ? Has he not described war for the most part, and the mutual intercourse of men, good and bad, lay and professional, and the ways of

411

ἀλλήλους καὶ πρὸς ἀνθρώπους ὁμιλούντων, ὡς
ὁμιλοῦσι, καὶ περὶ τῶν οὐρανίων παθημάτων καὶ
περὶ τῶν ἐν Ἅιδου, καὶ γενέσεις καὶ θεῶν καὶ
D ἡρώων; οὐ ταῦτά ἐστι περὶ ὧν Ὅμηρος τὴν
ποίησιν πεποίηκεν;

ΙΩΝ. Ἀληθῆ λέγεις, ὦ Σώκρατες.

ΣΩ. Τί δὲ οἱ ἄλλοι ποιηταί; οὐ περὶ τῶν αὐτῶν τούτων;

ΙΩΝ. Ναί, ἀλλ᾽, ὦ Σώκρατες, οὐχ ὁμοίως
πεποιήκασι καὶ Ὅμηρος.

ΣΩ . Τί μήν; κάκιον;

ΙΩΝ. Πολύ γε.

ΣΩ. Ὅμηρος δὲ ἄμεινον;

ΙΩΝ. Ἄμεινον μέντοι νὴ Δία.

ΣΩ. Οὐκοῦν, ὦ φίλη κεφαλὴ Ἴων, ὅταν περὶ
ἀριθμοῦ πολλῶν λεγόντων εἷς τις ἄριστα λέγῃ,
γνώσεται δήπου τις τὸν εὖ λέγοντα;

E ΙΩΝ. Φημί.

ΣΩ. Πότερον οὖν ὁ αὐτός, ὅσπερ καὶ τοὺς
κακῶς λέγοντας, ἢ ἄλλος;

ΙΩΝ. Ὁ αὐτὸς δήπου.

ΣΩ. Οὐκοῦν ὁ τὴν ἀριθμητικὴν τέχνην ἔχων
οὗτός ἐστιν;

ΙΩΝ. Ναί.

ΣΩ. Τί δ᾽; ὅταν πολλῶν λεγόντων περὶ ὑγιεινῶν
σιτίων, ὁποῖά ἐστιν, εἷς τις ἄριστα λέγῃ, πότερον
ἕτερος μέν τις τὸν ἄριστα λέγοντα γνώσεται ὅτι
ἄριστα λέγει, ἕτερος δὲ τὸν κάκιον ὅτι κάκιον, ἢ
ὁ αὐτός;

ΙΩΝ. Δῆλον δήπου, ὁ αὐτός.

ΣΩ. Τίς οὗτος; τί ὄνομα αὐτῷ;

ΙΩΝ. Ἰατρός.

the gods in their intercourse with each other and with men, and happenings in the heavens and in the underworld, and origins of gods and heroes? Are not these the subjects of Homer's poetry?

ION. What you say is true, Socrates.

soc. And what of the other poets? Do they not treat of the same things?

ION. Yes; but, Socrates, not on Homer's level.

soc. What, in a worse way?

ION. Far worse.

soc. And Homer in a better?

ION. Better indeed, I assure you.

soc. Well now, Ion, dear soul; when several people are talking about number, and one of them speaks better than the rest, I suppose there is some one who will distinguish the good speaker?

ION. I agree.

soc. And will this some one be the same as he who can distinguish the bad speakers, or different?

ION. The same, I suppose.

soc. And he will be the man who has the art of numeration?

ION. Yes.

soc. And again, when several are talking about what kinds of foods are wholesome, and one of them speaks better than the rest, will it be for two different persons to distinguish the superiority of the best speaker and the inferiority of a worse one, or for the same?

ION. Obviously, I should say, for the same.

soc. Who is he? What is his name?

ION. A doctor.

ΣΩ. Οὐκοῦν ἐν κεφαλαίῳ λέγωμεν, ὡς ὁ αὐτὸς γνώσεται ἀεὶ περὶ τῶν αὐτῶν πολλῶν λεγόντων, 532 ὅστις τε εὖ λέγει καὶ ὅστις κακῶς· ἢ εἰ μὴ γνώσεται τὸν κακῶς λέγοντα, δῆλον ὅτι οὐδὲ τὸν εὖ, περί γε τοῦ αὐτοῦ.

ΙΩΝ. Οὕτως.

ΣΩ. Οὐκοῦν ὁ αὐτὸς γίγνεται δεινὸς περὶ ἀμφοτέρων;

ΙΩΝ. Ναί.

ΣΩ. Οὐκοῦν σὺ φῂς καὶ Ὅμηρον καὶ τοὺς ἄλλους ποιητάς, ἐν οἷς καὶ Ἡσίοδος καὶ Ἀρχίλοχός ἐστι, περί γε τῶν αὐτῶν λέγειν, ἀλλ' οὐχ ὁμοίως, ἀλλὰ τὸν μὲν εὖ, τοὺς δὲ χεῖρον;

ΙΩΝ. Καὶ ἀληθῆ λέγω.

ΣΩ. Οὐκοῦν, εἴπερ τὸν εὖ λέγοντα γιγνώσκεις, Β καὶ τοὺς χεῖρον λέγοντας γιγνώσκοις ἂν ὅτι χεῖρον λέγουσιν.

ΙΩΝ. Ἔοικέ γε.

ΣΩ. Οὐκοῦν, ὦ βέλτιστε, ὁμοίως τὸν Ἴωνα λέγοντες περὶ Ὁμήρου τε δεινὸν εἶναι καὶ περὶ τῶν ἄλλων ποιητῶν οὐχ ἁμαρτησόμεθα, ἐπειδή γε αὐτὸς ὁμολογῇ τὸν αὐτὸν ἔσεσθαι κριτὴν ἱκανὸν πάντων, ὅσοι ἂν περὶ τῶν αὐτῶν λέγωσι, τοὺς δὲ ποιητὰς σχεδὸν ἅπαντας τὰ αὐτὰ ποιεῖν.

ΙΩΝ. Τί οὖν ποτὲ τὸ αἴτιον, ὦ Σώκρατες, ὅτι ἐγώ, ὅταν μέν τις περὶ ἄλλου του ποιητοῦ διαλέγηται, οὔτε προσέχω τὸν νοῦν ἀδυνατῶ τε καὶ C ὁτιοῦν συμβαλέσθαι λόγου ἄξιον, ἀλλ' ἀτεχνῶς νυστάζω, ἐπειδὰν δέ τις περὶ Ὁμήρου μνησθῇ, εὐθύς τε ἐγρήγορα καὶ προσέχω τὸν νοῦν καὶ εὐπορῶ ὅ τι λέγω;

ΣΩ. Οὐ χαλεπὸν τοῦτό γε εἰκάσαι, ὦ ἑταῖρε,

ION

soc. And so we may state, in general terms, that the same person will always distinguish, given the same subject and several persons talking about it, both who speaks well and who badly : otherwise, if he is not going to distinguish the bad speaker, clearly he will not distinguish the good one either, where the subject is the same.

ion. That is so.

soc. And the same man is found to be skilled in both ?

ion. Yes.

soc. And you say that Homer and the other poets, among whom are Hesiod and Archilochus, all speak about the same things, only not similarly ; but the one does it well, and the rest worse ?

ion. Yes, and what I say is true.

soc. And since you distinguish the good speaker, you could distinguish also the inferiority of the worse speakers.

ion. So it would seem.

soc. Then, my excellent friend, we shall not be wrong in saying that our Ion is equally skilled in Homer and in the other poets, seeing that you yourself admit that the same man will be a competent judge of all who speak on the same things, and that practically all the poets treat of the same things.

ion. Then what can be the reason, Socrates, why I pay no attention when somebody discusses any other poet, and am unable to offer any remark at all of any value, but simply drop into a doze, whereas if anyone mentions something connected with Homer I wake up at once and attend and have plenty to say ?

soc. That is not difficult to guess, my good friend ;

415

ἀλλὰ παντὶ δῆλον ὅτι τέχνῃ καὶ ἐπιστήμῃ περὶ
Ὁμήρου λέγειν ἀδύνατος εἶ· εἰ γὰρ τέχνῃ οἷός τε
ἦσθα, καὶ περὶ τῶν ἄλλων ποιητῶν ἁπάντων
λέγειν οἷός τ' ἂν ἦσθα· ποιητικὴ γάρ πού ἐστι
τὸ ὅλον. ἢ οὔ;

ΙΩΝ. Ναί.

D ΣΩ. Οὐκοῦν ἐπειδὰν λάβῃ τις καὶ ἄλλην τέχνην
ἡντινοῦν ὅλην, ὁ αὐτὸς τρόπος τῆς σκέψεώς ἐστι
περὶ ἁπασῶν τῶν τεχνῶν; πῶς τοῦτο λέγω, δέῃ
τί μου ἀκοῦσαι, ὦ Ἴων;

ΙΩΝ. Ναὶ μὰ τὸν Δί', ὦ Σώκρατες, ἔγωγε·
χαίρω γὰρ ἀκούων ὑμῶν τῶν σοφῶν.

ΣΩ. Βουλοίμην ἄν σε ἀληθῆ λέγειν, ὦ Ἴων·
ἀλλὰ σοφοὶ μέν πού ἐστε ὑμεῖς οἱ ῥαψῳδοὶ καὶ
ὑποκριταὶ καὶ ὧν ὑμεῖς ᾄδετε τὰ ποιήματα, ἐγὼ
δὲ οὐδὲν ἄλλο ἢ τἀληθῆ λέγω, οἷον εἰκὸς ἰδιώτην
E ἄνθρωπον. ἐπεὶ καὶ περὶ τούτου οὗ νῦν ἠρόμην
σε, θέασαι ὡς φαῦλον καὶ ἰδιωτικόν ἐστι καὶ
παντὸς ἀνδρὸς γνῶναι ὃ ἔλεγον, τὴν αὐτὴν εἶναι
σκέψιν, ἐπειδάν τις ὅλην τέχνην λάβῃ. λάβωμεν
γὰρ τῷ λόγῳ· γραφικὴ γάρ τίς ἐστι τέχνη τὸ
ὅλον;

ΙΩΝ. Ναί.

ΣΩ. Οὐκοῦν καὶ γραφῆς πολλοὶ καὶ εἰσὶ καὶ
γεγόνασιν ἀγαθοὶ καὶ φαῦλοι;

ΙΩΝ. Πάνυ γε.

ΣΩ. Ἤδη οὖν τινὰ εἶδες, ὅστις περὶ μὲν Πολυγνώτου τοῦ Ἀγλαοφῶντος δεινός ἐστιν ἀποφαίνειν, ἃ εὖ τε γράφει καὶ ἃ μή, περὶ δὲ τῶν
533 ἄλλων γραφέων ἀδύνατος; καὶ ἐπειδὰν μέν τις
τὰ τῶν ἄλλων ζωγράφων ἔργα ἐπιδεικνύῃ, νυστάζει

anyone can see that you are unable to speak on Homer with art and knowledge. For if you could do it with art, you could speak on all the other poets as well ; since there is an art of poetry, I take it, as a whole, is there not ?

ION. Yes.

SOC. And when one has acquired any other art whatever as a whole, the same principle of inquiry holds through all the arts ? Do you require some explanation from me, Ion, of what I mean by this ?

ION. Yes, upon my word, Socrates, I do ; for I enjoy listening to you wise men.

SOC. I only wish you were right there, Ion : but surely it is you rhapsodes and actors, and the men whose poems you chant, who are wise ; whereas I speak but the plain truth, as a simple layman might. For in regard to this question I asked you just now, observe what a trifling commonplace it was that I uttered—a thing that any man might know— namely, that when one has acquired a whole art the inquiry is the same. Let us just think it out thus : there is an art of painting as a whole ?

ION. Yes.

SOC. And there are and have been many painters, good and bad ?

ION. Certainly.

SOC. Now have you ever found anybody who is skilled in pointing out the successes and failures among the works of Polygnotus [1] son of Aglaophon, but unable to do so with the works of the other painters ; and who, when the works of the other painters are exhibited, drops into a doze, and is at a

[1] A celebrated painter who came from Thasos and adorned public buildings in Athens about 470 B.C. Cf. Gorg. 448 B.

τε καὶ ἀπορεῖ καὶ οὐκ ἔχει ὅ τι συμβάληται,
ἐπειδὰν δὲ περὶ Πολυγνώτου ἢ ἄλλου ὅτου βούλει
τῶν γραφέων ἑνὸς μόνου δέῃ ἀποφήνασθαι γνώμην,
ἐγρήγορέ τε καὶ προσέχει τὸν νοῦν καὶ εὐπορεῖ
ὅ τι εἴπῃ;

ΙΩΝ. Οὐ μὰ τὸν Δία, οὐ δῆτα.

ΣΩ. Τί δέ; ἐν ἀνδριαντοποιίᾳ ἤδη τιν' εἶδες,
ὅστις περὶ μὲν Δαιδάλου τοῦ Μητίονος ἢ Ἐπειοῦ
B τοῦ Πανοπέως ἢ Θεοδώρου τοῦ Σαμίου ἢ ἄλλου
τινὸς ἀνδριαντοποιοῦ ἑνὸς πέρι δεινός ἐστιν ἐξηγεῖσθαι ἃ εὖ πεποίηκεν, ἐν δὲ τοῖς τῶν ἄλλων
ἀνδριαντοποιῶν ἔργοις ἀπορεῖ τε καὶ νυστάζει,
οὐκ ἔχων ὅ τι εἴπῃ;

ΙΩΝ. Οὐ μὰ τὸν Δία, οὐδὲ τοῦτον ἑώρακα.

ΣΩ. Ἀλλὰ μήν, ὥς γ' ἐγὼ οἶμαι, οὐδ' ἐν αὐλήσει
γε οὐδὲ ἐν κιθαρίσει οὐδὲ ἐν κιθαρῳδίᾳ οὐδὲ ἐν
ῥαψῳδίᾳ οὐδεπώποτ' εἶδες ἄνδρα, ὅστις περὶ μὲν
C Ὀλύμπου δεινός ἐστιν ἐξηγεῖσθαι ἢ περὶ Θαμύρου
ἢ περὶ Ὀρφέως ἢ περὶ Φημίου τοῦ Ἰθακησίου
ῥαψῳδοῦ, περὶ δὲ Ἴωνος τοῦ Ἐφεσίου ἀπορεῖ
καὶ οὐκ ἔχει συμβαλέσθαι, ἅ τε εὖ ῥαψῳδεῖ καὶ
ἃ μή.

ΙΩΝ. Οὐκ ἔχω σοι περὶ τούτου ἀντιλέγειν, ὦ
Σώκρατες· ἀλλ' ἐκεῖνο ἐμαυτῷ σύνοιδα, ὅτι περὶ
Ὁμήρου κάλλιστ' ἀνθρώπων λέγω καὶ εὐπορῶ
καὶ οἱ ἄλλοι πάντες μέ φασιν εὖ λέγειν, περὶ δὲ
τῶν ἄλλων οὔ. καίτοι ὅρα τοῦτο τί ἔστιν.

---

[1] According to legend, the first sculptor : cf. *Euthyphro*
11, *Meno* 97 D.

ION

loss, and has no remark to offer ; but when he has to pronounce upon Polygnotus or any other painter you please, and on that one only, wakes up and attends and has plenty to say ?

ION. No, on my honour, I certainly have not.

SOC. Or again, in sculpture, have you ever found anyone who is skilled in expounding the successes of Daedalus[1] son of Metion, or Epeius[2] son of Panopeus, or Theodorus[3] of Samos, or any other single sculptor, but in face of the works of the other sculptors is at a loss and dozes, having nothing to say ?

ION. No, on my honour, I have not found such a man as that either.

SOC. But further, I expect you have also failed to find one in fluting or harping or minstrelsy or rhapsodizing who is skilled in expounding the art of Olympus[4] or Thamyras,[5] or Orpheus,[5] or Phemius,[6] the rhapsode of Ithaca, but is at a loss and has no remark to offer on the successes or failures in rhapsody of Ion of Ephesus.

ION. I cannot gainsay you on that, Socrates : but of one thing I am conscious in myself—that I excel all men in speaking on Homer and have plenty to say, and everyone else says that I do it well ; but on the others I am not a good speaker. Yet now, observe what that means.

[2] The maker of the wooden horse at Troy (Homer, *Od.* viii. 493).

[3] A metal-worker (Herodot. i. 51, iii. 41).

[4] One of the mythical inventors of music : *cf. Symp.* 215 E.

[5] A Thracian bard.

[6] The minstrel who was forced to sing to the suitors of Penelope (*Od.* i. 154, xxii. 330).

ΣΩ. Καὶ ὁρῶ, ὦ Ἴων, καὶ ἔρχομαι γέ σοι ἀπο-
D φανούμενος,[1] ὅ μοι δοκεῖ τοῦτο εἶναι. ἔστι γὰρ
τοῦτο τέχνη μὲν οὐκ ὂν παρὰ σοὶ περὶ Ὁμήρου εὖ
λέγειν, ὃ νῦν δὴ ἔλεγον, θεία δὲ δύναμις, ἥ σε
κινεῖ, ὥσπερ ἐν τῇ λίθῳ, ἣν Εὐριπίδης μὲν Μαγνῆτιν
ὠνόμασεν, οἱ δὲ πολλοὶ Ἡρακλείαν. καὶ γὰρ
αὕτη ἡ λίθος οὐ μόνον αὐτοὺς τοὺς δακτυλίους
ἄγει τοὺς σιδηροῦς, ἀλλὰ καὶ δύναμιν ἐντίθησι
τοῖς δακτυλίοις, ὥστ᾽ αὖ δύνασθαι ταὐτὸν τοῦτο
E ποιεῖν ὅπερ ἡ λίθος, ἄλλους ἄγειν δακτυλίους,
ὥστ᾽ ἐνίοτε ὁρμαθὸς μακρὸς πάνυ σιδηρίων καὶ
δακτυλίων ἐξ ἀλλήλων ἤρτηται· πᾶσι δὲ τούτοις
ἐξ ἐκείνης τῆς λίθου ἡ δύναμις ἀνήρτηται. οὕτω
δὲ καὶ ἡ Μοῦσα ἐνθέους μὲν ποιεῖ αὐτή, διὰ δὲ
τῶν ἐνθέων τούτων ἄλλων ἐνθουσιαζόντων ὁρμαθὸς ἐξαρτᾶται. πάντες γὰρ οἵ τε τῶν ἐπῶν
ποιηταὶ οἱ ἀγαθοὶ οὐκ ἐκ τέχνης ἀλλ᾽ ἔνθεοι ὄντες
καὶ κατεχόμενοι πάντα ταῦτα τὰ καλὰ λέγουσι
ποιήματα, καὶ οἱ μελοποιοὶ οἱ ἀγαθοὶ ὡσαύτως,
534 ὥσπερ οἱ κορυβαντιῶντες οὐκ ἔμφρονες ὄντες
ὀρχοῦνται, οὕτω καὶ οἱ μελοποιοὶ οὐκ ἔμφρονες
ὄντες τὰ καλὰ μέλη ταῦτα ποιοῦσιν, ἀλλ᾽ ἐπειδὰν
ἐμβῶσιν εἰς τὴν ἁρμονίαν καὶ εἰς τὸν ῥυθμόν,
βακχεύουσι καὶ κατεχόμενοι, ὥσπερ αἱ βάκχαι
ἀρύονται ἐκ τῶν ποταμῶν μέλι καὶ γάλα κατ-
εχόμεναι, ἔμφρονες δὲ οὖσαι οὔ, καὶ τῶν μελοποιῶν
ἡ ψυχὴ τοῦτο ἐργάζεται, ὅπερ αὐτοὶ λέγουσι.
λέγουσι γὰρ δήπουθεν πρὸς ἡμᾶς οἱ ποιηταί, ὅτι

[1] ἀποφανούμενος Cobet : ἀποφαινόμενος mss.

---

[1] Probably referring to Magnesia in Caria, south of which
was one of the many places called Heraclea. Μαγνῆτις λίθος
occurs in a fragment of Euripides' *Oeneus*.

soc. I do observe it, Ion, and I am going to point out to you what I take it to mean. For, as I was saying just now, this is not an art in you, whereby you speak well on Homer, but a divine power, which moves you like that in the stone which Euripides named a magnet,[1] but most people call " Heraclea stone." For this stone not only attracts iron rings, but also imparts to them a power whereby they in turn are able to do the very same thing as the stone, and attract other rings ; so that sometimes there is formed quite a long chain of bits of iron and rings, suspended one from another ; and they all depend for this power on that one stone. In the same manner also the Muse inspires men herself, and then by means of these inspired persons the inspiration spreads to others, and holds them in a connected chain. For all the good epic poets utter all those fine poems not from art, but as inspired and possessed, and the good lyric poets likewise ; just as the Corybantian[2] worshippers do not dance when in their senses, so the lyric poets do not indite those fine songs in their senses, but when they have started on the melody and rhythm they begin to be frantic, and it is under possession—as the bacchants are possessed, and not in their senses, when they draw honey and milk from the rivers—that the soul of the lyric poets does the same thing, by their own report. For the poets tell us, I believe, that the songs they

[2] The Corybantes were priests of Cybele or Rhea, mother of Zeus and other Olympian gods, and she was worshipped with wild music and frenzied dancing which, like the bacchic revels or orgies of women in honour of Dionysus, carried away the participants despite and beyond themselves. *Cf.* Eurip. *Bacchae.*

PLATO

B ἀπὸ κρηνῶν μελιρρύτων ἐκ Μουσῶν κήπων τινῶν
καὶ ναπῶν δρεπόμενοι τὰ μέλη ἡμῖν φέρουσιν
ὥσπερ αἱ μέλιτται, καὶ αὐτοὶ οὕτω πετόμενοι·
καὶ ἀληθῆ λέγουσι. κοῦφον γὰρ χρῆμα ποιητής
ἐστι καὶ πτηνὸν καὶ ἱερόν, καὶ οὐ πρότερον οἷός
τε ποιεῖν, πρὶν ἂν ἔνθεός τε γένηται καὶ ἔκφρων
καὶ ὁ νοῦς μηκέτι ἐν αὐτῷ ἐνῇ· ἕως δ' ἂν τουτὶ
ἔχῃ τὸ κτῆμα, ἀδύνατος πᾶς ποιεῖν ἐστιν ἄνθρωπος
καὶ χρησμῳδεῖν. ἅτε οὖν οὐ τέχνῃ ποιοῦντες
καὶ πολλὰ λέγοντες καὶ καλὰ περὶ τῶν πραγμάτων,
C ὥσπερ σὺ περὶ Ὁμήρου, ἀλλὰ θείᾳ μοίρᾳ, τοῦτο
μόνον οἷός τε ἕκαστος ποιεῖν καλῶς, ὃ ἡ ἐφ'
Μοῦσα αὐτὸν ὥρμησεν, ὁ μὲν διθυράμβους, ὁ δὲ
ἐγκώμια, ὁ δὲ ὑπορχήματα, ὁ δ' ἔπη, ὁ δ' ἰάμβους·
τὰ δ' ἄλλα φαῦλος αὐτῶν ἕκαστός ἐστιν. οὐ γὰρ
τέχνῃ ταῦτα λέγουσιν, ἀλλὰ θείᾳ δυνάμει, ἐπεί,
εἰ περὶ ἑνὸς τέχνῃ καλῶς ἠπίσταντο λέγειν, κἂν
περὶ τῶν ἄλλων ἁπάντων· διὰ ταῦτα δὲ ὁ θεὸς
ἐξαιρούμενος τούτων τὸν νοῦν τούτοις χρῆται
ὑπηρέταις καὶ τοῖς χρησμῳδοῖς καὶ τοῖς μάντεσι
D τοῖς θείοις, ἵνα ἡμεῖς οἱ ἀκούοντες εἰδῶμεν, ὅτι
οὐχ οὗτοί εἰσιν οἱ ταῦτα λέγοντες οὕτω πολλοῦ
ἄξια, οἷς νοῦς μὴ πάρεστιν, ἀλλ' ὁ θεὸς αὐτός
ἐστιν ὁ λέγων, διὰ τούτων δὲ φθέγγεται πρὸς
ἡμᾶς. μέγιστον δὲ τεκμήριον τῷ λόγῳ Τύννιχος
ὁ Χαλκιδεύς, ὃς ἄλλο μὲν οὐδὲν πώποτ' ἐποίησε
ποίημα, ὅτου τις ἂν ἀξιώσειε μνησθῆναι, τὸν δὲ
παίωνα ὃν πάντες ᾄδουσι, σχεδόν τι πάντων

---

bring us are the sweets they cull from honey-dropping founts in certain gardens and glades of the Muses— like the bees, and winging the air as these do.[1] And what they tell is true. For a poet is a light and winged and sacred thing, and is unable ever to indite until he has been inspired and put out of his senses, and his mind is no longer in him : every man, whilst he retains possession of that, is powerless to indite a verse or chant an oracle. Seeing then that it is not by art that they compose and utter so many fine things about the deeds of men—as you do about Homer—but by a divine dispensation, each is able only to compose that to which the Muse has stirred him, this man dithyrambs, another laudatory odes, another dance-songs, another epic or else iambic verse ; but each is at fault in any other kind. For not by art do they utter these things, but by divine influence ; since, if they had fully learnt by art to speak on one kind of theme, they would know how to speak on all. And for this reason God takes away the mind of these men and uses them as his ministers, just as he does soothsayers and godly seers, in order that we who hear them may know that it is not they who utter these words of great price, when they are out of their wits, but that it is God himself who speaks and addresses us through them. A convincing proof of what I say is the case of Tynnichus,[2] the Chalcidian, who had never composed a single poem in his life that could deserve any mention, and then produced the paean [3] which is in everyone's

praise of the early tragedian Phrynichus (*Birds* 750)—" he sipped the fruits of ambrosial lays, ever bringing away sweet song."

[2] Nothing else is known of this poet.

[3] A hymn in honour of a god, usually Apollo.

PLATO

μελῶν κάλλιστον, ἀτεχνῶς, ὅπερ αὐτὸς λέγει,
" εὕρημά τι Μοισᾶν." ἐν τούτῳ γὰρ δὴ μάλιστά
E ἐμοι δοκεῖ ὁ θεὸς ἐνδείξασθαι ἡμῖν, ἵνα μὴ δι-
στάζωμεν, ὅτι οὐκ ἀνθρώπινά ἐστι τὰ καλὰ ταῦτα
ποιήματα οὐδὲ ἀνθρώπων, ἀλλὰ θεῖα καὶ θεῶν, οἱ
δὲ ποιηταὶ οὐδὲν ἀλλ' ἢ ἑρμηνῆς εἰσι τῶν θεῶν,
κατεχόμενοι ἐξ ὅτου ἂν ἕκαστος κατέχηται.
ταῦτα ἐνδεικνύμενος ὁ θεὸς ἐξεπίτηδες διὰ τοῦ
φαυλοτάτου ποιητοῦ τὸ κάλλιστον μέλος ᾖσεν·
535 ἢ οὐ δοκῶ σοι ἀληθῆ λέγειν, ὦ Ἴων;

ΙΩΝ. Ναὶ μὰ τὸν Δία, ἔμοιγε· ἅπτει γάρ πώς
μου τοῖς λόγοις τῆς ψυχῆς, ὦ Σώκρατες, καί μοι
δοκοῦσι θείᾳ μοίρᾳ ἡμῖν παρὰ τῶν θεῶν ταῦτα οἱ
ἀγαθοὶ ποιηταὶ ἑρμηνεύειν.

ΣΩ. Οὐκοῦν ὑμεῖς αὖ οἱ ῥαψῳδοὶ τὰ τῶν ποιητῶν ἑρμηνεύετε;

ΙΩΝ. Καὶ τοῦτο ἀληθὲς λέγεις.

ΣΩ. Οὐκοῦν ἑρμηνέων ἑρμηνῆς γίγνεσθε;

ΙΩΝ. Παντάπασί γε.

B ΣΩ. Ἔχε δή μοι τόδε εἰπέ, ὦ Ἴων, καὶ μὴ ἀπο-
κρύψῃ ὅ τι ἄν σε ἔρωμαι· ὅταν εὖ εἴπῃς ἔπη καὶ
ἐκπλήξῃς μάλιστα τοὺς θεωμένους, ἢ τὸν Ὀδυσσέα
ὅταν ἐπὶ τὸν οὐδὸν ἐφαλλόμενον ᾄδῃς, ἐκφανῆ
γιγνόμενον τοῖς μνηστῆρσι καὶ ἐκχέοντα τοὺς
οἰστοὺς πρὸ τῶν ποδῶν, ἢ Ἀχιλλέα ἐπὶ τὸν Ἕκτορα
ὁρμῶντα, ἢ καὶ τῶν περὶ Ἀνδρομάχην ἐλεινῶν
τι ἢ περὶ Ἑκάβην ἢ περὶ Πρίαμον, τότε πότερον
ἔμφρων εἶ, ἢ ἔξω σαυτοῦ γίγνῃ καὶ παρὰ τοῖς

---

[1] *Od.* xxii. 2 foll.
[2] *Il.* xxii. 312 foll.

mouth, almost the finest song we have, simply—as he says himself—" an invention of the Muses." For the god, as it seems to me, intended him to be a sign to us that we should not waver or doubt that these fine poems are not human or the work of men, but divine and the work of gods ; and that the poets are merely the interpreters of the gods, according as each is possessed by one of the heavenly powers. To show this forth, the god of set purpose sang the finest of songs through the meanest of poets : or do you not think my statement true, Ion ?

ION. Yes, upon my word, I do : for you somehow touch my soul with your words, Socrates, and I believe it is by divine dispensation that good poets interpret to us these utterances of the gods.

soc. And you rhapsodes, for your part, interpret the utterances of the poets ?

ION. Again your words are true.

soc. And so you act as interpreters of interpreters ?

ION. Precisely.

soc. Stop now and tell me, Ion, without reserve what I may choose to ask you : when you give a good recitation and specially thrill your audience, either with the lay of Odysseus [1] leaping forth on to the threshold, revealing himself to the suitors and pouring out the arrows before his feet, or of Achilles [2] dashing at Hector, or some part of the sad story of Andromache [3] or of Hecuba,[4] or of Priam,[5] are you then in your senses, or are you carried out of yourself, and does your soul in an ecstasy suppose herself to be

[3] *Il.* vi. 370-502 ; xxii. 437-515.
[4] *Il.* xxii. 430-36 ; xxiv. 747-59.
[5] *Il.* xxii. 408-28 ; xxiv. 144-717.

C πράγμασιν οἴεταί σου εἶναι ἡ ψυχὴ οἷς λέγεις
ἐνθουσιάζουσα, ἢ ἐν Ἰθάκῃ οὖσιν ἢ ἐν Τροίᾳ ἢ
ὅπως ἂν καὶ τὰ ἔπη ἔχῃ;

ΙΩΝ. Ὡς ἐναργές μοι τοῦτο, ὦ Σώκρατες, τὸ
τεκμήριον εἶπες· οὐ γάρ σε ἀποκρυψάμενος ἐρῶ.
ἐγὼ γὰρ ὅταν ἐλεεινόν τι λέγω, δακρύων ἐμπίπλαν-
ταί μου οἱ ὀφθαλμοί· ὅταν τε φοβερὸν ἢ δεινόν,
ὀρθαὶ αἱ τρίχες ἵστανται ὑπὸ φόβου καὶ ἡ καρδία
πηδᾷ.

D ΣΩ. Τί οὖν; φῶμεν, ὦ Ἴων, ἔμφρονα εἶναι
τότε τοῦτον τὸν ἄνθρωπον, ὃς ἂν κεκοσμημένος
ἐσθῆτι ποικίλῃ καὶ χρυσοῖς στεφάνοις κλαίῃ τ᾽
ἐν θυσίαις καὶ ἑορταῖς, μηδὲν ἀπολωλεκὼς τούτων,
ἢ φοβῆται πλέον ἢ ἐν δισμυρίοις ἀνθρώποις ἑστηκὼς
φιλίοις, μηδενὸς ἀποδύοντος ἢ ἀδικοῦντος;

ΙΩΝ. Οὐ μὰ τὸν Δία, οὐ πάνυ, ὦ Σώκρατες, ὥς
γε τἀληθὲς εἰρῆσθαι.

ΣΩ. Οἶσθα οὖν ὅτι καὶ τῶν θεατῶν τοὺς πολλοὺς
ταὐτὰ ταῦτα ὑμεῖς ἐργάζεσθε;

E ΙΩΝ. Καὶ μάλα καλῶς οἶδα· καθορῶ γὰρ ἑκάστοτε
αὐτοὺς ἄνωθεν ἀπὸ τοῦ βήματος κλαίοντάς τε καὶ
δεινὸν ἐμβλέποντας καὶ συνθαμβοῦντας τοῖς λεγο-
μένοις. δεῖ γάρ με καὶ σφόδρ᾽ αὐτοῖς τὸν νοῦν
προσέχειν· ὡς ἐὰν μὲν κλαίοντας αὐτοὺς καθίσω,
αὐτὸς γελάσομαι ἀργύριον λαμβάνων, ἐὰν δὲ γελῶντας, αὐτὸς κλαύσομαι ἀργύριον ἀπολλύς.

ΣΩ. Οἶσθα οὖν ὅτι οὗτός ἐστιν ὁ θεατὴς τῶν
δακτυλίων ὁ ἔσχατος, ὧν ἐγὼ ἔλεγον ὑπὸ τῆς
Ἡρακλειώτιδος λίθου ἀπ᾽ ἀλλήλων τὴν δύναμιν
536 λαμβάνειν; ὁ δὲ μέσος σὺ ὁ ῥαψῳδὸς καὶ ὑποκριτής,
ὁ δὲ πρῶτος αὐτὸς ὁ ποιητής· ὁ δὲ θεὸς διὰ πάντων
τούτων ἕλκει τὴν ψυχὴν ὅποι ἂν βούληται τῶν

among the scenes you are describing, whether they be in Ithaca, or in Troy, or as the poems may chance to place them ?

ION. How vivid to me, Socrates, is this part of your proof! For I will tell you without reserve : when I relate a tale of woe, my eyes are filled with tears ; and when it is of fear or awe, my hair stands on end with terror, and my heart leaps.

soc. Well now, are we to say, Ion, that such a person is in his senses at that moment,—when in all the adornment of elegant attire and golden crowns he weeps at sacrifice or festival, having been despoiled of none of his finery ; or shows fear as he stands before more than twenty thousand friendly people, none of whom is stripping or injuring him ?

ION. No, on my word, not at all, Socrates, to tell the strict truth.

soc. And are you aware that you rhapsodes produce these same effects on most of the spectators also ?

ION. Yes, very fully aware : for I look down upon them from the platform and see them at such moments crying and turning awestruck eyes upon me and yielding to the amazement of my tale. For I have to pay the closest attention to them ; since, if I set them crying, I shall laugh myself because of the money I take, but if they laugh, I myself shall cry because of the money I lose.

soc. And are you aware that your spectator is the last of the rings which I spoke of as receiving from each other the power transmitted from the Heraclean lodestone ? You, the rhapsode and actor, are the middle ring ; the poet himself is the first ; but it is the god who through the whole series draws the

ἀνθρώπων, ἀνακρεμαννὺς ἐξ ἀλλήλων τὴν δύναμιν.
καὶ ὥσπερ ἐκ τῆς λίθου ἐκείνης ὁρμαθὸς πάμπολυς
ἐξήρτηται χορευτῶν τε καὶ διδασκάλων καὶ ὑπο-
διδασκάλων, ἐκ πλαγίου ἐξηρτημένων τῶν τῆς
Μούσης ἐκκρεμαμένων δακτυλίων. καὶ ὁ μὲν
τῶν ποιητῶν ἐξ ἄλλης Μούσης, ὁ δὲ ἐξ ἄλλης
B ἐξήρτηται· ὀνομάζομεν δὲ αὐτὸ κατέχεται· τὸ δέ
ἐστι παραπλήσιον· ἔχεται γάρ· ἐκ δὲ τούτων τῶν
πρώτων δακτυλίων, τῶν ποιητῶν, ἄλλοι ἐξ ἄλλου
αὖ ἠρτημένοι εἰσὶ καὶ ἐνθουσιάζουσιν, οἱ μὲν ἐξ
Ὀρφέως, οἱ δὲ ἐκ Μουσαίου· οἱ δὲ πολλοὶ ἐξ
Ὁμήρου κατέχονταί τε καὶ ἔχονται. ὧν σύ, ὦ
Ἴων, εἷς εἶ καὶ κατέχῃ ἐξ Ὁμήρου, καὶ ἐπειδὰν
μέν τις ἄλλου του ποιητοῦ ᾄδῃ, καθεύδεις τε καὶ
ἀπορεῖς ὅ τι λέγῃς, ἐπειδὰν δὲ τούτου τοῦ ποιητοῦ
φθέγξηταί τις μέλος, εὐθὺς ἐγρήγορας καὶ ὀρχεῖταί
C σου ἡ ψυχὴ καὶ εὐπορεῖς ὅ τι λέγῃς· οὐ γὰρ τέχνῃ
οὐδ' ἐπιστήμῃ περὶ Ὁμήρου λέγεις ἃ λέγεις, ἀλλὰ
θείᾳ μοίρᾳ καὶ κατοκωχῇ· ὥσπερ οἱ κορυβαντιῶντες ἐκείνου μόνου αἰσθάνονται τοῦ μέλους ὀξέως,
ὃ ἂν ᾖ τοῦ θεοῦ ἐξ ὅτου ἂν κατέχωνται, καὶ εἰς
ἐκεῖνο τὸ μέλος καὶ σχημάτων καὶ ῥημάτων εὐ-
ποροῦσι, τῶν δὲ ἄλλων οὐ φροντίζουσιν· οὕτω καὶ
σύ, ὦ Ἴων, περὶ μὲν Ὁμήρου ὅταν τις μνησθῇ,
εὐπορεῖς, περὶ δὲ τῶν ἄλλων ἀπορεῖς· τούτου δ'
D ἐστὶ τὸ αἴτιον, ὅ μ' ἐρωτᾷς, δι' ὅ τι σὺ περὶ μὲν
Ὁμήρου εὐπορεῖς, περὶ δὲ τῶν ἄλλων οὔ, ὅτι οὐ
τέχνῃ ἀλλὰ θείᾳ μοίρᾳ Ὁμήρου δεινὸς εἶ ἐπαινέτης.

ΙΩΝ. Σὺ μὲν εὖ λέγεις, ὦ Σώκρατες· θαυμάζοιμι
μέντ' ἂν εἰ οὕτως εὖ εἴποις, ὥστε με ἀναπεῖσαι,

souls of men whithersoever he pleases, making the power of one depend on the other. And, just as from the magnet, there is a mighty chain of choric performers and masters and under-masters suspended by side-connexions from the rings that hang down from the Muse. One poet is suspended from one Muse, another from another : the word we use for it is " possessed," but it is much the same thing, for he is *held*. And from these first rings—the poets— are suspended various others, which are thus inspired, some by Orpheus and others by Musaeus [1] ; but the majority are possessed and held by Homer. Of whom you, Ion, are one, and are possessed by Homer ; and so, when anyone recites the work of another poet, you go to sleep and are at a loss what to say ; but when some one utters a strain of your poet, you wake up at once, and your soul dances, and you have plenty to say : for it is not by art or knowledge about Homer that you say what you say, but by divine dis- pensation and possession ; just as the Corybantian worshippers are keenly sensible of that strain alone which belongs to the god whose possession is on them, and have plenty of gestures and phrases for that tune, but do not heed any other. And so you, Ion, when the subject of Homer is mentioned, have plenty to say, but nothing on any of the others. And when you ask me the reason why you can speak at large on Homer but not on the rest, I tell you it is because your skill in praising Homer comes not by art, but by divine dispensation.

ION. Well spoken, I grant you, Socrates : but still I shall be surprised if you can speak well enough to

[1] A legendary bard to whom certain oracular verses were ascribed.

ὡς ἐγὼ κατεχόμενος καὶ μαινόμενος Ὅμηρον
ἐπαινῶ. οἶμαι δὲ οὐδ' ἂν σοὶ δόξαιμι, εἴ μου
ἀκούσαις λέγοντος περὶ Ὁμήρου.

ΣΩ. Καὶ μὴν ἐθέλω γε ἀκοῦσαι, οὐ μέντοι
E πρότερον πρὶν ἄν μοι ἀποκρίνῃ τόδε· ὧν Ὅμηρος
λέγει περὶ τίνος εὖ λέγεις; οὐ γὰρ δήπου περὶ
ἁπάντων γε.

ΙΩΝ. Εὖ ἴσθι, ὦ Σώκρατες, περὶ οὐδενὸς ὅτου
οὔ.

ΣΩ. Οὐ δήπου καὶ περὶ τούτων, ὧν σὺ μὲν
τυγχάνεις οὐκ εἰδώς, Ὅμηρος δὲ λέγει.

ΙΩΝ. Καὶ ταῦτα ποῖά ἐστιν, ἃ Ὅμηρος μὲν
λέγει, ἐγὼ δὲ οὐκ οἶδα;

537 ΣΩ. Οὐ καὶ περὶ τεχνῶν μέντοι λέγει πολλαχοῦ
Ὅμηρος καὶ πολλά; οἷον καὶ περὶ ἡνιοχείας—ἐὰν
μνησθῶ τὰ ἔπη, ἐγώ σοι φράσω.

ΙΩΝ. Ἀλλ' ἐγὼ ἐρῶ· ἐγὼ γὰρ μέμνημαι.

ΣΩ. Εἰπὲ δή μοι ἃ λέγει Νέστωρ Ἀντιλόχῳ
τῷ υἱεῖ, παραινῶν εὐλαβηθῆναι περὶ τὴν καμπὴν
ἐν τῇ ἱπποδρομίᾳ τῇ ἐπὶ Πατρόκλῳ.

ΙΩΝ. Κλινθῆναι δέ, φησί, καὶ αὐτὸς ἐϋξέστῳ
ἐνὶ δίφρῳ
ἦκ' ἐπ' ἀριστερὰ τοῖιν· ἀτὰρ τὸν δεξιὸν ἵππον
B κένσαι ὁμοκλήσας, εἶξαί τέ οἱ ἡνία χερσίν.
ἐν νύσσῃ δέ τοι ἵππος ἀριστερὸς ἐγχριμφθήτω,
ὡς ἄν τοι πλήμνη γε δοάσσεται ἄκρον ἱκέσθαι
κύκλου ποιητοῖο· λίθου δ' ἀλέασθαι ἐπαυρεῖν.

ΣΩ. Ἀρκεῖ. ταῦτα δή, ὦ Ἴων, τὰ ἔπη εἴτε
C ὀρθῶς λέγει Ὅμηρος εἴτε μή, πότερος ἂν γνοίη
ἄμεινον, ἰατρὸς ἢ ἡνίοχος;

430

convince me that I am possessed and mad when I praise Homer. Nor can I think you would believe it of me yourself, if you heard me speaking about him.

soc. I declare I am quite willing to hear you, but not until you have first answered me this : on what thing in Homer's story do you speak well ? Not on all of them, I presume.

ion. I assure you, Socrates, on all without a single exception.

soc. Not, of course, including those things of which you have in fact no knowledge, but which Homer tells.

ion. And what sort of things are they, which Homer tells, but of which I have no knowledge ?

soc. Why, does not Homer speak a good deal about arts, in a good many places ? For instance, about chariot-driving : if I can recall the lines, I will quote them to you.

ion. No, I will recite them, for I can remember.

soc. Tell me then what Nestor says to his son Antilochus, advising him to be careful about the turning-post in the horse-race in honour of Patroclus.[1]

ion. Bend thyself in the polished car slightly to the left of them ;[2] and call to the right-hand horse and goad him on, while your hand slackens his reins. And at the post let your left-hand horse swerve close, so that the nave of the well-wrought wheel may seem to come up to the edge of the stone, which yet avoid to touch.

soc. Enough. Now, Ion, will a doctor or a charioteer be the better judge whether Homer speaks correctly or not in these lines ?

[1] *Il.* xxiii. 335 foll.
[2] *i.e.* one of the two white stones, set up at each end of the course, which had been mentioned six lines before.

PLATO

ΙΩΝ. Ἡνίοχος δήπου.

ΣΩ. Πότερον ὅτι τέχνην ταύτην ἔχει ἢ κατ᾽ ἄλλο τι;

ΙΩΝ. Οὔκ, ἀλλ᾽ ὅτι τέχνην.

ΣΩ. Οὐκοῦν ἑκάστῃ τῶν τεχνῶν ἀποδέδοταί τι ὑπὸ τοῦ θεοῦ ἔργον οἷά τε εἶναι γιγνώσκειν; οὐ γάρ που ἃ κυβερνητικῇ γιγνώσκομεν, γνωσόμεθα καὶ ἰατρικῇ.

ΙΩΝ. Οὐ δῆτα.

ΣΩ. Οὐδέ γε ἃ ἰατρικῇ, ταῦτα καὶ τεκτονικῇ.

ΙΩΝ. Οὐ δῆτα.

D ΣΩ. Οὐκοῦν οὕτω καὶ κατὰ πασῶν τῶν τεχνῶν, ἃ τῇ ἑτέρᾳ τέχνῃ γιγνώσκομεν, οὐ γνωσόμεθα τῇ ἑτέρᾳ; τόδε δέ μοι πρότερον τούτου ἀπόκριναι· τὴν μὲν ἑτέραν φῂς εἶναί τινα τέχνην, τὴν δ᾽ ἑτέραν;

ΙΩΝ. Ναί.

ΣΩ. Ἆρα ὥσπερ ἐγώ, τεκμαιρόμενος, ὅταν ἡ μὲν ἑτέρων πραγμάτων ᾖ ἐπιστήμη, ἡ δ᾽ ἑτέρων, οὕτω καλῶ τὴν μὲν ἄλλην, τὴν δὲ ἄλλην τέχνην, οὕτω καὶ σύ;

E ΙΩΝ. Ναί.

ΣΩ. Εἰ γάρ που τῶν αὐτῶν πραγμάτων ἐπιστήμη εἴη τις, τί ἂν τὴν μὲν ἑτέραν φαῖμεν εἶναι, τὴν δ᾽ ἑτέραν, ὁπότε γε ταὐτὰ εἴη εἰδέναι ἀπ᾽ ἀμφοτέρων; ὥσπερ ἐγώ τε γιγνώσκω ὅτι πέντε εἰσὶν οὗτοι οἱ δάκτυλοι, καὶ σύ, ὥσπερ ἐγώ, περὶ τούτων ταὐτὰ γιγνώσκεις· καὶ εἴ σε ἐγὼ ἐροίμην, εἰ τῇ αὐτῇ τέχνῃ γιγνώσκομεν τῇ ἀριθμητικῇ τὰ αὐτὰ ἐγώ τε καὶ σύ, ἢ ἄλλῃ, φαίης ἂν δήπου τῇ αὐτῇ.

ΙΩΝ. Ναί.

538 ΣΩ. Ὃ τοίνυν ἄρτι ἔμελλον ἐρήσεσθαί σε,

432

ion. A charioteer, of course.

soc. Because he has this art, or for some other reason ?

ion. No, because it is his art.

soc. And to every art has been apportioned by God a power of knowing a particular business ? For I take it that what we know by the art of piloting we cannot also know by that of medicine.

ion. No, to be sure.

soc. And what we know by medicine, we cannot by carpentry also ?

ion. No, indeed.

soc. And this rule holds for all the arts, that what we know by one of them we cannot know by another ? But before you answer that, just tell me this : do you agree that one art is of one sort, and another of another ?

ion. Yes.

soc. Do you argue this as I do, and call one art different from another when one is a knowledge of one kind of thing, and another a knowledge of another kind ?

ion. Yes.

soc. Since, I suppose, if it were a knowledge of the same things—how could we say that one was different from another, when both could give us the same knowledge ? Just as I know that there are five of these fingers, and you equally know the same fact about them ; and if I should ask you whether both you and I know this same fact by the same art of numeration, or by different arts, you would reply, I presume, that it was by the same ?

ion. Yes.

soc. Then tell me now, what I was just going to

νυνὶ εἰπέ, εἰ κατὰ πασῶν τῶν τεχνῶν οὕτω σοι
δοκεῖ, τῇ μὲν αὐτῇ τέχνῃ τὰ αὐτὰ ἀναγκαῖον
εἶναι γιγνώσκειν, τῇ δ' ἑτέρᾳ μὴ τὰ αὐτά, ἀλλ'
εἴπερ ἄλλη ἐστί, ἀναγκαῖον καὶ ἕτερα γιγνώσκειν.

ΙΩΝ. Οὕτω μοι δοκεῖ, ὦ Σώκρατες.

ΣΩ. Οὐκοῦν ὅστις ἂμ μὴ ἔχῃ τινὰ τέχνην, ταύτης τῆς τέχνης τὰ λεγόμενα ἢ πραττόμενα καλῶς
γιγνώσκειν οὐχ οἷός τ' ἔσται;

B   ΙΩΝ. Ἀληθῆ λέγεις.

ΣΩ. Πότερον οὖν περὶ τῶν ἐπῶν ὧν εἶπες, εἴτε
καλῶς λέγει Ὅμηρος εἴτε μή, σὺ κάλλιον γνώσῃ
ἢ ἡνίοχος;

ΙΩΝ. Ἡνίοχος.

ΣΩ. Ῥαψῳδὸς γάρ που εἶ, ἀλλ' οὐχ ἡνίοχος.

ΙΩΝ. Ναί.

ΣΩ. Ἡ δὲ ῥαψῳδικὴ τέχνη ἑτέρα ἐστὶ τῆς
ἡνιοχικῆς;

ΙΩΝ. Ναί.

ΣΩ. Εἰ ἄρα ἑτέρα, περὶ ἑτέρων καὶ ἐπιστήμη
πραγμάτων ἐστίν.

ΙΩΝ. Ναί.

ΣΩ. Τί δὲ δή, ὅταν Ὅμηρος λέγῃ, ὡς τετρω-
C μένῳ τῷ Μαχάονι Ἑκαμήδη ἡ Νέστορος παλλακὴ
κυκεῶνα πίνειν δίδωσι; καὶ λέγει πως οὕτως·

οἴνῳ Πραμνείῳ, φησίν, ἐπὶ δ' αἴγειον κνῇ τυρὸν
κνήστι χαλκείῃ· παρὰ δὲ κρόμυον ποτῷ ὄψον·

ταῦτα εἴτε ὀρθῶς λέγει Ὅμηρος εἴτε μή, πότερον
ἰατρικῆς ἐστι διαγνῶναι καλῶς ἢ ῥαψῳδικῆς;

---

[1] *Il.* xi. 639-40. The quotation, as Plato indicates, is not
accurate. Machaon was the son of Asclepius and physician
to the Greeks at Troy. Nothing is known of " Pramneian

434

ask you, whether you think this rule holds for all the arts—that by the same art we must know the same things, and by a different art things that are not the same ; but if the art is other, the things we know by it must be different also.

ION. I think it is so, Socrates.

SOC. Then he who has not a particular art will be incapable of knowing aright the words or works of that art ?

ION. True.

SOC. Then will you or a charioteer be the better judge of whether Homer speaks well or not in the lines that you quoted ?

ION. A charioteer.

SOC. Because, I suppose, you are a rhapsode and not a charioteer.

ION. Yes.

SOC. And the rhapsode's art is different from the charioteer's ?

ION. Yes.

SOC. Then if it is different, it is also a knowledge of different things.

ION. Yes.

SOC. Now, what of the passage where Homer tells how Hecamede, Nestor's concubine, gives the wounded Machaon a posset ? His words are something like this : [1]

Of Pramneian wine it was, and therein she grated cheese of goat's milk with a grater of bronze ; and thereby an onion as a relish for drink.

Is it for the doctor's or the rhapsode's art to discern aright whether Homer speaks correctly here or not ?

wine," except that it was " thick and nutritious " (Athen. i. 10 B).

ΙΩΝ. Ἰατρικῆς.

ΣΩ. Τί δέ, ὅταν λέγῃ Ὅμηρος·

D   ἡ δὲ μολυβδαίνῃ ἰκέλη ἐς βυσσὸν ἵκανεν,
ἥ τε κατ’ ἀγραύλοιο βοὸς κέρας ἐμμεμαυῖα
ἔρχεται ὠμηστῇσι μετ’ ἰχθύσι πῆμα φέρουσα·

ταῦτα πότερον φῶμεν ἁλιευτικῆς εἶναι τέχνης
μᾶλλον κρῖναι ἢ ῥαψῳδικῆς, ἄττα λέγει καὶ εἴτε
καλῶς εἴτε μή;

ΙΩΝ. Δῆλον δή, ὦ Σώκρατες, ὅτι ἁλιευτικῆς.

ΣΩ. Σκέψαι δή, σοῦ ἐρομένου, εἰ ἔροιό με·

E   “ ἐπειδὴ τοίνυν, ὦ Σώκρατες, τούτων τῶν τεχνῶν
ἐν Ὁμήρῳ εὑρίσκεις ἃ προσήκει ἑκάστῃ διακρίνειν,
ἴθι μοι ἔξευρε καὶ τὰ τοῦ μάντεώς τε καὶ μαντικῆς,
ποῖά ἐστιν ἃ προσήκει αὐτῷ οἵῳ τ’ εἶναι διαγιγνώσκειν, εἴτε εὖ εἴτε κακῶς πεποίηται ”—σκέψαι
ὡς ῥᾳδίως τε καὶ ἀληθῆ ἐγώ σοι ἀποκρινοῦμαι.
πολλαχοῦ μὲν γὰρ καὶ ἐν Ὀδυσσείᾳ λέγει, οἷον
καὶ ἃ ὁ τῶν Μελαμποδιδῶν λέγει μάντις πρὸς τοὺς
μνηστῆρας, Θεοκλύμενος·

539   δαιμόνιοι, τί κακὸν τόδε πάσχετε; νυκτὶ μὲν ὑμέων
εἰλύαται κεφαλαί τε πρόσωπά τε νέρθε τε γυῖα,
οἰμωγὴ δὲ δέδηε, δεδάκρυνται δὲ παρειαί·
εἰδώλων τε πλέον πρόθυρον, πλείη δὲ καὶ αὐλὴ
ἱεμένων ἔρεβόσδε ὑπὸ ζόφον· ἠέλιος δὲ
οὐρανοῦ ἐξαπόλωλε, κακὴ δ’ ἐπιδέδρομεν ἀχλύς·

B   πολλαχοῦ δὲ καὶ ἐν Ἰλιάδι, οἷον καὶ ἐπὶ τειχομαχίᾳ·
λέγει γὰρ καὶ ἐνταῦθα

---

[1] *Il.* xxiv. 80-82. The nature of this device is still in
dispute. Plutarch (*De sollertia animal.* 977) supports
Aristotle's view that the horn acted as a sheath to protect
the line from being bitten through by the fish.

ION. For the doctor's.

SOC. Well now, when Homer says :

And she passed to the bottom like a plummet[1] which, set on a horn from an ox of the field, goes in haste to bring mischief among the ravenous fishes.

are we to say it is for the fisherman's or for the rhapsode's art to decide what he means by this, and whether it is rightly or wrongly spoken ?

ION. Clearly, Socrates, for the fisherman's art.

SOC. Then please observe : suppose you were questioning me and should ask : " Since therefore, Socrates, you find it is for these several arts to appraise the passages of Homer that belong to each, be so good as to make out those also that are for the seer and the seer's art, and show me the sort of passages that come under his ability to distinguish whether they are well or ill done "; observe how easily and truly I shall answer you. For he has many passages, both in the *Odyssey*, as for instance the words of Theoclymenus, the seer of the line of Melampus, to the suitors : [2]

Hapless men, what bane is this afflicts you ? Your heads and faces and limbs below are shrouded in night, and wailing is enkindled, and cheeks are wet with tears : of ghosts the porch is full, and the court full of them also, hastening hell-wards 'neath the gloom ; and the sun is perished out of heaven, and an evil mist is spread abroad ;

and there are many passages in the *Iliad* also, as in the fight at the rampart,[3] where he says :

[2] *Od.* xx. 351-57. Melampus, the ancestor of Theoclymenus (*cf. Od.* xv. 225-56), was supposed to have been the first mortal who possessed the gift of prophecy.

[3] *Il.* xii. 200-7.

ὄρνις γάρ σφιν ἐπῆλθε περησέμεναι μεμαῶσιν,
αἰετὸς ὑψιπέτης, ἐπ' ἀριστερὰ λαὸν ἐέργων,
C φοινήεντα δράκοντα φέρων ὀνύχεσσι πέλωρον,
ζωόν, ἔτ' ἀσπαίροντα· καὶ οὔπω λήθετο χάρμης.
κόψε γὰρ αὐτὸν ἔχοντα κατὰ στῆθος παρὰ δειρὴν
ἰδνωθεὶς ὀπίσω, ὁ δ' ἀπὸ ἔθεν ἧκε χαμᾶζε
ἀλγήσας ὀδύνῃσι, μέσῳ δ' ἐγκάββαλ' ὁμίλῳ·
D αὐτὸς δὲ κλάγξας πέτετο πνοιῇς ἀνέμοιο.

ταῦτα φήσω καὶ τὰ τοιαῦτα τῷ μάντει προσήκειν
καὶ σκοπεῖν καὶ κρίνειν.

ΙΩΝ. Ἀληθῆ γε σὺ λέγεις, ὦ Σώκρατες.

ΣΩ. Καὶ σύ γε, ὦ Ἴων, ἀληθῆ ταῦτα λέγεις.
ἴθι δὴ καὶ σὺ ἐμοί, ὥσπερ ἐγὼ σοὶ ἐξέλεξα καὶ ἐξ
Ὀδυσσείας καὶ ἐξ Ἰλιάδος ὁποῖα τοῦ μάντεώς ἐστι
E καὶ ὁποῖα τοῦ ἰατροῦ καὶ ὁποῖα τοῦ ἁλιέως, οὕτω
καὶ σὺ ἐμοὶ ἔκλεξον, ἐπειδὴ καὶ ἐμπειρότερος εἶ
ἐμοῦ τῶν Ὁμήρου, ὁποῖα τοῦ ῥαψῳδοῦ ἐστίν, ὦ
Ἴων, καὶ τῆς τέχνης τῆς ῥαψῳδικῆς, ἃ τῷ ῥαψῳδῷ
προσήκει καὶ σκοπεῖσθαι καὶ διακρίνειν παρὰ
τοὺς ἄλλους ἀνθρώπους.

ΙΩΝ. Ἐγὼ μέν φημι, ὦ Σώκρατες, ἅπαντα.

ΣΩ. Οὐ σύ γε φῇς,[1] ὦ Ἴων, ἅπαντα· ἢ οὕτως
ἐπιλήσμων εἶ; καίτοι οὐκ ἂν πρέποι γε ἐπι-
λήσμονα εἶναι ῥαψῳδὸν ἄνδρα.

540 ΙΩΝ. Τί δὲ δὴ ἐπιλανθάνομαι;

ΣΩ. Οὐ μέμνησαι ὅτι ἔφησθα τὴν ῥαψῳδικὴν
τέχνην ἑτέραν εἶναι τῆς ἡνιοχικῆς;

ΙΩΝ. Μέμνημαι.

ΣΩ. Οὐκοῦν καὶ ἑτέραν οὖσαν ἕτερα γνώσεσθαι
ὡμολόγεις;

---

[1] φῄς Baiter: ἔφης mss.

ION

For as they were eager to pass over, a bird had crossed them, an eagle of lofty flight, pressing the host at the left hand, and bearing a blood-red monster of a snake, alive and still struggling; nor had it yet unlearnt the lust of battle. For bending back it smote its captor on the breast by the neck, and the bird in the bitterness of pain cast it away to the ground, and dropped it down in the midst of the throng; and then with a cry flew off on the wafting winds.

This passage, and others of the sort, are those that I should say the seer has to examine and judge.

ION. And you speak the truth, Socrates.

SOC. And so do you, Ion, in saying that. Now you must do as I did, and in return for my picking out from the *Odyssey* and the *Iliad* the kinds of passage that belong severally to the seer, the doctor, and the fisherman, you have now to pick out for me —since you are so much more versed in Homer than I—the kinds which belong to the rhapsode, Ion, and the rhapsode's art, and which he should be able to consider and distinguish beyond the rest of mankind.

ION. What I say, Socrates, is—" all passages."

SOC. Surely you do not say " all," Ion! Can you be so forgetful? And yet forgetfulness would ill become a rhapsode.

ION. Why, how am I forgetting?

SOC. Do you not remember that you said that the art of the rhapsode was different from that of the charioteer?

ION. I remember.

SOC. And you also admitted that, being different, it would know different things?

ΙΩΝ. Ναί.

ΣΩ. Οὐκ ἄρα πάντα γε γνώσεται ἡ ῥαψῳδικὴ κατὰ τὸν σὸν λόγον, οὐδὲ ὁ ῥαψῳδός.

ΙΩΝ. Πλήν γε ἴσως τὰ τοιαῦτα, ὦ Σώκρατες.

B ΣΩ. Τὰ τοιαῦτα δὲ λέγεις πλὴν τὰ τῶν ἄλλων τεχνῶν σχεδόν τι· ἀλλὰ ποῖα δὴ γνώσεται, ἐπειδὴ οὐχ ἅπαντα;

ΙΩΝ. Ἃ πρέπει, οἶμαι ἔγωγε, ἀνδρὶ εἰπεῖν καὶ ὁποῖα γυναικί, καὶ ὁποῖα δούλῳ καὶ ὁποῖα ἐλευθέρῳ, καὶ ὁποῖα ἀρχομένῳ καὶ ὁποῖα ἄρχοντι.

ΣΩ. Ἆρ᾽ ὁποῖα ἄρχοντι, λέγεις, ἐν θαλάττῃ χειμαζομένου πλοίου πρέπει εἰπεῖν, ὁ ῥαψῳδὸς γνώσεται κάλλιον ἢ ὁ κυβερνήτης;

ΙΩΝ. Οὔκ, ἀλλὰ ὁ κυβερνήτης τοῦτό γε.

C ΣΩ. Ἀλλ᾽ ὁποῖα ἄρχοντι κάμνοντος πρέπει εἰπεῖν, ὁ ῥαψῳδὸς γνώσεται κάλλιον ἢ ὁ ἰατρός;

ΙΩΝ. Οὐδὲ τοῦτο.

ΣΩ. Ἀλλ᾽ οἷα δούλῳ πρέπει, λέγεις;

ΙΩΝ. Ναί.

ΣΩ. Οἷον βουκόλῳ λέγεις δούλῳ ἃ πρέπει εἰπεῖν ἀγριαινουσῶν βοῶν παραμυθουμένῳ, ὁ ῥαψῳδὸς γνώσεται, ἀλλ᾽ οὐχ ὁ βουκόλος;

ΙΩΝ. Οὐ δῆτα.

ΣΩ. Ἀλλ᾽ οἷα γυναικὶ πρέποντά ἐστιν εἰπεῖν ταλασιουργῷ περὶ ἐρίων ἐργασίας;

D ΙΩΝ. Οὔ.

ΣΩ. Ἀλλ᾽ οἷα ἀνδρὶ πρέπει εἰπεῖν γνώσεται στρατηγῷ στρατιώταις παραινοῦντι;

440

ION. Yes.

soc. Then by your own account the rhapsode's art cannot know everything, nor the rhapsode either.

ION. Let us say, everything except those instances, Socrates.

soc. By " those instances " you imply the subjects of practically all the other arts. Well, as he does not know all of them, which kinds will he know ?

ION. Those things, I imagine, that it befits a man to say, and the sort of thing that a woman should say ; the sort for a slave and the sort for a freeman ; and the sort for a subject or for a ruler.

soc. Do you mean that the rhapsode will know better than the pilot what sort of thing a ruler of a storm-tossed vessel at sea should say ?

ION. No, the pilot knows better in that case.

soc. Well, will the rhapsode know better than the doctor what sort of thing a ruler of a sick man should say ?

ION. Not in that case either.

soc. But he will know the sort for a slave, you say ?

ION. Yes.

soc. For instance, if the slave is a cowherd, you say the rhapsode will know what the other should say to pacify his cows when they get fierce, but the cowherd will not ?

ION. That is not so.

soc. Well, the sort of thing that a woman ought to say—a spinning-woman—about the working of wool ?

ION. No.

soc But he will know what a man should say, when he is a general exhorting his men ?

441

ΙΩΝ. Ναί, τὰ τοιαῦτα γνώσεται ὁ ῥαψῳδός.

ΣΩ. Τί δέ; ἡ ῥαψῳδικὴ τέχνη στρατηγική ἐστιν;

ΙΩΝ. Γνοίην γοῦν ἂν ἔγωγε οἷα στρατηγὸν πρέπει εἰπεῖν.

ΣΩ. Ἴσως γὰρ εἶ καὶ στρατηγικός, Ἴων. καὶ γὰρ εἰ ἐτύγχανες ἱππικὸς ὢν ἅμα καὶ κιθαριστικός, ἔγνως ἂν ἵππους εὖ καὶ κακῶς ἱππαζομένους· Ε ἀλλ' εἴ σ' ἐγὼ ἠρόμην, "ποτέρᾳ δὴ τέχνῃ, ὦ Ἴων, γιγνώσκεις τοὺς εὖ ἱππαζομένους ἵππους; ἢ ἱππεὺς εἶ ἢ ᾗ κιθαριστής;" τί ἄν μοι ἀπεκρίνω;

ΙΩΝ. Ἦι ἱππεύς, ἔγωγ' ἄν.

ΣΩ. Οὐκοῦν εἰ καὶ τοὺς εὖ κιθαρίζοντας διεγίγνωσκες, ὡμολόγεις ἄν, ᾗ κιθαριστὴς εἶ, ταύτῃ διαγιγνώσκειν, ἀλλ' οὐχ ᾗ ἱππεύς.

ΙΩΝ. Ναί.

ΣΩ. Ἐπειδὴ δὲ τὰ στρατιωτικὰ γιγνώσκεις, πότερον ᾗ στρατηγικὸς εἶ γιγνώσκεις ἢ ᾗ ῥαψῳδὸς ἀγαθός;

ΙΩΝ. Οὐδὲν ἔμοιγε δοκεῖ διαφέρειν.

541 ΣΩ. Πῶς; οὐδὲν λέγεις διαφέρειν; μίαν λέγεις τέχνην εἶναι τὴν ῥαψῳδικὴν καὶ στρατηγικὴν ἢ δύο;

ΙΩΝ. Μία ἔμοιγε δοκεῖ.

ΣΩ. Ὅστις ἄρα ἀγαθὸς ῥαψῳδός ἐστιν, οὗτος καὶ ἀγαθὸς στρατηγὸς τυγχάνει ὤν;

ΙΩΝ. Μάλιστα, ὦ Σώκρατες.

ΣΩ. Οὐκοῦν καὶ ὅστις ἀγαθὸς στρατηγὸς τυγχάνει ὤν, ἀγαθὸς καὶ ῥαψῳδός ἐστιν.

ΙΩΝ. Οὐκ αὖ μοι δοκεῖ τοῦτο.

ION

ION Yes, that sort of thing the rhapsode will know.

soc. Well, but is the art of the rhapsode the art of the general?

ION. I, at any rate, should know what a general ought to say.

soc. Yes, since I daresay you are good at generalship also, Ion. For in fact, if you happened to have skill in horsemanship as well as in the lyre, you would know when horses were well or ill managed : but if I asked you, " By which art is it, Ion, that you know that horses are being well managed, by your skill as a horseman, or as a player of the lyre ? " what would your answer be ?

ION. I should say, by my skill as a horseman.

soc. And if again you were distinguishing the good lyre-players, you would admit that you distinguished by your skill in the lyre, and not by your skill as a horseman.

ION. Yes.

soc. And when you judge of military matters, do you judge as having skill in generalship, or as a good rhapsode ?

ION. To my mind, there is no difference.

soc. What, no difference, do you say ? Do you mean that the art of the rhapsode and the general is one, not two ?

ION. It is one, to my mind.

soc. So that anyone who is a good rhapsode is also, in fact, a good general ?

ION. Certainly, Socrates.

soc. And again, anyone who happens to be a good general is also a good rhapsode.

ION. No ; there I do not agree.

ΣΩ. Ἀλλ' ἐκεῖνο μὴν δοκεῖ σοι, ὅστις γε ἀγαθὸς
Β ῥαψῳδός, καὶ στρατηγὸς ἀγαθὸς εἶναι;

ΙΩΝ. Πάνυ γε.

ΣΩ. Οὐκοῦν σὺ τῶν Ἑλλήνων ἄριστος ῥαψῳδὸς
εἶ;

ΙΩΝ. Πολύ γε, ὦ Σώκρατες.

ΣΩ. Ἦ καὶ στρατηγός, ὦ Ἴων, τῶν Ἑλλήνων
ἄριστος εἶ;

ΙΩΝ. Εὖ ἴσθι, ὦ Σώκρατες· καὶ ταῦτά γε ἐκ
τῶν Ὁμήρου μαθών.

ΣΩ. Τί δή ποτ' οὖν πρὸς τῶν θεῶν, ὦ Ἴων,
ἀμφότερα ἄριστος ὢν τῶν Ἑλλήνων, καὶ στρατηγὸς
καὶ ῥαψῳδός, ῥαψῳδεῖς μὲν περιιὼν τοῖς Ἕλλησι,
C στρατηγεῖς δ' οὔ; ἢ ῥαψῳδοῦ μὲν δοκεῖ σοι
χρυσῷ στεφάνῳ ἐστεφανωμένου πολλὴ χρεία εἶναι
τοῖς Ἕλλησι, στρατηγοῦ δὲ οὐδεμία;

ΙΩΝ. Ἡ μὲν γὰρ ἡμετέρα, ὦ Σώκρατες, πόλις
ἄρχεται ὑπὸ ὑμῶν καὶ στρατηγεῖται καὶ οὐδὲν
δεῖται στρατηγοῦ, ἡ δὲ ὑμετέρα καὶ ἡ Λακεδαι-
μονίων οὐκ ἄν με ἕλοιτο στρατηγόν· αὐτοὶ γὰρ
οἴεσθε ἱκανοὶ εἶναι.

ΣΩ. Ὦ βέλτιστε Ἴων, Ἀπολλόδωρον οὐ γιγνώσκεις τὸν Κυζικηνόν;

ΙΩΝ. Ποῖον τοῦτον;

ΣΩ. Ὃν Ἀθηναῖοι πολλάκις ἑαυτῶν στρατηγὸν
D ᾕρηνται ξένον ὄντα· καὶ Φανοσθένη τὸν Ἄνδριον
καὶ Ἡρακλείδην τὸν Κλαζομένιον, οὓς ἥδε ἡ
πόλις ξένους ὄντας, ἐνδειξαμένους ὅτι ἄξιοι λόγου
εἰσί, καὶ εἰς στρατηγίας καὶ εἰς τὰς ἄλλας ἀρχὰς
ἄγει· Ἴωνα δ' ἄρα τὸν Ἐφέσιον οὐχ αἱρήσεται
στρατηγὸν καὶ τιμήσει, ἐὰν δοκῇ ἄξιος λόγου
εἶναι; τί δέ, οὐκ Ἀθηναῖοι μέν ἐστε οἱ Ἐφέσιοι

444

ION

soc. But still you agree that anyone who is a good rhapsode is also a good general?

ion. To be sure.

soc. And you are the best rhapsode in Greece?

ion. Far the best, Socrates.

soc. Are you also, Ion, the best general in Greece?

ion. Be sure of it, Socrates; and that I owe to my study of Homer.

soc. Then how, in Heaven's name, can it be, Ion, that you, who are both the best general and the best rhapsode in Greece, go about performing as a rhapsode to the Greeks, but not as a general? Or do you suppose that the Greeks feel a great need of a rhapsode in the glory of his golden crown, but of a general none at all?

ion. It is because my city,[1] Socrates, is under the rule and generalship of your people, and is not in want of a general; whilst you and Sparta would not choose me as a general, since you think you manage well enough for yourselves.

soc. My excellent Ion, you are acquainted with Apollodorus[2] of Cyzicus, are you not?

ion. What might he be?

soc. A man whom the Athenians have often chosen as their general, though a foreigner; and Phanosthenes[3] of Andros, and Heracleides[2] of Clazomenae, whom my city invests with the high command and other offices although they are foreigners, because they have proved themselves to be competent. And will she not choose Ion of Ephesus as her general, and honour him, if he shows himself competent? Why, you Ephesians are by

[1] Ephesus.   [2] Nothing else is known of this general.
[3] Captured the Thurian admiral Dorieus, 407 B.C.

445

τὸ ἀρχαῖον, καὶ ἡ Ἔφεσος οὐδεμιᾶς ἐλάττων
E πόλεως· ἀλλὰ σὺ γάρ, ὦ Ἴων, εἰ μὲν ἀληθῆ λέγεις,
ὡς τέχνῃ καὶ ἐπιστήμῃ οἷός τε εἶ Ὅμηρον ἐπαινεῖν,
ἀδικεῖς, ὅστις ἐμοὶ ὑποσχόμενος, ὡς πολλὰ καὶ
καλὰ περὶ Ὁμήρου ἐπίστασαι, καὶ φάσκων ἐπιδείξειν, ἐξαπατᾷς με καὶ πολλοῦ δεῖς ἐπιδεῖξαι,
ὅς γε οὐδὲ ἅττα ἐστὶ ταῦτα, περὶ ὧν δεινὸς εἶ,
ἐθέλεις εἰπεῖν, πάλαι ἐμοῦ λιπαροῦντος, ἀλλ᾽
ἀτεχνῶς ὥσπερ ὁ Πρωτεὺς παντοδαπὸς γίγνῃ
στρεφόμενος ἄνω καὶ κάτω, ἕως τελευτῶν διαφυγών
με στρατηγὸς ἀνεφάνης, ἵνα μὴ ἐπιδείξῃς ὡς
542 δεινὸς εἶ τὴν περὶ Ὁμήρου σοφίαν. εἰ μὲν οὖν
τεχνικὸς ὤν, ὅπερ νῦν δὴ ἔλεγον, περὶ Ὁμήρου
ὑποσχόμενος ἐπιδείξειν ἐξαπατᾷς με, ἄδικος εἶ·
εἰ δὲ μὴ τεχνικὸς εἶ, ἀλλὰ θείᾳ μοίρᾳ κατεχόμενος
ἐξ Ὁμήρου μηδὲν εἰδὼς πολλὰ καὶ καλὰ λέγεις
περὶ τοῦ ποιητοῦ, ὥσπερ ἐγὼ εἶπον περὶ σοῦ,
οὐδὲν ἀδικεῖς. ἑλοῦ οὖν πότερα βούλει νομίζεσθαι
ὑπὸ ἡμῶν ἄδικος ἀνὴρ εἶναι ἢ θεῖος.

ΙΩΝ. Πολὺ διαφέρει, ὦ Σώκρατες· πολὺ γὰρ
κάλλιον τὸ θεῖον νομίζεσθαι.

B ΣΩ. Τοῦτο τοίνυν τὸ κάλλιον ὑπάρχει σοι παρ᾽
ἡμῖν, ὦ Ἴων, θεῖον εἶναι καὶ μὴ τεχνικὸν περὶ
Ὁμήρου ἐπαινέτην.

origin Athenians,[1] are you not, and Ephesus is inferior to no city ? But in fact, Ion, if you are right in saying it is by art and knowledge that you are able to praise Homer, you are playing me false : you have professed to me that you know any amount of fine things about Homer, and you promise to display them ; but you are only deceiving me, and so far from displaying the subjects of your skill, you decline even to tell me what they are, for all my entreaties. You are a perfect Proteus in the way you take on every kind of shape, twisting about this way and that, until at last you elude my grasp in the guise of a general, so as to avoid displaying your skill in Homeric lore. Now if you are an artist and, as I was saying just now, you only promised me a display about Homer to deceive me, you are playing me false; whilst if you are no artist, but speak fully and finely about Homer, as I said you did, without any knowledge but by a divine dispensation which causes you to be possessed by the poet, you play quite fair. Choose therefore which of the two you prefer us to call you, dishonest or divine.

ION. The difference is great, Socrates ; for it is far nobler to be called divine.

soc. Then you may count on this nobler title in our minds, Ion, of being a divine and not an artistic praiser of Homer.

[1] Androclus of Attica founded Ephesus as the Ionian city known to the Greeks of Plato's time.

INDEX

Achilles, 425
Aërope, 48 n.
Ammon, 5
Anaxagoras, 269 n.
Androclus, 447
Andromache, 425
Anger, 331, 341 ; sometimes false, 307
Anticipation, 275
Antilochus, 431
Aphrodite, 207
Apollodorus, 445
Archilochus, 411, 415
Aristocracy, 157, 163
Arithmetic, two kinds, 361 ff.
Arts, 201
Asclepius, 407
Athena, 67 n.
Athenians, 123
Athens, 135

Beauty, 201, 343, 345, 389, 391, 393, 395
Biped, man a featherless, 71, 73, 75
Bonds, divine and human, 187 ff., 193
Book, 299

Callias, 199, 229
Captain of ship, 147 ff.
Carding, 89, 93, 185
Cause, 91, 243, 255, 257, 267, 269, 391 ; contingent, 91, 111, 119 ; actual, 91
Class and part, 25 f.
Cold, 273, 275
Comedy, 331, 339, 341
Corybants, 421, 429
Creative agent, 255
Cronus, 49, 57, 59, 61, 73
Cynics, 199

Daedalus, 419
Deficiency, 97, 99, 105
Demeter, 67 n.
Democracy, 125, 163, 164 n.
Desire, 283, 285, 309
Dialectic, 367
Diameter, 37 f.
Dionysus, 67 n., 379

Egypt, 123
Elements, 263, 265, 267
Envy, 331, 337, 339, 341
Epeius, 419
Ephesus, 445-7
Epidaurus, 407
Eucleides, 199
Euripides, 421
Excess, 97, 99, 105

Family, 191
Fear, 331 ; sometimes false, 307
Finite, 221, 243, 245, 249, 251, 253, 257, 259, 267
Fitness, 109, 201
Forgetfulness, 279
Fulling, 89

Glaucon, 409
Good, derived from beauty, proportion, and truth, 391
Gorgias, 291 n., 367, 369, 371
Government, forms of, 125 ff., 145, 157, 159, 161
Grammar, 225

Heat, 273, 275
Hecamede, 435
Hector, 425
Hecuba, 425
Hephaestus, 67, 379
Heraclea, 420-1

INDEX

Heracleides, 445
Heracleitus, 315 n.
Heracles, 57 n.
Herd, herding, herdsman, 21 ff., 59, 69 ff., 115
Hermes, 48 n.
Hesiod, 411, 415
Homer, 146 n., 331 n., 383, 409 ff.
Homeridae, 409
Hope, 275, 303
Hunger, 273, 283

Infinite, 221, 225, 243, 245, 247, 249, 251, 253, 257, 259, 267, 269, 309
Ion, 403 ff.
Isocrates, 404
Itch, 325

Jealousy, 331, 341
Judges, 173

King, 2-195 passim
Knowledge, 211 f., 259, 261, 345, 346, 359, 371, 395 ; pure and impure, 363, 379

Lamb, golden, 49
Laws, 133 ff., 145 ff., 159 ff., 173, 191
Letters, 79, 81, 105, 223, 225
Life, of pleasure, 235 f. ; of mind, 237 f. ; mixed, 239, 257, 377, 379 ff. ; three lives, 317
Limit, 253, 267
Love, 331, 341

Machaon, 435
Magnet, 421 ff.
Man, a featherless biped, 41
Mean, the, 99, 101, 103
Measure, 201, 389, 393
Measurement, 97 ff., 359
Melampus, 437
Memory, 203, 279 ff., 285, 291, 299, 377
Mending, 89
Menelaus, 56 n.
Metrodorus, 409
Mind, 201-397 passim
Mixture, of perfect life, 200, 379 ff. ; of pleasure and pain, 325 ff., 333, 335 ff., 371
Moderation, 201, 395
Monarchy, 125, 163, 164 n.
Mourning, 331, 339, 341

Musaeus, 429
Myrtilus, 48 n.

Nestor, 431, 435
Number, 251

Odysseus, 425
Oligarchy, 125, 157, 163, 164 n.
Olympus (musician), 419
Opinion, 79, 81, 201, 395 ; true and false, 291, 305, 369, 377
Orpheus, 419, 429

Paean, 423
Pain, 271 ff., 289, 309, 311, 313, 317, 319, 325, 343 ; caused by great changes, 315 ; true and false, 289 ff., 305
Painting, 417-19
Panathenaea, 407
Part and class, 25 f.
Patroclus, 431
Pelopidae, 48 n.
Perception, 279 f., 285, 291, 395
Perfection, 201, 395
Phanosthenes, 445
Phemius, 419
Philebus, 199-397 passim
Phrynichus, 423
Physician, 131, 139, 141, 147 ff.
Pictures, 77 ; in the soul, 301 f. ; 305
Pig, 39 n.
Pleasure, 201-399 passim ; kinds of, 207 ff., 229 ; true and false, 289 ff., 305, 306 ; caused by great changes, 315 ; intense, 321 ff., 347 ; pure and impure, 343 ff. ; a process or generation, 351 ff.
Pleiades, 48 n.
Plutarch, 436
Polygnotus, 417-19
Possessions in the state, 113 ff.
Pramneian wine, 434-5
Priam, 425
Prometheus, 67
Proportion. 201, 389, 391, 395
Protarchus, 199-399 passim
Proteus, 447

Recollection, 281 f.
Revolution, of universe, 51 ff.
Rhapsodes, 403 ff.
Rhetoric, 171
Ridiculous, 333 ff.

449

INDEX

Sciences, division of, 9 ff. ; kingly science, 9-195 *passim*; defined, 43, 127, 129, 131, 133, 155, 167, 169, 191, 201
Sculpture, 419
Shepherds, divine, 59, 69, 71, 75
Slaves and servants, 119 ff.
Smell, 345
Socrates, *passim*; young S., 2-195 *passim*
Sophist, 2, 3, 9, 39, 101, 107, 125, 151, 165, 167
Soul, 81, 187, 275, 279, 281, 283, 285, 299, 309, 327, 329, 331, 341, 357, 369, 395
Sound, 223, 225
Spinning, 93
Statesman, 2-195 *passim*
Statue-makers, 75
Stesimbrotus, 409
Stranger, Eleatic, 2-195 *passim*
Sun, change in course of, 49 ff.
Syllables, 79, 81

Thamyras, 419
Theaetetus, 2
Theoclymenus, 437
Theodorus, 2-195 *passim*

Theodorus (sculptor), 419
Thirst, 273, 283
Thyestes, 49
Tickling, 327
Tragedy, 331, 339, 341
Truth, 349, 369, 379, 387, 391
Tynnichus, 423
Tyranny, 127, 164 n.
Tyrant, 75

Unity, 213 ff., 225
Universe, revolution of, 51 ff.

Virtue, divisions of, 177 ff.

Warp, 95, 97, 187
Weaving, 83, 85 ff., 107, 111, 175, 185, 187
White, whiteness, 349 ff., 369
Wisdom, 201-397 *passim*; kinds of, 229
Woof, 95, 97, 187

Xenophon, 404

Yearning, 331, 341

Zeus, 48 n., 59, 267, 283, 395

Printed in Great Britain by R. & R. CLARK, LIMITED, *Edinburgh*

THE LOEB CLASSICAL LIBRARY

VOLUMES ALREADY PUBLISHED

LATIN AUTHORS

AMMIANUS MARCELLINUS. J. C. Rolfe. 3 Vols.

APULEIUS: THE GOLDEN ASS (METAMORPHOSES). W. Adlington (1566). Revised by S. Gaselee.

ST. AUGUSTINE: CITY OF GOD. 7 Vols. Vol. I. G. E. McCracken. Vol. VI. W. C. Greene.

ST. AUGUSTINE, CONFESSIONS OF. W. Watts (1631). 2 Vols.

ST. AUGUSTINE: SELECT LETTERS. J. H. Baxter.

AUSONIUS. H. G. Evelyn White. 2 Vols.

BEDE. J. E. King. 2 Vols.

BOETHIUS: TRACTS AND DE CONSOLATIONE PHILOSOPHIAE. Rev. H. F. Stewart and E. K. Rand.

CAESAR: ALEXANDRIAN, AFRICAN AND SPANISH WARS. A. G. Way.

CAESAR: CIVIL WARS. A. G. Peskett.

CAESAR: GALLIC WAR. H. J. Edwards.

CATO AND VARRO: DE RE RUSTICA. H. B. Ash and W. D. Hooper.

CATULLUS. F. W. Cornish; TIBULLUS. J. B. Postgate; and PERVIGILIUM VENERIS. J. W. Mackail.

CELSUS: DE MEDICINA. W. G. Spencer. 3 Vols.

CICERO: BRUTUS AND ORATOR. G. L. Hendrickson and H. M. Hubbell.

CICERO: DE FINIBUS. H. Rackham.

CICERO: DE INVENTIONE, etc. H. M. Hubbell.

CICERO: DE NATURA DEORUM AND ACADEMICA. H. Rackham.

1

THE LOEB CLASSICAL LIBRARY

CICERO : DE OFFICIIS. Walter Miller.
CICERO : DE ORATORE, etc. 2 Vols. Vol. I : DE ORATORE,
Books I and II. E. W. Sutton and H. Rackham. Vol. II :
DE ORATORE, Book III ; DE FATO ; PARADOXA STOI-
CORUM ; DE PARTITIONE ORATORIA. H. Rackham.
CICERO : DE REPUBLICA, DE LEGIBUS, SOMNIUM SCIPIONIS.
Clinton W. Keyes.
CICERO : DE SENECTUTE, DE AMICITIA, DE DIVINATIONE.
W. A. Falconer.
CICERO : IN CATILINAM, PRO MURENA, PRO SULLA, PRO
FLACCO. Louis E. Lord.
CICERO : LETTERS TO ATTICUS. E. O. Winstedt. 3 Vols.
CICERO : LETTERS TO HIS FRIENDS. W. Glynn Williams.
3 Vols.
CICERO : PHILIPPICS. W. C. A. Ker.
CICERO : PRO ARCHIA, POST REDITUM, DE DOMO, DE HA-
RUSPICUM RESPONSIS, PRO PLANCIO. N. H. Watts.
CICERO : PRO CAECINA, PRO LEGE MANILIA, PRO CLUENTIO,
PRO RABIRIO. H. Grose Hodge.
CICERO : PRO CAELIO, DE PROVINCIIS CONSULARIBUS, PRO
BALBO. R. Gardner.
CICERO : PRO MILONE, IN PISONEM, PRO SCAURO, PRO
FONTEIO, PRO RABIRIO POSTUMO, PRO MARCELLO, PRO
LIGARIO, PRO REGE DEIOTARO. N. H. Watts.
CICERO : PRO QUINCTIO, PRO ROSCIO AMERINO, PRO ROSCIO
COMOEDO, CONTRA RULLUM. J. H. Freese.
CICERO : PRO SESTIO, IN VATINIUM. R. Gardner.
[CICERO] : RHETORICA AD HERENNIUM. H. Caplan.
CICERO : TUSCULAN DISPUTATIONS. J. E. King.
CICERO : VERRINE ORATIONS. L. H. G. Greenwood. 2 Vols.
CLAUDIAN. M. Platnauer. 2 Vols.
COLUMELLA : DE RE RUSTICA ; DE ARBORIBUS. H. B. Ash,
E. S. Forster, E. Heffner. 3 Vols.
CURTIUS, Q. : HISTORY OF ALEXANDER. J. C. Rolfe. 2 Vols.
FLORUS. E. S. Forster : and CORNELIUS NEPOS. J. C. Rolfe.
FRONTINUS : STRATAGEMS AND AQUEDUCTS. C. E. Bennett
and M. B. McElwain.
FRONTO : CORRESPONDENCE. C. R. Haines. 2 Vols.
GELLIUS. J. C. Rolfe. 3 Vols.
HORACE : ODES AND EPODES. C. E. Bennett.
HORACE : SATIRES, EPISTLES, ARS POETICA. H. R. Fairclough.
JEROME : SELECT LETTERS. F. A. Wright.
JUVENAL AND PERSIUS. G. G. Ramsay.

2

THE LOEB CLASSICAL LIBRARY

Livy. B. O. Foster, F. G. Moore, Evan T. Sage, A. C. Schlesinger and R. M. Geer (General Index). 14 Vols.

Lucan. J. D. Duff.

Lucretius. W. H. D. Rouse.

Martial. W. C. A. Ker. 2 Vols.

Minor Latin Poets: from Publilius Syrus to Rutilius Namatianus, including Grattius, Calpurnius Siculus, Nemesianus, Avianus, with " Aetna," " Phoenix " and other poems. J. Wight Duff and Arnold M. Duff.

Ovid: The Art of Love and other Poems. J. H. Mozley.

Ovid: Fasti. Sir James G. Frazer.

Ovid: Heroides and Amores. Grant Showerman.

Ovid: Metamorphoses. F. J. Miller. 2 Vols.

Ovid: Tristia and Ex Ponto. A. L. Wheeler.

Petronius. M. Heseltine: Seneca: Apocolocyntosis. W. H. D. Rouse.

Plautus. Paul Nixon. 5 Vols.

Pliny: Letters. Melmoth's translation revised by W. M. L. Hutchinson. 2 Vols.

Pliny: Natural History. 10 Vols. Vols. I-V and IX. H. Rackham. Vols. VI-VIII. W. H. S. Jones. Vol. X. D. E. Eichholz.

Propertius. H. E. Butler.

Prudentius. H. J. Thomson. 2 Vols.

Quintilian. H. E. Butler. 4 Vols.

Remains of Old Latin. E. H. Warmington. 4 Vols. Vol. I (Ennius and Caecilius). Vol. II (Livius, Naevius, Pacuvius, Accius). Vol. III (Lucilius, Laws of the XII Tables). Vol. IV (Archaic Inscriptions).

Sallust. J. C. Rolfe.

Scriptores Historiae Augustae. D. Magie. 3 Vols.

Seneca: Apocolocyntosis. Cf. Petronius.

Seneca: Epistulae Morales. R. M. Gummere. 3 Vols.

Seneca: Moral Essays. J. W. Basore. 3 Vols.

Seneca: Tragedies. F. J. Miller. 2 Vols.

Sidonius: Poems and Letters. W. B. Anderson. 2 Vols.

Silius Italicus. J. D. Duff. 2 Vols.

Statius. J. H. Mozley. 2 Vols.

Suetonius. J. C. Rolfe. 2 Vols.

Tacitus: Dialogus. Sir Wm. Peterson: and Agricola and Germania. Maurice Hutton.

Tacitus: Histories and Annals. C. H. Moore and J. Jackson. 4 Vols.

3

THE LOEB CLASSICAL LIBRARY

TERENCE. John Sargeaunt. 2 Vols.
TERTULLIAN: APOLOGIA AND DE SPECTACULIS. T. R. Glover;
    MINUCIUS FELIX. G. H. Rendall.
VALERIUS FLACCUS. J. H. Mozley.
VARRO: DE LINGUA LATINA. R. G. Kent. 2 Vols.
VELLEIUS PATERCULUS AND RES GESTAE DIVI AUGUSTI. F. W.
    Shipley.
VIRGIL. H. R. Fairclough. 2 Vols.
VITRUVIUS: DE ARCHITECTURA. F. Granger. 2 Vols.

GREEK AUTHORS

ACHILLES TATIUS. S. Gaselee.
AELIAN: ON THE NATURE OF ANIMALS. A. F. Scholfield.
    3 Vols.
AENEAS TACTICUS, ASCLEPIODOTUS AND ONASANDER. The
    Illinois Greek Club.
AESCHINES. C. D. Adams.
AESCHYLUS. H. Weir Smyth. 2 Vols.
ALCIPHRON, AELIAN AND PHILOSTRATUS: LETTERS. A. R.
    Benner and F. H. Fobes.
APOLLODORUS. Sir James G. Frazer. 2 Vols.
APOLLONIUS RHODIUS. R. C. Seaton.
THE APOSTOLIC FATHERS. Kirsopp Lake. 2 Vols.
APPIAN'S ROMAN HISTORY. Horace White. 4 Vols.
ARATUS. Cf. CALLIMACHUS.
ARISTOPHANES. Benjamin Bickley Rogers. 3 Vols. Verse
    trans.
ARISTOTLE: ART OF RHETORIC. J. H. Freese.
ARISTOTLE: ATHENIAN CONSTITUTION, EUDEMIAN ETHICS,
    VIRTUES AND VICES. H. Rackham.
ARISTOTLE: GENERATION OF ANIMALS. A. L. Peck.
ARISTOTLE: METAPHYSICS. H. Tredennick. 2 Vols.
ARISTOTLE: METEOROLOGICA. H. D. P. Lee.
ARISTOTLE: MINOR WORKS. W. S. Hett. "On Colours,"
    "On Things Heard," "Physiognomics," "On Plants,"
    "On Marvellous Things Heard," "Mechanical Problems,"
    "On Indivisible Lines," "Situations and Names of
    Winds," "On Melissus, Xenophanes, and Gorgias."
ARISTOTLE: NICOMACHEAN ETHICS. H. Rackham.

4

THE LOEB CLASSICAL LIBRARY

ARISTOTLE: OECONOMICA AND MAGNA MORALIA. G. C. Armstrong. (With Metaphysics, Vol. II.)

ARISTOTLE: ON THE HEAVENS. W. K. C. Guthrie.

ARISTOTLE: ON THE SOUL, PARVA NATURALIA, ON BREATH. W. S. Hett.

ARISTOTLE: THE CATEGORIES. ON INTERPRETATION. H. P. Cooke; PRIOR ANALYTICS. H. Tredennick.

ARISTOTLE: POSTERIOR ANALYTICS. H. Tredennick; TOPICS. E. S. Forster.

ARISTOTLE: SOPHISTICAL REFUTATIONS. COMING-TO-BE AND PASSING-AWAY. E. S. Forster. ON THE COSMOS. D. J. Furley.

ARISTOTLE: PARTS OF ANIMALS. A. L. Peck; MOTION AND PROGRESSION OF ANIMALS. E. S. Forster.

ARISTOTLE: PHYSICS. Rev. P. Wicksteed and F. M. Cornford. 2 Vols.

ARISTOTLE: POETICS; LONGINUS ON THE SUBLIME. W. Hamilton Fyfe; DEMETRIUS ON STYLE. W. Rhys Roberts.

ARISTOTLE: POLITICS. H. Rackham.

ARISTOTLE: PROBLEMS. W. S. Hett. 2 Vols.

ARISTOTLE: RHETORICA AD ALEXANDRUM. H. Rackham. (With Problems, Vol. II.)

ARRIAN: HISTORY OF ALEXANDER AND INDICA. Rev. E. Iliffe Robson. 2 Vols.

ATHENAEUS: DEIPNOSOPHISTAE. C. B. Gulick. 7 Vols.

ST. BASIL: LETTERS. R. J. Deferrari. 4 Vols.

CALLIMACHUS: FRAGMENTS. C. A. Trypanis.

CALLIMACHUS: HYMNS AND EPIGRAMS, AND LYCOPHRON. A. W. Mair; ARATUS. G. R. Mair.

CLEMENT OF ALEXANDRIA. Rev. G. W. Butterworth.

COLLUTHUS. *Cf.* OPPIAN.

DAPHNIS AND CHLOE. *Cf.* LONGUS.

DEMOSTHENES I: OLYNTHIACS, PHILIPPICS AND MINOR ORATIONS: I-XVII AND XX. J. H. Vince.

DEMOSTHENES II: DE CORONA AND DE FALSA LEGATIONE. C. A. Vince and J. H. Vince.

DEMOSTHENES III: MEIDIAS, ANDROTION, ARISTOCRATES, TIMOCRATES, ARISTOGEITON. J. H. Vince.

DEMOSTHENES IV-VI: PRIVATE ORATIONS AND IN NEAERAM. A. T. Murray.

DEMOSTHENES VII: FUNERAL SPEECH, EROTIC ESSAY, EXORDIA AND LETTERS. N. W. and N. J. DeWitt.

DIO CASSIUS: ROMAN HISTORY. E. Cary. 9 Vols.

THE LOEB CLASSICAL LIBRARY

Dio Chrysostom. 5 Vols. Vols. I and II. J. W. Cohoon.
Vol III. J. W. Cohoon and H. Lamar Crosby. Vols. IV
and V. H. Lamar Crosby.

Diodorus Siculus. 12 Vols. Vols. I-VI. C. H. Oldfather.
Vol. VII. C. L. Sherman. Vol. VIII. C. B. Welles.
Vols. IX and X. Russel M. Geer. Vol. XI. F. R. Walton.

Diogenes Laertius. R. D. Hicks. 2 Vols.

Dionysius of Halicarnassus : Roman Antiquities. Spel-
man's translation revised by E. Cary. 7 Vols.

Epictetus. W. A. Oldfather. 2 Vols.

Euripides. A. S. Way. 4 Vols. Verse trans.

Eusebius : Ecclesiastical History. Kirsopp Lake and
J. E. L. Oulton. 2 Vols.

Galen : On the Natural Faculties. A. J. Brock.

The Greek Anthology. W. R. Paton. 5 Vols.

The Greek Bucolic Poets (Theocritus, Bion, Moschus).
J. M. Edmonds.

Greek Elegy and Iambus with the Anacreontea. J. M.
Edmonds. 2 Vols.

Greek Mathematical Works. Ivor Thomas. 2 Vols.

Herodes. Cf. Theophrastus : Characters.

Herodotus. A. D. Godley. 4 Vols.

Hesiod and the Homeric Hymns. H. G. Evelyn White.

Hippocrates and the Fragments of Heracleitus. W. H. S.
Jones and E. T. Withington. 4 Vols.

Homer : Iliad. A. T. Murray. 2 Vols.

Homer : Odyssey. A. T. Murray. 2 Vols.

Isaeus. E. S. Forster.

Isocrates. George Norlin and LaRue Van Hook. 3 Vols.

St. John Damascene : Barlaam and Ioasaph. Rev. G. R.
Woodward and Harold Mattingly.

Josephus. 9 Vols. Vols. I-IV. H. St. J. Thackeray. Vol.
V. H. St. J. Thackeray and Ralph Marcus. Vols. VI
and VII. Ralph Marcus. Vol. VIII. Ralph Marcus and
Allen Wikgren.

Julian. Wilmer Cave Wright. 3 Vols.

Longus : Daphnis and Chloe. Thornley's translation revised by J. M. Edmonds ; and Parthenius. S. Gaselee.

Lucian. 8 Vols. Vols. I-V. A. M. Harmon ; Vol. VI.
K. Kilburn ; Vol. VII. M. D. Macleod.

Lycophron. Cf. Callimachus.

Lyra Graeca. J. M. Edmonds. 3 Vols.

Lysias. W. R. M. Lamb.

MANETHO. W. G. Waddell. PTOLEMY: TETRABIBLOS. F. E. Robbins.

MARCUS AURELIUS. C. R. Haines.

MENANDER. F. G. Allinson.

MINOR ATTIC ORATORS. 2 Vols. K. J. Maidment and J. O. Burtt.

NONNOS: DIONYSIACA. W. H. D. Rouse. 3 Vols.

OPPIAN, COLLUTHUS, TRYPHIODORUS. A. W. Mair.

PAPYRI. NON-LITERARY SELECTIONS. A. S. Hunt and C. C. Edgar. 2 Vols. LITERARY SELECTIONS (Poetry). D. L. Page.

PARTHENIUS. *Cf.* LONGUS.

PAUSANIAS: DESCRIPTION OF GREECE. W. H. S. Jones. 5 Vols. and Companion Vol. arranged by R. E. Wycherley.

PHILO. 10 Vols. Vols. I-V. F. H. Colson and Rev. G. H. Whitaker; Vols. VI-X. F. H. Colson; General Index. Rev. J. W. Earp.
Two Supplementary Vols. Translation only from an Armenian Text. Ralph Marcus.

PHILOSTRATUS: IMAGINES: CALLISTRATUS: DESCRIPTIONS. A. Fairbanks.

PHILOSTRATUS: THE LIFE OF APOLLONIUS OF TYANA. F. C. Conybeare. 2 Vols.

PHILOSTRATUS AND EUNAPIUS: LIVES OF THE SOPHISTS. Wilmer Cave Wright.

PINDAR. Sir J. E. Sandys.

PLATO: CHARMIDES, ALCIBIADES, HIPPARCHUS, THE LOVERS, THEAGES, MINOS AND EPINOMIS. W. R. M. Lamb.

PLATO: CRATYLUS, PARMENIDES, GREATER HIPPIAS, LESSER HIPPIAS. H. N. Fowler.

PLATO: EUTHYPHRO, APOLOGY, CRITO, PHAEDO, PHAEDRUS. H. N. Fowler.

PLATO: LACHES, PROTAGORAS, MENO, EUTHYDEMUS. W. R. M. Lamb.

PLATO: LAWS. Rev. R. G. Bury. 2 Vols.

PLATO: LYSIS, SYMPOSIUM, GORGIAS. W. R. M. Lamb.

PLATO: REPUBLIC. Paul Shorey. 2 Vols.

PLATO: STATESMAN. PHILEBUS. H. N. Fowler: ION. W. R. M. Lamb.

PLATO: THEAETETUS AND SOPHIST. H. N. Fowler.

PLATO: TIMAEUS, CRITIAS, CLITOPHO, MENEXENUS, EPISTULAE. Rev. R. G. Bury.

PLUTARCH: MORALIA. 15 Vols. Vols. I-V. F. C. Babbitt;

THE LOEB CLASSICAL LIBRARY

Vol. VI. W. C. Helmbold; Vol. VII. P. H. De Lacy and B. Einarson; Vol. IX. E. L. Minar, Jr., F. H. Sandbach, W. C. Helmbold; Vol. X. H. N. Fowler; Vol. XII. H. Cherniss and W. C. Helmbold.

PLUTARCH: THE PARALLEL LIVES. B. Perrin. 11 Vols.

POLYBIUS. W. R. Paton. 6 Vols.

PROCOPIUS: HISTORY OF THE WARS. H. B. Dewing. 7 Vols.

PTOLEMY: TETRABIBLOS. *Cf.* MANETHO.

QUINTUS SMYRNAEUS. A. S. Way. Verse trans.

SEXTUS EMPIRICUS. Rev. R. G. Bury. 4 Vols.

SOPHOCLES. F. Storr. 2 Vols. Verse trans.

STRABO: GEOGRAPHY. Horace L. Jones. 8 Vols.

THEOPHRASTUS: CHARACTERS. J. M. Edmonds; HERODES, etc. A. D. Knox.

THEOPHRASTUS. ENQUIRY INTO PLANTS. Sir Arthur Hort. 2 Vols.

THUCYDIDES. C. F. Smith. 4 Vols.

TRYPHIODORUS. *Cf.* OPPIAN.

XENOPHON: CYROPAEDIA. Walter Miller. 2 Vols.

XENOPHON: HELLENICA, ANABASIS, APOLOGY, AND SYMPOSIUM. C. L. Brownson and O. J. Todd. 3 Vols.

XENOPHON: MEMORABILIA AND OECONOMICUS. E. C. Marchant.

XENOPHON. SCRIPTA MINORA. E. C. Marchant.

VOLUMES IN PREPARATION

GREEK AUTHORS

ARISTOTLE: HISTORIA ANIMALIUM. A. L. Peck.

PLOTINUS. A. H. Armstrong.

LATIN AUTHORS

BABRIUS (Greek) AND PHAEDRUS. B. E. Perry.

DESCRIPTIVE PROSPECTUS ON APPLICATION

CAMBRIDGE, MASS. LONDON
HARVARD UNIV. PRESS WILLIAM HEINEMANN LTD